CLINICAL AND DIAGNOSTIC INTERVIEWING

CLINICAL AND DIAGNOSTIC INTERVIEWING

Second Edition

Edited by
ROBERT J. CRAIG, PH.D., ABPP

JASON ARONSON
Lanham • Boulder • New York • Toronto • Oxford

Published in the United States of America
by Jason Aronson
An imprint of Rowman & Littlefield Publishers, Inc.

A wholly owned subsidiary of The Rowman & Littlefield Publishing Group, Inc.
4501 Forbes Boulevard, Suite 200, Lanham, Maryland 20706
www.rowmanlittlefield.com

PO Box 317
Oxford
OX2 9RU, UK

British Library Cataloging in Publication Information Available

Library of Congress Cataloging-in-Publication Data

Clinical and diagnostic interviewing / edited by Robert J.
Craig.—2nd ed.
    p. cm.
  Includes bibliographical references and index.
  ISBN 0-7657-0003-4 (cloth : alk. paper)
  1. Interviewing in psychiatry. 2. Interviewing in mental
health. 3. Mental illness—Diagnosis. 4. Psychology,
Pathological—Diagnosis. I. Craig, Robert J., 1941– II.
Title.
  RC480.7.C55 2004
  616.89'14—dc22   2004006034

Printed in the United States of America

♾™ The paper used in this publication meets the minimum requirements of
American National Standard for Information Sciences—Permanence of Paper for
Printed Library Materials, ANSI/NISO Z39.48-1992.

CONTENTS

Part III: Interviewing Patients with Specific Psychopathologies

Part IV: Interviewing Special Populations

Part V: Focused Interviews

PREFACE AND ACKNOWLEDGMENTS
(FIRST EDITION)

The idea for this book derived from my experiences in conducting yearlong seminars in clinical interviewing for graduate students in clinical psychology. Along with several of my colleagues at the Illinois School of Professional Psychology who were also conducting these intense, small group seminars, I experienced frustration in locating texts to use for this purpose. Although interviewing is essential to the role of all mental health professions, it is surprising to find so few resources devoted to this topic. Our course evaluations consistently requested a pragmatic textbook as an aid for training in clinical interviewing. Recently, a few books on interviewing have been published, but most have been tied to interviewing for DSM-III-R disorders. This is too narrow a focus for the kinds of knowledge and information needed by clinicians when faced with certain interviewing situations.

In discussing this dilemma with practicing clinicians, I found that they, too, had a need for source material on clinical interviewing. This was particularly true when they were faced with patients or problem areas in which they had limited training or experience. For these situations, they said they would prefer a sourcebook that provided a summary of the main issues or factors to be assessed, as well as guidelines that provided a systematic and comprehensive approach to the diagnostic and clinical interviewing process. Based on these evaluations and recommendations, I decided to undertake the endeavor.

Having edited a book before, I was fully cognizant of the difficulties that lay ahead. Once the idea took shape and the book's organization had been decided, the most crucial task was selecting clinicians who understood the nature of the patients and their problems, stayed abreast of contemporary developments in their fields of specialization, wrote well but pragmatically, and had the ability to put their expertise into writing against a deadline.

Assembled here is the work of clinicians who did meet these criteria and who truly deserve to be called "outstanding." This volume attests to the enthusiasm with which they approach their work.

ix

Many editors of contributed books provide their authors with a basic structure to follow to ensure that the book has a certain degree of coherence and organization. I feel, however, that such structuring may result in a loss of clinical richness. Therefore, each of my contributors was given the following directions: (1) Assume your audience knows nothing about your topic. If they were faced with a patient suspected of having a particular problem, what would they need to know to make a competent assessment? (2) Whenever possible, cite relevant research to substantiate your material so that clinical interviewing may be placed on a more empirical basis. And (3) cite case examples illustrating your concepts.

I felt that this structure would allow the reader to see how abstract concepts are dynamically expressed in actual clinical contexts. These directives provided organization while allowing contributors to develop the kinds of chapters they felt represented the "state-of-the-art" in their particular fields of clinical interviewing. The result, I think, is a readable and pragmatic contribution to the field of clinical interviewing.

This volume was not produced in a vacuum. Indeed, I received the assistance and cooperation of many people during this project. I want to particularly acknowledge the contributions of Patricia Bernbom, Psy.D., who facilitated the acquisition of several of the contributors, who gave me continued verbal support and encouragement during the entire process, and whose boundless energy, enthusiasm, and dedication to ethical practice is a model for us all. Eli Coleman, Ph.D., suggested one of the contributors. I am also deeply appreciative to the individual contributors, who met deadline requirements, and to their secretaries and typists for delivering a quality product to me in the requested format. Thanks to Joan Langs, consulting editor, who made many valuable suggestions that improved the quality of the manuscript, to Nancy Morgan Andreola, whose superb copyediting immeasurably improved this manuscript, to Dorothy Erstling, who kept the project moving along at a timely pace, and to Jason Aronson, M.D., for his faith in this volume. Finally, I thank my graduate students, colleagues, and professional friends for suggesting and supporting this work.

All of the material in this volume is original material except for my chapter on drug abuse, which is an expanded version of a paper that originally appeared in *Professional Psychology: Research and Practice* (1988), vol. 19, pp. 14–20, entitled "Diagnostic Interviewing with Drug Abusers," copyright 1988 by the American Psychological Association and reprinted and adapted by permission of the publisher.

PREFACE

I was quite pleased with the first edition of this book. While it did well from a publishing standpoint, I was most pleased by the general quality of the chapters and, most importantly, the consistently positive reviews this book received from the professional audience and from the students who used it for part of their curricular requirements. In firsthand discussions with some of these students in my own course on interviewing, this book was given extremely positive (blind) reviews as part of the course evaluation procedures.

Nevertheless, time marches on and, as with any field of endeavor, with the passage of time come new ideas, new innovations, new ways of thinking, new ways of approaching, and new products for consideration. Since this book was published, two significant developments have occurred in the field of clinical and diagnostic interviewing. First, the diagnostic manual of the American Psychiatric Association (DSM) was revised. Now, DSM-IV has become the standard document to use both for diagnostic criteria and to assign a clinical diagnosis on a psychiatric patient. Second, researchers have developed a plethora of *structured clinical interviews* (Craig, 2003; Rogers, 2001) for consideration in the diagnostic process. While most of these structured interviews have had their greatest utility in psychiatric research rather than in clinical practice, their publication has forced even clinicians to be more conscientious in forming diagnoses and assessing an array of signs and symptoms for given disorders.

These two significant trends also mean that material in the first edition has become somewhat outdated. Hence the need to revise this book with current thinking in the mental health disciplines. When I contacted many of the previous authors, all became excited about the opportunity to present the latest trends in their areas of expertise as they pertained to clinical and diagnostic interviewing. Most had been supplementing this text with newer material in their areas, anyway, as part of their teaching, writing, research, and supervising of students. This gave them the chance to present their ideas to the larger professional audience as well.

Also, mental health clinicians had begun to encounter problems more frequently in a number of areas in mental health (severe psychiatric disorders, anxiety disorders, adolescents, and so forth), and the previous edition did not include interviewing material in these areas. I wanted to enlist authors who would present state-of-the-art material on these additional areas.

Assembled here is the work of a confluence of national experts and practicing clinicians. All have maintained their clinical interests and activities with patients. All have kept abreast of developments in their fields. As in the first edition, all write well and pragmatically. None are merely teachers. They are clinicians in the widest sense.

As with the previous edition, I did not provide a rigid structure for these authors to follow. I felt this would result in a loss of clinical richness, though case examples were requested of each author. They were asked to assume that the reader knows nothing about the subject matter. Each was instructed to present material in his or her area that would represent a comprehensive assessment for the clinician who suspected that a patient had a particular problem. This would allow the reader to see how the richness of a clinical interview is dynamically expressed in the clinical context. Once again, I am extremely pleased with the overall quality of the chapters.

As in the previous edition, there are many people who provided me with assistance and cooperation. I want to thank Jason Aronson, M.D., who inspired me to produce a second edition and who convinced me that the extra work would be a rewarding experience (it has!). His administrative and production staff were extremely helpful in moving this project along to completion. Thank you one and all!

All of the material in this volume is original except for my chapter on drug abuse, which appeared in the first edition of this book and was an expanded version of a paper that originally appeared in *Professional Psychology: Research and Practice* (1988), vol. 19, pp. 14–20, entitled "Diagnostic Interviewing with Drug Abusers," copyright 1988 by the American Psychological Association and reprinted and adapted by permission of the publisher. This revised chapter is yet another expansion of these two sources. Also, occasional sexist language that appeared in the first edition has been excised in this edition. I hope the reader will find reading these chapters as exciting as the authors found writing them.

REFERENCES

Craig, R. J. (2003). Assessing personalty and psychopathology with interview. In J. R. Graham & J. A. Neglieri (Eds) "Assessment Psychology (vol. 10). In I. B. Weiner (Editor-in-Chief) *Handbook of Psychology*. New York: Wiley (pp 487–508).

Rogers, R. (2001). Handbook of diagostic and structured interviewing. New York: Guilford.

INTRODUCTION

This book is divided into five parts. Introductory chapters on clinical interviewing are presented in part I, chapters on philosophical orientations to interviewing are presented in part II, chapters on interviewing patients with specific psychopathologies are presented in part III, chapters on interviewing children and adolescents appear in part IV, and chapters on special, focused interviews appear in part V.

The first edition of this book evolved into one of two primary uses. First, many clinicians selected it to be read as part of course requirements for teaching graduate students about the techniques and processes of clinical interviewing. Second, practicing clinicians used it as a principal authoritative reference. This second edition continues to address the needs of the second group, but the initial outline of this revision did not fully address the needs of the first group. Accordingly, we added a chapter on teaching and learning about clinical interviewing that sets the tone for the remaining chapters. In chapter 1, Rudolph presents a metatheoretical model of teaching clinical and diagnostic interviewing, couched in a format for training in six diagnostic competencies. Her model proposes that we teach goals, tasks, and ways to enhance the therapeutic bond. Goals consist of three categories: skills, knowledge, and attitudes. Skills consist of the interviewing, conceptualization, and collaboration processes. Knowledge sets include the interview structure and phases, multicultural issues within the interview, ethical codes, knowledge of DSM utilization, alternate assessment methods, epidemiology of psychological and psychiatric disorders (especially pertinent when exploring for comorbidities), community resources, basic knowledge of psychopharmacology, and assessment and psychotherapy. This set is critically important when establishing a treatment plan and interventions. Her pantheoretical model of attitude development includes openness, compassion, self-respect, appreciation of diversity, a spirit of inquiry and self-reflection, awareness of the need for consultation, and the need to think critically. Rudolph proposes a lists of tasks that educators need to engage in to facilitate the learning of these knowledge areas and skills, and she also specifies a list of behaviors that can be used to evaluate the quality of the client–clinician bond. To accomplish these goals, Rudolph provides the reader with a stage–sequence process for teaching clinical interviewing and details the specific items and areas to be addressed within each of these processes. Finally, she details a list of six proposed interviewing competencies along with sample interviewer tasks that measure each of these major competencies. An excellent clinician and researcher in psychotherapy, Rudolph continues to develop measures that assess the degree to which students are attaining these skills, attitudes, and competencies.

In chapter 2, Craig discusses the generic process of clinical interviewing. He discusses the essential differences between clinical interviews and social interactions, discusses methods of obtaining information, compares structured and unstructured interview formats, discusses the physical setting as an ingredient in the interview process, and reviews different kinds of interviews. He presents and contrasts the ways patients and clinicians approach the interview process. He reviews basic interviewing techniques and notes the interpersonal qualities thought to be influencing variables toward an effective interview. While a novice clinician may view a basic clinical interview as an unstructured process, Craig presents the structure of the process of a clinical interview as consisting of the introduction, exploration, hypothesis testing, client feedback, and termination. This structure was initially proposed by the social psychiatrist Harry Stack Sullivan some six years ago and remains valid today. Interviewer biases and the role of race, culture, and ethnicity are also addressed. The dynamic nature of the clinical process and the interaction between client and clinician are stressed throughout the chapter. Craig stresses the notion that the clinician is in control of the process during all phases of the interview.

In chapter 3, Gruba-McCallister argues that the success of the interview—a relationship characterized by reciprocity and sharing—rests upon a particular stance and set of attributes in the clinician. In particular, it depends upon the quality of the relationship that the clinician is able to establish with the client. The interviewer tries to learn enough about the client to make an accurate diagnosis and appropriate recommendations, while at the same time, acting therapeutically. This relationship is the key to the interviewing process. By paying attention to the feelings created in the clinician by the client, the clinician can more accurately assess the way the client interacts in life. Gruba-McCallister uses the word "dialectic" to convey the mutuality that exists at multiple levels in the interview. Clinicians need to understand how their own presuppositions, attitudes, and beliefs can influence the nature and direction of the interview. The process of "bracketing" is recommended to reduce these biases. A receptive, participatory, observational approach is recommended to arrive at an assessment. From a phenomenological viewpoint, it is the perceptions and experiences of the client that the clinician needs to understand.

Part II presents the most contemporary theoretical orientations extant in the field of mental health. These chapters demonstrate that interviews are not aimless but rather stem from philosophical and theoretical positions concerning the nature of human behavior and that these orientations per se influence the interview itself.

In chapter 4, Yalof and Abraham detail the psychoanalytic model of clinical interviewing. This approach stresses unconscious processes, the importance of early developmental history and trauma in the formation of personality, coping and defenses, and self-esteem vulnerability in symptom formation. Psychoanalytically based clinical interviews may focus on psychodynamics and intrapsychic structures and concentrate on object relations and interpersonal functions. Thus interviewing from a psychoanalytic perspective is not one type of interview but several different kinds of interviews, depending on whether the clinician operates from drive theory—that classical psychoanalytic model, ego psychology, as exemplified by Hartmann, Anna Freud, and Mahler; object relations, as in Klein and Winnicott; or self-psychology, as exemplified by Kohut. These different perspectives of psychoanalytic theory are elucidated by the authors as a basic introduction to psychoanalytic theory.

A behavioral orientation is unique among the major approaches in that it does not require intervening variables or reified entities. This approach does not require an id, ego, or superego, nor does it require an empathic stance from the therapist (unless that *is* the response designated for reinforcement and modeling), nor does it deal with hypothetical constructs, such as role boundary disturbances and enmeshments. Behaviorists deal directly with overt behavior. Behavioral assessment assumes that all behavior is lawful and controlled by general principles of learning. In chapter 5, Beach explains classical and operant conditioning and provides examples of each. The topics of modeling, learned emotional responses, and verbal conditioning are addressed as they apply to the clinical interview. A behavioral epistemology assumes behavior is determined largely through differential rewards and punishments within the individual's learning history. The chapter concludes with the structure and content of the behavioral interview.

A philosophical orientation, now referred to as a humanistic or existential perspective, is a derivative of Rogerian philosophy and a nondirective approach to treatment. This orientation has traditionally eschewed diagnosis as "insufficiently appreciative of human subjectivity and unnecessary as a guide to psychotherapy." According to Maddi, however, in chapter 6, within the existential and humanistic tradition there are assessment goals and techniques that have relevance to the assessment process. Maddi reconceptualizes the psychological terms of psychopathology, maturity, and premorbidity into a humanistic and existential framework and sees these concepts as relevant in theorizing about human behavior. For example, humanists view psychopathology as a violation of what it means to be human, while existentialists see it as a chronic sense of meaninglessness. Psychological maturity is defined by the construct of "authenticity." Premorbidity, or what Maddi calls "conformism," stems from a relative lack of symbolization, imagination, judgment, and decision making (what the analysts would call "ego"). Stress undermines adjustment and results in psychopathology. Premorbidity and psychopathology result from receiving conditional positive regard. Symptom formation is the incongruence between the sense of self and the ideal self. Maddi describes the diagnostic assessment process from this humanistic/existential framework, which emphasizes current experiences, processes, and content and provides a detailed exposition of client statements that refer to relevant humanistic/existential concepts. There are even questionnaires that can be utilized for assessment from this perspective. Maddi makes a very strong case that the humanistic/existential framework is relevant to the diagnostic process and to clinical interviewing.

In chapter 7, van Dyke addresses interviewing from a family systems perspective. A family systems interviewing orientation, both for interviewing and for intervention, requires a different kind of thinking. Whereas all other orientations presume a linear causality between symptom and pathology, a family systems approach assumes a circular causality. Individual psychopathology, it is argued, plays a role in the homeostatic functioning of the family as a system. Relying on general systems theory and cybernetics, a variety of family systems theories and interventions have been developed. Van Dyke traces the history of these various approaches and elucidates their nuances. Beginning with the seminal contributions of the "communication" school, much of current family systems work strikes a middle ground, integrating the structural approach of Minuchin and the strategic approach of Jay Haley. The major tenet of all approaches within this framework is that every symptom or sign is, at its source, a sign of a dysfunctional family. A family systems orientation further diverges from other approaches in that the clinician, *at the onset of the initial interview,* is expected to begin interventions to change the family system. A sample family interview is provided to illustrate this approach. Keep in mind that the clinician does not necessarily have to see the entire family to do family therapy. One can intervene at the level of the individual and still change the family system.

Part III presents chapters addressing specific psychopathologies and presents interviewing techniques and suggestions for assessing the basic populations and problems that are frequently encountered by mental health clinicians. Since, according to recent epidemiological studies, anxiety is endemic to almost all forms of psychopathology and anxiety disorders are the most prevalent of the mental disorders, we begin this section with a discussion on interviewing patients with anxiety disorders. In chapter 8, Roth and Rauch outline the core features of the major anxiety disorders listed in DSM-IV and present guidelines for establishing rapport with these patients. Though they focus on the clinical interview as the major assessment source, the authors recognize that behavioral observation, self-report measures, consultation with significant others who may be knowledgeable about the person, and even physiological assessment may be used for a comprehensive assessment of the anxious client. They list some behavioral assessment measures that also may be used as a supplement to the clinical interview. Self-monitoring methods, where the patient keeps track of his/her own behavior (via log entries, daily recordings, and so forth), may also be part of the continuing assessment process. Since recent psychiatric interests have promoted the utilization of structured interviews, Roth and Rauch detail a number of general and also specific structured interviews for defined anxiety disorders. The chapter concludes with a number of practical suggestions for interviewing patients with anxiety disorders.

Substance abuse has become endemic in our society, and mental health clinicians are faced with the increasing responsibility of assessment and treatment of substance abuse. Also, many syndromes, including many anxiety and depressive disorders, may be drug induced and secondary to substance abuse. Finally, substance abuse is a comorbidity to many Axis I and II disorders, and it is a concomitant with many DSM-IV codes, such as child abuse, spousal abuse, and marital problems. In chapter 9, Craig presents principles of interviewing adult drug abusers and covers diagnostic classification, categories of abuse, changing concepts of addiction and dependence, determination of abuse liability, reliability of addict self-reports, structured and unstructured clinical interviews, available diagnostic instruments, dual diagnosis, special population considerations, confidentiality, and countertransference. A case example and a list of interview suggestions are included.

More so than other disorders, alcohol and drug problems are often assessed with both clinical interview and some type of self-report measurement tool. We would be remiss if we did not include a chapter detailing this routine comprehensive approach to substance-abuse assessment. Chapters 10 and 11 should be considered companion papers to chapter 9. Skinstad, Nathan, and Pizzini (chapter 10) discuss an overview of the interview and assessment process with alcoholics. Defining alcohol abuse versus alcoholism has been a major issue, since the syndrome is multivariate with many defining issues. Accordingly, there has been a proliferation of interview formats and questions recommended for use with problematic drinkers. These various formats differ in terms of the time frames (recent or long term, current or lifetime) and cognitive or personality trait, consumption patterns, or behavior consequences they focus on. Complicating the process is the fact that problematic drinking differs with such variables as age, gender, race, ethnicity, and culture. Furthermore, there are screening methods versus more comprehensive assessment tools. There are short-term and "pithy" screens (CAGE) and more detailed and expansive instruments that require up to an hour to complete. This makes it difficult to develop an interviewing tool or assessment measure that would capture the essence of the full range of the syndrome. In this chapter, the authors provide an exhaustive review of the various assessment measures that can be selected to compliment the clinical interview with alcoholics, which is not substantially different from the interview tool presented for use with substance abusers in chapter 9. Included here are measures that screen for the disorder, for problems associated with the disorder, for severity of dependence, for severity of withdrawal, and for personal assessments, such as readiness to change, alcohol-related expectancies, motivation models of etiology, family history tools, measures of social support, and cognitive and personality functioning.

In chapter 11, Isenhart introduces the subject of motivational interviewing, defined as a client-centered strategy to develop and promote a strong working alliance between therapist and patient to promote change in behavior. While the technique was originally introduced as a change method for addictions, it has been successfully used in a number of other areas (as referenced in this chapter). Isenhart defines motivational interviewing in depth, discusses stages of change, introduces the goals and principles of motivational interviewing, and details "therapeutic traps" to avoid as well as the basic strategies of this technique. A basic goal of motivational interviewing is to get clients to talk about change, and Isenhart discusses how to elicit and respond to change talk. Since resistance is endemic to all psychotherapies, ways to manage resistance within the motivational interviewing epistemology are also suggested. The chapter concludes with ways to learn this advanced interviewing skill.

Chapter 12, on eating disorders, concludes this section's submodule on abuse disorders. Within the spectrum of eating disorders, anorexia and bulimia have become the most prevalent. As Marshall notes, despite our increased knowledge about their assessment, diagnosis, and treatment, eating disorders are often omitted or given cursory treatment in introductory sources on diagnostic and clinical interviewing. Marshall presents the DSM-IV classification and criteria for anorexia and bulimia and discusses differential diagnosis and concurrent psychiatric conditions that have been linked with these two disorders. She details the medical, nutritional, and psychological aspects and presents the factors that should be considered in an initial evaluation. She stresses the need for history and a mental status exam. Specialized inventories are available to assess eating disorders, but the traditional mental health clinical interview remains the most popular method. The chapter concludes with a consideration of treatment recommendations.

No aspect of mental health has captured the attention of clinicians like the issue of personality. Discussions of personality seem to dominate case conferences, presentations, and reviews. Personality disorders are defined as patterns of inflexible, maladaptive personality traits that result in significant impairment in social or occupational functioning or subjective distress. They are receiving more attention since the inclusion of a separate diagnostic axis in DSM-III and the development of more objective criteria in DSM-III-R and DSM-IV. There is now a recognition that personality disorders can influence the course and treatment of Axis I disorders and be the focus of attention itself. In chapter 13,

Widiger argues that personality disorders are among the most difficult to assess and diagnose. He reviews techniques and principles of personality disorder interviewing and addresses the issues that complicate the diagnostic processes. These issues include unreliability, limited time and coverage, excessive diagnostic co-occurrence, traits versus states, distortions in self-description, and the issue of gender bias within the diagnostic criteria sets. To improve on the diagnostic process, a number of structured and semistructured clinical interviews for the assessment of personality disorders have been developed (along with a myriad of self-report inventories for the same purpose). Many of these measures are highlighted, contrasted, and evaluated in this chapter. Widiger recommends that both a self-report screening measure and a semistructured clinical interview should routinely be administered in order to improve the accuracy of personality disorder diagnoses.

The last chapter in part III (chapter 14) addresses the issue of interviewing patients with more severe psychiatric disorders, commonly referred to as mental illness. These disorders are characterized by major psychotic symptoms, disorders of uncommon breadth, and severe cognitive and interpersonal dysfunction, and at times, they may require treatment that encompasses a lifetime. Among these disorders are the schizophrenias, bipolar disorders, schizoaffective disorder, and major depression with psychotic features. Corrigan and Mc-Cracken summarize many of the problems that emerge when trying to interview patients with these severe disorders. The authors recommend a "personal empowerment approach" when interviewing patients with these disorders, and they recommend one of the major semistructured clinical interviews as well as one of the published symptom schedules for use with this population. The goal of diagnosis with severely impaired psychiatric treatments is not merely an accurate diagnosis but also one that provides the ability to target treatment to a specific symptom or symptom complex and to restore or improve functionality. The authors recommend some general interviewing strategies and provide case examples throughout the chapter to illustrate these introduced concepts. (As a teaching tool, I suggest the student wear earphones that play an audiotape of a conversation while being interviewed by the clinician. This will illustrate what it might be like for a patient to experience auditory hallucinations while receiving mental health services.)

The chapters in part III pertain to adult clinical interviews. In contrast, the three chapters in part IV address interviews with children and adolescents. In chapter 15, Logan suggests that, while the purpose of clinical interviews with children is not fundamentally different from those with adults—to arrive at an understanding of the presenting problems and the factors that contribute to them—children's behavior problems do differ from those of adults. While the DSM-IV classification system is the most frequently used nosological system for childhood disorders, there are other systems to consider, and many clinicians, especially those of the more psychodynamic persuasion, continue to rely on broader and more traditional classifications of child behavior problems. The author discusses assessment guidelines and formats, working with and involving parents, individual interviews with children, specialized evaluations, formulations of childhood problems, and treatment planning. Throughout the chapter, the focus remains on interviewing and *observing* the child. Logan reminds the clinician to place the presenting problem with the development stage and life circumstances of the child. A recommended evaluation format is provided, but it should not be followed in rote format, and suggestions are offered for preparing the child for the interview itself. The author raises the issue of confidentiality, which the clinician needs to give more thought to than in adult-focused interviews, because parents should be an integral part of the evaluation, while the child needs to feel free enough for self-expression without the fear of parental reprisals. Interviews with children can also take the form of play interviews and what Logan calls conversational interviews. Also, racial, cultural, and religious diversity need to be considered when formulating one's conclusions as to final assessment and intervention. The chapter concludes with a case history that illustrates chapter contents.

Chapter 16 presents clinical interviews with adolescents. Ball, Archer, and Hartmann discuss the developmental considerations and expected themes in working with adolescents and discuss the psychological "tasks" required of this age span. They address the ethical and legal concerns associated with gathering informed consent as a prelude to conducting the interview, and they present the emerging literature regarding the use of structured clinical interviews with adolescents. They also address the advantages of using supplementary survey and more formal, objective testing instruments and the need to gather data from multiple sources. They present interview methods and strategies that are useful with this population and end the chapter with a case example. The authors strongly recommend using adjunctive testing to supplement the clinical interview when dealing with adolescents.

The last chapter in part IV (17) addresses the growing problem of childhood abuse. This area of inquiry is becoming more sophisticated and specialized, and Wolf addresses the special skills needed by the clinician who initially evaluates a child or adolescent suspected of being a victim of child abuse or neglect. Methods to establish goals and rapport are initially presented, procedures for recognition and evaluation are outlined, and special techniques and aids for interviewing, such as anatomically correct dolls, are presented and debated. Clinicians are cautioned to control potential countertransference feelings that may arise in the context of these evaluations and to appreciate that some allegations are false.

Part V presents specialized chapters pertaining to specific kinds of interviews (mental status exams, assessment of suicidal risk) and clinical interviewing in medical settings. In chapter 18, Schwartz traces the development of the contemporary mental status exam (MSE) to the systematic observations of Emil

Kraeplin, which led to a psychiatric nosology based on observations and descriptions, culminating in DSM-IV. The author then provides guidelines for the general content categories one needs to assess a patient's mental status and highlights the major systems in each category. These categories include general appearance, behavior, affect and mood, speech and thought, perceptual processes, attention and concentration, memory, and intellectual functioning. Schwartz considers the MSE versatile because of its adaptability to different theoretical perspectives. He presents case histories as they apply to DSM diagnoses, neuropsychological evaluations, and the role of the MSE in psychopharmacological decisions.

Research has yet to establish a definitive indicator of suicide in patients at risk. The courts no longer expect clinicians to be able to predict a specific act of future suicide. Rather, the expectation is for the clinician to *evaluate the extent of suicidal risk and to take appropriate action based on that assessment*. This assessment is difficult because of the low base of occurrence of suicide in the general population (1 percent) and because the suicidal population is heterogeneous. Researchers speak of several subtypes of the suicidal risk population. There are those who intend to kill themselves and do so. There are those who threaten to commit suicide but never make an attempt. There are those who threaten to commit suicide without an accompanying intent to die (attention seekers). This group also contains a subgroup who make intended gestures without the intention to die but miscalculate the lethality of the attempt and do kill themselves. There are those who make multiple attempts of a nonlethal nature. And there may be more subgroups as well. Yufit (chapter 19) points out, however, that empirical studies and clinical observations have demonstrated that certain factors, if present, increase the probability of differentiating between an intent to die versus an attempt to communicate. He presents a Quantified Focused Interview that explores specific areas considered to be associated with increased suicidal potential and provides a quantification of these variables, deriving an index of suicidal potential. Yufit recommends both a structured, quantified approach and a clinical interview as aids to making these difficult judgments.

Health psychology and medical psychology have shown an exponential growth during the past two decades. Many clinicians are now themselves working primarily in medical settings and interviewing medical rather than primarily psychiatric patients. Wakely (chapter 20) points out that interviewing medical patients encompasses skills that are similar to those required for traditional mental health assessments, but also requires knowledge and skills specific to this population. Wakely emphasizes the biopsychosocial interview as the preferred approach with medical patients, discusses the kinds of patients one is likely to encounter in these settings and types of health psychology interviews, and offers a number of practical suggestions when working with these patients. Of course, collaboration with other medical health care providers is essential when working in such settings.

Many clinicians are now being trained in forensic issues such as fitness to stand trial, insanity pleas, and custody evaluations. These expanding roles provide exciting opportunities for the clinician and challenge our clinical skills. Meloy (chapter 21) elaborates on the basic characteristics of the forensic interview that distinguish it from other types of clinical interviews. These include the often coercive nature of the interview, the absence of privilege, the report as a tool to communicate to non–mental health professionals, the possible and even probable presence of distortion, the probability of disagreement and challenge to the basic findings during adversarial court proceedings, and the attitude and expectations of the interviewer. Meloy offers suggestions and recommendations to address each of these distinguishing characteristics.

The art of clinical interviewing is a dynamic process that incorporates the material presented in these chapters. For example, in assessing suicidal risk, one has to evaluate the extent of anxiety and depression, consider the role of alcohol and drug abuse, and perform a mental status evaluation while adhering to the general principles and suggestions presented in parts I and II of this book. The material necessarily requires separation for didactic purposes and the realization that there is no such separation in actual clinical practice.

I

BASIC ELEMENTS IN A
CLINICAL INTERVIEW

1

TEACHING DIAGNOSTIC AND CLINICAL INTERVIEWING

Bonnie A. Rudolph, Ph.D.

This chapter describes a method of teaching assessment interviewing based on twenty years of experience conducting and teaching such interviews. It describes the history, training contexts and contents, and a metatheoretical model of teaching diagnostic interviewing. The chapter also proposes a format of training and describes six diagnostic interviewing competencies.

Diagnostic interviewing is one of the most frequently practiced professional mental health activities. Counselors, psychologists, social workers, psychiatric nurses, and psychiatrists all utilize the first clinical interview to assess client needs and problems, identify strengths and weaknesses, suggest diagnoses, make referrals, plan treatment, form relationships, and make other interventions. Students from these professions are trained in the clinical interview using a variety of methods based on differing philosophical, pedagogical, and therapeutic orientations (Bootzin & Ruggil, 1988; Garb, 1989). Furthermore, there has been insufficient study of the processes of the first clinical interview and its outcomes (Rudolph et al., 1993). A review of the literature on evaluating the diagnostic interview by Smelson et al. (1998) recommended some strategies to strengthen first interview investigations. The thrust of this chapter, however, is to help teach students clinical interviewing.

To serve a diverse audience of trainers and trainees, a generic model that applies to different educational settings and theoretical orientations is offered. This model uses the concepts of goals, tasks, and bond suggested by Bordin (1979) as well as a developmental (phases) view of the assessment interview and training (Rudolph, 2004). A fundamental premise of the model is that given the variety of clients, assessment approaches, contexts, and purposes of clinical interviews, students should learn to utilize a discerning flexibility, an abiding respect for the person, and an appreciation for the many factors that influence the outcome of this first assessment interview. Below, relevant history, a context of training, and the diversity of content of diagnostic interviewing are introduced.

HISTORICAL INFLUENCES

Most training literature, the bulk of which comes from counseling psychology, has focused on intervention rather than assessment and has gradually moved over the past twenty-five years from an ill-defined and unstructured to a more clearly delineated approach (Baker & Daniels, 1989). Rogers (1957), Carkhoff (1969), and others popularized a didactic and experiential approach to training intervention skills; however, within this person–centered approach, assessment training was not emphasized. Ivy (1971) further systematized interview training with his microcounseling program, as did Hill (1986) with her response-mode categories. In addition, the move to "manualized" therapies within clinical psychology and psychiatry has made training more systematic within specific therapeutic approaches (e.g., Klerman et al., 1984; Strupp & Binder, 1984). Within mental health fields, efforts to identify professional competencies have also supported greater delineation of educational/training outcomes (Bourg et al., 1987; Coursey et al., 2000). However, with a few exceptions (Rosenberg, 1999; Bogels et al., 1995; Spitzer & Williams, 1986), the training literature on assessment interviewing has lagged behind this trend to greater specificity. Hence, trainers of the clinical and diagnostic interview have had to apply general therapy training principles as wells as concepts from their specific therapy approaches, many of which are untested or unsupported, when teaching the assessment interview. Acknowledging the variety in theories of therapy, professional associations have suggested broad ability categories such as knowledge, skills, and attitudes (American Psychological Association, APA, 1998; American Counseling Association, 1995). However, the specification of these categories is left to each theoretical school or training program. Most recently, APA (2002) has moved to use the terms *knowledge, skills,* and *competencies.*

Responding to these trends and recognizing the need to document training outcomes, one professional psychology program faculty in the mid-'90s focused on evaluating the assessment competency within its trainees (Rudolph et al., 1998). Over several years, the faculty developed a set of inventories to measure this competency. That process led to the identification of and agreement upon "floor-level" criteria for determining competency in assessment/diagnostic interviewing that could apply to the various therapeutic approaches of faculty and students, as well as to the range of clients and contexts where trainees were situated. Such agreement is noteworthy given the number of faculty (n = 32) and the diverse therapy orientations they espoused. These criteria are:

1. To structure the interview
2. To forge a working alliance
3. To facilitate interviewee participation and disclosure
4. To collect data and pursue the inquiry
5. To conduct the interview professionally

These and subsequent activities resulted in the development of the generic clinical interviewing teaching model described in this chapter.

TRAINING CONTEXT AND CONTENT

As this chapter is designed to serve trainers of various professional disciplines, some basic assumptions concerning the training context should be noted. My first assumption is that the training is occurring within an organized curriculum and program of study with an articulated training mission. The second assumption is that the trainees have at least a college education and are pursuing graduate studies with high motivation to provide good clinical/counseling services. The third assumption is that the learning outcomes of the training in clinical/diagnostic interviewing are clarified for students before training begins. That is, students should know the expected educational outcomes of successfully completing the training. The final assumption is that the trainer is an experienced assessment interviewer who is open to continuous learning, committed to self-reflection and collaborative learning processes, and operating within an adequately supportive educational environment. Faculty and students interacting in contexts where these assumptions are not met are encouraged to consider their situations and advocate for better training to best utilize this chapter.

Obviously, explicating assumptions about the qualities of the training context is an easier task than clarifying the "content" of what is taught concerning clinical interviewing. Different theories of therapy require specialized "knowledge bases" and suggest different assessment interview tasks, processes, and skills. Some models emphasize inquiry, others listening and sensitive reflection, yet others decision making and problem identification. The chapters that follow in this text explicate approaches of different therapeutic orientation toward the content and process of the clinical or diagnostic interview, while the beginning of this chapter describes a generic approach to teaching clinical interviewing. Although metatheoretical, the following model contains certain values and content that may be more or less compatible with different theoretical and pedagogic orientations. Thus I recommend the reader "keep the meat and throw out the bones" in applying the model to his or her own unique training situation.

A MODEL OF TEACHING CLINICAL OR
DIAGNOSTIC INTERVIEWING

The purpose of the model is to create a training environment in which all the participants learn, experiment, self-reflect, and collaborate in unique ways to achieve assessment-interviewing competence. The three concepts of goals, tasks, and bond articulated by Bordin (1979) help organize this teaching model. The model synthesizes literature on clinical and diagnostic interviewing (Benjamin, 1981; Craig, 1989; Sommers-Flanagan & Sommers-Flanagan, 1999; Cormier & Cormier, 1998), competencies (Bourg et al., 1987; Greenhalgh & Macfarlane, 1997; Freedheim & Overholser, 1998; Hansen et al., 2000; Peterson & Bry, 1980; Rychen & Salganik, 2001), assessment interview criteria (Rudolph et al., 1998), and learning outcomes (Edelstein & Berler, 1987).

Goals

Goals identify the specific desired learning outcomes of training and are conceptualized into the three categories of skills, knowledge, and attitudes. Within the skills category, three types of processes exist: interview processes, conceptualization processes, and collaboration processes. Table 1.1 depicts the skill goal category and the specific goals within each of the process subcategories for skills.

Table 1.1.   Skill Goals

Skill Goal Category	*Specific Goals*
Process Subcategory	
Interview Processes	Structure and focus the interview
	Forge an alliance
	Collect data and pursue inquiry
	Facilitate client engagement and disclosure
	Conduct interview professionally
	Perform enactment of participant-observer role
Conceptualization Processes	Provide coherent theoretical formulation of client and client difficulty
	Identify and consistently relate interview phase, content, and process to a particular theoretical model, verbally and in writing
	Articulate trainee intentions in interview and rationale (generate hypotheses)
	Describe therapeutic alliance valences
	Think critically
Collaboration Processes	Communicate self-reflection in training
	Offer timely, helpful feedback to fellow trainees and to clients in clinical interviews
	Attend respectfully to fellow trainee work
	Responding emphathically to client in interview
	Cooperate on common goals
	Share time and resources of training
	Receive feedback from fellow trainees and trainer/ supervisor and clients nondefensively
	Proactive efforts to seek appropriate consultation

Trainee skill development should be measured over time to reflect progressive changes. Generic inventories are available to measure the following areas: structuring and focusing the interview, forging an alliance, collecting data and pursuing inquiry, facilitating client engagement and disclosure, and conducting the interview professionally (Rudolph et al., 1998). Thus far, no specific instrument has been developed to measure the student's ability to enact the role of participant-observer. This skill, however, is readily observable in both the clinical interview behavior of the trainee and the trainee's behavior in the training/supervision context. There is enactment of the participant-observer role if the trainee performs two tasks at once: participating in an alert, responsive, and authentic manner, while also observing and commenting on the process. Fluency in this skill is especially difficult to develop for novice interviewers and for those with minimal psychological training. However, it is a fundamental diagnostic interview skill and significantly influences interview processes and other trainee skills.

The second goal category is made up of "knowledge sets" the trainee should master during training. The knowledge sets for this goal category are noted in table 1.2. Listing these knowledge sets emphasizes the depth and breadth of knowledge that trainees must acquire during clinical interview training. It also explains why both students and teachers in this area of training should expend so much effort and time. Clearly, this category of goals is most likely to require revision when teachers/trainers operate from a specific therapy orientation or specialized discipline such as biological psychiatry. Still, some of the sets noted in table 1.2 should be applicable to all orientations.

The final goal category includes development and enhancement of certain desirable professional attitudes. This category is perhaps the most difficult to measure, though there are good instruments available to measure values (Rokeach, 1979). Again, the specific discipline or therapeutic orientation will influence selection of specific attitudes. Table 1.3 depicts pantheoretical attitudes within the attitude goal category that hopefully would be compatible with most

Table 1.2.   Knowledge Goals

The Knowledge Goal Category	*Knowledge Sets*
	Interview structure and phases
	Multicultural issues in clinical interviews
	Ethical codes
	DSM Multi-axial system
	Alternate assessment methods
	Epidemiology of psychological disorders
	Community resources
	Basic knowledge of psychopharmacological agents
	A specific theory of assessment and therapy

Table 1.3.   Attitude Goals

Attitude Goal Category	Specific Attitudes
	Openness to experience
	Compassion for the human condition
	Disposition to self-reflect
	Appreciation for diverse peoples and cultures
	Spirit of inquiry
	Disposition to seek consultation
	Disposition to think critically

trainers' value systems and orientations. It is open to debate how much these attitudes can be "taught," and certainly some attitudes or dispositions may in fact be personality traits. (An example is openness to experience, Costa & McCrae, 1992). It has been argued that trainers merely reinforce or facilitate elaboration of attitudes that students bring with them to their career choice (Holland, 1996; Furnham, 2001). Nonetheless, it is useful both for students and researchers to articulate particular attitudes as desirable professional goals.

Tasks

Tasks are those activities in which the teacher engages to facilitate trainee goal attainment as well as those activities in which the trainee engages to attain the training goals and successfully complete the course of study. Tasks naturally vary depending on the academic context and the particular practice settings of the students. Tasks for both trainer and trainee change as the trainees progress through the training experience. Furthermore, it is the primary responsibility of the teacher/trainer to order the tasks in an effective manner, both for the group of trainees as a whole and for individual trainees. In general, the trainer is more task-oriented and active in the early stages and discriminatingly less so toward the end phases of training. Table 1.4 lists tasks that probably apply across a large number of settings and categorizes them according to who performs the tasks: teacher/trainer or student/trainee.

Bond

Bond is the term used to describe the interpersonal relationship between trainee and trainer where the specific purpose of the relationship is the growth and development of the trainee. The relationship among the various trainees also constitutes another type of bond and is often very important in the growth and development of individual trainees. This chapter focuses on the trainer–trainee bond. Creation of this bond is a developmental process, but it can be greatly enhanced by the trainer's special attention to the goals and tasks of training at its inception (Norcross, 2001). The bond must be deliberately fos-

Table 1.4. Tasks in Teaching Clinical Interviewing

Participant	Tasks
Teacher	Provide flexible, responsive structure for training
	Clarify training objectives and methods of measurement
	Encourage active student participation/engagement
	Model desired knowledge, skills, and attitudes (mentor)
	Assure opportunities for practice of learning activities
	Coordinate training with other teachers/supervisors
	Develop individualized learning goals with each trainee
	Monitor and evaluate student attainment of learning objectives and professional development
	Provide timely documentation and reporting to sanctioning agency
	Self-evaluate and identify areas for improvement
Trainee	Participate actively and ethically in learning
	Communicate honestly
	Collaborate with fellow trainees and teacher
	Complete assigned learning activities on time
	Receive feedback nondefensively
	Experiment with new behaviors
	Provide helpful feedback
	Study and integrate various of knowledge bases presented
	Self-evaluate and identify areas for improvement

tered by the trainer and be authentic and collaborative. When it fits these criteria, it will evolve in complexity and depth over time. Table 1.5 depicts the fundamental qualities of the professional bond between trainer and trainee within this teaching model. Again, specific therapy orientations may call for different or additional qualities.

Training Format

The recommended format for this model is group training and group supervision. Students may learn more in this format than in individual supervision meetings. However, individual meetings are used to augment and individualize

Table 1.5. Qualities of the Bond between Teacher and Trainee

Professional Training Bond	Fundamental Qualities
	Structured, consistent, but evolving in complexity
	Mutual respect and regard
	Focused on student training needs
	Evaluative functions are open and acknowledged
	Open and honest
	Nondefensive
	Emotionally expressive and expectant
	Ethical and cooperative

the training process. Teaching interviewing in small groups also fosters the learning of collaboration and consultation skills among the trainees. Weekly presentation of clinical interviews provides trainees multiple examples of processes. Regular meetings and repeated presentation of tapes is important because performance expertise is most often the result of extended practice and not innate talent (Ericsson et al., 1993).

Groups of four to eight are recommended. Even numbers of participants in groups are preferred when teaching individual clinical interviewing, as this permits maximal use of dyads in training role-plays. Training should occur over ten months to a year in weekly meetings of 90 to 120 minutes. If the groups are large (eight), meetings may need to occur twice a week. For the most part, these meetings should be devoted to reviewing the clinical interviewing work of students via audio or videotape, with videotaping preferred.

The first responsibility of the trainer in these group meetings is to communicate the learning objectives, structure, process, and schedule of evaluation of the training. Distribution of ethical codes, helpful feedback guidelines, training goals, and instruments to measure interviewing features should occur during this meeting. How and when these measures will be used should also be covered. If the trainer uses the interview process outcomes noted in the first part of table 1.1, he or she may want to use the Assessment Interview Skill Deployment Inventory and Global Impressions of the Diagnostic Interview (Rudolph et al., 1998).

Expectations of students and trainers alike should be clarified, including issues of confidentiality, consent for recording sessions, recording needs and problems, transcribing interviews, student interview presentation scheduling, characteristics of training sites, professional responsibilities of the trainer and other clinical interviewing supervisors, and ways to reach the teacher. Often, articulation of all these items as well as introduction of students and teacher and their initial goals for training require the entire first training meeting. This first meeting is also a good time for the trainer to outline his or her own clinical interviewing model and theoretical knowledge base and distribute a syllabus with required readings and other training resources. The more organized and straightforward this first meeting is, the more any student anxiety can be usefully addressed and channeled. Within this teaching model, ambiguity and stimulation of high levels of trainee anxiety are viewed as handicaps to learning.

In the second training meeting, the trainer might present a sample of his or her own clinical or diagnostic interviewing via videotape. This activity accomplishes a number of highly critical tasks at once. First, it models the open, reflective, and nondefensive behavior expected of students as they present their own work. It also encourages student engagement and feedback. Substantial time should be allowed for trainee critiques, reactions, and questions. The utility of feedback on performance improvement depends on the context, timing, and manner in which the feedback is delivered (Kluger & DeNisi, 1996). This is a good time to practice the use of the Assessment Interview Skill Deployment Inventory and the Global Impressions of the Diagnostic Interview by asking students to complete them by rating the trainer's taped interview. This activity demonstrates that "perfect performance" is not the goal of training. Furthermore, playing a substantial portion of a clinical interview also provides a base for early and graphic presentation of clinical interview tasks. The description and measurement of clinical interview tasks is an organizing device throughout the training year and is best presented at the initiation of training.

A good way to close the second meeting is to solicit volunteers to present a clinical interview at the next training meeting and then have volunteers schedule interview presentations over the next several meetings. Every student should present at least once before any student presents a second time. This approach models shared training time and resources as well as responsible student engagement. It also works against any procrastination that a student responding to anxiety about the interview presentation might engage in and allows students some control in when they present. For the trainer, this approach allows him or her to evaluate the initial skills of each student in the beginning stage of the training and identify any problems trainees may have with taping interviews.

After each student has presented a tape of a clinical interview, the trainer should schedule individual meetings with trainees. In the individual meeting, trainer and trainee identify initial individualized training goals. These targeted outcomes should be consistent with and subsumed within the general goal categories. It is useful for the trainer to record the goals for each trainee so they can be referred to when future samples of the trainee's interviews are reviewed and so student progress can be tracked.

Each week, a different student presents a taped interview. Trainees and trainer rate the skills deployed in the presented interview using the Assessment Interview Skill Deployment Inventory (Rudolph et al., 1998). Using this inventory, and their own subjective observations, students and trainer provide feedback on trainee skills, client problems, and a variety of formulations concerning client difficulties and symptoms. This process fosters the professional spirit of inquiry and appreciation for multiple perspectives on clinical material. Trainees can also role play such interview skills as making process observations and using silence. This practice enhances trainees' capacity to "sit" with their anxiety and not leap to inappropriate interview interventions. Initially, the trainer may offer the most feedback, but as the training group matures, fellow trainees offer more—and more sophisticated—feedback. As each trainee presents, the trainer considers not only the general training goals, but also that trainee's individualized learning objectives, tailoring his or her feedback to focus on both.

In this manner, the training continues. Feedback, which may be positive or negative, is given using guidelines of helpful feedback and may focus on the presented interview as well as interactions in the training group. Trainees are

Table 1.6.   Phases of Training: Clinical Interviewing

Phase of Training	Major Activities of Phase
Phase I	Orient, initiate, and address anxiety over exposure
Phase II	Risk exposure, development of trust, development of working style (creation of initial training alliance)
Phase III	Working to learn skills, clarification of individual goals Practicing skills, experimenting with new behaviors
Phase IV	Revising and refinement of skills; development of trainee as Participant–Observer; deepening of interpersonal feedback
Phase V	Development of initial trainee professional identity Final evaluation of learning outcomes and identification of future training and professional goals Summarize learning and meanings; letting go

also encouraged to experiment with new interview behaviors. Role-plays are used to provide "safe" practice of these behaviors in the training context. Presentation of interviews with clients of diverse racial, cultural, ethnic, sexual orientation, gender, and religious backgrounds foster discussion of multicultural issues, as do readings. Ethical issues are likewise addressed as client and site circumstances dictate, and students are required to demonstrate communication of confidentiality and its limits and statement of their credentials on tape so these skills can be verified. As trainees achieve their individualized training goals, new ones are set and the training cycle continues. Table 1.6 depicts the typical developmental phases that occur when this model and format are used.

Training Phases: The Clinical Interview

The phases of training are not discrete, and trainees will move through them at different paces. Trainees with considerable interview experience and supervision may initially progress quickly, if their experience has been well supervised and was of good quality. In addition, phases II, III, and IV are particularly fluid, but the observant trainer will be able to discern movement through these phases in training groups. During the first four phases, the trainer is involved in formative evaluation processes. Under normal circumstances, summative evaluation occurs only in phase V. However, if by phase IV any trainee is not adequately progressing toward the learning objectives, he or she should be so advised and remedial steps should be instituted.

UNIQUE CONTENT OF THE TRAINING

Some unique aspects of the content of this training model are described next. Other theories of assessment and therapy would call for different kinds of content, as would assessments focused on specific issues, such as neurological functioning, child custody, and competency to stand trail. The following content is offered to stimulate thinking and debate and to flesh out the model offered here.

Clusters of Therapeutic Tasks: Diagnostic Interview Competencies

No single therapist task or technique is consistently linked with successful outcomes (Messer & Wampold, 2002). However, categories of tasks related to the therapeutic alliance involving collaboration and empathy have been identified by an APA taskforce (Norcross, 2001). Using these categories, this model proposes six competencies. A competency is defined as a set of logically related tasks performed smoothly and consistently that facilitate therapeutic work. They are:

1. Setting the stage and structuring the interview
2. Engaging the client in disclosure
3. Deepening exploration and emotional expression
4. Reflecting and naming
5. Clarifying and testing focus
6. The megacompetency: forging a therapeutic alliance

Phases of the Clinical Interview

Trainees are introduced to these competencies in the first two weeks of training using items of the Assessment Interview Skill Deployment Inventory and other first interview measures (Bogels et al., 1995). Students are also introduced to the idea that clinical and diagnostic interviews can be divided into three phases, or stages, called (1) orienting and initiating, (2) working to understand, and (3) clarifying, contracting, and closing. Use of the task clusters and clinical interview stages facilitates student learning by helping to break down into smaller, more manageable "chunks" the immense amount of skills and knowledge trainees are trying to assimilate, deploy, and eventually master. The device of dividing the clinical interview into stages is not unique (Sullivan, 1954; Benjamin, 1981; Craig, 1989). However, within this model, the concept of interview phases is used to help trainees focus on learning tasks and competencies in a sequential manner. At the beginning of training, trainees focus on tasks that usually occur in the orienting and initiating phase. These tasks typically fall into the first two competencies: setting the stage and structuring the interview, and engaging the client in disclosure. Within the working to understand phase, the deepening exploration and emotional expression competencies tend to predominate, and trainees develop these competencies next. Finally, in the clarifying, contracting, and closing phase, the competencies of reflection and naming and of clarifying and testing occur. Throughout training, tasks having

Table 1.7. Proposed Clinical Interview Competencies and Sample Tasks

Competency	Sample Tasks
1. Set stage and structure interview	Interviewer discusses purpose(s) of interview Interviewer communicates confidentiality and limits to it Interviewer provides "safe and ample" environment for client disclosure Interviewer tracks time passage, alerts patient to impending close of interview Interviewer summarizes interview and communicates next steps in process
2. Engage patient and facilitate disclosure of problems	Interviewer inquires into reason(s) client is seeking help Interviewer inquires into past problems Interviewer responds empathically to client disclosures Interviewer uses paraphrase to assure accurate understanding and convey careful attending Interviewer attempts a variety of approaches to engage the reticent client
3. Deepen exploration and emotional expression	Interviewer pursues important material and encourages the client to elaborate Interviewer inquires into patient feelings and thoughts about the interview Interviewer communicates an observation of client behavior and inquires into its meaning Interviewer asks about the client's feelings and state of mind Interviewer allows for timely silences
4. Reflection & Naming	Interviewer offers a tentative interpretation of client material Interviewer offers a process observation of client interview behavior and links it to patient difficulties Interviewer names a feeling implicit in client communication, but not made explicit by client Interviewer observes and communicates a pattern in client relationships and seeks client reaction
5. Clarify and test focus	Interviewer educates or advises client about a condition, treatment, process, or risk Interviewer inquires into what the client would like to see change or be different as a result of clinical services Interviewer paraphrases a client goal for subsequent work such that it is more clear, measurable, or motivating Interviewer suggests a symptom, pattern, or conflict as the focus of further clinical work and elicits client reactions Interviewer communicates the next steps in the helping process and solicits client reactions and questions
6. Megacompetency: Forge a therapeutic alliance	Interviewer responds empathically to patient fears, anxieties, and hesitancies Interviewer accurately paraphrases patient material Interviewer accurately acknowledges patient feelings and states Interviewer responds with sensitivity to cultural differences Interviewer invites patient to share reactions to the interview

to do with the megacompetency, forging a therapeutic alliance, are emphasized. In these discussions, issues of diversity, such as gender effects on the alliance, are noted in an effort to help students become more multiculturally and gender-sensitive interviewers (Brown, 1990). Table 1.7 lists the six clinical interview competencies and gives examples of tasks within each.

Principles of Assessment and Data Collection

This model emphasizes certain principles of collecting client information and assessing clients in clinical interviews. These principles are repeated throughout the training:

- Use multiple data sets when doing assessments.
- Use multiple measures; never rely on only one measure.
- Attend carefully and empathically to the client's "story"; it is a rich source of data.
- Generate working hypotheses and then collect data to support or refute them.
- Pursue the inquiry; do not assume you know what is meant.
- Provide structure in the interview, but be flexible to respond to client needs.
- Always communicate to the client about confidentiality and its limits.
- Make every reasonable effort to create an atmosphere of sanctuary for the client in the interview and in the therapeutic relationship.
- Collaborate with other providers of data if possible, and do so with client consent.
- Conduct yourself professionally with all clients under all circumstances.
- Always attend to issues of safety, for your client, for the community, and for yourself.
- Always reflect on your assessment and regularly review your interview work.

EVALUATING TRAINING OUTCOMES

Traditionally, training programs have relied on student course evaluations, which are limited in validity and scope, and on rather distal outcomes to evaluate their educational outcomes. For example, how many students graduated, what employment did they gain after graduate study, how did they fare on licensing exams? These are reasonable, if gross, group measures. However, they do not provide a more fine-grained measurement of what learning outcomes were achieved, and they certainly cannot offer information on individual student learning outcomes or areas where the trainer may want to revise his or her teaching.

Researchers have studied the process and outcomes of supervision as well. Lambert and Ogles (1997) provide a fine review of the effectiveness of psychotherapy supervision and problems in researching this area, and there are several good measures of individual supervision that trainers may employ. See the review by Vonk and Thyer, (1997), who evaluate the measures. Unfortunately, these measures do not transfer well to group supervision/training processes. To meet the need for a measure of group supervision, White and Rudolph (2000) developed the Group Supervisory Behavior Scale (GSBS). The GSBS appears to have high rates of internal reliability, good content validity as judged by over one hundred psychologists and psychologists in training, and sound criterion validity using student rankings of supervisor excellence. The GSBS contains six subscales: professional understanding, clear communication, encouragement of self-evaluation, efficiency, clarity of evaluation, and overall quality. Trainers wanting student feedback on these dimensions may want to consider the GSBS as one among other measures.

Still, the use of measurable learning objectives provides perhaps the most useful and straightforward method of evaluating our teaching. By setting clear goals in each of the areas of knowledge, skills, and attitudes or competencies, and by measuring them at the inception of training and then during and after training, the trainer can evaluate the student's progress over time and, by extension, teaching effectiveness. This system has the advantage of allowing for both formative and substantive evaluation and also distinguishing the strengths and weaknesses of individual students.

SUMMARY

Utilizing Bordin's concepts of goals, tasks, and bond, I have suggested training goals, training tasks, and a training bond for teaching diagnostic interviewing. I have proposed goals in the areas of skills, knowledge, and attitudes. Three categories of "skill goals" for students of the diagnostic interview were outlined. The student must develop assessment interview skills. The student must develop skills in conceptualizing client problems; symptoms, and interview behavior; and the student must develop collaboration skills. Collaboration skills should be manifest not only with clients in interviews, but also with fellow trainees and the trainer. Nine "knowledge sets" were suggested within the knowledge goal area. These knowledge sets range from learning and applying ethical codes and the DSM Multi-axial system to knowing how to refer to other resources to assist clients. Seven attitudes within the attitudinal goal area were specified. Attitudes are critical to proper and genuine enactment of the professional role. I believe clinical interviewers are most effective when they are open, compassionate, self-reflective, sensitive to diverse peoples and cultures, and disposed to seek consultation, think critically, and express a respectful spirit of inquiry. These qualities are not unlike those Peterson and Bry (1980) reported when they surveyed other training professionals.

I also suggested tasks that the trainer and the trainee perform within this model. These tasks convey the active and collaborative efforts needed of both parties. Effective training doesn't just happen because a more senior clinician meets regularly with a novice. It happens when both are invested in learning and perform complimentary tasks. Ten tasks are listed for the teacher and nine for the trainee in this model. Clarification and measurement of training objectives, honest communication, nondefensive response to specific and timely feedback, and self-evaluation and identification of areas for further growth are essential tasks.

Five phases of successful training were also suggested: orienting and addressing student anxiety, creating a training alliance, clarifying goals, practicing and refining skills, and development of the trainee's initial professional identity. Three phases of the assessment interview were identified, and these three phases—orienting, working to understand, and clarifying, contracting, and closing—were related to specific interview task clusters.

Lastly, noting recent research (Rudolph, 2004), I described six diagnostic or clinical interview competencies and noted some specific tasks that occur within each. The six proposed competencies evolved out of the criteria developed at the Illinois School of Professional Psychology-Chicago in the mid-'90s. Further study is needed to determine the utility and accuracy of the proposed competencies. However, delineation of competencies for the assessment interview should spawn theoretical debate and empirical study.

Teaching clinical and diagnostic interviewing is a challenging activity. It requires trainers to continuously expand our knowledge and refine our skills. It is a very demanding occupation, best performed with a supportive group of colleagues engaged in similar endeavors. For me, it has been one of the most rewarding experiences of my professional life. Over and over again, it has taught me the training principles inherent in this model. For the sake of clarity, I reiterate them here.

- Create an open, supportive climate; self disclose when it facilitates learning.
- Provide clear objectives and expectations and a flexible, safe structure in which to learn.
- Model the knowledge, skills, and attitudes you want trainees to learn.
- Model toleration of painful affects and the ability to be quiet.
- Model process observations; facilitate collaboration and helpful feedback.
- Facilitate a proactive approach to trainee learning.
- Recognize anxiety, normalize it, and don't exacerbate it unnecessarily.
- Collect multiple samples of trainee performance before summative evaluation.

- Recognize individual trainee strengths, weaknesses, and training needs.
- Consider the developmental level of the training group and individual trainees.
- Acknowledge that perfection is not possible, but model consistent effort to improve (live lifelong learning).

REFERENCES

American Counseling Association (1995). *American Counseling Association Code of Ethics and Standards of Practice.* Washington, DC: American Counseling Association.

American Psychological Association, Board of Educational Affairs. (2002). Working Group 3: Core knowledge in doctoral education & training in psychology. Washington, DC: American Psychological Association.

American Psychological Association, Office of Program Consultation and Accreditation, Education Directorate. (1998). Guidelines and principles for accreditation of programs in professional psychology. Washington, DC: American Psychological Association.

Baker, S. B., & Daniels, T. G. (1989). Integrating research on the microcounseling program: A meta-analysis. *Journal of Counseling Psychology* 32(2):213–222.

Benjamin, A. (1981). *The Helping Interview,* 3rd ed. Boston: Houghton Mifflin.

Bogels, S. M., Van der Vleuten, C. P., Blok, G., Kreutzkamp, R., & Schmidt, H. G. (1995). Assessment and validation of diagnostic interviewing skills for the mental health professions. *Journal of Psychopathology and Behavioral Assessment* 17:217–230.

Bootzin, R. R., & Ruggil, J. S. (1988). Training issues in behavior therapy. *Journal of Consulting and Clinical Psychology* 56(5):703–708.

Bordin, E. (1979). The generalizability of the psychoanalytic concept of the working alliance. *Psychotherapy: Theory, Research and Practice* 16:252–260.

Bourg, E. F., Bent, R. J., Callan, J. E., Jones, N. F., McHolland, J., & Stricker, G., eds. (1987). *Standards, and Evaluation in the Education and Training of Professional Psychologists: Knowledge, Attitudes and Skills.* Norman, OK: Transcript.

Brown, L. S. (1990). Taking account of gender in the clinical assessment interview. *Professional Psychology: Research and Practice* 21(1):12–17.

Carkhoff, R. R. (1969). *Helping and Human Relations: A Primer for Lay and Professional Helpers,* Vols. 1 & 2. New York: Holt, Rinehart & Winston.

Cormier, W. H., & Cormier, L. S. (1998). *Interviewing Strategies for Helpers: Fundamental Skills and Cognitive Behavioral Interventions,* 3rd ed. Monterey, CA: Brooks/Cole.

Costa, P. T., & McCrea, R. R. (1992). *Revised NEO Personality Inventory (NEO-PI-R) and NEO Five Factor Inventory (NEO-FFI)* professional manual. Odessa, FL: Psychological Assessment Inventory.

Coursey, R. D., Curtis, L., Marsh, D. T., Campbell, J., Harding, C., Spaniol, L. (2000). Competencies for direct service staff members who work with adults with severe mental illnesses: Specific knowledge, attitudes, skills, and bibliography. *Psychiatric Rehabilitation Journal* 23:378–392.

Craig, R., ed. (1989). *Clinical and Diagnostic Interviewing.* Northvale, NJ: Jason Aronson.

Edelstein, B. A., & Berler, E. S., eds. (1987). *Evaluation and Accountability in Clinical Training.* New York: Plenum.

Ericsson, K. A., Krampe, R. Th., & Tesch-Romer, C. (1993). The role of deliberate practice in the acquisition of expert performance. *Psychological Review* 100(3):363–406.

Freedheim, D. K., & Overholser, J .C. (1998). Training in psychotherapy during graduate school. *Psychotherapy in Private Practice* 17:3–18.

Furnham, A. (2001). Vocational preferences and P-O fit: Reflections on Holland's theory of vocational choice. *Applied Psychology: An International Review* 50(1):5–29.

Garb, H. (1989). Clinical judgment, clinical training, and professional experience. *Psychological Bulletin* 105(3):387–396.

Greenhalgh, T., & Macfarlane, F. (1997). Towards a competency grid for evidence-based practice. *Journal of Evaluation in Clinical Practice* 3:161–165.

Hansen, N. B., Pepitone-Arreola-Rockwell, F., & Greene, A. F. (2000). Multicultural competence: Criteria and case examples. *Professional Psychology: Research and Practice* 31:652–660.

Hill, C. (1986). An overview of the Hill counselor & client verbal response modes category systems. In *The Psychotherapeutic Process: A Research Handbook*, eds. L. S. Greenberg & W. M. Pinsoff, pp. 131–160. New York: Guilford.

Holland, J. (1996). Exploring careers with a typology: What we have learned and some new directions. *American Psychologist* 51(4):397–406.

Ivy, A. (1971). *Micro-counseling: Innovations in Interview Training*. Springfield, IL: Thomas.

Klerman, G. L., Weissman, M. M., Rounsaville, B. J., & Chevron, E. S. (1984). *Interpersonal Psychotherapy of Depression*. New York: Basic Books.

Kluger, A., & DeNisi, A. (1996). The effects of feedback interventions on performance: A historical review, a meta-analysis and a preliminary feedback intervention theory. *Psychological Bulletin* 119(2):254–284.

Lambert, M. J., & Ogles, B. M. (1997). The effectiveness of psychotherapy supervision. In *Handbook of Psychotherapy Supervision*, ed. C. Watkins, pp. 421–446. New York: Wiley & Sons.

Messer, S. B., & Wampold, B. E. (2002). Let's face facts: Common factors are more potent than specific therapy ingredients. *Clinical Psychology: Science and Practice* 9(1):21–25.

Norcross, J. C. (2001). Purposes, processes and products of the task force on empirically supported therapy relationships. *Psychotherapy: Theory, Research, Practice, Training* 38(4):345–356.

Peterson, D. R., & Bry, B. H. (1980). Dimensions of perceived competence in professional psychology. *Professional Psychology: Research and Practice* 11:965–971.

Rogers, C. R. (1957). The necessary and sufficient conditions of therapeutic personality change. *Journal of Consulting Psychology* 21:95–103.

Rokeach, M. (1979). *Understanding Human Values: Individual and Societal*. New York: Free Press.

Rosenberg, J. L. (1999). Suicide prevention. An integrated training model using affective and action-based interventions. *Professional Psychology: Research and Practice* 30(1):83–87.

Rudolph, B. (2004). Therapist tasks in the first interview of brief psychodynamic psychotherapy. In *Core Concepts in Brief Psychodynamic Psychotherapy*, ed. D. P. Charmin. New York: Erlbaum.

Rudolph, B., Craig, R., Leifer, M., & Rubin, N. (1998). Evaluating competency in the diagnostic interview among graduate psychology students: Development of generic measures. *Professional Psychology: Research and Practice* 29(5):488–491.

Rudolph, B., Datz-Weems, H., Cusack, A., Beerup, C., & Kiel, S. (1993). Assessment interview processes: A successful and a failed brief psychotherapy. *Psychotherapy in Private Practice* 12(2):17–36.

Rychen, D. S., & Salganik, L. H., eds. (2001). *Defining and Selecting Key Competencies.* Seattle: Hogrefe & Huber.

Smelson, D., Kordon, M., & Rudolph, B. (1998). Evaluating the assessment interview: Obstacles and future directions. *Journal of Clinical Psychology* 53(5):497–505.

Sommers-Flanagan, R., & Sommers-Flanagan, J. (1999). *Clinical Interviewing,* 2nd ed. New York: Wiley & Sons.

Spitzer, R. L., & Williams, J. B.(1986). *Structured Clinical Interview for DSM-III.* New York: New York State Psychiatric Institute, Biometrics Research Department.

Strupp, H., & Binder, J. (1984). *Psychotherapy in a New Key: A Guide to Time-Limited Dynamic Psychotherapy.* New York: Basic.

Sullivan, H. S. (1954). *The Psychiatric Interview.* New York: Norton.

Vonk, M. E., & Thyer, B. A. (1997). Evaluating the quality of supervision: A review of instruments for use in field instruction. *Clinical Supervisor* 15:103–113.

White, J. H., & Rudolph, B. A. (2000). A pilot investigation of the reliability and validity of the Group Supervisory Behavior Scale (GSBS). *Clinical Supervisor* 19(2):161–171.

2

THE CLINICAL PROCESS
OF INTERVIEWING

Robert J. Craig, Ph.D., ABPP

The clinical interview is endemic to all mental health disciplines, yet it received surprisingly little attention in the literature prior to the introduction of DSM-III (American Psychiatric Association, 1980). Most classic psychiatry and psychology texts include a chapter on the topic (Stevenson, 1959; Strauss, 1995; Wiens & Tindall, 1995); research has been conducted and summarized on the anatomy of a clinical interview (Matarazzo, 1965; 1978; Wiens & Matarazzo, 1983); and more recently, literature has appeared on interviewing, but the latter has been tied rather specifically to the DSM (Endicott & Spitzer, 1978; Hersen & Turner, 1985; Othmer & Othmer, 1994). For example, recent citations on clinical interviews have averaged about sixty-three journal articles per year (Craig, 2003), but the overwhelming amount of these citations pertain to published interviews designed to assess DSM disorders. Here we try to discuss a more generic type of clinical interview. The purpose of this chapter is to provide a basic introduction to the clinical process of interviewing. Topics include the ways in which patients and clinicians approach an interview, techniques, phases, and a discussion of the last minutes of an initial interview.

SOCIAL VERSUS CLINICAL INTERACTIONS

A clinical interview has much in common with social interactions and contains elements of group and dyadic dynamics; however, there are fundamental differences between a clinical interview and other types of relationships. In a clinical interview, most rules of social etiquette do not apply. The conversation is focused on the patient and is often unidirectional. The relationship is primarily professional, and it is intimate only to the extent that personal material is conveyed with the expectation that such material is protected ethically and legally from evidentiary discovery (i.e., confidential). There are limits on time, place, and frequency of interaction imposed by both parties. The clinician's statements have a larger purpose than mere mutual dialogue, and the specific goals and expected outcomes are established as a result of the clinical interaction (Kanfer & Scheft, 1988).

METHODS OF OBTAINING INFORMATION

Most of the information contained in a clinical interview is based on patient self-report, combined with the interviewer's clinical observation. This is not to discount other sources of information, such as collateral reports from significant others, case records, psychological testing, or supplemental structured interviews. However, we will focus in this book on the direct interview of the individual patient because it is both the most common and the most clinically rich source of information.

STRUCTURED VERSUS UNSTRUCTURED INTERVIEWS

Interviews can be either structured or unstructured. Structured interviews prescribe a set of questions over defined content areas. Unstructured interviews are the more common types in clinical settings, while structured interviews are more common in research settings, especially to establish diagnoses on Axis I or Axis II. Unstructured interviews usually lack a rigid format, but they are not without structure. The clinical interview follows a sequence: one that will be described later in this chapter.

THE PHYSICAL SETTING

The physical setting of a clinical interview and its effect on the interviewing process is a subject that is often neglected in training, yet the *physical surround* is an important element in any clinical interview. The ideal physical setting is comfortable for both patient and clinician. The interviewing office should be attractively furnished, should be maintained at a comfortable temperature, and should contain all the elements required to properly conduct the interview (such as pen, pencil, notepad, or tape recorder).

The therapist should *schedule enough time* to devote full attention to the patient and to complete the interview in one sitting, if possible. *Interruptions are to be avoided.* Telephone calls should be transferred, cell phones should be on "silent" mode, a "do not disturb" sign should be placed on the door, or colleagues should otherwise be instructed not to interrupt you during the interview. If the therapist cannot ensure that the interview will not be interrupted, then the patient should be informed in advance that interruption is likely; but it should be kept to a minimum. *Privacy and confidentiality* should be maintained. This is sometimes difficult, such as when an interview must be conducted at a patient's bedside or in a prison cell, but every effort must be made to respect the patient's privacy.

Good interviewing requires that the clinician put the client at ease, get the required information for the task at hand, maintain control of the interview as well as rapport, and accomplish the purpose of the interview by the time the interview is completed. Therapists can put clients at ease by attending to privacy and confidentiality issues, reducing anxiety, avoiding interruptions, showing respect, and arranging seating configurations that promote observation and interaction. Getting the necessary information can be best accomplished by asking open-ended questions, avoiding unnecessary interruptions, demonstrating to the patient that you understand the problem, and clarifying any inconsistencies. Controlling the interview does not necessarily mean that a completely directive interview is given to the patient, but that the therapist has a purpose in mind for the interview and engages in behaviors that accomplish this purpose. Thus the therapist does not dominate the interview but guides it along a desired path. Rapport can be strengthened by showing nonjudgmental behavior, acting empathically, using language appropriate to the client, addressing salient client issues, and communicating a sense that the client's problems are understood and can be helped.

KINDS OF INTERVIEWS

There are many different kinds of interviews, differing in purpose, focus, and duration. Below, we present several types of interviews that have been discussed in the literature. They are not necessarily mutually exclusive, and several of the formats listed can be utilized within a single interview. However, there are settings and circumstances where one of these types of interviews is conducted separately or to the exclusion of the others. The list is somewhat arbitrary, but it affords the reader with a reasonable array of the kinds of interviews available for clinical use.

Diagnostic Interview

In diagnostic interviews, the clinician's primary task is to categorize the behavior of the client into some formal diagnostic system. In mental health, there are two official diagnostic classification systems in widespread use. The first is the official classification system of the World Health Organization— *International Classification of Disease*, 10th edition (WHO, 1992). The second is the *Diagnostic and Statistical Manual of Mental Disorders* (DSM), revised (American Psychiatric Association, 1980; 1987; 1994).

Forensic Interview

Forensic interviews are not just clinical interviews in a forensic setting. They differ from routine clinical interviews in a number of ways: (1) there is a legal purpose to the interview, which may include evaluations for competency to stand trial, custody evaluations, dangerousness, termination of parental rights, and evaluations of various insanity pleas, just to name a few; (2) these interviews are far more investigative, longer in duration, and tend to occur over multiple sessions; (3) often the person being interviewed is not the client at all, but the court, or perhaps private attorneys who retain these services on behalf of their clients; (4) privacy and confidentiality that is *sui generis* in clinical interviews is not applicable in forensic interviews. Forensic evaluations do not carry with them the same protection of privacy and confidentiality of material obtained in the evaluation that most other mental health interviews do.

Intake Interview

The purpose of the intake interview is to obtain preliminary information about a prospective patient. This type of interview usually occurs in agencies whose purposes may include the determination of the patient's eligibility in terms of the agency's mission. Other purposes of intake interviews are (1) to obtain sufficient information to present the case at a clinical conference, (2) to clarify the nature of the services that the agency provides or the nature of treatment that the patient will receive, (3) to communicate agency rules, regulations, and policies to a prospective patient, (4) to determine the type of treatment that would most benefit the patient (Woody & Sanderson, 1998) and the type of therapist that would be best for the patient, (5) to obtain general information for record-keeping purposes, and (6) to determine whether or not referral to a more appropriate resource is necessary.

Case History Interview

The case history is part of most clinical interviews. When more elaborate and detailed sequencing of this history is needed, an interview is conducted for the sole purpose of reviewing the nature of the patient's conflicts in historical sequence, with a focus on critical periods, antecedents, and precipitants. Case history interviews can be one of the richest sources of information about a patient. Case histories can also be obtained from the patient's family or friends. See Craig (2003) for a more detailed presentation of the nature of material and domains of inquiry in this type of interview.

Mental Status Exam

A mental status exam is conducted to determine the degree of mental impairment associated with the clinical condition under investigation. Among the content areas assessed are reasoning, thinking, judgment, memory, concentration, speech, hearing, and perception. This type of information is most often required when the symptoms suggest a major psychiatric disorder, neurological involvement, or substance abuse. Craig (2003) has provided a convenient outline that highlights the main content areas for a mental status exam, in worksheet format. These exams can be conducted formally, by systematically assessing the content domains of the mental status, or more commonly, by talking to the patient about other areas of the patient's life and thereby acquiring information pertinent to the content of the mental status interview.

Motivational Interviews

We can make a distinction between therapeutic versus assessment interviews. The former include generic activities within a session basically to obtain information leading to a diagnosis or clinical care decisions. The latter include a set of diverse activities designed to motivate a patient either to enter treatment or to advance some aspect of the treatment plan. Miller's *motivational interviewing* (1991) is the most prominently used example of therapeutic interviewing. Although it was developed with patients with addictive disorders, its principles can be applied to a number of assessment situations requiring behavior change.

Here, motivation is considered a dynamic concept and not a personality trait. The behavior of the clinician determines whether change in the patient will occur. The approach requires the clinician to give *feedback*, emphasize that clients take *responsibility* for change, give clients *advice* and a *menu* of treatment choices and strategies, be *emphatic*, and promote *self-efficacy*. The acronym FRAMES is used here as a mnemonic device. The clinician also has to avoid arguments, continually support self-efficacy, emphasize personal choice, point out discrepancies in behavior, reframe, roll with resistance, and use reflective listening.

Pre- and Posttesting Interviews

Psychological tests are often a part of a clinical workup. However, it is a basic misunderstanding of the nature of clinical tests to assume that a clinical report is based solely on test results. Administering a test or reporting the results is a psychometric assessment but not a clinical assessment. In fact, such a procedure is likely to miss important aspects of a patient's behavior. Modern psychological evaluations include reviews of a patient's record, consultation with relevant staff or patient family members, and a clinical interview with the patient. Some psychologists prefer to interview the patient prior to testing in order to explain the reasons for testing and its benefits to the client, and to cover certain administrative arrangements, such as time and place of testing and payment of fees. When the interview is conducted after the completion of testing, the psychologist has usually developed certain hypotheses as a result of testing and wishes to explore these ideas further with the patient to either confirm these ideas or to see if the patient has any insight with respect to the information provided.

Brief Screening Interview

The brief screening interview is distinguished by a time-limited, focused format. The clinician is interested only in a specific area and is willing to forgo other elements of the interview in order to screen for the desired information in a brief time period. This type of interview is conducted for the following purposes, among others: (1) to assess immediate suicidal risk in a depressed patient who is presenting in crisis, (2) to determine whether a patient needs to be involuntarily committed to a psychiatric hospital, (3) to determine whether medical referral is needed, (4) to determine whether a patient can be managed in an outpatient setting, (5) to determine dangerousness to others, and (6) to determine fitness to stand trial. The brief screening interview is followed by referral, and the patient is likely to participate in a more traditional clinical interview at a later date.

Discharge Interview

Some therapists conduct formal discharge interviews with patients who are about to leave an inpatient or outpatient program. The purpose of this type of interview is to learn from the patient's perspective what she or he has gained from treatment, to review aftercare plans, or to work through any unresolved problems the patient may have prior to termination or discharge.

Research Interview

As clinical research becomes increasingly valued, the research interview will be used more and more frequently in clinical settings. This kind of interview is specific to the nature of the research being conducted. It is usually part of a rigid protocol that has been approved by an institutional review committee. Such an interview is conducted with the patient's permission, which she or he grants by signing a document attesting to informed consent.

THE PATIENT'S APPROACH TO THE INTERVIEW

A clinical interview will be influenced by the patient's immediate reason for seeking the interview, which in turn depends on whether or not the patient has voluntarily sought help or has been referred by a third party. A voluntary patient presumably has noticed a problem, has made failed attempts at resolution, perhaps by discussing the problem with friends or using other self-help approaches, and then has sought professional direction. Most voluntary patients come with an expectation that their problem will be ameliorated through this professional assistance. Thus it is usually easier to elicit information and to establish a therapeutic alliance when the patient is self-referred. When a patient has been referred by a third party, the level of resistance generally tends to be higher. This makes it more difficult, but not impossible, to form a working alliance. It is the therapist's task to attempt to work through this resistance and at the same time conduct the interview so that the clinical task is accomplished despite this resistance. Motivational interviewing techniques (Miller, 1991) can be quite instrumental in this regard.

Whether the patient is self-or-other-referred, the patient's *purpose or motive* for coming to the session will also influence the clinical process. Even when a patient appears to be self-referred, there may be hidden agendas that serve to compromise the purity of the clinical interview. For example, a man who has committed incest may ask for treatment, but his true motive may be to present a remorseful facade to a judge at an upcoming court hearing. A woman may come to an interview ostensibly seeking relief from anxiety and depression resulting from back pain following an injury at work, but her true purpose may be to improve her chances of receiving workers' compensation by demonstrating the intractability of her condition and the psychological suffering it has caused. She may even have been sent there on instructions of her attorney, with no real intention at working toward improvement. A drug abuser may seek inpatient treatment to hide from people to whom he owes money. A chronic schizophrenic may seek hospitalization, reporting hallucinations, delusions, and suicidal ideation, merely to get off the street and be housed and fed. I once conducted an interview with a patient who complained of marital dissatisfaction. As the interview ended, the patient asked me if I thought she was crazy. When pressed for the reason for this question, she said her husband had told her she was crazy, so she wanted a letter from a professional attesting to the fact that she was sane. This was her real purpose for scheduling the interview. Thus it is the therapist's responsibility to determine the person's genuine purpose for seeking professional assistance, since this will affect not only the interview in progress but also future attempts at intervention.

The *patient's expectations* will also affect the interview. One family came to a therapist's office complaining about their daughter's behavior and demanding that the therapist give her an injection to make her behave. The family expected that medicine would be given and that obedience would be the result. All patients come to an interview with certain expectations about the role behaviors of the therapist, the interview process, and the potential outcome. It is a good idea early in the initial interview to clarify any misunderstanding about the nature and purpose of the session. Simply asking the patient "What do you think we are going to do here? or "Have you been told the reason for this interview?"

or "What do you want to be the outcome of your treatment?" are good ways to begin such clarification.

The patient's *perception of the therapist* can also affect the direction of the interview process, the information that is revealed in the session, and the therapist's response to the patient. The relationship between patient and therapist can be construed as one of parent to child, teacher to pupil, judge to accused, or lover to love object. These perceptions may be transferences, or they may be veridical assessments of the therapist's behavior. The patient's view of the therapist can affect the entire process. There is no easy way to assess such perceptions in the initial interview. They often remain unsaid, and they may even be outside the patient's awareness. However, it is important for the therapist to realize that such perceptions and misperceptions exist and affect the dynamic interaction between patient and therapist during the interview process.

In summary, voluntary or involuntary status of the patient, the purpose of the interview (manifest and latent), the patient's expectations, and the patient's perceptions of the therapist are salient factors that affect the patient's approach to an interview.

THE THERAPIST'S APPROACH TO THE INTERVIEW

Just as patients come to an interview with their own set of predispositions, so too do therapists. The first factor that influences a therapist's approach to an interview is *philosophical orientation*. Rarely does a therapist enter an interview as a blank slate. Therapists have theoretical frameworks that dictate the areas of inquiry, the method of inquiry, their assessments and evaluations, their goals, and how they understand the elicited information. An interview from a family systems perspective is quite different from an interview with a behavioral orientation. A therapist whose philosophy is psychodynamic and a therapist whose orientation is humanistic and nondirective are likely to offer different assessments of a clinical situation. (The nature of these differences is more fully explicated in section II of this book.)

Personal values and beliefs are a second factor that determines a therapist's approach to an interview. The therapist will select from the patient's material what is most important. This selection is formed in part by the therapist's orientation and also by one's values and beliefs as they relate to the content of inquiry. Research has repeatedly shown that patients improve in psychotherapy to the extent that they come to share or adopt the values and beliefs of their therapists. While one therapist may place a high value on expression of feelings, another may value a commitment to introspection or a willingness to look for antecedents and consequences of behavior. These areas will thus be given more attention by the therapist because they are believed to be more important.

A therapist eventually attempts to *understand the patient and the problem* in a way that is consistent with one's theoretical orientation. Thus most therapists make a diagnosis, but the frame of this assessment differs among the major theoretical philosophies. One therapist may describe the problem as "pre-oedipal," while to another the problem may be "faulty communication within a dysfunctional dyad designed to maintain a dominant–submissive relationship pattern," or "inadequate reinforcement when the patient tries to be assertive," or a "bipolar affective disorder." Similarly, the patient may be construed as narcissistic, as overadaptive, or as needing unconditional positive regard. By the end of every clinical interview, the therapist has made some evaluation or assessment of both the problem and the patient. On the basis of this assessment, goals are set and treatment methods are determined (Perry et al., 1987).

To summarize, the therapist approaches the interview with a philosophical orientation and a set of personal values and beliefs and then attempts to understand the patient and the problem. Goal setting and treatment planning, variously labeled as assessment, evaluation, or diagnosis, are then based on that understanding.

INTERVIEW TECHNIQUES

Therapists have an array of techniques that they use in an interview. Irrespective of theoretical orientation, all therapists use some of these approaches. Their philosophical orientation often dictates which ones they will use the most and the degree of emphasis they place on any one technique, but these techniques form the basis of the interview process. No single technique should be used to the exclusion of others. Rather, they are used in combination to form a dynamic interview. These techniques include direct questioning, reflection, restating (paraphrasing), confrontation, self-disclosure, silence, explanation, reframing (cognitive restructuring), interpretation, and humor.

Clarification

Clarification is usually done by using one of the other techniques (questioning, paraphrasing), but the purpose is to provide understanding of the client in the interview. This technique rarely evokes defensiveness in the patient because most patients want the therapist to understand their problems from their perspective. By seeking clarification, the therapist gives the patient an additional opportunity to tell her or his story so that it is fully understood.

Example
Patient: My mother is out most of the night, leaving me alone. She comes home at all hours. Sometimes she doesn't come home at all.
Therapist: What is your mother doing when she is out like this?

Confrontation

Confrontation is a technique whereby the therapist points out discrepancies between what is observed and what is stated. It is sometimes used when a patient says something different from what the therapist is experiencing or knows to be true or false, or when the patient's statements are inconsistent with their usual behavior. Confrontation is most often employed with substance abusers and other patients with character disorders to break through their denial and their rigid defenses. It usually has the effect of increasing anxiety and precipitating avoidance and denial that it was meant to address. *Confrontation* has evolved into a pejorative term because of the negative reports that have emanated from therapeutic communities, where the technique was used to the near exclusion of other approaches. While the technique has benefited many patients in such settings, others merely erect a defensive barrier so that the approach never reaches them. This is referred to as psychological reactance (Miller, 1991).

Confrontation can be constructive or destructive. It is most beneficial when it is based on factual content, devoid of hostile reference or affect, or focused on material that the patient should be addressing but isn't because of conscious or unconscious avoidance. Inexperienced therapists often have difficulty using confrontation because of their own insecurities, because of their (incorrect) concerns about being too intrusive, and because of their lack of skill in managing the patient's response if the technique is mishandled.

Example
Patient: I only drink a couple of times a day.
Therapist: Let's be honest! You drink every morning and every night after work! Face it! You're dependent on alcohol!

Exploration

Exploration is a technique whereby the therapist covers areas in a patient's life that require more in-depth review. It may also be used in a "testing-the-limits" approach, whereby the therapist tries to determine how much insight a patient has or how much pressure it takes before a patient experiences a given feeling. Most patients expect to be questioned about certain areas and activities and might wonder (usually to themselves) why these areas were not considered in the interview. Therapists should not be afraid to explore certain areas, even if they might be viewed as sensitive.

Example
Patient: My father used to beat me when I was a kid.
Therapist: How often did he beat you? How did he do it? Was he drunk at the time?

Questioning

This is the technique most often used in the initial clinical interview. The patient is asked direct questions in areas determined by the therapist. Questioning may be either *direct* or *open-ended*. A direct question may begin with words such as *how, what, where, when,* and *why,* but it invites a closed response when it is framed to elicit a yes-no response. Questions that are closed (for example, How old are you?) evoke a brief answer from the respondent, who then merely waits for the interviewer to ask another question. Too many closed questions become regressive. It is more desirable to ask open-ended questions (such as How does your spouse's behavior make you feel?). While neophyte therapists predominantly use the technique of direct questioning, it takes a skilled therapist to receive the maximum return from the question asked while still maintaining free-flowing communication.

Example
Patient: As a kid I was always in trouble.
Therapist: (closed-ended) How many times have you been arrested? (open-ended) What kind of trouble were you in?

Reflection

This technique requires the interviewer to skillfully restate the patient's cognitive or emotional material so as to demonstrate to the patient that feelings or statements have been heard and understood. Therapists who subscribe to the client-centered/Rogerian approach tend to rely heavily on reflection as a therapeutic tool and have made seminal clinical and research contributions toward our understanding of its usefulness and effectiveness. Once again, clinical skill is required if this technique is to be effective. The overuse of reflection in an initial interview is counterproductive because important areas are left unaddressed.

Example
Patient: I just can't seem to get anywhere in life.
Therapist: Your lack of progress is frustrating.

Reframing (Cognitive Restructuring)

This technique has either the patient or the therapist restate their beliefs, attitudes, or feelings in a manner more closely tied to reality. It provides a fresh perspective on a situation and serves to undercut negative self-statements and irrational thoughts that often accompany maladaptive behavior. It can promote new ways of thinking and new insights that can lead to behavior change. While a powerful technique, it does require practice and skill development before it will produce a full impact.

Example
Patient: I realize now he'll never change. I have to accept that.
Therapist: How can you take advantage of the situation so that it can bene-
fit you?

Restatement (Paraphrasing)

Restatement simply rephrases what a patient has said in a clearer or more articulate manner. This technique is also known as "paraphrasing," and it lets the patient know that the therapist is paying attention. It differs from reflection in purpose. Restatement is most often used to facilitate understanding or for clarification, while reflection is used as a therapeutic intervention.

Example
Patient: Thoughts are racing in my mind. I just can't concentrate. I'm so con-
fused.
Therapist: These strange things in your head are disturbing to you.

Self-Disclosure

In using self-disclosure, the therapist conveys personal experiences or feelings to the patient. Self-disclosure is intended to facilitate increments of patient self-disclosure within the interview to benefit the patient. Research has shown that self-disclosure by the therapist facilitates self-disclosure by the patient (Cozby, 1973). This technique should be used only sparingly, however, or it may set up a false expectation in the patient. The therapist must be judicious in determining what information will be disclosed and its probable effect on the patient.

Example
Patient: People don't understand what it's like not to be able to learn. I can't
get good grades in school. I'm stupid.
Therapist: When I was in school, I was dyslexic, too. But you can still do well
in life despite this problem. You're not stupid. You have special needs.

Silence

Neophyte therapists see silence as a dreadful experience, a product of their own inadequacies as interviewers. When silence occurs because of the interviewer's failure to lead the session along a predetermined course, these feelings are valid. However, silence can be an interviewing technique as well as a therapeutic tool. Silence provides the patient with an opportunity to process and understand what has been said, and it can thus appropriately move the interview in a positive direction. Silence must be timed appropriately and in such a way that the patient understands that the therapist is using silence for a reason. The reason is usually to promote introspection or to allow the patient to reassimilate emotions after release.

Example
Patient: I get so angry that I feel like kicking him where it hurts!
Therapist: (no response)

Interpretation

Here the therapist provides information in such a manner that behavior is explored and its motivation is understood by the patient. It derives historically from the psychoanalytic method, which is aimed at "making the unconscious conscious." It is the most difficult of all techniques to grasp because its use necessitates a comprehensive mastery of theory of personality and motivation, followed by supervised experience. Most therapists, regardless of persuasion (client-centered therapists may be an exception), use interpretation in one form or another. Some rely on it more exclusively than others. Therapists in training should use this technique with great care and only when they are certain that the formulation fits the facts and after consultation with their supervisor. Some patients merely accept clinician pronouncements, believing in the expertise, knowledge, and authority of the therapist. Therefore, we must be judicious and careful when offering interpretations.

Example
Patient: I got so mad at my father that I flushed his tranquilizers down the toilet.
Therapist: You play a role toward your mother that you feel your father should play. You want your father to stand up to your mother—that's why you did that. If he were more assertive, then maybe you wouldn't have to behave so aggressively toward her.

Humor

We are only beginning to understand the role of humor in clinical evaluations. Freud considered humor the highest form of defense but proffered no role for it in therapeutic work, other than to analyze it. However, humor can reduce anxiety, facilitate therapeutic movement, and enhance the interview. As with any technique, overreliance on its use will convey to the patient that the therapist is not taking the interview seriously. This is inappropriate and unprofessional. Timing is critical in the use of this technique. Humor should be delivered with the ultimate purpose of benefiting the patient.

Example
Patient: I was walking down the street and a neighbor yelled "Papa G—get over here!"
Therapist: What?
Patient: They call me "Papa G" in the neighborhood.
Therapist: Well, at least they don't call you Mother F.

THE THERAPIST'S INTERPERSONAL QUALITIES

Therapists bring with them more than a theoretical orientation, a set of personal values and beliefs, and a history of training that establishes a level of competence that continues to be enhanced by subsequence experience. They also bring to the interview a set of personal characteristics that some have argued are more important than any theoretical method or technique. These include the following:

- Empathy: the ability to understand the patient from the patient's perspective
- Genuineness: the freedom to be oneself; a lack of phoniness
- Warmth: the quality of being open, responsive, and positive toward a patient
- Respect: the ability to convey to patients that they have the power to change and to participate in that process
- Positive Regard: the ability to accept patients despite their negative behavior, attitudes, or demeanor

INTERVIEW PHASES

A good initial clinical interview develops in phase progression along predictable stages *that are controlled by the therapist.* Various authors have attempted to label these phases, but Harry Stack Sullivan (1954), the great interpersonal psychiatrist, was among the first to conceptualize the clinical interview as phase sequenced. He characterized these stages as the formal inception, the reconnaissance, the detailed inquiry, and termination. According to Sullivan, by the end of the *formal inception*, the therapist knows why the patient has come to the interview. The *reconnaissance*, the second stage, is the period in the interview during which the therapist obtains a brief sketch of the patient. Sullivan believed that this should take about twenty minutes. At the end of this stage, Sullivan recommended that the therapist tell the patient what he or she believes to be the nature of the problem. It is not presumed that the initial problem identified is the major problem in the patient's life; this may actually emerge much later, in subsequent sessions. According to Sullivan, however, identification of a problem gives both patient and therapist a direct path to follow and something concrete to work on. The *detailed inquiry* is the third stage, and it is the point in the interview when the initial impressions gained during the second stage are developed more thoroughly. Section III of this book contains many ideas, when interviewing specific psychopathologies, that normally occur within this stage of the initial interview process. The *termination* phase follows, during which the therapist makes a final statement summarizing what has been learned in the interview, giving the patient a behavioral prescription, making a final assessment (prognosis), and initiating formal leave-taking (miscellaneous business arrangements, such as appointments, fees, and policies, also tend to occur in this phase).

Benjamin (1969), operating from a psychosocial perspective, divided the interview into three main states, defined by the *initiation* or statement of the problem, followed by *development*, wherein both patient and therapist agree on the nature of the problem, and then by *closing*.

Kanfer and Scheft (1988), writing from a behavioral epistemology, subdivided the interview into *role structuring, creating a therapeutic alliance, developing a commitment for change, analyzing behavior, negotiating treatment objects, and planning or implementing*.

From a patient-centered perspective, the great psychologist Carl Rogers (1942) described the characteristic steps in a clinical interview as follows: the patient *comes for help*, the *situation is defined*, and through acceptance, clarification, and the expression of positive feelings, there is *development of insight*.

While most distinguished therapists from a variety of disciplines have attempted to capture the phases of the clinical interview, each has done so from a unique theoretical framework. Each then frames the analysis of the problem according to the assumptions and theorems provided by this philosophical orientation.

Irrespective of these philosophical differences, there are stages in an interview that most therapists would agree are the major points in the process. First, there is the *introduction*, which roughly corresponds to Sullivan's formal inception. The primary task of this phase is to understand the patient's reason for seeking the interview. The development of rapport and the establishment of trust begin in this stage.

Second, there is an *exploration* phase, corresponding to Sullivan's reconnaissance and detailed inquiry stages. Here, the therapist forms an initial hypothesis that is consistent with her or his theoretical orientation and that accounts for the presenting problem and explains the psychological adaptation to the precipitating stress in the light of historical and developmental issues. This could be described as "fixations," as "an unbalanced family hierarchy," or as "negative reinforcements." The crucial step is to form a hypothesis for the main facts in the case.

The third stage represents *hypothesis testing*. After the hypothesis has been formulated, the therapist develops a series of further inquiries to test the hypothesis within the interview by delving into other areas or situations in the patient's life. If the initial hypothesis is accurate, the material elicited should be consistent with and should elaborate upon the central hypothesis. The second and third stages are the most difficult for novice therapists, due to their lack of experience both with the process and with the breadth of qualitative analysis required.

During the fourth stage, *feedback* is offered. Here, the therapist tells the patient the conclusions drawn after talking with the patient. This stage, which corresponds to Sullivan's termination phase, is too often ignored even by seasoned therapists, who after asking a series of questions in the interview, leave the session without ever telling the patient anything. Note that this usually does not occur in medical interviews. There, a patient presents complaints or symptoms to the physician, who then tells the patient what is wrong (diagnosis). Perhaps more tests are needed to rule out several competing etiologies, but the patient usually leaves the physician's office with some idea about the direction that the physician is taking to address the problem. All too often, a mental health interview does not include this important step. Many patients no doubt fail to return for subsequent sessions (Baekeland & Lundwall, 1975) because they do not believe that the therapist understands them or their problem, or both; thus the patient believes that the therapist cannot be of help. The therapist simply telling the patient, in language that the patient can understand, what he or she thinks is causing the difficulties easily solves this problem. This will allow the therapist to determine the probable accuracy of the assessment and the level of the patient's resistance.

The final phase is *termination*. The task in this stage is to develop a treatment plan that is geared toward the attainment of mutually agreeable goals.

DYNAMIC INTERACTION

An interview is a dynamic interaction between patient and therapist. The nature of this interaction has been stressed by adherents of some orientations (such as psychoanalysis) and minimized by others (including nondirective and behavioral therapists), yet transferential processes must be attended to before the therapist can decide whether or not they should be addressed. Even Rogerian therapists admit that transference occurs; they just don't believe it is important to address it. Behaviorists agree that the relationship between patient and therapist is important in order to facilitate the implementation of behavioral strategies. Thus all schools recognize that there are processes occurring between patient and therapist that must be considered and that may become a focal point in the process.

THE LAST FIVE MINUTES

We noted that *termination* is the last stage of a clinical interview. I want to attend to that last few minutes of the interview here in greater detail.

In listening to interview tapes made by therapists in training, I have been horrified at the way some close their interviews. They too often end abruptly, without closure and without consideration of the important clinical information that can be obtained in the last few minutes. Just as a surgeon, after completing an operation, spends the last few minutes suturing the wound, so too must a clinical interviewer spend the last few minutes of a session ensuring there is closure by paying attention to important processes that may occur here, while simultaneously engaging in the final tasks that will complete the interview.

There are certain tasks that should be accomplished at this stage of the interview. By this time, the analysis has been made, goals should have been established, and a treatment plan should have been considered upon which the patient has agreed. The last part of the interview should be spent in decathecting from the emotional intensity of the interview and ensuring that all relevant information has been addressed. The therapist should ask some of the following questions at this point: Is there anything else you want to tell me or that I should know? Have we left anything out? Do you have any questions to ask me? This last question may be most important, because it allows the patient to ask important questions that may be lingering. During this time, the therapist should be *observing* how the *patient* handles the process of separation from the interview, because it may provide clues to how the patient handles these issues in real life.

Finally, some type of closing is appropriate. The therapist might want to thank the patient for participating in the interview or for sharing personal and sensitive information. Or the therapist might address certain administrative issues, such as the date and time of the next appointment.

INTERVIEW BIASES

Many sources of interviewer bias have been researched. These include client attractiveness, conceptualizing behavior as a static rather than a dynamic process, emphasizing trait, state, or situational determinants of behavior to the exclusion of the others, positive and negative halo, reliance on first impressions, and theoretical biases (e.g., insisting that one theory can explain all forms of behavior). One type of bias that we are becoming increasingly aware of is gender bias. To avoid gender bias, Brown (1990) has recommended that gender issues be integrated into the clinical interview. The model includes preassessment activities (familiarizing oneself with the relevant literature on gender and its relationship to clinical judgments) and self-monitoring activities within the interview itself. Therapists need to determine the meaning of gender membership for the client and the client's social and cultural environment, determine gender-role compliance or variation, notice how the client attends to the evaluator's gender, and guard against inappropriate gender stereotyping.

STRUCTURED, SEMISTRUCTURED, AND UNSTRUCTURED INTERVIEWS

A basic dimension of interviews is their degree of structure. Interviews can be thought of as structured, semistructured, or unstructured. Structured interviews follow rigid rules. The clinician asks specific questions in an exact sequence and includes well-defined rules for recording and judging responses. Structured interviews generally are more reliable than unstructured interviews, but they may overlook idiosyncrasies that add to the richness of personality. They also artificially restrain the topics covered within the interview and may reduce rapport between client and clinician. Semistructured interviews have more flexibility and provide guidelines rather than rules in fixed sequence. There are neither prepared questions nor required probes. Semistructured interviews may elicit more information than would emerge from a structured interview, because the therapist is allowed more judgment in determining what specific questions to ask. Semistructured interviews also may ascertain more detailed information about a specific topic. In completely unstructured interviews, the clinician assesses and explores conditions believed to be present within the interviewee. The interview discussed in this chapter is referred to as an unstructured interview, but even in the so-called unstructured interview there is a structure. In clinical practice settings, diagnoses are more often established using unstructured interviews, whereas in a research context diagnoses are more often established by using a structured or semistructured interview.

The introduction of criteria sets in DSM-III (American Psychiatric Association, 1980) ushered in renewed interest in the reliability of psychiatric diagnoses. At the same time, structured psychiatric interviews were developed to

Table 2.1. Selected Structured Interviews for Psychopathology and Personality

Name	Author(s)	Year
General Psychopathology		
Schedule of Affective Disorders and Schizophrenia	Endicott & Spitzer	1978
Diagnostic Interview Schedule	Robins et al.	1981
Structured Interview for DSM Disorders	Pfohl et al.	1983; 1995
Structured Clinical Interview for DSM-III-R	Spitzer et al.	1992
Personality Pathology Structured Interview for DSM	Stangl et al.	1985
Personality Disorders		
Personality Assessment Interview	Selzer et al.	1987
Diagnostic Interview for DSM-IV Personality Disorders	Zanarini et al.	1995
The International Personality Disorder Examination	Loranger et al.	1994
The Personality Disorder Interview	Widiger et al.	1995

assess psychopathology and personality pathology for both children (Edelbrock & Costello, 1984) and adults (Spiker & Ehler, 1984). Table 2.1 presents the major instruments that have appeared for this purpose. For a more expanded presentation of this material along with a more detailed listing of available psychiatric interviews for many psychopathologies and personality disorders, see Craig (2003).

RACE, CULTURE, AND ETHNICITY

Therapists must also appreciate the extent to which race, culture, and ethnicity may affect the course of the interview, as well as the conclusions drawn from it. We are only beginning to appreciate the extent to which these variables play a role in the expression of behavior, let alone in the clinical interview. Even if the same behaviors should be consistently identified across cultural groups, these behaviors might have different meanings based on the cultural context in which they occur. Unless you understand the culture of the patient, you can be adequately trained in psychopathology and personality pathology but still make erroneous interpretations and conclusions due to failing to understand how race, culture, or ethnicity affect the patient's response (Dana, 1993).

My goal in this chapter has been to acquaint the reader with some of the basic elements of a clinical interview. My hope is that the reader will have learned something from reading this chapter and will be motivated to read the remainder of this volume. So too with patients. As therapists, we hope that our patients will learn something from the initial interview that will motivate them to seek further understanding of their problems.

REFERENCES

American Psychiatric Association. (1980). *Diagnostic and Statistical Manual of Mental Disorders*, 3rd ed. Washington, DC: American Psychiatric Association.

American Psychiatric Association. (1987). *Diagnostic and Statistical Manual of Mental Disorders*, 3rd ed., revised. Washington, DC: American Psychiatric Association.

American Psychiatric Association. (1994). *Diagnostic and Statistical Manual of Mental Disorders*, 4th ed. Washington, DC: American Psychiatric Association.

American Psychological Association. (1980). Statement on DSM-III. Annual Meeting of the Council of Representatives, Montreal, August 31 and September 3.

Baekeland, F., & Lundwall, L. (1975). Dropping out of treatment: A critical review. *Psychological Bulletin* 82: 738–783.

Benjamin, A. (1969). *The Helping Interview*, 2nd ed. Boston: Houghton Mifflin.

Brown, E. (1990). Taking account of gender in the clinical interview. *Professional Psychology: Research and Practice* 21:316–327.

Cozby, P. C. (1973). Self-disclosure: A literature review. *Psychological Bulletin* 79:73–91.

Craig, R. J. (2003). Assessing personality and psychopathology with interview. In *Handbook of Psychology*, ed. I. Weiner. New York: Wiley & Sons.

Dana, R. H. (1993). *Multicultural Assessment Perspectives for Professional Psychology*. Boston: Allyn & Bacon.

Edelbrock, G., & Costello, A. J. (1984). Structured psychiatric interviews for children and adolescents. In *Handbook of Psychological Assessment*, ed. G. Goldstein & M. Hersen, pp. 276–290. New York: Pergamon.

Endicott, J., & Spitzer, R. L. (1978). A diagnostic interview: The schedule for affective disorders and schizophrenia. *Archives of General Psychiatry* 35:837–844.

Hersen, M. L., & Turner, S. M., eds. (1985). *Diagnostic Interviewing*. New York: Plenum.

Kanfer, F. H., & Scheft, B. K. (1988). *Guiding the Process of Therapeutic Change*. Champaign, IL: Research Press.

Loranger, A. W., Sartorius, N., Andreoli, A., Berger, P., Buchheim, P., Channabasavanna, S. M., Coid, B., Dahl, A., Diekstra, R. F., Ferguson, B., Jacobsberg, L. B., Mombour, W., Pull, C., & Regier, D. A. (1994). The International Personality Disorder Examination: The World Health Organization/Alcohol, Drug Abuse, and Mental Health Administration international pilot study of personality disorders. *Archives of General Psychiatry* 51:215–224.

Matarazzo, J. D. (1965). The interview. In *Handbook of Clinical Psychology*, ed. B. Wolman, pp. 403–450. New York: McGraw–Hill.

Matarazzo, J. D. (1978). The interview: Its reliability and validity in psychiatric diagnosis. In *Clinical Diagnosis of Mental Disorders*, ed. B. Wolman, pp. 47–96. New York: Plenum.

Miller, W. R. (1991). *Motivational Interviewing: Preparing People to Change Addictive Behavior*. New York: Guilford.

Othmer, E., & Othmer, S. C. (1994). *The Clinical Interview Using DSM-IV. Vol. 1: Fundamentals*. Washington, DC: American Psychiatric Association.

Perry, S., Cooper, A. M., & Michels, R. (1987). The psychodynamic formulation: Its purpose, structure, and clinical application. *American Journal of Psychiatry* 144:543–550.

Pfohl, B., Blum, N., & Zimmerman, M. (1995). *Structured Interview for DSM-IV*. Iowa City, IA: University of Iowa College of Medicine.

Pfohl, B., Stangl, D., & Zimmerman, M. (1983). *Structured Interview for DSM-III-R Personality SIDP-R*. Iowa City, IA: University of Iowa College of Medicine.

Robins, L. N., Helzer, J. E., Croughan, J., & Ratcliff, K. S. (1981). National Institute on Mental Health diagnostic interview schedule. *Archives of General Psychiatry* 38:381–389.

Rogers, C. R. (1942). *Counseling and Psychotherapy*. Cambridge: Houghton Mifflin.

Selzer, M. A., Kernberg, P., Fibel, B., Cherbuliez, T., & Mortati, S. (1987). The personality assessment interview. *Psychiatry* 50:142–153.

Spiker, D. G., & Ehler, J. G. (1984). Structured psychiatric interviews for adults. In *Handbook of Psychological Assessment*, ed. G. Goldstein and M. Hersen, pp. 291–304. New York: Pergamon.

Spitzer, R., Williams, J. B., Gibbon, M., & First, M. B. (1992). *Structured Clinical Interview for DSM-III-R (SCID-II)*. Washington, DC: American Psychiatric Association.

Stangl, D., Pfohl, B., Zimmerman, M., Bowers, W., & Corenthal, M. (1985). A structured interview for the DSM-III personality disorders: A preliminary report. *Archives of General Psychiatry* 42:591–596.

Stevenson, I. (1959). The psychiatric interview. In *American Handbook of Psychiatry*, Vol. 1, ed. S. Arieti, pp. 197–214. New York: Basic.

Strauss, G. S. (1995). The psychiatric interview, history and mental status examination. In *Comprehensive Textbook in Psychiatry*, ed. H. I. Kaplan & B. J. Sadock, 6th ed., pp. 521–531. Baltimore: Williams and Wilkens.

Sullivan, H. S. (1954). *The Psychiatric Interview*. New York: Norton.

Widiger, T., Mangine, S., Corbitt, E. M., Ellis, C. G., & Thomas, G. V. (1995). *Personality Disorder Interview—IV: A Semi-structured Interview for the Assessment of Personality Disorders*. Odessa, FL: Psychological Assessment Resources.

Wiens, A. N., & Tindall, A. G. (1995). Interviewing. In *Introduction to Clinical Psychology*, ed. L. Heiden & M. Hersen, pp. 173–190. New York: Plenum.

Wiens, A. N., and Matarazzo, J. D. (1983). Diagnostic interviewing. In *The Clinical Psychology Handbook*, ed. M. Hersen, A. Kazdin, & A. Bellak, pp. 309–328. Elmsford, NY: Pergamon.

Woody, S. R., & Sanderson, W. C. (1998). Manuals for empirically supported treatments: 1998 update. *Clinical Psychologist* 51:17–21.

World Health Organization. (1992). *The ICD-10 Classification of Mental and Behavioral Disorders*. Geneva: World Health Organization.

———. (1992). *International Classification of Diseases* (9th rev.). Geneva: World Health Organization.

Zanarini, M., Frankenburg, F. R., Sickel, A. E., & Yong, L. (1995). *Diagnostic Interview for DSM-IV Personality Disorders*. Laboratory for the Study of Adult Development, McLean Hospital, and the Department of Psychiatry, Harvard University.

3

PHENOMENOLOGICAL ORIENTATION TO THE INTERVIEW

Frank Gruba-McCallister, Ph.D.

Psychological instruments and tests proliferate, but the interview remains among the most important tools employed by therapists in the assessment of patients. It calls upon most, if not all, of the therapist's skills, diagnostic as well as therapeutic. The success of the interview rests upon a particular stance and a set of attitudes on the part of the therapist. This chapter elucidates the phenomenological orientation of the clinical interview and addresses processes inherent in it.

RECIPROCITY AND RAPPORT IN THE INTERVIEW

An important feature of the word *interview* is the reliance on *inter-*, which means "between," "reciprocal," and "shared." This prefix points to the first essential feature of the interview. It is a relationship between two persons and is characterized by reciprocity and sharing. The success of the interview depends upon the quality of the relationship that the interviewer is able to establish with the patient. What needs to be shared is a feeling of understanding and mutual trust. There is a giving and taking that occurs throughout the course of the interview around which a sense of mutuality evolves. Likewise, the degree of mutuality achieved in the interview influences the level of sharing that occurs.

This matter of mutuality refers to an issue often regarded as important not only to the interview situation, but also to other types of helping relationships: rapport. Rapport is characterized by a sense of being "on the same wavelength." As such, it implies a feeling shared by the participants in a relationship that allows for an open, easy sharing of information.

The manner in which this process occurs has been variously described. It can be thought of as working out of common purposes. Sullivan (1954) calls it an integration of reciprocal motivation. Other terms used are *working relationship* and *therapeutic alliance*. By any name, the relationship requires the achievement of some agreement between the interviewer and the interviewee regarding the purpose for and goals of their relationship. This goal, unfortunately, is often ill-defined and insufficiently stipulated. Much of the difficulty in establishing and maintaining rapport can be traced to this problem.

NEGOTIATION

Thus, negotiation of a set of common purposes or goals is part of the task of both therapist and patient in the interviewing process. As a result, some of the goals are made explicit, while others may remain implicit and unexpressed. The negotiation is based upon the different roles of interviewer and interviewee and the expectations, motivations, and needs that go along with these roles. As Sullivan (1954) notes, the interview, as an interpersonal situation, offers the opportunity for complementary needs to be resolved or aggravated, which will then affect the establishment of rapport.

THE PATIENT'S EXPECTATIONS

As Craig points out in chapter 2, the patient comes to the interview with a number of expectations and needs. Principal among these is the expectation of being helped. This expectation is often expressed as the desire for a remedy, a cure, a definitive answer to one's problems. This unrealistic attitude is prompted in part by the patient's keen distress and by the desire to be rid of this distress with the greatest expedience. It is also related to the authoritative role into which patients tend to place therapists, endowing them with this omnipotence or special powers.

While this belief in the therapist's omnipotence represents an extreme attitude, when expressed in its more moderate form it becomes the patient's expectation that he will derive some benefit from the interview. The therapist must take this expectation seriously; over the course of the interview, the patient should indeed come to some greater understanding of self that may then lead to an increased capacity for positive change. Correspondingly, the therapist must be careful not to be pulled into accepting the omnipotent role and becoming a rescuer. Steiner (1974, pp. 280–289) provides an excellent discussion of rescue and its hazards.

Learning

The need for the patient to learn something useful is stressed by Sullivan (1954) in his classic work on the interview, and yet it is still frequently neglected.

Since the interview is most often seen as a diagnostic tool and a form of psychological assessment, the patient is often regarded as responsible for providing information in response to a series of questions posed by the interviewer. That is, it is the therapist who is trying to learn something about the patient in order to make an accurate diagnosis and offer appropriate recommendations. However, the interview can no more be separated from therapeutic intervention than it can from psychodiagnosis. Questions posed by the therapist must be designed to promote greater understanding for the patient as well. The skill with which the therapist is able to frame questions has a substantial influence on the establishment of a good relationship with the patient. Questions must reflect a respect for patient's feelings, sensitivities, and strengths. They should be framed tactfully and with acknowledgment of the patient's defenses. Questions also perform a therapeutic function in that they can convey implicit suggestions designed to encourage the patient to consider alternative behaviors or to regard a problem from a different perspective. Finally, the patient is likely to be preoccupied with many questions from the very start of the interview, and it is good practice to allow the patient to ask some of these questions toward the end of the interview.

Ambivalence

Although the patient expects to learn something useful, there is an essential ambivalence characteristic of the patient seeking help. On the one hand, patients are experiencing distress and are motivated to share information and to reveal themselves in order to find relief. On the other hand, the very issues that patients need to share are often painful and embarrassing, so there is an opposing need to keep them hidden and unexpressed. The need to maintain one's self-esteem and the fear of losing the therapist's respect are two very powerful forces that operate throughout the course of the interview and interfere with the free expression of information and feelings. Here, again, the therapist's understanding, interest, respect, and tolerance are crucial to diminish this reluctance. The importance of building trust is likewise evident. The therapist's questions must enable the patient to maintain a sense of self-respect and dignity while also facilitating the sharing of information that may be painful and distasteful.

Thus, patients can learn something valuable in an interview from the way they are treated by the therapist. Patients expect to be treated with compassion and understanding, but as we have noted, they also come into the interview with unrealistic expectations born out of distortion and lack of information. The manner in which the therapist interacts teaches the patient something that works to correct not only misconceptions about the therapist and the nature of clinical work, but also misconceptions that the patients have about themselves. The hope is that the patients will increasingly see themselves as worthwhile people who possess the resources and abilities necessary to deal effectively with problems and to experience life as meaningful and enriching.

The Patient's Interpersonal Style

The relationship that the therapist establishes with the patient provides some valuable learning experiences for the patient, but the reverse is also true. Therapists must be sensitive to the sort of relationship that patients establish with them. Every patient has their own way of revealing themselves. From the very start of the interview, a patient conveys to the therapist how he wants to be treated. By picking up on these expectations and attitudes, the therapist develops a sense of how the patient will approach similar interpersonal situations.

One of the key areas that must be addressed during the interview is the way in which patients tend to interact with others and the basic beliefs and assumptions that guide how they approach interpersonal relationships. The relationship between the therapist and the patient is a microcosm of this broader sphere of relationships. The interview offers the distinct advantage of possessing a stronger interpersonal component than other forms of psychological assessment. The various dynamics that unfold as the relationship between therapist and patient evolves during the interview is thus a fertile source of information. The therapist must be alert to feelings that the patient arouses as well as to feelings that the patient displays (or does not display) in response to the therapist's interventions.

Psychoanalytic theorists who speak of development of transference during the interview make the latter point. In this case, the patient's response to the interview provides insights into unconscious feelings and behaviors based in relationships with significant figures from the past. However, this notion can be expended. An entire nexus of relationships—past and present—converge and play themselves out in the interview for both patient and therapist. Thus there are any number of "ghosts" in the room at any one time. Sensitivity to this fact enables the therapist to formulate a clearer sense of the patient's interpersonal sphere.

Interviews offer the patient a chance to experience a relationship that has the potential to encourage greater personal development and health. The mutuality and reciprocity so central to good therapeutic rapport are also the cornerstones of good relationships in general. This relationship between therapist and patient can be regarded as a dialectical one. The dialectic has many meanings (see Rychlak, 1976). Here it refers to an interaction in which the uniqueness and individuality of each person is respected while a deeper underlying bond that transcends such differences is also recognized. Laing (1960) talks of a dialectical relationship as one of "mutual enrichment and exchange of give-and-take between two beings 'congenial to each other'" (p. 92). Buber's description (1970) of the I–thou relationship is another example. Existentialists call it "encounter."

THE THERAPIST'S EXPECTATIONS

The therapist also brings certain expectations to the interview. These include expectations of being able to ask questions, make inquiries, and receive significant and relevant information. Expectations such as these are based on the role of the therapist as expert. In fact, certain aspects of the therapist's role can diminish the effectiveness of the interview. Therapists must be aware of the needs and motives that they bring to the interaction so they can be carefully monitored and thus not interfere with the goal of achieving objective, unbiased assessment of the patient.

Attention

This brings us to the second part of the word *interview*. One of the meanings of the word *view* is "to look at attentively." In the interview, the principal instrument of assessment and observation is the therapist. So we must look at factors that influence the therapist's ability to attend effectively to all facets of the interview and to gather the data needed to formulate a valid assessment.

The key word is *attention*. To describe the kind of attention needed by the therapist, we can again turn to the dialectic. One meaning of the dialectic is the bipolarity, or how meanings implicitly suggest the reverse. This is reflected in how human thought is structured around two poles that, while different, mutually define each other and are thus necessary to each other's existence. This is the dialectic of self versus other, subject versus object, knower versus known.

Human thought constantly fluctuates in its focus. At times, we are outer-directed and absorbed in the object of our attention. At other times, our awareness is reflected back upon ourselves as the knower and center of experience. When our attention is focused upon one of the poles, the other is always implicitly there and can emerge and come to the fore in the next instant. The shift from one pole to the other can be thought of as a figure-ground relationship.

The Therapist as Participant–Observer

The attention f the therapist conducting the interview is likewise organized around these poles. Sullivan (1954) describes the role of the interviewer as a participant–observer. In using the term, Sullivan stresses the interpersonal aspect of the interview. The therapist's personality inevitably enters into the processes, particularly since the therapist is the principal instrument for assessing the patient in the interview.

The role of participant–observer can be understood in terms of the dialectical structure of human thought. As participant, the therapist is absorbed in the process of the interview itself. This requires a receptive, open orientation that is basic to an empathic relationship. In such a state, the therapist loses the sense of being a separate individual and instead becomes absorbed in the patient. In so doing, the therapist conveys to the patient a sense of being understood and accepted.

As observers, therapists must be able to remove themselves from this process and analyze it from a more objective, third-person perspective. At these times, the therapist views the patient from a more detached stance that enables him to bring to bear clinical experience and theory in order to discern problematic patterns, conflicts, strengths, and supports that will eventually be integrated into a case conceptualization. From this perspective, the interviewer employs active listening, questioning, and probing to gather data needed to formulate hypotheses. (See the next chapter for a greater explication of interviewing techniques.) This represents the first dialectic that characterizes the interview process.

What has been described thus far is related to what Sullivan (1954) calls alertness to the patient. However, as he points out, the therapists must also maintain alertness regarding their own behavior within the interview. In addition to the constant fluctuation between an active versus passive attitude that occurs when the interviewer focuses attention on the patient, a second ever-present dialectic in the interview is alertness toward the patient versus alertness toward the self.

Therapists first need to be aware of what they do in the interview to monitor how this might impact the patient's behavior and the quality of the relationship that will be established. The key is to avoid any behavior or attitude that might prove to be disruptive to the interview process or might distort the therapist's concentration of the world view of the patient. The danger is that the interviewer's prejudices, beliefs, and preoccupations will so color his perceptions that all sense of the patient will be lost. This process is described by Dass and Gorman (1985), who comment that interviewers jump between listening and judging, and that when we are with our thoughts we are not with the patient.

To avoid this pitfall, therapists must be aware of their needs, motives, values, and prejudices and must not permit them to intrude upon the listening process. Maintaining this sort of awareness and control is a great challenge. How can we hope to achieve a view of the patient that is generally free of bias? While there is no definitive answer to this question, several valuable means can be proposed.

The mind of the therapist is the most important instrument that is employed in the interview. This instrument must be sharpened, focused, and carefully tuned. The resulting mental discipline enables the therapist to better screen out distractions, biases, and other intrusive attitudes in order to more accurately listen to what the client really has to say. A much deeper and more intense level of communication is made available to both the interviewer and the patient as a result. An additional benefit to the therapist is that mental discipline broadens self-awareness. As one's sense of self is expanded, new insights into oneself become possible.

Learning to concentrate, to quiet the mind sufficiently to enable oneself to focus accurately on what is being communicated by the patient and what is being communicated within, is thus the first means that can be proposed to achieve the awareness necessary for successful interviewing. Numerous methods and techniques have been proposed to develop the powers of mental concentration. Most are akin to meditation. The particulars of such methods lie outside the scope of this chapter, but the interested reader will have no problem obtaining additional sources of information on specific techniques.

The Phenomenological Stance

A second method, which is related in many respects to the discipline of meditation, is offered by the philosophical school known as phenomenology. As a philosophy, phenomenology seeks to study how human experience is influenced by various presuppositions or preexisting biases that the mind brings to bear in structuring experience and giving it meaning. The philosopher whose name has been most closely associated with phenomenology is Edmund Husserl (1962). He hoped to develop philosophy as a rigorous science. By this, he meant that he wanted to achieve absolutely valid knowledge. Such knowledge would have to be free of prejudice or presupposition. The quest for this knowledge might also lead to primary presuppositions that do not require clarification because they are immediately evident.

While the scope of phenomenology is much broader that the tasks involved in interviewing, the therapist can gain some insight and wisdom from phenomenology and its method. The therapist's task, like the phenomenologist's, is to come to a clearer understanding of his or her own basic or primary presuppositions. These might consist of attitudes, beliefs, and values that one regards as unquestionable and self-evident. They form a personal philosophy from which one regards and interprets all of one's own experience. These assumptions often operate subtly and outside of ones' awareness, which increases the risk of bias and distortion.

To rid oneself completely of these assumptions is a requirement that few, if any, can achieve. However, a method in phenomenology called "bracketing" provides an alternative approach. While the application of this method as proposed here departs in certain respects from the manner in which it is used in phenomenology, it does not depart from its spirit and intent. The idea behind bracketing is to temporarily suspend or put out of action one's presuppositions so that they do not interfere with the formation of an unbiased understanding of the patient's experience as it is revealed within the interview. In a sense, one's biases and presuppositions are placed within brackets and thus rendered inoperative. The interviewer who can then succeed in performing this operation of bracketing is likely to be more successful in differentiating the reality of the patient that is being constructed from the interview data from what is contributed to those data based on the interviewer's own interests, values, and biases.

To bracket these presuppositions, the interviewer must be aware of what they are. As previously noted, this self-knowledge can be achieved through the heightened awareness that comes with mental discipline. In many ways, what is being stressed here is the need for the therapist to make a careful study of experience, the structure in which it occurs, and the process through which experience develops and grows.

The resulting awareness of the patient that one achieves by suspending one's biases has been variously described. Maslow (1971) calls it Taoistic objectivity. In this state, we are noninterfering spectators. We allow patients to just be, and to unfold in all their various facets before our eyes. The goal of Taoist objectivity is not to try to interfere, control, or improve. Instead, it is characterized by loving perception in which the patient is regarded with intense interest and even fascination.

Staying within an Eastern-philosophy framework, Goldstein (1976) describes this awareness from a Zen perspective as "bare attention." We observe things and persons as they are, without choosing, comparing, or evaluating. It is awareness that is focused in the present moment and that is open, passive, and receptive.

This open, receptive attitude goes a long way toward enabling the therapist to enter the world view of the patient. It also conveys to the patient an acceptance and understanding that are conducive to positive changes within the helping relationship. Within the dialectical framework that we have been following, however, we need to remember that we must also direct this sort of awareness back toward ourselves. In so doing, we make available still more sources of valuable information.

There is first greater willingness on the part of the therapist to accept these deeper-level responses and feelings that have been stirred in the interaction with the patient. More trust is placed in this intuitive sense. Second, the feelings that are experienced are in response to what the patient says and does during the interview, if not colored by the therapist's own prejudices, lead to a clearer sense of the ways in which others experience the patient and the type of interpersonal relations the patient typically develops. From this assessment, the patient's basic beliefs and assumptions can be inferred.

Thus a passive and receptive attitude is essential to the success of the interview. Nevertheless, such an attitude alone is not enough. Returning to the therapist's participant–observer role, the need to detach oneself from the interview process and critically appraise and evaluate it is equally necessary. The passive, receptive attitude enables the therapist to gather the necessary information to capture the patient's world view. These data must then be submitted to the therapist's clinical experience and knowledge of theory if he or she is to look beyond this information and discover within it deeper levels of meaning and significance.

The interview process thus represents an ongoing balancing act for the therapist. Attention may be directed toward the patient or reflected back upon the interviewer. This attention may take the form of being passive, receptive, and noninterfering, or it may be more detached, critical, and evaluative. The process is a dynamic, ever-changing one, taking one form and then another from moment to moment. It is not surprising, therefore, that interviewing is hard, demanding work requiring flexibility and the constant attention of the therapist.

Clinical Judgment

The need to critically analyze the interview data brings us to a second meaning of the word *view* that is "judgment." Interviewing involves the exercise of judgment by the therapist in order to arrive at an assessment based on a theoretical perspective. As data from what the patient says together with what the therapist observes are gathered, hypotheses are generated to make sense of and to order these data. These hypotheses are the product of a critical, analytic attitude.

The hypotheses, or educated guesses, made by the interviewer are a means whereby what appear to be discrete pieces of information become related and interwoven in a meaningful fashion. The therapist's task is to use hypotheses in order to make connections and to discern patterns. The patient is often unaware of these patterns or is aware of them but feels locked into them and unable to break free. The therapist's ability to introduce order by identifying patterns and relationships helps the patient to become more aware of them. The therapist's ability to see beyond these patterns and to creatively reorganize them into new ones helps the patient to change them.

Hypotheses are tentative and must be tested. While this idea seems self-evident, the tendency to forget this tenet is perhaps one of the most common problems to which clinicians fall prey. The same tendency of the mind that leads us to introduce order and stability into our experience can also, if unchecked, lead us to come to premature closure regarding a belief or assumption and can make us unwilling to challenge or alter a position that we have settled upon. One of the most common reasons the patients seek our help is that they have become frozen in distressing patterns for which they see no alternatives. A therapist who does likewise is of little value to the patient.

Multiple Hypotheses

For this reason, the therapist must engage in still another balancing act while conducting the interview. The therapist should try to entertain more than one hypothesis at all times. The process of the interview becomes one of testing these hypotheses, rejecting some, supporting others, and generating new ones. At no point should only one hypothesis be entertained. Even at the end of the interview, one may settle upon a number of hypotheses in which one can place considerable confidence, but there should still be enough room for doubt that further exploration and inquiry would either strengthen these hypotheses or suggest others.

Hypotheses play an important role in guiding assessment. They tell the interviewer what additional information should be acquired either during the interview or at a later time. They point the interviewer in the direction of other areas of the patient's life that should be discussed. If the interviewer has a firm hold on the hypotheses he wishes to test, then the task of developing a systematic line of inquiry becomes simpler. However, this line of inquiry need not be rigid and ritualized as is the case when one follows some preordained or prescribed outline of questions. Rather, by being guided by the data provided by the patient, and by constantly challenging and modifying one's hypotheses, one can accommodate any patient's individuality.

The goal of the interview is to arrive at a case conceptualization. Here again the therapist's judgment and command of theory is critical to success. It is theory that guides the creation of hypotheses used to explain the data. Large amounts of information can be condensed and integrated within the framework provided by one's theory of human behavior. Again, this is frequently expressed in terms of basic themes or patterns that seem to prevail in the patient's life. The value of a good theory is that it provides the therapist with a sense of the critical issues, themes, and problems with which humans must come to terms through the course of their lives. Indeed, the case conceptualization must ultimately come to reflect the patient's personal philosophy and the basic premises and beliefs that guide the patient's thoughts, feelings, and behavior.

A dialectical relationship must exist between the data provided by the patient and the theoretical perspective applied by the clinician to these data if the resulting case conceptualization is to be valid. Again, one must avoid imposing one's world view on the patient while at the same time not accepting uncritically the data the patient provides.

SHARING THE PATIENT'S WORLD VIEW

The patient's view of experience is made preeminent in the establishment of a case conceptualization. It is this world of experience that the therapist seeks to capture. The role of theory and the hypotheses it generates is to provide the means whereby the patient's world view can be described in a manner that makes sense (not only to the therapist and the patient but to others as well), lends meaning (by the relationships it draws from the data), and offers new insights (by making new relationships possible).

The value of arriving at the fullest possible appreciation of the patient's world view is that it makes the patient's thoughts, feelings, and behavior more understandable. There is nothing that a patient says or does that is "crazy" in the sense that it has no meaning or is illogical. Its meaning and logic can be understood only once the case conceptualization we develop captures the experience of the patient. This approach is exemplified by the work of Laing (1960; 1967). From the perspective of what he calls the social-phenomenological approach, Laing maintains that the bizarre and crazy behavior of the schizophrenic can be made socially intelligible when viewed within the patient's original family context and ongoing life situation, thereby permitting understanding of the patient's existential position.

The therapist's attitude should be concerned not so much with whether the patient's behavior or thinking is accurate, correct, or real. Instead, the therapist must bracket or suspend the issue of the "reality" of the client's experience and accept it as having validity and meaning in the light of the patient's existential situation (Boss, 1963).

Thus the exercise of judgment by the interviewer in applying theory to the data acquired from the interview is not intended to be the imposition of the interviewer's world view upon the patient's. There can be little hope of rapport in an interview when such a process occurs. The result will be the patient's feeling misunderstood and perceiving the therapist as coming from another world. In this sort of situation, the therapist can likewise feel irritated because the patient is "not catching on"; the therapist may ascribe failure to the patient who does not embrace that world view.

A situation in which the therapist and patient agree on many basic assumptions and beliefs likewise poses problems. The interview becomes an exercise in mutual confirmation of views, and a critical part of the therapist's capacity to help the patient to change is lost. Some challenge to the patient's dearly held beliefs and expectations is required in order to generate the alternatives that make change possible.

Respect for the patient's experience must therefore be central to the therapist's attitude. The invalidating of one's experience is one of the most potent factors contributing to psychopathology. It would thus be a serious disservice to the patient for the therapist to engage in a similar pathogenic process. The recognition of the validity of the patient's experience communicates the sense of acceptance that is needed in the interview situation. The therapist must not hide behind theory to transform the patient into a diagnosis, a syndrome, or some other set of abstractions. The purpose is to provide the means whereby we can appreciate the patient as alive, real, dynamic, and unique.

In this chapter I have described a particular stance and related attitudes important to the success of the interview. This stance requires an understanding of certain basic facets of the human condition, including the structure of human thought and the dilemmas with which all humans must struggle. The human condition provides the common base upon which the interview rests, for both the therapist and the patient are joined in the endeavor of making sense of their experience—experience that is grounded for both in the human condition they share. Thus the interview holds promise for growth in self-awareness and understanding not only for the patient, but for the therapist as well.

REFERENCES

Boss, M. (1963). *Psychoanalysis and Daseinsanalysis*, trans. L. Lefebre. New York: Basic.

Buber, M. (1970). *I and Thou*, trans. W. Kaufmann. New York: Scribner's Sons.

Dass, R., & Gorman, P. (1985). *How Can I Help?* New York: Knopf.

Goldstein, J. (1976). *The Experience of Insight*. Boulder: Shambhala.

Husserl, E. (1962). *Ideas*, trans. W. R. Boyce Gibson. New York: Collier.

Laing, R. D. (1960). *The Divided Self*. Baltimore: Penguin.

Laing, R. D. (1967). *The Politics of Experience*. New York: Ballantine.

Maslow, A. H. (1971). *The Farther Reaches of Human Nature*. New York: Viking.

Rychlak, J. F., ed. (1976). *Dialectic: Humanistic Rationale for Behavior and Development*. Basel, Switzerland: Karger.

Steiner, C. (1974). *Scripts People Live*. New York: Bantam.

Sullivan, H. S. (1954). *The Psychiatric Interview*. New York: Norton.

II

PHILOSOPHICAL APPROACHES
TO INTERVIEWING

4

PSYCHOANALYTIC INTERVIEWING

Jed Yalof, Psy.D., ABPP, and Pamela Pressley Abraham, Psy.D., NCSP

This chapter presents a psychoanalytic model for conducting an initial clinical interview. Gabbard (1990) and Iennarella and Frick (1997) have also presented models for conducting an initial psychoanalytic interview. We view this chapter as an extension of their contributions.

The initial interview challenges the therapist's thoughtful, systematic, and empathic application of a rich base of theory and technique in a time-limited period. In an initial consultation, the therapist listens, interacts, and evaluates the client's motivation, mental status, ego strength, current stresses, experience of self and others, defenses, superego integrity, support system, potential for response to different interventions, and quality of relationship to the therapist. Typically, the initial interview has to be accomplished within a forty-five to sixty-minute time frame and provides a real test to the therapist's ability to work flexibly and skillfully within a psychoanalytic orientation.

The first part of this chapter addresses some of the central themes that shape the direction of an initial psychoanalytic interview with an adult client, including theory, assessment of mental status and ego functions, intervention strategies, diagnosis, and treatment planning. The second part focuses on the application of psychoanalytic principles to the initial parent consultation and child therapy interview. Case illustrations are presented to highlight these points.

THEORY

Case formulation is shaped by theory. In psychoanalytic theory, the roles of early developmental history and trauma, self-esteem vulnerability, and unconscious conflict in symptom formation help to shape case formulation. Major theoretical contributions to psychoanalytic theory and their relation to each other have been reviewed and summarized thoroughly by Greenberg and Mitchell (1983),

Guntrip (1971), Levine, (1996), and Mitchell and Black (1995). Drive psychology, ego psychology, object relations theory, and self psychology have emerged as the central theoretical positions. We agree with Gabbard (1990), who advocates a thoughtful, open-minded, pluralistic approach to psychoanalytic theory when evaluating a patient. Each theory has much to contribute to a comprehensive clinical assessment.

Drive Theory

Sigmund Freud proposed a biologically oriented drive theory model of personality development (Mitchell and Black, 1995). In Freud's model, there is a basic desire for pleasure and a drive to discharge tension in response to the buildup of internal drive pressure. The essence of drive theory posited the emergence of personality as a compromise between the wish to discharge tension on demand and social prohibition against such expression. The ego emerges in response to the demands of external reality and strives to contain the sexual and aggressive drive pressure emanating from the most primitive part of the mind, which Freud termed the "id." The higher-level defenses of the ego, such as displacement, reaction formation, intellectualization, isolation, introjection, and undoing, begin to supercede reliance on use of primitive defenses, such as denial and splitting. Individual character takes shape through a series of psychosexual and, as Erik Erikson (1963) later described, psychosocial developmental stages that interact with emergent defense mechanisms and influence the quality of reality adaptation. The child negotiates different developmental conflicts related to oral, anal, phallic, and genital psychosexual stages that correspond, respectively, to Erikson's psychosocial crises of trust versus mistrust, autonomy versus shame and doubt, and initiative versus guilt. During the oedipal crises, children begin to move away from dyadic, need-driven ways of relating and toward triadic interactions. The resolution of the oedipal conflict in boys involves the repression of longing for their mother as a primary love object secondary to fear of rivalry and castration by their father. The resolution of oedipal conflict in girls is more complex, involving disappointment in the mother upon discovering the absence of a penis (i.e., penis envy) and turning to the father as primary love object as phallic substitute. In both boys and girls, the repression of primitive wishes during the oedipal period leads to the development of the superego and internalization of social values and prohibitions. Anxiety associated with unconscious drive pressure can lead to symptom formation and developmental regressions (e.g., inhibitions, interpersonal conflicts, and reliance on primitive defenses) that color the intrapsychic and interpersonal dynamics of adult personality. Freud's model can be understood as representing a biopsychosocial approach to personality development because of the role that internalized values play in shaping and subordinating drive expression in accordance with a refinement of social consequence.

Ego Psychology

Heinz Hartmann and Anna Freud each further developed Sigmund Freud's drive theory by developing a psychology of the ego (Mitchell & Black, 1995). Anna Freud's main contribution to ego psychology was to describe how the ego's defense mechanisms were interwoven with drives into the structure of personality. The unconscious workings of defense mechanisms became the focus of psychoanalytic attention and led to therapeutic strategies that were designed to identify and modify defenses. In Sigmund Freud's therapy approach, interpretations of underlying drive content were viewed as the primary intervention. In Anna Freud's therapy approach, influenced by an expanded understanding of the role of the ego's defenses in shaping personality (and not just resisting drives), the interpretation of defense mechanisms was seen as the primary intervention.

Hartmann further developed ego psychology by focusing on the ego's autonomous functions and its facilitating adaptation to the environment (Mitchell & Black, 1995). Whereas Sigmund Freud posited the ego as being subordinate to the id, Hartmann saw the ego as representing an autonomous and adaptive mental structure. Hartmann viewed the ego as being vulnerable to drive pressure, but not exclusively so; instead, the ego was, by its intricate biological design, primed to regulate drives and facilitate adaptation. Various autonomous ego functions such as memory, planning, motility, and visualization could be affected by drive conflict in a way that compromised adaptive strivings; however, adaptational and mastery strivings were important determinants of personality. Thus, Hartmann's interpretation of the ego as having an autonomous motivational direction represented a change from Freud's purely tension-reduction theory of motivation. Ego deficits result in excessive reliance on defenses, and rigid defenses limited the flexibility of psychological operations, adaptation, resiliency, and response to treatment.

Mitchell and Black (1995) also cast Margaret Mahler and Edith Jacobson as influential theorists in ego psychology. Both Mahler and Jacobson focused on the role of the environment in shaping object relations, thereby moving psychoanalytic theory further away from a tension-reduction, biological drive theory of motivation and closer to a motivational theory that emphasized the interaction between child and environment. Mahler's work identified different points of stage-related object relational subphases (e.g., hatching, practicing, rapprochement) for the child to navigate in relation to the maternal figure. Each phase had its own series of developmental tasks, with the outcome of each subphase influencing the quality of the child's experience of self and others. Mahler's work has been especially influential in understanding ego functions and object relations of pre-oedipal patients with borderline level psychopathology. Mahler's sensitive portrayal of early interactional patterns in the mother–child dyad allowed for a deeper understanding of pre-oedipal, adult patients and their therapeutic needs. Jacobson used the notion of the child's subjective evaluation of experience to describe how the tone and tenor of resonance between child and mother influenced the child's experience and shaped the experience of drive states. Taken together, the ego psychology made significant contributions to an understanding of psychoanalytic personality theory by focusing on the role of the ego in adaptation, defense, self-protection, and subjective interpretation of interaction with the maternal figure. In this sense, both Mahler and Jacobson could easily fit into an object-relations model.

Object Relations

Object-relations theorists continued to develop the idea of an interpersonal emphasis as the cornerstone of psychoanalytic theory. Melanie Klein combined elements of drive and object theories into her psychoanalytic schema. Klein focused on the role of innate aggression as the primary drive, but understood aggression in a relational context. For Klein, the projection of primitive aggression into the maternal object helped to organize, through maternal containment, the intensity of aggressive fantasies. Fantasies of the object/self and object relations, however rudimentary and ill-defined, were embedded in drive states, rather than emerging/being discovered in response to ungratified drive states, as had been suggested by Sigmund Freud. The aggressive drive matured, according to Klein, because it was contained by the maternal object. Maturity of the aggressive drive resulted in a shift in object relations from paranoid-schizoid position, persecutorial fantasies directed toward a part-object were dominant. In the depressive position, themes of loss, disappointment, anger, guilt, and reparation directed toward a whole object were dominant. Ronald Fairbairn underscored the striving of the ego for attachment and elevated relational considerations to primary levels in psychoanalytic theory and therapy. Fairbairn's model posited that psychological growth occurred when relationship patterns were changed and new connections were established. Donald Winnicott saw the child as being at the center of his or her experience and maturing in response to good-enough mothering. Good-enough mothering provided the child with the transitional space to discover himself or herself through relationship to the maternal figure. In Winnicott's model, the child's healthy sense of self emerged gradually from the dialectal tension between subjective omnipotence and objective reality. Winnicott was also interested in understanding preoedipal pathology manifested in "false self disorders." False self disorders represented severe disturbances of self experience in which the individual felt disconnected from his or her own true sense of being. These were disorders that emerged in response to chronic maternal failure, which led the child to become prematurely concerned with the external world and with his or her own sense of separateness from the maternal figure. Winnicott's therapy model, couched in a flexible approach to accommodate the needs of the patient, focused on the quality of interaction between patient and analyst in bringing about a change in the overall quality of the patient's experience of self.

Self Psychology

Heinz Kohut's self psychology developed in response to the needs of patients who were not able to tolerate interpretations, silence, and other classically oriented analytic interventions without feeling rage, shame, or humiliation (Mitchell & Black, 1995). These were patients who presented with acute vulnerability in self-esteem regulation and whose psychological symptoms and acting-out behaviors reflected disturbances in the cohesiveness of the self structure that emanated from one of two primary sectors of the personality: archaic exhibitionism and archaic idealism. Kohut was also concerned with the development of the maturity of these two sectors of the personality, respectively, into healthy exhibitionism and mature ideals. Kohut viewed the primitive exhibitionism and grandiose ideals that characterized the child's perception of self and others as reflective of distinct lines of psychological development that had the potential to mature throughout the life span. Where Freud posited a single line of development leading from narcissism to object relations, Kohut posited a dual developmental line that led to the development of mature narcissism and object relations. Kohut saw the emergence of disturbances in either area in adulthood not as regressions secondary to oedipal conflicts and thwarted libidinal strivings, but as deficits in self structure secondary to the failure of caretakers to provide specific psychological functions. In Kohut's model, the absence of timely mirroring responses stifled the maturity of healthy exhibitionism, and chronic disappointment in nonsoothing adults fostered a failure to develop mature ideals. Parental figures were understood as providing "selfobject" functions in which, ideally, their response to the child's incipient needs was timely and appropriate to regulate levels of stimulation, disappointment, or despair. The patient's symptomatic expression (e.g., depressed mood, agitation, anxiety, vulnerable self-esteem) was understood as being secondary to deficiencies in the selfobject environment, while the exacerbation of sexual and aggressive drives reflected efforts to reestablish vibrancy and purpose to the defective self. A Kohutian therapist approached treatment not with an interpretive focus, but with an empathic and supportive tone that paid attention to the patient's need for mirroring and idealizing selfobject experiences.

CONDUCTING THE INTERVIEW

Theory helps to place observation into context. Iennarella and Frick (1997) classify psychoanalytic interviewing strategies into two general approaches— one that emphasizes psychodynamics and intrapsychic structure (e.g., drive and ego psychology) and one that emphasizes object relations and interpersonal processes (e.g., object relations and self psychology). However, they also note that it would not be unusual to find elements of both strategies included in the same diagnostic interview. This is the type of integrative approach that we advocate when responding to material in the initial interview.

The Interview Context

The application of psychoanalytic principles to clinical interviewing and case formulation requires an approach that is conceptually and technically sound, flexible, and sensitive to context. When conducting an initial interview, it is important for the therapist to tailor the interview approach to the needs of the patient, while also considering the context in which the patient is being seen. Psychoanalytic psychotherapists work in many different settings, including residential, medical, outpatient clinic, day treatment, forensic, group practice, and independent practice. Each setting sets different parameters around the interview and its frame. The presence or absence of third-party payers is one example of how the frame of therapy will influence the direction of the interview (Barron & Sands, 1996; Stutman, 1991).

The initial interview has to be adapted to fit the particular clinical environment and patient population. Psychoanalytic theory and therapy has been adapted for patients with severe character pathology (Kernberg, 1975) and self disturbances (Kohut, 1971) as well as for patients who are learning disabled (Rothstein & Glenn, 1999), developmentally disabled (Campbell & Ladner, 1999), intellectually limited (Juni, 2001), and brain injured (Freed, 2002). In addition, the interviewer needs to remain sensitive to ways in which gender, race, and sexual orientation are integrated into a psychoanalytic formulation (e.g., Cornett, 1993; Fast, 1984; Frosh et al., 2000; Thompson, 1995; Yi, 1998). Thus, an approach to the initial interview strives to understand the patient in multiple contexts—developmental-historical, psychodynamic, and sociocultural—and draws upon concepts from different psychoanalytic models to do so.

The Patient–Therapist Relationship

The diagnostic interview process generates a wealth of data. The type of information that is generated during the interview will depend on the relative balance in the interviewer's approach—open-ended versus structured—in conjunction with the patient's interpersonal style, verbal skills, psychological mindedness, empathy, self-esteem, reality testing, defensiveness, and so on.

The first goal of the interview is to communicate a sense of respect, concern, and attentiveness to the patient's unique problems (Gabbard, 1990). Establishing a positive rapport, explaining general parameters of the interview, and inviting the patient's collaboration in the interview process are important features of the relationship developed between patient and therapist. The therapist can observe the patient's ease of disclosure and responses to questions and interventions and can monitor transference and countertransference reactions that occur during the interview.

The quality of alliance developed in the first interview can be key to determining the patient's ability to work in a psychoanalytically informed treatment. The following example illustrates how a therapist can draw on transference–countertransference issues in the first session that are related to a patient's ego strength and ability to benefit from interpretation.

A patient who came for therapy because of increasing negativity toward her husband felt intimidated by a therapist's interpretation toward the end of the first meeting. The interpretation addressed the patient-therapist interaction. The therapist noted how the patient's excessive questioning of his motives for asking questions sounded similar to the way she described her nitpicking at her husband because she wanted him to become, in her words, "a better man." Throughout the interview, the therapist had felt badgered by having to qualify his reasons for asking questions, but was able to develop a trial interpretation after analyzing his countertransference reaction to the patient. With the therapist's encouragement, the patient was able to process her initial reaction to the interpretation and reported feeling relief that the therapist was comfortable enough to actually raise the issue and talk to her about her aggressive style, which she knew was problematic. She then described its origins in her childhood relationship with a critical father. The patient agreed to further sessions and, over the course of therapy, would periodically refer back to the therapist's calm and accurate assessment of her style in their first session as a turning point in her realization that she truly needed help.

Mental Status and Ego Functioning

Both mental status data and ego functioning are important to assay when developing an initial impression of the patient. An initial diagnostic interview that involves process and structure can cover a significant amount of territory in a way that respects the patient's needs and helps the therapist make an informed diagnosis and treatment plan. Gabbard (1990) and Schwartz (1997) described the importance of making an evaluation of mental status and ego functioning one part of the first meeting.

The therapist who conducts an initial diagnostic interview need not solicit specific information on all fronts, but may be able to derive valuable data through observation and inference based upon the patient's physical appearance and self-report. Areas that are important to note include orientation to person, place, and time; dress; manner; physical anomalies; gait; volume of speech; verbal facility; and speech comprehension. In addition, the therapist attends to appropriateness of mood, range of affect, thought content, ability to abstract and self-reflect, defensive style, and ease of rapport. The therapist also makes a mental note of the patient's reality testing, presence of hallucinations, ideas of reference, persecutorial ideation, suicidal or aggressive ideation, phobias or anxiety, work history, current support system, superego maturity, self-esteem vulnerability, and prior therapy history and its outcomes. Information about the patient's judgment, abstract reasoning, insight, self-image, perception of relationships, frustration tolerance, defenses, and sublimations add valuable information to the initial diagnostic formulation (Iennarella & Frick, 1997). The therapist might make a direct inquiry, if not referenced spontaneously, about the patient's physical health, relationship to parents and siblings, and family mental health history. The patient's goals for therapy would be identified as part of the initial meeting.

There might be a need to inquire in areas that are not always articulated openly by the patient, such as a history of drug and alcohol use, any history of learning disability or attention-deficit disorder, and forensic history. The therapist might also choose to invite the patient to comment on his or her experience of the interview. As part of the evaluation process, the therapist assesses the patient's need for other types of intervention that would provide additional direction and support to the psychotherapy experience, including psychological testing, neurological assessment, and medication. A psychological test battery, assessment of the patient's neurological status, and medical evaluation for pharmacological intervention can strengthen an understanding of the patient's needs and help to refine diagnosis and treatment planning.

Interventions

The combination of structured and semistructured interviewing techniques organized around specific intervention strategies can elicit a wealth of diagnostic data in the initial session. Psychoanalytic interventions can be classified along a supportive–exploratory continuum (Gabbard, 1990; Josephs, 1995; Perry, 2002). Supportive intervention does not seek to uncover and resolve unconscious conflict. Instead, supportive comments provide the patient with a sense of feeling validated and understood, while not pressing defenses beyond their threshold. Exploratory interventions encourage the patient's reflection and insight into underlying conflicts. In reality, many therapists use both approaches with the same patient, emphasizing one over the other depending upon the patient's needs at any given time.

Supportive Interventions

Holinger (1999) has outlined a systematic approach to the application of noninterpretive interventions that issues from developmental theory, infant research, and an evolving body of clinical theory. Noninterpretive interventions are stimulus-regulating techniques that include validation, confirmation, mirroring, clarification, and providing a holding environment. They are meant to be synthesized with, rather than displace, an interpretive focus in psychoanalytic work. Noninterpretive interventions offer a model for providing patients who are vulnerable to intense affect states and prone to regression in self-esteem and object relations with supportive, reality-orienting, affirming, encouraging, and calming therapeutic responses that are offered in an atmosphere of psychological safety. Gabbard (1990) has included affirmation, empathic validation, and advice and praise in his schema of noninterpretive, supportive interventions.

An example of the application of a noninterpretive intervention approach is illustrated in the following vignette.

> A college sophomore with attention-deficit hyperactivity disorder, mixed type, had difficulty staying focused in the first interview. She had difficulty organizing her thoughts and listening to the therapist. Her inattentiveness so interfered with listening that she often felt herself responding to the last few words of what people said in conversation, and thus seemed—and was—out of sync socially. She felt depressed, angry, and misunderstood. People responded to her as if she was odd, and she had internalized a view of herself as defective, "weird," and unappealing. She had started using drugs and hanging out with other students who did not take their studies seriously. She placed herself at risk sexually on a number of occasions. She had begun taking stimulant medication prior to beginning college at the recommendation of her pediatrician, but was still socially awkward and always seemed agitated. In the first session, she spoke loudly and had difficulty modulating her voice tone as the therapist sought to clarify details about her history. The therapist asked for many clarifications and the patient experienced the questions as making her feel even more confused. The therapist heard the patient's comment as reflecting a sense of cognitive overload. She modified her style of interviewing and began offering supportive and explanatory comments as the patient continued to talk about her problems. The therapist helped the patient reframe her feelings, empathized with her frustration, and validated her positive strivings. The patient settled down and was able to describe her experiences in a way that was easy to understand.

Exploratory Interventions

Clarifications and confrontations each direct the patient's attention to particular aspects of the therapy process (Gabbard, 1990). A therapist might ask questions in order to clarify information or invite the patient's exploration of specific content in order to deepen the flow of material. An example of a clarification is, "Try to help me understand more about how you understood why your father insists on your calling him every night after work?" Or, "See if you can explain how her reaction to your comment made you feel?" A confrontation would endeavor to help the patient see inconsistencies in his or her description of people or events. An example of a confrontation is: "Earlier in the session, you described your girlfriend as very caring, and now you are talking about her as being selfish and devaluing. How can we understand these two descriptions as they apply to the same person?"

Interpretive intervention provides the groundwork for working through the layering of defenses that block conscious understanding of underlying conflict. The content of interpretation is built upon the patient's associations or the therapist's processing of an internal reaction to the patient's material, whereas the presentation of an interpretation is sensitive to the patient's ability to both hear and use the interpretation to gain insight and feel understood. Material presented in the first interview can provide the therapist with an opportunity to test the patient's response to an interpretation as a way of furthering the diagnostic process. There are different types of interpretations that a therapist might consider offering a patient during a first interview.

Transference interpretation is directed toward helping the patient understand the unconscious conflicts that shape perception toward significant people in the patient's life and is directed toward distortions in the patient's reaction to the therapist. These conflicts have a basis in the patient's early development. In a transference interpretation, the therapist draws the patient's attention to content in a way that illuminates an underlying conflict emergent with the therapist, with the goal of making this information conscious and accessible to working through.

Here-and-now transference interpretations (Gill, 1982; Gill & Hoffman, 1982) focus on the immediacy of the patient's reaction to the therapist as embedded in disguised allusions or references to the relationship. For example, a patient who talks about his father as a disappointment might be presented with an interpretation that addresses the therapist's sense that the patient is sensitive to similar qualities in the therapist.

Selfobject transference interpretations (Rowe & Mac Isaac, 1989) address disturbances in the patient's experience of the therapist. *Mirror transference interpretations* address the patient's narcissistic vulnerability in response to the therapist's perceived lack of empathy. *Twinship transference interpretations* address the patient's narcissistic vulnerability upon perceiving the therapist as having interests that are different from those of the patient. *Interpretations of the idealizing transference* address the patient's disappointment in the therapist's ability to live up to the patient's grandiose ideals. These interpretations would seek to restore cohesion to the temporary disruption of self structure experienced by the patient. An interpretation that reflects a selfobject disturbance in the idealizing transference might take the following form: "What I hear you saying is that it was disappointing and painful, upon getting my name from your friend whom you respect, not to see my name listed among 'top doctors' in the local newspaper when you went to check my credentials. It seemed to remind you, based upon what you've told me thus far, of your father's failure to achieve and the disappointment that you felt over his behavior."

Extratransference interpretations encourage the patient's understanding of connections that are outside of immediate conscious awareness, but are accessible to reflection through the interpretive process, without drawing attention to the way in which unconscious perceptions of the therapist might also be represented in the material. For example, a therapist might draw the patient's attention to the relationship between her reactions to a teacher and to a parent, but not to the relationship between teacher, parent, and therapist.

Projective identification communications develop from the therapist's processing of his or her emotional reaction to the patient's material. Tansey and Burke (1989) presented an extensive model for understanding and working with projective identifications in therapy. In projective identification, the patient projects conflicted material into the therapist. The therapist has a reaction to the material, which is then processed and developed into a communication to the patient. An example of a *transference-based communication* might be stated as follows: "You've been very clear in your expression of anger at me for not offering you several options for scheduling. You also mentioned that you accepted your wife's apology without discussion after she cursed at you in front of the kids because you couldn't make their school play because of work obligations. She doesn't see how hard you are trying to be everything to everyone, and the toll that it takes. Right now, it seems that is easier for you to be angry at me than to discuss your hurt and your disappointment and anger at your wife." In a *countertransference-based communication*, the therapist makes an explicit reference to his or her emotional knowledge (i.e., countertransference disclosure) derived from having processed the projective identification. An example of a countertransference-based communication, using the vignette noted above and defining countertransference as the totality of the therapist's reaction, might be stated as follows: "I realize that things have not been easy at home and that you have feelings about where you stand. It is not an easy situation to cope with. However, your anger at me is making me feel caught in the middle between your wife and you." In a *transference–countertransference-based communication* derived from a projective identification, the therapist combines the transference and countertransference interpretations based upon further deliberation about the possible meanings of the projective identification. In a transference–countertransference interpretation, the therapist might state: " I sense that you are trying to get me to be annoyed with you because you feel that I let you down by not offering a make-up time. It also tells me that you feel that you let your wife and child down, and that this is even harder for you to experience because of the anger that is involved in her response to you. I wonder if it is easier to create distance than to tell me that you really needed me to be there for you, that you felt vulnerable. If you told me this, it would have risked a lot, maybe more than you felt I could give."

Framework-based interpretations derive from Langs's communicative psychotherapy model (1982), in which the patient's reactions to deviations from an ideal therapeutic framework (e.g., set fee, total privacy, total confidentiality, interpretive interventions, therapist's anonymity, set time, set place) are given primacy for organizing the material in a session. Framework breaks are the basis for interpretive work because they disrupt the ideal therapeutic hold. The therapist listens for manifest references to issues related to the status of the therapy framework (e.g., comments about fees, shared waiting rooms, therapist cancellations, third-party payment), indicators of disturbance (e.g., anxiety, sleep disturbance, anger), and derivative perceptions (e.g., references to people in the client's life). Upon hearing an adaptive context, a few symptomatic indicators, and a few derivative perceptions, the therapist would offer an interpretation along very specific lines. In relation to an initial interview, an interpretation about the framework might take the following form: "You mentioned that I was a few minutes late in coming to meet you in the waiting area right when we began. You've been open in sharing with me why you are here, and you've been telling me about feeling depressed, anxious, and displaced by your husband, who works all of the time, and underappreciated by your boss. I think that you are telling me that you fear the same thing could happen here; that is, that I will not be able to give you full attention, which will only add to your anxiety and depression."

Within the communicative approach, therapists can also offer *secure-frame interpretations* (Langs, 1982). When the therapy frame is secure, the client experiences increased anxiety because of the stability of the therapy relationship. The stable therapy frame is unconsciously perceived as a threatening situation, because the relative absence of therapist input stimulates primitive anxiety in the patient. For example, in a secure-frame therapy, a client asks to leave the first session early. The therapist encourages the client's associations, and the client associates to a back pain, to a television show depicting someone who committed fraud, and to a depressed friend whose spouse cheated because he was never around. The therapist would then have the option of interpreting the associations in relation to the fears associated with a tightly controlled therapy, which makes the patient anxious, scared, and vulnerable to the problems that would arise if the therapist supported a frame break. A secure frame interpretation might take the following form: "You're indicating that if I were to support your leaving early, it would lead you to see me as a fraud and a cheat, and this would hurt and lead you to feel depressed." In short, when the frame is stable, there is more of an emphasis on the patient's conflicts operating with greater freedom from the therapist's conflicts than is the case when the therapeutic setting is highly unstable. Trawinski (1990) has argued for a flexible approach within a communicative model, emphasizing the integration of self psychology principles in certain circumstances that include sensitivity to severity of patient diagnosis, rather than a reliance on a purely interpretive model of intervention.

VALIDATION

Strategies for validating the success of interventions are important (Langs, 1982). How a therapist validates interventions will vary depending on approach, but there are some general guidelines that can help the therapist determine the patient's reaction to key interventions. Indications that an intervention has led to a positive identification with the therapist might include any of various observations. The patient might seem calmer and evidence reduced behavioral agitation in the session. The patient might manifest an increased ability to talk or associate without resistance or anxiety. The patient might comment about feeling less tense or more understood. There might be comments, either direct or displaced, about reduced symptomatic expression. The patient's associations might include images of well-functioning people. There might also be new disclosures that deepen the therapist's understanding of the patient's experience.

Conversely are indications that a particular intervention was not successful. The patient's thinking might become blocked. The patient might become more agitated or anxious in the session. There might be comments, either direct or displaced, suggestive of symptomatic tension. There might be images of people embedded in the associative flow who are hurtful or inaccessible, or there might be a flattening of associations. In addition, the therapist's own sense of increased understanding or anxiety and confusion might, respectively, provide additional information about the degree to which an intervention has helped or hindered the patient.

DIAGNOSIS AND TREATMENT PLANNING

Data from the initial interview shape diagnosis and treatment planning. Diagnosis and treatment planning influence each other (Gabbard, 1990). Diagnosis has multiple meanings within a psychoanalytic model. It can include the diagnosis of character (Lerner, 1991; McWilliams, 1994; Shapiro, 1965), disorders of self (Rowe & Mac Isaac, 1989), level of ego functioning (Kernberg, 1975), "if-then" contingency predictions in strategic diagnostic understanding (Bachrach, 1974), and maturity of psychosexual stage (Trimboli & Farr, 2000). Psychoanalytic theory can also accommodate the comprehensive symptom and personality clusters in the *Diagnostic and Statistical Manual* of the American Psychiatric Association, fourth edition (DSM-IV-TR; American Psychiatric Association, 2000). Gabbard (1990) has recommended a descriptive diagnosis based upon DSM criteria and a psychodynamic diagnosis that strives to help understand how the patient developed his or her problems and what purposes are served by the maintenance of these problems. A model for developing a descriptive and psychodynamic formulation that lends to decisions about treatment planning (e.g., ability to work in intensive or supportive psychoanalytic therapy, need for medication, need for hospitalization) is presented below.

Level of Ego Functioning and Core Dynamics

Trimboli and Farr (2000) have presented a comprehensive model for guiding psychoanalytic treatment planning that integrates drive and ego psychology. The model takes into account the patient's level of ego organization (psychotic, borderline, and neurotic), core dynamics, character style, and level of psychosexual development (oral, anal, and phallic). The diagnosis of level of ego organization is based upon Kernberg's three main structural criteria (1975)—degree of identity integration, maturity of defensive operations, and adequacy of reality testing—and the relative weighting of the nonspecific ego factors of anxiety tolerance, impulse control, and sublimatory channels. Degree of identity integration reflects the extent to which positive and negative images of self and objects are synthesized and continuous over time. Maturity of defensive operations covers a continuum ranging from the use of nonrepressive defenses of splitting, projection, and other lower defense mechanisms to reliance on repression, reaction formation, undoing, and intellectualization as examples of higher-level defenses. Reality testing refers to accuracy of perception under varying degrees of external structure.

Psychotic-level ego organization is characterized by deficits in identity integration, defense maturity, and reality testing. Core conflicts at the psychotic level of ego organization include annihilation, engulfment, and loss of self. Borderline-level ego organization is characterized by fluctuations in reality testing, with temporary, conflict-sensitive regressions related to themes of loss and aggression more likely to occur when structure declines and more likely to reconstitute with support and structure. Identity is intact and defenses are organized around splitting (e.g., devaluation, idealization). Core borderline conflicts include themes of separation, abandonment, and betrayal. Neurotic individuals function with consistent intrapsychic stability. Core neurotic conflicts include guilt and shame. There are other nonspecific manifestations of ego weakness that influence diagnosis. The psychosexual developmental level considers the prominence of oral, anal, and phallic traits. Patients organized at the psychotic, borderline, and neurotic levels of ego organization can be primarily oral, anal, or phallic in character orientation. According to Trimboli and Farr (2000), oral characters are concerned mainly with gratification of their own needs, anal characters struggle with themes of control and domination, and phallic characters are conflicted around themes of wanting what and whom others have.

Character Diagnosis

Psychoanalytic character style (McWilliams, 1994; Shapiro, 1965) can be integrated within a model of psychosexual and ego levels of development. For example, patients with hysterical, obsessive-compulsive, and depressive personality characteristics each present with a unique cluster of symptoms, core dynamics, and defenses that can be integrated within a model of psychosexual and ego levels of development. The hysteric is emotional, intuitive, seductive, competitive, and prone to naïveté and repression. The obsessive compulsive is rigid, ideational, inhibited, precise, conscientious, and prone to intellectualization, undoing, and reaction formation. The depressive is somber, sensitive, serious, critical, controlled, self-conscious and prone to defensive self-blame/introjection. In Trimboli and Farr's model (2000), hysterics are more phallic–neurotic, obsessive compulsives are more anal–neurotic, and depressives are more oral–neurotic. Other patients with different personality styles, such as sadistic–masochistic, infantile, narcissistic, antisocial, schizotypal, schizoid, and paranoid, each have different sensitivities and defensive patterns that place them within the borderline or psychotic range.

Disorders of Self

Disorders of self have a different theoretical base than either ego disturbance or psychosexual character disturbance, but the phenomenological description of self disorders can be diagnostic in highlighting narcissistic vulnerability (Rowe & Mac Issac, 1989). Narcissistically vulnerable patients will often require interventions that respond to self-esteem variance as a prelude to interpretive work. The *understimulated self* is related to a developmental history of inadequate mirroring, which leads these patients to present as apathetic, bored, and lacking a sense of vitality. To compensate for this sense of understimulation, patients may resort to high-risk behaviors, including suicidal gestures, to escape the empty and depressed feeling that underlies the agitated behavior. The *fragmenting self* portrays the patient who is vulnerable to severe disruptions in self-cohesion secondary to empathic lapse and to chronic states of exaggerated health concerns, including severe hypochondriacal concerns. The *overstimulated self* describes patients who received excessive or phase inappropriate stimulation in the grandiose or idealizing sectors of the personality. These patients can present with intense excitability or with grandiose fantasies. If the grandiose sector of the personality is overstimulated, then the patient will experience a vulnerability to acute states of anxiety and fear if she is the recipient of public recognition for achievements. Consequently, the creative potential of patients with excessive grandiosity is often underdeveloped because of the fear associated with heightened states of accomplishments. If the idealizing sector of the personality is overstimulated, then the patient will experience a longing for merger with an idealized other. However, fear of being overstimulated by this contact will lead the patient to shun opportunities for contact with admired others, thereby relinquishing opportunities for enjoyment and collaboration with people whose values she admires. The *overburdened self* describes patients who were deprived of an opportunity to merge with an idealized object. The absence of contact with soothing and calm people during formative development can result in a spread of anxiety and heightened affect, a perception of the self as burdened, and a view of the world as fraught with danger.

ADULT CASE ILLUSTRATION

Interview Data

The following vignette is a hypothetical composite of different patients, but the general content and themes would be a fair portrayal of themes and content that emerge in an initial session.

The patient is Caucasian male in his late twenties who was referred for therapy by his wife's psychotherapist. His wife had been in therapy for many years secondary to a history of childhood abuse at the hands of her stepfather. Her father had died young, and her mother remarried to a volatile man who was mentally and physically cruel to the client's wife during her formative years. The patient had periodically participated in joint sessions at his wife's request for support, but felt ambivalent about doing so and that he would benefit from his own therapy. His stress level was increasing, and he needed to talk some things out. He expressed this thought to his wife's therapist in the context of also describing his own desire to speak with someone professionally. He requested a male therapist and was referred to a Caucasian, male psychologist who was older than the patient.

After some back and forth with voice messages, the patient spoke directly to the therapist (the therapist had given the patient a set time to call) and explained the basis for the referral and the referral source. They discussed a time and date to meet. The patient knew the area where the therapist's office was located. The patient also inquired about the therapist's involvement with managed care. The therapist stated that he was not on any provider panels and asked if this would pose a problem to the patient. The patient said that he was fine with this and asked for the therapist's fee. The therapist stated his usual fee and the patient stated that the fee would not be a problem. They agreed to a forty-five-minute initial interview to explore the patient's problem.

The patient arrived five minutes late for the session and introduced himself upon being met in the waiting area. The therapist greeted him, stating that he was glad that the patient made it. He motioned the patient to a chair; as he sat down, the patient apologized, stating that there had been unexpected traffic.

The therapist asked the patient how he could be of help. The patient stated that his stress level was going up. The therapist asked the patient to explain more about what he meant. The patient stated that his spouse and he had been married for five years and had a two-and-one-half-year-old son. Their marriage had its ups and downs, due mainly to his wife's mood, but he was also concerned with the fact that his son required seemingly endless limit setting, which made him feel guilty. He felt that he was always the one setting limits. The patient often lost his temper with his son, which made him feel very guilty and led him to overeat. He noted that he had always had a weight problem and had been unable to commit to an exercise program. His wife, like the patient, was college educated, but not working. She always seemed stressed, near tears, and doubted her parenting skills. The patient knew that her needs were extensive and realized that he would have to bear the brunt of things in order to help keep the house settled. The patient's wife was doing better in her therapy. However, the patient noted that he had started to express resentments, including openly critical remarks about her parenting, despite her progress. He questioned his behavior toward his wife. Admittedly, he also doubted his own parenting skills. He also had begun to feel a sense of dread when it was time to leave work and come home for the evening, but was losing interest in his job as a computer programmer. His wife was talking about wanting another child, but he did not see them as being ready for it and had noticed that he was withdrawing from sexual opportunities with his wife for fear that she would become pregnant. He reported feeling burdened, sleeping fitfully, and feeling unhappier than ever before. He had been feeling down in mood and physically tired for a few years, had difficulty concentrating at work or at home, and could never relax.

The therapist asked the patient if he had ever been in therapy before. The patient initially said "No," but then recalled having had a few sessions with a college counselor right after his father had suddenly died from cardiac arrest when the patient was a college junior. The therapist asked the patient to talk more about his memory of his relationship with his father. The patient described his father with mixed emotions—the patient loved him because he was his father, but felt torn because his father was a "mean man." The therapist asked the patient to clarify what he meant by a "mean man." The patient stated that his father was tense, a bully, and never happy. He worked nonstop, seemed miserable and grouchy, and was mean to the patient and to his mother, but not to the patient's older sister, for whom the father had a special fondness. The patient also described his mother's sadness when the patient left for college and his guilt about leaving her alone with his father.

The therapist asked the patient to describe more about his recollection of his family. The patient focused on how his mother was "an abused housewife— he was always critical of her"—and described how he would spend long periods talking with his mother to keep her spirits up. He felt like the man of the family in many ways, even though he was just a teenager at the time.

The patient's eyes welled up. He reached for a tissue. After a brief silence, the therapist said that he noted similarities between the patient and his father; the patient felt on edge, stressed, and not at peace with his wife and was not reacting to his son in a way that he felt good about. The patient reacted somewhat defensively, stating, "Well, I can see your point, but it's really not the same at all. He was a mean s.o.b. and I am trying to deal with a lot without flipping out. He never would have come for therapy." The therapist stated, "Let me check this out with you. Did you feel that my question was a criticism?" The patient responded by stating, "Maybe a bit, but that's just me. It's not your fault. I always get my back up when I feel criticized. Your question made sense. I just have to work on this." The therapist responded that he was glad that the patient was able to tell him how he felt and that he would be attentive to this in the future.

At this point, the interview was coming to a close. The therapist stated, "I'm glad you came in; you have a lot on your mind and a lot to talk about. You do seem to need a space for yourself." He asked the patient if he wanted to set up weekly appointments at a set date and time. The patient agreed. The therapist then asked the patient what he wanted to attain from therapy. The patient stated that he wasn't exactly sure; talking had been helpful and he wanted to feel less stress, but beyond that, he couldn't really say. He paused and then asked if the therapist would be willing to consider lowering the fee. He stated: "I think that it could be more expensive than I originally thought, with both my wife and me in therapy. I hadn't really thought the money piece through." The therapist stated that he would be willing to consider a small reduction in the stated fee, but added that it might be helpful to talk more about the fee when they had more time. The patient agreed. The therapist then explained his policy on confidentiality, cancellations, record keeping, and the open-ended nature of therapy. They shook hands, and the session ended.

Analysis of the Session

The therapy setting is a private, nonmanaged care practice in which the therapist operates with a reasonable amount of autonomy and control over patient selection, fee structure, and conditions of the treatment. That the therapist is able to represent a level of autonomous functioning can serve as a positive identification for a patient who feels easily sapped by the needs of others.

The referral was motivated by the patient's decision to seek his own psychotherapy. His history included a period of overinvolvement with his mother and an emotionally unavailable father. It is possible that his periodic presence in his wife's therapy sessions also made him feel overly involved and stimulated his own need for contact with a male in whom he could confide.

The therapist needed to set a limit around the phone-tag process that was evolving around setting up the appointment. The need to set a limit has the positive quality of presenting a clear and firm statement to the patient that is boundaried and direct. It also leads the therapist to speculate about whether or not this patient has difficulty with limit setting with coworkers and at home.

In introducing a discussion of the fee during the initial phone contact, the patient showed a practical side to his character—if he could not pay the therapist's fee, then there might be little value in setting up a first meeting. The therapist responded honestly and the patient agreed to the initial meeting. However, introducing the fee also suggested the possibility that the patient might feel a sense of guilt about starting therapy on his own; for example, could he make himself a priority without feeling that his wife, like his mother, would have difficulty once he moved into his own therapy? Or would he be overstimulated by his own initiative and set up obstacles to the treatment that would undo his independent strivings, including feeling conflicted about having to pay for what he might privately have felt was his entitlement? Or, given the fact that his wife was getting better, was he now more anxious than before about his own issues? That is, in the past, he could easily blame many of his frustrations on his wife, but now he might have to attend more to his own needs, which might create additional ambivalence about beginning therapy. There was also a hidden test of the therapist's style embedded in the fee question: Would the therapist be forthright or defensive? Thus, the patient also sought to garner important diagnostic information about the therapist right from the start of the interview process.

The patient arrived five minutes late for the first session. The lateness might be taken as a sign of anxiety about beginning therapy, although there was also the reality of unpredictable traffic patterns that are not always easy to anticipate, even when one is familiar with a particular area. The therapist's greeting was appropriate, but possibly belied a reaction-formation ("glad you made it") as a defense against anger associated with the patient's lateness. The patient's apology spoke to a mature sense of guilt, but might also have been motivated by a desire to appease an unconscious perception of the therapist's annoyance.

The therapist began with a standard opening about how he might be of help; it is important to note, however, that hypotheses had already been generated silently about the patient's guilt, his need for more autonomy, and possibly a passive-aggressive form of resistance as areas that would probably require attention in therapy. The patient then offered a clear description of his concerns. The comments about marital tension, his sleep disturbance, unhappiness, burden, overeating, wife's mental health needs, son's need for limits, dread of coming home, sexual withdrawal, fear of losing his job, and critical attitude each say something about the patient's needs and anxieties as he entertained the onset of treatment. He portrayed himself as needing relief from an inner crisis, including the need for help in setting boundaries internally, and the presence of a calm and soothing relationship with a therapist who would lift away some of the weight and burden associated with anxiety, guilt, inhibition, anxiety, and self-blame.

It was easy to feel an emergent projective identification—the patient was late, the therapist worried, felt anxious, and felt angry. These reactions might have spoken to the therapist's having identified with the patient's own anxieties about his wife becoming pregnant (i.e., worry, possible concern about her being "late"), his reaction to his son (i.e., anxiety, worry, anger), and his anxiety around loss (i.e., the patient was not present when expected). Through the projective identification, the therapist identified a heightening of affect states and evaluated their fit with the patient's life in order to determine if a communication would be helpful to the patient at this point in time.

Rather than respond overtly to the projective identification, the therapist, in keeping with his interest in gathering a range of information about the patient, chose to inquire about the patient's prior therapy history. The patient's initial reaction was "No," suggesting a temporary repression of his having participated in therapy with his wife. Indeed, both patient and therapist appeared to have jointly repressed the fact that the patient had indeed been in therapy, albeit sporadically, with the therapist who saw the patient's wife. The patient may have had discomfort over his role in that relationship, and the therapist's own sensitivities may have been stirred by the triadic dynamics of the conjoint marital therapy as well. The patient's recollection of his father revealed a rivalrous, aggressive relationship that rendered the patient vulnerable to the moods of his father and his mother. His relationship to his wife and own son had some of the same features that were present in his early relationship to his parents—a sense of burden related to his wife's mental health needs, outbursts toward his son, and longing for respite.

The therapist offered an extratransference interpretation by linking the patient to his father. The interpretation followed the patient becoming openly sad in the interview. The therapist's response can be understood as a reaction to his own discomfort with the emergence of sadness. He responded with an aggressive comment with which the patient immediately took umbrage. The therapist's guilt became aroused; he immediately noted the patient's reaction, acknowledged a lapse in empathy, and conveyed in a promissory way that he would try to take his lead from the patient. The patient then became self-blaming to take the heat off of the therapist.

The session ended with the therapist offering a gentle comment that summarized the essence of the patient's needs. They agreed to meet, but the fee issue again cropped up. Its reemergence at this point raises a question about whether the patient wanted compensation for the therapist's ill-timed interpretation, in addition to the earlier noted themes of guilt and anxiety associated with beginning therapy. The therapist, while willing to renegotiate the fee within reason, is able to contain the patient's request without overreacting by rapidly undoing his sense of having injured the patient's self-esteem.

Theory

The following discussion highlights some of the main theoretical concepts from different models that help to illuminate the patient's psychodynamics. The oedipal theme is salient in this session. The patient had a serious conflict with his father, who was shaming and dismissive, which stimulated an intense, adult-like attachment to his mother at an early age. Symptoms of guilt and sexual inhibition may be reflective of superego prohibitions associated with an unresolved oedipal conflict. A control theme with his son may have been a vestige of anal conflicts, whereas his overeating may have reflected strong oral needs. The impulse-defense configurations that shaped the patient's ego structure appeared to organize around undoing (going overboard to take responsibility), reaction formation (guilt over breakthrough of anger associated with not being good enough), and introjection (self-blame). The patient's internal object representations show a reasonably high level of maturity and separation, but he appeared to struggle to distance an unconscious identification with his father's sadism toward his son and wife. He was capable of warm and loving feelings, but also had selected a spouse whose mental health needs were prominent and symbolically representative of his mother's upset. In the initial interview, he arrived late and expressed the theme of absent other that characterized his relationship with his father. With his mother, using Winnicott's terms, he felt contained, but also functioned as a container. He was able to see positive and negative qualities in the same person, suggesting the capacity for relatively consistent whole-object relations. In the area of self-esteem regulation, it appears that he received sufficient mirroring and affirmation of his talents from his mother, but the absence of a consistently regulating idealizing object had rendered him vulnerable to states of heightened affect, somatic anxiety related to weight control, and dysphoric mood.

Mental Status and Ego Functioning

The patient was oriented to person, place, and time. He was responsive to questions, evidenced no obvious physical anomalies, and was able to present his thoughts in an organized and articulate way that responded directly to the therapist's inquiry. Mood was somber if not depressed. Primary affects appeared to be sadness, anger, and anxiety. Affect was appropriate to content. There were no apparent disturbances in reality testing. He appeared to be capable of insightful thought.

The patient's superego appeared to be mature, but vulnerable to harsh self- and other judgments. There was conflict around anger expression and around the expression of sexual feelings. His frustration tolerance appeared to be reasonably intact, without evidence of frank impulse disorders related to drugs or alcohol, promiscuity, or other forms of acting out, but with evidence of impulse control vulnerability in the areas of aggression and overeating. He seemed capable of whole-object relations on a consistent basis. His identity was stable and continuous over time. His primary defense mechanisms were organized around higher-level defenses, but he also evidenced the potential to use projective identification as a defense mechanism in response to his conflict with his wife (he agitated her and then reacted) and his son.

Diagnosis and Treatment Planning

The patient exhibited DSM-IV-TR (American Psychiatric Association, 2000) descriptive symptomatology reflective of a dysthymic disorder (e.g., sadness, fatigue, decreased concentration; sleep and appetite dysregulation as symptoms; duration of depressed mood for a few years). His level of ego functioning was neurotic (i.e., stable reality testing, identity, primary reliance on depressive defenses), but with a concern about few sublimation channels (i.e., difficulty relaxing, work dissatisfaction). His psychosexual character orientation appeared to reflect a mixture of oral (e.g., overeating), anal (e.g., control theme, shame), and oedipal (e.g., rivalry with father) conflicts. His personality type appeared to be depressive (e.g., somber mood, self-critical, self-conscious, quick to feel judged). His history of a disappointing and nonsoothing relationship with his father and his depressed, depleted, and anxious symptoms bear similarity to Kohut's description of the overburdened self.

Treatment planning for this patient would suggest that he had the potential to benefit from a combination of supportive and exploratory interventions. He was somewhat resistant to starting therapy and had a history of disappointment in his father, whose death he never mourned. He was also sensitive to criticism and was experiencing an uncomfortable level of stress that included being a young father, having a wife with a history of trauma at the hands of an abusive stepparent, job uncertainty, and an incomplete mourning of his relationship with his father. Themes that were likely to influence his core sensitivities to the therapist's interventions: Was he good enough? Could he tolerate interpretation without feeling criticized and judged? Would he regress into states of ruminative self-blame in the absence of having his mother's needs to buffer his pain? Would he look to cut deals and withhold as a way of keeping the anxiety attached to mature discussion and reflection at bay? He was also intelligent, was able to introspect, had a strong conscious, and could probably respond favorably to interpretations once a solid foundation was established. He did not require medication to reduce symptom intensity.

DIFFERENCES BETWEEN ADULT AND CHILD INTERVIEWING

There are several key differences in the type of diagnostic interview approach used with children and adolescents and with adults. With child and adolescent clients, there is less emphasis on verbal communication, especially in younger children. There is collateral involvement with parents/caregivers that influences the treatment process and the ascendance of child and adolescent comorbid disorders (e.g., Attention Deficit Hyperactivity Disorder and learning disabilities) that can introduce challenges into the process of assessment and treatment. Chethik (1989) highlights the emotional dependency of children, a greater need for action through play, fluctuating ego states, and involvement with parents when comparing child and adult diagnostic and treatment considerations. In child and adolescent therapy, and more so with child therapy, the therapist's language must be adapted carefully to the developmental stage/level of the child as well as to the child's receptive and expressive language skill. Adults, in contrast, typically enter therapy with knowledge about presenting complaints that reflects a higher level of insight than seen in younger clients. Adults are generally self-referred, whereas children are often referred for therapy at the request of adults. Adults also have a richer vocabulary for expressing concerns, whereas children may prefer to express thoughts and feelings through play. Through the process of play, a child may express wishes, fears, and fantasies as well as inner reality, whereas the adult conveys his or her inner reality primarily through the use of language. The relationship between the child and adult is more influenced by ongoing developing dependency needs, while the adult functions at different levels of independence and interaction. The therapist often plays a role designated by the child, whereas therapists who interview adults do not engage in a change of role. Sanville (1991) indicated that children process experiences through play without a long accumulation of memories to influence experience, whereas the adult client has acquired an accumulation of memories over time that influence verbalizations during the interview.

ORIGINS OF PSYCHOANALYTIC CHILD INTERVIEWING

Analytic contributions to the psychiatric/psychological assessment of children began in 1921, when von Hug-Hellmuth introduced the concept that children communicate through play. Melanie Klein (1932) later recognized the importance of fantasy and the play technique when diagnosing and treating children. Child analytic therapy is sensitive to developmental stages and their impact on the psyche of a child. Developmental stage theory in psychoanalytic psychology includes Sigmund Freud's psychosexual stages (1905; 1916–1917), Anna Freud's concept of the diagnostic profile using developmental norms (1963), Erikson's psychosocial stages (1963), and the stages of maturation proposed by Mahler et al. (1975). Kernberg (1975) and Kohut (1971; 1977) have presented different views on the developmental factors that place individuals at risk for serious personality disturbances. Rapaport (1957) and Stern (1985) have contributed to understanding the adaptive functioning of the child's dynamics, including reality testing and an evolving sense of self.

The clinical approach of Greenspan (1997) incorporates developmental theory with a psychoanalytic understanding of development. Greenspan encourages spontaneous and semistructured interactions when evaluating children. His assessment process places an emphasis on the child's capacity for representation, representation differentiation, shared attention efforts, engagement, intentional signaling, and representational elaboration. Other analytic concepts that have contributed to understanding the assessment process include the importance of the child/caregiver relationship, how symbolism and representation are manifested in a child's play, separation/individuation issues, attachment, the role of the unconscious, and the importance of transference.

Morrison and Anders (1999) have also identified the significance of the play interview and direct and indirect interview styles when assessing children. Differences in open-ended questions and questions that request specific information as well as the play interview were noted and viewed as equally important in the process of collecting information from the child.

INTERVENTIONS

The diagnostic interview with children includes a process of collecting information from a variety of sources. Common sources of information about the child include parents/significant family members and teachers. Depending on the nature of the referral, the therapist might also have contact with a pediatrician. In addition, the actual child interview may include structured and unstructured questions in addition to play sessions as complementary methods of gathering diagnostic information while observing and interacting with the child (Morrison & Anders, 1999). Responses to projective questions and play provide a window into understanding of the child's sense of self, strengths, and weaknesses within the relational outside world and of internal conflicts that hamper development and influence experience.

The ability to conduct a skilled diagnostic interview requires an understanding of theory and technique, as well as an effective style of communicating with the child. The relationship is established in the interview through rapport building, providing a secure environment, and verbal and nonverbal communication. Technique involves establishing a "holding environment" (Winnicott, 1965), listening and observing, and using play, words, empathic engagement, gestures, expressions, voice intonations, and reciprocal exchanges (Greenspan, 1997). Through the identification and understanding of transference, of how past interactions interfere with current relationships, of the function the child delegates to the therapist, and of developmental markers, resistance, and defenses, the interviewer organizes and assigns meaning to clinical information. Developing and strengthening adaptive coping skills through noninterpretive and interpretive intervention can lead to the modification of defenses and behaviors that interfere with coping. Developing positive rapport with parents, teachers, and other individuals who are significant in the child's daily life can support and strengthen the continuity of therapy and facilitate the child's ability to benefit from direct therapeutic intervention.

The therapist might begin the intervention process by conducting a formal consultation with the parent(s) or guardian/caregiver(s). The purpose of the consultation is to meet the parent(s) or guardian/caregiver(s), gather background information, explain therapy, and assess potential fit with the client. History taking includes the chief complaint, past psychiatric/psychological and medical problems, neurological history, developmental history (e.g., fine and gross motor development, language development, temperament, nutritional status), educational history, and family history. Once an agreement to begin therapy is made, the therapist sees the child for a first session, during which essential diagnostic information is gathered. Observations of the child begin upon initial contact and may include how the child separates from the parent/guardian/caregiver, what the child brings into the session, questions the child asks, and how the child uses the therapist when communicating. The therapist observes the child for signs of anxiety, exaggeration, or grandiosity; identifies the child's preference for seating and play materials; and monitors the child's need for verbal and nonverbal reassurance. A decision about whether or not to request a psychological evaluation might also be made in response to the first therapy session.

CHILD CASE ILLUSTRATION

The following case is presented to illustrate one strategy for conducting an initial diagnostic interview in child therapy from a psychoanalytic perspective. As an orientation to the interview, it will help to highlight in advance the therapist's role and approach in the session. The therapist in this session conducted a history that included an assessment of cultural factors between the interviewer, child and mother and cultural components associated with the mother's understanding of the problem, and utilized observation and clinical inferencing while assessing the child's internal capacities and needs in relation to the external environment. The therapist sustained contact, reframed, clarified, reflected, and explored themes with the child and attempted to build rapport with verbal and nonverbal communications. These points will be noted below.

The Parent Consultation

This case is a composite of symptoms of similar patients and demonstrates how their problems may be revealed in an initial psychoanalytic child therapy interview.

Martin is an African American seven-year-old boy referred for therapy by his school district and mother. The therapist is a Caucasian female similar in age to Martin's mother. Martin's mother called up the therapist. They discussed some basics about therapy, including the main problem area. Martin's father, a physician, had been killed by a drunken driver one year earlier, and Martin was struggling to cope. After leaving the hospital where he worked as a physician, Martin's father had proceeded to walk toward the parking garage where his car was parked. As he crossed a major intersection one block from his car, he was struck and killed. Martin was six at the time of his father's death. The therapist empathized with Martin's situation. The case was under litigation at the time of initial consultation. The therapist and Martin's mother agreed to meet for a consultation during which the therapist could gather background information and decide, along with Martin's mother, about whether or not Martin would be comfortable meeting with the therapist.

Martin's mother met the therapist in the therapist's private office, which was a short drive from Martin's home. The therapist's office was equipped with toys, crayons, dolls, and other accoutrements to accommodate play therapy sessions. The therapist greeted Martin's mother in the waiting area, motioned her to a chair, and invited her to share more about why she was seeking therapy for her son.

The therapist first asked about the main areas of concern. Martin's mother stated that he was an only child who had recently begun to ask excessive questions and express worries about the strength of objects, animals, and people. Other concerns included preoccupations with a magnet collection, limited peer relationships, and fears of going to school. Martin's mother was also interested in knowing if taking her son to Africa to visit relatives (particularly male uncles) would help alleviate her son's feelings of pain regarding the loss of his father. Martin had begun to talk about feeling sad and about how he missed his father.

The therapist then asked about Martin's relationship to his father. Martin's mother became teary as she described Martin's close relationship to his father prior to his father's death. Following this event, Martin went through a period of denial, but then became tense, exhibited fears, and repeatedly asked questions about the strength of objects, animals, and people. He also began making get well cards for anyone he heard had become ill (whether he knew them or not). He also began to have difficulty making friends easily and "lost his spontaneity."

The therapist then inquired about Martin's relationship to his mother and extended family. His mother stated that they were close and that she wanted to make sure that Martin spent considerable time with extended family in order to provide him with support. Martin's mother was concerned that Martin would suffer because their extended family in America consisted mostly of females, and she was concerned there were not enough adult males in his life to help provide him with male bonding. His mother did indicate their strong association with the community church and pastor. Martin's mother stated that she was still grieving and had no desire to date. She felt that her life had to be focused on Martin's needs.

The therapist asked about Martin's early development. Regarding developmental milestones, Martin walked at thirteen months, was toilet trained at twenty-four months, and spoke in sentences at two and one-half years of age. As an infant and toddler, Martin startled easily but was able to be comforted by both mother and father. At family parties and events, Martin was described as "interactive" and "intense." When home movies were taken, people would say "smile Martin, you look so serious." Martin was very coordinated and played well on gym equipment.

Martin's mother shared insights provided by Martin's teacher, who had also been his preschool–kindergarten teacher. Martin's teacher had commented that during the past year he seemed "worried" and had recently started biting his lips, sometimes making them bleed. She noticed that Martin was hesitant to enter the classroom and required coaxing to join the other students. She also shared that he appeared "anxious" and "fearful." When in reading group, Martin would frequently interrupt the readings with questions regarding the strength of the animals or buildings mentioned in the stories.

When asked how she would like for Martin to improve, the mother commented, "I would like for him to blend in with the other children, not ask so many strange questions, and learn to stand on his own two feet; I know that is what his father would have wanted."

Martin's mother asked the therapist if she had worked with African American clients. The therapist stated that she had, and she shared a bit of her background as a therapist who did multicultural consultation as part of her practice. The therapist asked Martin's mother if Martin would be comfortable with the therapist. Martin's mother stated that she felt that Martin would feel comfortable with the therapist.

The session ended with a discussion of how therapy would proceed. The therapist explained the role of play in therapy and gave Martin's mother a general idea of the type of questions she might ask and how the session might proceed. She indicated that she would communicate with Martin's mother about her initial impression and then as needed, and she also explained confidentiality and its parameters. They also discussed the fee. Martin's mother agreed to the therapist's fee. The therapist was not on an insurance provider panel and agreed to submit a bill to Martin's mother at the end of the month for the previous month's sessions. Martin's mother wanted to submit the bill to her insurance company. Martin would be seen in an independent private practice. Martin's mother was open about her concerns and felt that the therapist would be a good match for Martin. Martin's mother stated that she was in counseling herself and was coping better now than last year. Her primary concern was for Martin. The therapist gave Martin's mother some general guidance on how to prepare Martin for the meeting. Overall, Martin's mother and the therapist developed the type of comfortable rapport that was needed to support Martin's therapy.

The Play–Diagnostic Interview

Martin's mother brought him on time to the first session. Following greetings in the waiting room, the therapist asked Martin to join her in the office to talk and play. He readily separated from the mother; however, he pulled out several metal pieces of his magnet collection from a small satchel he was carrying and asked that the mother hold them.

Upon entering the therapist's office, Martin quickly surveyed the area and immediately walked over to the toys and sat down. He said, "I like turtles and frogs," while at the same time picking up a hard plastic turtle and holding it. "I wish I had a real one."

> Therapist: Oh you have been thinking about turtles and frogs and would like to have one of your very own.
>
> Martin: Yes. [He then adds] "How do they eat?"
>
> Therapist: What do you think?
>
> Martin: I think frogs have a long, special tongue. Do other animals eat them? Can they feel it when they die?
>
> Therapist: Sounds like you are wondering if they will be OK and what it feels like when someone dies.
>
> Martin: I think turtles must be safer than frogs.
>
> Therapist: Oh?
>
> Martin: Yea, they have a hiding place and can store food in their hard shell [knocks on the shell with his knuckles]. You can die without food. I don't know how they eat [turns turtle over and looks at the mouth]. Do they feel things?
>
> Therapist: Feel things?
>
> Martin: You know, when the other animals eat them, can they feel it when they die?
>
> Therapist: How can we figure that out?
>
> Martin: See how hard the turtle is? How does he get so strong? If he is strong, maybe he won't die. I heard turtles live a long, long time. Do you think he is stronger than a snake?
>
> Therapist: Um, you are thinking about who is stronger?
>
> Martin: Yeah, a snake is very, very strong. But I touched one before and they are soft. They can get squashed but they can squeeze very hard. They are soft but strong. They have poison inside them so they won't get hurt. The poison makes them strong so they won't let anyone kill them.
>
> Therapist: Being strong might be something very important to you.
>
> Martin: Yes, it is!!!! A wolf is strong. Do you think a wolf is dangerous?
>
> Therapist: Maybe you have heard something about wolves; I am wondering what that is.
>
> Martin: There are small ones, medium-sized ones, and big ones.
>
> Therapist: What might a small one be like?
>
> Martin: They have a heart. I think it may be better to be a cold-blooded animal. They can't feel and they don't have hearts. Maybe it is better so their heart won't break. If a bullet lands there, he won't have a heart and he would not die.
>
> Therapist: Is it important for you to know more about death?
>
> Martin: I wonder about how animals die.
>
> Therapist: That's right, and how animals stay strong is something we can talk more about when we meet again, if you'd like to do that?
>
> Martin: Uh-huh.
>
> Therapist: Good, me too. We have to stop for today in a few minutes. There are just a few questions that I'd like to ask before we end, if that's okay.
>
> Martin: Uh-huh.

The Semistructured Interview

At this point in the interview, the therapist asked a few questions in order to refine her diagnostic impression of Martin.

Therapist: If you could have three wishes, what would they be?

Martin: Not let people do bad things, work in an animal shelter, and run real fast.

Therapist: If you had three bags of money to spend, what would you do?

Martin: Help my mother buy a new house, build more animal shelters, and fix all the tall buildings so they stay strong and not fall down.

Therapist: If you could take someone with you to a desert island, who would it be?

Martin: My mother to help me search for all the strong animals on the island.

Therapist: If you could be any type of animal, what kind of animal would you choose?

Martin: An elephant, because nobody tries to hurt elephants! I think about big elephants, how they are huge and strong and take *big heavy steps!* [Demonstrates. Then he adds] Sometimes I pretend I'm in Africa taking care of the elephants.

Therapist: What animal would you least want to be like?

Martin: An alligator; they surprise the wildebeests. They jump up out of the water and scare the animals getting a drink.

Therapist: If you could change someone in your family, who would you change?

Martin: My mother, so she could not be lonely.

Therapist: How would you change yourself if you could?

Martin: I would get big muscles or be a cold-blooded animal.

Therapist: Do you ever have dreams that wake you up?

Martin: Sometimes I dream something's going to kill me. I don't pay attention to it.

Therapist: How do you keep from paying attention to the nightmare?

Martin: I hold my breath and keep my head straight on the pillow.

Therapist: Martin, what are you most bothered by?

Martin: I don't know.

Therapist: Thanks for answering all those questions. I have just one more. Martin, why do you think your mom brought you to see me?

Martin: To help me not feel sad.

Analysis of the Session

In the interview, what became manifest was that Martin's verbalizations and play were prompted by his fears and unresolved issues related to the unexpected death of the father. For a latency child, the resolution of the Oedipus complex involves shifts in libido energy, object relations, and self-image (Blos, 1962; 1970), occurs through identification. In this case, the negotiation of the oedipal complex has been compromised, resulting in much tension and inner turmoil. The father's unexpected death interrupted Martin's ability to identify with the father, threatening his security and arousing tremendous anxiety. The death of the father did not allow him to work through the oedipal rivalry with the father and subsequent identification with him. Unresolved and in conflict, he remained torn by the guilt he felt about the father's death and by the lack of the protective shield of the father, thereby exposing him to danger.

Martin could not feel strong and confident to engage in school and peer interactions, because there was an unconscious need to come back to a dependency type of situation (e.g., neediness for the mother, magnet attraction, fears of going to school). He was afraid to leave the mother who was available to him because the father as a rival had ceased to exist. Stimulated by anxiety, he experienced a regressive shift as his drives and energy did not push him toward the outside world whereby he could replace the mother or father with a teacher and friendships with peers.

Martin's preoccupation with strong animals can be understood as representing a displacement of his earlier identification with a strong father whom he desperately misses. These attempts were efforts to avoid feeling helpless and unprotected. Separation anxieties were manifested in obsessive worries about objects, animals, and people's strength and safety and were viewed as displacement for the safety of a loved object.

Martin's superego was taxed by guilt associated with his own rivalrous feelings toward his father, who died. Martin's wish to find a protective role (working in animal shelters, building more animal shelters, fixing tall buildings, pretending he is in Africa taking care of elephants) can be understood as reflecting a projection of his own desires for protection and as an effort to provide support in a symbolic parental role.

Martin's primary defenses were regression, undoing, denial, projection, and displacement. Wishes for mastery and competence were compromised by regressive pulls as seen in unresolved dependency issues (e.g., fears of going to school). In addition, Martin's fears perhaps represented repressed anger toward the father for perceived abandonment or rejection. Manifestations of undoing and reparative efforts in response to underlying anger can be seen in his anxious questioning about the strength of objects (e.g., "Do you think he is stronger than a snake?" "How does he get so strong?"). Denial was manifested when he was unable to absorb the implications of his father's death. Projection was also utilized. He projected out his own wishes to be strong as well as his own fear of death with questions about how strong the animals are and how the animals experience death ("Can they feel it when they die?). He projected onto the animals his wishes for strength and security. The desire to help others get well by making get well cards represented a wish to help himself get well. This restitutional effort and the projection of the wish for others to get well reflected Martin's attempts to feel less vulnerable.

Considerations When Assessing Minority Children

When assessing minority children, the interviewer must determine the cultural elements of the relationship between the child and the interviewer. This assessment includes evaluating cultural factors related to social stresses, the family's support system, cultural components associated with the parent's explanation of the problems, and an open-mindedness to the role of cultural racism affecting a family's perception of itself. Moreover, the interviewer's cultural sensitivity is increased by a self-assessment of biases/prejudice as well as ongoing professional training in multiculturalism (Paniagua, 1998; 2001). The interviewer must not only pursue additional training when assessing culturally diverse children, but also seek guidance and consultation from multicultural experts. Moreover, an understanding of sociopolitical aspects of the child and family as well as understanding the child's world view assist the interviewer in providing professional and ethical services to individuals of culturally diverse backgrounds (Gopaul-McNicol & Thomas-Presswood, 1998; Gopaul-McNicol & Amour-Thomas, 2002). With regard to this case study, cultural considerations for Martin and his mother included assessing the implications of the child/ interviewer racial and ethnic differences (openly discussing feelings about the differences) and the mother's understanding of the cultural components associated with Martin's problems (importance of the extended family, community, and church). Ongoing and frequent contact with extended family members would be an important aspect of Martin's treatment and would be encouraged and supported. Because the mother specifically asked if Martin should visit the uncles in Africa, the therapist might suggest ways to prepare Martin for the travel and continue ongoing contacts with the uncles through the exchange of pictures and letters, phone contact, or e-mail and visits.

Diagnosis and Treatment Planning

Martin's case suggests an adjustment disorder with mixed anxiety and depressed mood (American Psychiatric Association, 2000). Therapeutic interventions (talking and play) would help Martin explore the connection between symptoms of anxiety and his unexpressed feelings of loss and fears of inadequacy. Martin was attempting to rationally understand his world (e.g., "I think turtles must be safer than frogs?" "Do you think a wolf is dangerous?"). However, he had difficulty emotionally integrating the pain he has experienced regarding the sudden loss of his father (e.g., "Can they feel it when they die?" "I think it may be better to be a cold-blooded animal").

Treatment would assist Martin in verbalizing feelings and associating affect with real events. It would be important to support the mother and son's strong identification with their cultural heritage, family and community networks, and ethnic identity. Weekly sessions for the mother were recommended to assist her in recognizing ways she might continue to enhance her son's sense of mastery and feelings of competence. Martin's reality testing was good and he had no problems with impulsive behavior. He was cooperative, able to symbolize, and could use humor. Both parents were emotionally available to him early in his life, and he felt sufficiently close to them until the unfortunate, unexpected death of the father. It also appears as though stress initiated Martin's difficulties with loss and separation, and his treatment would need to address the mourning process and dealing with being without a father.

It is important to note the unconscious sensitivities that were aroused by this interview. The interaction was organized around structured questions versus a more open-ended process approach, which may have affected Martin's sense of control and security during the interview. For example, anxiety about safety may be inferred from Martin's comments about dangerous animals. His wish for muscles might reflect his effort to "muscle his way" through the stress of the interview questions as well as his hope that the therapist can help him grow stronger over time. These less conscious reactions to the therapist might become more of a focus of the therapist's attention as the treatment shifts to a process-oriented approach. Such an approach would move beyond data gathering and attend further to the latent meaning of Martin's manifest comments and play activity. Primary interventions would be both supportive and exploratory, including interventions that sensitively address the client-therapist interaction.

CONCLUSION

A psychoanalytic approach to initial diagnostic interviewing with adults and children is challenging on multiple levels. It requires an understanding of psychoanalytic developmental theory, different approaches to clinical intervention, an introspective attitude toward the therapy process, and an ability to organize a diagnosis in a way that lends to treatment planning that is sensitive to the patient's age, life context, motivation, personal resources, and goals.

REFERENCES

American Psychiatric Association. 2000. *Diagnostic and Statistical Manual of Mental Disorders*, 4th ed., text revised. Washington, DC: American Psychiatric Association.

Bachrach, H. (1974). Diagnosis as understanding. Bulletin of the Menninger Clinic, 38:390–405.

Barron, J. W., & Sands, H. (1996). *Impact of Managed Care on Psychodynamic Treatment*. Madison, CT: International Universities Press.

Blos, P. (1962). *On Adolescence*. New York: Free Press.

Blos, P. (1970). *The Young Adolescent*. New York: Free Press.

Campbell, A., & Ladner, L. (1999). *Bridges of Compassion: Insight and Interventions in Developmental Disabilities*. Northvale, NJ: Aronson.

Casement, P. J. (1985). *On Learning from the Patient.* New York: Guilford.

Chethik, M. (1989). *Techniques of Child Therapy: Psychodynamic Strategies.* New York: Guilford.

Cornett, C., ed. (1993). *Affirmative Dynamic Psychotherapy with Gay Men.* Northvale, NJ: Aronson.

Erikson, E. (1963). *Childhood and Society.* New York: Norton.

Fast, I. (1984). *Gender Identity: A Differentiation Model.* Hillsdale, NJ: Analytic Press.

Freed, P. (2002). Meeting of the minds: Ego reintegration after traumatic brain injury. *Bulletin of the Menninger Clinic* 66:61–78.

Freud, A. (1963). The concept of developmental lines. *Psychoanalytic Study of the Child* 18:245–265.

Freud, S. (1905). Three essays on the theory of sexuality. *Standard Edition* 7:123–245.

Freud, S. (1916–1917). Introductory lectures on psychoanalysis, general theory of the neurosis, the development of the libido and the sexual organizations (Lecture 21). *Standard Edition* 15.

Frosh, S., Phoenix, A., & Pattman, R. (2000). "But it's racism I really hate": Young masculinities, racism and psychoanalysis. *Psychoanalytic Psychology* 17:225–242.

Gabbard, G. O. (1990). *Psychodynamic Psychiatry in Clinical Practice.* Washington, DC: American Psychiatric Press.

Gill, M. M. (1982). *The Analysis of the Transference*, Vol. 1. New York: International Universities Press.

Gill, M. M., & Hoffman, I. Z. (1982). *The Analysis of the Transference*, Vol. 2. New York: International Universities Press.

Gopaul-McNicol, S., & Amour-Thomas, E. (2002). *Assessment and Culture: Psychological Tests with Minority Populations.* San Diego, CA: Academic.

Gopaul-McNicol, S., & Thomas-Presswood, T. (1998). *Working with Culturally and Linguistically Different Children: Innovative Clinical and Educational Approaches.* Needham Heights, MA: Allyn & Bacon.

Greenberg, J. R., & Mitchell, S. A. (1983). *Object Relations in Psychoanalytic Theory.* Cambridge, MA: Harvard University Press.

Greenspan, S. I. (1997). *Developmentally Based Psychotherapy.* New York: International Universities Press.

Guntrip, H. (1971). *Psychoanalytic Theory, Therapy and the Self.* New York: Basic.

Holinger, P. C. (1999). Noninterpretive interventions in psychoanalysis and psychotherapy: A developmental perspective. *Psychoanalytic Psychology* 16: 233–253.

Hug-Hellmuth, H. von (1921). On technique of child analysis. *International Journal of Psychoanalysis* 2:287–305.

Iennarella, R. S., & Frick, E. (1997). Psychoanalytic interviewing. *Clinical and Diagnostic Interviewing*, ed. R. J. Craig, pp. 35–56. Northvale, NJ: Aronson.

Josephs, L. (1995). *Balancing Empathy and Interpretation.* Northvale, NJ: Aronson.

Juni, S. (2001). Indirect communication as an insight-oriented technique with the resistant and intellectually limited. *Journal of Psychotherapy Integration* 11:453–480.

Kernberg, O. F. (1975). *Borderline Conditions and Pathological Narcissism.* New York: Aronson.

Klein, M. (1932). *The Psychoanalysis of Children*, 3rd ed. London: Hogarth.

Kohut, H. (1971). *The Analysis of the Self.* New York: International Universities Press.

Kohut, H. (1977). *The Restoration of the Self.* New York: International Universities Press.

Langs, R. (1982). *Psychotherapy: A Basic Text.* New York: Aronson.

Lerner, P. M. (1991). *Psychoanalytic Theory and the Rorsach.* Hillsdale, NJ: Analytic Press.

Levine, S. S. (1996). *Useful Servants: Psychodynamic Approaches to Clinical Practice*. Northvale, NJ: Aronson.

Mahler, M., Pine, F., Bergman, A. (1975). *The Psychological Birth of the Human Infant*. New York: Basic.

McWilliams, N. (1994). *Psychoanalytic Diagnosis*. New York: Guilford.

Mitchell, S. A., & Black, R. J. (1995). *Freud and Beyond: A History of Modern Psychoanalytic Thought*. New York: Basic.

Morrison, J., & Anders, T. (1999). *Interviewing Children and Adolescents: Skills and Strategies for Effective DSM-IV Diagnosis*. New York: Guilford.

Paniagua, F. A. (1998). *Assessing and Treating Culturally Diverse Clients: A Practical Guide*, 2nd ed. Thousand Oaks, CA: Sage.

Paniagua, F. A. (2001). *Diagnosis in a Multicultural Context: A Casebook for Mental Health Professionals*. Thousand Oaks, CA: Sage.

Perry, C. J. (2002). Development of the therapeutic alliance: Current research. *Psychologist–Psychoanalyst* 22:21–24.

Rapaport, D. (1957). The theory of ego autonomy: A generalization. In *The Collected Papers of David Rapaport*, ed. M. M. Gill, pp. 22–724. New York: Basic, 1967.

Rothstein, A. A., & Glenn, J. (1999). *Learning Disabilities and Psychic Conflict: A Psychoanalytic Casebook*. Madison, CT: International Universities Press.

Rowe, C. E., Jr., & Mac Issac, D. S. (1989). *Empathic Attunement: The "Technique" of Psychoanalytic Self Psychology*. Northvale, NJ: Aronson

Sanville, J. (1991). *The Playground of Psychoanalytic Therapy*. New York: Analytic Press.

Schwartz, E. (1997) The mental status exam. In *Clinical and Diagnostic Interviewing*, ed. R. J. Craig, pp. 269–288. Northvale, NJ: Aronson.

Shapiro, D. (1965). *Neurotic Styles*. New York: Basic.

Stern, D. (1985). *The Interpersonal World of the Infant: A View from Psychoanalysis and Developmental Psychology*. New York: Basic.

Stutman, G. (1991). Insurance reimbursement: The impossible necessity? *Bulletin of the Society for Psychoanalytic Psychotherapy* 6:3–10.

Tansey, M. J., & Burke, W. F. (1989). *Understanding Countertransference: From Empathy to Projective Identification*. Hillsdale, NJ: Analytic Press.

Thompson, C. L. (1995). Self-definition by opposition: A consequence of minority status. *Psychoanalytic Psychology* 12:533–545.

Trawinski, C. J. (1990). An analysis of a shift in intervention style. *Bulletin of the Society for Psychoanalytic Psychotherapy* 5:5–20.

Trimboli, F., & Farr, K. L. (2000). A psychodynamic guide for essential treatment planning. *Psychoanalytic Psychology* 17: 336–359.

Winnicott, D. W. (1965). *The Maturational Processes and the Facilitating Environment*. New York: International Universities Press.

Yi, K. Y. (1998). Transference and race: An intersubjective conceptualization. *Psychoanalytic Psychology* 15:245–261.

5

THE BEHAVIORAL INTERVIEW

Daniel A. Beach, Ph.D.

BEHAVIORAL PRINCIPLES

Behavioral psychology, or behaviorism, has gained in popularity and respect as an approach to clinical treatment over the past several decades. However, many clinicians fail to understand its basic principles or the way in which these principles can be applied in a clinical setting.

Many treatment approaches are included under the rubric of behaviorism. They differ in many ways, but they all operate from the same set of fundamental assumptions. One assumption is that behavior is lawful; that is, identifiable laws influence behavior, whether or not the individual is aware of their influence. Behaviorists do not create the laws—they discover them. The behavioral therapist attempts to provide patients with the opportunity to take control of the contingencies that affect their lives.

A second assumption is that behavior is primarily learned. Adaptive behavior as well as manipulative behavior can be learned, unlearned, and modified. Certain kinds of learning can be more resistant to change than others, and they may require various forms of intervention to modify the resultant behavior. Maladaptive behavior is not qualitatively different from adaptive behavior, and it can be understood by applying our general understanding of the acquisition of any behavior pattern.

A third assumption is that both public behavior (which can be viewed by others) and private behavior (thought) are influenced by the same basic laws. An individual's cognitions are controlled by contingencies in much the same way that public behavior is controlled. Anxieties, fears, and other thoughts can be learned, unlearned, and modified just as public behaviors, such as table manners, driving skills, and social skills, can be altered.

There are three primary modes by which we acquire behavior: classical conditioning, operant conditioning, and modeling.

Classical Conditioning

Ivan Pavlov, an early-twentieth-century Russian physiologist, was interested in studying the process of digestion. His research methods included feeding dogs and measuring the amount of saliva they produced while eating. He noted that they salivated not only when they were being fed, but also when the laboratory assistant who regularly fed them entered the room. They even salivated to the sound of the laboratory door opening. The study of this phenomenon so intrigued Pavlov that he abandoned his research in digestion and spent the rest of his life studying this process.

He found that many behaviors involving the smooth muscles of the body (nonskeletal) could be conditioned to occur in the presence of an apparently unrelated stimulus. This learning process begins with an *unlearned stimulus* (US) being associated with the elicitation of an *unlearned response* (UR). For example, salivating is an unlearned response to the presence of food in the mouth. This is a behavior that is natural to the organism; it is not learned, but is present in the organism at birth. A new stimulus is then presented by the researcher in the presence of the unlearned stimulus. The organism experiences both of them at the same time. The new, learned stimulus is referred to as the *conditioned stimulus* (CS). When these two stimuli (US and CS) are experienced together over multiple pairings, the organism will respond to the new stimulus (the CS) in much the same way it responded to the US. When the behavior is produced in the presence of the CS alone, we call it a learned response, or a *conditioned response* (CR).

To use Pavlov's research as an example, we can say that the US (the food), which produces the UR (salivation), was frequently presented at the same time that the CS (the laboratory assistant) happened to be nearby. Thus, later, when the dog saw the CS, it salivated, producing a CR that was similar to the one it produced in the presence of the food. Pavlov showed that bells, tones, light, and many other stimuli, when paired with the unlearned stimulus, could be made to elicit this same response.

Behaviors learned through classical conditioning can be unlearned. This learning reversal is known as *extinction*. A behavior is extinguished when the CS is presented often enough without being paired with the US. The association between the two stimuli is thus weakened, and the CR will fail to occur in the presence of the CS. Extinction can be produced more quickly by classically conditioning a new response (CR) to the CS. The new CR must be incompatible with the old CR. That is, it should not be possible for the subject to produce the new response and the old response at the same time. This process of rapid extinction through new learning is called *counterconditioning*.

Many different kinds of behavior have been shown to be learned according to the principles of classical conditioning as discovered by Pavlov. Not only simple reflex behavior, but also more complex forms of human behavior are subject to these same laws. Such behaviors can include the flushed or weak feeling one has when an examination is being returned by a teacher or the sinking feeling in the pit of the stomach when one hears a noise in a dark, empty house.

Operant Conditioning

Several psychologists in the United States contributed to the discovery and understanding of another form of learning called *operant conditioning*. The foremost researcher in this area was B. F. Skinner, whose discoveries came from laboratory research, primarily with rats and pigeons. This type of learning affects what we refer to as voluntary behavior.

To understand operant conditioning we must have a fundamental understanding of another concept, namely, reinforcement. *Reinforcement* is the consequence of a behavior that always *increases* the probability that a behavior will occur again. There are two types of reinforcement: positive and negative. *Positive reinforcement* is equivalent to a reward. A reward can be something tangible, such as money, food, or awards, or it can be intangible, such as attention from others, a smile, or a pleasurable feeling.

Negative reinforcement involves the termination or avoidance of a negative stimulus. It is not the negative stimulus itself. Remember that reinforcement always increases the probability of the occurrence of a behavior. A negative stimulus (punishment, pain) does not typically result in one's desiring to repeat the behavior that resulted in that experience. Rather, when one is about to experience the negative situation or is currently experiencing it, one will usually attempt to terminate it or avoid it. Whatever behavior works to avoid or terminate that experience will be reinforced, and we call that type of reinforcement negative reinforcement.

For example, it you were to step into a darkened room off a hallway to avoid seeing someone with whom you had had an argument earlier in the day, your avoidance of that individual and the awkward or aversive experience that would accompany that encounter would have been negatively reinforced. The next time you saw that person, you would be even more likely to take steps to avoid contact.

When we are dealing with simple organisms, it is not difficult to determine in advance what will be reinforcing. In dog training, we often use food or praise and a scratch behind the ear. Few people would be willing to accept that as sufficient reward for a week's labor. A paycheck is the usually expected reinforcement. Because humans are so much more complex, we can never be sure what will be reinforcing and what will not. Reinforcement is always in the eye of the receiver.

In any give circumstance, there are various behaviors in which we might engage, ranging from those that are most likely to occur to those that might occur rarely. We could rank order these behaviors, with those that are most probable at the top of a column and those that are least probable at the bottom. If we chose a low-probability behavior and reinforced it when it occurred, we could raise its probability of occurring by a slight amount each time reinforcement was received. If we continue this process, the probability of occurrence would be raised sufficiently to make the behavior much more likely to occur, and therefore we would see the behavior being performed more frequently. When this behavior becomes the most probable behavior to occur in the set of circumstances, we say that the behavior is conditioned, or learned. Nonreinforced behavior tends to drop in terms of its probability of occurrence. By identifying a target behavior and selectively reinforcing or not reinforcing it, we can affect its probability of occurrence and the frequency with which it is performed.

Reversal of an operantly conditioned behavior is also called *extinction*. Extinction is produced by withdrawal of reinforcement. when a behavior occurs in the absence of reinforcement, its probability of recurrence drops. When it has been nonreinforced often enough, it drops very low in the individual's repertoire of behavior. At this point, we refer to the behavior as having been extinguished.

In a classroom, we might wish to have a particular child remain in his seat more frequently. If this were a low-frequency behavior, we could provide reinforcement each time we noticed the child sitting in the seat. The reinforcement could be a positive verbal statement, eye contact and a smile, a tangible reward, or another method that the child perceives as reinforcing. After sufficient reinforcement, the probability of occurrence will increase, and we will see more in-seat behavior. As a by-product, we will also see less disruption of others, a more organized classroom, a less frustrated teacher, and a child who views the teacher as a source of reward rather than punishment.

Modeling

A third mode of behavior acquisition that is stressed by behaviorally oriented psychologists is *modeling*, which is a process of learning through imitation. It is a method that we all use in everyday life to acquire skills. When we see another person performing a behavior that appears to be effective or that is reinforcing for that person, we are likely to attempt that behavior ourselves. The learning does not come from merely observing the behavior, but from practicing our imitation of that behavior until we have mastered it. The mere observation of a model being reinforced for a particular behavior increases the probability that one will imitate the behavior. Whether it is learned, and hence repeated, will depend on the consequences.

Such a process places great emphasis upon the individual's thoughts and perceptions rather than upon external factors, as is the case in classical and operant conditioning. In addition, through modeling, as compared to conditioning techniques, rather complex behaviors can be acquired in a relatively short period.

LEARNED EMOTIONAL RESPONSES

Although our emotional responses feel natural to us and appear to most of us to be innate responses to various experiences, they are learned in much the same way that other behaviors are learned.

Watson, who classically conditioned a fear response in the now famous "little Albert," conducted the first demonstration of this. In this study, Watson placed Albert in a chair and put a cage containing a white rat on a table top immediately in front of the young child. The child had previously exhibited no fear of the animal; in fact, he exhibited curiosity and some enjoyment in its presence. The cage was then covered with a cloth. Watson's assistant stood behind Albert and struck an iron bar with a hammer each time the cloth was raised from the cage. Not surprisingly, Albert was startled and began to cry at the sound of the hammer striking the iron. After a number of such trials, the cloth was raised without the loud noise. Albert became fearful and cried. This demonstration was a success for Watson, if not for Albert, in showing that fears can be learned through the process of classical conditioning.

Albert not only learned a fear response to this previously neutral stimulus, but also maintained this same fear response to a whole class of stimuli, including white mice, white rabbits, and a white ball of cotton. He generalized his learned fear to an entire class of stimuli that he perceived as being similar to the original CS (the white rat). We refer to this process as *stimulus generalization*. What is most important here is that the person perceives the stimuli to be similar whether or not most other people might agree that a similarity exists. Once again, as in reinforcement, the judgment is made by the one affected.

How does such learning affect individuals who enter the therapeutic situation? Many behavioral disorders, particularly those that fall into neurotic categories, are associated with learned fear or anxiety responses.

Sara, for example, came to see her psychologist with a complaint that many of her relationships had fallen apart and that she was unable to maintain relationships, especially those with men, for very long. She desired to be close to others, but it never worked out for her. After several sessions, she revealed that she had been physically and emotionally abused by her alcoholic father, to whom she had been very close during her early childhood years.

A behavioral analysis of this situation would first describe the learned fear response. Sara learned to fear her father, who had inflicted pain upon her. The physical violence and emotional rejection are the US. Under these conditions, the associated pain is the UR. The presence of the father who inflicts this pain is the CS, and the subsequent fear of closeness with the father becomes the CR. In Sara's case, we find that she has learned to fear not only her father's closeness, but also the closeness of any other individual. Through stimulus generalization, she has learned that emotional closeness, or even the possibility of it, is a cue for her to begin to experience anxiety. This cuts her off from the possibility of engaging others and developing intimacy.

If that was all there was to it, then Sara could simply live her life without being close to others, finding enjoyment in solitary activities. However, Sara has a serious "flaw." She is human. Sara possesses the same needs that we all have for closeness, love, affection, caring, and understanding, and these needs can be satisfied only through interpersonal relationships. Because of these human needs, Sara approaches others with the desire to establish relationships despite her fear.

The anxiety-producing stimulus (closeness) now requires her to find some way of reducing her anxiety. She is in an operant-conditioning situation in which, through trial and error, she attempts to discover ways to reduce anxiety. Those behaviors that are effective will be negatively reinforced, since she is attempting to terminate or avoid the negative stimulus (anxiety or fear). Such behaviors might include keeping people at a distance through polite, nonrevealing conversation, continued use of humor to prevent serious discussion, engaging only others who have similar fears of closeness, or thousands of other possibilities that keep her insulated from the dangers of emotional vulnerability. Not all, or even most, close relationships result in pain. By continuing to avoid the anxiety-provoking situation, Sara prevents herself from experiencing interpersonal closeness in the absence of pain. Thus she is not allowing extinction of the fear response to take place.

Sara may eventually feel that she has exposed too much of herself or has reached a point at which she is pressured by another to develop a closer relationship. This is a cue for strong feelings of anxiety that might only be reduced by ending the relationship. If either person ends the relationship, Sara is likely to feel pain, which serves to strengthen the original classical-conditioned experience and to justify her feelings that closeness inevitably leads to pain and must be guarded against.

The fear of intimacy described in this example could develop from a classical-conditioning experience that does not necessarily include physical pain or abuse. Rejection, disapproval, and other responses could have similar effects and result in fear of closeness. In addition, Sara might not generalize her response to the entire population; rather, she might be somewhat selective and experience such responses only to men, older men, men who look or act like her father, people who act in an authoritative manner, or any other individuals or group that she might perceive as being similar to her father.

Psychoanalytic theory recognizes that such responses may occur in the therapeutic situation, and its literature has documented such occurrences and has named them *transferences*. That is, the patient feels the same way toward the therapist as the patient felt toward some other significant individual. *Counter-transference* is a similar process, whereby the therapist begins to experience feelings toward the patient that are similar to feelings the therapist had toward someone else. A behaviorist would say that both the patient and the therapist are experiencing stimulus generalization. Such generalization appears to have survival value for our species. If every situation in which we found ourselves were unique, so that previous adaptive behaviors could not be used, we would find life exceedingly stressful. Just as adaptive behaviors can be generalized, so maladaptive behaviors (including emotional responses) can be generalized to new situations, causing problems and nonadaptive responses.

Humans are able to symbolize the events in their lives. We can think about our experiences and relive them in a very powerful way through imagery. In a sense, we can replay our experiences so that they have virtually the same emotional impact that the real-life experience had. By reexperiencing life events through imagery, one can repeat trials, much as the repeated trials that we use in classically conditioning a laboratory subject. As a consequence, the learned emotional response becomes well fixed and very resistant to extinction.

The process just described is referred to as the *two-factor theory* of avoidance learning. It involves the classical conditioning of a fear (anxiety) response to a previously neutral stimulus, the generalization of that stimulus to a variety of situations, and then an operantly conditioned response to reduce that anxiety. These two factors, when working together in this manner, can describe a wide range of maladaptive behaviors that are frequently seen by therapists in the therapeutic situation.

VERBAL CONDITIONING: A PROCESS ISSUE

When we speak to others, we selectively reinforce statements that we may agree with or may be interested in hearing more about. Reinforcement in this setting usually involves such actions as statements of agreement, attention, smiles, nods of the head, maintenance of eye contact, and nonverbal vocalizations.

In Greenspoon's well-known study (1955) on this topic, subjects were asked to say as many words as they could think of in an allotted period. In one group, the experimenter said "mmm-hmm" every time the subject mentioned a plural noun and said nothing when other words were mentioned. A second group of subjects heard "huh-uh" (a statement of disapproval) after each plural noun. A control group received no verbal responses at all from the experimenter.

The results showed that the subjects reinforced with "mmm-hmm" produced the largest number of plural nouns. In second place came the control group, and the group receiving disapproval produced the least amount of plural nouns. The results of this study and others like it (Isaacs et al., 1960; Konecni & Slamecka, 1972; Verplanck, 1955) have provided clear evidence for the process of conditioning of verbal responses.

In therapy, especially in the more traditional forms, verbal exchanges between the patient and therapist are critical. The therapist may express concern about the patient's feelings of depression and rejection, suicidal ideation, and low self-esteem. At the same time, the patient may receive little or no response when speaking of more positive issues. To the extent that the therapist's remarks are reinforcing to the patient, the therapist may be reinforcing the patient's negative self-statements, while positive self-statements may be extinguished.

Attention from another person, particularly one who is in a powerful position, can be highly reinforcing. In therapy, as in institutional mental health settings, problem behaviors tend to receive more attention than positive behaviors. This is referred to as the "squeaky wheel" principle: the part that makes the most noise (negative behavior) get the most grease (attention and reinforcement). By attending to problems, which, of course, is what therapists are trained to do, we risk more firmly solidifying these negative self-statements and making the process damaging rather than therapeutic. Such occurrences may not be rare.

Careful attention must be paid by the therapist in the clinical interview to those statements that are in need of reinforcement and those that are not. Of course, the therapist's theoretical orientation will influence the decision as to which statements are reinforced. In the initial portions of the interview, when the patient is presenting his or her formulation of the problem, the therapist must not take control prematurely and risk losing valuable information by directing the patient away from salient issues. By ignoring the effects of verbal conditioning, the therapist may restrict conversations to topics with which the therapist may feel comfortable or to those that are related to the therapist's biases.

Verbal conditioning affects all forms of therapy, not only the form used by behaviorists. The analytically oriented therapist who chooses to positively reinforce a statement made by the patient reinforces that statement and can expect to hear others similar to it. When Carl Rogers smiled at his client and nodded his head, he was manipulating (unintentionally) the direction of conversation in his own, nondirective way. When the family therapist fails to respond positively to an observation made by a family member, that person may be less likely to speak out in future sessions. Verbal reinforcement occurs whether or not the therapist decides to take advantage of the contingencies of reinforcement.

Verbal reinforcement is an important process in therapy, and it deserves the therapist's continuous attention. Maintenance or extinction of problem behavior can be closely related to the contingencies of reinforcement involved in the verbal exchange between therapist and patient.

CAUSATION

All therapists, regardless of theoretical orientation, look for the cause of the behavior that the patient defines as problematic. What is meant by *cause* and how it affects the behavior in question is what separates the various therapeutic schools.

When the general public looks at behavioral causation, the approach, for the most part, tends to be rather simplistic. A recent television news program reported that a man had been found unconscious on the street and was taken to a local hospital. The cause of this incident was reported to be an overdose of heroin. Was this indeed the case? In part, yes. But this is neither the whole picture nor an accurate description of the actual cause of the incident.

Behavior is multicausal. Usually, no single event can be isolated as *the* cause. To understand the causal aspects of a behavior and to develop an intervention strategy, we must understand the importance of the causal chain leading to the behavior in question. In the example just noted, the drug overdose was clearly related to the fact that the man was found unconscious, but it was one of many causes that put him in that position. It was *a* cause, but not *the* cause.

One effective means of understanding the causal chain of events is to organize it into chronological order. There are three types of causes: predisposing, precipitating, and perpetuating. The three P's of causality are a way of conceptualizing the important variables necessary for the production of any behavior. All three must occur before the behavior is manifested. No one of these events is solely responsible for the behavior we see. In other words, each is a necessary cause, but none is sufficient by itself to cause the behavior.

Predisposing causes are the historical antecedents of the behavior. They set the stage, as it were, for the other causes. They establish the general conditions that permit the individual to engage in the behavior. Predisposing causes can include such factors as genetic endowment, physical illness, reinforcement history, various life experiences, environmental variables, and the person's history of learned emotional responses.

The *precipitating cause* is the triggering mechanism of the behavior. It is the immediate, observable event that sets the behavior in motion. This is the occurrence that people usually point to as *the* cause of a behavior.

The *perpetuating* cause is the set of contingencies that sustains the behavior. Unless the behavior is maintained in some fashion, it will not continue to be produced. Perpetuating causes are responsible for the fact that the problem continues to affect the patient's quality of life adversely.

At what point should the therapeutic intervention take place? Since all three forms of causation are necessary to produce the behavior, an intervention strategy aimed at any one of the three causes would result in the termination (extinction) of the behavior. The clinical interview seeks to identify these factors so that treatment can be directed to intervene at any one of these three points.

How can we intervene with a predisposing cause? Most traditional forms of therapy have this as their goal. Their emphasis upon underlying causes of behavior presumes that the predisposing cause is the primary and determining cause of the behavior. Behaviorists recognize the importance of early experiences and other predisposing factors but do not view them as the only or primary point of intervention.

Genetic predispositions, physical disease, and environmental variables indigenous to a patient's community setting may not be fruitful points of intervention. More effective strategies might involve the elimination of learned emotional responses to various types of interpersonal situations.

Wolpe's use of systematic desensitization (1973) is a form of intervention directed at predisposing causes. It seeks to extinguish a classically conditioned fear or anxiety that in the past has placed the patient in the position of avoiding or terminating that anxiety through a behavior that has proven to be maladaptive or unsatisfying. In such an approach, the behavioral therapist uses a counterconditioning technique to have the CS evoke a relaxation response rather than an anxiety response. The reversal of early learning through conditioning or modeling techniques can reduce or eliminate the effectiveness of the predisposing cause.

As mentioned earlier, we can replay painful life events through imagery and thus strengthen a classically conditioned emotional response. Positive visualization, thought-stoppage techniques, relaxation techniques, quieting-reflex techniques, and others can be employed to extinguish this response and thus intervene at the level of the predisposing cause.

The precipitating cause is often obvious or can be clarified through the interview. Sometimes, the precipitating event can be controlled or managed in a very direct manner. The patient who feels most depressed when alone on a Sunday night can plan community, church, or family activities at such times. The patient who feels most frustrated after six consecutive hours with the children can arrange a short period of child care in the middle of the day with a neighbor. The student who experiences tremendous stress at exam time can practice more effective study habits through the semester and thus feel more confident when the exam date arrives. The precipitating cause may not always be identifiable or may have occurred only once at some time in the distant past. In such cases, an intervention at this point may not be profitable or practical.

In examining the perpetuating cause, the behavioral therapist is evaluating the system of reinforcement that maintains the behavior at a sufficiently high level to be identifiable and problematic. Based upon the principles of reinforcement, we know that when the behavior is reinforced by reward or by avoidance of an aversive experience, it tends to be repeated. Reinforcement maintains behavior, since behavior is under the control of the consequences of the reinforcement. The withdrawal of reinforcement reduces the occurrence of a behavior. In the clinical interview, the behaviorist seeks to identify those sources of reinforcement that are sustaining the problem behavior. Such sources can include attention from others, satisfaction of physical needs, avoidance of learned anxiety responses, or a myriad of other forms of reinforcement. Therapeutic strategy is then aimed at eliminating the reinforcement from the problem behavior. Such withdrawal leads to the extinction of the behavior in question. Verbal reinforcement in the therapeutic setting can maintain negative self-statements, or their extinction can be produced by the elimination of reinforcement. At the same time, positive self-statements can be strengthened by their selective reinforcement.

In a social system, the identification of cause-and-effect relationships is made more difficult by the fact that an individual's action may be both a cause of another's behavior and an effect of some behavior of that other individual. This circularity of causation is certainly present in family systems. To understand interactive patterns, the therapist must be aware that every behavior is both a cause and an effect.

INTERVIEW ASSESSMENT

The therapist's approach to assessment defines the nature of the interview. As previously mentioned, the major point of departure between the behavioral and traditional assessment approaches appears to be in the understanding of the nature of the causes of the patient's behavior. Traditional assessment views these causes as essentially intrapsychic. Consequently, the traditionalist would view the behaviors as symptoms of an underlying cause and only of trivial significance in their own right. These causes produce a generalized response and therefore can produce behaviors across a variety of situations.

Behavioral assessment emphasizes *response specificity*. Behaviorists believe that a behavior is produced in relation to the environmental and personal variables that are present in specific circumstances. The behaviors themselves may be problematic, but they are not symptomatic. The behavior itself is the problem; it is not a symptom of a hypothetical construct. The orientation of the behavioral interview is derived from this position. A behaviorist addresses problem behavior in detail rather than attempting to paint the patient with a broad brush that seeks to describe the patient's entire personality functioning (Goldfried & Pomeranz, 1968).

The primary goal of the clinical assessment is to find out what the patient's problem is and develop a working hypothesis about what actions can relieve the problem. This involves gathering relevant data and deciding which variables can be effectively addressed in therapy. The interview has been advocated by many behaviorally oriented therapists as one of the various methods of acquiring such information (Kanfer & Saslow, 1969; Lewinsohn et al., 1976). Although other purposes have been associated with the use of this technique, most behaviorists agree that its primary use is to assess specific behavioral targets (Lichtenstein,

1971). Traditional approaches have oriented the interview to the individual patient, whereas behavioral interviewing may include many significant others in the patient's environment in order to gather additional data and to clarify hypotheses about variables that may be contributing to the patient's behavior.

The clinical interview is seen as one part of the behavioral assessment. Aside from interviews with significant others, the assessment may include observations in vivo, observations in structured situations, self-monitoring, role playing, review of records, or any other method of assembling information about possible variables contributing to the patient's behavior.

The behavioral interview should include:

1. The identification of the behaviors that are perceived to be problematic;
2. A determination of the variables related to the causal chain of events;
3. The identification of those characteristics of the patient that may facilitate or interfere with a method of treatment;
4. The assessment of environmental variables that may facilitate or interfere with treatment, particularly the sources of positive or negative reinforcement; and
5. The choice of a treatment intervention technique. Such an approach may not differ dramatically from the elements of other theoretical approaches. The types of variables that are attended to as salient factors will differ depending upon orientation.

With respect to points 3 and 4, the interview is used to evaluate the effectiveness of the variables used to treat the target behavior. For example, if we plan to use a certain form of reinforcement to increase the frequency of a behavior that is incompatible with the problem behavior, we must be certain that the patient perceives the reinforcement to be reinforcing or it will not have the desired effect. Similarly, we must assess whether or not the system in which the patient lives can provide this source of reinforcement. Through the interview, we can gather information that can lead to a conclusion on these issues.

The clinical interview is often used to determine the likelihood of being able to establish a productive relationship with the patient. The quality of the interaction may be predictive of future behavior patterns. The quality of the relationship is directly related to the effectiveness of information gathering (Cozby, 1973).

The clinical interview is not only effective in aiding the patient to conceptualize the problem he is experiencing, but it also may be therapeutic in and of itself (Linehan, 1977). For a patient who is experiencing feelings of desperation, lack of control, or guilt, a behavioral explanation of the variables contributing to this behavior can bring immediate relief and assurance. Such information can raise expectations and feelings of self-efficacy, which are closely tied to treatment effectiveness. The knowledge that the patient has a clear definition of the situation and can potentially gain control of the contingencies that affect these problem behaviors can go a long way toward alleviating the patient's immediate distress. In this way, the initial interview can serve not only as a method for making an assessment for future intervention, but also as an intervention itself.

CONTENT OF THE BEHAVIORAL INTERVIEW

Many formats for the structure of the behavioral interview have been proposed. Among the most influential of these approaches have been those of Kanfer and Saslow, Wolpe, and Lazarus. Kanfer and Saslow (1969) suggest an evaluation of past and present patterns of behavior and environmental influences. Their model consists of assembling information in seven primary areas:

1. An analysis of the presenting problem
2. A clarification of the problem and the causes of the behavior
3. A motivational analysis
4. A developmental analysis
5. An analysis of self-control
6. An analysis of social relationships
7. An analysis of the social–cultural–physical environment

Wolpe (1973) also recommends securing a large amount of data about past and present functioning in five areas:

1. Early family history
2. Education
3. Employment history
4. Sexual history
5. Current relationships with others

Lazarus (1973; 1976) suggests a comprehensive assessment of the important facets of the patient. He used the helpful acronym BASIC ID to organize the information that needs to be assessed in the behavioral interview:

B: identification of *behavioral* deficiencies and excesses
A: *affective* responses that require modification
S: *sensory* deficits, oversensitivities, or pain
I: *imagery* in which the patient habitually engages
C: *cognitions* that are illogical or mistaken and lead to emotional disturbance
I: patterns of *interpersonal* relationships
D: *drugs*, which also includes fitness and general well-being

The contents of the aforementioned models should be viewed as salient areas to search for important information rather than as critical outlines of information that must be filled in for every patient.

STRUCTURE OF THE INTERVIEW

Based upon the preceding discussion, a general structure emerges for the behavioral interview. The first step involves defining the patient's presenting problem. The patient is not likely to offer a list of various stimulus–response situations or to divide the problem between those that were conditioned and those that were modeled. Nor is it necessary at this point to translate the patient's complaints into behavioral terms. It is important that the therapist attend carefully to specific behavioral situations that have generated the patient's concerns and refrain from overdirecting the conversation by verbally reinforcing those points that may be of interest to the patient but may have no relevance to the patient's presenting problem.

The second step involves collecting broad-based information that might relate to the problem. Models, such as those by Kanfer and Saslow, Wolpe, and Lazarus, are helpful in identifying major areas in which information collection should be concentrated.

The third step requires the gathering of more precise data from those areas that appear most salient based on the forgoing process. Close inspection of the problem behavior from this perspective will help to establish preliminary hypotheses that can be supported or disconfirmed through the acquisition of additional information.

In the fourth step, we establish a working hypothesis regarding the variables affecting the patient's behavior, with emphasis on the three P's of causation. By examining the causal chain and identifying the elements that operate at these three critical junctures, we can begin to think about potential points of intervention. Such hypotheses involve the understanding of the origins and maintenance of the behavior through the processes of conditioning and modeling.

The fifth step requires that we conduct an initial test of this hypothesis. This test can begin with a detailed questioning of the patient's perceptions of the contingencies that are controlling the behavior. Beyond this, the therapist can use role-playing to assess skills and imagined-exposure techniques to evaluate beliefs and emotional reactivity to particular events. Interviews with significant others can also be used to evaluate environmental contingencies. This step requires flexibility on the part of the therapist, since the original hypothesis may be disconfirmed or require some modification.

The sixth and final step in the interview involves the design of a treatment approach that permits the patient to gain control of those variables affecting the problem behavior. An understanding of the behavioral approaches to treatment is necessary in order to design the most effective strategy possible.

The behavioral interview is based upon the understanding of the acquisition of behavior through the processes of conditioning and modeling. Behaviorally oriented therapists attempt to determine the causes of the problem behavior with respect to the predisposing, precipitating, and perpetuating events that are necessary for the production of such behavior. The goal of the interview is to define the contingencies that control the behavior and to establish a treatment plan that permits the patient to gain more control over those contingencies.

As research increasingly supports the efficacy of behavioral interventions (Chambless et al., 1996; 1998), behavioral approaches to treatment are gaining in popularity. The roots of the behavioral approach are in the psychology laboratory, and its value is established both by convincing research evidence and by clinical observations of its effectiveness in treating human problems.

REFERENCES

Chambless, D. L., et al. (1996). An update on empirically validated therapies. *Clinical Psychologist* 49:5–18.

Chambless, D. L., et al. (1998). Update on empirically validated therapies II. *Clinical Psychologist* 51:3–16.

Cozby, P. (1973). Self-disclosure. *Psychological Bulletin* 79:73–91.

Goldfried, M., & Pomeranz, D. (1968). Role of assessment in behavior modification. *Psychological Reports* 23:75–87.

Greenspoon, J. (1955). The reinforcing effect of two spoken sounds on the frequency of two responses. *American Journal of Psychology* 68:409–416.

Isaacs, J., Thomas, M., & Golddiamond, I. (1960). Application of operant conditioning to reinstate verbal conditioning. *Journal of Speech and Hearing Disorders* 25:8–12.

Kanfer, F., & Saslow, G. (1969). Behavioral diagnosis. In *Behavior Therapy: Appraisal and Status*, ed. C. M. Franks, pp. 417–444. New York: McGraw–Hill.

Konecni, J., & Slamecka, N. (1972). Awareness in verbal nonoperant conditioning: An approach through dichotic listening. *Journal of Experimental Psychology* 94:248–254.

Lazarus, A. (1973). Multimodal behavior therapy: Treating the "BASIC-ID." *Journal of Nervous and Mental Disease* 156:404–411.

Lazarus, A. (1976). *Multimodal Behavior Therapy*. New York: Springer.

Lewinsohn, P., Biglan, A., & Zeiss, A. (1976). Behavioral treatment for depression. In *The Behavioral Management of Anxiety, Depression, and Pain*, ed. P. O. Davidson, pp. 91–146. New York: Bruner/Mazel.

Lichtenstein, E. (1971). Techniques for assessing outcomes of psychotherapy. In *Advances in Psychological Assessment*, ed. P. McReynolds, pp. 178–197. Palo Alto, CA: Science and Behavior Books.

Linehan, M. (1977). Issues in behavioral interviewing. In *Behavioral Assessment: New Directions in Clinical Psychology*, ed. J. Cone and R. Hawkins, pp. 30–51. New York: Brunner/ Mazel.

Verplanck, W. S. (1955). The control of the content of conversation: Reinforcement of statements of opinion. *Journal of Abnormal and Social Psychology* 51:668–676.

Wolpe, J. (1973). *The Practice of Behavior Therapy*. New York: Pergamon.

6

THE EXISTENTIAL/HUMANISTIC INTERVIEW

Salvatore R. Maddi, Ph.D.

It may seem odd to be writing about assessment interviewing from an existential/humanistic perspective, as this position has eschewed diagnosis as insufficiently appreciative of human subjectivity, and as unnecessary as a guide to psychotherapy. This deemphasis of assessment has been coextensive with an unwillingness to theorize elaborately, for fear of rendering human experience as static and complete rather than pulsating and becoming, and as predictable and conventional rather than free and individualistic (e.g., Schneider, 1998). Despite what might be called this romantic or deconstructionist bias, there is in the existential/humanistic position some bona fide personality theorizing and some screening or intake interviewing. Scrutinizing these efforts permits explication of assessment goals and techniques that are existential/humanistic in spirit and that can serve as a guide to those interested in applying this position.

In the pages that follow, I will first consider existential/humanistic theorizing and then proceed to how these thoughts are expressed in interviewing practice. As in any clinical position on human behavior, the most relevant theorizing concerns the assumptions framing the views of psychopathology, premorbidity, and maturity (Maddi, 1996). It is how the patient is doing with regard to these three evaluative criteria that gives direction to assessment interviewing.

EXISTENTIAL THEORY

It must be said at the outset that terms such as *psychopathology, premorbidity*, and even *maturity* sound foreign to existential psychologists. The connotations of these terms are objectionable to them for reasons already mentioned. I will use these terms nonetheless, in order to facilitate comparisons with other approaches more accepting of them.

To define psychopathology, we must have a sense of normal behavior and of what constitutes deviations from normal that are so contradictory as to appear sick. There is little resembling objectivity in this matter of defining psychopathology, and different positions arrive at different conclusions. When we are dealing with adults, normalcy is usually described in the language of maturity. Psychological maturity is the result of sound development. One whose development has not been ideal may be vulnerable to psychopathology. Not themselves actual illnesses, these vulnerabilities, or premorbidity, only result in psychopathology when certain precipitating factors or stressors are encountered. As you can see, my introduction of the terms *psychopathology, premorbidity,* and *maturity* is deceptively simple. Actually, these terms are so embedded in and critical to any approach that they must be completely explicated. So let us get on with the task, as the existential approach is no exception.

Psychopathology

A behavior is regarded as psychopathological by any well-developed approach when it violates assumptions about what it means to be human (Maddi, 1988). Sometimes these inhuman actions are deviations from social convention. Often, however, they are common, everyday behaviors. It is an important function of the various approaches to alert us to actions that may be damaging to ourselves and others even though they are accepted by society (Maddi, 1988). Indeed, when an approach appears to define psychopathology as social deviance, you can expect that the approach is not conceptually well developed, because it substitutes socially conventional views of what is acceptable for considered assumptions about maturity and failures to reach it.

The existential approach has a very definite position on what constitutes psychopathology. The common denominator is that psychopathology involves a strong, chronic sense of meaninglessness. Underlying this view is the belief that humans are unique among living beings because of the ability to construct meaning through self-reflective thought and through decision making (Binswanger, 1963; Boss, 1963; Frankl, 1965; Maddi, 1970; 1998; May et al., 1959). Thus to feel a chronic, desperate sense of meaninglessness is to fail to be human, and this is serious enough to be regarded as psychopathological.

Various existentialists have depicted states of meaninglessness. The philosopher Søren Kierkegaard (1954) spoke of "the sickness unto death," by which he meant a kind of psychological death in which persons feel that their lives have been wasted and there is nothing of value left. Among psychologists, Frankl (1965) delineates the noogenic neurosis, a state of emptiness similar to that described by Kierkegaard. Incorporating much in other existential positions, my position (Maddi, 1967; 1970) attempts to be both comprehensive and detailed by distinguishing three forms of existential sickness, or meaninglessness.

In order of decreasing severity, they are *vegetativeness, nihilism*, and *adventurousness*. Each has cognitive, affective, and behavioral components.

In *vegetativeness*, the cognitive element is that the person cannot find anything in whatever is being done or can be imagined that seems interesting or worthwhile; the emotional element is apathy and boredom, punctuated by bouts of depression that become less frequent as the disorder is prolonged; and the behavioral element is indolence and aimlessness. Vegetativeness is the most severe existential pathology because there is little or no sense of meaningfulness left. Persons suffering vegetativeness go through their days in a lost, aimless, empty way, doing only what they have to, and often not even that. The disorder can become severe enough to render sufferers incapable of caring for themselves. Much in what is called burnout, depression, and simple schizophrenia is covered by the vegetative syndrome.

In contrast, *nihilism* is a less severe sickness because some sense of meaning persists. But it is paradoxical meaning, or antimeaning. In nihilism, the cognitive element is the cynical conviction that nothing purporting to have meaning is really meaningful, that nothing is what it seems. This belief is accompanied at the emotional level by frequent feelings of disgust and anger, and at the behavioral level by competitiveness and ungenerosity. Sufferers of this syndrome are quick to expose whatever appears to have face validity, and they revel in the angry, competitive exposure of the naïveté in others whose beliefs are more straightforward. They are often quite skilled in developing diabolically effective negativistic accounts of experience. But have them encounter something manifestly meaningless and they will be equally agile in insisting on its meaningfulness. Episodes such as these show the nihilistic process at the heart of this disorder. The nihilism syndrome bears some similarity to paranoid, obsessive-compulsive, and aggressive states.

Finally, the *adventurousness* syndrome involves the least severe form of pathology because those suffering from it retain a partial sense of meaning (in contrast to vegetativeness), and that meaning is positive rather than paradoxical (in contrast to nihilism). In adventurousness, it is common, everyday life that has lost meaning, and the sufferer is forced to ever greater risk and deviancy in order to experience satisfaction and vitality. At the cognitive level, adventurers are attracted to that which is dangerous, believing the rest to be banal. At the emotional level, there are mood swings between the poles of boredom or apathy, and there is exhilaration or anxiety, depending on whether it is everyday life or risk that is being encountered. Similarly, at the action level, adventurers are indolent or decisive, depending on whether the circumstances of the moment are challenging or routine. Sufferers of this syndrome can be soldiers of fortune and perennial joiners of causes, on the one hand, or addicted gamblers and substance abusers, on the other hand. Traditionally defined mood disorders have much in common with adventurousness. Many respected industrialists and professionals fall into this category, regardless of the socially acceptable nature of their activity.

Maturity

The existential viewpoint on maturity is in many ways the opposite of the viewpoint on psychopathology. It is the nature of humans to construct meaning; then to quality as mature, one must be able to do this regularly and effectively. The mature lifestyle is called *authenticity* by existentialists. Summarizing the thinking of several relevant philosophers and psychologists, I have elsewhere (Maddi, 1967; 1970) delineated the characteristics of authenticity as including (1) the tendency to choose the future rather than the past in decision-making situations; (2) self-definition as a person who can influence social and biological experience through use of wits; (3) the belief that society is the creation of humans and is therefore best considered in their service; (4) vigorous expression of symbolization, imagination, and judgment; (5) the belief that life is best when there is continual growth through learning; (6) the knack for finding something interesting and worthwhile in whatever one is doing; (7) the willingness to tolerate the anxiety normally surrounding new experience in order to choose the future; (8) a minimum of guilt over missed opportunities; (9) decisiveness of actions; and (10) a tendency to conduct interpersonal relationships intimately rather than contractually.

As you can tell from the foregoing characteristics, the authentic lifestyle involves persons in vigorous interaction with their social, physical, and biological surroundings; a rather continual growth process; and a cognitive, emotional, and behavioral definiteness that is aptly called *individuality* (Maddi, 1970).

To appreciate why authenticity is the epitome of maturity for existentialists, it is important to reflect on the associated assumptions concerning human nature or the core of personality (Maddi, 1996). Existentialists assume that humans are by their nature not only *social* and *biological,* but also *psychological* (Maddi, 1998; 2002). Their psychological side is expressed in an active propensity for *symbolizing* (generalizing specific experiences into abstract categories, such as words), *imagining* (combining and recombining symbols without the requirement of external experience), and *judging* (taking a preferential or ethical stance toward the fruits of symbolizing and imagining). This symbolizing, imagining, and judging lends the character of *decision making* to experiencing that has extensity in time.

Persons who symbolize, imagine, and judge vigorously are proficient at differentiating experiences from one another (have many categories or symbols), at formulating ideas about change (have a rich imagination), and at developing preferences and ideals (form definite judgments). This certainly makes them individualistic (Maddi, 1988; 1998; 2002), but it also gives them heightened awareness that they formulate the meaning in their lives by the decisions they make. In decision-making circumstances, they recognize that they can launch themselves into the future or stay with what is already familiar. Choosing the future is the way of growing through learning, whereas choosing the familiar (the past) teaches one little or nothing. Concomitantly, choosing the future is anxiety provoking, because the unknown is unpredictable. However safe choosing the past may seem, it brings with it the guilt of missed opportunity.

To achieve the lifestyle of authenticity, one must learn to tolerate anxiety sufficiently that one can choose the future regularly and thereby continue to grow and have a sense of vitality, control, and satisfaction. What one needs to do this is *courage*, and this is learned by youngsters in interaction with parents who reward them the largest proportion of the time, encourage them to try tasks that exceed their capacities just a little, and expose them to a wide variety of experiences interpreted as richness rather than chaos (Kobasa & Maddi, 1977). Recent research (Khoshaba & Maddi, 1999) has also shown that being designated by one's parents as the hope of the family is also a factor facilitating authenticity.

Premorbidity

Persons not fortunate enough to experience the ideal developmental conditions just summarized will develop a premorbid lifestyle instead. If parents punish more than reward, set tasks that are either too difficult or too easy, and protect their offspring from variety and change while showing little appreciation of their capabilities, the result is a lifestyle aptly characterized as *conformism* (Maddi, 1970; 1998).

The dimensions of conformism are (1) definition of self as a player of social roles in which it is important to be pragmatic and acceptable in a conventional sense; (2) a belief in the paramount importance of biological needs, in the sense of physical comfort, materialism, and survival; (3) a sense of powerlessness to influence events; (4) chronic feelings of alienation and a sense of missed opportunity; (5) an inability to tolerate the uncertainty of change, preferring the status quo; and (6) a tendency to conduct interpersonal relationships on a contractual rather than intimate basis (Maddi, 1970; 1998).

The premorbidity, or vulnerability, to psychopathology constituted by conformism stems from a relative lack of symbolization, imagination, and judgment and from a concomitant choice of the familiar rather than the new in decision-making circumstances. As time goes by, conformists consequently feel that life has passed them by and that they are frail and inadequate.

Certain stressors can undermine the conformist adjustment (Maddi, 1967), precipitating the psychopathologies of meaning mentioned earlier. These stressors include (1) social upheavals (such as economic depression, war, political changes, job loss), (2) threats to physical well-being (such as illness or physical attack), and (3) confrontations with one's own superficiality (this is usually forced by some significant other who is suffering because of this superficiality). Social upheavals can undermine adjustment because the conformist's underlying assumption is that it is the social system (institutions, norms, reference groups) that lends meaning to life. In effect, the conformist is treating society as if it were perfect enough never to change, so when it does, trouble ensues. Similarly, threats to physical well-being undermine adjustment because the conformist's underlying assumption is that physical well-being is the most important thing lending meaning to life. Forced recognition of superficiality undermines adjustment because it confirms the conformist's worst fears, fears carefully guarded against.

HUMANISTIC THEORY

As in the existential approach, humanistic theory does not accept the traditional emphasis on psychopathology and assessment. Indeed, there is even less basis in humanistic approaches for discerning implicit assumptions about psychopathology, maturity, and premorbidity. Nonetheless, let us plunge in.

Maturity

A rather clear position on maturity is contained in the theories of Rogers and Maslow. According to Rogers (1959; 1961), ideal or *fully functioning persons* are (1) open to experience rather than defensive, (2) spontaneous rather than rigidly planful (flexible, adaptive, and inductive), (3) organismically trusting (tend to listen to cues from their bodies rather than subscribing to conventional values), (4) experientially free (have a subjective sense of free will), and (5) creative (productive of new ideas and things). Theorizing similarly, Maslow (1955, 1962) describes ideal or self-actualized persons as having (1) realistic orientation, (2) acceptance of self, others, and the natural world, (3) spontaneity, (4) task orientation (rather than self-preoccupation), (5) a sense of privacy, (6) independence, (7) appreciativeness, (8) spirituality (not necessarily in a formal religious sense), (9) identity with humankind, (10) feelings of intimacy with a few loved ones, (11) democratic values, (12) recognition of the difference between means and ends, (13) humor (that is, philosophical rather than hostile), (14) creativeness, and (15) nonconformism.

In general, Maslow's characteristics of maturity emphasize cognitive functioning (such as democratic values, identity with humankind, recognition of the difference between means and ends) more than do those of Rogers. The characteristics developed by Rogers emphasize process, emotionality, and intuition more than is true for those developed by Maslow. Nonetheless, both depictions are humanistic in that they render maturity as a rich, sensitive, intuitive openness to experience and a nondefensive ability to reflect on this experience.

In all conceptions of personality, maturity is considered a joint product of expressions of the core or basic innate tendency that defines humanness and an ideal reaction to such expressions on the part of significant others. Humanistic positions are no exception. According to Rogers and Maslow, the core tendency is to *actualize inherent potential*. This tendency underlies all human behavior. If youngsters are to become mature, their natural efforts to express their potential must receive *unconditional positive regard* (uncritical appreciation and support) from significant others. If they have this, they will have no need to modify their natural behavioral tendencies to conform to values imposed by significant others. Thus they will grow by ever greater expression of their inherent potential and will accept themselves readily, without imposing on themselves conventional conditions of worth.

Premorbidity and Psychopathology

It is particularly difficult to discern humanistic distinctions between premorbid and psychopathological states. Both Rogers (1959) and Maslow (1962) are clear that if youngsters encounter *conditional* (rather than unconditional) *positive regard* from significant others (that is, if these others impose their own or conventional standards of evaluation on the youngsters' behavior), then maturity is jeopardized. The resulting lifestyle, called *maladjustment* by Rogers (1959), includes:

1. Conditions of worth
2. Incongruence between the subjective self and the inherent potential
3. Defensiveness, rather than openness to experience
4. Living according to an inflexible plan rather than existentially
5. Disregarding organismic messages rather than trusting them
6. Feeling manipulated rather than free
7. Behaving conventionally rather than creatively

Maslow (1962) appears to endorse such theorizing, adding notions of cognitive rigidity and authoritarian values.

From these theorists' views on how the maladjusted lifestyle develops, one would conclude that it expresses premorbidity. But there is no formal humanistic theorizing about additional factors, such as stressors, that can undermine this lifestyle and lead to frank psychopathology. Nor do Rogers and Maslow detail conceptions of psychopathology per se. There are only three possible meanings to this state of affairs: (1) the maladjusted lifestyle is regarded as psychopathology; (2) some different viewpoint on psychopathology (for example, that contained in the fourth edition of the *Diagnostic and Statistical Manual of Mental Disorders*, DSM-IV) is endorsed in understanding mental illness; or (3) there is disbelief in the existence of psychopathology altogether.

Rogerians appear to reject number 2 and endorse either 1 or 3 with some inconsistency. When they endorse number 1, they are operating as if psychopathology inheres in lifestyles rather than in breakdowns in the face of pressures (this is like using Axis II rather than Axis I of DSM-IV). When they endorse 3, they join forces with other critics of the idea of mental illness as a form of victimization imposed by conventional society on persons having nothing more than problems in living. On the whole, Maslovians also tend to endorse 1 and 3, rather than 2. Early in his career, however, Maslow did appear to regard traditional bases for considering psychopathology (of the sort that have culminated in DSM-IV) rather useful. So it is possible that he and others like him might find alternative 2 congenial, although their writings are not at all clear on this.

DIAGNOSTIC ASSESSMENT

Now we have the theoretical underpinnings of diagnostic interviewing in existential and humanistic approaches. On the one hand, there is more specificity than might have been expected from the general deemphasis on systematization of human behavior that exists in these approaches. On the other hand, there are certain obstacles to heavy reliance on diagnostic assessment.

Existential Psychology: Overview

As is the case in assessment generally, the existential approach focuses on psychopathological states, premorbidity, stressors, and maturity. Regarding psychopathology, the emphasis is on determining degrees and qualities of meaninglessness. With premorbidity, what is searched for are various characteristics of a conforming lifestyle that express (1) a reliance on conventional society and organismic biology as that which defines living, (2) a sense of powerlessness and threat in coping with complexity and change, and (3) feelings of boredom and sadness about missed opportunities. As for stressors that might have precipitated psychopathology, one looks for social and interpersonal upheavals, threats to physical survival, and confrontations with one's own superficiality. Determining maturity, or authenticity or individuality, involves the search for lifestyle characteristics that are in many ways the opposites of those defining premorbidity.

Needless to say, premorbidity and maturity are lifestyles that are rooted in developmental experience. But existential psychology does not emphasize identification of these developmental experiences as a key to sound diagnostic assessment.

Existential Psychology: Diagnostic Interviewing

It is typical for the therapist to ask patients to talk about their problems or themselves and to probe as needed. In this regard, the therapist is not particularly passive and can be confrontational as needed, giving feedback to patients on how they sound to another person. The emphasis is on current experiences and problems rather than the past, unless interviewee's insistence suggest that something in the past is of paramount importance. Further, there is no special focus on dreams; in existential psychology, these nighttime experiences have no greater validity as a diagnostic guide than do daytime experiences.

The therapist is after both experiential process and content. As for process, the therapist listens carefully to patients to determine how they make the inevitable decisions that mark human life. The interviewer is trying to determine (1) the level of awareness in the patient that personal experience is constructed by the decisions we make and (2) whether decisions tend to be made for the future or the past. Thus a patient who says the following expresses little awareness of the personal decisions made, however implicitly, that led to that person's problem: "My life is like a treadmill. I'd like to get off, but you can't do that, what with all the obligations and responsibilities you have. For once in my life, I'd like to be able to plan something, or just to take it easy." In contrast is the high level of awareness in the following statement: "As I think about my divorce, I realize all the little things I did, and failed to do, that contributed to the problem that finally did us in. I wish I could blame it all on my spouse, but I know that's not right."

Whether decisions are made for the future or the past depends on what, in any particular circumstance, is new and what is familiar for the patient. A patient who is choosing the past might make the following statement:

> As the time of the cocktail party approached, I began to wonder whether I wanted to go. Even though I was feeling lonely and bored, I wasn't sure I'd have a good time. The thought of meeting all those new people seemed daunting. What would I have to say to people like that? It began to seem more and more attractive to stay home and watch a movie. I felt like I was finking out on my friend, who was nice enough to try to help me meet new people, but finally I stayed home, anyway. I felt a little inadequate, but it was so comfortable to be warm and cozy in bed watching that movie.

This statement also contains the anxiety that attends thinking about choosing the future, and the guilt resulting from shrinking from it by choosing the past. Contrast that with a clear choice of the future:

> I couldn't decide whether to take the job or not. Taking it meant leaving my friends and relatives and the city I knew so well. I even began to think that the old job wasn't so bad after all, even though I had done so much complaining about it. But I always came back to thinking about how exciting this new job opportunity was—just the kind of thing I had been preparing for. And I kind of knew that I had been in a rut for quite a while, not learning anything, seeing the same people, doing the same things. Finally, I screwed up my courage and decided to take the new job. After all, the worst that could happen is that I wouldn't like it.

This person also experiences anxiety in facing the future, but finds that path developmentally valuable enough to take it. Understandably, there is no sign of the guilt of missed opportunity. What is important diagnostically is not whether any one decision is made for the future or the past, but whether the pattern or regularity over time favors one or the other direction.

Diagnostically, a low level of decisional awareness and a tendency to choose the past are characteristic of the premorbid lifestyle, of conformism, and of the various psychopathological states of meaninglessness. In contrast, high decisional awareness and regular choices of the future suggest the mature or authentic lifestyle.

The content of experience, as shown in beliefs about self and world, in actions, and in continuing moods, also aid in diagnosing mature and premorbid lifestyles and psychopathological states.

The following are examples of relevant expressions of conformism.

PLAYER OF SOCIAL ROLES

"Whenever I go to a party, I always try to find out what everyone will be wearing, because I always want to fit in."

"At work meetings, I take my cue from my superiors and the older workers, so that I can give them what they want."

EMBODIMENT OF BIOLOGICAL NEEDS

"I read everything I can about diet and exercise, because the most important thing you have is your health."

"As I get older, I live in fear of having a stroke or a heart attack."

"I love my wife, but I'd take every opportunity for a little free sex, if there were no strings attached."

MATERIALISM

"When I graduated from college, I took the job offer that made me the most money, even though the other one might have been more interesting."

"I admit that it made me feel lower than low when Joe showed up in his white Rolls–Royce."

PRAGMATISM

"As a lawyer, my sense of ethics is to help my client get off rather than to worry about what might or might not be just."

"There's no point in worrying about abstract problems that you can't do anything about, anyway. It's enough to do what you can."

CONTRACTUAL RELATIONSHIPS

"I spend my time with my customers and the others in the office, and although we usually talk about work-related matters, we sometimes talk about other things—you know, the weather, sports—but never controversial things like politics or religion."

"I don't like to meet with people unless I know what they want from me and how that fits into my goals."

POWERLESSNESS

"What's the sense of trying hard at work—someone else always gets the glory anyway."

"It's one of the more foolish ideas we humans have that we can influence what's going on around us."

ALIENATION AND MISSED OPPORTUNITY

"I'm halfway through my life, and nothing has happened. The days just come and go, and all that's happened is that I get older and more bored."

"I could have become an artist, but somehow it just didn't happen, and now what do I have to show for all these years of life?"

FEAR OF CHANGE

"Every day I feel like I'd like to stop the world and get off."

"This crazy technological race is leading us to chaos. Soon we're going to blow ourselves up or something."

The following are examples of expressions of the authentic lifestyle.

SELF-DEFINITION AS INFLUENCE

"I find that when I try to take a part in town meetings, people generally listen to me as long as I am not all tied up in my own little problems."

"I've noticed that I enjoy sex more when it's with someone who excites my imagination."

SOCIETY AS HUMAN INSTRUMENT

"After all, where did society come from, if not from our own efforts to cooperate or compete together?"

"Society isn't some monolithic, God-given thing out there. It's up to us to make it work for us."

INTIMATE RELATIONSHIPS

"I really like meeting someone and trying to get to know them on a real, personal basis."

"I like to know all sorts of things about people, not in order to control them, but because it's more fun sharing secrets than just talking about the weather or politics."

VALUE OF CONTINUAL GROWTH

"When I think about how much I've learned, and how much remains to be learned, it makes me very happy to be alive."

"Whatever happens, even if it's painful, I feel that if you can learn something for your future, you're way ahead."

KNACK OF FINDING INTEREST AND MEANING

"When the lecturer started droning on and on, I was dismayed, but then I concentrated on making a list of all the ways he had of being boring, so that I could learn never to be that way myself."

"At work, when I have to do routine tasks, I try to determine how to reorganize the job so that it can be done faster and with more value."

TOLERATING ANXIETY IN ORDER TO CHOOSE THE FUTURE

"My relationship with Al was at least comfortable, if unfulfilling, and that made it very hard to leave—but finally I was stagnating so much that it seemed as if my life was over, so I had to gulp twice and leave."

"My heart was in my mouth as I began to sign the contract that brought the new company to me. Suppose I failed and lost everything? But I had researched it too well to turn back. It could be the turning point of my life."

DECISIVE ACTIONS

"By the time I got home after the argument with my boss, I had thought the problem through enough to want to talk with her about it, so I just called her apartment."

"Whenever I have a problem, I'm the kind of person who wants to deal with it sooner rather than later."

The following are examples of expressions of psychopathological states.

ADVENTUROUSNESS

"I'm like an ambulance chaser, only with me it's causes. As soon as I finish working for one cause, I feel uncomfortable, bored, and empty until another comes along. I'm a creature of crisis, I suppose."

"I don't know why I keep breaking the law. All I know is that when I'm breaking into that house at night, or when I'm trying to get away from the cops chasing me, that's when I feel really alive."

"You know, being a commodities broker is really asinine. You can make a lot of money, but you can lose even more. And the tension is not to be believed. It's enough to make you a junkie. But it's the only thing that cancels out humdrum, everyday routines. Being a broker, you don't even need friends or lovers."

NIHILISM

"We can say whatever we want to about why things happen or don't happen—theories, religions, romance. But when you come right down to it, we don't understand anything because there's nothing to understand. There's no scientific or religious order. There's only chaos, if you can make that into a religion."

"We think of humans as the triumph of evolution, as so much more advanced than the animals. That's baloney. We are just like so many apes, or sharks, or cockroaches, nothing better."

"Amy took me to church, and it disgusted me so much to sit through that sermon. I should have walked out. What drivel about rising above pressures and being tested by God. I'm amazed that Amy and the others could be so naïve."

VEGETATIVENESS

"I don't have any reason to get out of bed in the morning. If anything in my day had the least bit of meaning, I'd bolt up, but it's the same emptiness day after day."

"I don't even feel anything any more. There are no reds or yellows, just gray. Nothing matters, nothing is now. I wish I could even get angry at it all."

"I sit there at my desk at the office and try to be pleasant and get something done. But I just don't care about the work, or the others, or myself, I guess. I'd commit suicide, but even that seems dumb."

As with any diagnostic approach, it is difficult to determine whether one is confronted with the premorbidity of conformism or with some outright psychopathological state. Patients often express aspects of conformism, adventurousness, nihilism, and vegetativeness within the same session. As with other approaches, the therapist must decide on a diagnosis based on the weight of evidence and be prepared to revise conclusions as additional information becomes available.

A further complication is that patients do not always express themselves elaborately. In such cases, it behooves the therapist to ask questions designed to elicit relevant material. Interviewing techniques designed to provoke particular responses are sometimes useful. Binswanger (1963), for example, would insistently ask "Why?" or "Why not?" when patients appeared unable to communicate or experience richly. No sooner was one insistent "Why" answered then another would confront the respondent. Frankl's primary therapeutic technique (1965) of *paradoxical intention* can also be used for assessment interviewing. This technique involves listening discerningly to the patient and then suggesting some behavior that is a logical extension of the behavioral theme but seems paradoxical nonetheless. Thus, someone who complains about the emptiness and worthlessness of life can be asked "Why haven't you committed suicide?" The answer to such a question is often quite revealing of underlying assumptions about the self and the world.

I have employed a technique called *situational reconstruction* in a diagnostic (as well as therapeutic) manner (Maddi, 1986). In this technique, patients are asked to describe a current stressful event in their own words. Then they must imagine three versions of the event that would have been even worse, from their viewpoint, and three versions that would have been better. They are then invited to investigate the plausibility of the three better and worse versions of the event by imagining others who might be involved, the roles they all play, and the relevant tasks and social forces that would have been necessary for these alternative versions to occur. If they have not covered this already, they are then asked to imagine what they themselves could do to increase the likelihood of the better versions of the event and to decrease the likelihood of the worse versions. It is helpful to record this entire exercise or take notes, because in answering the questions, patients usually reveal much about their beliefs concerning themselves and their world that is relevant to existential diagnosis.

Take, for example, the case of Arthur, whose stressful event was the denial of an expected job promotion based on a negative evaluation from his supervisor. Arthur was so angry and hurt that he resisted my efforts to have him imagine better and worse versions of what had happened. This difficulty suggested that he did not make vigorous use of imagination in daily life (possible evidence for conformism or psychopathology). However much he tried, he could come up with only two worse versions of the event, suggesting just how bad what had happened was in his view (this suggests conformism, as the event provoked strong negative emotions and involved being rejected by an authority figure). Arthur's two worse versions of the event were combining the negative job evaluation with being fired, or with no salary increase. Both more negative versions suggest materialism (being without a job or money seemed as bad as he could imagine things getting). It was somewhat easier for Arthur to imagine three better versions of the event. They were (1) if the negative evaluation had been presented as tentative rather than definite, (2) if it had not been believed by the officers of the company, and (3) if it had occurred at a time when he had another attractive job offer. Versions 1 and 3 suggest some mature initiative on Arthur's part (he could perhaps influence a tentative negative evaluation or take another job entirely), but 2 suggests the powerlessness of conformism (he is subject to the whims of officers' beliefs). As the emphasis shifted to considering the plausibility of the better—and worse—event versions, the simple, almost stereotypical nature of his views of self and world became more apparent. He emerged as an ordinary, passive, fearful person buffeted about by the forces in the world, such as power-hungry peers, indifferent supervisors, incompetent officers, and crass, "bottom-line" thinking. There was little in all this to suggest psychopathological tendencies of adventurousness, nihilism, or vegetativeness. On balance, the diagnosis reached was conformism.

Existential Psychology: Questionnaires

There are also some questionnaires that are useful in assessment from an existential viewpoint. There are, for example, several measures of powerlessness, often called Internal-versus-External-Locus-of-Control Scales (LOC) (Bialer, 1961, Crandall et al., 1965, Rotter et al., 1962). There is also the Purpose-in-Life Test (PIL) (Crumbaugh, 1968; 1971; 1972; Crumbaugh & Henrion, 1988; Crumbaugh & Maholik,1964; Crumbaugh et al., 1970), a questionnaire aimed at assessing Frankl's concept of the existential vacuum (meaninglessness). Crumbaugh (1977) has also developed another measure, the Seeking of Noetic Goals Test (SONG), which assesses the will to (motivation for) meaning, and is meant to supplement the PIL. Another related test, the Existential Study (ES), is under development by Thorne (Thorne, 1973; Pishkin and Thorne, 1973; Thorne & Pishkin, 1973).

The PIL, SONG, and ES are short, have face validity, and have benefited from some research. But more research must be done with them before they are accepted as reliable and valid enough for clinical use. Also, although much research has been reported using the various versions of the LOC Scale, complications abound concerning reliability, homogeneity, and validity. It, too, must be used with caution.

Over the years, Maddi and his associates (cf. Maddi, 1997; Maddi & Khoshaba, 2001a) have developed a promising measure of hardiness, called the Personal Views Survey, now in its third edition, revised (PVS III-R). Hardiness (Maddi & Kobasa, 1984) is a composite of three sets of beliefs about self and world concerning commitment (versus alienation), control (versus powerlessness), and challenge (versus threat). Considered a version of existential courage (Maddi, 1986; 1996; 1998; 2002) especially useful in coping with stressful events, hardiness has evidenced a buffering, or health-preserving, effect on subjects experiencing much stress (Maddi, 1997; 1998; 2002; Maddi & Kobasa, 1984). Although earlier versions of the PVS had homogeneity problems when used with adolescents and (sometimes) with females, the most current version (PVS III-R), which consists of eighteen rating-scale items balanced for positive and negative content, shows consistently adequate reliability and validity (Maddi & Khoshaba, 2001a). Persons high in hardiness can be expected to reflect the authentic lifestyle, whereas those achieving low scores will probably do so either out of existential premorbidity (conformism) or actual existential psychopathology. Also available is the HardiSurvey III-R (Maddi & Khoshaba, 2001b), a sixty-five rating-scale item questionnaire of adequate reliability and validity that adds to hardiness the stress, strain, coping, and social support measures relevant to determining overall functioning from an existential perspective.

Humanistic Psychology: Overview

There are both similarities and differences between existential and humanistic approaches to assessment. Among the similarities are the encouragement to patients to relate their current (rather than past) experiences, a deemphasis on dreams, and a generally supportive stance on the part of the therapist. As for differences, the humanistic interviewer will reflect rather than confront, and in asking questions, will take special care not to appear confrontational.

For some humanistic psychologists, there is no point to diagnostic assessment; the decision as to whether therapy is desirable is the patient's alone, and the nature of the therapy is the same regardless of the presenting symptoms. Other humanistic psychologists will find it a matter of interest to determine whether the patient is fully functioning (self-actualized) or maladjusted. For the latter practitioners, some diagnostic procedures can be specified.

Humanistic Psychology: Diagnostic Interviewing

The major task is to determine from patients' material whether they are maladjusted or fully functioning (self-actualized). The following are examples of maladjustment.

CONDITIONS OF WORTH

"I hate myself when I fritter away the whole day and get nothing of value done."
"I don't care what other people do, but I have to stay calm and collected no matter what."

INCONGRUENCE BETWEEN SELF AND POTENTIAL

"I work so hard, and for what? Just money. At the end of the day, I'm so tired, but also so dissatisfied. I don't even know what I want any more, but I know I'm not happy."
"Sometimes I have this vague sense that I could have done all sorts of things instead of having the orderly, mundane life I'm stuck with."

DEFENSIVENESS

"I don't understand myself. I try and try to figure things out, but the more I try, the less clear it all becomes."
"I'm just like other people; I do all the things you're supposed to do. So why am I having all these problems? Why am I the one who gets left behind all the time?"

RIGID, PRECONCEIVED PLANS

"Ever since graduating from college, I've had this schedule for myself: start as a junior exec, maybe making $40,000 a year, move up the ladder and make assistant VP by age thirty, and be a major force in the company by forty, with a salary of $120,000."

"I always wanted a normal American life. You know, two children, a house in the suburbs, a Mercedes in the driveway, good standing in the community. What's so wrong with that?"

ORGANISMIC DISREGARD

"When I get that tightness in the chest, I just shrug it off. I've always been a little cowardly, and I'm not about to give in to it."

"When I'm with Amy, we have pleasant times, but I can't always think of things to say. On the other hand, Laura and I always have a ball, without ever making any plans, without ever feeling bored. But I'm going to see if Amy will marry me, because I respect her education and career too much, and I see myself as needing that."

FEELINGS OF MANIPULATION

"Life is a rat race. You just keep running to try to reach your goals before the guy behind you beats you out."

"I'm a loser. I've never won anything or been in the least bit lucky."

CONFORMITY

"I love shopping in Harold's because it has all the latest, trendy styles that you need in order to look acceptable."

"At staff meetings, it's important to know who the power brokers are so that you can say the right things and get on their side."

The following are examples of the fully functioning lifestyle (Rogers, 1961).

OPENNESS TO EXPERIENCE

"When I meet a person, it's as if it's the first person I've ever met. I'm so excited about getting to know him."

"When Joe hurt me so much, I thought I'd never want anything to do with him again. But then, whenever we'd get together, I realized that despite my hurt pride, I enjoyed and appreciated what we could have together. I began to realize that life and relationships are complicated, and you have to let them go wherever they go."

EXISTENTIAL LIVING

"When people ask me where I'm going on vacation next year, I never know what to say. I don't feel like making big, unchangeable future plans. Who knows what I'll want to do next year?"

"I know I change my mind a lot, but it's not just arbitrary. There's always a lot of input that I mull over before I decide what to do and think."

ORGANISMIC TRUSTING

"I know everyone was counting on me to marry Jim. All the plans were made, and we seemed to be such a nice couple. But, when push came to shove, I just didn't feel right enough or excited enough down deep."

"You know, all the odds were against making a success of that business. But something in me kept saying I should give it a shot, so I did."

EXPERIENTIAL FREEDOM

"You know, if you try to influence what's going on around you, you often can. Not always, but many times."

"Sometimes I have this great sense of power, like I can do anything I want to if I believe in it and am willing to work at it."

CREATIVITY

"When I am assigned a task at work, I always start by asking myself what's the best solution to the problem. I have to discard the usual ways the problem has been approached. Sometimes it's best to think of some way that seems outlandish, because it may turn out to be the best."

"I don't like to do things the same way twice. Better to explore new solutions."

Note that the implications of Maslow's version of maturity (1962), the self-actualized person, are sufficiently different from those just explicated to warrant separate treatment.

REALISTIC ORIENTATION

"Relationships are two-way streets. When I try to understand some problem I have with another person, I try to listen to his point of view and understand it as well as I understand my own."

"Every piece of information on some topic has truth to it. You have to consider it all."

ACCEPTANCE OF SELF, OTHERS, AND WORLD

"The older I get, the more I realize that my limitations are as important in making me who I am as are my strengths. Finally, it's all me, and that's okay."

"It doesn't make sense to blame everything on the politicians and bosses. Everyone more or less tries their best sometimes and goofs around sometimes. People aren't perfect, but they're all we have."

SPONTANEITY

Same as Rogers's Existential Living.

TASK ORIENTATION

"When there's a job to be done, that pulls me out of myself. It doesn't much matter how I and the others are feeling that day or who likes whom. There's work to be done."

"Even at times when I've been really down, I can get into working with the tasks at hand."

SENSE OF PRIVACY

"I really get a kick out of people. But sometimes I just need to be alone, to hear my inner voice."

"Just because I can open up to my intimate friends doesn't mean that I wear my heart on my sleeve wherever I go."

INDEPENDENCE

"Although it's more fun to travel with someone you like a lot, I also enjoy going places by myself."

"More and more, I find that I have my own point of view on various matters."

APPRECIATIVENESS

"Last night, the sunset was unbelievably beautiful. I just felt the whole power of the universe and it made me happy to be part of it."

"When I think of my past, I realize how wonderful people have been to me."

SPIRITUALITY

"Sometimes I'm overwhelmed at the ability of people—artists, writers, even ordinary people—to take giant steps forward."

"We all have such power in us, for good or evil."

INTIMACY

Same as in existential psychology.

DEMOCRATIC VALUES

"We are all brothers under the skin, as the saying goes."

"I like having all sorts of friends—rich, poor, educated, uneducated—it makes for a more meaningful life."

DIFFERENCE BETWEEN MEANS AND ENDS

"It's fine to want to rise to the top of the heap, but it's not fine to do so by lying and cheating."

"I care too much about my family's well-being to cast them aside and pursue my own freedom."

PHILOSOPHICAL HUMOR

"It's funny to see how we all try to cover up those wrinkles as we get older. We primp and preen and spend all that money on oils and massages. I guess we just don't want to part with life."

"Here we are telling each other lies about ourselves, for fear that we aren't acceptable to each other. We humans are so frightened and yet so wonderful."

CREATIVITY

Same as in Rogers.

NONCONFORMISM

Same as in existential psychology.

In the humanistic approach, there is little reliance on aids to interviewing such as Binswanger's "Why?" technique and Maddi's situational reconstruction. Such techniques would appear too manipulative of the patient to be acceptable to humanistic psychologists. But these psychologists have found the Experiencing Scale (Gendlin & Tomlinson, 1967) useful. Experiencing is described as "the quality of an individual's experiencing of himself, the extent to which his ongoing, bodily, felt flow of experiencing is the basic datum of his awareness and communications about himself, and the extent to which this inner datum is integral to action and thought" (Klein et al., 1969, p. 1). Although the name may imply it, the Experiencing Scale is not a questionnaire to be filled out by the patient. Rather, the patient verbalizes in the interview, and then these verbalizations are rated by the therapist on a scale of degree of experiencing. There are seven stages of experiencing, ranging from the lowest, in which the patient seems distant or remote from feelings; through the middle range, in which feelings are brought into clearer perspective as the patient's own; to the highest, in which feelings have been scrutinized and explored such that they become a trusted and reliable source of self-awareness. Clearly, low experiencing is akin to maladjustment, whereas high experiencing suggests a fully functioning lifestyle. Klein and her colleagues (1969) provide a scoring manual for the Experiencing Scale and report adequate interscorer reliability after practice. More recently, Klein and others have extended the Experiencing Scale to apply not only to individual patients, but to group interactions and therapist behavior as well (Klein et al., 1986), and added on to it the Adjective Check List (Thomas et al., 1982). Unfortunately, the research evidence with which to be sure of the validity and reliability of these measures appears insufficient and problematic at this time.

Humanistic Psychology: Questionnaires

There is a questionnaire aimed at measuring the components of self-actualization included in Maslow's theories. Called the Personal Orientation Inventory (POI) (Shostrom, 1965; 1966), this test consists of 150 paired, opposing statements. Responses yield scores on two major scales (inner-directedness and time competence) and ten complementary scales (self-actualizing values, existentiality, feeling reactivity, spontaneity, self-regard, self-acceptance, nature of man, synergy, acceptance of aggression, and capacity for intimacy). Adequate reliability is reported for the scales. There is also evidence for construct validity in that persons appearing to be self-actualized tend to score higher on the scales than those who do not appear self-actualized (Shostrom et al., 1976) and that group therapy appears to increase POI scores (Knapp & Shostrom, 1976).

CONCLUSION

Not all existential and humanistic psychologists will agree with the position I have taken in this chapter—namely, that there is an assessment technology inherent in these approaches. Admittedly, there is little acceptance in these approaches of DSM-IV as a guide to psychopathology; nor is there even general acceptance of the concept that psychopathology is of value. Nonetheless, it seems to me that there is a surprising amount of conceptual and technical material relevant to existential and humanistic practice. I have tried to highlight this material.

REFERENCES

Bialer, I. (1961). Conceptualization of success and failure in mentally retarded and normal children. *Journal of Personality* 29:303–320.

Binswanger, L. (1963). *Being-in-the-World: Selected Papers of Ludwig Binswanger,* trans. J. Needleman. New York: Basic.

Boss, M. (1963). *Psychoanalysis and Daseinsanalysis,* trans. L. B. Lefebre. New York: Basic.

Crandall, V. C., Katkovsky, W., & Crandall, V. J. (1965). Childrens' beliefs in their own control of reinforcement in intellectual–academic achievement situations. *Child Development* 36:91–109.

Crumbaugh, J. C. (1968). Cross-validation of the Purpose-in-Life Test based on Frankl's concepts. *Journal of Individual Psychology* 24:74–81.

Crumbaugh, J. C. (1971). Frankl's logotherapy: A new orientation in counseling. *Journal of Religion and Health* 10:373–386.

Crumbaugh, J. C. (1972). Aging and adjustment: The applicability of logotherapy and the Purpose-in-Life Test. *Gerontologist* 12:418–420.

Crumbaugh, J. C. (1977). The Seeking of Noetic Goals Test (SONG): A complementary scale to the Purpose in Life Test (PIL). *Journal of Clinical Psychology* 33:900–907.

Crumbaugh, J. C., & Henrion, R. (1988). The PIL Test: Administration, interpretation, uses, theory and critique. *International Forum for Logotherapy* 11:76–88.

Crumbaugh, J. C., & Maholik, L. T. (1964). An experimental study in existentialism: The psychometric approach to Frankl's concept of noogenic neurosis. *Journal of Clinical Psychology* 20:200–207.

Crumbaugh, J. C., Raphael, M., & Shrader, R. R. (1970). Frankl's will to meaning in a religious order. *Journal of Clinical Psychology* 26:206–207.

Frankl, V. (1965). *The Doctor and the Soul*, 2nd ed., trans. R. Winston and C. Winston. New York: Knopf.

Gendlin, E. T., and Tomlinson, T. M. (1967). The process conception and its measurement. In *The Therapeutic Relationship and Its Impact: A Study of Psychotherapy with Schizophrenics*, ed. C. R. Rogers et al., pp. 109–131. Madison: University of Wisconsin Press.

Khoshaba, D. M., & Maddi, S. R. (1999). Early experiences in hardiness development. *Consulting Psychology Journal* 51:106–116.

Kierkegaard, S. (1954). *Fear and Trembling and the Sickness unto Death*, trans. W. Lowrie. Garden City, NY: Doubleday Anchor.

Klein, M. H., et al. (1969). *The Experiencing Scale: A Research and Training Manual*, Vol. 1. Madison: Wisconsin Psychiatric Institute.

Klein, M. H., Mathieu-Coughlan, P., & Kiesler, D. J. (1986). The Experiencing Scales. In *The Psychotherapeutic Process: A Research Handbook*, ed. L. S. Greenberg & W. M. Pinsof, pp. 21–71. New York: Guilford.

Knapp, R. P., & Shostrom, E. L. (1976). POI outcomes in studies of growth groups: A selected review. *Group and Organizational Studies* 2:187–202.

Kobasa, S. C. (1979). Stressful life events, personality, and health: An inquiry into hardiness. *Journal of Personality and Social Psychology* 37:1–11.

Kobasa, S. C., & Maddi, S. R. (1977). Existential personality theory. In *Current Personality Theory*, ed. R. Corsini, pp. 243–276. Itasca, IL: Peacock.

Kobasa, S. C., Maddi, S. R., & Kahn, S. (1982). Hardiness and health: A prospective study. *Journal of Personality and Social Psychology* 42:168–177.

Laing, R. D. (1967). *The Politics of Experience*. New York: Ballantine.

Maddi, S. R. (1967). The existential neurosis. *Journal of Abnormal Psychology* 72:311–325.

Maddi, S. R. (1970). The search for meaning. In *Nebraska Symposium on Motivation*, ed. M. Page, pp. 137–186. Lincoln: University of Nebraska Press.

Maddi, S. R. (1986). Existential psychotherapy. In *Contemporary Psychotherapies: Models and Methods*, ed. S. Lynn and J. Garske, pp. 191–215. New York: Merrill.

Maddi, S. R. (1988). On the problem of accepting facticity and pursuing possibility. In *Hermeneutics and Psychological Theory: Interpretive Perspectives on Personality, Psychotherapy, and Psychopathology*, ed. S. B. Messer, L. A. Sass, and R. L. Woolfolk, pp. 182–209. New Brunswick, NJ: Rutgers University Press.

Maddi, S. R. (1996). *Personality Theories: A Comparative Analysis*, 6th ed. Prospect Heights, IL: Waveland.

Maddi, S. R. (1997). Personal Views Survey II: A measure of dispositional hardiness. In *Evaluating Stress*, ed. C. P. Zalaquett & R. J. Wood, pp. 293–309. Lanham, MD: Scarecrow.

Maddi, S. (1998). Creating meaning through making decisions. In *The Human Quest for Meaning*, ed. P. T. Wong and P. S. Fry, pp. 3–26. Mahwah, NJ: Erlbaum.

Maddi, S. (2002). The story of hardiness: Twenty years of theorizing, research, and practice. *Consulting Psychology Journal* 54: 173–185.

Maddi, S. R., & Kobasa, S. C. (1984). *The Hardy Executive: Health Under Stress*, Chicago: Dorsey.

Maddi, S. K. & Khoshaba, D. M. (2001a). Personal Views Survey-III-R: Test development and inernet instruction manual. Newport Beach, CA: Hardiness Institute.

Maddi, S. R. & Khoshaba, D. M. (2001b). HardiSurvey III-R: Test development and internet instruction manual. Newport Beach, CA: Hardiness Institute.

Maslow, A. H. (1955). Deficiency motivation and growth motivation. In *Nebraska Symposium on Motivation*, ed. M. R. Jones, pp. 1–30. Lincoln: University of Nebraska Press.

Maslow, A. H. (1962). Some basic propositions of a growth and self-actualization psychology. In *Perceiving, Behaving, Becoming: A New Focus for Education*. Washington, DC: Yearbook of the Association for Supervision and Curriculum Development.

May, R., Angel, E., & Ellenberger, H. F., eds. (1959). *Existence: A New Dimension in Psychiatry and Psychology*. New York: Basic.

Pishkin, V., & Thorne, F. C. (1973). A factorial study of existential state reactions. *Journal of Clinical Psychology* 29:392–402.

Rogers, C. R. (1959). A theory of therapy, personality, and interpersonal relationships, as developed in the client-centered framework. In *Psychology: A Study of a Science*, Vol. 3, ed. S. Koch, pp. 184–256. New York: McGraw-Hill.

Rogers, C. R. (1961). *On Becoming a Person*. Boston: Houghton Mifflin.

Rotter, J. B., Seeman, M., & Liverant, S. (1962). Internal versus external control of reinforcements: A major variable in behavior theory. In *Decisions, Values, and Groups*, Vol. 2, ed. N. F. Washburne, pp. 473–516. London: Pergamon.

Schneider, K. J. (1998). Toward a science of the heart. *American Psychologist* 53:277–289.

Shostrom, E. (1965). An inventory for the measurement of self-actualization. *Educational and Psychological Measurement* 24:207–218.

Shostrom, E. (1966). *Manual for the Personal Orientation Inventory (POI): An Inventory for the Measurement of Self-Actualization*. San Diego: Educational and Industrial Testing Service.

Thomas, J. T., Stein, L. I., & Klein, M. H. (1982). A comparative evaluation of changes in basic clinical pastoral education students in different types of clinical settings as measured by the Adjective Check List and the experience scale. *Journal of Pastoral Care* 3:181–193.

Thorne, F. C. (1973). The existential study: A measure of existential status. *Journal of Clinical Psychology* 29:387–392.

Thorne, F. C., & Pishkin, V. (1973). The existential study. *Journal of Clinical Psychology* 29:389–410.

Zalaquett, C. P., & R. J. Woods, ed. (1997). *Evaluating Stress: A Book of Resources*. New York: University Press.

7

THE FAMILY
THERAPY INTERVIEW

David van Dyke, Ph.D.

FAMILY SYSTEMS HISTORICAL CONTEXT

The concept of working with families to foster therapeutic change grew simultaneously at different locations during the 1950s (Nichols, 1992). Two pivotal scholars, Gregory Bateson and Ludwig von Bertalanffy, in collaboration with dozens of other clinicians, provided the theoretical foundation for the practice of marital and family therapy.

General Systems Theory

Bertalanffy was a biologist who sought to develop a theory that would explain all living systems. He proposed that all living organisms are part of open systems where information flows in and out (Bertalanffy, 1968). This flow of information helps organisms reach higher levels of organization. From a general systems orientation, the focus is on the interaction of the parts rather than the individual parts themselves (Bertalanffy, 1968). This "refocusing" highlights the mutual influence and relationships that are central in family systems thinking. Instead of looking at the individual person and their deficits, the clinician attends to the interactions of the individual with the various contexts in their life and the mutual influences that are creating the current structure (i.e., presenting problem).

Cybernetics

Norbert Wiener (1961) provided the name cybernetics for a new paradigm of "behavior" that addressed communication, feedback, and control. Cybernetics had a profound impact on the social sciences. Cybernetics was the product of the 1942 conference funded by the Josiah Macy Foundation to explore the various disciplines' understandings of control and communication. Anthropologist Gregory Bateson attended this conference and brought the concepts of cybernetics to the marital and family therapy field. In their study "Toward a Theory of Schizophrenia," Bateson and colleagues (1956) introduced the concept of symptom functionality as a means for understanding behavior. In 1958, Richard Fisch, Jay Haley, Don Jackson, Virginia Satir, Paul Watzlawick, and John Weakland joined together to form the Mental Research Institute (MRI) in Palo Alto, California, which was greatly influenced by Bateson's ideas about communication and system organization.

Family Therapy Theories

Clinical work with families grew out of the scientific ethos that both cybernetics and general systems theory established. There are numerous family approaches (cf. Piercy et al., 1996); the Mental Research Institute and Murray Bowen were among those of the first generation. The MRI model of intervention emphasizes communication and problem solving (Fisch et al., 1982; Watzlawick et al., 1974). This style of therapy has been described as interactional and brief (Gale & Long, 1996), and the focus is on how family members communicate, both verbally and nonverbally. This communication shapes the interactional sequences and behavioral response. Change occurs by disrupting the communication style and sequences. In assessing a family with a behavior problem, the clinician would study the words of the family members, their nonverbal communication, and the congruency between the verbal and nonverbal messages. Gale & Long (1996) point out how Bateson's work with cybernetics and its application by the MRI group differ. Some in the MRI group have focused on strategic interventions intended to nudge the system's homeostasis (Haley, 1973; 1987). Those who have reinterpreted Bateson's work urge an approach that attends to the system's wisdom, and how the system makes sense of its process (cf. Anderson, 1987; Dell, 1989; Hoffman, 1985; Keeney, 1983). Family therapy frameworks that have arisen from the MRI group are the Milan Team (Selvini Palazolli et al., 1978), Structural Family Therapy (Minuchin, 1974; Minuchin & Fishman, 1981), Strategic Family Therapy (Haley, 1987; Madanes, 1991), Conjoint Family Therapy (Satir, 1964), and Solution-Focused Family Therapy. Assessment in the MRI model involves communication patterns (both verbal and nonverbal). The interaction sequences in communication create trajectories of meaning and behavior for the individual. The clinician's responsibility was to assess the elaborate interactions and disrupt them, creating space for new interactions with different meanings and behavior.

While MRI's applications developed from Bateson's work, Murray Bowen's Systems Theory originated from Bertalanffy's work. Bowen noticed that families seek organization. This organization exists in patterned behaviors.

In the 1950s, Bowen was working on a psychiatric ward with schizophrenics and their families. He noticed predictable patterns of behavior, specifically in response to anxiety (Bowen, 1960). Later, Bowen moved beyond working with just schizophrenic families and sought to understand behavior within all families and their contexts (Friedman, 1991). Bowen noticed that interdependency existed for both families and other organisms (from cells to society). The way groups organize, especially the repetitive nature of the organization, is the emotional system (Kerr & Bowen, 1988). Bowen, working from an evolutionary perspective, argued that the emotional system is necessary to deal with perceived threats from without (i.e., anxiety). The instinctual, emotional response to perceived anxiety is fight or flight. Most individuals/families fight or flee the anxiety through the process of triangulation. When anxiety increases between two individuals in a relationship, a third entity is "pulled" into the relationship to provide stability and bind the anxiety (Kerr & Bowen, 1988). Triangulation takes many forms. One form is the pathologized child. If marital conflict is perceived as a threat to the relationship, attention may turn to a child's behavior to decrease the anxiety in the marriage. In assessing an individual's functioning and need for intervention, Bowen would look at the level of differentiation and the historical organization in the family emotional system. Differentiation is the process an individual continually goes through to define the self within the family emotional system (Bowen, 1978). Bowenian assessment looks across the generations at the transmission of the family emotional system. How has the family organized (in repetitive patterns) to deal with anxiety? What is the level of differentiation for the individual within the family system? How is the current problem part of the repetitive pattern in dealing with anxiety within the family?

FAMILY THEORIES AND WORKING WITH INDIVIDUALS

Family system conceptualization of behavioral/emotional problems is based in the reciprocal nature of interaction. Walter Buckley (1968) emphasizes the mutual causality and interdependence of each family member: I affect and am affected by others in my environment. This mutual influencing leads to a certain homeostasis of functioning. An individual's behavior serves some function or meaning for the individual, and the family and is thus maintained. Determining these patterns, functions, and meanings is done through gathering the history of the individual and family, observing interactional behavior patterns, and studying the language used in the family's conversation. Each family theorist has his or her own way of assessing families. Some family theories focus on working with the family in the session (Haley, 1987; Minuchin, 1974; Whitaker & Ryan, 1989). Others conceptualize change through work with an individual, parts of the family, or the entire family (Anderson & Goolishian, 1992; Hoffman, 1991; White & Epston, 1990). The systemic reason for working with the family is that the family homeostasis (Jackson, 1965) will seek to maintain the status quo. An individual trying to change his or her behavior will bump up against the reoccurring family patterns that have provided stability when change (often perceived as a threat to the system) occurs. For the individual to successfully change his or her behavior, the context (e.g., family structure, family interactional sequences, family meaning of behavior) must change. A systemic reason for working with an individual is based in the idea of mutual influence. The change in one of the parts will have a ripple affect through the entire system, and it will need to reorganize. Two ways of interviewing and assessing the family are structural family therapy and Bowenian family therapy.

Structural Family Interview

The structural family approach invites the entire family to attend the session. Structural family therapy focuses on the organization issues in the family and how they maintain the presenting problem (Minuchin, 1974). A structural therapist assesses the relational structures in terms of subsystems, hierarchy, and boundaries between individuals, subsystems, and the family in society. Assessment and intervention are typically done focusing on the in-session behavioral sequences (Piercy & Wetchler, 1996). This in-session, directive approach works well when the entire family is present. During the interview, the structural family therapist gathers information about the presenting problem. The attention, however, is focused on the process of the answer. Who answers? What are the other family members doing while this person talks? Does this perspective get challenged? Where are family members located physically in the room? What happens when the power balance in the family is disturbed? Some of these questions are addressed by having the family participate in an enactment. The therapist may encourage the family to have an argument. Through this activity, the therapist assesses communication patterns, family structure, and interaction patterns. The interview is based on the assumption that the structure frames each individual's feelings, thoughts, and behavior.

Bowenian Family Interview

A Bowenian family interview can involve either the family or just the identified client. The focus of the interview is the level of differentiation and the relational settings in which the individual gets pulled into the family's emotional system (Bowen, 1978). Much of the information needed comes from historical patterns of relating within the immediate family and across the generations. There are eight processes that are assessed: differentiation of self, triangles, nuclear family emotional system, family projection process, emotional cutoff, multigenerational transmission process, sibling position, and emotional process in society (Hall, 1991). The best interview technique of collecting this information is called intergenerational family genogram (McGoldrick & Gerson, 1985). Genograms are graphical depictions of family structure, history, and relationships across at least three generations. The therapist asks questions that track the presenting problem (who knows about it, how they have responded, what has/hasn't worked to resolve the situation), the family's relationships and how they affect/are affected by the problem (the family's ability to reorganize given the current situation, the close/distant relationship, and whether relationships have changed in the given context), the family history (anniversaries of transitions, family patterns, birth order, history of physical and emotional illness), and the individual functioning of each family member (e.g., behavioral problems, substance abuse, employment, legal problems, and physical problems). This assessment helps the therapist understand the historical and relational context of the presenting problem. It can also provide insight for the family into the dynamics that may contribute to the presenting problem. The multiple generational perspective allows the therapist to identify triangles, that is, patterns of relationships that detour conflict and anxiety through a third party. Often, these are children who become the identified client.

Including the context (e.g., the family) in the interview remains a core supposition in family systems perspective. Regardless of the theory or approach used in the interview, the systemic conceptualization is that the presenting problem is relationally maintained and not solely an intrinsic problem of the individual.

FIRST INTERVIEW

This section includes important content areas to include in your first interview, regardless of your therapeutic approach. (It is more or less an integrative approach; cf. McHolland, 1995; Pinsof, 1981. Theoretical purists from each of these orientations would stress or delete certain areas listed below.)

Who to Interview?

Family interview. There are various assessment instruments for families; however, the most common form of assessment is the family interview (Thomlison, 2002). For most family therapists, attendance at the first session provides important information. Therapists who seek to work with the entire family will notice who attends and who elects not to attend, and they will discuss this with the family. For instance, after all family members are urged to attend during the initial phone contact, an adolescent is brought to therapy by his mother alone. "He is the one who has the problem, and he is the one who needs to be here," says Mom. A family therapist conceptualizing the situation systemically will wonder if this demonstrates how the family functions, issues of power in the family, and implicit roles and rules of the family. Some therapists, such as Carl Whitaker, have been known to refuse to see clients without the entire family, due to their theory of change (Napier & Whitaker, 1988). As a clinician, whom you invite to the first session and who attends are important data, depending on your theoretical orientation. The emphasis on all family members attending also creates an intervention by reframing the concept of an individual problem to a family issue (Nichols & Schwartz, 1998). McGoldrick and Gerson (1985) describe the *Rashomon effect*, "based on a famous Japanese movie where one event is shown from the perspective of a number of different characters" (p. 30). Multiple reporters, versus an individual self-report, can provide a fuller description of behaviors, family dynamics, and emotional responses. Family interviews are simultaneously assessment and intervention. An additional benefit for conducting a family interview is the behavioral observations that can be made by the therapist. There are four times when interviewing the entire family is vital: in binding and exploitative family relationships, when talking to an "outsider" violates the family's invisible loyalties, when therapy leads to alienation of family relationships, and in issues of isolation and rejection (Stierlin et al., 1980). The following is an example of the initial session/interview of a child struggling with anxiety.

A family was referred to therapy through the father's employee assistance program. The father was missing work and becoming increasingly stressed over family issues with his son. This was impacting his job performance. The son was a five year old who was three weeks from beginning kindergarten. The boy had had significant separation anxiety for the past year. He would throw up at preschool, was unable to sleep well on nights before school, and was throwing tantrums hours before leaving for school. The mother stated that it had been occurring for the past two years, which correlated with the birth of the boy's younger brother. Since that time, the mother had slept in his room to pacify him and the family. However, things began to escalate as "real" school approached. Over the phone during the initial contact, the mother stated that she and the son would come. The therapist stated that he needed to talk to the whole family, since it affected everyone. The initial session was informative because of the content provided by the family, but even more so because of the observations of family patterns. After a half an hour, the therapist requested to see the child alone. The first to speak was the mother, who said that she doubted he would be able to tolerate that situation. The father waited to be told what to do. The child then began screaming and grabbing on to the family. The patterns of this family were more helpful in the development of a treatment plan than was the information they supplied. The interview led to work with parents on their responses to the child and how to deal with their worries of lack of influence in their child's life. There was also work with the child in learning the new patterns of interaction and ways to think about events in his life.

Individual interview. Occasionally, whether due to theoretical orientations, limits of the clinical settings, or geographical limitations (the family lives out of state), the family interview occurs with only the client. The context of the presenting problem can be gathered from the self-report of the individual. The client's perceptions of the context are important, because this shapes their responses in those relationships (Jacob & Tennenbaum, 1988). Jay Haley (1987) and Karl Tomm (1984) provide four stages to the family interview that structures the therapist's thought process. The stages suggested here are simple but involve important content area for a family therapist. The four stages involve joining/engagement, family interaction/assessment, intervention/developing a plan, and ending the session. The joining stage involves the presenting problems: why therapy is being sought now, when the problems began, what hasn't worked, who is most affected. This is the point when the therapist gathers symptoms and medical, psychological, and relational history. Clinical interviews gather developmental data to place the individual within a continuum of normalcy. Families have developmental stages and tasks that are important in understanding the family functioning and the individual's coping. Family life cycle stage (Carter & McGoldrick, 1989) provides six stages with important tasks: leaving (moving from family home to establishing financial and emotional differentiation), marriage (redefining relationships and reorganizing roles), family with young children (space for children and readjustment of roles), family with adolescents (encouraging autonomy and refocusing the marital relationship), launching (developing an adult–adult relationship with the child), and later in life (dealing with losses and accepting shifts in roles). Problems can be caused or maintained by these tasks. Both individual and family development are important in forming a course of treatment.

The interactional stage involves the context of the family, how each person responds, boundaries, communication, and how previous generations would deal with the current situation. When interviewing a client from a family perspective, it is important to use the client's language, metaphors, and so forth to connect with each family member and gain a shared frame of reference. The final stage is developing the course of action (e.g., therapy modality, further diagnostic testing, available resources, and specific goals for treatment). Stierlin et al. (1980) provide detailed questions for the therapist while interviewing the entire family. Some suggested questions and the sequencing are located in table 7.1.

A clinical interview from a family therapy perspective involves understanding the context for the problem and developing consensus for the treatment plan (Stierlin et al., 1980). Just as the family therapist values understanding the context of the problem, the therapist is also mindful of establishing a context that can foster change and growth. The following is an example of a family that would seek therapy and a way of interviewing with the individual. Italics represent metacomments by the author.

Table 7.1.   Content of First Interview

Content Area	Sample Questions
Presenting Problem	What is it?
	When did it start?
	Why are you coming in for therapy now?
	Who does the problem bother most?
	How does each family member respond to the situation?
	What are the symptoms?
	What is the history of this situation in the family?
Family Structure Subsystems	Are there teams in your family?
	Who is on your team?
	Do these teams/alliances change? When?
Communication	What happens in the family when the problem is addressed?
Power	Who do you talk with about this problem?
	What would "X" say about this situation?
	Often best observed by interactions
	Who has the final say?
	Who are you afraid will find out? Why?
Family Roles	Evoke and listen for comments about the roles each family member embraces in given situations. A Bowenian family therapist would listen for issues of differentiation from the emotional family system. Satir would listen for congruency between thoughts and feelings of the individual and her interactions/roles in the family. Minuchin would listen and observe the family structure, its flexibility, and issues of distance in relationship.
Family Life Cycle Stage	Family members, ages, who is in the home
Contextual Issues	
Culture	Ask questions about impact—looking at both
Gender	tension and resiliency regarding presenting
Religion	problem.

A FAMILY INTERVIEW: JERRY'S RAGE

Jerry's mother called to make an appointment. She was concerned with Jerry's behavior at home and at school. She stated on the phone that over the past two years he had been more aggressive and got angry "at the drop of a hat." From the phone contact, it was learned that Jerry was an eleven-year-old boy who lived with his family in suburbia. Jerry's family was affluent and consisted of Jerry, his mother, his father, and his younger sister. Most of Jerry's problem be–

havior occurred at home; however, he did demonstrate a lot of aggression while playing hockey.

An appointment was set for the family to attend the session. At the time of the appointment, Jerry and his mother, who were finishing the required paperwork, were the only people in the waiting room. The therapist greeted the family and asked about the rest of the family. The reply was that the father was unable to attend because of an emergency at work and that the mother was not able to stay because of chronic pain.

At this initial stage of the interview, the therapist should be cataloguing the following: chronic illness in the family, normal developmental tasks for an eleven year old, family patterns of parents.

Mom went to rest in the car during the session. Jerry entered the therapy room and sat, waiting for instructions. The therapist explained confidentiality and its limits. Then the therapist stated that he had talked with the client's mother and discussed the information that was shared. The therapist then asked the client why he thought he was in therapy. He stated, "I have been getting angry and yelling at my mom and my sister." Jerry discussed his love for hockey, which was evident in his Red Wings jersey. He stated that his outlet was hockey. The therapist spent time joining briefly with Jerry by talking about his favorite team. Jerry was asked about when the problem started, who noticed most, when it didn't occur, and what had been helpful in keeping it from happening. Jerry stated that he had been mad since his mother's illness started. She had a car accident and lived in constant pain. Jerry stated, "She has ruined my life!" He continue by saying that she no longer went to all his games and did not do the things she used to do with him. He also stated that she yelled a lot and then they got into it. He reported that he was better when he could do something physical such as hitting people on the ice.

The reason Jerry was willing to come to therapy was that he got in trouble with his coach for getting into a fight on the ice (hitting another player repeatedly with his stick), costing the team a game and placing the other child in the hospital. Jerry stated that when he was busy at school he did not have any behavior problems. He stated that his mother is most bothered by his behavior.

An important question in this section would be how the other family members respond to the conflict between Jerry and his mother. Also, how do other family members respond to Mom's diminished capacities? Without this information, the problem becomes framed in a limited way: "The problem is either me or its Mom." But it appears that the family is having difficulty coping and adjusting to the transition of chronic illness.

After joining with Jerry and gathering the presenting problem information, the interviewer turned to relational questions: What happens between family members when he "explodes"? What does each family member do when he gets angry? What would happen in the family if the behavior stayed the same? How do Mom and Dad respond to him and to each other? Two significant relational issues arose from this questioning. Jerry noticed that the family focused less on

Mom's pain when he was getting into trouble. He also noted that his Dad would calm his Mom down and "referee" the situation. He was asked about the roles when he "acted up" and when things were "normal" in the family. The family organized around his anger, and it appeared to provide an outlet for the anger the family had regarding Mom's loss of physical health.

This anger appears to be functional for the family. The problem has become, as reported in Jerry's answer to why he was coming to therapy, now, that Jerry has become aggressive and violent outside of the family. The family relationships and emotional process need to change to allow space for Jerry to try new behaviors.

Jerry was asked about Mom's health, and he stated that he hated her because she had become grumpy and unable to do anything with him. The final family questions were about how both his parents and grandparents dealt with their emotions. Specifically, how did they express their emotions and how did it work for them? Jerry stated that his dad never cried, that he would just get quiet and go to work on the house. Jerry stated that his mom yelled and cried "way too loud." He stated that he didn't know his grandparents. When asked if they were alive, he was unsure and didn't know why the family wouldn't spend time with them if they were alive.

After the family questions, the therapist asked Jerry about his individual functioning. He did not have any physical problems and was appropriate in his developmental milestones. He was in the normal functioning in terms of mood and thought disorders. The school counselor stated to Jerry that because of his behavior in hockey he might be diagnosed as having oppositional defiant disorder.

The individual questions in the case are held until last in an effort to frame the presenting problem as relational instead of just Jerry's.

The interview ended with a discussion of what Jerry would like changed and what the family would look like if those changes happened. Jerry said that he would like to be calm and not explode. He stated that if he could change his mother, she wouldn't be so angry and she would be able to do more things he wanted, instead of being grounded. He also said that his mom and dad would probably argue more. Jerry and the therapist agreed on working on developing new skills to express his feelings.

SUMMARY

The interview with Jerry is an example of how a systemic perspective might be used in a clinical interview. The paradigmatic shift is thinking about emotional problems as relationally based. From this perspective, the clinician must address the context of the individual (e.g., family life cycle, individual development, issues of loss, transitions, family cohesion and adaptability to new life events, family history in dealing with communication and emotions, resources available to the family, and structure of the family system). Family systems view behavior as a function of the relationship and as an antecedent of the relationships. Behavior change is based on greatest likelihoods versus causal models. Thus relationships in the family can maintain and constrain certain choices and behavioral options. A clinical interview from a family systems perspective is not only data collection but also an intervention.

REFERENCES

Andersen, T. (1987). The reflecting team: Dialogue and metadialogue in clinical work. *Family Process* 21:415–428.

Anderson, H., & Goolishian, H. A. (1992). The client is the expert: A not-knowing approach to therapy. In *Therapy as a Social Construction*, ed. S. McNamee & K. J. Gergen. Newbury Park, CA: Sage.

Bateson, G., Jackson, D. D., Haley, J., & Weakland, J. (1956). Toward a theory of schizophrenia. *Behavioral Science* 1:251–264.

Bertalanffy, L. von. (1968). *General Systems Theory: Foundations, Development, Applications.* New York: Braziller.

Bowen, M. (1960). A family concept of schizophrenia. In *The Etiology of Schizophrenia*, ed. D. D. Jackson. New York: Basic.

Bowen, M. (1978). *Family Therapy in Clinical Practice*. New York: Jason Aronson.

Buckley, W. (1968). Society as a complex adaptive system. In *Modern Systems Research for the Behavioral Scientist*, ed. W. Buckley. Chicago: Aldine.

Carter, B. & McGoldrick, M. (1989). *The Changing Family Life Cycle: A Framework for Family Therapy*, 2nd ed. Boston: Allyn & Bacon.

Dell, P. (1989). Violence and the systemic view: The problem of power. *Family Process* 28:1–14.

Fisch, R., Weakland, J., & Segal, L. (1982). *The Tactics of Change: Doing Therapy Briefly*. San Francisco: Jossey-Bass.

Friedman, E. H. (1991). Bowen theory and therapy. In *Handbook of Family Therapy*, Vol. 2, ed. A. S. Gurman & D. P. Kniskern. New York: Brunner/Mazel.

Gale, J. E., & Long, J. K. (1996). Theoretical foundations of family therapy. In *Family Therapy Sourcebook*, 2nd ed., ed. F. P. Piercy et al. New York: Guilford.

Haley, J. (1973). *Uncommon Therapy*. New York: Norton.

Haley, J. (1987). *Problem-Solving Therapy*, 2nd ed. San Francisco: Jossey-Bass.

Hall, C. M. (1991). *The Bowen Family Theory and Its Uses*. New Jersey: Jason Aronson.

Hoffman, L. (1985). Beyond power and control: Toward a second-order family systems therapy. *Family Systems* 3:381–396.

Hoffman, L. (1991). A reflexive stance for family therapy. *Journal of Strategic and Systemic Therapies* 10:4–17.

Jackson, D. D. (1965). The study of the family. *Family Process* 4:1–20.

Jacob, T., & Tennenbaum, D. L. (1988). *Family Assessment: Rationale, Methods, and Future Directions*. New York: Plenum.

Keeney, B. P. (1983). *Aesthetics of Change*. New York: Guilford.

Kerr, M. E., & Bowen, M. (1988). *Family Evaluation: An Approach Based on Bowen Therapy.* New York: W. W. Norton.

Madanes, C. (1991). Strategic family therapy. In *Handbook of Family Therapy*, Vol. 2, ed. A. S. Gurman & D. P. Kniskern. New York: Brunner/Mazel.

McGoldrick, M., & Gerson, R. (1985). *Genograms in Family Assessment*. New York: Norton.

McHolland, J. (1995). *An Integrative Eclectic Therapy: A Bio-psycho-social Model for Utilizing Diverse Therapeutic Modalities*. Chicago: Illinois School of Professional Psychology.

Minuchin, S. (1974). *Families and Family Therapy*. Cambridge, MA: Harvard University Press.

Minuchin, S., & Fishman, H. C. (1981). *Family Therapy Techniques*. Cambridge, MA: Harvard University Press.

Napier, A. Y., & Whitaker, C. A. (1988). *The Family Crucible: The Intense Experience of Family Therapy*. New York: HarperCollins

Nichols, W. C. (1992). *Fifty Years of Marital and Family Therapy*. Washington, DC: American Association for Marriage and Family Therapy.

Nichols, M. P., & Schwartz, R. C. (1998). *Family Therapy: Concepts and Methods*, 4th ed. Needham Heights, MA: Allyn & Bacon.

Piercy, F., et al. (1996). *Family Therapy Sourcebook*, 2nd ed. New York: Guilford.

Piercy, F., & Wetchler, J. (1996). Structural, strategic, and systemic family therapies. In *Family Therapy Sourcebook*, 2nd ed., ed. F. Piercy et al. New York: Guilford.

Pinsof, W. (1981). *Problem Centered Systems Therapy: Toward an Integrative Model for the Conduct of a Comprehensive Psychotherapy*. Chicago: Center for Family Studies.

Satir, V. (1964). *Conjoint Family Therapy*. Palo Alto, CA: Science and Behavior Books.

Selvini Palazolli, M., Boscolco, L., Cecchin, G., & Prata, G. (1978). *Paradox and Counterparadox*. New York: Jason Aronson.

Stierlin, H., Rucker-Embenden, I., Wetzel, N., & Wisching, M. (1980). *The First Interview with the Family*. New York: Brunner/Mazel.

Thomlison, B. (2002). *Family Assessment Handbook: An Introductory Practice Guide to Family Assessment and Intervention*. Pacific Grove, CA: Brooks/Cole.

Tomm, K. (1984). One perspective on the Milan systemic approach: Part II. Description of session format, interviewing style and interventions. *Journal of Marital and Family Therapy*, 10, 253–271.

Watzlawick, P., Weakland, J., & Fisch, R. (1974). *Change: Principles of Problem Formation and Problem Resolution*. New York: Norton.

Whitaker, C. A., & Ryan, M. O. (1989). *Midnight Musings of a Family Therapist*. New York: Norton.

White, M., & Epston, D. (1990). *Narrative Means to Therapeutic Ends*. New York: Norton.

Wiener, N. (1961). *Cybernetics or Control and Communication in the Animal and the Machine*. Cambridge, MA: MIT Press.

III

INTERVIEWING PATIENTS WITH SPECIFIC PSYCHOPATHOLOGIES

8

ANXIETY DISORDERS

Deborah Roth Ledley, Ph.D., and Sheila A. M. Rauch, Ph.D.

OVERVIEW OF THE ANXIETY DISORDERS

The anxiety disorders are the most prevalent of the mental disorders. According to the National Comorbidity Survey (NCS), the lifetime prevalence of anxiety disorders is almost 25 percent (Kessler et al., 1994). This total does not include posttraumatic stress disorder (which in a separate report of NCS data was reported to have a lifetime prevalence of 7.8 percent; see Kessler et al., 1995) or obsessive-compulsive disorder, suggesting that clinically significant anxiety is an experience shared by well over one-quarter of Americans at some time in their lives. Given this high prevalence, it is not surprising that anxiety disorders place a great economic burden on the American economy, estimated at over 42 billion dollars per year (Greenberg et al., 1999).

Before outlining techniques for interviewing clients with anxiety disorders, it is important to review the core features of these disorders as set forth by *The Diagnostic and Statistical Manual of Mental Disorders*, 4th edition (DSM-IV, American Psychiatric Association, 1994). *Panic disorder* is characterized by recurrent, unexpected ("out of the blue") panic attacks accompanied by at least one month or more of concern about having additional attacks, worry about the consequences of having attacks (e.g., worrying about having a heart attack or going crazy), or change in behavior due to the attacks. The lifetime prevalence of panic disorder is about 5 percent in women and 2 percent in men (Kessler et al., 1994).

Panic disorder can be diagnosed with or without agoraphobia, a term used to describe fear or avoidance of situations that might bring on panic attacks. This fear and avoidance is due to concern that if an attack were to happen, escaping the situation would be difficult or embarrassing or help would not be available. Commonly feared situations include using public transportation, going to movie theaters, being away from home, and being in crowds. Most clients with panic disorder have at least mild agoraphobia (White & Barlow, 2002).

145

DSM-IV includes two types of phobias: simple phobia and social phobia. *Simple phobia* is characterized by a "marked or persistent fear . . . of a specific object or situation" (American Psychiatric Association, 1994, p. 410). To be diagnosed with a simple phobia, the client must realize that his or her fear is excessive or unreasonable; this criterion is not applied to children, although they must exhibit symptoms of the specific phobia for at least six months in order to differentiate a clinically significant phobia from the common transient fears of childhood. Specific phobia is diagnosed only when clients report that their fears cause them significant distress or impairment in functioning. DSM-IV includes five specific phobia subtypes: animal type, natural environment type (e.g., fear of storms, water, heights), blood-injection-injury type, situational type (e.g., flying, driving, bridges), and other type (e.g., fear of choking or vomiting). Simple phobias are quite common, affecting 15.7 percent of women and 6.7 percent of men over their lifetimes (Kessler et al., 1994).

Social phobia shares similar diagnostic criteria with specific phobia, but the focus is on social or performance situations. The core concern of clients with social phobia is that they will do or say something embarrassing (or exhibit anxiety symptoms) that will lead to negative evaluation from others. DSM-IV requires clinicians to specify whether or not the social phobia is "generalized," meaning that the individual fears most social situations. In contrast with individuals whose social anxiety is more circumscribed (e.g., fear limited to public speaking), clients with generalized social phobia tend to experience more severe social phobia symptoms and tend to suffer greater impairment in functioning (Mannuzza et al., 1995). The lifetime prevalence rate for social phobia is 13.3 percent (Kessler et al., 1994). Although the disorder is more common among women in community samples, it tends to affect women and men at equal rates in clinic samples (see Chapman et al., 1995).

Obsessive-compulsive disorder (OCD) is characterized by the presence of obsessions or compulsions. Typically, obsessions and compulsions occur together and are functionally related. Obsessions are defined as "recurrent and persistent thoughts, impulses, or images that are experienced . . . as intrusive and inappropriate and that cause marked anxiety or distress" (American Psychiatric Association, 1994, p. 422). Common obsessions include fear of contamination, fear of acting on unwanted sexual or aggressive impulses, fear of throwing things away, and fear of making mistakes. In response to the anxiety caused by obsessions, clients with OCD engage in compulsions or rituals. Rituals are meant to decrease or prevent the experience of anxiety and prevent the occurrence of feared consequences. Rituals can be overt behaviors (e.g., washing hands after touching something contaminated to prevent oneself from getting sick) or mental acts (e.g., saying a prayer to ward off the possibility of stabbing a loved one while making dinner). While OCD was not assessed in the NCS, the Epidemiological Catchment Area Study (ECA), which was based on DSM-III diagnostic criteria, found a lifetime prevalence rate for OCD of 2.5 percent (Karno & Golding, 1991). Similar prevalence rates were found in epidemiological studies conducted in Germany (Wittchen, 1988) and Canada (Kolada et al., 1994). OCD may be slightly more common among women than men, although some studies suggest that there are no significant sex differences in prevalence of the disorder (see Antony et al., 1998).

The core feature of *generalized anxiety disorder* (GAD) is excessive worry about a number of events or activities that occurs more days than not, for six months or more. Typical areas of worry include health of self and others, relationships, minor matters (e.g., getting to places on time, fixing things around the house), and world affairs. Clients with GAD find it difficult to control their worry, and they experience accompanying somatic and affective symptoms such as muscle tension, irritability, and sleep disturbance (American Psychiatric Association, 1994). GAD affects approximately 5.1 percent of the population during their lifetimes and is about two times more common in women than in men (Kessler et al., 1994).

Posttraumatic stress disorder (PTSD) is the only anxiety disorder with a required precipitant. To be diagnosed with PTSD, clients must have been exposed to a traumatic event that "involved actual or threatened death or serious injury, or a threat to the physical integrity of self or others" that the person responded to with "intense fear, helplessness, or horror" (American Psychiatric Association, 1994, pp. 427-428). Individuals with PTSD reexperience the trauma (e.g., in nightmares or flashbacks), avoid stimuli associated with the trauma, and experience increased arousal (e.g., sleep and concentration difficulties). As noted above, approximately 7.8 percent of Americans have met criteria for PTSD during their lifetimes (Kessler et al., 1995).

In the process of assessing clients with anxiety disorders, it is not sufficient to simply gather information on *what* they fear. There is a great deal of overlap across the anxiety disorders, not only in terms of what clients fear, but also in terms of the symptoms they experience (e.g., panic attacks can occur in all of the anxiety disorders). It is essential, then, to get a clear picture of *why* clients fear a specific object or situation. Consider, for example, a client who reports having a fear of flying. This client might fear having a panic attack while flying, since escape from that situation is impossible. This would point to a diagnosis of panic disorder. A person who fears being in a plane crash may meet criteria for a specific phobia of flying. Although less likely, clients might fear flying because they are anxious about making casual conversation with a seat mate (social phobia) or because they had a traumatic experience in the past while on an airplane (PTSD). It is essential to ask the right questions to arrive at the right diagnosis, and the best way to ensure this is to be very familiar with the diagnostic criteria for each anxiety disorder.

ESTABLISHING RAPPORT

It is important in the process of assessment to attend not only to the client's symptoms, but also to establishing a solid rapport. Even for clients who have seen a therapist before, coming to speak to a new person about one's problems can be stressful. It is more likely that an accurate diagnosis will be established if clients feel comfortable sharing the details of the difficulties that they are having.

While each client may be different in what he or she needs in order to feel comfortable and safe in an assessment environment, some general guidelines can be applied for the majority of clients. As described in Morrison (1995), rapport is best developed through the presentation of a relaxed, interested, nonjudgmental, and sympathetic environment to aid the client in feeling comfortable and safe. These issues of comfort and safety may be especially salient for anxiety disorder clients. For instance, with PTSD clients, the clinician is often working against many of the reactions that people have to trauma, including lack of trust, anger, shame, and avoidance (Newman et al., 1996). Clients with PTSD may require more time and encouragement to feel safe enough during the interview to discuss their trauma history. The projection of empathy and sensitivity through the pacing of questions to fit the client's comfort level is a key to successful interviewing. Clarification of the expectations for the interview and the roles of the clinician and client along with a discussion of confidentiality can assist in establishing trust with the client. The clinician may begin by explaining confidentiality and its limits. Then, the clinician may proceed to orient the client to the assessment process by explaining in general what the client can expect as far as time, general areas for examination, and goals for the assessment (e.g., diagnosis, specific treatment plan) are concerned. Letting the client know that, while some of their concerns may sound weird or even "crazy" to them, many of them are common symptoms of anxiety disorders, and it is important for the client to be straightforward in discussing his or her concerns in order to receive the best assistance possible.

Clinicians must be careful to monitor their facial expressions and balance eye contact to help the client feel comfortable during the assessment. For instance, clients with social phobia may feel more uncomfortable than other clients with prolonged periods of eye contact. Monitoring the client's nonverbal behavior to detect discomfort is especially important in these cases in order to allow the client to disclose the difficulties that he or she may be having. In cases where discomfort is apparent, modification of procedures to calm the client may be necessary. For instance, the clinician might want to make more frequent breaks in eye contact or have more general discussion before proceeding to the key difficulties. In cases where the client is evidencing discomfort, normalizing the client's symptoms within your experience as a clinician can be helpful in putting the client at ease. For instance, letting a client with social phobia know that while thinking that other people are always talking about you in social situations may sound unusual to the client, this is a common symptom of social anxiety. This also provides an opportunity to reinforce clients for taking the first step toward working on their problems by coming in for treatment.

The need for clinicians to monitor their own feelings and behavior toward the client (e.g., discomfort, nonverbal behavior) has also been presented as an important component of establishing rapport (Morrison, 1995). For instance, many clients with generalized social phobia may have difficulties with common communication skills, either due to anxiety or because of true social skills deficits. They might fail to make appropriate eye contact, or might respond to questions in an overly abrupt manner. Clients with PTSD may express anger toward others in situations that provoke anxiety (e.g., anger at having to wait for the clinician prior to their first interview). OCD clients may engage in rituals during the interview that can interfere with gathering information or be interpreted as socially inappropriate if not identified as a component of the disorder. For instance, clients who are concerned with saying "just the right thing" may have a difficult time answering yes or no questions. With these clients, identifying the pattern and briefly discussing the source may assist the client in returning to the purpose of the interview. However, modifications of the interview procedures and methods, such as setting a time guide on responding or going with the first answer only, may be necessary as well.

Throughout the interview process, identifying the client's language and using it can assist in establishing rapport. This helps the client feel that the clinician is empathetic and listening. If the client describes his or her anxiety as "the jitters," the clinician can obtain a clear description of the "the jitters" and determine whether this is congruent with anxiety. If it is, using this term through the assessment may help the client to more accurately report symptoms and help establish a rapport as the client has confirmation that the clinician is listening.

The appropriate use of humor with some clients can assist in establishing a comfortable and safe environment. However, the clinician should be very careful with the use of humor, since some clients may easily take offense or personalize comments. Damage to the rapport may be difficult to repair. Thus humor may be best left for after a clinician has established a basic trust and rapport with the client.

While the main purpose of the interview is information gathering, another important function of interviewing is psychoeducation. As an interviewer proceeds to gather information regarding clients' difficulties, taking the opportunity to discuss their concerns within the context of anxiety disorders may help clients to perceive that the clinician is listening and that they are not alone in having these problems. Simply knowing that the problems they are experiencing are a part of an anxiety disorder and not a sign of psychosis can provide hope for people who are often feeling isolated and hopeless. Occasionally relating clients' problems to other anxiety disorder cases or predicting difficulties that clients may be experiencing but not reporting may help to open them up to discuss their difficulties. For instance, a rape survivor with PTSD may not spontaneously report difficulties in her sexual relationship with her husband, but knowing that these difficulties are common in rape survivors with PTSD may help the client to feel comfortable talking about this difficult issue.

THE ASSESSMENT PROCESS

Gathering Information from Multiple Sources

While the current chapter focuses on interviewing, effective assessment of anxiety disorders, as with any psychological difficulty, requires the use of multiple tools (Beck & Zebb, 1994). While the interview is a key component of this process, behavioral observation, self-report measures, consultation with others who might be knowledgeable about the client's conditions (e.g., parents, spouse, doctor), and even physiological assessment may be used to obtain a more complete picture of the client. For instance, some clients may feel anxious about sharing personal information with a stranger and more comfortable revealing such information in self-reports. Self-reports can then be used to facilitate and focus the assessment process (see Antony et al., 2001, for an excellent guide to self-report measures for anxiety disorders). Further, self-report measures can provide a baseline for use throughout treatment to examine changes in symptoms more quickly than can repeated clinical interviews.

Another compelling reason to gather information from multiple sources is that it is often difficult for anxious clients to describe the ways in which their anxiety affects their lives, either because they avoid anxiety-provoking situations or because they engage in habitual behaviors when such situations are encountered. For example, a person with OCD might not accurately judge how much time they spend in a typical day doing rituals, since these behaviors are so habitual for them. In such situations, a family member can provide useful information about how much time the rituals are taking and how they interfere in the client's life.

Behavioral assessment is another useful tool. While the current chapter does not allow for a full discussion of behavioral assessment, Bellack and Hersen (1998) offer more complete coverage of behavioral assessment as it applies to the anxiety disorders. Two commonly used behavioral assessment techniques are behavioral tests and self-monitoring. Behavioral tests include formal situational tasks that have been empirically examined, such as the Multitask Behavioral Avoidance Test (M-BAT, Beurs et al., 1991) for agoraphobic avoidance and informal situations such as asking an OCD client with contamination concerns to touch his or her shoe. Both types of behavioral tests can provide information on the severity of avoidance and anxiety produced by the phobic situations, places, or other content that might not be immediately accessible through interview. Such information can be critical when formulating a treatment plan. For instance, clients with specific phobias may have avoided their feared stimuli for so long that they no longer know how they would react to encountering it. Setting up a behavioral test in the clinician's office can be helpful in establishing the severity of the fear and can serve as a useful measure of progress over the course of treatment.

Self-monitoring of target difficulties or symptoms is a common and often useful form of assessment. With this technique, the client keeps a record of the occurrence of target behaviors (e.g., nightmares, angry outbursts). Such recording often includes the date and time of the occurrence, the situation during which the symptom is apparent, thoughts at the time of the symptom, and the client's emotional reactions during the occurrence of the symptom. These reactions are often measured using the Subjective Units of Distress scale (SUDs), where 100 indicates panic level distress and 0 indicates no distress. The information obtained by self-monitoring (e.g., symptom triggers, avoidance, dysfunctional thoughts, and reaction patterns) can be used in both assessment and treatment to pinpoint anxiety triggers and thoroughly examine frequency, intensity, and duration of symptoms. In the case of a client with panic disorder, for instance, a week of self-monitoring might reveal that she experiences panic symptoms most often on her subway ride to work and that, if she has a panic attack on her way to work, she tends to choose to walk home from work and then experience more extreme anticipatory anxiety the following day when she has to get back on the subway. Gathering such information will be helpful when educating the client about the maintenance of panic disorder over time and, as with behavior tests, will prove very useful in treatment planning. Despite the rich information obtained from self-monitoring, it is underutilized because it requires a lot of effort during both recording and reviewing. Despite the effort, self-monitoring is a very useful tool in assessment and treatment, providing rich information for diagnosis and treatment planning.

Structured Interviews

Some clinicians are averse to the idea of "structured" clinical interviews, assuming that they are delivered in a staid and impersonal way. In reality, the two interviews most commonly used to assess the anxiety disorders—the Structured Clinical Interview for DSM-IV (SCID-IV, First et al., 1997) and the Anxiety Disorders Interview Schedule for DSM-IV (ADIS-IV, Brown et al., 1994) are actually "semistructured." Structured interviews, such as those used in epidemiological studies, can be administered by lay people and basically require respondents to give "yes" or "no" answers. In contrast, semistructured interviews require clinical judgment and must be administered by people familiar with the diagnostic system. While questions should be read as written in the manual, it is perfectly appropriate for clinicians to then deviate and ask questions that they deem necessary for carefully establishing diagnoses.

The SCID and the ADIS differ somewhat, but both are excellent tools for assessing anxiety and related disorders. In addition to the anxiety disorders, the SCID covers the mood disorders, substance use disorders, somatoform disorders, and eating disorders, and it also includes a screen for psychotic symptoms. A separate SCID (SCID-II) is available to assess for personality disorders. A decision tree approach is used in the SCID such that a section can be "skipped out" of once it is evident that full criteria for the disorder will not be met (e.g., if a client reports having experienced panic attacks, but has not experienced at least four panic symptoms during attacks, the interviewer will be prompted to skip to the next section of the SCID). The SCID assesses for the presence or absence of disorders and asks that current severity be specified (mild, moderate, or severe).

The ADIS, assessing only for the anxiety disorders, mood disorders, substance use disorders, hypochondriasis, and somatization disorder, is slightly more limited in its scope than the SCID. The ADIS, like the SCID, includes a screen for psychotic symptoms. Despite its slightly more limited scope in terms of coverage of disorders, the ADIS provides much more information about the disorders that are assessed—particularly with respect to the anxiety disorders. For each positive diagnosis, a severity rating is given based on a 0 (absent) to 8 (very severe) scale, with a rating of 4 or greater being indicative of a clinically significant diagnosis. This rating system allows for a clearer assessment of change over time than does the SCID, which focuses primarily on the presence or absence of a disorder.

The ADIS facilitates the gathering of additional information beyond the DSM criteria for each disorder. For example, in the social phobia section, clients are asked to rate the degree to which they fear and avoid situations that are commonly difficult for clients with the disorder. Similarly, clients are asked to rate the degree to which they experience panic attack symptoms when they are in social situations. Both of these sections provide valuable information for treatment planning and can serve as useful measures of change from pre- to posttreatment. The ADIS also asks about feared consequences (e.g., what clients with social phobia think will happen if they enter their feared social situations), beliefs that clients hold about the etiology of their difficulties, and ways in which the difficulties have interfered in their lives. Again, this information can be useful for treatment planning and can also be helpful for building rapport, since the interviewer expresses interest in the client beyond simple symptoms.

Disorder-Specific Interviews

While the ADIS provides a great deal of useful information on each anxiety disorder, disorder-specific interviews can also be very helpful for gathering information, establishing diagnoses, and providing indices of severity. In the next section, commonly used interviews for each anxiety disorder are reviewed.

PANIC DISORDER

The most commonly used semistructured interview for assessing panic disorder is the Panic Disorder Severity Scale (PDSS, Shear et al., 1997). The PDSS is a seven-item measure that assesses for panic symptoms over the past month. Clients are asked about the frequency of their panic attacks, the distress that they experience during panic attacks, the severity of their anticipatory anxiety, fear and avoidance of agoraphobic situations, fear and avoidance of panic-related symptoms, and impairment in work and social functioning. The scale has been shown to have good interrater reliability ($r = .88$), but low internal consistency ($\alpha = .65$, see Shear et al., 1997). The PDSS correlates strongly with other measures that assess similar constructs (e.g., the item on the PDSS that assesses for agoraphobic fear/avoidance correlates highly with the agoraphobia scale of the Albany Panic and Phobia Questionnaire, Rapee et al., 1994/1995) and is sensitive to treatment-related changes (see Shear et al., 1997).

When interviewing a client with panic disorder, the clinician must be aware that the client may have panic symptoms or a panic attack during the interview. Should this happen, the clinician's reaction should be one of controlled sympathy. The clinician can use this as an opportunity to get information on the sensations experienced by the client and educate the client about panic symptoms and panic disorder. The clinician can convey this by expressing that it may have seemed unpleasant, but that those types of experiences are common in anxiety disorder clients and that the client got through the attack without his or her feared consequences coming to pass.

SOCIAL PHOBIA

There are two commonly used interviewer-rated measures of social phobia. The Brief Social Phobia Scale (BSPS, Davidson et al., 1991) is an eighteen-item interviewer-rated scale that assesses for the symptoms of social phobia that the client has experienced in the past week. Clients are first presented with seven broadly defined social/performance situations (e.g., speaking in public, talking to strangers) and are asked to rate on a five-point scale how much they have feared each situation and the degree to which they have avoided each situation in the past week. If clients have not encountered a particular situation in the past week (due to avoidance or because it simply didn't come up), they are asked to provide hypothetical ratings (e.g., "If you had been invited to a party this week, to what degree would you have feared it?"). In the second part of the interview, clients are asked to rate the severity of four physiological symptoms (e.g., sweating, blushing) that clients sometimes experience when they are in social/performance situations or even when they are just thinking about such situations.

The BSPS yields three subscales—fear, avoidance, and physiological arousal. The scale has been shown to have strong internal consistency (α = .81 for the total scale) and good retest reliability (r = .91 for the total scale over one week, Davidson et al., 1997b), but there is some concern with its convergent validity, particularly with respect to the physiological subscale (Davidson et al., 1997b). The BSPS has been shown to be sensitive to medication-related changes in social anxiety symptoms (Stein et al., 1999).

The Liebowitz Social Anxiety Scale (LSAS, Liebowitz, 1987) is a twenty-four-item interviewer-rated scale that includes eleven items pertaining to social interactions and thirteen items pertaining to performance situations. Clients are asked to rate on a four-point scale the degree to which they have feared each situation and the degree to which they have avoided each situation over the past week.

The LSAS yields many useful indices. In addition to a total score (sum of fear and avoidance ratings for all situations), the following subscale scores can also be computed: fear of social interaction, fear of performance situations, avoidance of social interaction, avoidance of performance situations, total fear, and total avoidance. However, psychometric studies suggest that fear and avoidance are not independent constructs (see Cox et al., 1998). The scale has excellent internal consistency (α = .96) and good convergent and discriminate validity and is sensitive to treatment-related changes (see Heimberg et al., 1999).

When conducting assessments with clients with social phobia, clinicians should be sensitive to the fact that the clients' core concern is of being judged negatively by others. Admitting the degree to which they fear and avoid social situations can be embarrassing for clients and can make them feel concerned that the clinician will judge them as negatively as they think others judge them. To alleviate these concerns, clinicians should normalize the experience of social anxiety, noting that most people feel anxious in some social situations. They can also draw parallels between the client's experience and the experience of other clients that they have seen who have similar concerns (e.g., "A lot of clients who we see are also worried about sweating a lot in social situations"). For clients who seem particularly reluctant to share personal information, it can be helpful to reinforce them for coming in for the assessment and encourage them that sharing information is the first step in getting help for their social anxiety.

OBSESSIVE-COMPULSIVE DISORDER

The Yale-Brown Obsessive Compulsive Scale (YBOCS, Goodman et al., 1989a; 1989b) is the most commonly used clinician-administered measure of the symptoms of OCD. The YBOCS includes a checklist of commonly experienced obsessions and compulsions as well as ten items, five that assess for the severity of obsessions and five that assess for the severity of compulsions. When the internal consistency of the YBOCS has been explored, divergent results have been reported with alphas ranging from .69 (Woody et al., 1995) to .91 (Goodman et al., 1989a, b). The YBOCS has been found to have excellent interrater reliability (see Goodman et al., 1989a, b) and test retest reliability (Kim et al., 1990).

Prior to administering the YBOCS, it is important to define "obsessions" and "compulsions" according to the definitions provided in the YBOCS. In reviewing these definitions, it is helpful to delineate for clients the functional relationship between obsessions and compulsions. Throughout the interview, it is often necessary to reiterate the distinction between obsessions and compulsions to distinguish the five specific obsession items from the five specific compulsion items.

OCD symptoms can influence the way that clients respond to the YBOCS. Some clients with OCD are very concerned with saying "just the right thing" and will sometimes spend quite a lot of time mentally formulating a response before saying it out loud. Similarly, some clients will provide a response but then start to mentally review it to make sure they said it correctly or provided exactly accurate information, distracting them from responding to subsequent questions. Clients who have these sorts of difficulties can sometimes take a long time to make it through the YBOCS. It can be helpful for clinicians to ask clients if their OCD is getting in the way of them responding and provide them with some pointers for more efficiently getting through the interview (e.g., "Go with your first response" or "I will prompt once, and then I need the answer you think best fits"). This should be done in a sensitive manner so that clients do not feel criticized or undermined. In our experience, clients appreciate when clinicians pick up on these difficulties and offer them some guidelines on resisting their rituals within the assessment session.

Another guideline to keep in mind when assessing clients with OCD is to be observant of their behavior during the assessment. For some clients with OCD, their rituals are so habitual that it is difficult for them to recall all of them or accurately describe them. Clinicians can inquire about within-session behaviors as a way of facilitating the assessment process. In a recent assessment, a client declined to shake hands with us when we met in the waiting room, and as we walked down the hall to the office, we observed that he held his arms very close to his body. During the initial part of the session, he held his briefcase on his lap rather than placing it on the floor and sat very rigidly so that his back and arms did not make contact with the chair. The client was extremely reluctant to discuss his OCD symptoms, and we were able to use the behaviors that we had observed as a starting point. Not wanting to make the client feel uncomfortable, we normalized his behaviors within the context of others clients that we had seen and offered him a number of potential explanations for the behavior that we had seen him exhibit thus far (e.g., "Are you worried about getting sick from dirt and germs or are you concerned just about the way that things feel?").

POSTTRAUMATIC STRESS DISORDER

In assessing PTSD, the first step is to assess the client's trauma history. Many measures have been created to do this in both interview and self-report forms (for a thorough review of available measures, see Antony et al., 2001). Two of the most commonly used measures are the Posttraumatic Diagnostic Scale (PDS, Foa et al., 1997) and the Trauma Events Questionnaire (TEQ, Vrana & Lauterbach, 1994). Both of these self-report forms assess exposure to a number of potentially traumatic events along with questions targeting the individual's reaction to the traumatic event (i.e., fear, horror, and helplessness). While the PDS also includes assessment of PTSD symptom severity for a target trauma, the TEQ simply assesses exposure to potentially traumatic events. In general, when assessing trauma exposure, specific questions about potential categories of traumatic experiences have tended to yield more sensitive assessment of trauma history than simply asking a general question about trauma exposure or categories, such as rape (Resnick et al., 1993): for instance, asking, "Has someone forced you to have unwanted sexual contact through verbal or physical force?" rather than asking, "Have you ever been raped?"

Once a positive trauma history has been determined, it should not be assumed that exposure to trauma invariably results in PTSD (Newman et al., 1996). While PTSD is more common following certain traumatic experiences than others (e.g., interpersonal violence versus natural disasters), studies have demonstrated that the majority of people do not develop PTSD following trauma (e.g., Kessler et al., 1995; Breslau et al., 1998). Newman et al. (1996) suggest that interviewers should consider the nature of the trauma and individual difference variables (e.g., social support, history of anxiety or depression, external stressors) when examining symptoms. For instance, interpersonal violence, such as rape or severe physical assault, is more likely to result in PTSD than are natural disasters, such as flood or hurricane (e.g., Breslau et al., 1999). Also, personal exposure to a trauma places the client at higher risk for PTSD than indirect exposure, such as witnessing a physical assault or motor vehicle accident (e.g., Breslau et al., 1999).

It is also important to note that the relationship between symptoms and trauma may not be easily apparent (Newman et al., 1996). Assessment of symptom onset, symptom cueing, and symptom content may help to elucidate the relationship. Gathering information on any behavior changes following trauma exposure is especially important. Therefore, a careful assessment of pre- and posttrauma adjustment is critical to the assessment of PTSD. For instance, a client who has always had problems with concentration and continues to have the same type of difficulty after a trauma with no increase in severity would not be considered to have the PTSD symptom of concentration difficulty. If the person developed concentration problems following the trauma, this would be considered a symptom of PTSD.

Once the client's trauma history has been assessed, assessment of PTSD symptoms can be accomplished. Several options for structured PTSD interviews are available.

The thirty-item Clinician-Administered PTSD Scale (CAPS, Blake et al., 1990) assesses frequency and intensity of individual PTSD symptoms as well as associated features. The associated features assessed by the CAPS include guilt, depression, and functional impairment in job and social performance. The three subscales (reexperiencing, avoidance and numbing, and arousal) coincide with the three symptom clusters of PTSD. Interrater reliability of the CAPS in combat veterans is excellent for all three subscales ($r = .92-.99$; Blake et al., 1990). Internal consistency is also high (α's $= .87-.95$; Hyer et al., 1996). High correlations with other measures of PTSD symptoms—PK scale of the MMPI ($r = .77$, Keane et al., 1984) and Mississippi Scale for Combat-related PTSD ($r = .91$, Keane et al., 1988)—indicate good convergent validity. Nine distinct scoring rules for the CAPS have been developed (for a review of these methods and their appropriate use, see Weathers et al., 1999). The CAPS has been found to be sensitive to changes with treatment (e.g., van der Kolk et al., 1994). Studies on the psychometric properties of the CAPS in nonveteran trauma populations are scarce. While CAPS is a psychometrically sound instrument, the length of its administration has been criticized (between forty and sixty minutes; Foa & Tolin, 2000; Newman et al., 1996).

The Posttraumatic Stress Disorder Symptom Scale-Interview (PSS-I, Foa et al., 1993) is a seventeen-item scale that assesses the presence of a PTSD diagnosis and the frequency/severity of each PTSD symptom. Each item is rated on a scale of 0 ("not at all") to 3 ("very much") with ratings incorporating both frequency and severity. The three subscales represent each of the three DSM-IV symptom clusters of reexperiencing, avoidance, and arousal. Test-retest reliability is excellent over one month ($r = .80$). Interrater reliability is excellent, with a kappa of .91 for PTSD diagnosis. Foa et al. (1993) reported high correlations of the PSS-I with other measures of PTSD symptoms demonstrating good concurrent validity: Impact of Event Scale (IES)-Intrusion ($r = .69$, Horowitz et al., 1979) and IES-Avoidance ($r = .56$, Horowitz et al., 1979). The PSS-I correlates highly with other measures of psychological distress, including the Beck Depression Inventory (BDI, $r = .72$, Beck et al., 1961) and State-Trait Anxiety Inventory-State (STAI-S, $r = .48$; Spielberger et al., 1970). Finally, the PSS-I is sensitive to changes with treatment (Foa et al., 1999). The interview takes approximately twenty minutes to administer. In a psychometric study comparing the CAPS and the PSS-I, Foa and Tolin (2000) found that the PSS-I and CAPS performed equally well with regard to diagnosis and psychometrics properties, with the PSS-I taking an average of twenty minutes and the CAPS thirty-three minutes.

The Structured Interview for PTSD (SIP, Davidson et al., 1997a) includes seventeen items covering DSM-IV symptoms of PTSD along with two items assessing survivor and behavioral guilt. Items are scored on a five-point scale (0 = not at all, 4 = extremely severe, daily, or produces so much distress the client cannot function at work or socially). The SIP takes ten to thirty minutes to administer and yields both a dichotomous categorization for PTSD diagnosis and a symptom-severity score. The internal consistency of the scale is good (α = .80, .94, Davidson et al., 1989; 1997a). Interrater reliability is excellent for total score, symptoms in the past four weeks, and worst period ever (Davidson et al., 1997a). Convergent validity is found in high correlations with other measures of PTSD and anxiety and no correlations with combat exposure (Davidson et al., 1989; Davidson et al., 1997a). High correlations are also found between the SIP and measures of depression (Davidson et al., 1989).

SPECIFIC PHOBIA AND GENERALIZED ANXIETY DISORDER

At present, there is no broad measure available for assessing specific phobias. Similarly, there is no standardized interview for assessment of GAD. Both disorders can be assessed using the ADIS or the SCID, and the assessment can be rounded out through the use of self-report measures.

PRACTICAL SUGGESTIONS

Below is a summary of suggestions provided in this chapter:

- Know the diagnostic criteria for each of the anxiety disorders and understand how to differentiate one anxiety disorder from another.
- When doing assessments with anxious clients, set a tone that is relaxed, interested, nonjudgmental, and sympathetic. Allow time to establish rapport.
- Prior to beginning an assessment, orient clients to the assessment process (e.g., what will happen, how long it will take, what the purpose is). While the clinician may have done hundreds of assessments, this is likely a new experience for the client.
- Normalize the experience of anxiety. Without minimizing clients' difficulties, reassure them that anxiety is an experience common to most people, and that as a clinician, you have a great deal of experience dealing with clients who have similar problems.
- Clinicians should be attentive to shifts that they might need to make in their behavior, depending on the kind of client they are assessing.
- While the clinical interview is an essential part of the assessment process, assessments will be more complete if clinicians gather information from multiple sources.

• Be vigilant in looking for areas of avoidance. Clients who have suffered with anxiety disorders for long periods may be unaware that some of their daily routine may be influenced by avoidance of anxiety triggers (e.g., taking the bus rather than driving for a person with a driving phobia).

REFERENCES

American Psychiatric Association. (1994). *Diagnostic and Statistical Manual of Mental Disorders*, 4th ed. Washington, DC: American Psychiatric Association.

Antony, M. M., Downie, F., & Swinson, R. P. (1998). Diagnostic issues and epidemiology in obsessive-compulsive disorder. In *Obsessive-Compulsive Disorder: Theory, Research, and Treatment*, ed. R. P. Swinson, M. M. Antony, S. Rachman, & M. A. Richter, pp. 3–32. New York: Guilford.

Antony, M. M., Orsillo, S. M., & Roemer, L., eds. (2001). *Practitioner's Guide to Empirically Based Measures of Anxiety: AABT Clinical Assessment Series.* New York: Kluwer Academic/Plenum.

Beck, A. T., Ward, C. H., Mendelson, M., Mock, J., & Erbaugh, J. (1961). An inventory for measuring depression. *Archives of General Psychiatry* 4:53–63.

Beck, J. G., & Zebb, B. J. (1994). Behavioral assessment and treatment of panic disorder: Current status, future directions. *Behavior Therapy* 25:581–611.

Bellack, A. S., & Hersen, M. (1998) *Behavioral Assessment: A Practical Handbook*, 4th ed. Needham Heights, MA: Allyn & Bacon.

Beurs, E. de, Lange, A., Van Dyck, R., Blonk, R., & Koele, P. (1991). Behavioral assessment of avoidance in agoraphobia. *Journal of Psychopathology and Behavioral Assessment* 13(4):285–300.

Blake, D. D., Weathers, F. W., Nagy, L. N., Kaloupek, D. G., Klauminzer, G., Charney, D. S., & Keane, T. M. (1990). A clinical rating scale for assessing current and lifetime PTSD: The CAPS-1. *Behavior Therapist* 18:187–188.

Breslau, N., Chilcoat, D., Kessler, R. C., Peterson, E. L., & Lucia, V. C. (1999). Vulnerability to assaultive violence: Further specification of the sex difference in post-traumatic stress disorder. *Psychological Medicine* 29:813–821.

Breslau, N., Kessler, R. C., Chilcoat, H. D., Schult, L. R., Davis, G. C., & Andreski, P. (1998). Trauma and posttraumatic stress disorder in the community: The 1996 Detroit area survey of trauma. *Archives of General Psychiatry* 48:216–222.

Brown, T. A., DiNardo, P. A., & Barlow, D. H. (1994). *Anxiety Disorders Interview Schedule for DSM-IV, Lifetime Version.* San Antonio, TX: Psychological Corporation.

Chapman, T. F., Mannuzza, S., Fyer, A. J. (1995). Epidemiology and family studies in social phobia. In *Social Phobia: Diagnosis, Assessment, and Treatment*, ed. R. G. Heimberg, M. R. Liebowitz, D. A. Hope, & F. R. Schneier, pp. 21–40. New York: Guilford.

Cox, B. J., Ross, L., Swinson, R. P., & Direnfeld, D. M. (1998). A comparison of social phobia outcome measures in cognitive-behavioral group therapy. *Behavior Modification* 22:285–297.

Davidson, J. R. T., Malik, M. A., & Travers, J. (1997a). Structured Interview for PTSD (SIP): Psychometric validation for DSM-IV criteria. *Depression and Anxiety* 5:127–129.

Davidson, J. R. T., Miner, C. M., De Veaugh-Geiss, J., Tupler, L. A., Colket, J. T., & Potts, N. L. S. (1997b). The Brief Social Phobia Scale: A psychometric evaluation. *Psychological Medicine* 27:161–166.

Davidson, J. R. T., Potts, N. L. S., Richichi, E. A., Ford, S. M., Krishnan, R. R., Smith, R. D., & Wilson, W. (1991). The Brief Social Phobia Scale. *Journal of Clinical Psychiatry* 52:48–51.

Davidson, J., Smith, R., & Kudler, H. (1989). Validity and reliability of the DSM-III criteria for posttraumatic stress disorder: Experience with a structured interview. *Journal of Nervous and Mental Disease* 177:336–341.

First, M. B., Spitzer, R. L., Gibbon, M., & Williams, J. B. W. (1997). *Structured Clinical Interview for DSM-IV, Axis I Disorders (SCID-I), Clinician Version.* Washington, DC: American Psychiatric Publishing.

Foa, E. B., Cashman, L., Jaycox, L., & Perry, K. (1997). The validation of a self-report measure of posttraumatic stress disorder: The Posttraumatic Diagnostic Scale. *Psychological Assessment* 9:445–451.

Foa, E. B., Riggs, D. S., Dancu, C. V., & Rothbaum, B. O. (1993). Reliability and validity of a brief instrument for assessing post-traumatic stress disorder. *Journal of Traumatic Stress* 6:459–473.

Foa, E. B., Dancu, C. V., Hembree, E. A., Jaycox, L. H., Meadows, E. A., & Street, G. P. (1999). The efficacy of exposure therapy, stress inoculation training and their combination in ameliorating PTSD for female victims of assault. *Journal of Consulting and Clinical Psychology* 67:194–200.

Foa, E. B., & Tolin, D. F. (2000). Comparison of the PTSD Symptom Scale-Interview Version and the Clinician Administered PTSD Scale. *Journal of Traumatic Stress* 13(2):181–191.

Goodman, W. K., Price, L. H., Rasmussen, S. A., Mazure, C., Delgado, P., Heninger, G. R., & Charney, D. S. (1989a). The Yale-Brown Obsessive Compulsive Scale: II. Validity. *Archives of General Psychiatry* 46:1012–1016.

Goodman, W. K., Price, L. H., Rasmussen, S. A., Mazure, C., Fleischmann, R. L., Hill, C. L., Heninger, G. R., & Charney, D. S. (1989b). The Yale-Brown Obsessive Compulsive Scale: I. Development, use, and reliability. *Archives of General Psychiatry* 46:1006–1011.

Greenberg, P. E., Sisitsky, T., Kessler, R. C., Finkelstein, S. N., Berndt, E. R., Davidson, J. R. T., Ballenger, J. C., & Fyer, A. J. (1999). The economic burden of anxiety disorders in the 1990s. *Journal of Clinical Psychiatry* 60:427–435.

Heimberg, R. G., Horner, K. J., Juster, H. R., Safren, S. A., Brown, E. J., Schneier, F. R., & Liebowitz, M. R. (1999). Psychometric properties of the Liebowitz Social Anxiety Scale. *Psychological Medicine* 29:199–212.

Horowitz, N. Wilner, N., & Alvarez, W. (1979). Impact of Event Scale: A measure of subjective distress. *Psychosomatic Medicine* 41:209–218.

Hyer, L., Summers, M. N., Boyd, S., Litaker, M., & Boudewyns, P. (1996). Assessment of older combat veterans with the clinician administered PTSD scale. *Journal of Traumatic Stress* 9(3):587–594.

Karno, M., & Golding, J. M. (1991). Obsessive compulsive disorder. In *Psychiatric Disorders in America: The Epidemiological Catchment Area Study,* ed. L. N. Robins & D. A. Regier, pp. 204–219. New York: Free Press.

Keane, T. M., Caddell, J. M., & Taylor, K. L. (1988). Mississippi Scale for Combat-related PTSD: Three studies in reliability and validity. *Journal of Consulting and Clinical Psychology* 56:85–90.

Keane, T. M., Malloy, P. F., & Fairbank, J. A. (1984). Empirical development of an MMPI subscale for the assessment of combat-related posttraumatic stress disorder. *Journal of Consulting & Clinical Psychology* 52:888–891.

Kessler, R. C., McGonagle, K. A., Zhao, S., Nelson, C. B., Hughes, M., Eshleman, S., Wittchen, H.-U., & Kendler, K. S. (1994). Lifetime and 12-month prevalence of DSM-III-R psychiatric disorders in the United States: Results from the National Comorbidity Survey. *Archives of General Psychiatry* 51:8–19.

Kessler, R. C., Sonnega, A., Bromet, E., Hughes, M., & Nelson, C. (1995). Posttraumatic stress disorder in the National Comorbidity Survey. *Archives of General Psychiatry* 52(12):1048–1060.

Kessler, R. C., Sonnega, A., Bromet, E., Hughes, M., Nelson, C. B., & Breslau, N. (1999). Epidemiological risk factors for trauma and PTSD. In *Risk factors for posttraumatic stress disorder*, ed. R. Yehuda, pp. 23–59. Washington, DC: American Psychiatric Press.

Kim, S., Dysken, M., & Kuskowski, M. (1990). The Yale-Brown Obsessive Compulsive Scale: A reliability and validity study. *Psychiatry Research* 41:37–44.

Kolada, J. L., Bland, R. C., & Newman, S. C. (1994). Obsessive-compulsive disorder. *Acta Psychiatrica Scandinavica* supplement 376:24–35.

Liebowitz, M. R. (1987). Social phobia. *Modern Problems in Pharmacopsychiatry* 22:141–173.

Mannuzza, S., Schneier, F. R., Chapman, T. F., Liebowitz, M. R., Klein, D. F., & Fyer, A. J. (1995). Generalized social phobia: Reliability and validity. *Archives of General Psychiatry* 52:230–237.

Morrison, J. (1995). *The First Interview: Revised for DSM-IV.* New York: Guilford.

Newman, E., Kaloupek, D. G., & Keane, T. M. (1996). Assessment of posttraumatic stress disorder in clinical and research settings. In *Traumatic Stress: The Effects of Overwhelming Experience on Mind, Body, and Society*, ed. B. A. van der Kolk & A. C. McFarlane, pp. 242–275. New York: Guilford.

Rapee, R. M., Craske, M. G., & Barlow, D. H. (1994/1995). Assessment instrument for panic disorder that includes fear of sensation-producing activities: The Albany Panic and Phobia Questionnaire. *Anxiety* 1:114–122.

Resnick, H. S., Kilpatrick, D. G., Dansky, B. S., Saunders, B. E., & Best, C. L. (1993). Prevalence of civilian trauma and posttraumatic stress disorder in a representative national sample of women. *Journal of Consulting and Clinical Psychology* 61:984–991.

Shear, M. K., Brown, T. A., Barlow, D. H., Money, R., Sholomskas, D. E., Woods, S. W., Gorman, J. M., & Papp, L. A. (1997). Multicenter collaborative panic disorder severity scale. *American Journal of Psychiatry* 154:1571–1575.

Shear, M. K., Brown, T. A., Sholomskas, D. E., Barlow, D. H., Gorman, J. M., Woods, S. W., & Cloitre, M. (1992). *Panic Disorder Severity Scale (PDSS).* Pittsburgh, PA: Department of Psychiatry, University of Pittsburgh School of Medicine.

Spielberger, C. D., Gorsuch, R. L., & Lushene, R. E. (1970). Manual for the State-Trait Anxiety Inventory (self-evaluating questionnaire). Palo Alto, CA: Consulting Psychologists Press.

Stein, M. B., Fyer, A. J., Davidson, J. R. T., Pollack, M. H., & Wiita, B. (1999). Fluvoxamine treatment of social phobia (social anxiety disorder): A double-blind placebo-controlled study. *American Journal of Psychiatry* 156:756–760.

van der Kolk, B. A., Dreyfuss, D., Michael, M., Shera, D., et al. (1994). Fluoxetine in posttraumatic stress disorder. *Journal of Clinical Psychiatry* 55(12):517–522.

Vrana, S., & Lauterbach, D. (1994). Prevalence of traumatic events and post-traumatic psychological symptoms in a nonclinical sample of college students. *Journal of Traumatic Stress* 7:289–302.

Weathers, F. W., Ruscio, A., & Keane, T. M. (1999). Psychometric properties of nine scoring rules for the Clinician Administered PTSD Scale (CAPS). *Psychological Assessment* 11:124–133.

White, K. S., & Barlow, D. H. (2002). Panic disorder and agoraphobia. In *Anxiety and Its Disorders: The Nature and Treatment of Anxiety and Panic*, ed. D. H. Barlow, 2nd ed., pp. 328–379. New York: Guilford.

Wittchen, H. U. (1988). Natural course and spontaneous remissions of untreated anxiety disorders: Results of the Munich Follow-up Study (MFS). In *Panic and Phobias 2: Treatment and Variables Affecting Course and Outcome*, ed. I. Hand & H.-U. Wittchen, pp. 3–17. New York: Springer-Verlag.

Woody, S. R., Steketee, G., & Chambless, D. L. (1995). Reliability and validity of the Yale-Brown Obsessive Compulsive Scale. *Behaviour Research and Therapy* 33:597–605.

9

SUBSTANCE ABUSE

Robert J. Craig, Ph.D., ABPP

Mental health clinicians are increasingly faced with the need to assess substance abuse, as a primary disorder, as a comorbid condition associated with other psychiatric disorders, and as a condition affecting significant others, such as family members who may be the focus of treatment. The purpose of this chapter is to provide a broad overview of clinical interviewing with substance abusers, emphasizing drug (not alcohol) abuse in adult patients. However, much of the content of this chapter is applicable to the assessment of alcoholics as well.

DSM-IV CLASSIFICATION OF SUBSTANCE USE DISORDERS

DSM-IV (American Psychiatric Association, 1994) provides descriptions and classification of substance-related disorders in two groups: substance use disorders, including substance abuse and substance dependence, and substance-induced disorders, including substance (specific) intoxication, substance (specific) withdrawal, substance-induced delirium, persisting dementia, psychotic disorders, mood disorders, anxiety disorders, sexual dysfunction, and sleep disorder. The criteria set for substance dependence requires a maladaptive pattern of substance use that results in impairment within the past year in at least three of the seven criteria specified in the manual. There is a four-criteria set for a diagnosis of substance abuse of which only one needs to be satisfied to establish the diagnosis.

There are eleven types of drugs mentioned (alcohol, amphetamines, caffeine, cannabis, cocaine, hallucinogens, inhalants, nicotine, opioids, phencyclidine, or PCP, and sedatives, hypnotics, or anxiolytics) with six course specifiers (early full remission, early partial remission, and sustained partial remission, on agonist therapy and in a controlled environment). Any substance dependence diagnosis must also be accompanied by a specification of "with" (or "without") physiological dependence. The "remission" specifiers are applicable if the patient has

been drug free for at least one month, but do not apply if the patient is on agonist therapy or in a controlled environment (e.g., prison, hospital, or a therapeutic community). The manual also contains some data on age, gender, culture, and
familial aspects of these disorders.

ABUSE LIABILITY

The addiction potential of abused drugs has been well research and is well understood (Erickson et al., 1990). The Controlled Substances Act was passed to
enable the federal government to minimize the quantity of drugs that are available to persons prone to abuse them. Responsibility for enforcing this act lies
primarily with the Drug Enforcement Administration but also with the Substance Abuse Mental Health Services Administration. This law set up a five-tier

Table 9.1.   The Controlled Substances Act Schedule of Drugs

Schedule	Basic Requirements	Examples
I	Substances with high potential for abuse and no currently accepted medical use. They are available for research only.	heroin LSD marijuana
II	Substance with high potential for abuse, but with a currently accepted medical use. These drugs may lead to severe physical and psychological dependence. They are available only by written prescription with no refills.	morphine methadone amphetamines PCP cocaine Demorol
III	Substances with potential for abuse, but less so than for drugs in Class II. They have an accepted medical use. Abuse may result in low to moderate physical dependence or high psychological dependence. They are available only by written or oral prescription, with five refills permitted in six months with medical authorization.	Dilantin Doriden Preludin
IV	Substances with less potential for abuse and with an accepted medical use. Abuse may lead to low physical or psychological dependence. Refills are permitted as in Class III drugs.	Dalmane chloral hydrate
V	Substances with low potential for abuse and accepted medical use. Abuse may lead to limited physical or psychological dependence. Some may be available without a prescription, depending on state laws.	Cough syrup with codeine

system to classify psychoactive drugs in terms of their potential and accepted use in medicine. Each class of drugs may also differ in terms of registration requirements, record keeping, manufacturing quantity, distribution restrictions, dispensing limits, security precautions, reporting mechanisms, and criminal penalties for trafficking. Table 9.1 presents this Schedule of Controlled Drugs.

RELIABILITY OF ADDICT SELF-REPORTS

Since most life-history and information on patterns of use come from the drug-abusing patient, based on clinical interview and self-report data, a major question is whether this information can be trusted. Surprisingly, research has shown there is a high degree of correspondence between addict self-reported history information and that same data obtained from family, criminal records, and other significant sources (Bale, 1979; Bale et al., 1981; Ben-Yehuda, 1980; Bonito et al., 1976; Maddux and Desmond, 1975; Maisto et al., 1982/1983; Pompi and Shreiner, 1979; and Rounsaville et al., 1981). Similar findings have been reported in the alcohol literature. When the patient is interviewed in clinical or research contexts in an alcohol-free state and assured that the information provided is confidential, alcohol abuser's self-reports are reasonably accurate (Babor et al., 1987; O'Farrell and Maisto, 1987; Rankin, 1990; Sobell and Sobell, 1986; 1990; and Sobell et al., 1988). Discrepancies have been attributed to normal memory decay and the possible masking of specific crimes. Additionally, addicts tend to exaggerate the amount of drugs they use, while alcoholics tend to underreport the amount of alcohol they use. The latter is particularly important when evaluating the need for medical detoxification. When the patient–therapist relationship is based on trust and rapport, when the patient believes that the therapist will keep information confidential, and when the patient understands that the information obtained will be used to benefit him or her, then the patient can give reliable and valid life-history information.

DIAGNOSTIC INTERVIEW SCHEDULES FOR ADDICTIVE DISORDERS

Diagnostic interviews may be structured, semistructured, or unstructured. As argued in chapter 2, even the so-called unstructured interviews have a structure. Several structured interviews have been published that assess general psychopathology (e.g., Axis I disorders; see chapter 1 and Craig, 2003a) and all of these have a section or module that assesses for substance use disorders. The Addiction Severity Index (see below) has become the most popular of the structured diagnostic interviews for both alcohol and drug abuse, and it is in widespread use in both clinical and research contexts. Before we discuss the recommended content for a comprehensive clinical assessment interview with substance abusers, we will mention the most popular structured diagnostic interview with this population.

Addiction Severity Index (ASI)

The ASI (McLellan et al., 1992) is a structured clinical interview designed to assess areas known to be affected by substance abuse. Its administration time is about thirty minutes, and it allows the examiner to assign a nine-point severity rating in each of six areas (substance abuse, employment, medical, legal, family/social, and psychiatric/psychological functioning). The patient also assigns a severity rating in these areas. Where there is discrepancy between the patient's severity rating and the clinician's, that is presumptive evidence of denial. The ASI has good reliability and validity (McLellan et al., 1985; Kosten et al., 1985) and is "in the public domain" and may be reproduced for clinical use (Craig, 2003a).

DIAGNOSTIC INSTRUMENTS

Laboratory Tests

In settings in which medical tests are available, the most useful tests are a toxicology screen for the presence of illicit drugs and either a blood alcohol test or a Breathalyzer test for alcohol.

Urinalysis (Toxicology Screen)

There are many analytic drug-screening methods, but the most frequently used are the enzyme multiplied immunoassay technique (EMIT), the radioimmunoassay (RIA), and the thin-layer chromatography (TLC). Each method has advantages and disadvantages. Most urine samples are tested with one procedure. If confirmation is necessary, they are confirmed with another, more sensitive procedure.

Before accepting laboratory test results on urine, the clinician should ensure that the test (1) was taken under direct observation and (2) has been confirmed with another procedure. Even with confirmation, there are many problems associated with mass urine-screening programs, such as sensitivity levels, lack of specificity, cross-reactivity to other drugs, and human error, that can produce false positive or false negative results (DeAngelis, 1973; Morgan, 1984). Furthermore, patients will attempt to influence urine results by trying to dilute their urine with water or vinegar, by using a drug immediately before the test to ensure positive results if it suits their interest, by substituting "clean" (i.e., drug-free) urine for "dirty" (i.e., drug-positive) urine up to and including attempts to bribe the sampling technician. There are also products available that purportedly allow a person to pass a urine drug test screen. However, the efficiency of these claims is unsubstantiated. All urine samples from addicts should be taken under direct observation. However, the half-life (i.e., the time it takes for half of the drug to be metabolized and excreted) of psychoactive drugs varies, and hence the detectability of drugs in urine also varies. Some drugs (including barbiturates, marijuana, and opiates) are stored longer in tissue than are others (such as cocaine). A positive urine test may indicate past use (seven to ten days ago) but not necessarily current use. A negative result could mean that the patient has not used a psychoactive drug, or it could indicate a low dose or low purity levels that go undetected with mass screening procedures. Also, patients may believe they are buying and using one drug but actually get another.

The urine test itself may be invalid for other reasons. Hansen and colleagues (1985) evaluated the performance of thirteen laboratories servicing 262 methadone clinics. These labs were sent preanalyzed urine as if it were from routine patient samples. The error rate ranged from 0 to 100 percent, which suggests that these labs were often unable to detect drugs at clinically useful concentration levels. There are also ethical and sociopolitical aspects of drug tests (Craig, 2003a; Lewis et al., 1972) that must be understood.

Alcohol Testing

Blood-alcohol-level (BAL) tests measure the concentration of alcohol in blood. Readings of .8 and above are set as the legal definition of intoxication in most states. The tests are extremely accurate. Breathalyzer tests are available to detect alcohol concentration levels excreted through the lungs. BALs are somewhat intrusive and more costly, since they require a sample of blood to be drawn; alcohol Breathalyzers are much cheaper and easily adapted to most substance abuse treatment programs.

Psychological Tests

Omnibus screening inventories often contain scales that assess for substance abuse. The Minnesota Multiphasic Personality Inventory (MMPI) is the most frequently used psychological test for assessing substance abuse. Both drug addicts and alcoholics tend to have T-Scores above 65 on the MMPI/MMPI-2 clinical scale of psychopathic deviation (Pd). They also often have moderate elevations on the F (validity) scale and on the D (depression) scale. Common profile code types with substance abusers include combinations of Psychopathic Deviation and Hypomania (49/94), Depression (42/24), and Schizophrenia (48/84) clinical scales (Craig, 1984a; Graham and Strenger, 1988).

The MacAndrew Alcoholism Scale (MAC) of the MMPI (MAC-R-MMPI-2) was developed to detect alcoholism among psychiatric outpatients. A large body of research indicates that the MAC is a generic substance abuse scale and can detect both alcohol and drug abuse (Craig, 1984b; Preng and Clopton, 1986). Patients with elevated MAC scores should be interviewed specifically for substance abuse. Low scores on the MAC among known substance abusers usually suggest a milder form of substance abuse that may be more responsive to treatment.

The Millon Clinical Multiaxial Inventory, as revised, has both a drug abuse and an alcohol abuse scale with good validity and reveals distinct personality patterns and styles among substance abusers. The test has been well researched and has acceptable levels of detectability for both alcohol and drug abuse (Craig and Weinberg, 1992a; 1992b) ‹

Concurrent Psychiatric Diagnosis

Substance abuse may be a primary disorder, it may be a disorder secondary to other psychiatric conditions, or it may coexist independently with other disorders. It is essential that the clinician evaluate for the presence of other Axis I disorders in a routine assessment of the substance abuser. Research has shown that depression, alcoholism (in a drug addict), and antisocial personality disorders are frequently associated with substance abuse (Gawin and Kleber, 1986; Khantzian and Treece, 1985; O'Brien et al., 1984; Rounsaville et al., 1982), although the full range of DSM-IV personality disorders can be expected (Craig, 1985b; 2003c). Consideration of concurrent psychiatric conditions has important treatment implications because substance abusers rated high in psychiatric severity tend to have lower rates of improvement, despite various kinds of treatment (McLellan et al., 1983).

ALCOHOLISM AND DRUG ABUSE

Alcohol plays a significant role for many drug addicts. Some were alcoholic before developing a drug habit; others use alcohol (1) to maintain or intensify a high, (2) to ease or forestall withdrawal, or (3) as a substitute when their preferred drug is not available. Prevalence estimates of alcoholism among drug addicts range from 10 percent to 50 percent, with modal prevalence at around 20 percent (Belenko, 1979; Green and Jaffe, 1977). Thus drug addicts should be routinely assessed for alcohol abuse and alcoholics should be routinely assessed for drug abuse, especially for cocaine.

CONFIDENTIALITY

It is extremely important for clinicians dealing with substance abusers to become familiar with the federal regulations governing patient records for alcohol and drug abusers (U.S. Department of Health and Human Services, 1987). These regulations are considered the most restrictive and the most protective and are a model for other medical and mental health records (Lanman, 1980). As a general rule, all patient records related to the assessment and treatment of drug or alcohol abuse are considered confidential, although this status may be waived by the patient's written informed consent. Recipients of the information may not redisclose the information without obtaining another signed consent. Medical emergencies, audits, and court orders are situations in which these regulations allow for disclosure of information without consent. Of course, in situations pertaining to child abuse and neglect, and when the patient has become a danger to oneself or to others, aspects of the regulations do not apply. The regulations also prohibit undercover agents or informants being enrolled in drug or alcohol programs unless they have been granted permission by a court order. If a law enforcement agent wants to know whether a patient is attending a program, the program is prohibited by these same regulations from acknowledging or denying the patient's participation. The regulations provide a very specific format and content for "consent to release information" documents, and the reader is urged to obtain a complete copy of these regulations.

COUNTERTRANSFERENCE

Drug addicts have the capacity to engender powerful countertransferential reactions, even in brief diagnostic interviews. These patients are often aggressive, demanding, confronting, or defensive, and they enjoy exposing the therapist's vulnerabilities (Levine and Stephens, 1971). This "oral insatiability" is further complicated by the behaviors and lifestyle that accompany drug abuse, especially criminal activity. It strains the most objective clinician not to experience emotional reactions to these processes.

Common countertransferential reactions evoked by the drug-abusing population include (1) acting in the role of a good parent rescuing a bad, impulsive child, (2) reacting with anger when the patient challenges the therapist's knowledge or authority, (3) aligning with the patient by identifying with anti-authority stories or by vicariously romanticizing the drug addict lifestyle, and (4) emotionally withdrawing, becoming indifferent, or feeling bored, angry, or burned out (Imhof et al., 1983).

It is recommended that clinicians constantly monitor their emotional reactions when interviewing drug addicts and seek consultation or supervision for catharsis and growth. Some of the therapist's reactions may have important therapeutic implications and may form the basis of treatment recommendations for the future management of the patient.

RECOMMENDED INTERVIEW FORMAT

Table 9.2 suggests an interview format to be used with drug addicts. This format should not be followed in a rote, sequential manner; it merely depicts the content areas that should be covered by the time the interview process has been completed.

Table 9.2.   Recommended Assessment Content Areas for Diagnostic Interviews with Substance Abusers

General Assessment
    Conduct a (formal or informal) mental status exam
    Evaluate for the presence of concurrent psychiatric disorders

Presenting Complaint
    Assess the patient's motivation for treatment
    Determine why the patient is seeking treatment now
    Determine the patient's goals (look for a hidden agenda)

Drug Use
    Identify drugs used
    Determine the amount and frequency of use (currently and over time)
    Determine the route of administration (the way drugs are taken)
    Identify the amount and time of last use
    Determine the pattern and context of use
    Assess tolerance, dependence, and withdrawal states
    Include an assessment for alcohol if the patient is a drug addict and for drugs if
        the patient is an alcoholic

Effects of Alcohol/Drug Abuse
    Assess the patient's work history
    Inquire about legal problems
    Explore the nature and quality of interpersonal and family relationships and
        interactions
    Assess the patient's psychological state for subjective distress
    Explore leisure use and recreation
    Determine the presence of physical problems or symptoms
    Look for enabling situations or relationships
    Look for changes in spirituality

Special Considerations
    Evaluate sexual dysfunction
    Do an AIDS risk assessment
    Review for history of suicide
    Inquire about the history of physical and sexual abuse
    Inquire about the history of domestic violence

Treatment Considerations
    Explore any prior attempts at self-treatment
    Identify previous treatment episodes for both alcohol and drugs
    Determine modalities of prior treatments (detoxification, methadone
        maintenance, outpatient counseling, residential programs, etc.)

Determine whether there were any previous psychiatric treatments and the
 reasons for them
Check for overdose history
Explore the patient's history of abstinence or sobriety (length and circumstances)

DSM-IV Diagnosis
 Expect multiple diagnoses to be present on Axis I
 Expect at least one personality disorder on Axis II and perhaps one or more "V"
 codes

Treatment Recommendations
 Review with the patient your recommend treatment plan
 Attempt to reach mutually agreeable goals

General Assessment

Because drugs affect cognitive processes, it is necessary to evaluate the patient's mental status and psychiatric condition. The mental status exam need not be a formal one. One can obtain most of the necessary information from the patient by asking content questions in other areas.

Presenting Complaint

Drug addicts rarely seek treatment out of a desire to change themselves. Their motivation for treatment is almost always external and precipitated by pressure or crisis. Loss of residence; the threat of some type of action by a spouse, partner, employer, or parents unless the person stops using drugs; unexpected physical symptoms; running out of drugs; and pending legal difficulties are typical reasons that drug addicts seek treatment. Many have hidden agendas, and it is important to identify them early in the treatment relationship.

Drug Use

The therapist must determine whether the patient needs medical referral for detoxification, withdrawal, or possible delirium tremens (DTs). Table 9.2 provides a list of content areas that should be assessed for in the area of drug use. For treatment purposes, information about the pattern and context of drug use is particularly useful and can lead to meaningful intervention strategies.

Effects of Drugs

Alcohol and drugs affect cognitive, social, and familial relationships, affect the ability to function at work and play, and result in legal difficulties or illegal activities. They also lead to an array of physical problems, most commonly abscesses, cellulitis, chest pains, seizures, hepatitis C+, toxic psychotic states, panic reactions, flashbacks, substance-induced mood and anxiety disorders, and aggressive behavior.

Male substance abusers tend to structure their relationships in certain kinds of ways. Some get women to take care of them, satisfying their unresolved dependency needs (many marry women in the nursing professions), but all the while manifesting a pseudoassertive demeanor (Ganger and Shugart, 1966; Wellish et al., 1970). They tend to be enmeshed with the parents or parent surrogates in alliances that cross generational lines and are in reversal of the hierarchical organization of their families. This may serve to perpetuate addictive behavior (Kaufman, 1981; Kosten et al., 1982; Madanes et al., 1980).

Addicts create enabling relationships with others that are characterized by family behaviors that perpetuate drug abuse. Awareness of the relationship patterns can form the basis of an individualized treatment plan that may also involve the family.

Special Considerations

Alcohol and drugs interfere with sexual performance in both genders and produce a variety of sexual dysfunctions (Abel, 1984; Buffum, 1982). Addicts may present with suicidal histories or recent overdoses (Murphy et al., 1983) and sometimes have been abused as children. Although suicide history is frequently assessed, many clinicians ignore sexual functioning and child-abuse history in routine assessment. A complete assessment should include these important treatment variables, including an HIV assessment risk.

Treatment Considerations

Table 9.2 lists many key variables to explore when assessing for treatment history. Especially important is an assessment for previous sobriety and abstinence, which gives good clues as to ego strength and alerts the therapist to possible recalcitrant and refractory behaviors.

Diagnosis and Treatment

After a diagnosis has been made and a tentative treatment plan has been considered, the plan should be explored with the patient. The therapist should check for resistance and attempt to reach mutually agreeable goals. The most common treatment modalities for substance abusers include detoxification, maintenance (methadone) or antagonist (antabuse) treatment, therapeutic communities, outpatient counseling, and group or family therapy, although a multimodal approach is the most popular (Craig, 1985a).

CASE HISTORY

The patient was a thirty-two-year old, married, unemployed, white man in stable condition who was seen in consultation in a medical intensive care unit after an overdose of Valium. He had a history of one previous outpatient psychiatric treatment and two previous inpatient treatment episodes for drug abuse. He also had been on methadone maintenance as an outpatient for several years.

An immediate precipitant for his request for another treatment attempt was the fact that his methadone maintenance clinic had been closed, and the patient, having no other legal source of methadone, had begun to buy street methadone to avoid withdrawal. He called me to arrange an admission to outpatient methadone treatment, but before coming in for an assessment, he was in a car accident that caused a seizure disorder. He was placed on methadone to avoid withdrawal, barbiturates to control his seizures, and Vicodan for pain and was then released from the hospital.

The patient telephoned again to arrange a screening interview, this time requesting detoxification from methadone. His speech was slurred and he sounded confused and lethargic, but his reasoning was intact. Arrangements were made for him to come to the admissions area the following morning.

He reported to the hospital not on the prearranged day, but on the following day. He arrived too late to be processed and was told by the physician to return the next day. Instead, he went to a local public hospital, where he was placed in the alcoholic ward, despite the fact that he did not drink. He left the next day and claimed that he had walked thirty miles (he probably hitched rides also) back to our hospital and applied for admission to our drug abuse program. Upon arriving, he experienced significant delays in processing. His medical records could not be located quickly, and he was sent to several locations in the hospital. He was among the last patients scheduled to be seen that day and reported feeling "depressed and anxious; I wasn't being taken care of." He began to experience withdrawal symptoms, so he went into the bathroom and took twenty-five Valium tablets. He took another twenty-five Valium tablets shortly thereafter. He was brought to the emergency room and treated for a drug overdose. He denied this was a suicide attempt, claiming he had taken the Valium to calm down.

His history included a father who was a functional alcoholic, but who provided for his family and was not abusive. The patient had been in several race riots while in high school, and his parents sent him to live out of state. He had several brothers who were career military men, so he enlisted in the army after graduation. While in service he was gang raped by civilians who didn't like the military base in their community. Since he was a medic, he had access to drugs, and he quickly became addicted. Subsequently, he experienced a psychotic episode and had to be hospitalized. He was given a medical discharge and had been using drugs almost continually since leaving the service.

The patient reported a history of nightmares (twice a year), mildly intrusive thoughts, and occasional but infrequent flashbacks. He refused to talk about his military experiences. He denied other symptoms of posttraumatic stress disorder (PTSD) and said he had no current symptoms.

He had not worked since leaving service, but had a financial interest in a family business that provided support for him and his wife and children. He said there was a communication problem between him and his wife, and he admitted to delayed ejaculation, of which his wife was not complaining. He said that his wife was talking about leaving him, but he denied there was a "conflict," because, he said, he was the problem. He blamed the doctors for causing his problems, saying that a doctor had called his wife and told her that he had overdosed and was in intensive care and that doctors had not successfully treated his drug abuse problem. He had taken a temporary job to get out of the house once in a while and to show his wife that he was "trying." He denied any history of legal problems.

His urine tests were positive for methadone, barbiturates, and benzodiazepines and negative for all other drugs.

DSM-IV Diagnosis

Axis I: Opiate dependence
Sedative, hypnotic, or anxiolytic abuse
Posttraumatic stress disorder (chronic, with delayed onset) by history
Axis II: Diagnosis deferred on Axis II
Axis III: Status posttrauma seizure disorder, controlled with medication
Axis IV: Problems related to social environment (closing of methadone clinic)
Problems with primary support group (marital conflict due to use of drugs)
Occupational problems (no steady employment)
Axis V: Global assessment function: 40 (current)

Treatment Plan

1. Detoxify patient from opiates
2. Observe for signs of PTSD
3. Observe for suicidal ideation

4. (Individual and group therapy to) Improve patient's ability to deal with stress and frustrations
5. Reduce his internalized anger and hostility
6. Reduce externalization of blame
7. Address relapse prevention
8. Contact wife for further history; evaluate for possible marital therapy
9. Maintain patient on barbiturates for seizure disorder

SPECIAL POPULATIONS

Interview format and content are generally applicable to most substance abusers but need to be adapted when considering special populations of abusers. The populations that have been given special attention in the literature include adolescents, women, African Americans, Hispanic Americans, Native Americans, gays and lesbians, the elderly, and the military. Several articles have been published that discuss their specific issues and needs (Council on Scientific Affairs, American Medical Association, 1996; Bray et al., 1999; Bux, 1996; Caetano and Clark, 1998; Chavez and Mora, 1994; De La Rosa et al., 1990; Shedler and Block, 1990) and most introductory texts summarize this literature (Craig, 2003a). The reader is urged to consult these and other recent sources when assessing these special populations.

SOME PRACTICAL SUGGESTIONS FOR THE THERAPIST: SUBSTANCE ABUSE REFERRALS

When should a therapist refer a patient to a substance abuse program or to a treating clinician who specializes in substance abuse? Until research establishes reliable guidelines, the following clinical indicators are offered:

Therapists should refer patients to a substance abuse program when

- the therapist does not possess the expertise to treat the primary or secondary substance abuse problem,
- the patient's drug abuse is out of control,
- the patient's drug abuse becomes a serious danger to the patient, friends or family, or the general public,
- the patient has medical problems associated with drug abuse, or
- the patient cannot be managed on an ambulatory basis.

Therapists should refer patients to a substance abuse specialist (e.g., psychologist, psychiatrist, clinical social worker)

- when the therapist does not possess the expertise to treat the primary or secondary substance abuse problem,
- as part of a plan to follow the patient after release from inpatient care for relapse prevention, and
- when the patient's substance abuse is reactive to other primary problems that can be resolved by psychotherapy.

REFERENCES

Abel, E. L. (1984). Opiates and sex. *Journal of Psychoactive Drugs* 16:205–216.

American Psychiatric Association. (1994). *Diagnostic and Statistical Manual of Mental Disorders*, 4th ed. Washington, DC: American Psychiatric Association.

Babor, T. F., Stephens, R. S., and Marlatt, G. A. (1987). Verbal report methods in clinical research on alcoholism: Response bias and its minimization. *Journal of Studies on Alcohol* 48: 410–424.

Bale, R. N. (1979). The validity and reliability of self-reported data from heroin addicts: Mailed questionnaires compared with face-to-face interviews. *International Journal of the Addictions* 14:993–1000.

Bale, R. N., Van Stone, W. W., Engelsing, T. M., and Zarcone, V. P. (1981). The validity of self-reported heroin use. *International Journal of the Addictions* 16:1387–1398.

Belenko, S. (1979). Alcohol abuse by heroin addicts: Review of research findings and issues. *International Journal of the Addictions* 14:965–975.

Ben-Yehuda, N. (1980). Are addict self-reports to be trusted? *International Journal of the Addictions* 15:1265–1270.

Bonito, A. J., Nurco, D. N., and Shaffer, J. W. (1976). The veridicality of addict self-reports in social research. *International Journal of the Addictions* 11:719–724.

Bray, R. M., Fairbank, J. A., and Marsden, M. E. (1999). Stress and substance abuse among military women and men. *American Journal of Drug and Alcohol Abuse* 25:239–256.

Buffum, J. (1982). Pharmacosexology: The effects of drugs on sexual function. A review. *Journal of Psychoactive Drugs* 14:5–44.

Bux, D. A. (1996). The epidemiology of problem drinking in gay men and lesbians: A critical review. *Clinical Psychology Review* 16: 277–298.

Caetano. R., & Clark, C. L. (1998). Trends in alcohol consumption among whites, blacks and Hispanics: 1984–1995. *Journal of Studies on Alcohol* 59:659–668.

Chavez, E. L., and Mora, J., eds. (1994). Special issue on substance use patterns in latinas. *International Journal of the Addictions* 29:1079–1204.

Council on Scientific Affairs, American Medical Association. (1996). Alcoholism in the elderly. *Journal of the American Medical Association* 275:797–801.

Craig, R. J. (1984a). A comparison of MMPI profiles of heroin addicts based on multiple methods of classification. *Journal of Personality Assessment* 48:115–120.

Craig, R. J. (1984b). MMPI substance abuse scales on drug addicts with and without concurrent alcoholism. *Journal of Personality Assessment* 48:495–499.

Craig, R. J. (1985a). Multimodal treatment package for substance abuse treatment programs. *Professional Psychology: Research and Practice* 16:271–285.

Craig, R. J. (1985b). A psychometric study of the prevalence of DSM-III personality disorders among treated opiate addicts. *International Journal of the Addictions* 23:115–124.

Craig, R. J. (2003a). *Counseling the Alcohol and Drug Abuser: A Practical Approach*. Boston: Allyn & Bacon.

Craig, R. J. (2003b). Assessing psychopathology and personality with interview. In *Handbook of Psychology*, ed. I. Weiner. New York: Wiley and Sons.

Craig, R. J. (2003c). *Prevalence of Personality Disorders among Cocaine and Heroin Addicts*. Long Island City, New York: Hatherleigh Comp.

Craig, R. J., & Weinberg, D. (1992a) Assessing alcoholics with the Millon Clinical Multiaxial Inventory: A review. *Psychology of Addictive Behaviors* 6:200–208.

Craig, R. J., & Weinberg, D. (1992b) Assessing drug abusers with the Millon Clinical Multiaxial Inventory: A review. *Journal of Substance Abuse Treatment* 9:249–255.

DeAngelis, G. G. (1973). Testing for drugs: Techniques and issues. *International Journal of the Addictions* 8:997–1014.

De La Rosa, M. R., Khalsa, J. H., and Rouse, B. (1990). Hispanics and illicit drug use: A review of recent findings. *International Journal of the Addictions* 25:665–691.

Erickson, C. K., Javors, M. A., Morgan, W. W., and Stimmel, B. (1990). *The Addiction Potential of Abused Drugs and Drug Classes*. New York: Haworth.

Ganger, R., and Shugart, G. (1966). The heroin addict's pseudoassertive behavior and family dynamics. *Social Casework* (December):643–649.

Gawin, F. H., and Kleber, H. D. (1986). Abstinence symptomatology and psychiatric diagnosis in cocaine abusers: Clinical observations. *Archives of General Psychiatry* 43:107–113.

Graham, J. R., and Strenger, V. E. (1988). MMPI characteristics of alcoholics: A review. *Journal of Consulting and Clinical Psychology* 656:197–205.

Green, J., and Jaffe, J. H. (1977). Alcohol and opiate dependence: A review. *Journal of Studies on Alcohol* 38:1274–1293.

Hansen, H. J., Caudill, S. P., and Boone, J. (1985). Crisis in drug testing: Results of CDC blind studies. *Journal of the American Medical Association* 253:2382–2387.

Imhof, J., Hirsh, R., & Terenzi, R. E. (1983). Countertransferential and attitudinal considerations in the treatment of drug abuse and addiction. *International Journal of the Addictions* 18:491–510.

Kaufman, E. (1981). Family structure of narcotic addicts. *International Journal of the Addictions* 16:273–282.

Khantzian, E. J., and Treece, C. (1985). DSM-III psychiatric diagnosis of narcotic addicts. *Archives of General Psychiatry* 42:1067–1071.

Kosten, T. R., Jalali, B., and Kleber, H. D. (1982). Complimentary marital roles of male heroin addicts: Evaluation and intervention tactics. *American Journal of Drug and Alcohol Abuse* 9:155–169.

Kosten, T. R., Rounsaville, B. J., and Kleber, H. D. (1985). Concurrent validity of the Addiction Severity Index. *Journal of Nervous and Mental Disease* 171:606–610.

Lanman, R. B. (1980). The federal confidentiality protections for alcohol and drug abuse patient records: A model for mental health and other medical records? *American Journal of Orthopsychiatry* 50:666–677.

Levine, S., and Stephens, R. (1971). Games addicts play. *Psychiatric Quarterly* 45:584–592.

Lewis, V. S., Petersen, D. M., Geis, G., and Pollack, S. C. (1972). Ethical and sociopsychological aspects of urinalysis to detect heroin use. *British Journal of Addictions* 67:303–307.

Madanes, C., Lic, J. D., and Harbin, H. (1980). Family ties of heroin addicts. *Archives of General Psychiatry* 37:889–894.

Maddux, J. F., and Desmond, D. P. (1975). Reliability and validity of information from chronic heroin users. *Journal of Psychiatric Research* 12:87–95.

Maisto, S. A., Sobell, L. C., and Sobell, M. D. (1982/1983). Corroboration of drug abusers' self-reports through the use of multiple data sources. *American Journal of Drug and Alcohol Abuse* 9:301–308.

McLellan, A. T., Kushner, H., Metzger, D., Peters, R., Grissom, G., Pettinati, H., and Argeriou, M. (1992). The fifth edition of the Addiction Severity Index. *Journal of Substance Abuse Treatment* 9:1–15.

McLellan, A. T., Luborsky, L., Cacciola, J., & Griffith, J. E. (1985). New data from the Addiction Severity Index: Reliability and validity in three centers. *Journal of Nervous and Mental Diseases* 173:412–423.

McLellan, A. T., Luborsky, L., Woody, G. E., et al. (1983). Predicting response to alcohol and drug abuse treatments: Role of psychiatric severity. *Archives of General Psychiatry* 40:620–625.

Morgan, J. P. (1984). Problems of mass urine screening for misused drugs. *Journal of Psychoactive Drugs* 16:305–317.

Murphy, S. L., Rounsaville, B. J., Eyre, S., and Kleber, H. D. (1983). Suicide attempts in treated opiate addicts. *Comprehensive Psychiatry* 24:79–89.

O'Brien, C. P., Woody, G. E., and McLellan, A. T. (1984). Psychiatric disorders in opioid-dependent patients. *Journal of Clinical Psychiatry* 45:9–13.

O'Farrell, T. J., and Maisto, S. A. (1987). The utility of self-report and biological measures of alcohol consumption in alcoholism treatment outcome studies. *Advances in Behavior Research and Therapy* 9:91–125.

Pompi, K. F., and Shreiner, S. C. (1979). The reliability of biographical information from court-stipulated clients newly admitted to treatment. *American Journal of Drug and Alcohol Abuse* 6:79–95.

Preng, K. W., and Clopton, J. R. (1986). The MacAndrew scale: Clinical application and theoretical issues. *Journal of Studies on Alcohol* 47:228–236.

Rounsaville, B. J., Kleber, H. D., Wilber, C., et al. (1981). Comparison of opiate addicts' reports of psychiatric history with reports of significant other informants. *American Journal of Drug and Alcohol Abuse* 8:51–69.

Rounsaville, B. J., Weissman, M. M., Kleber, H. D., and Wilber, C. (1982). Heterogeneity of psychiatric diagnosis in treated opiate addicts. *Archives of General Psychiatry* 38:161–166.

Rankin, H. (1990). Validity of self-reports in clinical settings. *Behavioral Assessment* 12:107–116.

Shedler, J., and Block, J. (1990). Adolescent drug use and psychological health: A longitudinal inquiry. *American Psychologist* 45:612–603.

Sobell, L. C., and Sobell, M. B. (1986). Can we do without alcohol abusers' self-reports? *Behavior Therapist* 7:141–146.

Sobell, L. C., and Sobell, M. B. (1990). Self-report issues in alcohol abuse: State of the art and future directions. *Behavioral Assessment* 12:91–106.

Sobell, L. C., Sobell, M. B., and Nirenberg, T. N. (1988). Behavioral assessment and treatment planning with alcohol and drug abusers: A review with an emphasis on clinical application. *Clinical Psychology Review* 8:19–54.

U.S. Department of Health and Human Services (1987). Confidentiality of alcohol and drug abuse patient records. *Federal Register* 52:2796–2814.

Wellish, D. K., Gay, G. R., and McEntee, R. (1970). The easy rider syndrome: A pattern of hetero-and homosexual relationships in a heroin addict population. *Family Process* 9:425–430.

10

ALCOHOLISM

Anne Helene Skinstad, Ph.D., Peter E. Nathan, Ph.D.,
and Nicole Pizzini, Ph.D.

DEVELOPMENT OF THE CONCEPT OF ALCOHOLISM

The concept of addiction or dependence upon alcohol is at least 2,000 years old (Caetano, 1985). Until the beginning of the twentieth century, the concept was influenced in large part by the belief that alcoholism was a moral default—a willful disorder—that the alcoholic could control if he or she chose to. This view of alcohol dependence rendered thorough assessment of abusive drinking unnecessary since, regardless of the special issues and circumstances clients faced, their appropriate treatment was always the same, namely, total abstinence; efforts to enhance the willpower required to refuse alcohol for the rest of their lives.

Jellinek (1960) rearticulated the concept of alcoholism and reintroduced the biological bases of alcoholism. Schuckit (1994) has observed that Jellinek brought a combination of "armchair philosophy, clinical observations, and some aspects of scientific method to the question of what might most appropriately be called alcoholism." Jellinek developed a theory, based on his research among Alcoholics Anonymous members, that posited a series of subtypes of alcoholism. Two forms of alcoholism, gamma and delta alcoholism, were thought to be associated with high levels of impairment, including evidence of tolerance, withdrawal, and either loss of control over use of the drug or the inability to abstain from drinking alcoholic beverages. Jellinek's theory represented what has come to be called the "disease model" of alcoholism, in part, because it recognized the existence of a unique disorder with clear physical manifestations that, if not appropriately treated, could run a very serious course.

The development of a standard U.S. nomenclature for mental disorders paralleled the development and ultimate publication in 1960 of Jellinek's disease model of alcoholism. The first edition of the *Diagnostic and Statistical Manual of Mental Disorders* (DSM-I) was published in 1952; the second edition (DSM-II) was published in 1968. Both were consensus documents that were not research based. In DSM-I (American Psychiatric Association, 1952), alcoholism was categorized along with antisocial behavior and the sexual deviations as evidence of sociopathy, a disorder of personality rather than a disease. DSM-II (American Psychiatric Association, 1968) did not continue to view alcoholism as a personality disorder subtype, but viewed it as one of a group of "certain other nonpsychotic mental disorders," together with the sexual deviations and drug dependence (Caetano, 1985). In both instances, alcohol dependence was seen as a voluntary behavior worthy of stigmatization.

DSM-III (American Psychiatric Association, 1980) was the first of these manuals to base the diagnosis of alcohol abuse and dependence on research findings—specifically, on the Research Diagnostic Criteria (RDC) proposed by Spitzer and his colleagues in 1975. These criteria yielded a kappa coefficient of reliability (using the Diagnostic Interview Schedule (DIS, Robins et al., 1981) ranging from .80 to .86; these figures were substantially higher than those for the reliability of alcohol abuse and dependence in DSM-I and DSM-II.

DSM-IV (American Psychiatric Association, 1994) clarified divergent concepts of alcohol abuse and dependence by making adverse social and occupational consequences of alcohol use principal criteria for alcohol abuse and making compulsive use/loss of control principal criteria for alcohol dependence. When the syndrome included tolerance or withdrawal, it was designated as "with physiological dependence"; when it did not include tolerance or withdrawal, it was "without physiological dependence" (Nathan, 1992).

The development of a valid, useful concept of alcohol/substance abuse and dependence, admittedly, has taken a long time. However, the diagnosis now appears to show both adequate reliability and some predictive validity in that it reflects future differences in the course of treatment and helps in the assignment of appropriate treatments (Schuckit, 1994).

In recent years, influenced in part by data from the DSM-IV field trials, alcoholism and drug addiction have come to be considered biopsychosocial disorders (Grant and Dawson, 1999). Understandably, this view of alcohol abuse and dependence requires interviews and assessments of alcoholism that incorporate items from all three domains. Accordingly, the methods discussed in this chapter focus on one or more of the three elements of the biopsychosocial model. In this regard, it is also important to note the declining numbers of individuals who suffer only from alcohol dependence, without additional substance dependencies or other DSM-IV disorders; more and more clients are both polysubstance dependent and clinically anxious or depressed, a phenomenon that, understandably, influences how these individuals ought to be interviewed and assessed.

THE INTERVIEW/ASSESSMENT PROCESS

Assessment methods are designed to serve both as means by which to understand specific disorders and as a common language for clinicians and researcher

(Rounsaville, 1996). Accurate and comprehensive assessment is fundamental to both treatment and research. Predictably, the assessment needs of researchers and clinicians differ. The clinician is primarily concerned with the clinical utility of an assessment, specifically, how clearly it identifies the treatment needs of a given client and hence will guide treatment planning. The clinician must also weigh how long an interview or assessment will take, the setting in which it takes place, and the likelihood that it will be followed by the opportunity to undertake treatment. Clinicians are also concerned about the concurrent and predictive validity of an assessment, availability of norms for an instrument, and its psychometric properties. Given current efforts to manage health care costs and service utilization, clinicians also care about the ease of administration, scoring, and interpretation of an instrument as well as its cost, time, and acceptability to clients. Researchers may be less concerned about an assessment measure's cost-benefit ratio so long as it provides the information they seek for the purposes for which they seek it.

Clinicians working in community-based substance abuse treatment centers typically carry very large client caseloads and have very little time to spend selecting the most appropriate assessment instruments. As a result, many institutions use a standard assessment battery for every client. If further assessment then appears warranted, specific instruments can be chosen or other professionals can be asked to supplement the assessment. Use of the standard battery enables clinicians to compare their clients' responses to those of others treated at the same institution. If a statewide assessment system is in place, as is sometimes the case, institutions can also compare their clientele to that of other state institutions.

Clinical interviews and assessment procedures may also be chosen with an eye to the expectations of insurance companies and other third party payers. In this regard, assessments may be chosen above all to reflect the effectiveness of treatment at the institution. Since funding for substance abuse treatment may be driven by an institution's ability to present convincing financial and clinical data in support of its funding requests, assessments that demonstrate clinical effectiveness help convince funding agencies that the institution merits their support.

The Institute of Medicine (1990) suggests a threefold division of the goals of substance abuse assessment: screening, problem assessment, and personal assessment. In determining how extensive an assessment should be, clinicians should be able to answer the following questions (Allen et al., 1995):

- Do I need a screening tool for alcohol or drug abuse?
- Do I need an assessment tool that yields a formal alcohol/substance-related diagnosis or quantifies symptoms central to the alcohol dependence syndrome?
- Do I need an assessment method for drinking behavior, including quantity, frequency, intensity, and pattern of alcohol consumption?

- Do I need a scale that can assist me in developing a client-specific treatment plan?
- Do I need an assessment instrument that will assist me in understanding the process of treatment, such as treatment atmosphere, degree of treatment structure, and immediate or proximal outcomes of treatment?
- Do I need an assessment instrument designed specifically to assess the end result of treatment?
- What are the purposes and clinical utility of the instrument?
- What is the purpose of the assessment? Is it consistent with prior use of the instrument?

Assessment Time Frame and Timing of Test/Interview Administration

Assessment instruments differ according to time frame. Some interview and assessment strategies are designed to measure recent drinking behavior; others reflect long-term, chronic alcohol use. Screening and diagnostic scales can also reflect either lifetime or current diagnostic conditions. Understandably, it is important to administer tests or interviews in line both with intended time frame and with awareness of factors that might affect the reliability of the assessment. For instance, tests that are designed to tap neuropsychological functioning may need to be delayed until a client has fully recovered from withdrawal (e.g., after at least a month), while trait-focused personality measures can be administered after a week or two, when acute withdrawal has been completed (Donovan & Marlatt, 1988; Rourke & Løberg, 1996; Sherer et al., 1984). It is rarely appropriate to evaluate clients shortly after admission to an inpatient unit, before they have completed acute withdrawal. While substance withdrawal can cause cognitive impairment, it also affects emotional status; if the client is also dependent on other substances, appropriate timing of assessment may be even more difficult to determine. Benzodiazepine abusers' very serious withdrawal syndrome may last for up to three months. In general, for most clients, postponing assessment for three weeks to permit acute withdrawal symptoms to subside makes good sense.

Age of Target Population

Most alcohol measures have been developed for adult populations between the ages of eighteen and sixty. Relatively few focus on clients under eighteen, even though adolescents have specific issues around sexuality, life goals, and aspirations that may loom large in planning treatment. As a consequence, clinicians may be forced to use assessment instruments designed for adults that also have norms for adolescents (Winters et al., 1993). Happily, in recognition of the fact that older substance abusers have different treatment needs than those who are younger, a variety of specific interview strategies and assessment instruments have been developed for use with older substance abusers (Allen et al., 1995).

Gender of Target Population

Problem drinking in men and women differs. Women and men also have different treatment needs and experience different social, familial, and medical consequences of abusive drinking. Although some assessment tools—for example, the Addiction Severity Index (McLellan et al., 1980; McLellan et al., 1992; Stoffelmayr et al., 1994)—are normed for women (Brown et al., 1993), interviews and assessment instruments for adults have generally been developed based on men's issues. As a consequence, they are not wholly appropriate for women (McCrady & Raytek, 1996). Moreover, it is questionable whether gender-based norming would significantly augment the utility of most treatment planning measures, which often are individual in nature (Allen et al., 1995).

Race and Ethnicity of Target Population

Few substance abuse assessment instruments provide ethnicity-based norms. This fact needs to be taken into consideration when assessments of clients who are not Caucasian are contemplated. This is because different cultural groups may understand the questions posed differently than clients from the dominant culture (Huff, 1999). Also, to more fully understand the impact of problem drinking on a particular client, clinicians ought to be familiar with the drinking patterns and cultural context in which alcohol consumption takes place for ethnic groups they are called upon to assess. Research on these issues, unfortunately, is in its infancy (Columbus & Allen, 1995).

Collateral Sources of Information

Clients who abuse substances are not always willing or able to provide accurate information about their disorders (Donovan, 1999). The client's memory of how much of the substance he or she consumed is the principal source of information on quantity and frequency of consumption in clinical interview. Because the consumption usually leads to intoxication, memory for this information may not be accurate. Further, clients may have a need to under- or overestimate consumption. As a result, family members may have a clearer picture of how much a client has consumed (Donovan, 1995).

Also, the client sometimes is simply unable to provide a valid self-report of quantity and frequency of consumption. Chronic abusers may have suffered sufficient cognitive impairment to be unable to remember the details of con-sumption, even recent consumption. Or the client may have been admitted to the emergency room unconscious as the result of an overdose or a serious traf-fic accident. In the latter instance, when it is essential to start treatment (in-cluding withdrawal) immediately, family members, friends, or others who can provide collateral information are especially important sources of information.

Intoxication during the Interview

It is sometimes difficult to know whether the client is under the influ-ence of alcohol or another drug during an assessment session. Clinical experi-ence has shown that even trained clinicians may overlook or underestimate a client's level of intoxication (Schuckit, 1995). It is not a good idea to interview clients when they are intoxicated, both because the resultant information may not be reliable and because the client may choose to disclose information he or she otherwise would not reveal (Donovan, 1995). To be absolutely certain the client is sober during the assessment, consideration of the use of a Breath-alyzer is recommended.

Computerized Assessment Instruments

A number of assessment instruments now have computerized versions. The Addiction Severity Index and the Alcohol Use Inventory, both very well-regarded and widely used assessments, have such versions (Allen, Columbus & Fertig, 1995). While computerized assessments sometimes save time, in part be-cause their scoring can be instantaneous, they are difficult to use if the client is not computer literate. As well, it is unclear whether an instrument's standards are changed when its computerized version is used (Allen et al., 1995).

Recent studies (Collins, 2000) suggest that the reliability of self-reports of alcohol consumption is enhanced when clients are asked to enter information on consumption immediately, either into a small Palm Pilot, by e-mail, or by daily telephone contact, rather than by recalling the information hours or days later. Collins (2000) has developed computerized methods for assessing daily al-cohol consumption. She gives clients a Palm Pilot computer, into which they en-ter data on consumption immediately after they have had a drink. Before this computerized version of self-monitoring was developed, clients completed daily "drinking charts," which were not as accurate. Searles (2000) has provided clients with a telephone number they were to use to provide drinking information on a daily basis. However, clients provided much more accurate data on consump-tion when they recorded data on consumption immediately (Collins, 2000; Sear-les, 2000). Collins (2000) concludes both that clients previously tended to un-derreport their consumption level, because of their inability to remember accurately how many drinks they had consumed, and that a computerized self-monitoring system may be even more reliable than consumption information from collaterals.

Assessment of Co-occurring Psychopathology

Persons with substance abuse problems, including those seeking treatment for alcoholism, are more likely than those who are not substance abusers to merit concurrent mood or anxiety disorder diagnoses (Schuckit et al., 1997). In turn, these comorbid conditions may impact the client's ability to understand and respond to questions about quantity and frequency of alcohol consumption, as well as short- and longer-term consequences of the substance use disorder. Depending on the nature of the co-occurring disorder, these clients may also distort or conceal their substance use (Cocco & Carey, 1998). Standard interviews or questionnaires may not be adequate for this group of clients.

Alcohol abuse is associated with a number of serious medical, neurological, and psychiatric consequences. Accordingly, it is important when planning treatment to undertake a comprehensive evaluation of the likelihood of co-occurring disorder. This assessment should include urine and blood tests to examine the status of liver enzymes and blood components that tend to be affected by heavy alcohol consumption. These tests complement psychological, psychiatric, and substance use assessments by providing an evaluation of the seriousness of the physical consequences of alcohol abuse.

If psychiatric comorbidity seems likely, a thorough DSM-IV diagnostic evaluation indicated. As indicated above, the diagnostic interview should take place after detoxification has been completed: differentiating symptoms of withdrawal, especially severe withdrawal, from those of diverse psychiatric conditions can be quite difficult.

The CNS consequences of long-term alcoholism can be quite serious; they include both alcohol-induced persisting dementia and alcohol-induced persisting amnesic disorder. Women tend to experience these results of chronic alcohol abuse earlier and, often, more severely than men (Gomberg, 1999; Hill, 1995). Cognitive impairment hinders the clinician's treatment planning by making it difficult for the client to participate fully in making informed decisions about treatment. Also, memory loss can make self-reports of consumption level and its consequences very unreliable.

It is important to evaluate literacy before asking a client to complete either a paper-and-pencil test or a computerized assessment instrument. Reading difficulties will seriously impact the validity of the results. Unfortunately, clients are often embarrassed to admit to their inability to read or to a dyslexia problem (Center for Substance Abuse Treatment, 1998; Donovan, 1995). Clients are typically not forthcoming about these issues, so clinicians need routinely to ask about issues of reading, writing, and visual disabilities/impairment.

A SUGGESTED APPROACH TO ASSESSMENT

At the beginning of a diagnostic interview/assessment, the clinician should tell the client why it is taking place, the purposes for which its results will be used, and how it will benefit treatment. The client also needs to know how this information will be treated; limits on confidentiality should be clearly articulated. Taking the time to answer clients' questions about the assessment process helps create rapport with the client that facilitates assessment. While describing what is to come during the assessment process, the interviewer should also suggest a feedback session: it is easier to elicit cooperation when it is clear that the client will receive feedback on the results of the assessment.

Motivational interviewing, a component of Motivational Enhancement Therapy (MET, Miller, 1991), was designed as a brief intervention in the Project MATCH RCT for alcohol abuse and dependence (Project MATCH Research Group, 1997). MET is directive and client centered; it brings about behavior change by helping clients explore and resolve their ambivalence about whether or not to stop drinking. Five general principles underlie the process of motivational interviewing (Miller & Rollnick, 1991). They are valuable guides for effective interviewing of alcohol-abusing clients, regardless of the specific focus or method.

- *Avoid Argumentation.* Arguing with patients can cause them to feel attacked and redouble their efforts to resist change. For these reasons, the clinician avoids arguing with the client during the motivational interview.
- *Express Empathy.* Try to see the world through the patient's eyes. When clinicians demonstrate accurate understanding of the client, the client feels understood and is able to share his or her experiences. In such an instance, client and clinician are at liberty to explore the client's ambivalence toward change.
- *Support Self-Efficacy.* Believing one can change is an important motivator of successful change. Clinicians can assist clients by helping foster hope that change can occur, does occur, and will occur.
- *Roll with Resistance.* Do not challenge the client. Instead, try to explore his or her views. Clinicians may invite clients to explore new perspectives, but do not impose these views on them.
- *Develop Discrepancy.* Help patients identify discrepancies between their future goals and current behaviors.

SCREENING METHODS

Screening methods are designed to identify quickly and inexpensively individuals who may have alcohol-related problems or be at risk for such problems. They are not designed to diagnose or explain the client's alcohol problems in detail, but to suggest that a problem with alcohol may exist. Ideally, screening should be done in such a way as to facilitate subsequent, more definitive assessment and referral to treatment. A screening instrument needs to have high sensitivity. That is, it should correctly identify a substantial proportion of persons with alcohol-related disorders and rarely label as alcoholic a person who is not. The screening instrument also needs to have a high level of specificity, as shown by the capacity to identify persons who are not likely to meet criteria for alcohol-related disorders. Ideally, screening instruments should also be sensitive to alcohol-related disorders in special populations. The most widely used alcoholism screening instruments are the CAGE, the TWEAK and T-ACE, the AUDIT, and the MAST (Allen, Columbus & Fertig, 1995).

The CAGE consists of four questions designed to be used in a primary care physician's office. They include:

- Have you ever felt that you need to Cut down on your drinking?
- Have people Annoyed you by criticizing your drinking?
- Have you ever felt bad or Guilty about your drinking?
- Have you ever had a drink first thing in the morning to steady your nerves or to get rid of a hangover (Eye opener)?

The TWEAK (Russell et al., 1991) and T-ACE (Sokol et al., 1989) are similar screening methods originally developed for women, especially pregnant women. The TWEAK consists of the following five questions:

- How many drinks can you hold (Tolerance)?
- Have close friends or relatives Worried or complained about your drinking?
- Do you sometimes take a drink in the morning when you first get up (Eye-opener)?
- Has a friend or family member ever told you about things you said or did while you were drinking that you could not remember (Amnesia or blackouts)?
- Do you sometimes feel the need to cut down on your drinking (K[C]— Cut Down)?

The T-ACE is similar to the CAGE and the TWEAK.

- How many drinks does it take to make you feel high (Tolerance)?
- Have people Annoyed you by criticizing your drinking?
- Have you felt you ought to Cut down on your drinking?

• Have you ever had a drink first thing in the morning to steady your nerves or get rid of a hangover (*E*ye opener)?

The Michigan Alcoholism Screening Test (MAST, Selzer, 1971) is a paper-and-pencil test that, in its original form, included twenty-five items. The MAST is the oldest, most extensively studied, and most widely used screening test for alcoholism. The Brief-MAST consists of ten items (Pokorny et al., 1972). There is also a geriatric version of the MAST called the G-MAST; it was developed for people over sixty (Mudd et al., 1993).

Typical MAST questions include:

• Do you enjoy a drink now and then?
• Do you feel guilty about your drinking?
• Are you able to stop drinking when you want to?
• Do you drink before noon fairly regularly?
• Have you ever gone to anyone for help about your drinking?

The Alcohol Use Disorders Identification Test is an easily administered paper-and-pencil screening instrument developed for adults that consists of three subscales and ten items. Designed to be culture fair, it was developed by the World Health Organization to identify persons whose alcohol consumption has become hazardous to their health. The client is asked to respond to the ten questions on five-point Likert-type scales. Examples of AUDIT questions include:

• How often do you have a drink that contains alcohol?
• How often do you have six or more drinks on one occasion?
• How often in the past year have you needed a first drink in the morning to get yourself going after a heavy drinking session?

While all of these screening methods are paper-and-pencil tests, all can also be administered as interviews. The MAST is the most extensively studied and validated of these methods, followed by the AUDIT. The TWEAK, T-ACE, and CAGE have only recently begun to be studied.

Few options are available to screen adolescents for alcohol abuse and alcohol-related problems. One of the few instruments for this purpose, the Adolescent Alcohol Involvement Scale, consists of fourteen items organized in a multiple-choice format (Mayer & Filstead, 1979; Putnins, 1992). Another such screening instrument is the twenty-three-item Rutgers Alcohol Problem Index (White & Labouvie, 1989; Thombs & Beck, 1994). Both are paper-and-pencil instruments that can be used for both research and clinical purposes; each takes about five minutes to administer. Neither, however, has an extensive research literature thus far.

PROBLEM ASSESSMENT

Problem assessment involves efforts to diagnose the alcohol problem and identify its correlates and consequences. Problem assessment requires a more extensive assessment of behavior than screening assessment (Institute of Medicine, 1990).

Diagnostic Measures

A number of assessment methods have been developed to diagnose alcohol dependence according to DSM criteria. The diagnosis of substance dependence according to DSM-IV (American Psychiatric Association, 2000) requires the individual to meet three or more of nine dependence criteria over a twelve-month period. Specifically, it means that the client has demonstrated symptoms of tolerance, withdrawal, and/or compulsive use/loss of control of the substance. Because DSM-IV is a polythetic system, clients do not have to meet all of these equally weighted criteria to merit this diagnosis.

There is a longstanding, unresolved controversy over the validity of psychiatric (syndromal) diagnosis that, in essence, asks whether diagnosing on the basis of signs and symptoms is as helpful to the client as assessment by other means. While the reliability of diagnoses based on DSM-III and DSM-IV criteria, including those for substance abuse, is significantly higher than the reliability of diagnoses based on DSM-I and DSM-II, the utility of these diagnoses for treatment planning continues to be widely debated (Maisto & McKay, 1995). In particular, a good deal more than the diagnosis is taken into account when planning treatment, including treatment for substance abuse (Todd & Reich, 1989). In particular, the antecedents and consequences of the target symptoms and behaviors that constitute the diagnosis are important in planning treatment for substance abuse (e.g., Carroll, 1999; O'Farrell & Fals-Stewart, 1999; Sheehan & Owen, 1999; Yahne & Miller, 1999).

Nonetheless, syndromal diagnosis continues to be a major component of a comprehensive assessment, in part because it enhances communication about clients among professionals. Moreover, the diagnosis of alcohol abuse or dependence suggests the degree of severity of an alcohol problem and therefore has some utility in the assignment of treatments. A number of interviews and assessment instruments for this purpose have been developed. The most widely used include the following.

Diagnostic Interview Schedule for DSM-III-R (DIS-III-R), *Alcohol Module.* This structured interview, which closely follows the DSM-III-R diagnostic criteria for alcohol abuse and dependence, was originally designed for use in epidemiological research by trained laypersons; it was later modified as a briefer instrument (Quick-DIS). In the latter form, it consists of thirty interview items designed to lead to a DSM-III-R diagnosis of alcohol abuse or dependence. In addition to determining whether criteria for a DSM-III-R diagnosis have been met, information about onset and course of drinking problems and the time course of the disorder is provided.

Structured Clinical Interview for DSM-IV (SCID-IV, Spitzer et al., 1996). This semistructured diagnostic interview provides a comprehensive diagnostic assessment that also permits the exercise of clinical judgment by mental health professionals. While the SCID-IV, based on the DSM-IV diagnostic criteria, is time-consuming to administer, it enables a comprehensive picture of a client's symptoms. Many consider this instrument the diagnostic instrument of choice by virtue of its comprehensiveness, reliability, and usefulness.

The Substance Use Disorder Diagnostic Schedule has been computerized for use with adults. Clients complete the interview on a computer by themselves in thirty to forty-five minutes. The SUDDS is based on DSM-III-R diagnostic criteria for substance abuse. Other diagnostic instruments are the Drinking Inventory of Consequences (DrInC, Tonigan, Miller & Brown, 1997) for adults, a paper-and-pencil test that takes about ten minutes to complete, and the Drinking Problem Index, a test for adults over fifty-five years of age that takes about five minutes to administer and is also done with paper and pencil.

Severity of Dependence

In their comprehensive overview of alcoholism assessment instruments, Allen, Columbus & Fertig (1995) described a number of assessment instruments designed to evaluate the severity of alcohol dependence. We will briefly describe four of these instruments.

Alcohol Dependence Scale (ADS, Skinner & Allen, 1982). The ADS is a self-report, paper-and-pencil test for adults. It includes twenty-five items and takes about five minutes to complete. It can be used to assess severity of an alcohol problem in a variety of settings, including health care, corrections, and general population surveys. Sample questions from the ADS include:

- How much did you drink the last time you drank?
- Have you had the "shakes" when sobering up?
- Do you panic because you fear you may not have a drink when you need it?
- Do you drink throughout the day?
- As a result of drinking, have you "felt things" crawling on you that are not really there (e.g., bugs, spiders)?

Adolescent Diagnostic Interview (ADI, Winters & Henly, 1993, Winters et al., 1993) is designed for adolescents between twelve and eighteen years of age. It consists of 213 questions, not all of which are asked during every interview. Answers to "gateway" questions determine the specific course of the interview. An example of a gateway question is "Have you ever used cannabis, whether in the form of marijuana, hashish, or THC?" If the answer is yes, the interviewer will continue with specific follow-up questions designed to capture the dimensions of this behavior, including the severity of addiction. If the answer to the question is no, the interviewer will continue with questions from the next section of the interview. The interview takes fifteen to twenty minutes to administer. Results can assist professionals in identifying, referring, and treating adolescents with substance abuse problems.

Severity of Alcohol Dependence Questionnaire. The SADQ is a self-administered, paper-and-pencil test of twenty items. Designed to reflect the severity of alcohol dependency according to the alcohol dependence syndrome, the test takes only about five minutes to complete. Sample items include:

- During a heavy drinking period, I wake up feeling sweaty.
- When I'm drinking heavily, I dread waking up in the morning.
- During a heavy drinking period, I drink more than a quart of a bottle of spirits per day.

The Short Alcohol Dependence Questionnaire can be completed as either an interview or a paper-and-pencil test. It consists of fifteen items and takes two to five minutes to administer. The test is "suitable for patients seeking help for their drinking problem; [it is] a measure of present alcohol dependence, sensitive across the full range of dependence, sensitive to changes over time, and also relatively free of socio-cultural influence." (Sample questions from the SADD include:

- Do you find difficulty in getting the thought of drinking out of your mind?
- Do you drink for the effect of alcohol without caring what the drink is?
- The morning after a heavy drinking session, do you wake up with a definite shakiness of your hands?

Severity of Withdrawal

If a goal of assessment includes evaluating the severity of the alcohol withdrawal syndrome, the Clinical Institute Withdrawal Assessment-Revised is most often used. This assessment tool is an observational system of eight items that takes about two minutes complete. A range of different professional groups can learn to complete the instrument. Its scales identify the clinical features of withdrawal and convert DSM-III-R items into scores that reflect the severity of withdrawal symptoms over time. A clinician using this instrument takes the client's pulse and observes sweating, hand tremor, agitation, and anxiety level (by asking "Do you feel nervous?"). The clinician also observes transient tactile, auditory, and visual disturbances (by asking "Have you any itching, pins and needles sensations, any burning, any numbness, or do you feel bugs crawling on or under your skin?) The client's potential for nausea, vomiting, and headaches is also assessed. Responses are scored on a seven-point scale from not present to severe.

PERSONAL ASSESSMENT

Personal assessment is the third and most comprehensive stage in the assessment of alcohol problems (Institute of Medicine, 1990). While the principal goal of a comprehensive alcoholism assessment is the alcohol use disorder itself, evaluation of its medical, emotional, social, vocational, and familial consequences is also of considerable interest. While some of these problems are directly related to alcohol use, others may be less directly related or unrelated completely. Distinguishing among consequences and problems in relation to the fundamental alcohol use disorder is helpful, above all, in planning treatment. This section of the chapter reviews interviews and other assessment tools designed both to reflect alcohol consumption and its consequences and to provide additional information of value in treatment planning.

Alcohol Consumption Measures

Most of these measures were developed to facilitate cognitive behavioral treatment and thus are heavily influenced by social learning theory. Goals of nonproblem drinking as well as abstinence are envisioned within this framework. These assessment methods are designed to be relevant to treatment planning by providing thorough descriptions of the problem behaviors, their antecedents, and their consequences.

In choosing a measure to assess alcohol use, the clinician needs to make a number of important decisions. Among them, almost invariably, are:

- What do I want to do with this information?
- For what time interval do I need drinking data?
- How much time do I have to administer the measure?
- What level of precision of data do I need?
- What are the psychometric characteristics of the measure when used for this purpose?

Alcohol consumption measures are summary or aggregated measures of consumption, often referred to as measures of quantity–frequency (QF). Development of these methods began in the 1970s, when the first broad-spectrum behavioral treatment programs with nonproblem drinking as a treatment option were implemented. However, concerns about how best to reflect alcohol consumption were expressed by Pearl fifty years earlier, in 1926.

Although concerns about the reliability and validity of self-report measures of drinking, noted earlier in the chapter, have continued, Sobell and Sobell (e.g., 1996) have claimed that self-reports of alcohol consumption are generally accurate when clients are interviewed when they are sober and they do not anticipate negative consequences for valid self-reports. The accuracy of self-reports of alcohol consumption can be enhanced by the clinician in several ways, including assuring the client that the information provided will remain confidential, wording questions clearly and understandably, and conducting the interview in a setting that encourages honesty about alcohol use, such as outside a correctional setting (Sobell & Sobell, 1990).

A number of measures that assess "average" or "typical" consumption patterns have been developed. These measures typically require the client to provide detailed information on drinking patterns over varying periods of time. Two major types of QF measures exist. Single dimensional measures provide information on average number of drinks per drinking day (Q) and average number of days on which alcohol is consumed (F). Multidimensional measures (MD) assess volume variability and volume pattern. The latter measure classifies individuals into drinking categories based on cross-classification dimensions of usual quantity and frequency. Room (1990) offers a very comprehensive summary of the major quantity/frequency measures used in both research and clinical practice. The following instruments provide detailed information on consumption patterns; several also ask for information on antecedents, correlates, and consequences of these drinking patterns.

Daily drinking measure. The Alcohol Time-Line Follow-Back (TLFB, Sobell & Sobell, 1992) is a widely used consumption measure for evaluating specific changes in drinking before, during, and after treatment, when estimates need to be very precise. The TLFB can be administered as either a self-report paper-and-pencil instrument or as an interview. In either case, the client is asked: "What we would like you to do is recall your drinking for the past — days. We want you to get an idea of how much alcohol you consumed on each day during this time." The client is then presented with the past week's, month's, or year's calendar, depending on the time frame in question, and asked to fill in consumption data for every day. The client is asked to use his or her appointment book as a reference and to start the process with holidays and major family events, if the client finds it difficult to recall consumption. Extensive suggestions for the conduct of this interview are provided. The instrument is time-consuming to administer, but is said to provide valid information about consumption up to a year before the start of treatment, by day, week, and month (Sobell & Sobell, 1992). It is demanding for both the client and assessor to complete.

Drinking self-monitoring log. Daily monitoring of drinking behavior is appropriate when more accurate information about frequency of drinking is needed. It provides information about progress following treatment and can also be used to identify situations that represent high risk for relapse. If the client is not motivated to do the work required to self-monitor drinking on a daily basis, the resultant data will be unreliable (Sobell et al., 1994). However, self-monitoring of drinking behavior is time-consuming, some clients do not follow instructions, and many others are simply not motivated to undertake this assessment (Sanchez-Craig & Annis, 1982).

Lifetime drinking histories. These measures obtain information about lifetime or long-term alcohol consumption, generally representing a summary of more than a year's alcohol consumption. Data on lifetime drinking history are relevant when information over a longer assessment interval is needed, such as during the period from adolescence to adulthood. However, these measures generally do not yield accurate information about recent alcohol consumption since they cover such a span of time (Skinner & Sheu, 1982; Sobell et al., 1993).

The Chemical Dependency Assessment Profile (Harrell et al., 1991), a lengthy paper-and-pencil questionnaire, permits a comprehensive assessment of substance use history, patterns of use, client's self-concept, and interpersonal relations. In addition, it gives information about quantity and frequency of use, physiological consequences, situational stresses, antisocial behavior, interpersonal skills, affective dysfunction, attitudes toward treatment, and degree of impact the substance abuse has had on the client's life.

The Comprehensive Drinker Profile (CDP, Miller & Marlatt, 1984b) is a widely used structured intake interview of eighty-eight items. It can be administered by either an experienced clinician or a trained technician. The interview provides data on the quantity and frequency of alcohol and drug use, symptoms and consequences of alcohol use and abuse, other life problems, medical and family history, and motivation for treatment. The CDP incorporates the MAST (Selzer, 1971). The CDP is also available in a short version and has a follow-up form, Follow-up Drinker Profile (Miller & Marlatt, 1984a).

The Computerized Lifestyle Assessment incorporates brief versions of the Family Assessment Measure, the Alcohol Dependency Scale (ADS, Skinner & Allen, 1982), and the Drug Abuse Screening Test (DAST, Skinner, 1982). Consisting of 350 items and twenty subscales, the CLA examines a broad range of lifestyle activities, provides graphic feedback during the assessment situation, and generates a profile of lifestyle strengths, concerns, and risks. An additional virtue of its incorporation in the routine intake assessment is that it is computerized and requires minimum administration time.

Assessment in the Treatment Planning Process

Assessment of alcohol-related disorders is also meant, of course, to aid in treatment planning and to help predict treatment outcome. A number of methods, including those listed below, have been developed for these purposes; some are questionnaires and others are interview guides.

MOTIVATIONAL READINESS TO CHANGE MODEL

This model for motivational readiness for change was originally developed from observations of smoking cessation and later applied to other addictive behaviors (Prochaska et al., 1986; Prochaska et al., 1992). The "stages of change" model describes six possible stages of change in a problem behavior. The first, precontemplation, describes a person who does not see the behavior as a problem and, accordingly, does not want to change it. Contemplation, the second stage, involves initial realization that the behavior may be causing problems. In the third stage, preparation/determination, the person has begun to consider options for change and may actually have begun to make preparations to change. In the fourth stage, action, the person has begun to take concrete steps to change the problem behavior in specific ways. During maintenance, the fifth stage, the person strives to avoid relapse back into the problem behavior; he or she may take specific precautions to avoid relapse. The final stage in this model is relapse, during which the client may slip back into problematic use or abuse of alcohol. Of course, relapse into problem use of alcohol can occur during any of the previously mentioned stages. The assumption is that by reducing the extent of the relapse, the client can learn from the experience and reenter the stage in which the relapse occurred by continuing to deal with the problem behaviors. The assessment tools and interview guides mentioned below are designed both to reflect the stage of change the client is in and to guide the clinician in treatment planning.

The Readiness to Change Questionnaire (RTCQ, Rollnick et al., 1992) is a paper-and-pencil test that takes only a few minutes to complete and is appropriate for both adolescents and adults. It consists of twelve items; when scored, results are displayed on three subscales (Heather et al., 1991). Clients are asked to grade their responses on a five-point Likert-type scale; sample items include:

- I do not drink too much.
- It is a waste of time to think about my drinking.
- My drinking is a problem sometimes.

RTCQ responses provide information on the drinker's readiness to change drinking behaviors, specifically, on the stage of change the client is in at the time of the assessment.

The University of Rhode Island Change Assessment (URICA, McConnaughy et al., 1983) was developed specifically to evaluate the change process in therapy. It has been used for this purpose for treatment of smoking

(DiClemente et al., 1991). The scale includes twenty-eight items, each assessed on a five-point Likert-type scale, and seven subscales (DiClemente & Hughes, 1990).

Stages of Change Readiness and Treatment Eagerness (SOCRATES, Miller et al., 1990; Miller & Tonigan, 1994) was developed to assess stage of readiness to change within the framework of Prochaska and DiClemente's model of change (1986). It consists of two versions, one with twenty items and the other with forty items. SOCRATES also asks clients to respond on a five-point Likert-type scale. A factorial analysis of the instrument yielded three empirically derived scales: readiness for change, taking steps for change, and contemplation (Miller & Tonigan, 1994).

ALCOHOL-RELATED EXPECTANCIES AND REASONS FOR DRINKING

Cognitive factors in both decisions to drink and drinkers' responses to drinking situations (Goldman et al., 1987) may play a role in both drinking pattern and relapse. Alcohol-related expectancies refer to the beliefs and cognitive representations held by the individual concerning the anticipated effects of alcohol consumption.

The Alcohol Expectancy Questionnaire (AEQ) is the most widely used instrument to assess alcohol expectancies. The adult version (Brown et al., 1987) consists of 120 self-reported items; the adolescent version (cited in Miller et al., 1995) includes 90 items. Both versions possess high levels of internal consistency and test-retest reliability. The client is asked to respond to each item with either agreement or disagreement. The very extensive research done on alcohol expectancies over the past two decades suggests AEQ predicts drinking pattern as well as response to treatment (Sher et al., 1996; Smith et al., 1995). Examples of items from the adult version are:

- Alcohol can transform my personality.
- Alcohol lets my fantasies flow easily.
- If I am nervous about having sex, alcohol makes me feel better.
- Alcohol makes women more sensuous.
- Drinking makes the future seem brighter.
- Alcohol makes me more tolerant of people I do not enjoy.

The Alcohol Expectancy Questionnaire (AEFQ, Brown et al., 1987), a related expectancy measure by the same research group, assesses both desirable and undesirable effects of alcohol (impairment and irresponsibility) as well as positive reinforcement effects (beliefs about the effects of alcohol on oneself). Eight alcohol effect subscales were developed from the items of the questionnaire, including positive, social, and physical pleasure, sexual enhancement, power and aggression, social expressiveness, relaxation and tension reduction, cognitive and physical impairment, and careless unconcern. The instrument is normed on students and alcoholics. Sample items include:

- Drinking makes me feel flushed.
- I am more romantic when I drink.
- Drinking makes me feel good.
- I am a better lover after a few drinks.

The Drinking Expectancy Questionnaire (DEQ, Young & Knoght, 1989) assesses the positive expectancies an adult person might hold about the effects of alcohol. Consisting of forty-three items and six subscales, it is a self-administered pencil-and-paper test that takes about fifteen minutes to complete. Clients can score the instrument themselves. Sample items include:

- I get better ideas when I am drinking.
- I get more self-confidence when drinking.
- Alcohol makes me more sexually responsive.
- I am less concerned about my actions when I'm drinking.

The Alcohol Beliefs Scale (ABS, Connors & Maisto, 1988) is a paper-and-pencil test that assesses beliefs about the effects of three levels of alcohol consumption on behaviors and feelings. The instrument also assesses the ability of these levels of consumption to produce desired behavioral or emotional outcomes. The instrument, which includes forty-eight items and seven subscales, has been used with problem drinkers as well as clients in treatment.

MOTIVATIONAL MODELS

Motivational models posit that people drink excessively because of the purpose and function of alcohol in their lives. The common pathway toward alcoholism is seen as motivational, even though biological, psychological, and social factors are also assumed to influence abusive drinking.

The Motivational Structure Questionnaire (MSQ, Klinger & Cox, 1986) is a self-administered semistructured questionnaire that requires about two hours to complete. Clients are asked to identify general and specific concerns in major life areas, including interests, activities, goals, joys, disappointments, hopes, and fears. A motivational profile is then generated that is supposed to reveal the significant features of the individual's motivational structure and identify problematic motivational patterns. This profile can in turn be used as a tool in treatment planning.

The Inventory of Drinking Situations (IDS, Annis, 1982; Annis et al., 1987) has two versions: IDS-100 and IDS-42. Both are paper-and-pencil, self-report questionnaires designed to reflect heavy drinking situations over the past year. Eight general categories of drinking situations are assessed based on Marlatt's relapse classification system (Marlatt & Gordon, 1985): unpleasant emotions, physical discomfort, pleasant emotions, testing personal control, urges and temptations to drink, conflicts with others, social pressure to drink, and pleasant times with others. The questionnaire attempts to determine the relative cue strength for drinking in each situation—essentially, the extent to which each situation represents a risk for relapse. While the IDS has demonstrated adequate reliability, factor analysis at the item level has failed to support the existence of eight rationally derived factors.

The Situational Confidence Scale (SCQ, Annis, 1982; Annis & Graham, 1988) is a thirty-nine-item self-report questionnaire that attempts to determine a client's current level of confidence in his or her ability to encounter a range of high-risk situations without drinking. The instrument has been used to monitor the development of self-efficacy for coping with different risk situations. Because the instrument is not appropriate for use in abstinence-focused treatment centers, DiClemente and his colleagues developed the Alcohol Abstinence Self-Efficacy Scale (AASE), composed initially of forty-nine items and subsequently shortened to twenty items (DiClemente et al., 1994). The AASE assesses the client's confidence that he or she will be able to abstain from alcohol in a wide range of high-risk situations. The questionnaire has been used to evaluate treatment progress and outcome, since it reflects both temptation to drink and confidence in remaining abstinent.

PERCEIVED LOCUS OF CONTROL OF DRINKING BEHAVIOR

The concept of locus of control, originally developed by Rotter (1966), refers to the belief that important life events are either under personal control (internal locus of control) or under the influence of fate, chance, or the powers of others (external locus of control). Rotter (1966) suggested that the predictive utility of this construct was increased by using measures directly related to the behavior under consideration, which in this case is problem drinking.

The Drinking Related Locus of Control Scale (DRIE, Koski-Jannes, 1994; Lettieri et al., 1985) was developed to assess the person's perception of control with respect to alcohol, drinking behavior, and recovery. The DRIE is a twenty-five-item paper-and-pencil self-report questionnaire with three subscales that uses a forced choice format; it takes about ten minutes to complete. The measure shows high reliability, has empirically defined factors, including intrapersonal factors and general factors associated with drinking, and has shown the capacity to differentiate between alcohol–dependent and nondependent drinkers (Donovan, 1995). The questionnaire can be used to assess perception of personal control over alcohol and abusive drinking behaviors and recovery from them. The client is asked to choose between two alternative questions for each item. Examples include:

- One of the major reasons why people drink is because they cannot handle their problems, or People drink because circumstances force them to.
- Without the right breaks one cannot stay sober.
- Alcoholics who are not successful in curbing their drinking often have not taken advantage of help that is available.

FAMILY HISTORY OF ALCOHOL PROBLEMS

Clinicians and researchers agree that, in addition to assessing factors that are relatively proximal to relapse episodes, a comprehensive assessment should also tap factors in the abuser's life that are distal, including family history of alcoholism. These predisposing factors have been shown to impact on involvement with alcohol, patterns of drinking, and potential for relapse (Cadoret, 1990; Lawson & Lawson, 1998). Information on family history has usually been determined from self-report, retrospective data. Some questionnaires, such as the CDP (Miller & Marlatt, 1984b), also include questions about family history of alcoholism. A number of instruments have been developed specifically to assess family history of alcoholism.

The Family Tree Questionnaire (FTQ, Mann et al., 1985) was developed specifically to assess family history of alcohol problems. It is easy and quick to administer. The client is given a family tree that includes siblings, parents, and grandparents. He or she is then to categorize family members into four categories: (1) never drank, (2) social drinker, (3) possible problem drinker, and (4) definitely a problem drinker. The measure has shown high validity and reliability and has proven useful in determining the extent of a client's family history of alcohol-related problems.

The Adapted Short Michigan Alcoholism Screening Test for Fathers (F-SMAST) and the Adapted Short Michigan Alcoholism Screening Test for Mothers (M-SMAST) were developed by Crews and Sher. Their target population is adults and adolescents. Separate forms are provided for mothers and fathers. Each form consists of thirteen items and has a dichotomous response format; the items describe alcohol-related consequences that father or mother might have experienced. In addition, the client is asked to make a global judgment about whether or not his or her mother or father was/is an alcoholic. Both forms show a relatively high level of reliability and internal consistency.

SOCIAL SUPPORT

Social support is important for recovery from alcoholism. Feeling supported by friends, family, and coworkers may moderate the relationship between a positive family history of alcoholism and the development of alcohol problems (Ohannessian & Hesselbrock, 1993). Longabaugh and colleagues (1993) developed several measures designed to assess different areas of alcohol-specific social support, by separately exploring the support persons feel in their workplace, support from their family and support from friends. These scales have been shown to have predictive validity for success in treatment eighteen months after discharge from treatment (Longabaugh et al., 1993).

Your Workplace (YWP, Beattie et al., 1993) is a thirteen-item measure that can either be given as a self-administered questionnaire or as an interview. The instrument has three subscales: adverse effects of drinking on work performance, cues and support for consumption, and support for abstinence. The second and third subscales have been found to be related, respectively, to higher and lower levels of consumption at seven- to twelve-month follow-ups.

Important People and Activities (IPA) is an interview-administered instrument developed by Beattie et al. (1993) to reflect support from family, friends, and people with whom the client may have frequent interactions. The client is asked to rate how important presumably significant people in the person's environment are to him or her, how much he or she likes these individuals, and how they respond both to the client's abstinence and drinking. The instrument is designed to assess attitudinal and behavioral support from members of the social network for drinking, lack of sanctions against drinking, and attitudinal and behavioral support for abstinence (Beattie et al., 1993).

The Significant Other Behavior Questionnaire (SBQ, Love et al., 1993) was developed to evaluate responses by a significant other to drinking and abstinence by an alcohol-involved person. This twenty-four-item questionnaire requires the client to rate the likelihood that a significant other would respond each of a number of ways to the client's drinking behaviors on a five-point Likert-type scale. Four factors have been identified in the SBQ: the client's perception of the likelihood that the significant other will punish drinking, support sobriety, support drinking, and withdraw from the client when he or she is drinking. This questionnaire has two versions, one that reflects the client's perceptions and another that reflects the perceptions of significant others.

MULTIDIMENSIONAL ASSESSMENT

Drinking behavior and alcohol problems are multidimensional. For this reason, they warrant comprehensive biopsychosocial evaluation (Adesso, 1995; Grant & Dawson, 1999). Two semistructured interviews are often used for this purpose.

The most widely used of these interviews is the Addiction Severity Index (ASI, McLellan et al., 1980; 1992). Many states have adopted this semistructured questionnaire as the basic instrument for the assessment of all substance-abusing clients. ASI items (approximately 200) address seven rationally developed potential problem areas for substance abusers: medical status, employment status and support, drug use, alcohol use, legal status, family/social status, and psychiatric status. Factor analysis has revealed four independent empirically derived factors: chemical dependence, criminality, psychological distress, and health-related problems (Rogalski, 1987). The ASI has been normed for a number of treatment groups, including women, men, pregnant substance users, substance abusers with co-occurring disorders, gamblers, homeless persons, probationers, and alcohol, cocaine, and opiate abusers (Hodgins & El-Ghubaly, 1992; McLellan et al., 1992). The ASI is lengthy, and training in its administration is required so that it is used in a standardized way. The ASI yields two scores: a substance abuse severity rating—and related subjective evaluation of the need for treatment—and a composite score that gives a more objective portrayal of problem severity during the thirty days preceding the interview. The ASI and its subscales have achieved a high degree of concurrent validity.

The Alcohol Use Inventory (AUI, Horn et al., 1987; Wanberg et al., 1977) has been validated on large samples of alcoholics admitted to substance abuse treatment centers, on both genders, and on several different ethnic groups. It consists of 228 items and has multiple alternative items; when scored, the items contribute to a set of twenty-four scales. The twenty-four scales are intended to serve as operational indicators of constructs from a multiple condition theory about how people differ in their perceptions of the consequences of alcohol dependence, how they deal with their alcohol problems, how they express their different drinking styles, and how they perceive the advantages of their drinking. The AUI can be administered either as a self-report questionnaire or on a computer. It was developed primarily as a research instrument, but is now used widely in clinical settings. It is often used to make decisions about most appropriate treatment modality.

DIFFERENTIAL TREATMENT PLACEMENT

Client-treatment matching involves attempts to place clients in the treatment modalities most appropriate for their needs. While the results of Project MATCH (Project MATCH Research Group, 1997) failed to support the validity of patient-treatment matching, attempts to do so continue. Project MATCH findings notwithstanding, it is widely believed that treatments vary on dimensions that ought to be considered when assigning clients to treatment (Institute of Medicine, 1990). The treatment dimensions on which clients are often matched include treatment setting (inpatient, residential, outpatient), treatment intensity, specific treatment modality, and degree of structure in the treatment.

The American Society of Addictive Medicine (ASAM) has established a set of rationally developed criteria for the administration, placement, discharge, and transfer of individuals with alcohol problems at different levels of care (Hoffman et al., 1991). The ASAM criteria are based on an assessment of six general problem areas: (1) acute intoxication or withdrawal; (2) biomedical conditions and complications; (3) emotional and behavioral conditions or complications; (4) treatment acceptance or resistance; (5) relapse potential; and 6) recovery environment. Based on this assessment, one of four levels of care is selected as most appropriate: (1) outpatient treatment of less than nine hours a week; (2) intensive outpatient or partial hospitalization for a minimum of nine hours per week; (3) medically monitored intensive inpatient treatment; and (4) medically managed inpatient treatment (Finney & Moos, 2002).

Even though clinicians have long considered patient-treatment matching an ethical and clinical imperative, there is relatively little empirical support for the practice (Finney & Moos, 2002). Besides the failure of Project MATCH to confirm a series of patient-treatment matches (Project MATCH Research Group, 1997), Rychtarik and his colleagues (2000) failed to find any support for the clinical assumption that clients who come from an environment with excessive drinking would profit more from being treated in an inpatient treatment setting (because of the structure and protection such environments typically provide) than an outpatient treatment program. Thus, while the ASAM criteria are widely used, there are minimal data to support the reliability and validity of assessment instruments based on these criteria. Nonetheless, the instruments can also be used as tools to observe and categorize clients after an intake interview. Two complementary instruments, one administered as an interview and the other as a self-report questionnaire, have been developed to provide a standardized assessment of the dimensions included in the ASAM criteria. Recovery Attitude and Treatment Evaluator–Clinical Evaluator (RAATE-CE) and Recovery Attitude and Treatment Evaluator–Questionnaire I (RAATE-QI) were developed to help place clients into the correct level of care at admission, to make continued stay and transfer decisions during treatment, and to document the appropriateness of discharge.

The RAATE-CE (Mee-Lee, 1988; Smith et al., 1992) is a thirty-five–item structured clinical interview designed to be administered by a trained technician or counselor. The instrument incorporates five scales. They measure constructs of resistance to treatment, resistance to continued care, severity of biomedical problems, severity of psychiatric/psychological problems, and social and environmental support. By interviewing clients regularly with the RAATE-CE, clinicians can monitor changes in their responses to these constructs as a function of treatment. The lowest level of the interview's interrater reliability was found to be associated with the severity of psychiatric problems scale, while the biomedical acuity scale showed the highest interrater reliability (Smith et al., 1992).

The *RAATE-QI* (Smith et al., 1995) is a ninety-four-item true-false, self-report questionnaire. It is intended to confirm findings from the RAATE-CE from the client's point of view. The instrument's test-retest reliability ranged from .73 to .83, and its internal consistency ranged from .63 to .78 (Donovan, 1995; McKay et al., 1992; Smith et al., 1995). Since both the RAATE-CE and the RAATE-QI are intended to be compatible with the ASAM criteria, a conversion table is available to translate the clients' severity scores to ASAM criteria.

MMPI AND MMPI-2

The Minnesota Multiphasic Personality Inventory (Hathaway & McKinley, 1983) and the MMPI-2 (Butcher et al., 1989; Butcher et al., 1990; Graham, 1993) have been used extensively to study a variety of disorders, including substance dependence. The MMPI-2, a revision of the MMPI, consists of 567 true-false items. The MMPI first appeared in 1943 (Hathaway & McKinley, 1943); it contained three validity scales and ten basic scales. The MMPI was normed on Minnesota residents who were relatives of and visitors to patients at the University of Minnesota Hospitals, as well as on a clinical sample of psychiatric patients (Graham, 1993). The MMPI has also been normed in a variety of countries (Butcher & Pancheri, 1976), as well as for several different ethnic groups in the United States (Butcher et al., 1983). The MMPI and MMPI-2 have been used for many purposes, including as clinical tools for evaluation of psychopathology and treatment planning (Butcher, 1990), as well as for personnel screening (Butcher, 1988).

A characteristic MMPI pattern for alcoholics is a profile with a primary elevation on scale 4 (psychopathy) and secondary elevations on scale 2 (depression) and scale 7 (psychasthenia) (Owen & Butcher, 1979; Skinstad, 1994). The MacAndrew Alcoholism Scale (MAC) of the MMPI (MacAndrew, 1965; Allen, 1991) was developed specifically to differentiate alcoholics from psychiatric patients. The MAC scale includes forty-nine items keyed in the direction selected most often by alcoholics. The major content dimensions of the MAC scale are cognitive impairment, school maladjustment, interpersonal competence, risk taking, extroversion and exhibitionism, and moral indignation (Schwarz & Graham, 1979). Although the scale has recently been revised, neither its internal consistency nor its test–retest reliability is particularly high (Graham, 1993).

The revised MMPI-2 (Butcher et al., 1989; Butcher et al., 1990; Graham, 1993) includes two new scales that are directly relevant to addiction and alcoholism. The Addiction Admission Scale (AAS, Greene et al., 1992; Weed et al., 1992) is a thirteen-item scale that includes such items as "I have a drug or alcohol problem" and "I can express my true feeling only when I drink." The scale discriminates between normal and substance abusing subjects much better than the MacAndrew Alcoholism Scale-Revised (MAC-R) (Butcher et al., 1989; Levitt et al., 1992). The Addiction Potential Scale (APS, Svanum et al., 1994; Weed et al., 1992) is a thirty-nine-item scale that includes quite heterogeneous items without obvious relevance to substance use and abuse; nonetheless, the scale covaries considerably with the AAS. Items have to do with extroversion, excitement seeking, and risk taking, as well as self-doubts, self-alienation, and cynical attitudes about other people. The APS discriminates well between normal and substance-abusing samples, as well as between substance abuse and psychiatric samples (Greene et al., 1992).

ASSESSMENT OF COGNITIVE FUNCTIONING

Substance abusers, especially chronic substance abusers, are at risk for cognitive impairment. As a consequence, neuropsychological assessment ought to be a component of the personal assessment for comprehensive treatment planning. Psychologists who wish to evaluate the cognitive functioning of an alcohol abuser can choose among a number of methods; all, however, require prior training and experience. If the psychologist does not possess this training and experience, he or she may wish to refer the client to a neuropsychologist experienced in the evaluation of cognitive dysfunction as a function of long-term alcohol abuse.

The most widely used of these neuropsychological instruments, the Halstead-Reitan Neuropsychological Battery (Davison, 1974; Parsons, 1987), contains subtests that are sensitive to cognitive impairment in chronic substance abusers, prominently including the Category Test (which taps abstraction and problem-solving abilities) and Tactual Performance (which reflects perceptual-motor deficits). A neuropsychologist might also choose to use subtests of the WAIS to look for patterns of intellectual impairment as a result of long-term alcoholism. Subtests that assess memory, abstract reasoning, attention and concentration span, cognitive flexibility, and nonverbal and subtle verbal memory functions (Parsons, 1987; Ryan & Butters, 1983) are often impaired by chronic alcoholism. The Digit Symbol and Block Design subtests of the WAIS have shown serious impairment after long-term drinking (Donovan et al., 1987). The Shipley-Hartford Vocabulary Test, the Shipley-Hartford Abstraction test, the Trail-Making Test (Form A and Form B), and the Symbol Digit Modality Test, are included in the MET assessment of neuropsychological impairment (Miller et al., 1994).

CONCLUSION

When assessing clients who may suffer from alcohol abuse or dependence, a number of decisions have to be made. First, the purposes of the assessment must be determined. That determination will, in part, then determine the necessary extent of the assessment. Specifically, a decision should be made on whether screening for possible alcohol abuse or dependence will be sufficient or more extensive assessments, either problem assessment or extensive personal assessment, should be undertaken. When the extent of the assessment has been decided upon, a decision on whether to use a standardized assessment instrument should be made. If the decision is to do so, the instrument or instruments that best fit the purpose of the assessment must be chosen. In this context, thorough understanding of the purpose, utility, and psychometric properties of available assessment instruments is a necessity. Also, a number of the instruments described in this chapter require additional training, which must also be considered in making these decisions.

REFERENCES

Adesso, V. J. (1995). Cognitive factors in alcohol and drug use. In *Determinants of Substance Abuse: Biological, Psychological, and Environmental Factors*, ed. M. Galizio & S. A. Maisto, pp. 179–208. New York: Plenum.

Allen, J. P. (1991). Personality correlates of the MacAndrew Scale: A review of the literature. *Psychology of Addictive Behaviors* 5:59–65.

Allen, J. P., Columbus, M., & Fertig, J. B. (1995). Assessment in alcoholism treatment: An overview. In *Assessing Alcohol Problems: A Guide for Clinicians and Researchers*, ed. J. P. Allen & M. Columbus. Treatment Handbook Series no. 4, NIH Publication no. 95-3745. Washington, DC.: National Institute on Alcohol Abuse and Alcoholism.

American Psychiatric Association. (1952). *Diagnostic and Statistical Manual of Mental Disorders*, 1st ed. Washington, DC: American Psychiatric Association.

American Psychiatric Association. (1968). *Diagnostic and Statistical Manual of Mental Disorders*, 2nd ed. Washington, DC: American Psychiatric Association.

American Psychiatric Association. (1980). *Diagnostic and Statistical Manual of Mental Disorders*, 3rd ed. Washington, DC: American Psychiatric Association.

American Psychiatric Association. (1987). *Diagnostic and Statistical Manual of Mental Disorders*, 3rd ed. (revised). Washington, DC: American Psychiatric Association.

American Psychiatric Association. (1994). *Diagnostic and Statistical Manual of Mental Disorders*, 4th ed. Washington, DC: American Psychiatric Association.

American Psychiatric Association. (2000). *Diagnostic and Statistical Manual of Mental Disorders*, 4th ed., text revised. Washington, DC: American Psychiatric Association.

Annis, H. M. (1982). *Inventory of Drinking Situations*. Toronto: Addiction Research Foundation.

Annis, H. M., & Graham, J. M. (1988). *Situational Confidence Questionnaire User Guide*. Toronto: Addiction Research Foundation.

Annis, H. M., Graham, J. M., & David, C. S. (1987). *Inventory of Drinking Situations (IDS) Users Guide*. Toronto: Addiction Research Foundation.

Barnes, G. E. (1979). The alcoholic personality. A reanalysis of the literature. *Journal of Studies on Alcohol* 40:570–634.

Beattie, M., Longabaugh, R., Elliot, G., Strout, R. L., Fava, J., & Noel, N. E. (1993). Effect of the social environment on alcohol involvement and subjective well-being prior to alcoholism treatment. *Journal of Studies on Alcohol* 54:283–296.

Brown, L. S., Alterman, A. I., Rutherford, M. J., Cacciola, J. S., & Zaballero, A. R. (1993). Addiction Severity Index scores of four racial/ethnic and gender groups of methadone maintenance patients. *Journal of Substance Abuse* 5:269–279.

Brown, S. A., Christiansen, B. A., & Goldman, M. S. (1987). The Alcohol Expectancy Questionnaire: An instrument for the assessment of adolescent and adult expectancies. *Journal of Studies on Alcohol* 48:483–491.

Butcher, J. N. (March, 1988). Use of MMPI in personnel screening. Paper presented at the 23rd Annual Symposium on Recent Developments in the Use of the MMPI. St. Petersburg Beach, FL.

Butcher, J. N. (1990). *MMPI-2 in Psychological Treatment.* New York: Oxford University Press.

Butcher, J. N., Braswell, L., & Raney, D. (1983). A cross-cultural comparison of American Indian, black, and white inpatients on the MMPI and presenting symptoms. *Journal of Consulting and Clinical Psychology* 51:587–594.

Butcher, J. N., Dahlstrom, W. G., Graham, J. R., Tellegen, A., & Kaemmer, B. (1989). *Minnesota Multiphasic Personality Inventory–2 (MMPI): Manual for Administration and Scoring.* Minneapolis: University of Minnesota Press.

Butcher, J. N., Graham, J. R., Williams, C. L., & Ben-Porath, Y. S. (1990). *Development and Use of the MMPI Content Scales.* Minneapolis: University of Minnesota Press.

Butcher, J. N., & Pancheri, P. (1976). *A Handbook of Cross-national MMPI Research.* Minneapolis: University of Minnesota Press.

Cadoret, R. J. (1990). Genetics of alcoholism. In *Alcoholism and the Family: Research and Clinical Perspectives*, ed. R. L. Collins, K. E. Leonard, J. S. Searles, pp. 39–78. New York: Guilford.

Caetano, R. (1985). Two versions of dependence: DSM-III and the Alcohol Dependence Syndrome. *Drug and Alcohol Dependence* 15:81–103.

Carroll, K. M. (1999). Behavioral and cognitive behavioral treatments. In *Addictions: A Comprehensive Guidebook*, ed. B. S. McCrady, & E. E. Epstein, pp. 250–267. New York: Oxford University Press.

Center for Substance Abuse Treatment. (1998). *Substance Use Disorder Treatment for People with Physical and Cognitive Disabilities.* Treatment Improvement Protocol (TIP) Series, No. 29. DHHS Pub. No. (SMA) 98. Washington, DC: U.S. Government Printing Office.

Cocco, K. M., & Carey, K. B. (1998). Psychometric properties of the Drug Abuse Screening Test in psychiatric outpatients. *Psychological Assessment* 10:408–414.

Collins, R. L. (2000). Electronic diary for drinking assessment. Symposium paper at the Annual Convention of the American Psychological Association.

Columbus, M., & Allen, J. P. (1995). Introduction to assessing alcohol problems. In *Assessing Alcohol Problems: A Guide for Clinicians and Researchers*, ed. J. P. Allen & M. Columbus. NIH Publication No. 95-3745. Washington DC: National Institute on Alcohol Abuse and Alcoholism.

Connors, G. J., & Maisto, S. A. (1988). The Alcohol Belief Scale. In *Dictionary of Behavioral Assessment Techniques*, ed. M. Hersen & A. S. Bellack, pp. 24–26. New York: Pergamon.

Davison, L. A. (1974). Current status of clinical neuropsychology. In *Clinical Neuropsychology: Current Status and Applications*, ed. R. M. Reitan & L. A. Davison, pp. 325–363. New York: Wiley & Sons.

DiClemente, C. C., Carbonari, J. P., Montgomery, R. P. G., & Hughes, S. O. (1994). The Alcohol Abstinence Self-Efficacy Scale. *Journal of Studies on Alcohol* 55:141–148.

DiClemente, C. C., & Hughes, S. O. (1990). Stages of change profiles in outpatient alcoholism treatment. *Journal of Substance Abuse* 2:217–235.

DiClemente, C. C., Prochaska, J. O., Fairhurst, S. K., Velicer, W. F., Velasquez, M. M., & Rossi, J. S. (1991). The process of smoking cessation: An analysis of precontemplation, contemplation, and preparation stages of change. *Journal of Consulting and Clinical Psychology* 59:295–304.

Donovan, D. M. (1995). Assessment to aid in the treatment planning process. In *Assessing Alcohol Problems: A Guide for Clinicians and Researchers*, ed. A. P. Allen & M. Columbus, pp. 75–122. Treatment Handbook Series 4, NIH Publication No. 95-3745. Washington DC: National Institute on Alcohol Abuse and Alcoholism.

Donovan, D. M. (1999). Assessment strategies and measures in addictive behaviors. In *Addictions: A Comprehensive Guidebook*, ed. B. S. McCrady & E. E. Epstein, pp. 189–215. New York: Oxford University Press.

Donovan, D. M., & Marlatt, G. A. (1988). *Assessment of Addictive Behaviors*. New York: Guilford.

Donovan, D. M., Walker, R. D., & Kivlahan, D. R. (1987). Recovery and remediation of neuropsychological functions: Implications for alcoholism rehabilitation process and outcome. In *Neuropsychology of Alcoholism: Implications for Diagnosis and Treatment*, ed. O. A. Parsons, N. Butters, & P. E. Nathan, pp. 339–360. New York: Guilford.

Exner, J., Jr. (2000). *2000 Alumni Newsletter from the Rorschach Workshops*. Asheville, NC: Rorschach Workshops.

Finney, J. W., & Moos, R. H. (2002). Psychosocial treatments for alcohol use disorders. In *A Guide to Treatments That Work*, 2nd ed., ed. P. E. Nathan & J. M. Gorman, pp. 157–168. New York: Oxford University Press.

Goldman, M. S., Brown, S. A., & Christiansen, B. A. (1987). Expectancy theory: Thinking about drinking. In *Psychological Theories of Drinking and Alcoholism*, ed. H. T. Blane & K. E. Leonard, pp. 181–226. New York: Guilford.

Gomberg, E. S. L. (1999). Women. In *Addictions: A Comprehensive Guidebook*, ed. B. S. McCrady & E. E. Epstein, pp. 527–541. New York: Oxford University Press.

Graham, J. R. (1993). *MMPI-2: Assessing Personality and Psychopathology*, 2nd ed. New York: Oxford University Press.

Grant, B. F., & Dawson, D. A. (1999). Alcohol and drug use, abuse and dependence: Classification, prevalence, and comorbidity. In *Addictions: A Comprehensive Guidebook*, ed. B. S. McCrady & E. E. Epstein, pp. 9–29. New York: Oxford University Press.

Greene, R. C., Weed, N., Butcher, J. S., Arredondo, R., & Davis, H. (1992). A cross-validation of MMPI-2 substance abuse scales. *Journal of Personality Assessment* 58:405–410.

Harrell, T. H., Honsker, L. M., & Davis, E. (1991). Cognitive and behavioral dimensions of dysfunction in alcohol and poly-drug abusers. *Journal of Substance Abuse* 3:415–426.

Hathaway, S. R., & McKinley, J. C. (1943). *The Minnesota Multiphasic Personality Inventory Manual*. New York: Psychological Corporation.

Heather, N., Gold, R., & Rollnick, S. (1991). *Readiness to Change Questionnaire: User's Manual*. Technical Report 15. Kensington, Australia: National Drug and Alcohol Research Center, University of New South Wales.

Hill, S. Y. (1995). Vulnerability of alcoholism in women: Genetic and cultural factors. In *Recent Developments in Alcoholism: Volume 12, Alcoholism in Women*, ed. M. Galanter, pp. 9–28. New York: Plenum.

Hodgins, D. C., & El-Ghubaly, G. N. (1992). More data on the Addiction Severity Index: Reliability and validity with mentally ill substance abusers. *Journal of Nervous and Mental Disease* 180:187–201.

Hoffman, N. G., Halikas, J. A., Mee-Lee, D., & Weedman, R. D. (1991). *Patient Placement Criteria for the Treatment of Psychoactive Substance Use Disorders*. Washington, DC: American Society of Addictive Medicine.

Horn, J. L., Wanberg, K. W., & Foster, F. M. (1987). *Guide to the Alcohol Use Inventory*. Minneapolis: National Computer Systems.

Huff, R. M. (1999). Cross-cultural concepts of health and disease. In *Promoting Health in Multicultural Populations: A Handbook for Practitioners*, ed. R. M. Huff, & M. V. Kline, pp. 23–40. Thousand Oaks, CA: Sage.

Institute of Medicine (1990). *Broadening the Base of Treatment for Alcohol Problems*. Washington, DC.: National Academy Press.

Jellinek, E. M. (1960). *The Disease Concept of Alcoholism*. New Haven, CT: College and University Press.

Klinger, E., & Cox, W. M. (1986). Motivational predictors of alcoholics' responses to inpatient treatment. *Advances in Alcohol and Substance Abuse* 6:35–44.

Koski-Jannes, A. (1994). Drinking-related locus of control as a predictor after treatment. Addictive Behavior, 19m, 491–491.

Lawson, A., & Lawson, G. (1998). *Alcoholism and the Family: A Guide to Treatment and Prevention*, 2nd ed. Gaithersburg, MD: Aspen.

Lettieri, D. J., Nelson, J. E., & Sayers, M. A. (1985). *Alcoholism Treatment Assessment Research Instruments*. Treatment Handbook Series no. 2, DHHS Publication no. (85–1380). Washington, DC: U.S. Government Printing Office.

Levitt, E. E., Browning, J. M., & Freeland, L. J. (1992). The effect of MMPI-2 on the scoring of special scales derived from MMPI-1. *Journal of Personality Assessment* 59:22–31.

Longabaugh, R., Beattie, M., Noel, N., Stout, R., & Malloy, P. (1993). The effect of social investment on treatment outcome. *Journal of Studies on Alcohol* 54:465–478.

Love, C. T., Longabaugh, R., Clifford, P. B., Beattie, M., & Peaslee, C. F. (1993). The significant-other behavior questionnaire (SBQ). An instrument for measuring the behavior of significant others toward a person's drinking and abstinence. *Addiction* 88:1267–1279.

MacAndrew, C. (1965). The differentiation of male alcoholic outpatients from nonalcoholic psychiatric outpatients by means of the MMPI. *Quarterly Journal of Studies on Alcohol* 26:238–246.

Maisto, S. A., & McKay, J. R. (1995). Diagnosis. In *Assessing Alcohol Problems: A Guide for Clinicians and Researchers*, ed. J. P. Allen & M. Columbus, pp. 41–54. NIH Publication No. 95–3745. Washington, DC: National Institute for Alcohol Abuse and Alcoholism.

Mann, R. E., Sobell, L. C., Sobell, M. B., & Pavan, D. (1985). Reliability of a family tree questionnaire for assessing family history of alcohol problems. *Drug and Alcohol Dependence* 15:61–67.

Marlatt, G. A., & Gordon, J. R., eds.) (1985). *Relapse Prevention: Maintenance Strategies in the Treatment of Addictive Behaviors*. New York: Guilford.

Mayer, J., & Filstead, W. J. (1979). The Adolescent Alcohol Involvement Scale: An instrument for measuring adolescents' use and misuse of alcohol. *Journal of Studies on Alcohol* 40:291–300.

McConnaughy, J. E., Prochaska, J. O., & Velicer, W. F. (1983). Stages of change in psychotherapy: Measurement and sample profiles. *Psychotherapy: Theory, Research and Practice* 20:368–375.

McCrady, B. S., & Raytek, H. (1996). Women and substance abuse: Treatment modalities and outcomes. In *Women and Substance Abuse*, ed. E. S. L. Gomberg & T. D. Nirenberg, pp. 314–338. Norwood, NJ: Ablex.

McKay, J. R., McLellan, A. T., & Alterman, A. I. (1992). An evaluation of the Cleveland Criteria for inpatient treatment of substance abuse. *American Journal of Psychiatry* 149:1212–1218.

McLellan, A. T., Kushner, H., Peters, F., Smith, I., Corse, S. J., & Alterman, A. I. (1992). The Addiction Severity Index ten years later. *Journal of Substance Abuse Treatment* 9:199–213.

McLellan, A. T., Luborsky, L., O'Brian, C. P., & Woody, G. E. (1980). An improved diagnostic instrument for substance abuse patients: The Addiction Severity Index. *Journal of Nervous and Mental Disorders* 168:26–33.

Mee-Lee, D. (1988). An instrument for treatment progress and matching: The Recovery Attitude and Treatment Evaluator (RAATE). *Journal of Substance Abuse Treatment* 5:183–186.

Miller W. R. (1991). *Motivational Inteviewing: Preparing People to Change Addictive Behavior.* New York: Guilford Press.

Miller, W. R., & Marlatt, G. A. (1984a). *Comprehensive Drinker Profile Manual Supplement for Use with Brief Drinker Profile: Follow-up Drinker Profile. Collateral Interview Form.* Odessa, FL: Psychological Assessment Resources.

Miller, W. R., & Marlatt, G. A. (1984b). *Manual for the Comprehensive Drinker Profile.* Odessa, FL: Psychological Assessment Resources.

Miller, W. R., & Rollnick, S. (1991). Using assessment results. In *Motivational Interviewing*, ed. W. B. Miller & S. Rollick, pp. 89–99. New York: Guilford.

Miller, W. R., & Tonigan, J. S. (1994). Assessing drinkers' motivation for change: The Stages of Change Readiness and Treatment Eagerness Scale (SOCRATES). Unpublished manuscript, Center on Alcoholism, Substance Abuse and Addictions, University of New Mexico, Albuquerque.

Miller, W. R., Tonigan, J. S., Montgomery, H. A., Abbott, P. J., Meyers, R. J., Hester, R. K., & Delaney, H. D. (1990). Assessment of client motivation for change: Preliminary validation of the SOCRATES instrument. Paper presented at the Annual meeting of the Association for the Advancement of Behavioral Therapy, San Francisco.

Miller, W. R., Westerberg, V. S., & Waldron, H. B. (1995). Evaluating alcohol problems in adults and adolescents. In *Handbook of Alcoholism Treatment Approaches*, ed. R. K. Hester & W. R. Miller, pp. 61–88. Boston: Allyn & Bacon.

Miller, W. R., Zweben, A., DiClemente, C. C., & Rychtarik, R. G. (1994). *Motivational Enhancement Therapy Manual: A Clinical Research Guide for Therapists Treating Individuals with Alcohol Abuse and Dependence.* NIH Publication No. 94–3723. Rockville, MD: National Institute on Alcohol Abuse and Alcoholism.

Mudd, S. A., Blow, F. C., Hill, E. M. Demo-Dananberg, L., Young, J. P., & Jacob, A. (1993). Differences in symptom reporting between older problem drinkers with and without a history of major depression. *Alcohol Clinical and Experimental Research*, 17, 489.

Nathan, P. E. (1988). The addictive personality is the behavior of the addict. *Journal of Consulting and Clinical Psychology* 56:183–188.

Nathan, P. E. (1992). Substance abuse disorders in the DSM-IV. *Journal of Abnormal Psychology* 100:356–361.

O'Farrell, T. J., & Fals-Stewart, W. (1999). Treatment models and methods: Family models. In *Addictions: A Comprehensive Guidebook*, ed. B. S. McCrady & E. E. Epstein, pp. 287–305. New York: Oxford University Press.

Ohannessian, C. M., & Hesselbrock, V. M. (1993). The influence of perceived social support on the relationship between family history of alcoholism and drinking behaviors. *Addiction* 88:1651–1658.

Owen, P., & Butcher, J. N. (1979). Personality factors in problem drinking: A review of the evidence and some suggested directions. In *Psychiatric Factors in Drug Abuse*, ed. R. Pickens, & L. Heston, pp. 67–91. New York: Grune & Stratton.

Parsons, O. A. (1987). Neuropsychological consequences of alcohol abuse: Many questions—Some answers. In *Neuropsychology of Alcoholism: Implications for Diagnosis and Treatment*, ed. O. A. Parsons, N. Butters, & P. E. Nathan, pp. 153–175. New York: Guilford.

Pearl, R. (1926). *Alcohol and Longevity*. New York: Knopf.

Pokorny, A. D., Miller, B. A., & Kaplan, H. B. (1972). The brief MAST: A shortened version of the Michigan Alcoholism Screening Test. *American Journal of Psychiatry* 129:342–345.

Prochaska, J. O., DiClemente, C. C., & Norcross, J. C. (1986). Towards a comprehensive model of change. In *Treating Addictive Behaviors: Process of Change*, ed. W. B. Miller, & N. Heather, pp. 3–27. New York: Plenum.

Prochaska, J. O., DiClemente, C. C., & Norcross, J. C. (1992). In search of how people change: Application to addictive behaviors. *American Psychologist*, 47, 1102–1114.

Project MATCH Research Group (1997). Matching alcohol treatment to client heterogeneity: Project MATCH post-treatment drinking outcomes. *Journal of Studies on Alcohol* 58:7–29.

Putnins, A. L. (1992). The Adolescent Alcohol Involvement Scale: Some findings with young offenders. *Drug and Alcohol Review* 11:253–258.

Robins, L. H., Helzer, J. E., Croughan, J., & Ratcliff, K. S. (1981). National Institute of Mental Health Diagnostic Interview Schedule: Its history, characteristics, and validity. *Archives of General Psychiatry* 38:381–389.

Rogalski, C. J. (1987). Factor structure of the Addiction Severity Index in an inpatient detoxification sample. *International Journal of Addictions* 22:981–992.

Rollnick, S., Heather, N., Gold, R., & Hall, W. (1992). Development of a short "readiness change" questionnaire for use in brief, opportunistic interventions among excessive disorders. *British Journal of Addiction*, 87, 743–754.

Room, R. (1990). Measuring alcohol consumption in the United States: Methods and rationales. In *Research Advances in Alcohol and Drug Problems*, Vol. 10, ed. L. T. Kozlowski, H. M. Annis, H. D. Cappell, F. B. Glaser, M. S. Goodstadt, Y. Israel, H. Kalant, E. M. Sellers, & E. R. Vingilis, pp. 39–80. New York: Plenum.

Rotter, J. B. (1966). Generalized expectancies for internal versus external locus of control of reinforcement. *Psychological Monographs* 80 (1, Whole No. 609):1– 28.

Rourke, S. B., & Løberg, T. (1996). The neurobehavioral correlates of alcoholism. In *Neuropsychological Assessment of Neuropsychiatric Disorder*, ed. I. Grant & K. Adams, pp. 423–485. New York: Oxford University Press.

Rounsaville, B. J. (1996). Overview: Rationale and guidelines for using comparable measures to evaluate substance abusers. In *Diagnostic Sourcebook on Drug Abuse Research and Treatment*, B. J. Rounsaville, F. M. Tims, A. M. Horton, & B. J. Sowder, pp. 1–10. NIH Publication No. 96–3 508. Rockville, MD: National Institute on Alcohol Abuse and Alcoholism.

Russell, M., Martier, S. S., Sokol, R. J., Jacobson, S., Jacobson, J., & Bottoms, S. (1991). Screening for pregnancy risk drinking: TWEAKING the test. *Alcoholism: Clinical and Experimental Research* 15:638.

Ryan, C., & Butters, N. (1983). Cognitive deficits in alcoholics. In *The Biology of Alcoholism: Vol. 7. The Pathogenesis of Alcoholism: Biological Factors*, ed. B. Kissin & H. Begleiter, pp. 485–538. New York: Plenum.

Rychtarik, R. G., Connors, G. J., Whitney, R. B., McGillicuddy, N. B., & Fitterling, J. M., Wirtz, P. W. (2000). Treatment settings for persons with alcoholism: Evidence for matching clients to inpatient versus outpatient care. *Journal of Consulting and Clinical Psychology* 68:277–289.

Sanchez-Craig, M., & Annis, H. M. (1982). "Self-monitoring" and "recall" measures of alcohol consumption: Convergent validity with biological indices of liver function. *British Journal of Alcohol and Alcoholism* 17:117–121.

Schuckit, M. A. (1994). DSM-IV: Was it worth all the fuss? Paper presented at the International Society for Biomedical Research on Alcoholism, Queensland, Australia, June 29.

Schuckit, M. A. (1995). *Drug Abuse and Alcohol Abuse: A Guide to Diagnosis and Treatment*, 4th ed. New York: Plenum Medical Book Company.

Schuckit, M. A., Tipp, J. E., Bergman, M., Reich, W., Hesselbrock, V. M., & Smith, T. L. (1997). Comparison of induced and independent major depressive disorders in 2,945 alcoholics. *American Journal of Psychiatry* 154:948–957.

Schwartz, M. F., & Graham, J. R. (1979). Construct validity of the McAndrew Alcoholism Scale. *Journal of Consulting and Clinial Psychology*, 47, 1090–1095.

Searles, J. S. (2000). Interactive voice response technology for collecting information about daily drinking. Paper presented at Symposium: Use of Technology in Addiction Research and Treatment. The 108th Annual Convention of the American Psychological Association Washington, DC, August 4.

Selzer, M. L. (1971). The Michigan Alcoholism Screening Test: The quest for a new diagnostic instrument. *American Journal of Psychiatry* 127:1653–1658.

Sheehan, T., & Owen, P. (1999). The disease model. In *Addictions: A Comprehensive Guidebook*, ed. B. S. McCrady, & E. E. Epstein, pp. 268–286. New York: Oxford University Press.

Sher, K. J., Wood, M. D., Wood, P. K., & Raskin, G. (1996). Alcohol outcome expectancies and alcohol use: A latent variable cross-lagged panel study. *Journal of Abnormal Psychology* 105:561–574.

Sherer, M., Haygood, J. M., & Alfano, A. (1984). Stability of psychological test results in newly admitted alcoholics. *Journal of Clinical Psychology* 40:855–857.

Skinner, H. A. (1982). Drug abuse screening test. *Addictive Behaviors* 7:363–371.

Skinner, H. A., & Allen, B. A. (1982). Alcohol dependence syndrome: Measurement and validation. *Journal of Abnormal Psychology* 91:199–209.

Skinner, H. A., & Sheu, W. J. (1982). Reliability of alcohol use indices: The Life-Time Drinking History and the MAST. *Journal of Studies on Alcohol* 43:1157–1170.

Skinstad, A. H. (1994). MMPI characteristics of alcoholics with borderline personality disorder. *European Journal of Psychological Assessment* 10:34–42.

Smith, G. T., Goldman, M. S., Greenbaum, P. E., & Christiansen, B. A. (1995). Expectancy for social facilitation from drinking: The divergent paths of high-expectancy and low-expectancy adolescents. *Journal of Abnormal Psychology* 104:32–40.

Smith, M. B., Hoffman, N. G., & Nederhoed, R. (1992). The development and reliability of the RAATE-CE. *Journal of Substance Abuse* 4:355–363.

Smith, M. B., Hoffman, N. G., & Nederhoed, R. (1995). Development and reliability of the Recovery Attitude and Treatment Evaluator-Questionnaire I (RAATE-QI). *International Journal of Addiction* 30:147–160.

Sobell, L. C., & Sobell, M. B. (1990). Self-report issues in alcohol abuse: State of the art and future directions. *Behavioral Assessment* 12:91–106.

Sobell, L. C., & Sobell, M. B. (1992). Timeline follow-back: A technique for assessing self-reported alcohol consumption. In *Measuring Alcohol Consumption: Psychosocial and Biochemical Methods*, ed. R. Z. Litten & J. P. Allen, pp. 41–72. Totowa, NJ: Humana.

Sobell, L. C., & Sobell, M. B. (1996). Timeline Followback Instructional Training Video for Alcohol (videotape). Toronto: Addiction Research Foundation.

Sobell, L. C., Sobell, M. B., Toneatto, T., & Leo, G. I. (1993) What triggers the resolution of alcohol problems without treatment? *Alcoholism: Clinical and Experimental Research* 17:217–224.

Sobell, L. C., Toneatto, T., & Sobell, M. B. (1994). Behavioral assessment and treatment planning for alcohol, tobacco, and other drug problems: Current status with an emphasis on clinical applications. *Behavioral Treatment* 25:533–580.

Sokol, R. J., Martier, S. S., & Anger, J. W. (1989). T-ACE questions: Practical prenatal detection of risk-drinking. *American Journal of Obstetrics and Gynecology* 160:863–870.

Spitzer, R. L., Williams, J. B., Gibbon, M., & First, M. B. (1996). *Structured Clinical Interview for DSM-IV*. Washington, DC: American Psychiatric Association.

Stoffelmayr, B. E., Mavis, B. E., & Kasim, R. M. (1994). The longitudinal stability of the Addiction Severity Index. *Journal of Substance Abuse Treatment* 11:373–378.

Svanum, S., McGrew, J., & Ehrmann, L. (1994). Validity of the substance abuse scales of the MMPI-2 in a college student sample. *Journal of Personality Assessment* 64:427–439.

Thombs, D. L., & Beck, K. H. (1994). Social context of four adolescent drinking patterns. *Health Education Research* 9:13–22.

Todd, T. D., & Reich, T. (1989). Linkage markers and validation of psychiatric nosology: Toward an etiologic classification of psychiatric disorders. In *The Validity of Psychiatric Diagnosis*, ed. L. N. Robins & Barrett, J. E., pp. 163–175. New York: Raven.

Tonigan, J. S., Miller, W. R., & Brown, J. M. (1997). The reliability of the SUDDS: An instrument for assessing alcohol treatment outcomes. Journal of Studies on Alcohol. 58, 358–364.

Wanberg, K. W., Horn, J. L., & Foster, F. M. (1977). A differential assessment model of alcoholism. *Journal of Studies on Alcohol* 38:512–543.

Weed, N., Butcher, J. S., McKenna, T., & Ben-Povath, Y. (1992). New measures for assessing alcohol and drug abuse problems with the MMPI-2: The APS and AAS. *Journal of Personality Assessment* 58:389–404.

White, H. R., & Labouvie, E. W. (1989). Towards the assessment of adolescent problem drinking. *Journal of Studies on Alcohol* 50:30–37.

Winters, K., & Henley, G. (1993). *Adolescent Diagnostic Interview (ADI) Manual*. Los Angeles: Western Psychological Services.

Winters, K., Stinchfield, R., Fulkerson, J., et al. (1993). Measuring alcohol and cannabis use disorders in an adolescent clinical sample. *Psychology of Addictive Behaviors* 7:185–196.

World Health Organization. (1975). Manual for the International Statistical Classification of Diseases, Injuries, and Causes of Death (ICD-9-Revision). Geneva: World Health Organization.

Yahne, C. E., & Miller, W. R. (1999). Enhancing motivation for treatment and change. In *Addictions: A Comprehensive Guidebook*, ed. B. S. McCrady & E. E. Epstein, pp. 235–249. New York: Oxford University Press.

Young, R. McD., & Knoght, R. G. (1989). The Drinking Expectancy Questionnaire: A revised measure of alcohol related beliefs. *Journal of Psychopathology and Behavioral Assessment* 11:99–112.

Young, R. McD., Knoght, R. G., & Oei, T. P. S. (1991). The stability of alcohol related expectancies. *Australian Psychologist* 43:321–330.

11

MOTIVATIONAL INTERVIEWING

Carl Isenhart Psy.D., L.P., MBA

Imagine the following scenario in a therapist's office:

> Therapist: I see from the records you're here to talk about your alcohol problem.
> Client: I don't know if I'd call it a problem. . . . I have some concerns about the amount I've been drinking.
> Therapist: It looks to me like you're an alcoholic, and you need to totally abstain from alcohol and all mood-altering drugs.
> Client: I think that's a bit strong, I should probably drink less, but. . . .
> Therapist: You're in denial . . . come back and see me when you're ready to cooperate and do what you're told.

The preceding interaction is based on actual observed interactions between therapist and client. This interaction is an example of a missed opportunity to engage a person who is ambivalent about his/her alcohol use and who was at least interested in considering some level of change. However, because the client's priorities did not match the therapist's priorities, the client was summarily dispatched and, in addition to not receiving any help, very likely developed a tainted view of the health care system that is supposed to offer help.

Motivational interviewing (MI) is an empirically supported therapeutic approach that, at its core, seeks to build a strong working alliance with the client that thereby allows the client to change by resolving his/her ambivalence. Miller and Rollnick (2002), the developers of MI, have stated that therapists can "wrestle" with clients or "dance" with them (figuratively speaking). Wrestling with clients results in resistance, while dancing with clients can result in the client talking about change (what is called "change talk") and consequently being more likely to make changes.

The scenario at the start of this chapter is an example of wrestling; typically, at best it results in temporary and superficial change, and at worst it results in little or no change and reactance. Reactance is the concept whereby people attempt to regain their freedom of choice when they perceive their ability to freely choose is being threatened (Janis & Mann, 1977). This concept explains why many people become contrary and oppositional, refuse to comply, or even become aggressive or abusive when being pressured to follow somebody else's advice. In addition, in the person's mind the "restricted" act becomes more valued and the alternative into which they feel pressured is depreciated (Janis & Mann, 1977). Applying the concept of reactance to the opening example, not only will the interaction likely result in the client engaging in limited behavior change, if any, but also s/he is less likely to consider abstinence as a goal. Essentially, the therapist has created the type of interaction that yields the opposite result from what is intended.

The MI approach is to "dance" with the client, that is, work with the client in a collaborative and collegial manner to "move" the client toward the goals to which s/he aspires and, by doing so, encourage the client to consider making changes over and beyond their initial goal. By following the MI philosophy and using the MI strategies, the therapist allows the client to spontaneously talk about making changes (i.e., change talk). Because there is a strong working alliance, the therapist is in a position to be directive and actively elicit change talk statements from the client. Change talk is critical in MI because the more change talk the client verbalizes, the greater the likelihood of the client making actual changes.

Miller (2002) describes new research where it was found that clients receiving MI therapy in a drug abuse treatment program who verbalized more change-talk statements during the sessions tended to have higher levels of abstinence at follow-up. Specifically, the stronger the commitment language (change talk), the better the outcome. The researchers found that commitment language consisted of client statements of desire and ability to change and reasons and need to change. The more the clients were allowed and encouraged to verbalize change-talk statements (i.e., the desire, ability, reasons, and need to change), the stronger was the commitment language and the better was the outcome. This is the major goal in MI: to create the therapeutic atmosphere in which the client can engage in change talk. Change-talk statements that occur in MI include the client verbalizing recognition of the disadvantages of the status quo (i.e., verbalizing recognition of problems associated with the current behavior and concern about the possible ongoing negative consequences of his/her behavior), verbalizing recognition of the advantages of making changes, verbalizing intentions to change, and verbalizing optimism for being able to make changes (Miller & Rollnick, 2002). In the opening example, the client was never given the opportunity to engage in change talk (except for spontaneous phrases about concern about drinking too much and perhaps cutting down). Because of the high level of reactance created by the interaction, the client was too busy defending him-/herself and salvaging his/her freedom to independently make personal decisions.

The MI philosophy challenges the traditional approaches used in the area of treating substance use disorders. However, the MI approach is very consistent with the original writings of Bill W. and Dr. Bob in the *Big Book*: "If he does not want to stop drinking, don't waste time trying to persuade him. You may spoil a later opportunity" (Alcoholics Anonymous, 1976, p. 90). Miller and Rollnick have discussed the principles and practice of MI in two books (1991; 2002) and other writings (Miller, 1995; 1998); in addition, much of the information about MI has been promulgated through workshops, seminars, and the MI website. The goal of this chapter is to provide to the reader an understanding of the basics of MI. Although in practice it is helpful to read the materials, to truly learn to do MI requires completing a formal training program and receiving supervision and consultation with an experienced MI practitioner.

As clinicians read or hear about MI, a typical response is, "I already do all that"; this refrain is heard during most MI training seminars. This type of comment is expected, for example, when considering the basic MI strategies: reflective listening, affirmations, summarizing, and asking open-ended questions. These all sound like very basic, "counseling 101" skills, and most clinicians like to think that they incorporate these skills into their practice. However, there are two factors that make the practice of MI a challenge, even for the most seasoned practitioners. First, many clinicians get into a trap of trying to "figure out" what the client has and its etiology and then "fix it." This trap and others will be discussed later in this chapter. The practice of MI requires the practitioner to temporarily suspend these attempts of figuring out and fixing the problem and instead focus on two things: building a collaborative therapeutic relationship with the client and allowing and encouraging the client to engage in change talk. The second issue that makes MI a challenge is that the therapist simply does not reflect, affirm, and summarize everything; rather the MI therapist strategically uses these skills to respond selectively to the client in order to increase the client's change talk.

The chapter begins by providing the philosophy and definition of MI. The stages of change and how those concepts apply to MI will then be reviewed. The guiding goals and principles of MI will be discussed along with various "traps" that can occur when working with clients. The three "levels" of MI will be reviewed: basic MI strategies (including "roadblocks" to working with clients), defining and eliciting change talk, and handling resistance. Various studies from the outcome literature on MI will be highlighted. Finally, the chapter will describe a typical MI training seminar.

DEFINITION AND PHILOSOPHY OF MI

MI can be defined as a directive, client-centered counseling style for eliciting behavior change by helping clients to use their ambivalence to engage in change talk. Change talk has already been discussed, but there are three other important parts of this definition: *directive, client-centered,* and *ambivalence.* MI is *directive* in that the therapist is aware of healthy changes the client should be considering. Although the client may not share the therapist's goal (e.g., the therapist may think that abstinence from alcohol is the best goal, but the client may believe that an appropriate goal would be to reduce his/her alcohol use), the MI therapist begins working with the client where s/he "is at" and attempts to "move" the client toward the healthiest goal (e.g., abstinence). Abstinence is a goal and not a requirement for treatment, and this is consistent with the harm reduction approach (Marlatt, 1998). *Client-centered* means that the client determines the therapeutic goals and priorities, strategies to achieve those goals, and the time frame for starting and completing the strategies to achieve the goal. This does not mean the therapist has no input or cannot provide advice or feedback; on the contrary, the therapist is very active and directive in providing feedback and advice; however, what happens regarding behavior change is ultimately the client's decision.

Ambivalence is the focus of the work in MI. As was shown in the example at the beginning of the chapter, in traditional treatments it was not uncommon for therapists to perceive ambivalence as resistance and to actively confront resistance in an attempt to "break it down" and motivate the client to change. However, in MI, the goal is to allow and encourage the client to discuss the "prochange side" of the ambivalence, which represents change talk. As a consequence of the change talk, the client becomes more likely to change. It is the client's task, not the counselor's, to articulate and resolve ambivalence; essentially, the goal is to "normalize" ambivalence and to let the client know that it is natural to be ambivalent.

In MI, level of motivation is not a client trait, but a fluctuating product of interpersonal interaction. Reviews of "personality variables" of substance abusers have not yielded consistent results: no substance abuse personality style exists where a major factor is denial or resistance to change (Sher et al., 1999). Motivation is a function of the quality of the therapeutic relationship (i.e., the working alliance): the better the working alliance, the more change will occur. A strong therapeutic relationship is a strong predictor of positive outcome (Project MATCH Research Group, 1998) and is associated with low levels of client resistance (Peterson et al., 1996; Miller et al., 1993). Therefore, in MI the goal is to establish and maintain a strong therapeutic alliance, and the client/counselor relationship is respectful, collaborative, and nonjudgmental.

MI is nonprescriptive. The MI counselor elicits goals, strategies, and methods or techniques from the client. Once this information is obtained, the therapist can provide direction and advice to the client after asking for permission to do so. This approach shows respect for the client by communicating that the client's ideas and thoughts are important and valuable, which enhances the therapeutic relationship. The therapist may have concerns about the client's goals, strategies, and time lines. When this occurs, the therapist asks permission to share these concerns (again showing respect), then verbalizes these concerns: "that is an interesting plan you have. . . . Can I share with you some thoughts I have about it?" If a relationship has been established, the client will not decline the offer.

Finally, MI involves monitoring the client's motivation level to ensure the therapist doesn't jump ahead of the client, generating resistance. The focus in MI is on what the client does want to change or at least is willing to consider changing. Many times, this is not what the therapist or others in the client's life believe s/he should change; however, therapy begins where the client is willing to start.

STAGES OF CHANGE

The stages-of-change concept is consistent with MI. Briefly, the theory states that people go through different stages or phases when considering and completing change (Prochaska et al., 1992). First, people are *precontemplative* (what typically has been called denial): the person sees no reason to change and believes that there is no problem. The next stage is *contemplative*: the main feature is ambivalence; the person is "on the fence" and at some level may be aware of the possibility of a problem. Such a person can argue both sides of change: the reasons not to change and the reasons to change. The next stage is *determination*: the person has decided that there is a problem and that there needs to be some changes. The person has not initiated any of those changes yet, but s/he has determined that the problem cannot continue and that something needs to be different. Next is the *action* stage, when the individual is taking steps to make changes. The "final" stage is *maintenance*, where the person has made changes and is maintaining those changes and attempting to avoid relapse. One issue with the stage model is that ambivalence is more than a specific phase, that even in determination and action the client may continue to feel some ambivalence about making changes. Consequently, MI is applicable to even "action"-oriented clients as they continue to struggle with ambivalence.

The stage at which the client is located along the change continuum is influenced by the here-and-now, that is, the events surrounding the client at the time. This includes the provider who is working with the client. Consequently, the services offered to the client should "meet" the patient where s/he is at on the continuum. If the client is contemplative (i.e., ambivalent), then the therapist needs to work with the client's ambivalence; to discuss the client taking action to change would be premature and would risk increasing the client's level of resistance.

GOALS AND PRINCIPLES OF MI

There are four general principles in MI (Miller & Rollnick, 2002). The first is *express empathy*: the therapist expresses acceptance of the client's feelings, attitudes, and point of view. This does not necessarily mean condoning or agreeing with the client's perspective, but letting the client know that s/he is understood and is being listened to in a nonjudgmental and supportive manner. Expressing empathy is crucial for developing the therapeutic relationship that in turn allows the client to verbalize ambivalence about change and engage in change talk. An MI therapist communicates empathy by reflective listening, which is the cornerstone technique in MI and will be discussed in detail later.

The next principle is *develop discrepancy*: the therapist highlights and allows the client to verbalize the "gap" between the client's current behavior and his/her primary goals, values, and priorities. The inconsistency between the client's current circumstances and his/her ideal situation creates stress that may be reduced by changing current behavior to be more consistent with future aspirations. The "size" of that gap determines the level of the client's motivation. It is imperative, therefore, for the therapist to listen to the client to understand what is important to him/her and what his/her priorities are. By being aware of these priorities, the therapist can highlight inconsistencies between the client's behavior and values and reflect them back to the client for his/her consideration.

Another principle is *roll with resistance*: this is consistent with the stages-of-change philosophy, in which the goal is to provide services that are consistent with the client's stage of change. The goal is for the therapist to avoid arguing for change; if the therapist argues for the "change side" of the client's ambivalence, that leaves the client to argue for the "not to change side" of the ambivalence (i.e., to make resistance statements). In MI, it is critical for the therapist to be constantly monitoring the client's resistance and to use resistance as a signal that the therapist is moving too rapidly along the stages of change and that the therapist needs to respond differently. By rolling with resistance, the therapist enhances the therapeutic alliance and helps the client feel more accepted, less defensive, and therefore more likely to make change-talk statements spontaneously.

Finally, the last principle is to *support self-efficacy*: many times, clients may not believe they have it in them to make changes even if they want to. The goal is to support and affirm the client to help build his/her belief in his/her ability to carry out change. By building a strong, trusting, and nonjudgmental therapeutic relationship, the client develops a sense of hope and optimism that s/he can make changes.

THERAPEUTIC TRAPS TO AVOID

There are a number of "traps" the MI therapist attempts to avoid (Miller & Rollnick, 2002); these traps interfere with the therapeutic alliance and, because s/he is focusing on defending his/her point of view, prevent the client from engaging in change talk. The first is the *question–answer trap*, in which the therapist peppers the client with yes/no questions. This style does not allow the therapeutic alliance to develop, because it feels more like an interrogation than it does a collaborative relationship. In addition, the client is only allowed to answer "yes" or "no" so that s/he does not have the opportunity to discuss his/her ambivalence, and there are no opportunities to engage in change talk. Finally, this style does not allow the client to discuss his/her priorities; therefore, the therapist is not able to develop discrepancies within the client.

In the *confrontation–denial trap*, or *the taking sides trap*, the therapist confronts the client with the need to change and/or with a particular label (e.g., "addict" or "alcoholic"). In this type of situation, because of reactance, the tendency is for the client to defend him-/herself and deny that there is a problem, essentially arguing for the reasons not to change. By arguing for not changing, the client is engaging in resistance talk rather than change talk and, consequently, is less likely eventually to engage in change.

In the *premature focus trap*, the therapist jumps too far ahead of the client along the stages-of-change continuum: the therapist begins to work a goal, using his/her own strategy and time frame with minimal input from the client. The therapist assumes to know what is best for the client and assumes the client is ready to actively participate in an "action-oriented" treatment plan.

In the *blaming trap*, the therapist blames the client for not following through with previous arrangements or for not following the therapist's advice and direction from the past. This creates huge barriers and greatly interferes with the therapeutic process. A related trap is the *expert trap*: the therapist assumes to know what is best for the client and is not open to the client's views or opinion, but rather focuses on his/her own agenda and treatment priorities for the client.

In the *cheerleader trap*, the therapist tries to "cheer up" the client by being overly encouraging and optimistic. To the client, particularly in the early phase of therapy, the therapist may sound naïve (as if the therapist does not have a true grasp of the client's plight), superficial, or disingenuous. One tenet of MI is to be affirming, but this involves having the client define for him-/herself what s/he can feel encouraged about from his/her own perspective. The MI therapist wants the client to start verbalizing optimism, when s/he is ready, then start from the client's perspective.

In the *righting reflex*, the therapist prematurely attempts to "fix things" or "make things right." Although the goal of therapy is to make things better eventually, from the MI perspective, this is done within a collaborative therapeutic alliance using the client's time frame. The therapist may understand and "diagnose" the problem and have a range of potential solutions to it; however, no matter how quick the therapist is, the client is the one determining when or if s/he is ready to change. In addition, in trying to fix the problem, the therapist is making the assumption that s/he knows what the problem is, what the most appropriate goal is, what strategies would work best, and what the time frame should be. However, these are all decisions that have to come from the client in collaboration with the therapist. Therapists often feel frustrated with what appears to be (and may actually be) the client's lack of movement or direction and feel pressured to "get the client moving"; it may feel as though therapy is a waste of time. The problem is that by pressuring the client to initiate change before s/he is ready to do so, the therapist is being inefficient because, as the therapist is "pushing," the client is resisting, and the process of change is impeded and delayed.

BASIC STRATEGIES

Four basic strategies are used in MI (Miller & Rollnick, 2002). The primary tool in MI is *reflective listening*. The MI therapist attempts to reflect more than the content of the client's statements; the goal is to reflect the meaning behind what the client is saying. This requires a high level of listening, empathy, and understanding on the therapist's part. Reflective listening communicates to the client that s/he is being listened to, that s/he is being understood in a non-judgmental way, and that what the client is saying is important. The result is that the client is less likely to feel defensive and demonstrate resistance. Consequently, reflective listening is crucial in developing and maintaining a strong therapeutic alliance with the client. In doing reflective listening, the therapist makes a "therapeutic presumption" about the meaning of what the client is saying and verbalizes that meaning back to the client. The assumption is that there is "more" to what the client is saying than the superficial meaning, and the goal of the MI therapist is to figure out what that meaning is and reflect it back to the client. Miller and Rollnick (2002) refer to the process of anticipating the client's next statement and reflecting it back to the client as "continuing the paragraph." Skillfully placed reflections, therefore, are more than mere echoes of the client's statement; they provide momentum to the client by drawing him/her through the stages-of-change continuum by anticipating and verbalizing the "prochange" side of the client's ambivalence.

In addition, reflective listening involves more than the client's words; the therapist can also reflect the client's unspoken feelings, facial expression, behavior, and body posture. Reflective listening is a "win–win" situation: if the therapist is "correct" with the reflection (from the client's point of view), the therapist gives voice to the client's thoughts and feelings, which builds the alliance and encourages the client to verbalize more change talk. If the therapist is "wrong," the client will correct the therapist and clarify the meaning. The client "correcting" the therapist is helpful in a couple of ways. First, it provides the therapist with new and accurate information about the client that can allow the change process to continue. Second, the extent to which a client can "correct" a therapist is a good barometer of the strength of the therapeutic relationship. If a client is able to disagree with and correct the therapist, an authority figure, this shows that the client feels a high level of trust and safety within the relationship.

Gordon (1970) has described a number of "Roadblocks to Reflective Listening" that interfere with the development and maintenance of a therapeutic relationship, that prevent the client from exploring his/her ambivalence, and that discourage the client from engaging in change talk. If a therapist engages in any of these "roadblock" behaviors, the client is forced to defend him-/herself rather than engage in change talk. These roadblocks include:

- Ordering or commanding
- Warning or threatening
- Giving advice or making suggestions too soon
- Persuading with logic or lecturing
- Moralizing, preaching, telling clients what to do
- Judging or blaming

The next basic MI tool is *affirming* the client: affirmations build the therapeutic relationship and instill a sense of hope and optimism for the client. Affirmations include *complimenting* the client ("It's great that you are putting this much effort into changing"), understanding the client's challenges ("I realize how hard it is for you to talk about this"), appreciating the client's efforts ("I appreciate you putting so much time and effort into this"), and *reframing* apparent "shortcomings" ("You seem to be spirited and strong-willed," in response to the client saying that s/he is impulsive and stubborn). In this last example, the goal is not to candy-coat problematic thinking or behavior, but to provide a frame that acknowledges some aspect of the client that may demonstrate strength or a positive feature.

The next MI basic strategy is to *summarize*: summary statements consist of a series of reflective statements. There are three kinds of summarizing statements: collecting, linking, and transitional. Just as with reflections, summary statements allow the MI therapist to highlight the client's change talk, communicate that the client is being heard, and thereby strengthen the therapeutic relationship. *Collecting summaries* allows the therapist to gather several of the client's change-talk statements, then summarize them back to the client. In this way, the client hears his/her change-talk statement three times: when s/he says it, when the therapist initially reflects it, and finally, when the therapist summarizes it. For example, a collecting summary may be: "You are tired of wasting money on cocaine and feeling tired and depressed. You want more out of life and have higher expectations for yourself that are inconsistent with your use of cocaine." *Linking summaries* allows the therapist to link comments or phrases made by the client in such a way as to create discrepancies for the client, which generates motivation on the client's part. For example: "You've said that it is important for you to be a good father. But it seems that since you've been stopping at the tavern after work you've been missing your son's soccer games." Finally, the *transitional links* allow the therapist to move on from one topic to another; this is a particularly helpful tool during structured interviews or protocols.

The final MI tool is to ask *open-ended questions*, questions that cannot be answered with simple "yes" or "no" responses. Open-ended questions encourage the client to continue talking, which gives the client more opportunity to discuss his/her ambivalent feelings and to verbalize change talk spontaneously. Setting up the kind of interaction in which all the client is allowed to do is answer "yes" or "no" restricts the client and does not allow him/her to talk about making changes; the client is being forced into answering questions.

ELICITING AND RESPONDING TO CHANGE TALK

By using the basic MI strategies, the therapist is setting up a therapeutic relationship in which the client is likely to make change-talk statements spontaneously, which facilitates behavioral change. To review, change talk consists of the client verbalizing recognition of the disadvantages of staying the same (i.e., verbalizing recognition and concern), verbalizing recognition of the advantages of making changes, verbalizing intentions to change, and verbalizing optimism for change. Although spontaneous change talk from the client is good, the goal in MI is to encourage as much change talk from the client as possible. Therefore, in addition to using the basic MI strategies to allow clients to engage in change talk, Miller and Rollnick (1991; 2002) have identified several change-talk strategies that can be used, in conjunction with the basic strategies, to encourage the client to talk about making changes.

Before discussing the strategies to elicit change talk, it is important to highlight the need for therapists to know how to identify change-talk statements. Frequently, therapists hear and respond to the resistance talk, but in MI, the goal is to listen for and respond to spontaneous change talk. For example, consider the following client's statement: "There is no need for me to stop smoking pot. . . . I should cut down . . . but there is no reason for me to stop totally." Typically, therapists focus on the first and last phrases and likely challenge the client's assertion that s/he does not need to stop his/her cannabis use. However, in MI, the therapist would emphasize the change talk part of the statement ("I should cut down") with, for example, a reflection: "There's a part of you that is concerned about the amount of pot you are smoking, and you think it would be a good idea to smoke less." Although smoking less cannabis may not be the optimal goal, it is a way to at least engage the client, start developing a therapeutic relationship, and "move" the client toward the optimal goal of abstinence.

The first strategy to elicit change talk is to have the client describe the *benefits and costs of staying the same*. This is typically done by first having the client describe the benefits of their unhealthy behavior; this is a way to engage the client by having him/her talk about something that he/she enjoys doing or at least invests a lot of time and energy in doing (e.g., "What do you like about drinking alcohol?"). After the client has been encouraged to verbalize two or three benefits, s/he can be ask about "the other side," or what is the "not so good" part, of his/her behavior (e.g., "What is the other side of your alcohol use?"). It is good to avoid using evaluative or judgmental terms, but the client typically knows the intention even when using neutral language (e.g., "What else do you notice"). It is not uncommon for clients spontaneously to start verbalizing the negative aspects of their behavior after talking about the benefits of their behavior: "I like the way pot makes me relax . . . but it is really getting expensive." The "really getting expensive" phrase represents change talk in which the client has verbalized awareness of the disadvantage of the status quo (i.e., continuing to smoke pot is expensive), to which the therapist can respond by reflecting: "Because of your pot smoking, you are unable to spend money on other things that are important for you." By asking what the client likes about smoking pot, the therapist has set up the circumstances in which the client can tell the therapist the disadvantages of the behavior. By discussing the disadvantages, the client is engaging in change talk and, consequently, s/he is more likely to begin making changes.

By having the client describe some of the "negative" side of his/her behavior, the therapist is then set up to engage in the next series of strategies to evoke change talk. The next strategy is to encourage the client to verbalize the *benefits and costs of changing*. This strategy can be initiated by the therapist reflecting on the down side of continuing the behavior. Using the example given above, the therapist may summarize that smoking pot is getting too expensive and that one benefit to stopping smoking pot would be saving money. The therapist would then continue to use open-ended questions to ask for other benefits to stopping smoking pot and ask what the client could do with the money saved: "What would you spend the money on if you weren't buying pot?" The goal would be to elicit from the client as many additional benefits to changing his/her behavior as possible. It is also important to have the client verbalize the costs or negative side of making change; doing so acknowledges the client's ambivalence about making changes, it identifies potential high-risk situations for relapse ("I'm afraid that I'll be lonely), and it helps to build the therapeutic relationship in that the therapist is showing an interest in the client's concerns and potential struggles.

Another strategy is *forward looking*: the therapist asks the client to look into the future and describe what the future may be like if s/he changes and if s/he does not change. This would involve asking, for example, "If you don't stop using cocaine, what would your life be like in one year?" or "If you do decide to stop using cocaine, what would your life be like in one year?" By asking these open-ended questions, the therapist puts the client in a position to engage in change talk: "If I don't stop using cocaine, I won't be as good a parent as I would like to be" (the disadvantages of maintaining the status quo) and "if I stop using cocaine, I'll have fewer legal and financial problems" (the advantages of changing). Because the therapist asks these questions, the client, not the therapist, is providing the costs for not changing and the benefits for changing.

Another strategy is *backward looking*: having the client look back to when his/her life was going well and when it was not going so well. For example, the therapist might ask the client, "What did you notice two years ago when you were sober for six months?" (Notice the "neutral" term of "notice"). This sets up the circumstance where the client can say something such as, "Well, when I was sober, I didn't get into arguments and I was less depressed." This encourages the client to start verbalizing the benefits for not using alcohol. Another example would be asking the client, "What did you notice starting to happen after your relapse?" The client would likely verbalize, "I starting feeling ill physically and my anxiety went sky-high." Here, again, the client is providing reasons to change.

Forward and backward looking also allow the therapist to highlight discrepancies between the client's current circumstances and his/her aspirations. Using the examples from above, the therapist could respond with, "It is very important for you to be the best parent you can be to your children, but your cocaine use gets in the way of that," or "You see yourself as a responsible person, but when you use cocaine you aren't able to fulfill your financial responsibilities," or finally, "You don't like feeling anxious and physically ill, yet your alcohol use makes you sick and nervous." In almost every situation, the client has to agree with the therapist in response to these observations because the priorities and observations came from the client; the therapist is simply "linking" the observations and reflecting them back to the client to create the discrepancy.

Another way to elicit change talk is to ask directly *evocative questions*. These open-ended questions are used to examine the client's awareness, concerns, intentions, and levels of optimism. As discussed with reflective listening, it is important for the therapist to make therapeutic assumptions with this strategy also: the therapist does not ask whether or not the client has concerns or intentions; the therapist assumes that the client does have such concerns and intentions and asks about them.

Exploring the client's goals can be another way to elicit change talk. The therapist asks the client to describe the things that are most important in his/her life, that is, what goals or priorities does the client hold most important? The purpose is to develop discrepancies by identifying ways in which the client's current behavior is inconsistent with his/her goals or priorities.

Just as it is critical to elicit change talk, the therapist needs to respond to the change talk in order to reinforce the client's continued change talk. One way to respond is through *elaboration*, that is, asking the client to elaborate or expand on his/her change-talk statement. This may include making such comments as, "Tell me more about that" or "In what way?" or "Give me an example of that." Other ways to respond include using the basics: reflecting ("You can't go on this way"), summarizing ("You are tired of living this way and you have decided that now is the time to make some changes"), and affirming ("This is a huge decision; not everybody has been able to decide what you are deciding to do."). Because the therapist responds to the client's change talk in these ways, the client is encouraged to continue engaging in change talk that increases the chances of actually making changes.

MANAGING RESISTANCE

Clients who are thinking about, or should be thinking about, making changes typically demonstrate some level of resistance. In MI, when resistance is encountered, it is seen as a signal to the therapist to respond to the client differently. That is, the therapist is moving too far ahead of the client on the stages-of-change continuum, and therefore it is important to "move back" and engage the client where s/he is. One of the benefits of using the basic MI strategies and focusing on eliciting change talk is that the conditions that lead to resistance on the part of the client are eliminated or at least minimized. For example, a client may show resistance by disagreeing with the therapist; if the therapist focuses on the MI basics, there is little with which the client to disagree. However, even when MI strategies are used, resistance can occur, and when it does there are MI strategies to manage it (Miller & Rollnick, 1991; 2002). It should be noted also that these strategies can be used even when the client is not being resistant; these are good strategies to use to continue building the therapeutic relationship and to elicit change talk from the client.

The primary way to manage resistance is through *reflection*. This may involve reflecting the client's reluctance to change or even to be assessed or interviewed (e.g., "You're angry about being here and have other things you'd rather be doing"). Another strategy is the *double-sided reflection*. This involves reflecting both sides of the client's ambivalence (e.g., "On the one hand, alcohol helps you relax, but on the other, you're tired of your husband's complaints about your drinking"). This technique is particularly useful because the first part of the statement acknowledges the client's concerns and therefore communicates that his/her issues are being heard and understood. The second part of the reflection elicits change talk from the client because it is a reflection of a concern that he/she has already communicated to the therapist. *Shifting focus* means to move away from the area in which the resistance is being encountered and instead to encourage the client to discuss what his/her concerns or priorities are. This serves to encourage the therapeutic alliance in that it communicates to the client that his/her ideas, values, and priorities are important and that the therapist is ready and interested in hearing them. Once the client feels that s/he has been heard and understood, the client is more willing to discuss and explore the possibility of making changes.

Many times when a client is considering making changes, s/he has been given much advice and pressure to change, and the client is typically tired of being subjected to others' opinions. Also, the client may feel that s/he is being pressured to do what others want him/her to do, with little consideration with what the client wants to do. For example, the pressure may be coming from a spouse or partner, judge, probation officer, employer, or any number of other people who may be telling the client what to do. Consequently, one way to reduce resistance is to *ask the client what s/he wants*; unfortunately, this may be the first time anybody has asked the client what his/her priorities or goals are. This can go a very long way in reducing the client's resistance and building the therapeutic alliance. This strategy shows the client that somebody really is interested in them and is willing to listen. Related to this is *emphasizing the client's personal control and choice*: "It is all up to you. . . . I can't make you change; whether you change or not and what you change is totally in your control." In many ways, this is simply acknowledging reality, since it is ultimately the client's decision to change or not, and it is important to verbalize that.

Finally, two related strategies are *reframe* and *agreement with a twist* (a reflection followed by a reframe). A reframe is when the therapist provides the client with an alternative interpretation of the client's circumstances in order to reduce the resistance. For example, if a client is angry about his/her employer making him/her come for an assessment, the therapist may say something such as, "It sounds as though your employer really cares about you and wants to keep you on the job." The agreement with a twist involves adding a reflection to the reframe, such as, "You're angry at your boss for sending you here and think it's a waste of time, but it sounds as though your boss really values you and wants to keep you on the job." Or a client may be angry about his/her spouse forcing him/her in for an evaluation, in which case an agreement with a twist could be: "You're upset with your spouse, but it sounds as though s/he loves you very much and really wants the best for you." The client almost always agrees with the twist (reframe), if grudgingly at times, and it goes a long way in reducing the resistance the client may be demonstrating.

RESEARCH LITERATURE

Miller et al. (1995) have reported empirical support for MI, and there is a growing research literature supporting MI's effectiveness. MI strategies have been applied to and have demonstrated some level of effectiveness in a number of different problem areas. These areas include addictive behaviors: alcohol abuse in college students (Marlatt et al., 1998), adolescent substance abusers (Aubrey, 1998), marijuana use (Stephens et al., 2000), cocaine use (Stotts et al., 2001), opiate abuse (Saunders et al., 1995), gambling problems (Hodgins et al., 2001), and relapse prevention (Allsop et al., 1997). MI has been used with patients with substance use and other mental disorders (Daley et al., 1998; Swanson et al., 1999), and it has been effective in use with alcohol-dependent patients with high levels of anger (Project MATCH Research Group, 1997). MI has improved participation in substance abuse treatment programming (Brown & Miller, 1993; Connors et al., 2002), and it has been used to integrate interventions for alcohol abuse in primary-care settings (Senft et al., 1997; Heather et al., 1996) and to address alcohol-related problems with adolescents receiving treatment in emergency rooms (Monti et al., 1999). MI is used in primary medicine to address obesity and diabetes (Smith et al., 1997). In addition, Resnicow et al. (2002) have reviewed the application of MI to health promotion, and Bombardier and Rimmele (1999) discuss the application of MI in reducing alcohol use after a traumatic brain injury.

LEARNING MOTIVATIONAL INTERVIEWING

This chapter is meant to be an introduction to and overview of MI. By reading this chapter, the clinician may become more aware of and sensitive to his/her style and consider receiving formal MI training. MI training typically involves a two-day training that is very experiential and oriented to skill building. The training involves the presentation of the MI concepts (i.e., stages of change, basic strategies, eliciting and responding to change talk, and managing resistance), viewing training videos and live demonstrations, and then practicing the strategies. Practicing the techniques typically involves working in triads where each learner role-plays the therapist (practicing the particular strategy), the client, and the observer; the observer monitors the therapist's behavior and the client's responses. After a period of practicing the strategy, the triad debriefs and gives feedback to the therapist regarding his/her style, then the roles change. Each learner in the triad has the opportunity to engage in each of the roles. An MI trainer should be a practitioner of MI and should be trained as an MI trainer; a worldwide list of MI trainers is available on the MI website (www.motivationalinterview.org). This website also has abstracts or research articles and ways to contact individuals who are applying MI to various clinical problem areas (e.g., couples or groups).

SUMMARY

MI is a client-centered strategy that is based on the development of a strong working alliance and allows the therapist to utilize a client's own ambivalence, no matter how little there is, to encourage the client to engage in change talk. Although the MI principles and strategies appear to run counter to traditional substance abuse interventions, MI is consistent with the initial writings in Alcoholics Anonymous, and it is continuing to develop a strong empirical base. Also, MI principles are consistent with and incorporate the stages of change and the harm reduction approaches (by engaging the client at whatever level of change s/he is ready to pursue and working with the client to reduce the harm associated with his/her behavior). By using the basic MI strategies, the therapist encourages the client to talk about the "change side" of his/her ambivalence (i.e., change talk) and, by so doing, increases the likelihood that the client will actually make behavioral changes. In addition to responding to spontaneous change talk, the therapist is actively directing the client by eliciting change talk. Because these strategies focus on engaging the client and building the therapeutic relationship, the potential for resistance on the part of the client is reduced; however, resistance still does occur. When resistance does occur, it is a signal to the therapist to alter his/her style and to reassess the client's level of motivation. There are MI tools that are very helpful in reducing the level of resistance the client is experiencing. MI has been applied to a number of "problematic areas" in which the individual is considering, or should be considering, making changes in his/her life. In addition to the substance abuse area, MI has been used within the broader mental health area, and it has application in dual disordered and primary medical care settings. Finally, MI continues to develop a strong empirical base that supports its effectiveness in promoting behavior change across a wide range of areas.

REFERENCES

Alcoholics Anonymous. *Big Book* (1976). 3rd ed. New York.

Allsop, S., Saunders, B., Philips, M., & Carr, A. (1997). A trial of relapse prevention with severely dependent male problem drinkers. *Addiction* 92:61–74.

Aubrey, L. (1998). Motivational interviewing with adolescents presenting for outpatient substance abuse treatment. Unpublished doctoral dissertation, University of New Mexico. *Dissertation Abstracts International* 59-03B:1357.

Bombardier, C. H., & Rimmele, C. T. (1999). Motivational interviewing to prevent alcohol abuse after traumatic brain injury: A case series. *Rehabilitation Psychology* 44:52–67.

Brown, J. M., & Miller, W. R. (1993). Impact of motivational interviewing on participation in residential alcoholism treatment. *Psychology of Addictive Behavior* 7:211–218.

Connors, G. J., Walitzer, K. S., & Dermen, K. H. (2002). Preparing clients for alcoholism treatment: Effects on treatment participation and outcomes. *Journal of Consulting and Clinical Psychology* 70:1161–1169.

Daley, D. C., Salloum, I. M., Zuckoff, A., Kirisci, L., & Thase, M. E. (1998). Increasing treatment adherence among outpatients with depression and cocaine dependence: Results of a pilot study. *American Journal of Psychiatry* 155:1611–1613.

Gordon, T. (1970). *Parent Effectiveness Training.* New York: Wyden.

Heather, N. , Rollnick, S., Bell, A., & Richmond, R. (1996). Effects of brief counseling among heavy drinkers identified on general hospital wards. *Drug and Alcohol Review* 15:29–38.

Hodgins, D. C., Currie, S. R., & el-Guebaly, N. (2001). Motivational enhancement and self-help treatments for problem gambling. *Journal of Consulting & Clinical Psychology* 69:50–57.

Janis, I. L., & Mann, L. (1977). *Decision Making: A Psychological Analysis of Conflict, Choice, and Commitment.* New York: Free Press.

Marlatt, G. A. (1998). *Harm Reduction: Pragmatic Strategies for Managing High-Risk Behaviors.* New York: Guilford.

Marlatt, G. A., Baer, J. S., Kivlahan, D. R., Dimeff, L. A., Larimer, M. E., Quigley, L. A., Somers, J. M., & Williams, E. (1998). Screening and brief intervention for high-risk college student drinkers: Results from a 2-year follow-up assessment. *Journal of Consulting and Clinical Psychology* 66:604–615.

Miller, W. R. (1995). Increasing motivation for change. In *Handbook of Alcoholism Treatment Approaches: Effective Alternatives.* 2nd ed. Boston: Allyn and Bacon.

Miller, W. R. (1998). Enhancing motivation for change. In *Treating Addictive Behaviors,* 2nd ed. New York: Plenum.

Miller, W. R. (2002). A streetcar named desire. *Motivational Interviewing Newsletter: Updates, Education and Training* 9:1–4.

Miller, W. R., Benefield, R. G., & Tonigan, S. (1993). Enhancing motivation in problem drinking: A controlled comparison of two therapist styles. *Journal of Consulting and Clinical Psychology* 61:455–461.

Miller, W. R., Brown, J. M., Simpson, T. L., Handmaker, N. S., Bien, T. H., Luckie, L. F., Montgomery, H. A., Hester, R. K., & Tonigan, J. S. (1995). What works? A methodological analysis of the alcohol treatment outcome literature. *Handbook of Alcoholism Treatment Approaches: Effective Alternatives.* 2nd ed. Boston: Allyn and Bacon.

Miller, W. R., & Rollnick, S., eds. (1991). *Motivational Interviewing: Preparing People to Change Addictive Behavior.* New York: Guilford.

Miller, W. R., & Rollnick, S., eds. (2002). *Motivational Interviewing: Preparing People for Change.* 2nd ed. New York: Guilford.

Monti, P. M., Colby, S. M., Barnett, N. P., Spirito, A., Rohsenow, D. J., Myers, M., Woolard, R., and Lewander, W. (1999). Brief interventions for harm reduction with alcohol-positive older adolescents in a hospital emergency department. *Journal of Consulting and Clinical Psychology* 67:989–994.

Peterson, T. R., Waldron, H. B., & Miller, W. R. (1996) A sequential analysis of client and therapist behaviors during motivational enhancement therapy for problem drinking.

Prochaska, J. O., DiClemente, C. C., & Norcross, J. C. (1992). In search of how people change: Applications to addictive behaviors. *American Psychologist* 47:1102–1114.

Project MATCH Research Group. (1997). Project MATCH secondary a priori hypotheses. *Addiction* 92:1671–1698.

Project MATCH Research Group. (1998). Therapist effects in three treatments for alcohol problems. *Psychotherapy Research* 8:455–474.

Resnicow, K., DiIorio, C., Soet, J. E., Borrelli, B., Hecht, J., & Ernst, D. (2002). Motivational interviewing in health promotion: It sounds like something is changing. *Health Psychology* 21: 444–451.

Saunders, B., Wilkinson, C., & Philips, M. (1995). The impact of a brief motivational intervention with opiate users attending a methadone program. *Addiction* 90:415–424.

Senft, R. A., Polen, M. R., Freeborn, D. K., & Hollis, J. F. (1997). Brief intervention in a primary care setting for hazardous drinkers. *American Journal of Preventive Medicine* 13:464–470.

Sher, K. J., Trull, T. J., Bartholow, B. D., & Vieth, A. (1999). Personality and alcoholism: Issues, methods, and etiological processes. In *Psychological Theories of Drinking and Alcoholism.* 2nd ed. New York: Guilford.

Smith, D. E., Heckemeyer, C. M., Kratt, P. P., & Mason, D. A. (1997). Motivational interviewing to improve adherence to a behavioral weight-control program for older obese women with NIDDM: A pilot study. *Diabetes Care* 20:52–54.

Stephens, R. S., Roffman, R. A., & Curtin, A. (2000). Comparison of extended versus brief treatments for marijuana use. *Journal of Consulting and Clinical Psychology* 68:898–908.

Stotts, A. L., Schmitz, J. M., Rhoades, H. M., & Grabowski, J. (2001). Motivational interviewing with cocaine-dependent patients: A pilot study. *Journal of Consulting and Clinical Psychology* 69:858–862.

Swanson, A. J., Pantalon, M. V., & Cohen, K. R. (1999). Motivational interviewing and treatment adherence among psychiatric and dually-diagnosed patients. *Journal of Nervous & Mental Disease* 187:630–635.

12

ANOREXIA AND BULIMIA

Cheryl A. Marshall, Psy.D.

The eating disorders—anorexia nervosa and bulimia nervosa—have become the focus of much research in the past thirty-five years, resulting in a dramatic expansion in our knowledge base about their assessment, diagnosis, and treatment. These disorders are particularly evident in industrialized societies. In the United States, they represent a significant health problem, especially among adolescent and young adult females (American Psychiatric Association, 1994; Stice, 2001). Specialized evaluation centers and treatment programs continue to become available, even though third-party payers are increasingly reducing or refusing payment for the treatment of eating disorders (Andersen et al., 1997). There is also an impressively large and ever growing body of literature on anorexia nervosa and bulimia nervosa to guide clinicians in their work with persons struggling with these disorders. It is likely that eating disorders will continue to be encountered in a variety of settings, making it incumbent upon health care professionals to have a working understanding of these potentially life-threatening ailments so that effective evaluation, accurate diagnosis, and treatment recommendations can be made. Given these developments, it is surprising that assessment of the eating disorders is often either omitted or granted cursory review in general or introductory compendia on diagnostic interviewing.

The eating disorders are among the most frequently occurring mental disorders afflicting young women today, probably owing to the fact that females are influenced by sociocultural values stressing slimness (Pawluck & Gorey, 1998). Even with this obvious sociocultural contribution to their development, anorexia nervosa and bulimia nervosa are believed to be multidetermined disorders, with each also having significant medical, nutritional, and psychological implications and consequences. There is a much lower prevalence rate in males, which most likely accounts for how little is known about males with eating disorders. It is possible that more males are affected than clinical and community samples would suggest, and that categorizing these disorders as feminine afflictions has deterred men from admitting problematic eating behaviors (Johnson

& Connors, 1987) and from seeking treatment. Although the data are sparse, there is also some evidence that the eating disorders in males and females represent different phenomena. For example, there are differences in measured characteristics of anorexic males as compared with anorexic females (e.g., males show markedly less drive for thinness), so it is possible that gender-specific differences may be operating in causal ways and that effective treatment approaches with each population may differ (Andersen, 1995).

The eating disorders often are chronic and complex, with concomitant medical complications and frequently observed comorbid psychopathology. The clinician who has a serious interest in working in this field is advised to refer to the vast number of articles and handbooks exclusively devoted to furthering our knowledge about care of persons who suffer with these syndromes. This chapter provides only an introduction to diagnostic procedures for the assessment of eating disorders. It is organized into three sections. First, diagnostic categories and issues will be reviewed. Next, various medical, nutritional, and psychological complications and consequences of these disorders will be presented, with an eye toward holistic understanding. Finally, an interview format will be put forth, along with suggestions for treatment planning.

DSM-IV CLASSIFICATION OF EATING DISORDERS

The eating disorders are a subclass of disorders characterized by a significant disturbance in eating behavior (American Psychiatric Association, 1994). The focus here will be on anorexia nervosa and bulimia nervosa, disorders that typically begin in adolescence and early adulthood and that predominantly affect females (approximately 95 percent of these patients are female).

Anorexia Nervosa

The essential features of anorexia nervosa include low body weight, morbid fear of becoming overweight, disturbance in body image, and amenorrhea. A great deal has been written about body image in women in general, and about body image in anorexia nervosa in particular. We have learned that the expressions of disturbance in the patient's experience of his or her shape and weight may vary across patients. Body size may be *perceived* accurately, but *judgments* about these perceptions may be distorted (Walsh & Garner, 1997). For example, patients may become fixedly preoccupied with certain body parts and express great dissatisfaction toward these parts (e.g., stomach, hips), even though they accurately perceive their overall body size.

Patients with anorexia nervosa are significantly, and sometimes profoundly, underweight. Weight loss (or, in children and young adolescents, the failure to gain weight as expected) is achieved via restrictive dieting or fasting, sometimes with the additional weight-reduction methods of self-induced vomiting, laxative or diuretic abuse, and vigorous exercise. Amenorrhea (absence of menstruation for three consecutive cycles) typically follows excessive weight loss, but it can also occur prior to noticeable reduction in weight (American Psychiatric Association, 1994; Garfinkel et al., 1996; Ohlrich & Stephenson, 1986; Walsh & Garner, 1997). The amenorrhea criterion also is satisfied when menstrual periods have been stimulated by ovarian steroids, such as birth control pills, in girls or women who otherwise would not menstruate spontaneously (Walsh & Garner, 1997). In males, the reproductive system is also similarly affected by anorexia nervosa, although unlike girls who manifest a dramatic sign in the abrupt cessation of menses, males have no immediately obvious outward signs of these changes. Whereas in females there is too little estrogen, in males there is an underproduction of testosterone, which gradually affects healthy growth, sexual desire, and potency (Andersen, 1995).

Once a diagnosis of anorexia nervosa has been determined, then the patient must be further diagnosed as meeting the criteria for one or another of the two subtypes: restricting type or binge eating/purging type. In the *Diagnostic and Statistical Manual of Mental Disorders*, third edition, revised (DSM-III-R, American Psychiatric Association, 1987), if the anorexic patient also engaged in binge-eating behavior, then the diagnosis of bulimia nervosa was also applied. Not so in the current nomenclature. It is necessary for the clinician to assess in anorexic patients whether or not there is binge-eating or purging behavior. A patient presenting with both anorexic and bulimic behaviors is classified as anorexia nervosa, binge–purge subtype. According to Herzog and Delinsky (2001), this change in the DSM-IV was made because of reliable evidence that anorexia nervosa poses greater medical danger to patients than bulimia nervosa and is consistently associated with less-favorable outcomes. The diagnostic criteria for this disorder are listed in table 12.1.

Clinically, anorexic patients often deny having any problems (Szmukler & Tantam, 1984), and they are known to be unreliable informants. They begin the assessment process in an avoidant stance, and typically they have been forced to be there by circumstances. There may be motivation to give false information because the patient does not want interference with an approach to coping that, for the time being at least, he or she experiences as positively reinforcing. Upon inquiry, anorexics are likely to say that they are "fine" and that other aspects of their lives are "fine," too. Not surprisingly, they are unlikely to be self-referred. Frequently observed, however, is an emaciated-looking person whose excessive thinness belies disavowal of a problem. The pervasive denial encountered in these patients can make the assessment interview challenging for the therapist interested in understanding the patient.

Many diverse theoretical models exist to explain how anorexia nervosa develops, and applications of these models to psychotherapeutic treatment exist also. However, phenomenologically speaking, the onset of anorexia nervosa

Table 12.1.   Diagnostic Criteria for 307.1, Anorexia Nervosa

A. Refusal to maintain body weight at or above a minimally normal weight for age and height (e.g., weight loss leading to maintenance of body weight less than 85 percent of that expected, or failure to make expected weight gain during period of growth, leading to body weight less than 85 percent of that expected).
B. Intense fear of gaining weight or becoming fat, even though underweight.
C. Disturbance in the way in which one's body, weight, or shape is experienced, undue influence of body weight or shape on self-evaluation, or denial of the seriousness of the current low body weight.
D. In postmenarcheal females, amenorrhea, i.e., the absence of at least three consecutive menstrual cycles. (A woman is considered to have amenorrhea if her periods occur only following administration of hormone, e.g., estrogen.)

Specify type:

Restricting Type: during the current episode of anorexia nervosa, the person has not regularly engaged in binge eating or purging behavior (i.e., self-induced vomiting or the misuse of laxatives, diuretics, or enemas).

Binge-Eating/Purging Type: during the current episode of anorexia nervosa, the person has regularly engaged in binge-eating or purging behavior (i.e., self-induced vomiting or the misuse of laxatives, diuretics, or enemas).

American Psychiatric Association (1994). *Diagnostic and Statistical Manual of Mental Disorders*, 4th ed. Washington, DC: American Psychiatric Association.

symptoms may follow a stressor (Cooper, 1995) that is accompanied by loss of appetite and related weight loss, or it sometimes follows a "successful" restrictive diet in which desired weight loss is found to be particularly reinforcing. In some cases, the disorder may also appear consequent to exposure to media coverage (Chiodo & Latimer, 1983), where along with heightened awareness of the problem, an attraction emerges to the idea of developing the disorder. Bruch (1986) has noted that the latter phenomenon is seen in "me-too" anorexia, in which the imitative basis of the problem may represent a syndrome clinically distinct from the primary anorexia nervosa seen prior to the 1970s. She has also speculated that the traditional psychodynamic conceptualization of the disorder as an original, passionate, and fierce expression of independent strivings may come to lose its meaning, as the "me-too" anorexic begins to predominate. Genuine primary anorexia nervosa may in fact disappear until cultural conditions are once again right for its emergence.

Bulimia Nervosa

The essential feature of bulimia nervosa is binge eating, coupled with overconcern about body weight and shape. There is a feeling of lack of control over eating behavior during the binges, and compensatory activities are used in an attempt to prevent weight gain as a result of the binges. These methods typically include self-induced vomiting, laxatives or diuretics, strict fasting or restrictive dieting, and excessive exercise. Bulimia nervosa often develops out of anorexia nervosa (Keel et al., 2000; Russell, 1979), and while it shares symptoms with this disorder, the essential distinction is that in bulimia nervosa normal weight is often maintained. Often one sees a pattern of alternation between fasting and episodes of binge eating. Compensatory activities designed to prevent weight gain from the binge eating are then instituted. Bulimia nervosa, like anorexia nervosa, also has two subtypes: purging and nonpurging. In the nonpurging subtype, there is no regular use of vomiting, laxatives, or diuretics to control weight. Fasting and excessive exercise are used instead. The diagnostic criteria for bulimia nervosa are listed in table 12.2.

As with the onset of anorexia nervosa, bulimia nervosa often develops following a restrictive diet. In contrast to anorexic patients, though, bulimics typically view their symptoms as pathological. Also, unlike anorexics who may secretly take pride in their eating disordered behavior, bulimic patients often feel quite ashamed of their aberrant behaviors. In addition, the bulimic patient is more likely to be self-referred, openly unhappy, and longing for more effective solutions to personal problems.

Table 12.2.   Diagnostic Criteria for 307.51 Bulimia Nervosa

A. Recurrent episodes of binge eating. An episode of binge eating is characterized by both of the following:
  (1) eating, in a discrete period of time (e.g., within any two-hour period), an amount of food that is definitely larger than most people would eat during a similar period of time and under similar circumstances
  (2) a sense of lacking control over eating during the episode (e.g., a feeling that one cannot stop eating or control what or how much one is eating)
B. Recurrent inappropriate compensatory behavior in order to prevent weight gain, such as self-induced vomiting; misuse of laxatives, diuretics, enemas, or other medications; fasting; or excessive exercise.
C. The binge eating and inappropriate compensatory behaviors both occur, on average, at least twice a week for three months.
D. Self-evaluation is unduly influenced by body shape and weight.
E. The disturbance does not occur exclusively during episodes of anorexia nervosa.

Specify type:

Purging Type: during the current episode of bulimia nervosa, the person has regularly engaged in self-induced vomiting or the misuse of laxatives, diuretics, or enemas.

Nonpurging Type: during the current episode of bulimia nervosa, the person has used other inappropriate compensatory behaviors, such as fasting or excessive exercise, but has not regularly engaged in self-induced vomiting or the misuse of laxatives, diuretics, or enemas.

American Psychiatric Association (1994). *Diagnostic and Statistical Manual of Mental Disorders,* 4th ed. Washington, DC: American Psychiatric Association.

Eating Disorder Not Otherwise Specified

Sometimes it happens that a patient shows prominent disturbances in eating behavior but does not meet the criteria for a specific eating disorder. In atypical cases such as this, the residual category of eating disorder not otherwise specified (NOS) is used. There are two common misconceptions about this diagnostic category. The first is that somehow a more minor or less clinically significant form of eating disorder is implied by the NOS diagnosis. The second is that eating disorder NOS accounts for only a small minority of patients with eating disorders. However, studies show that this diagnosis is given to up to half or more of persons with eating disorder symptoms (Bunnel et al., 1990; Mitrany, 1992). DSM-IV examples are listed in table 12.3.

Differential Diagnosis

The process of identifying the correct diagnosis from among conditions with similar features is known as *differential diagnosis* (Maxmen, 1986). For any apparent psychiatric problem with physiological involvement, etiological distinction must be made between organic and functional conditions. When there is no known physiological cause for a disorder, it is said to be *functional*. Thus, even though biological factors are involved in the eating disorders, they are considered to be functional because no known biological cause is necessary to produce the disorder. In this case, the etiology is believed to be primarily psy-

---

Table 12.3.   307.50, Eating Disorder Not Otherwise Specified

The Eating Disorder Not Otherwise Specified category is for disorders of eating that do not meet the criteria for any specific eating disorder. Examples include:

1. For females, all of the criteria for anorexia nervosa are met except that the individual has regular menses.
2. All of the criteria for anorexia nervosa are met except that, despite significant weight loss, the individual's current weight is in the normal range.
3. All of the criteria for bulimia nervosa are met except that the binge eating and inappropriate compensatory mechanisms occur at a frequency of less than twice a week for a duration of less than three months.
4. The regular use of inappropriate compensatory behavior is displayed by an individual of normal body weight after eating small amounts of food (e.g., self-induced vomiting after the consumption of two cookies).
5. Repeatedly chewing and spitting out, but not swallowing, large amounts of food.
6. Binge-eating disorder: recurrent episodes of binge-eating in the absence of the regular use of inappropriate compensatory behaviors characteristic of bulimia nervosa.

American Psychiatric Association. (1994). *Diagnostic and Statistical Manual of Mental Disorders*, 4th ed. Washington, DC: American Psychiatric Association.

chosocial. The eating disorders are a unique type of psychopathology because the culture, as an environmental variable, appears to be a major etiological factor in their development (Mitchell & Eckert, 1987). Even though functional in etiology, a thorough physical evaluation is always mandatory, due to the medical consequences of the disorders and because some medical illnesses can mimic the physiological aspects of anorexia nervosa and bulimia nervosa (American Psychiatric Association, 1994; Mitchell, 1986).

Once an organic basis for the illness has been ruled out, eating-disordered patients must be distinguished from weight-preoccupied dieters. Dieting and concern about weight have become "normative," and researchers have pointed out that these two groups share some pathological attitudes and behavior, such as binge eating, purging, body-image dissatisfaction, and a drive for thinness (Garner et al., 1984; Polivy & Herman, 1987). Fortunately, the weight-loss criterion for anorexia nervosa and the frequency and duration criteria for bulimia nervosa will help clarify the issue.

Experimental research on starvation in normal subjects (Keys et al., 1950) has found cognitive and behavioral effects (such as irritability, poor concentration, anxiety, emotional lability, and obsessive thinking) that are also observed in the semistarvation associated with anorexia nervosa and bulimia nervosa (Garner et al., 1985; Garner, 1995). This research has clarified the contribution of the effects of starvation to the symptoms of eating disorders, while highlighting the importance of weight gain as fundamental to the treatment process (Andersen, 1983; Garfinkel & Dorian, 2001).

There are also some noteworthy populations to keep in mind when evaluating patients. There are some groups of patients who are at higher risk for developing eating disorders, such as people whose career choices demand that they be thin (e.g., models, dancers, gymnasts). Also at greater risk are persons with severe psychopathology and those who have a history of sexual abuse. There is also the need to be mindful of cultural differences. African American and Asian American women seem to be at lower risk for eating disorders than middle-class white females. However, the risk for minority women increases with more education and greater identification with white middle-class culture (Crago et al., 1996).

Regarding differential diagnosis among psychiatric disorders, there may be weight loss and anorexia (loss of appetite) in depressive disorders, but there is rarely a genuine loss of appetite in anorexia nervosa except in the late stages. Also assisting with the distinction is the fact that depressed patients without anorexia nervosa will not manifest a disturbance in body image or a morbid fear of obesity. In bulimia nervosa, there may be a fear of obesity, and weight loss may be significant, but the patient will not meet the 85 percent of expected body weight criterion.

Past research differentiated "bulimic anorexics" from "restricting anorexics," based on evidence that the former subgroup resembled bulimics more than anorexics. Although these terms are not used in the DSM-IV, the conceptual distinctions they represent have been incorporated into formal diagnosis in the anorexia nervosa subtypes (i.e., the restricting subtype versus the binge-eating/purging subtype). Perhaps a deeper awareness of research findings on these subgroups may be helpful. Of particular interest are the symptoms of bulimia—binge eating and purging—that may have important clinical implications in anorexia nervosa patients with bulimic symptoms (Garner at al., 1993; Johnson & Connors, 1987). The symptoms have been associated with impulse-dominated behavior, indirect expression of aggression, stereotypical views of femininity (Norman and Herzog, 1983), and affective instability (DaCosta & Halmi, 1992; Johnson & Connors, 1987). Overall, however, this subgroup is believed to have the greatest degree of psychopathology (Garner et al., 1993), and according to earlier studies, the poorest prognosis (Casper et al., 1980, Hsu et al., 1979). More severe affective instability may be present, with suicidal ideation (Casper et al., 1980), self-mutilation, sexual acting out, shoplifting, history of sexual abuse, and substance abuse. Persons afflicted with anorexia nervosa binge/purge subtype have a higher rate of suicide attempts and a higher death rate (Garner et al., 1993) Their mortality rate has been identified as 10 percent, much higher than in the other subgroup. Pryor et al. (1996) believe that the clinical utility of these subgroups remains to be seen, because the research is mixed. Other than mortality rates and suicide attempts, some investigators have found no differences between the groups on the impulsive behavior dimension.

CONCURRENT PSYCHIATRIC DIAGNOSIS

Although there appear to be broad similarities among patients diagnosed as manifesting anorexia nervosa and bulimia nervosa, several writers have associated these disorders with specific personality traits and psychopathologies. In anorexia nervosa without bulimic symptoms, obsessiveness, social inhibition, and emotional restraint are common. Bulimia nervosa, in contrast, has been associated with impaired impulse control, although recent research has not supported this finding (Wonderlich, 1995). Heterogeneity is being stressed here in the interest of the patients whom the therapist will be assessing. Knowledge of research suggesting apparent uniformity of personality correlates is important, but only in conjunction with efforts to understand the individual with whom one is working. The eating disorders are best understood from a biopsychosocial framework, and as with any patient, a thorough diagnostic assessment is indispensable to effective treatment planning.

Some research has revealed a link between the eating disorders and the primary affective disorders, particularly for bulimic patients (Johnson, 1985). Both affective disorders and substance abuse disorders have been found to be prevalent among first- and second-degree relatives of eating-disordered patients

(American Psychiatric Association, 1994; Strober et al., 1982, Winokur et al., 1980). However, the role of depression in bulimia nervosa is controversial. It was once believed that bulimia may be a symptom of a biologically mediated affective disorder that might respond to pharmacotherapy. More current thinking includes the alternative notion that an affective disorder may develop as a result of the low self-worth and related feelings of shame that are triggered by the eating disordered behaviors themselves. When a mood disorder is observed, it should be diagnosed on Axis I.

BEYOND THE DSM-IV

Diagnostic labels by themselves do not begin to capture the wide spectrum of behaviors, implications, and consequences found in the eating disorders. The classification of anorexia nervosa and bulimia nervosa as "mental disorders" immediately suggests psychological and social impairment, but omits biological facets of the problem. Since careful assessment based on holistic understanding of the eating disorders is essential to responsible and ethical treatment, the therapist must be familiar with medical, nutritional, and psychological perspectives on the problem.

Medical Aspects of Assessment

The medical consequences of eating disorders differ significantly depending on the particular symptom. Minimally, a comprehensive assessment should include a medical evaluation, both to rule out an organic basis for the disturbed eating and to evaluate for the presence of physical effects of an eating disorder. The potential physical consequences of various eating-disordered behaviors are quite numerous, with the most medically dangerous combination of behavior being restriction of calorie intake and vomiting. In 1986, Ohlrich and Stephenson compiled a list, which is as useful now as it was then, that cites the range of medical complications that can result from each of the specific eating disorder behaviors (see table 12.4).

Among the more common physical side effects of the eating disorders are menstrual difficulties or absence of menses, electrolyte imbalance, dehydration, edema, dental decay, parotid gland enlargement, and gastrointestinal difficulties. The physical consequences can range from minor, reversible problems to death. There are also certain higher-risk situations that may be encountered in clinical practice with the eating disorders, such as with patients who manipulate their medicines to lose weight. For example, persons with hypothyroidism may take doses of their thyroid hormone in excess of the prescribed amount. Diabetic patients may withhold insulin to take off weight, an especially dangerous situation that requires expert understanding and intervention. Involvement of a

Table 12.4.   Major Medical Consequences of Behaviors Associated with Eating Disorders

Restrictive eating—low weight	*Vomiting*
Amenorrhea	Electrolyte problems
Lanugo	Dehydration: dizziness, syncope
Bradycardia	Muscle weakness
Acrocyanosis	Dental enamel erosion, caries
Dehydration: dizziness, syncope	Cardiac arrhythmias
Hypothyroidism: coldness, constipation,	Sore throat; sores in mouth,
gums, dry skin, coarse hair	Nasal congestion
Osteoporosis	Enlarged salivary glands
Retardation of growth in height	Hematemesis
Edema of feet, legs, hands, body	Calluses
Congestive heart failure	*Laxative abuse*
Depression, suicide	Dehydration: dizziness, syncope
Kidney stones	Electrolyte problems
Decreased kidney function	Cardiac arrhythmias
Binge eating	Muscle weakness
Obesity	Rectal bleeding
Edema of feet, legs, hands	Feel constipated upon
Acute stomach dilation; rupture	discontinuing laxatives
possible	Edema of feet, legs, hands upon
Depression, suicide	discontinuing laxatives
Diet pill abuse	Depression, suicide
Elevation of blood pressure	*Diuretic abuse*
Stroke	Electrolyte problems
Myocardial infarction	Dehydration
Seizures	Cardiac arrhythmias
Restlessness, anxiety	Muscle weakness

Ohlrich, S. E., and Stephenson, J. N. (1986). Pitfalls in the care of patients with anorexia nervosa and bulimia. In *Seminars in Adolescent Medicine* 2:81–88. Reprinted by permission from Thieme Medical Publishers, Inc., New York.

physician who is knowledgeable in the assessment and treatment of eating disorders is an absolute necessity in the overall care of all eating disorder patients. A thorough physical examination should be conducted, along with standard laboratory tests such as complete blood count, urinalysis, and a multiple channel chemistry analysis. Additional diagnostic tests should be ordered by a well-informed physician on an individual basis depending on the patient's symptomatic presentation (Goldbloom & Kennedy, 1997; Mitchell, 1995).

Nutritional Aspects of Assessment

Assessment of nutritional status is an integral part of the comprehensive evaluation of an eating-disordered patient. If your clinical setting does not afford opportunity for collaboration with a multidisciplinary team, an outside registered dietician should be consulted. A dietary assessment will reveal in-depth information about the patient's past and present eating patterns, activity level, food dislikes and preferences, and knowledge about nutrition. To understand the patient's degree of nutritional compromise, the nutritionist will conduct a thorough evaluation and determine the patient's body mass index (BMI). Much of the recent research uses Quetelet's body mass index for determining target weights for eating disordered patients (Beaumont et al., 1988). The BMI formula is expressed as weight (in kilograms) divided by height (in meters) squared. Guides to minimum acceptable weights (expressed as BMI) will be determined according to age and other factors by the nutritionist.

The nutritionist's interventions incorporate a great deal of psychoeducation, which is an essential component of comprehensive treatment for the eating disorders (Beaumont et al., 1997; Garner, 1995). The main purpose of nutritional management is the patient's return to, or attainment of, normal body weight. In addition, normal eating behavior will be facilitated and healthy attitudes toward food will have a chance to develop.

Psychological Aspects of Assessment

The eating disorders have profound psychosocial implications, and it is the therapist's task to assess the patient's overall occupational, intrapsychic, and interpersonal functioning. The therapist should inquire in depth about eating patterns, weight history, and related life events. Also evaluated are the type and degree of psychopathology, assets and strengths, and motivation for treatment. In the care of eating-disordered patients, the therapist generally determines the diagnosis, develops a working conceptual understanding of the patient and his or her behavior, and makes treatment recommendations. Hypotheses should be developed regarding the adaptive, functional role of the patient's symptoms as a misfired solution to underlying needs, issues, and conflicts.

THE INITIAL ASSESSMENT

The therapist's approach will differ depending on the setting and availability of professional resources. In a formal program dedicated to the assessment and treatment of eating disorders, there is typically found a multidisciplinary professional team, usually comprising a physician, a nurse, a dietician, and a psychologist. The solitary practitioner should not attempt diagnosis or treatment in the absence of collaborative relationships with other professionals. When outside professionals are consulted, an alliance must be formed so that the therapeutic aspects of a "team" might be simulated. The team approach provides a Winnocottian "holding environment" for the patient, in which clinical management is based on developmental object relations theory (Stern, 1986). Most major programs for eating disorders adhere to some guiding team philosophy in their assessment, treatment, and management of the eating disorders.

Assuming that eating and weight difficulties are known and are part of the presenting complaint, it is essential that the therapist understand the circumstances of the referral. The initial few minutes of the interview are important in understanding attitudes that might affect data collection as well as motivation for subsequent treatment (Johnson, 1985). Generally speaking, patients with anorexia nervosa appear for evaluation at the behest of others in their lives; thus they may be resistant or, at best, reluctant to engage in the assessment process. Patients with bulimia nervosa tend more often to be self-referred and to have some self-awareness as to the pathological nature of their behavior. Consequently, despite their shame and embarrassment, bulimics may be more motivated to provide reliable information. In assessing anorexics, particularly adolescents, it's a good idea to interview parents about the youngster's eating patterns. Some experts also recommend that the clinician spend some time preparing the patient and family for the highly involved assessment process and for the enormous commitment to treatment that may be required for return to health (Strober, 1997).

Significant countertransference reactions may be evoked in working with eating-disordered patients, even in the initial consultation (Johnson, 1985; Johnson, 1992). The term *countertransference* refers to the emotional reactions that arise in the therapist as a result of the patient's influence on the therapist's unconscious feelings (Freud, 1910). Interviewers, in keeping with traditional technique, are advised to monitor their own reactions so as to avoid any deleterious effects of countertransference on the patient and to humanize the situation as a two-party encounter to help understand the patient (Johnson, 1992). The interviewer can "maintain perspective" in the face of provocative or resistant behavior by understanding the "adaptive context" of the eating disorder—that is, by conceptualizing the eating disorder as an attempt to adapt to desperate circumstances (Johnson, 1985). Garfinkel and Dorian (2001) emphasize the importance of seeing the limitations of the DSM-IV system and moving beyond it in our work to truly understand the individual who is being evaluated.

EATING AND WEIGHT HISTORY

Once a medical examination has ruled out an organic basis for abnormal eating behavior, the therapist is free to investigate the psychosocial contributions to the problem. Inquiry will be made into the patient's weight history, including weight fluctuation and methods of weight control, and body image. Onset of weight and food preoccupation should be explored, and the patient should be encouraged to reconstruct the life circumstances that coincided with the development of overconcern with food and weight. Patterns of subsequent problematic eating can be explored in a similar vein. Weight-control methods tried by the patient must be investigated in detail, since this information may bear significantly on the patient's physical health and on degree of medical risk involved. Methods of weight control may include any one of the following activities or some combination thereof: (1) restrictive dieting; (2) self-induced vomiting (possibly with use of syrup of ipecac); (3) laxatives, diuretics, and diet pills; and (4) physical exercise. Vomiting and use of laxatives and diuretics are considered to be purging behaviors. All have serious side effects, and the extent of the behaviors should be ascertained. Patients who use syrup of ipecac, in particular, are at risk for cardiac arrest and sudden death (Adler et al., 1980). The patient's phenomenological experience of all food- and weight-related behaviors can be explored, including dieting behavior, binge eating, and purging. Similarly, the perception of body image can be explored. Body-image difficulties among these patients can range from mild dissatisfaction to severe distortion, and the extent to which such difficulties interfere with life adjustment should be assessed.

SOCIAL HISTORY

The nature of patients' interpersonal functioning is assessed by inquiring about their relationships with family and friends. An interview with the family of the patient provides an opportunity to observe the family in action and to note styles of relating, ways in which members manage the stress of the interview, and the patient's apparent role in the family. In the context of an interpersonal assessment, sexual adjustment can be assessed via inquiry into significant romantic relationships in the individual's life. In this context, sexual attitudes can come to be understood as part of the patient's overall adjustment.

MENTAL STATUS EXAMINATION

It is a sound practice to conduct a mental status examination on all patients seen for an eating disorders assessment. Much of the mental status examination for this population can be informal, ascertained by observations of the patient when covering background history. However, because of the established relationship between increased risk for suicide attempts and eating disorders, a more direct assessment of mood and affect should be made. Any history of suicidal ideation or attempts should be noted, along with any current suicidal thinking or inclinations. Potential for insight is best determined by offering patients a few interpretations during the assessment. Patients' reactions can provide some data from which to conjecture about openness to the therapeutic process. See table 12.5 for a recommended interview format. In addition to the clinical interview, the clinician may want to administer self-report questionnaires as part of the assessment

Table 12.5. Suggested Format for the Assessment of Eating Disorders

1. Background information
   Inform patient and family what to expect from comprehensive assessment and what will be asked of them.
   Establish rapport.
   Determine circumstances of the referral and patient's attitudes about coming for an evaluation.
2. Eating and weight history
   Explore history of the problem.
   Determine onset of weight preoccupation.
   Assess for unusual eating patterns, including binge eating and restrictive dieting.
      (Determine frequency and duration, as well as information about onset of each.
      Also explore patient's perception of control of binge eating and caloric restriction.)
   Note any significant weight fluctuations.
   Inquire about life events that have coincided with any of the foregoing items.
3. Weight-control methods
   Account for nature of restrictive dieting.
   Identify purging methods used by the patient. (Determine frequency and duration for each method.)
      —Vomiting (Self-induced? Reflexive? How induced? Ipecac used?)
      —Laxatives (Type used?)
      —Diuretics (Over-the-counter or prescription?)
      —Diet pills or appetite suppressants (Over-the-counter or prescription?)
   Evaluated activity level and use of exercise to control weight.
   Assess patient's past and current patterns with foregoing information.
4. Self-image
   Explore perceptions of body-image, including perceptions and patient's beliefs about other people's perceptions.
   Explore patient's judgments about his or her own perceptions.
   Assess feelings of self-efficacy.
   Explore issues, concerns, complaints not related to food or weight.
5. Social history
   Gather family history, assessing quality of patient's relationships with parents and siblings.
   Inquire about family environment, past and present.
   Ask patient to tell you something about his or her early youth.
   Explore with patient his or her relationships with peers.
   Explore sexual history, which may range from total retreat from sexual maturation to self-destructive acting out.
   Inquire about history of sexual abuse.
6. Mental status examination
   Evaluate patient formally when sufficient data have not been obtained informally during the interview.
   Determine history and current patterns of substance abuse.
   Identify disturbances in mood and affect.
   Conduct a suicide assessment, including any history of self-mutilation or self-harm.
   Explore any past experiences with treatment.
   Explore long-term goals and goals for current treatment.
7. Treatment recommendations
   Discuss patient's diagnosis.
   Provide feedback on medical, nutritional, and psychological needs.
   Make treatment recommendations.

process. There are several instruments available that assess the behavioral and psychological facets of eating disorders, for example, the Eating Disorder Inventory (EDI-2 [Garner, 1991]) and the Eating Attitudes Test (EAT [Garner & Garfinkel, 1979]). These instruments can never substitute for a thorough and competent clinical interview, but they can provide specific data about problematic behaviors and attitudes, and they can be readministered as a measure of treatment outcome (Crowther & Sherwood, 1997).

TREATMENT RECOMMENDATIONS

When a diagnosis has been determined, feedback is given to the patient and, if they have been involved, to the family as well. Any concerns raised by the diagnosis can then be discussed. Specific medical, nutritional, and psychological needs are highlighted, followed by discussion of a treatment plan. Patient and family must be prepared by the clinician for the involved nature of the upcoming treatment (Strober, 1997). The most obvious treatment decision to be made is between inpatient, partial hospitalization, and outpatient care. The recommendation to hospitalize is based on the following criteria: serious medical compromise resulting from the eating disorder, suicide risk, and failure of previous outpatient treatment to assist the patient with refeeding or with interruption of the binge-purge cycle.

Treatment recommendations should be based on the individual patient's needs, which may require a variety of treatment modalities, such as individual, group, or family psychotherapy; nutritional counseling; medical care; and psychiatric consultation for pharmacotherapy. There is a great deal of research on specific types of psychotherapies used with the eating disorders, and a variety of them are useful. Because of the nature of these disorders, however, psychotherapy alone is not enough; the symptoms must be treated, too (Johnson, 1992). Even though the efficacy of symptom management as a treatment for eating disorders has not been established in the research literature, it is widely accepted that it should be a component of every patient's treatment. Ideally, this is a medically monitored program conducted by a health care professional who regularly checks patient weight and vital signs while also providing psychoeducational material to assist patients toward behavior change. Symptom management is primarily psychoeducational and is conducted as part of, or in conjunction with, ongoing psychotherapies, with attention given to coordinating psychological and medical treatment. Ultimately, these patients need to be in a relationship with an empathic therapist, regardless of theoretical approach, who sees their symptoms as desperate attempts to hang on to hope of growth and self-enhancement. The therapist, by incorporating symptom management into treatment, does not ignore symptoms that hurt the patient physically. In so doing, the therapist ensures the patient is cared for as a whole person—body and soul—and a meaningful relationship can develop in which there is hope and the possibility for true healing.

REFERENCES

Adler, A. G, Walinsky, P., Kroll, R. A., & Cho, S. Y. (1980). Ipecac syrup poisoning. *Journal of the American Medical Association* 243:1927–1928.

American Psychiatric Association (1987). *Diagnostic and Statistical Manual of Mental Disorders*, 3rd ed., rev. Washington, DC: American Psychiatric Association.

American Psychiatric Association (1994). *Diagnostic and Statistical Manual of Mental Disorders*, 4th ed. Washington, DC: American Psychiatric Association.

Andersen, A. E. (1983). Anorexia nervosa and bulimia: A spectrum of eating disorders. *Journal of Adolescent Health Care* 4:15–21.

Andersen, A. E. (1995). Eating disorders in males. In *Eating Disorders and Obesity,* ed. K. D. Brownell and C. G. Fairburn, pp. 177–182. New York: Guilford.

Andersen, A. E., Bowers, W., & Evans, K. (1997). Inpatient treatment for anorexia nervosa. In *Handbook of Treatment for Eating Disorders,* 2nd ed., ed. D. M. Garner and P. E. Garfinkel, pp. 327–348. New York: Guilford.

Beaumont, P. J. V., Al-Alami, M., & Touyz, S. W. (1988). Relevance of a standard measurement of undernutrition to the diagnosis of anorexia nervosa: Use of Quetelet's body mass index. *International Journal of Eating Disorders* 7:399–406.

Beaumont, P. J., Beaumont, C. C., Touyz, S. W., & Williams, H. (1997). Nutritional counseling and supervised exercise. In *Handbook of Treatment for Eating Disorders,* 2nd ed., ed. D. M. Garner and P. E. Garfinkel, pp. 178–187. New York: Guilford.

Bruch, H. (1986). Four decades of eating disorders. In *Handbook of Psychotherapy for Anorexia Nervosa and Bulimia,* ed. D. M. Garner and P. E. Garfinkel, pp. 7–18. New York: Basic.

Bunnel, D. W., Shenker, I. R., Nussbaum, M. P., Jacobson, M. S., & Cooper, P. (1990). Subclinical versus formal eating disorders: Differential psychological features. *International Journal of Eating Disorders* 9:357–362.

Casper, R. C., Eckert, E. D., & Halmi, K. A., et al. (1980). Bulimia: Its incidence and significance in patients with anorexia nervosa. *Archives of General Psychiatry* 37:1030–1035.

Chiodo, J., & Latimer, P. R. (1983). Vomiting as a learned weight-control technique in bulimia. *Journal of Behavior Therapy and Experimental Psychiatry* 14:131–135.

Cooper, Z. (1995). The development and maintenance of eating disorders. In *Eating Disorders and Obesity,* ed. K. D. Brownell and C. G. Fairburn, pp. 199–206. New York: Guilford.

Crago, M., Shisslak, C. M., & Estes, L. M. (1996). Eating disturbance among American minority groups: A review. *International Journal of Eating Disorders* 19:239–248.

Crowther, J. H., & Sherwood, N. E. (1997). Assessment. In *Handbook of Treatment for Eating Disorders,* 2nd ed., ed. D. M. Garner and P. E. Garfinkel, pp. 34–49. New York: Guilford.

DaCosta, M., & Halmi, K. A. (1992). Classification of anorexia nervosa: Question of subtypes. *International Journal of Eating Disorders* 11:305–313.

Freud, S. (1910). The future prospects of psychoanalytic therapy. *Standard Edition* 3:43–68.

Garfinkel, P. E., Lin, E., Goering, P., Spegg, C., Goldbloom, D. S., Kennedy, S., Kaplan, A. S., & Blake Woodsie, D. (1996). Should amenorrhea be necessary for the diagnosis of anorexia nervosa? Evidence from a Canadian community sample. *British Journal of Psychiatry* 168: 500–506.

Garfinkel, P. E., & Dorian, B. J. (2001). Improving understanding and care for the eating disorders. In *Eating Disorders*, ed. R. H. Striegel-Moore and L. Smolak, pp. 9–26. Washington, DC: American Psychological Association.

Garner, D. M. (1991). EDI-2. Odessa, FL. Psychological Assessment Resources.

Garner, D. M. (1995). Measurement of eating disorders psychopathology. In *Eating Disorders and Obesity*, ed. K. D. Brownell and C. G. Fairburn, pp. 117–121. New York: Guilford.

Garner, D. M., & Garfinkel, P. E. (1979). The Eating Attitude Test: An index of symptoms of anorexia nervosa. *Psychosomatic Medicine* 9:273–279.

Garner, D. M., Garner, M. V., & Rosen, L. W. (1993) Anorexia nervosa "restrictors" who purge: Implications for subtyping anorexia nervosa. *International Journal of Eating Disorders* 13:171–186.

Garner, D. M., Olmsted, M. P., Polivy, J., & Garfinkel, P. E. (1984) Comparison between weight-preoccupied women and anorexia nervosa. *Psychosomatic Medicine* 46:255–260.

Garner, D. M., Rockert, W., & Olmsted, M. P., et al. (1985). Psychoeducational principles in the treatment of bulimia and anorexia nervosa. In *Handbook of Psychotherapy for Anorexia Nervosa and Bulimia*, ed. D. M. Garner and P. E. Garfinkel, pp. 19–51. New York: Basic.

Goldbloom, D. S., & Kennedy, S. H. (1995). Medical complications of anorexia nervosa. In *Eating Disorders and Obesity*, ed. K. D. Brownell and C. G. Fairburn, pp. 266–269. New York: Guilford.

Herzog, D. B., & Delinsky, S. S. (2001). Classification of eating disorders. In *Eating Disorders: Innovative Directions in Research and Practice*, ed. R. H. Striegel-Moore and L. Smolak, pp. 31–50. Washington, DC: American Psychological Association.

Hsu, L. K. G., Crisp, A. H., & Harding, B. (1979). Outcome of anorexia nervosa. *Lancet* 1:61–65.

Johnson, C. (1985). Initial consultation for patients with bulimia and anorexia nervosa. In *Handbook of Psychotherapy for Anorexia Nervosa and Bulimia*, ed. D. M. Garner and P. E. Garfinkel, pp. 19–51. New York: Basic.

Johnson, C. (1992). Psychodynamic treatment of bulimia nervosa. In *Psychodynamic Technique in the Treatment of Eating Disorders*, ed. C. P. Wilson, C. G. Hogan, & I. L. Mintz, pp. 349–353. New York: Jason Aronson.

Johnson, C., and Connors, M. E. (1987) *The Etiology and Treatment of Bulimia Nervosa*. New York: Basic.

Keel, P. K., Mitchell, J. E., Miller, K. B., Davis, T. L., & Crow, S. J. (2000) Predictive validity of bulimia nervosa as a diagnostic category. *American Journal of Psychiatry* 157: 136–138.

Keys, A., Brozek, J., Henschel, A., et al. (1950). *The Biology of Human Starvation*. Minneapolis: University of Minnesota Press.

Maxmen, J. S. (1986) *Essential Psychopathology*. New York: Norton.

Mitchell, J. E. (1986). Anorexia nervosa: Medical and physiological aspects. In *Handbook of Eating Disorders*, ed. K. D. Brownell and J. P. Foreyt, pp. 247–265. New York: Basic.

Mitchell, J. E. (1995). Medical complications of bulimia nervosa. In *Eating Disorders and Obesity*, ed. K. D. Brownell and C. G. Fairburn, pp. 271–275. New York: Guilford.

Mitchell, J. E., and Eckert, E. D. (1987). Scope and significance of eating disorders. *Journal of Consulting and Clinical Psychology* 55:628–634.

Mitrany, E. (1992). Atypical eating disorders. *Journal of Adolescent Health* 13:400–402.

Norman, D. K., & Herzog, D. B. (1983). Bulimia, anorexia nervosa, and anorexia nervosa with bulimia: A comparative analysis of MMPI profiles. *International Journal of Eating Disorders* 2:43–52.

Ohlrich, S. E., & Stephenson, J. N. (1986). Pitfalls in the care of patients with anorexia nervosa and bulimia. *Seminars in Adolescent Medicine* 2:81–88.

Pawluck, D. E., & Gorey, K. M. (1998) Secular trends in the incidence of anorexia nervosa: Integrative review of population-based studies. *International Journal of Eating Disorders* 23:347–352.

Polivy, J., & Herman, C. P. (1987). Diagnosis and treatment of normal eating. *Journal of Consulting and Clinical Psychology* 55:635–644.

Pryor, T., Wiederman, M. W., & McGilley, B. (1996). Clinical correlates of anorexia nervosa subtypes. *International Journal of Eating Disorders* 19:371–379.

Russell, G. F. M. (1979). Bulimia nervosa: An ominous variant of anorexia nervosa. *Psychological Medicine* 9:429–448.

Stern, S. (1986). The dynamics of clinical management in the treatment of anorexia nervosa and bulimia: An organizing theory. *International Journal of Eating Disorders* 5:233–254.

Stice, E. (2001). Risk factors for eating pathology: Recent advances and future directions. In *Eating Disorders: Innovative Directions in Research and Practice*, ed. R. H. Striegel-Moore and L. Smolak, pp. 51–73. Washington, DC: American Psychological Association.

Strober, M. (1997). Consultation and therapeutic engagement in severe anorexia nervosa. In *Handbook of Treatment for Eating Disorders*, 2nd ed., ed. D. M. Garner and P. E. Garfinkel, pp. 229–247. New York: Guilford.

Strober, M., Salkin, B., Burroughs, J., & Morrell, W. (1982). Validity of the bulimia-restrictor distinction in anorexia nervosa: Parental personality characteristics and family psychiatric morbidity. *Journal of Nervous and Mental Diseases* 170:345–351.

Szmukler, G. I., & Tantam, D. (1984). Anorexia nervosa: Starvation dependence. *British Journal of Medical Psychology* 57:303–310.

Walsh, B. T., & Garner, D. M. (1997). Diagnostic issues. In *Handbook of Treatment for Eating Disorders*, 2nd ed., ed. D. M. Garner and P. E. Garfinkel, pp. 25–33. New York: Guilford.

Winokur, A., March, V., & Mendels, J. (1980). Primary affective disorder in relatives of patients with anorexia nervosa. *American Journal of Psychiatry* 137:695–698.

Wonderlich, S. (1995). Personality and eating disorders. In *Eating Disorders and Obesity*, ed. K. D. Brownell and C. G. Fairburn, pp. 171–176. New York: Guilford.

13

PERSONALITY DISORDERS

Thomas A. Widiger, Ph.D.★

PERSONALITY DISORDERS

"Personality traits are enduring patterns of perceiving, relating to, and thinking about the environment and oneself that are exhibited in a wide range of social and personal contexts" (American Psychiatric Association, 2000, p. 686). Every individual, including every person with some form of psychopathology, will have had a characteristic manner of thinking, feeling, behaving, and relating to others prior to and during the course of his or her current disorder. In addition, "when personality traits are inflexible and maladaptive and cause significant functional impairment or subjective distress, . . . they constitute Personality Disorders" (American Psychiatric Association, 2000, p. 686). Some persons obtaining treatment within clinical settings will be there primarily because of their personality disorders.

Personality disorders were first placed on a separate diagnostic axis (Axis II) in the influential third edition of the American Psychiatric Association's (APA's) *Diagnostic and Statistical Manual of Mental Disorders* (DSM-III; American Psychiatric Association, 1980). Most other mental disorders were placed on Axis I. This distinction has been retained with the fourth, text revision edition of the APA diagnostic manual (DSM-IV-TR, American Psychiatric Association, 2000) in order to continue to encourage the recognition of maladaptive personality traits in virtually every patient for whom a diagnosis might be provided, because personality disorders will affect the occurrence, expression, course, or treatment of most other mental disorders (Dolan-Sewell et al., 2001; Frances, 1980; Widiger, 2001) and are the potential focus of effective treatment themselves (Perry et al., 1999; Salekin, 2002; Sanislow & McGlashan, 1998).

★ Correspondence concerning this chapter should be sent to Thomas A. Widiger, Ph.D., Department of Psychology, 115 Kastle Hall, University of Kentucky, Lexington, Kentucky, 40506-0044; e-mail: widiger@uky.edu.

Personality disorders, however, are among the most difficult to assess and diagnose (Farmer, 2000; Perry, 1992; Westen, 1997; Widiger, 2002; Widiger & Coker, 2001; Zimmerman, 1994). This chapter reviews techniques and principles of personality disorder interviewing, organized with respect to the major issues that complicate the obtainment of valid diagnoses: unreliability, limited time and coverage, excessive diagnostic co-occurrence, traits versus states, distortions in self-description, and gender bias.

UNRELIABILITY

One of the major innovations of DSM-III (American Psychiatric Association, 1980) was the provision of behaviorally specific diagnostic criterion sets (Spitzer et al., 1980): "The order of inference [was] relatively low, and the characteristic features [consisted] of easily identifiable behavioral signs or symptoms" (American Psychiatric Association, 1980, p. 7). These behaviorally specific diagnostic criteria improved substantially the reliability of clinicians' diagnoses (Nathan & Langenbucher, 1999; Rogers, 2001; Segal, 1997). However, the development of behaviorally specific diagnostic criterion sets has been problematic for the personality disorders. It is difficult, perhaps even impossible, to provide a brief list of specific diagnostic criteria for the broad and complex behavior patterns that constitute a personality disorder. As acknowledged in DSM-III-R, "for some disorders, . . . particularly the Personality Disorders, the criteria require much more inference on the part of the observer" (American Psychiatric Association, 1987, p. xxiii). Narcissistic lack of empathy and borderline identity disturbance, for example, are abstract clinical constructs that can be interpreted in a variety of ways by different clinicians and can be inferred on the basis of a variety of behaviors (Widiger, 1991). As a result, personality disorders typically fail to be diagnosed reliably in general clinical practice (Mellsop et al., 1982; Nazikian et al., 1990; Spitzer et al., 1979). The only personality disorder to be diagnosed reliably in general clinical practice has been the antisocial, largely because its diagnostic criterion set is the most behaviorally specific (Blais et al., 1996; Shea, 1992); yet, the validity of this diagnosis has been questioned precisely because of its emphasis on overt and behaviorally specific acts of criminality, irresponsibility, and delinquency (Hare et al., 1991; Widiger & Corbitt, 1995).

The authors of DSM-IV (American Psychiatric Association, 1994) attempted to address this problem in part by providing more discussion of the meaning of each personality disorder diagnostic criterion in the text of the manual (Frances et al., 1995). The section of the diagnostic manual that will be most familiar to clinicians is the table providing the diagnostic criterion set. However, a substantial amount of additional information that can be helpful in assessment and diagnosis is provided in other sections of the text. More specifically, the text description of each personality disorder begins with a section that describes narratively the "diagnostic features" of that disorder. In DSM-III (American Psychiatric Association, 1980) and DSM-III-R (American Psychiatric Association, 1987) this material did no more than reiterate the diagnostic criterion sets in a narrative format. No additional examples, elaboration, or clarification of the criterion sets were provided, because it was believed that the criterion sets should be self-explanatory (Frances et al., 1995; Spitzer et al., 1980). If additional information was necessary to understand or apply them, it was believed that this information should have been included within the criterion set. However, the authors of DSM-IV took a different view and used the diagnostic features section of the text to provide additional information, clarification, and elaboration of each diagnostic criterion in order to increase the likelihood that clinicians would be accurate and consistent in their understanding, interpretation, and application of the criterion.

A good example of this effort is provided by the diagnostic criterion for antisocial recklessness. In DSM-III-R, this criterion was: "Is reckless regarding his or her own or others' personal safety, as indicated by driving while intoxicated, or recurrent speeding" (American Psychiatric Association, 1987, p. 345). This criterion was assessed reliably in general clinical practice because it was quite behaviorally specific, being confined to just two possible behaviors: (1) driving while intoxicated and (2) recurrent speeding. However, it was apparent to clinicians and researchers that limiting the assessment of antisocial recklessness to just these two behaviors provided an inadequate (invalid) assessment. The criterion was in fact useless for persons who rarely used a car (e.g., persons living in cities where cabs and public transportation are commonly used). Therefore, the authors of DSM-IV broadened the criterion to a "reckless disregard for safety of self or others" (American Psychiatric Association, 1994, p. 650) and indicated within the text discussion that this recklessness involved not only driving but also sexual behavior (e.g., multiple and indiscriminately selected sexual partners without using protection), drug behavior (e.g., use of dirty needles), and parental behavior (e.g., involving children in drug usage).

Researchers and many clinicians have also addressed unreliability in the assessment of personality disorders by using semistructured interviews (Widiger & Coker, 2001). Semistructured interviews are the preferred method for assessing personality disorders in clinical research (Rogers, 2001; Segal, 1997; Zimmerman, 1994). Semistructured interviews improve the reliability of assessments by providing an explicit set of required questions for each diagnostic criterion and, in some instances, a detailed manual for the interpretation of the answers to these questions, for interpreting vague or inconsistent symptomatology, and for resolving diagnostic ambiguities. Adequate levels of reliability are generally (although not necessarily) obtained when semistructured interviews are used (Kaye & Shea, 2000; Widiger & Coker, 2001; Zimmerman, 1994).

Clinicians will find semistructured interviews to be constraining. They may prefer to follow leads that arise during the course of an interview and to adjust questioning to facilitate rapport and personal style (Westen, 1997). However, a major strength of a semistructured interview is the assurance through an explicit structure that each relevant diagnostic criterion is in fact systematically assessed (Rogers, 2001; Segal, 1997).

Semistructured interviews have been described as providing only a superficial and mindless symptom counting (Westen & Shedler, 1999a). However, semistructured interviews are not simply a series of direct questions as to the presence of each DSM-IV-TR diagnostic criterion. Semistructured interviews are *semi*structured because they include many open-ended questions, indirect inquiries, and observations of a respondent's manner of relating to the interviewer, in addition to relatively more direct questions. Furthermore, interviewers administering semistructured interviews do not simply record respondents' answers to queries. Interviewers must use their clinical expertise to rate each diagnostic criterion based on the substantial amount of information that is generated by a semistructured interview. In some instances, interviewers will code a diagnostic criterion as present even though a respondent is denying its presence.

DSM-IV-TR SEMISTRUCTURED INTERVIEWS

There are currently five semistructured interviews coordinated explicitly with the diagnostic criteria provided within DSM-IV-TR (American Psychiatric Association, 2000): (1) Diagnostic Interview for Personality Disorders (DIPD, Zanarini et al., 1987); (2) International Personality Disorder Examination (IPDE, Loranger, 1999); (3) Personality Disorder Interview-IV (PDI-IV, Widiger et al., 1995); (4) Structured Clinical Interview for DSM-IV Axis II Personality Disorders (SCID-II, First et al., 1997); and (5) Structured Interview for DSM-IV Personality Disorders (SIDP-IV, Pfohl et al., 1997).

Each of these interviews has particular advantages and disadvantages relative to one another (Kaye & Shea, 2000; Rogers, 2001; Widiger, 2002). The SIDP-IV and PDI-IV were the first to be developed. The SIDP-IV, SCID-II, and IPDE have been used in the most studies and have more empirical support than either the DIPD or PDI-IV. The manuals for the SIDP-IV, SCID-II, and DIPD are relatively limited in the amount of information and guidance provided. A valid interview assessment of the personality disorders is facilitated substantially by a sophisticated understanding of the criterion sets. The manual for the PDI-IV is the most thorough, providing a detailed history, the rationale, and the major assessment issues for every one of the ninety-four DSM-IV-TR personality disorder diagnostic criteria. Even if a researcher or clinician prefers to use another semistructured interview, the PDI-IV manual will be helpful in the training of interviewers. Some researchers use the PDI-IV manual in conjunction with the administration of the SCID-II, SIDP-IV, or IPDE. The IPDE takes the most time to administer, as it includes the largest number of required and recommended inquiries per diagnostic criterion. The IPDE and SIDP-IV include guidelines for the assessment of the World Health Organization's International Classification of Diseases (ICD-10; World Health Organization, 1992) personality disorder diagnostic criteria, but it should be noted that neither interview provides separate questions for their assessment. They simply indicate which questions developed for the assessment of the DSM-IV-TR personality disorders could also be used for the assessment of respective ICD-10 diagnostic criteria. The SCID-II might be considered by most researchers as the most straightforward to administer, and it might be the easiest and briefest to administer, but it might also be the most superficial in its questioning.

An additional instrument to consider is the Shedler-Westen Assessment Procedure (SWAP-200, Westen & Shedler, 1999a; 1999b). The SWAP-200 is a set of 200 items, approximately half of which are the ninety-four DSM-IV-TR personality disorder diagnostic criteria, the remainder being additional personality disorder symptoms, defense mechanisms, and adaptive personality traits. The SWAP-200 items can be scored by a clinician on the basis of an interview. However, the SWAP-200 does not provide any required or recommended questions for the assessment of each item, nor does it include a manual for their interpretation or assessment. The SWAP-200 is essentially a checklist that includes the DSM-IV-TR diagnostic criteria as well as additional diagnostic criteria that could be useful and informative.

The extent of convergence among the semistructured interviews is difficult to determine because there have been only two studies that have administered more than one of these interviews to the same respondents. This remarkable lack of concurrent validity research is a testament to the amount of time it takes to administer them (an issue discussed further below). The two published studies were by O'Boyle and Self (1990) and Skodol and colleagues (1991). O'Boyle and Self administered the DSM-III-R versions of the IPDE and the SCID-II to twenty psychiatric inpatients (a limited sample size for a study concerned with the convergent validity of ten personality disorder diagnoses). The IPDE and SCID-II were administered on average three days apart by interviewers blind to the results of the other interview. Order of administration was staggered. Only twelve of the twenty patients met the criteria for at least one personality disorder. Agreement for the three personality disorders for which at least five patients received a diagnosis ranged from a kappa of only .18 for the diagnosis of paranoid personality disorder to .23 for dependent and .62 for borderline. Overall kappa across all diagnoses was only .38.

The results of O'Boyle and Self (1990) are not encouraging, although the findings should be tempered by the very low number of participants. In addition, four of the twenty patients were psychotic during their interviews. Eighteen of the twenty patients were subsequently readministered both interviews at the time of discharge (mean of sixty-three days later, median of seventeen days). The interviews were this time administered on average within .5 mean days of one another (median 1.7 days). Agreement for any particular personality disorder at the readministration was considerably better (i.e., kappa =.78).

Skodol and colleagues (1991) administered the DSM-III-R versions of the IPDE and SCID-II to one hundred inpatients of a personality disorders treatment unit. Both interviews were administered blind to one another on the same day (one in the morning, the other in the afternoon). Order of administration was staggered. Rates of agreement for categorical diagnoses were statistically significant for all but two of the disorders (schizoid and passive–aggressive), but were still lower than the authors' expectations. Kappa for individual diagnoses ranged from a low of .14 (schizoid) to a high of .66 (dependent), with a median kappa of .53 (borderline). The authors considered the agreement for half of the categorical diagnoses to be inadequate. "It is fair to say that, for a number of disorders (i.e., paranoid, schizoid, schizotypal, narcissistic, and passive-aggressive) the two [interviews] studied do not operationalize the diagnoses similarly and thus yield disparate results" (Skodol et al., 1991, p. 22). They also indicated that, in general, the SCID-II yielded appreciably more personality disorder diagnoses than the IPDE (thirty-five versus fifteen diagnoses). However, it should also be noted that the median agreement was comparable to agreement rates typically obtained for the diagnosis of Axis I mental disorders when their assessments are conducted blind to one another (Loranger, 1992). In addition, agreement with respect to a more quantitative assessment of the extent to which each personality disorder was present was considerably better, with correlations ranging from a low of .58 (schizoid) to a high of .87 (antisocial). Skodol and colleagues concluded that "the greater agreement shown by comparing dimensions of disorder than by comparing strict categorical diagnoses suggests that patients are providing interviewers with reliable information about areas of difficulty in personality functioning and interviewers are able to judge when at least some of these reports indicate clinically significant psychopathology" (Skodol et al., 1991, p. 22).

ADDITIONAL SEMISTRUCTURED INTERVIEWS

There are also interviews for the assessment of individual personality disorders, including (but not limited to) the Revised Diagnostic Interview for Borderlines (DIB-R, Zanarini et al., 2002), the Diagnostic Interview for Narcissism (DIN, Gunderson et al., 1990), and the Hare Psychopathy Checklist-Revised (PCL-R, Hare, 1991). There is currently only one interview for the assessment of a dimensional model of personality disorder: the Structured Interview for the Five-Factor Model (SIFFM, Trull & Widiger, 1997).

The DIB-R, DIN, and PCL-R are very useful when the clinician's or researcher's interest is confined to the borderline, narcissistic, or psychopathic personality disorder, respectively (Kaye & Shea, 2000). However, each of these interviews can require as much time to assess the individual personality disorder as the SIDP-IV, SCID-II, or PDI-IV would use to assess all ten of the DSM-IV-TR personality disorders. The individual personality disorder interviews provide more fidelity (specificity, detail); the DSM-IV-TR interviews provide more bandwidth (coverage). For example, the DIB-R will provide a more thorough assessment of borderline symptomatology than is provided by the SIDP-IV, including subscales for affective instability, interpersonal relationships, impulsivity, and cognitive aberrations, but the DIB-R will fail to assess for the presence of other personality disorder symptomatology assessed by the SIDP-IV that might also be of substantial clinical or scientific importance.

Psychopathy is a personality disorder that is of particular importance to clinicians and researchers working within forensic settings. Psychopathy is closely related to the DSM-IV-TR antisocial personality disorder, but it includes a few additional personality traits, notably glib charm, arrogance, shallow affect, and lack of empathy (Widiger et al., 1996). Other personality traits included within the PCL-R (i.e., lack of remorse, deceitfulness, and irresponsibility) are included within the DSM-IV-TR antisocial diagnostic criteria (arrogance and lack of empathy are included within the DSM-IV-TR criterion set for narcissistic personality disorder).

The PCL-R is a well-validated instrument and PCL-R psychopathy does appear to have more validity within prison and forensic settings than the DSM-IV-TR antisocial personality disorder (American Psychiatric Association, 2000; Hare et al., 1991; Lilienfeld, 1994; Widiger et al., 1996). However, as suggested by its title, the PCL-R is better described as a checklist than as a semistructured interview. Many of its items are scored primarily (if not solely) on the basis of a person's criminal record rather than on the basis of interview questions (e.g., a history of murders or rapes is used to indicate a lack of empathy; Hare, 1991). The purported advantage of the PCL-R in providing an assessment that is not based simply on a criminal or legal record (Hare et al., 1991) is compromised by PCL-R's reliance on this same history to score most of its items, including the key psychopathic traits of callousness, lack of empathy, deceitfulness, and lack of remorse. The availability of a detailed criminal history within prison settings has probably been the major reason for PCL-R's excellent interrater reliability and predictive validity. An application of the PCL-R within other clinical settings (e.g., outpatient clinics, private practice, and psychiatric hospitals) will have to rely heavily, if not solely, on an interview, yet no interview questions are provided for many of the PCL-R items.

LIMITED TIME, LIMITED COVERAGE

An additional issue is the amount of time it takes to provide a thorough and accurate assessment of personality disorder symptomatology. Eighty diagnostic criteria are provided for the ten personality disorders included in DSM-IV-TR (American Psychiatric Association, 2000). Even if one spent two hours devoted to their assessment, that would still allow (on average) only ninety seconds to assess for a borderline identity disturbance or a narcissistic lack of empathy, and one would not have left any time for the assessment of the two personality disorders included in the appendix to DSM-IV-TR (depressive and negativistic) or for the assessment of any other maladaptive personality traits that could be of considerable clinical importance (Westen & Arkowitz, 1998; Bagby et al., 1994).

Clinicians often fail to assess adequately the full range of personality disorder symptomatology that is in fact present in their patients (Zimmerman & Mattia, 1999b). Morey and Ochoa (1989) provided 291 clinicians with the 166 DSM-III (American Psychiatric Association, 1980) personality disorder diagnostic criteria and asked them to indicate which DSM-III personality disorder(s) were present in one of their patients and indicate which of the 166 DSM-III personality disorder diagnostic criteria were present. Kappa for the agreement between their diagnoses and the diagnoses that would be given based upon the diagnostic criteria they indicated to be present was poor, ranging from .11 (schizoid) to .58 (borderline), with a median kappa of only .25. In other words, their clinical diagnoses agreed poorly with their own assessments of the diagnostic criteria for each of the personality disorders. These findings were subsequently replicated by Blashfield and Herkov, who concluded that "the actual diagnoses of clinicians do not adhere closely to the diagnoses suggested by the [diagnostic] criteria" (Blashfield & Herkov, 1996, p. 226).

One of the advantages of a semistructured interview relative to an unstructured interview is that a semistructured interview compels the clinician to assess systematically each diagnostic criterion, ensuring that all of the disorders are comprehensively assessed (Kaye & Shea, 2000; Rogers, 2001; Segal, 1997; Widiger, 2002). If clinicians are provided with the systematic and comprehensive assessments of personality disorder symptomatology provided by a semistructured interview, they do recognize the value of this information. For example, Zimmerman and Mattia (1999a) reported that a large sample of clinicians diagnosed only .4 percent of patients with borderline personality disorder, whereas 14.4 percent were diagnosed with this disorder when a semistructured interview was implemented. Zimmerman and Mattia then provided the clinicians with the additional information obtained by the semistructured interview. They found that "providing the results of [the] semistructured interview to clinicians prompts them to diagnose borderline personality disorder much more frequently" (Zimmerman & Mattia, 1999a, p. 1570). The rate of diagnosis increased from .4 percent to 9.2 percent. "This is inconsistent with the notion that personality disorder diagnoses based on semistructured interviews are not viewed as valid by clinicians" (p. 1570).

The administration of an entire semistructured personality disorder interview, however, is unrealistic in general clinical practice, particularly in these days of severely limited funding for clinical assessments. The PDI-IV (Widiger et al., 1995) and SIDP-IV (Pfohl et al., 1997) require, on average, two hours for their administration; the IPDE (Loranger, 1999) typically requires much more time. One approach to this problem has been to develop screening interviews. Pfohl and his colleagues are exploring whether just eleven questions from the SIDP-IV can be used to identify whether any one of the DSM-IV-TR personality disorders is likely to be present (Langbehn et al., 1999). However, their findings are too limited to date to recommend this approach in clinical practice or research.

Another approach is to use a self-report screening measure (Dowson, 1992). Pilkonis and his colleagues have been conducting studies to try to reduce the 127-item Inventory of Interpersonal Problems (Horowitz et al., 1988) to a much briefer set of items (e.g., twenty-five) that would identify effectively whether any one of the ten DSM-IV-TR personality disorders is likely to be present (e.g., Kim & Pilkonis, 1999). A hypothesis of this project is that personality disorders are primarily disorders of interpersonal relatedness (Pilkonis, 1997); therefore, an instrument that provides a comprehensive assessment of the different ways in which a person can be interpersonally dysfunctional might serve as an effective screening device. A limitation of this effort is that a substantial proportion of personality disorder symptomatology (e.g., borderline) may not be adequately represented by maladaptive interpersonal functioning (Widiger & Hagemoser, 1997).

A more effective screening device would be a self-report inventory developed for the purpose of identifying the presence of the DSM-IV-TR personality disorders. The amount of time required for the administration of a semistructured interview can be reduced substantially by first administering this screening instrument to identify which personality disorders should be emphasized during the interview and which disorders could be ignored with minimal risk. For example, the interviewer might focus on just the two to four diagnoses that obtained the highest elevations on the screening measure (one or more of which might not have been anticipated by the clinician), thereby reducing considerably the amount of time needed for the interview, yet still covering disorders that might have been missed with an unstructured interview. A potential advantage of the SCID-II (First et al., 1997) and the IPDE (Loranger, 1999) relative to the other semistructured interviews is that they provide easily hand-scored, self-report screening instruments constructed to err in the direction of false positives (Jacobsberg et al., 1995). However, if the clinician intends to use a screening questionnaire, he or she might as well use a self-report inventory that was constructed to provide a comprehensive, valid, and independent assessment of the personality disorders and for which a substantial amount of validity data have been obtained, such as the Millon Clinical Multiaxial Inventory-III (Millon et al., 1997) or the relatively briefer and less expensive Personality Diagnostic Questionnaire-4 (Hyler, 1994) or Coolidge Axis II Inventory (Coolidge & Merwin, 1992).

EXCESSIVE DIAGNOSTIC CO-OCCURRENCE

The intention of the DSM-IV-TR diagnostic manual is to help clinicians determine which particular disorder is present, the diagnosis of which would purportedly indicate the presence of a specific pathology that would explain the occurrence of all of the symptoms and suggest a specific treatment that would ameliorate the patient's suffering (Frances et al., 1995). Ideally, patients would then meet DSM-IV-TR diagnostic criteria for only one personality disorder.

To facilitate the effort to identify which personality disorder is present, one of the sections of the text of DSM-IV-TR is devoted to differential diagnosis. "This section discusses how to differentiate the disorder from other disorders that have some similar presenting characteristics" (American Psychiatric Association, 2000, p. 10). For example, many patients who meet the DSM-IV-TR criteria for dependent personality disorder will also meet the DSM-IV-TR criteria for avoidant personality disorder (Widiger & Trull, 1998). To facilitate the differentiation of these disorders, it is noted in the text of DSM-IV-TR that although both are characterized by feelings of inadequacy, hypersensitivity to criticism, and a need for reassurance, "the primary focus of concern in Avoidant Personality Disorder is avoidance of humiliation and rejection [whereas] in Dependent Personality Disorder the focus is on being taken care of" (American Psychiatric Association, 2000, p. 720). Some of the personality disorder semi-structured interview manuals go further than DSM-IV-TR and provide additional suggestions for how each personality disorder might be effectively differentiated from others. For example, fights are included within the diagnostic criterion sets for both the antisocial and borderline personality disorders (American Psychiatric Association, 2000), but it is suggested in the manual for the PDI-IV that the fights of an antisocial person are likely to be more calculated or premeditated and are more likely to serve the purpose of subjugation, control, humiliation, or exploitation, whereas the fights of a person with a borderline personality disorder will tend to be more impulsive, explosive, provocative, and self-harmful (Widiger et al., 1995).

However, despite the best efforts of the authors of each edition of the diagnostic manual to construct criterion sets that would optimize differential diagnosis, comprehensive and systematic assessments of the DSM-IV-TR personality disorders have repeatedly indicated that multiple diagnoses are the norm rather than the exception (Clark et al., 1997; Oldham et al., 1992; Bornstein, 1998; Lilienfeld et al., 1994). Nevertheless, clinicians generally provide only one personality disorder diagnosis for each patient (Gunderson, 1992; Zimmerman & Mattia, 1999b). Clinicians appear to diagnose personality disorders hierarchically (Gunderson, 1992). Once a patient is identified as having a particular personality disorder (e.g., borderline or antisocial), the clinician tends to fail to assess whether additional maladaptive personality traits are present (Herkov & Blashfield, 1995). Adler et al. (1990) provided forty-six clinicians with case histories of a patient that met the DSM-III (American Psychiatric Association,

1980) criteria for four personality disorders (histrionic, narcissistic, borderline, and dependent). "Despite the directive to consider each category separately, . . . most clinicians assigned just one [personality disorder] diagnosis" (Adler et al., 1990, p. 127). Sixty-five percent of the clinicians provided only one diagnosis, 28 percent provided two, and none provided all four.

The Collaborative Longitudinal Personality Disorders multisite study (Gunderson et al., 2000) has formally adopted a hierarchical decision rule for their personality disorder diagnoses. If a patient meets the DSM-IV-TR criteria for a borderline or schizotypal personality disorder, then no additional personality disorder diagnoses (e.g., antisocial, narcissistic, or avoidant) are recorded. This approach is useful in removing excessive diagnostic co-occurrence from data analyses, but it may only address the problem by fiat. That antisocial or avoidant personality traits are simply not included in the data analyses does not mean that they are not in fact present and would not have a meaningful impact on treatment, course, or outcome. Diagnostic comorbidity does appear to have clinically meaningful and theoretically significant implications for the etiology, course, and treatment of mental disorders (Mineka, Watson, & Clark, 1998; Widiger & Clark, 2000).

The application of the SWAP-200 (Westen, 1997) typically results in substantially fewer multiple diagnoses than are obtained by semistructured interviews (Westen & Shedler, 1999a, 1999b), but this finding is largely the result of the artifactual requirement of the SWAP-200 to record as many as half of its items as being absent and only a very small number as being highly descriptive. For example, Westen and Shedler (1999b) required the clinicians in their study to identify no more than eight of the two hundred items as being highly descriptive and one hundred of them as being entirely absent. Requiring that a specific distribution of personality disorder ratings be provided is advantageous in minimizing the occurrence of undesirable and problematic results, but it may also fail to provide the most accurate descriptions. The SWAP-200 fixed distribution is equivalent to requiring that persons administering a DSM-IV-TR personality disorder semistructured interview rate half of the diagnostic criteria as being absent, no matter what behaviors or symptoms are observed by the clinician.

The optimal solution to the occurrence of multiple diagnoses may not be ignoring their presence or even more effort at obtaining a differential diagnosis. The problem might be the assumption that multiple diagnoses are failing to provide an accurate description of the patient. Multiple diagnoses may simply reflect the fact that persons are best characterized by a variety of adaptive and maladaptive personality traits. The reason that patients meet the criteria for more than one personality disorder might be that one diagnostic label is inadequate in describing any particular person's idiosyncratic constellation of maladaptive personality traits (Livesley, 1998; Widiger, 1993; Widiger & Frances, 1985). There are over a thousand personality trait terms within the English language, many of which would be necessary to describe adequately any particular individual (Goldberg, 1990). A patient might be dependent, but he or she can also be introverted, exhibitionistic, alexithymic, impulsive, hostile, excitement seeking, negligent, or hedonistic. The DSM-IV-TR personality disorder diagnoses provide a substantial amount of useful and valid information concerning the maladaptive personality functioning of a patient, but single diagnoses will often fail to describe adequately the full range of maladaptive functioning that is in fact present in any particular patient (Widiger, 1993).

A proposal for the next edition of the diagnostic manual is to provide the diagnosis of "extensive personality disorder" when the person meets criteria for two or more personality disorders (Oldham & Skodol, 2000). One might say, for instance, that one patient has a dependent personality disorder (if he or she fails to meet diagnostic criteria for any other personality disorder), whereas another patient has an extensive personality disorder, characterized by dependent, histrionic, and borderline personality traits. One could also provide a dimensional profile description of a patient in terms of all of the DSM-IV-TR personality disorders, indicating which disorders are absent, subthreshold, threshold, moderately present, or severely present (Oldham & Skodol, 2000; Widiger & Sanderson, 1995). The manuals for some semistructured interviews (SCID-II, SIDP-IV, and PDI-IV) already encourage the use of profile descriptions. The PDI-IV includes a profile scoring summary sheet for this dimensional description (Widiger et al., 1995).

A more radical alternative is to abandon the DSM-IV-TR diagnostic categories altogether and convert to a more comprehensive dimensional system of classification. Many such proposals are being developed, including the seven-factor model of Cloninger (2000), the four-factor models of Livesley and Clark (Livesley & Jang, 2000; Clark & Livesley, 2002), and the five-factor model of Costa and Widiger (2002). Each of these systems includes broad domains of personality functioning (e.g., neuroticism versus emotional stability, introversion versus extraversion, openness versus closedness to experience, agreeableness versus antagonism, and conscientiousness versus undependability within the five-factor model) and more specific underlying facets (e.g., the facets of agreeableness versus antagonism are gullible versus mistrusting, naïve versus deceptive, sacrificial versus exploitative, docile versus combative, meek versus arrogant, and softhearted versus callous). These alternative dimensional models may not in fact replace the personality disorder diagnostic categories in DSM-V, but they will likely be given some recognition and may in fact be the future of personality disorder diagnosis (First et al., in press; Widiger, 2001; Widiger et al., 2002).

PERSONALITY TRAITS VERSUS
MOOD STATES AND AXIS I DISORDERS

Personality disorders are typically assessed during a patient's initial days of clinical treatment, but this is probably the most difficult time to obtain an accurate self-description of personality functioning. Persons who are significantly depressed, anxious, or angry are unlikely to provide accurate descriptions of their characteristic, ongoing manner of thinking, feeling, and relating to others. Persons who are depressed will describe themselves as being more dependent, introverted, self-conscious, vulnerable, and pessimistic than they would have prior to their depressed mood.

Clinical interviews have the potential of being relatively more resistant to the distorting effects of mood states than self-report inventories (Loranger et al., 1991; Widiger & Coker, 2001), but they are not immune to this problem (e.g., O'Boyle & Self, 1990; Stuart et al., 1992). An interviewer can easily fail to appreciate the extent to which patients' self-descriptions are being distorted by their mood. In fact, the one study that claimed to demonstrate the resilience of a semistructured interview to mood-state distortions obtained results equivalent to mood-state distortion findings reported for self-report inventories (e.g., Piersma, 1989). Loranger and his colleagues compared IPDE assessments obtained at the beginning of an inpatient admission to those obtained one week to six months later and found that "there was a significant reduction in the mean number of criteria met on all of the personality disorders except schizoid and antisocial" (Loranger et al., 1991, p. 726). They argued that the apparent reduction in personality disorder symptomatology was not due to an artifactual inflation of scores secondary to a depressed or anxious mood, because the changes were not correlated with anxiety or depression. However, an alternative perspective is that the study lacked sufficiently sensitive or accurate measures to explain why there was a substantial decrease on ten of the twelve personality disorder scales over a brief period of time. It is unlikely that one week to six months of treatment resulted in the extent of changes to personality that were indicated by the IPDE (the change scores also failed to correlate with length of treatment). In fact, four of the patients were diagnosed with a histrionic personality disorder by the IPDE at admission, whereas eight were diagnosed with this disorder at discharge. If the change in scores on the IPDE reported by Loranger et al. (1991) represented valid changes in personality functioning, then treatment apparently created histrionic personality disorders in some patients. It is unlikely that the changes in IPDE scores would have been supported by the clinicians' discharge diagnoses.

One approach to the distortion provided by comorbid Axis I disorders is to request that someone who knows the patient well provide a description of his or her personality. Spouses, friends, and close colleagues will not provide an entirely accurate description of an identified patient, as they will not be familiar with all aspects of the person's functioning and they may have their own axes to grind. Nevertheless, they do provide a useful source of additional information, they may have known a patient's characteristic manner of functioning well before the onset of a recently developed mental disorder, and their descriptions may lack the particular distortions, denials, and exaggerations that characterize accounts by someone with the patient's personality disorder. Agreement between self-descriptions and peer descriptions of normal personality traits has been good to excellent (Costa & McCrae, 1992). Agreement between self-descriptions and informant descriptions of personality disorders has been poor to adequate (Klonsky et al., 2002). The reasons for the poor agreement are many (e.g., distortion of self-descriptions secondary to personality and mood disorder or biased and inadequate bases for informant descriptions), but the disagreement does at least indicate the importance of obtaining multiple sources of input for a diagnostic assessment.

Adequate differentiation of a personality disorder from an Axis I disorder requires that the clinician assess whether the maladaptive behavior pattern has been evident since late childhood or early adulthood. Personality disorders must have an age of onset that "can be traced back at least to adolescence or early adulthood" (American Psychiatric Association, 2000, p. 689). Self-report inventories fail to make adequate distinctions between Axis I and personality disorders, in part because they fail to even make reference to age of onset. Semi-structured and unstructured clinical interviews typically make a more concerted effort to determine whether the behavior pattern has been characteristic of adult life prior to the onset of the Axis I disorder, although interviews will vary considerably in how closely they adhere to the DSM-IV-TR age of onset requirement. The PDI-IV encourages the interviewer to document that each diagnostic criterion was evident in young adulthood and has remained evident throughout much of the person's adult life but does not provide any specific requirements to do so (Widiger et al., 1995). The IPDE is more explicit in its requirements but also more liberal, as it requires that only one of the diagnostic criteria for a respective personality disorder be present since the age of twenty-five; all of the others can be evident only within the past few years (Loranger, 1999). The SCID-II is confined largely to the past five years (First et al., 1997), the SIDP-IV is concerned with the person's usual self but emphasizes the past five years (Pfohl et al., 1997), and the DIPD is confined largely to the past two years (Zanarini et al., 1987).

Verifying that a behavior pattern has been evident since young adulthood will usually be sufficient in differentiating a personality disorder from most Axis I disorders. For example, one of the more problematic differential diagnoses is antisocial personality disorder and substance dependence. The requirement in DSM-IV-TR that antisocial features be evident prior to the age of fifteen will usually assure that the onset of the personality disorder came prior to the onset of a substance-related disorder. If both disorders are present within adulthood and both were evident prior to the age of fifteen, then both diagnoses should be provided. Antisocial personality disorder and substance-dependence will often interact, exacerbating and escalating each other's development (Millon et al., 1986).

However, the differentiation between some Axis I disorders and Axis II personality disorders will be complicated by the absence of a meaningful distinction between them within DSM-IV-TR (American Psychiatric Association, 2000). No conceptual or operational definition of a mood or an anxiety disorder is even provided in DSM-IV-TR, and the boundaries of these sections of the diagnostic manual have been expanding with each edition. What was once diagnosed as a depressive personality disorder is now diagnosed as an early onset variant of a depressive mood disorder (Keller, 1989; Widiger, 1999). Social phobia in DSM-III (American Psychiatric Association, 1980) was a quite circumscribed disorder but has since been expanded to include a generalized subtype that "typically has an onset in the mid-teens, sometimes emerging out of a childhood history of social inhibition or shyness. . . . Duration is frequently lifelong" (American Psychiatric Association, 2000, p. 453). There might be no meaningful distinction between a generalized social phobia and an avoidant personality disorder (Alden et al., 2002; Widiger, 2001).

DISTORTIONS IN SELF-DESCRIPTION

Inherent to the pathology of most, if not all, of the personality disorders are distortions in self-image or self-presentation (Millon et al., 1996; Stone, 1993). Just as depressed persons will be overly pessimistic and self-critical, antisocial persons will be dishonest, histrionic persons might exaggerate their symptomatology, paranoid persons will withhold information, dependent persons can be overly self-denigrating, and narcissistic persons might deny the existence of faults and inadequacies. The self-description of persons with personality disorders should not be taken at face value (Bornstein, 1995; Westen, 1997).

A criticism of personality disorder semistructured interviews is that they can degenerate into simplistic queries as to the presence of each diagnostic criterion (Perry, 1992; Westen, 1997). Support for this concern is perhaps provided by the curious finding that semistructured interview assessments of narcissistic personality disorder often fail to find one instance of this disorder within community samples (e.g., Coryell & Zimmerman, 1989; Maier et al., 1992; Moldin et al., 1994; Samuels et al., 1994) and that narcissistic personality disorder is among the least frequently diagnosed personality disorders in clinical practice (Gunderson et al., 1991). There are a number of compelling explanations for the failure to identify many cases of this disorder (e.g., the disorder is exceedingly rare, the diagnosis is illusory, or the criterion set is inadequate), but one possibility is that the disorder is difficult to identify in a one- to two-hour semistructured interview (Hilsenroth et al., 1996; Westen, 1997). Many persons with narcissistic self-esteem conflicts are unlikely to simply say "yes" when asked if they are arrogant, have a grandiose sense of self-importance, are preoccupied with fantasies of unlimited success, require excessive admiration, have a sense of entitlement, are interpersonally exploitative, are envious of others, or lack empathy. Some semistructured interviews attempt to address this problem by asking respondents if others have ever accused them of being arrogant, exploitative, or lacking in empathy, but this approach might be just as transparent and ineffective as a direct query.

Most semistructured interviews, however, do not rely on direct queries to assess the narcissistic and other personality disorder diagnostic criteria. Each of the interviews does in fact use a substantial number of indirect and subtle queries to probe for the presence of maladaptive personality traits that the patient might be reluctant or unable to acknowledge. For example, the PDI-IV assesses for the presence of a grandiose sense of self-importance in part by asking respondents if they have any special talents or abilities and to describe their future ambitions and goals (Widiger et al., 1995). Narcissistic grandiosity can be suggested by observing whether the resulting description is markedly inflated. Lack of remorse is assessed in part by determining what expressions of remorse have in fact been made by respondents. Antisocial persons will often express verbally quite strong feelings of remorse but will have never in fact even attempted any reparation, penance, or direct apology outside of the requirements of their conviction or probation. Lack of empathy is assessed in part by asking the person to describe the feelings of another person who has recently suffered a loss. The interviewer then judges whether the person does appear to be capable of understanding and appreciating this other person's pain and suffering. Many other examples of indirect assessments, probes, and clinical observations can be found in the PDI-IV (Widiger et al., 1995), SIDP-IV (Pfohl et al., 1997), IDPE (Loranger, 1999), and even the SCID-II (First et al., 1997) and DIPD (Zanarini et al., 1987).

Interviews of persons who know the respondent well can also be helpful in circumventing patients' distortions in self-presentation. Interviews with a spouse or close friend are likely to result in the discovery of more maladaptive personality functioning than is identified through the interview of the patient (Klonsky et al., 2002). Persons who know the patient well will likely be quite personally familiar with the patient's tendency to deny, exaggerate, deceive, idealize, devalue, or exploit. They may have observed firsthand the need for excessive admiration, the sense of entitlement, or the lack of empathy. Their description might itself be distorted by their own emotional involvement with the patient, but such interviewers will at least be a useful source of additional information and alternative perspective (Klonsky et al., 2002).

Endorsements of personality disorder symptomatology, whether obtained from the patient or by someone who knows the patient well, should not be based solely on the opinions of the respondents. The responsibility of the clinical interviewer is to assess for the presence of the personality disorder symptomatology, not just obtain to the opinions and perceptions of respondents. Another reason that direct queries can be inadequate is that patients and informants will have an inadequate appreciation of the clinical meaning or significance of the diagnostic criteria and may not be the best judges (for example) of whether they have a clinically significant lack of empathy or sense of entitlement (Frances, 1998). For example, persons with a schizoid personality disorder may at times claim that they have close friends or confidants, but they never confide in them, never visit them at their homes, never invite them over to visit, and never telephone them just to talk. As stated in the manual for the PDI-IV, "a rule of thumb that will apply to almost all of the PDI-IV item assessments is to ask for examples or illustrations" (Widiger et al., 1995, p. 22). An assessment of a diagnostic criterion should be based on the interviewer's judgments concerning examples or incidents described by the patient, rather than simply the patient's opinions. The interviewer can then determine whether the behaviors or incidents do in fact exemplify a respective diagnostic criterion.

GENDER BIAS

Gender bias has been one of the more difficult and heated controversies in the diagnosis of mental disorders (Garb, 1997; Hartung & Widiger, 1998). Three of the personality disorders in DSM-IV-TR (borderline, dependent, and histrionic) are diagnosed more often in women, but questions of gender bias have been raised for each of them. Gender bias can occur with respect to the conceptualization of personality disorders, the wording of individual diagnostic criteria, the assessment by self-report inventories, and of particular concern for this chapter, the assessment of the diagnostic criteria by clinical interviews (Widiger, 1998).

Biased applications of the diagnostic criteria have been repeatedly demonstrated in analogue studies (e.g., Adler et al., 1990; Becker & Lamb, 1994; Fernbach, et al., 1989; Ford & Widiger, 1989; Gilbertson et al., 1986; Hamilton et al., 1986; Slavney & Chase, 1985; Warner, 1978). Clinicians do appear to favor diagnosing female patients with histrionic personality disorder (and, to a lesser extent, male patients with antisocial personality disorder) in the presence of subthreshold symptomatology.

Some authors have blamed the diagnostic manual for the gender-biased diagnoses demonstrated in these analogue studies (Caplan, 1991; Walker, 1994). However, it was the failure to adhere to the diagnostic criterion sets that resulted in the gender-biased diagnoses (Widiger, 1998). These studies did not indicate that the histrionic diagnostic criteria inappropriately favored women over men. These studies indicated that clinicians either failed to apply the histrionic diagnostic criteria to males who presented with histrionic symptomatology or failed to consider all of the diagnostic criteria when applying the diagnosis to women. If the clinicians had adhered to the diagnostic criteria (e.g., systematically considered each diagnostic criterion and applied the required diagnostic threshold), no bias in the diagnoses would have been observed. This was the explicit conclusion in the analogue study of Ford and Widiger (1989). They first replicated the common finding that clinicians are more likely to diagnose histrionic personality disorder in females than in males when provided with a subthreshold case. However, when the clinicians were required systematically to consider each of the histrionic diagnostic criteria, no evidence of bias occurred. Ford and Widiger concluded that "sex biases may best be diminished by an increased emphasis in training programs and clinical settings on the systematic use and adherence to the criteria and diagnostic rules presented in the DSM-III" (Ford & Widiger, 1989, p. 304).

However, it should also be noted that clinicians are more likely to over-diagnose histrionic personality disorder in females than to overdiagnose antisocial personality disorder in males (e.g., Ford & Widiger, 1989; Hamilton et al., 1986). This could be due in part to a closer relationship of the histrionic diagnostic criteria to the feminine gender than the antisocial criteria to the masculine gender (Sprock et al., 1990). The tendency of clinicians to overdiagnose histrionic personality disorder in females does reflect a failure to adhere to the criterion sets, but the direction of this error could be due in part to the gender-related nature of the diagnostic criteria. Gender-related errors may occur more often for the histrionic diagnosis than for the antisocial diagnosis because of a closer association of the histrionic criterion set to stereotypic feminine personality traits, relative to the association of the antisocial criterion set to stereotypic masculine traits.

Alternatively, the greater magnitude of error in the unstructured, clinical diagnoses of histrionic personality disorder relative to antisocial may simply reflect the greater behavioral specificity of the antisocial criterion set. The personality disorder diagnostic criteria vary substantially in their degree of explicitness, complexity, and subjectivity, with the antisocial criterion set being relatively more specific and clear than the histrionic (Blais et al., 1996; Shea, 1992). If the histrionic criterion set were less ambiguous, or at least as behaviorally specific as the antisocial, perhaps fewer diagnostic errors would occur. Clinicians might then apply the histrionic criteria to males when they evidence the symptomatology, and avoid applying the criteria to females when they do not, in a manner comparable to the more successful application of the antisocial criterion set.

Gender-biased applications of diagnostic criterion sets will occur much less frequently when semistructured interviews are used, because the interviewers must consider each histrionic diagnostic criterion when interviewing both male and female patients (Ford & Widiger, 1989). In fact, it was the conclusion of the authors of the dependent and histrionic diagnostic criterion sets of the DSM-IV (American Psychiatric Association, 1994) that the differential sex prevalence rates reported in prior editions of the manual were due largely to inaccurate, biased assessments and that more systematic, comprehensive assessments did not indicate the presence of a differential sex prevalence rate for these two personality disorders (Hirschfeld et al., 1991; Pfohl, 1991). "When standardized measures are used, women are not more frequently diagnosed with

Dependent Personality Disorder" (Hirschfeld et al., 1991, p. 141). It was therefore stated in the DSM-IV text discussions of the dependent and histrionic personality disorders that "studies using structured assessments report similar prevalence rates among males and females" (American Psychiatric Association, 1994, pp. 656, 667).

The empirical bases for these conclusions, however, were unclear. For example, Hirschfeld et al. (1991) cited only one semistructured interview study (Reich, 1987) to support their conclusion that dependent personality disorder occurs as frequently in men as in women, and this study had in fact reported that 75 percent of the persons diagnosed with dependent personality disorder by a semistructured interview were female. Corbitt and Widiger (1995) identified published studies that used semistructured interviews and indicated that "the proportion of those with dependent personality disorder who were female ranged from 65% to 100%" (p. 228). Bornstein (1996) conducted a meta-analysis of studies comparing prevalence rates of dependent personality disorder in males and females. He noted that "all dependent personality disorder prevalence rate studies published before 1993 that (a) used structured interviews to derive dependent personality disorder diagnoses and (b) involved random samples of psychiatric inpatients, outpatients, or community subjects were included in this analysis (n of studies = 18)" (Bornstein, 1996, p. 4). He found "a highly significant difference that indicates that a woman is nearly 40% more likely than a man to receive a dependent personality disorder diagnosis" (p. 4). In other words, clinicians using unstructured clinical interviews do appear to overdiagnose the dependent personality disorder, and an unbiased, systematic assessment might then reduce the differential sex prevalence rate to some extent. However, the reduction does not appear to be to the point of no differential sex prevalence rate. More women than men do appear to meet the diagnostic criteria for dependent personality disorder, even when semistructured interviews are used (Bornstein, 1996; Corbitt & Widiger, 1995). The statement in DSM-IV (American Psychiatric Association, 1994) that dependent personality disorder is as likely to occur in males as in females when standardized measures are used was therefore deleted in DSM-IV-TR (American Psychiatric Association, 2000). It is now stated that "this disorder has been diagnosed more frequently in females although [it is still acknowledged that] some studies report similar prevalence rates among males and females" (American Psychiatric Association, 2000, p. 723).

CONCLUSION

A useful procedure for the clinical assessment of personality disorders is to first administer a self-report screening measure, followed by a semistructured interview for the assessment of the two to four personality disorders that obtained the highest elevations on the screening device. Semistructured interviews are not often used in general clinical practice, in part because they can be so time-consuming. However, the amount of time required for their administration can be reduced substantially by first using a screening measure that identifies which personality disorders most likely warrant the systematic and comprehensive assessment.

Many semistructured interviews are now being used in general clinical practice when the results of the clinical assessment might be subsequently questioned or reviewed (e.g., custody, disability, and forensic assessments). The administration of a semistructured interview can be very useful in documenting that the interview was indeed systematic, comprehensive, and objective. A highly talented clinician can provide a more valid assessment than can be provided in a semistructured interview, but it is risky to assume that one is indeed this talented clinician. It would at least seem desirable for a talented and insightful clinician to be fully informed by a systematic and comprehensive assessment.

Semistructured interviews are not fully structured and are not simply a matter of recording respondents' answers to simplistic questions regarding the presence of each diagnostic criterion. They rely substantially on the clinical experience, training, and knowledge of the interviewer to render a valid assessment. Semistructured interviews should not be administered without adequate training and expert clinical supervision.

Semistructured interviews are used routinely in general clinical research and perhaps someday will be used routinely in general clinical practice. Individually administered intelligence tests are comparable to a fully structured clinical interview, particularly an assessment of verbal intelligence that involves a series of specified questions, the responses to which are scored according to a test manual. Very few clinicians would attempt to diagnose mental retardation in the absence of the administration of one of these structured interviews. Perhaps in the future no clinician will attempt to diagnose an anxiety, mood, psychotic, dissociative, personality, or other mental disorder without at least considering the results obtained by the administration of a respective semistructured interview.

REFERENCES

Adler, D. A., Drake, R. E., & Teague, G. B. (1990). Clinicians' practices in personality assessment: Does gender influence the use of DSM-III Axis II? *Comprehensive Psychiatry* 31:125–133.

Alden, L. E., Laposa, J. M., Taylor, C. T., & Ryder, A. G. (2002). Avoidant personality disorder: Current status and future directions. *Journal of Personality Disorders* 16:1–29.

American Psychiatric Association. (1980). *Diagnostic and Statistical Manual of Mental Disorders*, 3rd ed. Washington, DC: American Psychiatric Association.

American Psychiatric Association. (1987). *Diagnostic and Statistical Manual of Mental Disorders*, 3rd ed., revised. Washington, DC: American Psychiatric Association.

American Psychiatric Association. (1994). *Diagnostic and Statistical Manual of Mental Disorders*, 4th ed. Washington, DC: American Psychiatric Association.

American Psychiatric Association. (2000). *Diagnostic and Statistical Manual of Mental Disorders*. 4th ed., text revised. Washington, DC: American Psychiatric Association.

Bagby, R. M., Taylor, G. J., & Parker, J. D. A. (1994). The twenty-item Toronto Alexithymia Scale-II. Convergent, discriminant, and concurrent validity. *Journal of Psychosomatic Research* 38:23–32.

Becker, D., & Lamb, S. (1994). Sex bias in the diagnosis of borderline personality disorder and posttraumatic stress disorder. *Professional Psychology: Research and Practice* 25:53–61.

Blais, M. A., Benedict, K. B., & Norman, D. K. (1996). The perceived clarity of the Axis II criteria. *Journal of Personality Disorders* 10:16–22.

Blashfield, R. K., & Herkov, M. J. (1996). Investigating clinician adherence to diagnosis by criteria: A replication of Morey and Ochoa (1989). *Journal of Personality Disorders* 10:219–228.

Bornstein, R. F. (1995). Sex differences in objective and projective dependency tests: A meta-analytic review. *Assessment* 2:319–331.

Bornstein, R. F. (1996). Sex differences in dependent personality disorder prevalence rates. *Clinical Psychology: Science and Practice* 3:1–12.

Bornstein, R. F. (1998). Reconceptualizing personality disorder diagnosis in the DSM-V: The discriminant validity challenge. *Clinical Psychology: Science and Practice* 5:333–343.

Caplan, P. J. (1991). How do they decide who is normal? The bizarre, but true, tale of the DSM process. *Canadian Psychology* 32:162–170.

Clark, L. A., & Livesley, W. J. (2002). Two approaches to identifying the dimensions of personality disorder: Convergence on the five-factor model. In *Personality Disorders and the Five-Factor Model of Personality*, ed. P. T. Costa and T. A. Widiger, 2nd ed., pp. 161–176. Washington, DC: American Psychological Association.

Clark, L. A., Livesley, W. J., & Morey, L. (1997). Personality disorder assessment: The challenge of construct validity. *Journal of Personality Disorders* 11:205–231.

Cloninger, C. R. (2000). A practical way to diagnosis personality disorders: A proposal. *Journal of Personality Disorders* 14:99–108.

Coolidge, F. L., & Merwin, M. M. (1992). Reliability and validity of the Coolidge Axis II Inventory: A new inventory for the assessment of personality disorders. *Journal of Personality Assessment* 59:223–238.

Corbitt, E. M., & Widiger, T. A. (1995). Sex differences among the personality disorders: An exploration of the data. *Clinical Psychology: Science and Practice* 2:225–238.

Coryell, W. H., & Zimmerman, M. (1989). Personality disorder in the families of depressed, schizophrenic, and never-ill probands. *American Journal of Psychiatry* 146:496–502.

Costa, P. T., & McCrae, R. R. (1992). *Revised NEO Personality Inventory (NEO PI-R) and NEO Five-Factor Inventory (NEO-FFI) Professional Manual*. Odessa, FL: Psychological Assessment Resources.

Costa, P. T., & Widiger, T. A., eds. (2002). *Personality Disorders and the Five Factor Model of Personality*. Washington, DC: American Psychological Association.

Dolan-Sewell, R. G., Krueger, R. F., & Shea, M. T. (2001) Co-occurrence with syndrome disorders. In *Handbook of Personality Disorders*, ed. W. J. Livesley, pp. 84–104. New York: Guilford.

Dowson, J. H. (1992). Assessment of DSM-III-R personality disorders by self-report questionnaire: The role of informants and a screening test for co-morbid personality disorders (SCTCPD). *British Journal of Psychiatry* 161:344–352.

Farmer, R. F. (2000). Issues in the assessment and conceptualization of personality disorders. *Clinical Psychology Review* 20:823–852.

Fernbach, B. E., Winstead, B. A., & Derlega, V. J. (1989). Sex differences in diagnosis and treatment recommendations for antisocial personality and somatization disorders. *Journal of Social and Clinical Psychology* 8:238–255.

First, M. B., Bell, C. B., Krystal, J. H., Reiss, D., Shea, M. T., Widiger, T. A., & Wisner, K. L. (In press). Gaps in the current system: Recommendations. In *A Research Agenda for DSM-V*, ed. D. J. Kupfer, M. B. First, and D. A. Regier. Washington, DC: American Psychiatric Press.

First, M., Gibbon, M., Spitzer, R. L., Williams, J. B. W., & Benjamin, L. S. (1997). *User's Guide for the Structured Clinical Interview for DSM-IV Axis II Personality Disorders.* Washington, DC: American Psychiatric Press.

Ford, M., & Widiger, T. A. (1989). Sex bias in the diagnosis of histrionic and antisocial personality disorders. *Journal of Consulting and Clinical Psychology* 57:301–305.

Frances, A. J. (1980). The DSM-III personality disorders section: A commentary. *American Journal of Psychiatry* 137:1050–1054.

Frances, A. J. (1998). Problems in defining clinical significance in epidemiological studies. *Archives of General Psychiatry* 55:119.

Frances, A. J., First, M. B., & Pincus, H. A. (1995). *DSM-IV Guidebook.* Washington, DC: American Psychiatric Press.

Garb, H. N. (1997). Race bias, social class bias, and gender bias in clinical judgment. *Clinical Psychology: Science and Practice* 4:99–120.

Gilbertson, A. D., McGraw, L. K., & Brown, N. E. (1986). A different empirical perspective on sex bias in the diagnosis of DSM-III Axis II disorders. *Psychiatric Quarterly* 58:144–147.

Goldberg, L. R. (1990). An alternative "description of personality": The Big Five factor structure. *Journal of Personality and Social Psychology* 59:1216–1229.

Gunderson, J. G. (1992). Diagnostic controversies. In *Review of Psychiatry*, Vol. 11, ed. A. Tasman and M. B. Riba, pp. 9–24. Washington, DC: American Psychiatric Press.

Gunderson, J. G., Ronningstam, E., & Bodkin, A. (1990). The diagnostic interview for narcissistic patients. *American Journal of Psychiatry* 47:676–680.

Gunderson, J. G., Ronningstam, E., & Smith, L. E. (1991). Narcissistic personality disorder: A review of data on DSM-III-R descriptions. *Journal of Personality Disorders* 5:167–177.

Gunderson, J. G., Shea, M. T., Skodol, A. E., McGlashan, T. H., Morey, L. C., Stout, R. L., Zanarini, M. C., Grilo, C. M., Oldham, J. M., & Keller, M. B. (2000). The Collaborative Longitudinal Personality Disorders Study: I. Development, aims, design, and sample characteristics. *Journal of Personality Disorders* 14:300–315.

Hamilton, S., Rothbart, M., & Dawes, R. (1986). Sex bias, diagnosis, and DSM-III. *Sex Roles* 15:269–274.

Hare, R. D. (1991). *The Hare Psychopathy Checklist-Revised Manual.* North Tonawanda, NY: Multi-Health Systems.

Hare, R. D., Hart, S. D., & Harpur, T. J. (1991). Psychopathy and the DSM-IV criteria for antisocial personality disorder. *Journal of Abnormal Psychology* 100:391–398.

Hartung, C. M., & Widiger, T. A. (1998). Gender differences in the diagnosis of mental disorders: Conclusions and controversies of DSM-IV. *Psychological Bulletin* 123:260–278.

Herkov, M. J., & Blashfield, R. K. (1995). Clinicians' diagnoses of personality disorder: Evidence of a hierarchical structure. *Journal of Personality Assessment* 65:313–321.

Hilsenroth, M. J., Handler, L., & Blais, M. A. (1996). Assessment of narcissistic personality disorder: A multi-method review. *Clinical Psychology Review* 16:655–683.

Hirschfeld, R. M. A., Shea, M. T., & Weise, R. (1991). Dependent personality disorder: Perspectives for DSM-IV. *Journal of Personality Disorders* 5:135–149.

Horowitz, L. M., Rosenberg, S. E., Baer, B. A., Ureno, G., & Villasenor, V. S. (1988). Inventory of interpersonal problems: Psychometric properties and clinical applications. *Journal of Consulting and Clinical Psychology* 56:885–892.

Hyler, S. E. (1994). *Personality Diagnostic Questionnaire-4 (PDQ-4)*. New York: New York State Psychiatric Institute.

Jacobsberg, L., Perry, S., & Frances, A. (1995). Diagnostic agreement between the SCID-II screening questionnaire and the Personality Disorder Examination. *Journal of Personality Assessment* 65:428–433.

Kaye, A. L., & Shea, M. T. (2000). Personality disorders, personality traits, and defense mechanisms. In *Handbook of Psychiatric Measures*, ed. A. J. Rush, H. A. Pincus, and M. B. First, pp. 713–749. Washington, DC: American Psychiatric Association.

Keller, M. (1989). Current concepts in affective disorders. *Journal of Clinical Psychiatry* 50:157–162.

Kim, Y., & Pilkonis, P. A. (1999). Selecting the most informative items in the IIP scales for personality disorders: An application of item response theory. *Journal of Personality Disorders* 13:157–174.

Klonsky, E. D., Oltmanns, T. F., & Turheimer, E. (2002). Informant reports of personality disorder: Relation to self-reports and future directions. *Clinical Psychology: Science and Practice* 9:300–311.

Langbehn, D. R., Pfohl, B. M., Reynolds, S., Clark, L. A., Battaglia, M., Bellodi, L., Cadoret, R., Grove, W., Pilkonis, P., & Links, P. (1999). The Iowa Personality Disorder Screen: Development and preliminary validation of a brief screening interview. *Journal of Personality Disorders* 13:75–89.

Lilienfeld, S. O. (1994). Conceptual problems in the assessment of psychopathy. *Clinical Psychology Review* 14:17–38.

Lilienfeld, S. O., Waldman, I. D., & Israel, A. C. (1994). A critical examination of the use of the term "comorbidity" in psychopathology research. *Clinical Psychology: Science and Practice* 1:71–83.

Livesley, W. J. (1998). Suggestions for a framework for an empirically based classification of personality disorder. *Canadian Journal of Psychiatry* 43:137–147.

Livesley, W. J., & Jang, K. L. (2000). Toward an empirically based classification of personality disorder. *Journal of Personality Disorders* 14:137–151.

Loranger, A. W. (1992). Are current self-report and interview methods adequate for epidemiological studies of personality disorders? *Journal of Personality Disorders* 6:313–325.

Loranger, A. W. (1999). *International Personality Disorder Examination (IPDE)*. Odessa, FL: Psychological Assessment Resources.

Loranger, A. W., Lenzenweger, M. F., Gartner, A. F., Susman, V. L., Herzig, J., Zammit, G. K., Gartner, J. D., Abrams, R. C., & Young, R. C. (1991). Trait-state artifacts and the diagnosis of personality disorders. *Archives of General Psychiatry* 48:720–729.

Maier, W., Lichtermann D., Klingler, T., Heun, R., & Hallmayer, J. (1992). Prevalences of personality disorders (DSM-III-R) in the community. *Journal of Personality Disorders* 6:187–196.

Mellsop, G., Varghese, F. T. N., Joshua, S., & Hicks, A. (1982). The reliability of Axis II of DSM-III. *American Journal of Psychiatry* 139:1360–1361.

Millon, T., Davis, R. D., Millon, C. M., Wenger, A. W., Van Zuilen, M. H., Fuchs, M., & Millon, R. B. (1996). *Disorders of Personality. DSM-IV and Beyond*. New York: Wiley & Sons.

Millon, T., Millon, C., & Davis, R. (1997). *MCMI-III Manual*, 2nd ed. Minneapolis, MN: National Computer Systems.

Mineka, S., Watson, D., & Clark, L. A. (1998). Comorbidity of anxiety and unipolar mood disorders. *Annual Review of Psychology* 49:377–412.

Moldin, S. O., Rice, J. P., Erlenmeyer-Kimling, L., & Squires-Wheeler, E. (1994). Latent structure of DSM-III-R Axis II psychopathology in a normal sample. *Journal of Abnormal Psychology* 103:259–266.

Morey, L. C., & Ochoa, E. S. (1989). An investigation of adherence to diagnostic criteria: Clinical diagnosis of the DSM-III personality disorders. *Journal of Personality Disorders* 3:180–192.

Nathan, P., & Langenbucher, J. W. (1999). Psychopathology: Description and classification. *Annual Review of Psychology* 50:79–107.

Nazikian, H., Rudd, R. P., Edwards, J., & Jackson, H. J. (1990). Personality disorder assessments for psychiatric inpatients. *Australian and New Zealand Journal of Psychiatry* 24:37–46.

O'Boyle, M., & Self, D. (1990). A comparison of two interviews for DSM-III-R personality disorders. *Psychiatry Research* 32:85–92.

Oldham, J. M., & Skodol, A. E. (2000). Charting the future of Axis II. *Journal of Personality Disorders* 14:17–29.

Oldham, J. M., Skodol, A. E., Kellman, H. D., Hyler, S. E., Rosnick, L., & Davies, M. (1992). Diagnosis of DSM-III-R personality disorders by two semistructured interviews: Patterns of comorbidity. *American Journal of Psychiatry* 149:213–220.

Perry, J. C. (1992). Problems and considerations in the valid assessment of personality disorders. *American Journal of Psychiatry* 149:1645–1653.

Perry, J. C., Banon, E., & Ianni, F. (1999). Effectiveness of psychotherapy for personality disorders. *American Journal of Psychiatry* 156:1312–1321.

Pfohl, B. (1991). Histrionic personality disorder: A review of available data and recommendations for DSM-IV. *Journal of Personality Disorders* 5:150–166.

Pfohl, B., Blum, N., & Zimmerman, M. (1997). *Structured Interview for DSM-IV Personality*. Washington, DC: American Psychiatric Press.

Piersma, H. L. (1989). The MCMI-II as a treatment outcome measure for psychiatric inpatients. *Journal of Clinical Psychology* 45:87–93.

Pilkonis, P. A. (1997). Measurement issues relevant to personality disorders. In *Measuring Patient Change in Mood, Anxiety, and Personality Disorders: Toward a Core Battery*, ed. H. H. Strupp, M. J. Lambert, and L. M. Horowitz, pp. 371–388. Washington, DC: American Psychological Association.

Reich, J. H. (1987). Sex distribution of DSM-III personality disorders in psychiatric outpatients. *American Journal of Psychiatry* 144:485–488.

Rogers, R. (2001). *Diagnostic and Structured Interviewing. A Handbook for Psychologists*. New York: Guilford.

Salekin, R. T. (2002). Psychopathy and therapeutic pessimism: Clinical lore or clinical reality? *Clinical Psychology Review* 22:79–112.

Samuels, J. F., Nestadt, G., & Romanoski, A. J. (1994). DSM-III personality disorders in the community. *American Journal of Psychiatry* 51:1055–1062.

Sanislow, C. A., & McGlashan, T. H. (1998). Treatment outcome of personality disorders. *Canadian Journal of Psychiatry* 43:237–250.

Segal, D. L. (1997). Structured interviewing and DSM classification. In *Adult Psychopathology and Diagnosis*, ed. S. M. Turner and M. Hersen, pp. 24–57. New York: Wiley & Sons.

Shea, M. T. (1992). Some characteristics of the Axis II criteria sets and their implications for the assessment of personality disorders. *Journal of Personality Disorders* 6:377–381.

Skodol, A. E., Oldham, J. M., Rosnick, L., Kellman, H. D., & Hyler, S. E. (1991). Diagnosis of DSM-III-R personality disorders: A comparison of two structured interviews. *International Journal of Methods in Psychiatric Research* 1:13–26.

Slavney, P. R., & Chase, G. A. (1985). Clinical judgments of self-dramatisation. A test of the sexist hypothesis. *British Journal of Psychiatry* 146:614–617.

Spitzer, R. L., Forman, J. B. W., & Nee, J. (1979). DSM-III field trials: I. Initial interrater diagnostic reliability. *American Journal of Psychiatry* 136:815–817.

Spitzer, R. L., Williams, J. B. W., & Skodol, A. E. (1980). DSM-III: The major achievements and an overview. *American Journal of Psychiatry* 137:151–164.

Sprock, J., Blashfield, R. K., & Smith, B. (1990). Gender weighting of DSM-III-R personality disorder criteria. *American Journal of Psychiatry* 147:586–590.

Stone, M. H. (1993). *Abnormalities of Personality: Within and Beyond the Realm of Treatment.* New York: Norton.

Stuart, S., Simons, A. D., Thase, M. E., & Pilkonis, P. (1992). Are personality disorders valid in acute major depression? *Journal of Affective Disorders* 24:281–290.

Trull, T. J., & Widiger, T. A. (1997). *Structured Interview for the Five-Factor Model of Personality.* Odessa, FL: Psychological Assessment Resources.

Walker, L. E. A. (1994). Are personality disorders gender biased? In *Controversial Issues in Mental Health*, ed. S. A. Kirk and S. D. Einbinder, pp. 22–29. New York: Allyn & Bacon.

Warner, R. (1978). The diagnosis of antisocial and hysterical personality disorders. *Journal of Nervous and Mental Disease* 166:839–845.

Westen, D. (1997). Divergences between clinical and research methods for assessing personality disorders: Implications for research and the evolution of Axis II. *American Journal of Psychiatry* 154:895–903.

Westen, D., & Arkowitz-Westen, L. (1998). Limitations of Axis II in diagnosing personality pathology in clinical practice. *American Journal of Psychiatry* 155:1767–1771.

Westen, D., & Shedler, J. (1999a). Revising and assessing Axis II, part I: Developing a clinically and empirically valid assessment method. *American Journal of Psychiatry* 156:258–272.

Westen, D., & Shedler, J. (1999b). Revising and assessing Axis II, part II: Toward an empirically based and clinically useful classification of personality disorders. *American Journal of Psychiatry* 156:273–285.

Widiger, T. A. (1991). Definition, diagnosis, and differentiation. *Journal of Personality Disorders* 5:42–51.

Widiger, T. A. (1993). The DSM-III-R categorical personality disorder diagnoses: A critique and an alternative. *Psychological Inquiry* 4:75–90.

Widiger, T. A. (1998). Sex biases in the diagnosis of personality disorders. *Journal of Personality Disorders* 12:95–118.

Widiger, T. A. (1999). Depressive personality traits and dysthymia: A commentary on Ryder and Bagby (1999). *Journal of Personality Disorders* 13:135–141.

Widiger, T. A. (2001). Official classification systems. In *Handbook of Personality Disorders*, ed. W. J. Livesley, pp. 60–83. New York: Guilford.

Widiger, T. A. (2002). Personality disorders. In *Handbook of Assessment, Treatment Planning, and Outcome for Psychological Disorders*, ed. M. M. Antony and D. H. Barlow, pp. 453–480. New York: Guilford.

Widiger, T. A., Cadoret, R., Hare, R., Robins, L., Rutherford, M., Zanarini, M., Alterman, A., Apple, M., Corbitt, E., Forth, A., Hart, S., Kultermann, J., Woody, G., & Frances, A. (1996). DSM-IV antisocial personality disorder field trial. *Journal of Abnormal Psychology* 105:3–16.

Widiger, T. A., & Clark, L. A. (2000). Toward DSM-V and the classification of psychopathology. *Psychological Bulletin* 126:946–963.

Widiger, T. A., & Coker, L. A. (2001). Assessing personality disorders. In *Clinical Personality Assessment: Practical Approaches*, ed. J. N. Butcher, 2nd ed., pp. 407–434. New York: Oxford University Press.

Widiger, T. A., & Corbitt, E. M. (1995). Antisocial personality disorder in DSM-IV. *The DSM-IV Personality Disorders*, ed. W. J. Livesley, pp. 103–126. New York: Guilford.

Widiger, T. A., Costa, P. T., & McCrae, R. R. (2002). A proposal for Axis II: Diagnosing personality disorders using the five factor model. In *Personality Disorders and the Five Factor Model of Personality*, ed. P. T. Costa and T. A. Widiger, 2nd ed., pp. 431–456. Washington, DC: American Psychological Association.

Widiger, T. A., & Frances, A. (1985). The DSM-III personality disorders: Perspectives from psychology. *Archives of General Psychiatry* 42:615–623.

Widiger, T. A., & Hagemoser, S. (1997). Personality disorders and the interpersonal circumplex. In *Circumplex Models of Personality and Emotions*, ed. R. Plutchik and H. R. Conte, pp. 299–325. Washington, DC: American Psychological Association.

Widiger, T. A., Mangine, S., Corbitt, E. M., Ellis, C. G., & Thomas, G. V. (1995). *Personality Disorder Interview-IV: A Semistructured Interview for the Assessment of Personality Disorders. Professional Manual.* Odessa, FL: Psychological Assessment Resources.

Widiger, T. A., & Sanderson, C. J. (1995). Towards a dimensional model of personality disorders in DSM-IV and DSM-V. In *The DSM-IV Personality Disorders*, ed. W. J. Livesley, pp. 380–394. New York: Guilford.

Widiger, T. A., & Trull, T. J. (1998). Performance characteristics of the DSM-III-R personality disorder criteria sets. In *DSM-IV Sourcebook*, Vol. 4, ed. T. A. Widiger, A. J. Frances, H. A. Pincus, R. Ross, M. B. First, W. W. Davis, and M. Kline, pp. 357–373. Washington, DC: American Psychiatric Association.

World Health Organization. *The ICD-10 Classification of Mental and Behavioural Disorders: Clinical Descriptions and Diagnostic Guidelines* (1992). Geneva: World Health Organization.

Zanarini, M. C., Frankenburg, F. R., Chauncey, D. L., & Gunderson, J. G. (1987). The Diagnostic Interview for Personality Disorders: Interrater and test-retest reliability. *Comprehensive Psychiatry* 28:467–480.

Zanarini, M. C., Frankenburg, F. R., & Vujanovic, A. A. (2002). Inter-rater and test-retest reliability of the Revised Diagnostic Interview for Borderlines. *Journal of Personality Disorders* 16:270–276.

Zanarini, M. C., Gunderson, J. G., Frankenburg, F. R., & Chauncey, D. L. (1989). The Revised Diagnostic Interview for Borderlines: Discriminating BPD from other Axis II disorders. *Journal of Personality Disorders* 3:10–18.

Zimmerman, M. (1994). Diagnosing personality disorders. A review of issues and research methods. *Archives of General Psychiatry* 51:225–245.

Zimmerman, M., & Mattia, J. I. (1999a). Differences between clinical and research practices in diagnosing borderline personality disorder. *American Journal of Psychiatry* 156:1570–1574.

Zimmerman, M., & Mattia, J. I. (1999b). Psychiatric diagnosis in clinical practice: Is comorbidity being missed? *Comprehensive Psychiatry* 40:182–191.

14

SEVERELY MENTALLY ILL

Patrick W. Corrigan, Psy.D., and Stanley G. McCracken, Ph.D.

INTERVIEWING PEOPLE WITH SERIOUS MENTAL ILLNESS

There are a lot of people with serious mental illness in the United States. About 1 percent of the population has schizophrenia (Kessler et al., 1994; Regier et al., 1993), which in a metropolitan area the size of Chicago equals eighty thousand people, as many as live in most small cities in the country. The number of people who are considered seriously mentally ill increases exponentially when adding twelve-month diagnostic rates for people with bipolar disorder (about 1.3 percent of the population) or major depression (10.3 percent). Despite the prevalence of people with serious psychiatric disorders, less than a third obtain adequate care (Kessler et al., 2001; Narrow et al., 2000). A variety of factors account for this shortfall, but prominent among these are mental health care providers who are ill prepared to work with this population. In this chapter, we summarize some of the problems that emerge during interviews with people with serious mental illness and some of the strategies that may help interviewers deal with these difficulties. We begin by briefly reviewing what it means to be considered seriously mentally ill. Included in this discussion are some of the stereotypes that cloud professional understanding of schizophrenia and other disorders; these must be understood so that mental health counselors can fully partner with their client in a meaningful interview. We then segue into a review of cognitive and interpersonal problems that are experienced frequently by people with serious mental illness and that might interfere with the clinical interview. Finally, we review three general strategies that, when applied to work with serious mental illness, greatly facilitate the interview.

WHAT IS SERIOUS MENTAL ILLNESS?

Serious mental illness is defined by three factors: psychiatric diagnosis, breadth of disability, and course of the disorder. Each of these factors needs to be considered when conducting clinical interviews for people with serious mental illness.

Relevant Diagnoses

The diagnoses most frequently considered serious include the psychotic disorders, such as schizophrenia and schizoaffective disorder; recurring severe mood disorders, such as bipolar disorder (formerly known as manic–depressive disorder); and major depression (Pratt et al., 1999). Individuals with psychotic disorders experience symptoms such as hallucinations and delusions that challenge one's experience of reality. Individuals with severe mood disorders experience debilitating depression that may lead to suicidal ideation or suicide attempts. Alternatively, they may have periods of mania in which they feel invulnerable and are unable to control behavioral excesses, such as high-risk behaviors or foolish extravagance. Psychotic and mood symptoms, when severe, can markedly influence both the content and the process of interviewing. For example, experiencing auditory hallucinations, disordered thinking, or flight of ideas may make it difficult for the individual to concentrate on the interview or to provide coherent answers to questions. Consider this interviewer's experiences with Randy.

> Interviewer: Randy, what are your goals for attending the rehab program?
> Randy: (Looks at the table in front of him. Does not answer.)
> Interviewer: Randy, do you understand my question?
> Randy: Did you say that I was stupid and funny looking?
> Interviewer: No, Randy. I asked you what are your goals for attending rehab.
> Randy: Oh, I thought you said that I was stupid and funny looking.
> Interviewer: Are you having problems with voices today?
> Randy: Sometimes they call me names.

Individuals with psychotic disorders experience symptoms such as delusions, hallucinations, disorganized speech, and catatonic behavior. These are known as positive symptoms because they manifest as an excess or distortion of normal function. They are contrasted to negative symptoms such as flat affect, reduced fluency and content of speech, and difficulty in initiating goal-directed behavior. Negative symptoms are so named because they appear as deficits in normal functioning. During the acute phase of a psychotic disorder, positive symptoms tend to predominate. In periods of partial remission, or the residual phase of the illness, negative symptoms are frequently dominant and positive symptoms may be experienced in an attenuated form. Schizophrenia and schizoaffective disorder are the psychotic disorders most frequently encountered in individuals with severe mental illnesses. Delusional disorder is seen less commonly in this population because intellectual and occupational functioning are less likely to be impaired than social and marital functioning

(American Psychiatric Association, 2000). Schizophreniform disorder and brief psychotic disorder, though psychotic disorders, are not usually considered severe, since by definition they are not chronic.

As we discussed above, mood disorders, such as recurrent unipolar major depression and bipolar disorder, may also be included among the serious mental disorders. The mood disorders consist of three types of episodes: major depressive, manic, and mixed. People with one of these episodes may experience psychotic symptoms, though the mood symptoms predominate. Interviewing people with severe depression may be difficult due to psychomotor symptoms, such as psychomotor retardation in which there may be long speech latencies and a reduced amount of speech or psychomotor agitation in which the individual may have difficulty sitting and may need to pace.

> Interviewer: Margaret, you don't look so good. How are things going for you?
> Margaret: (Long pause. When she speaks it is with obvious effort.) Not so good.
> Interviewer: What's going on?
> Margaret: (Long pause.) I feel really bad.
> Interviewer: Could you say more?
> Margaret: (No response.)
> Interviewer: It seems like even talking is an effort for you.
> Margaret: (Nods, says nothing.)

On the other hand, individuals experiencing a manic episode may be difficult to interview due to racing thoughts, flight of ideas, or pressured speech.

> Interviewer: How have things been going at work?
> Terry: (Speaking rapidly in a nearly steady stream.) Things have been great; I've been getting plenty of overtime and I've been exercising again at the gym and rollerblading in the park. Man, the parks are getting really messy; it's about time that someone does something about the mess they're in; people throw things around and no one cares any more—they have no pride. I've got pride; I take care of my body, my spirit, and my mind. Body, spirit, and mind, that's what you need; once you've got that, you've got everything. I mean money's good don't get me wrong; without money. . . .
> Interviewer: (Interrupts with some difficulty.) Terry, have you been having trouble with your thoughts racing again?

Dual diagnoses. By convention, two diagnoses from the *Diagnostic and Statistical Manual of Mental Disorders* (DSM)—developmental disabilities and substance abuse disorders—are typically not included in the range of serious mental illnesses, despite the presence of a chronic course as well as both broad and severe disabilities. Nevertheless, interviewers must be aware of the presence of these problems in what clinicians frequently call dual disorders, that is, people with serious mental illnesses who also are challenged by another significant disorder. Developmental disabilities including mental retardation (MIDD) and various substance abuse behaviors (MISA) are the most prominent disorders combining with serious mental illness. Other dually diagnosed disorders might include a combination of severe mental illnesses and secondary mental disorders, such as anxiety disorders and personality disorders, general medical conditions, traumatic brain injury, or learning disabilities. Some people suffer from multiple disabilities, for example, serious mental illness along with developmental disabilities and substance abuse (Drake et al., 2001).

Dually disabled individuals provide a special challenge to the mental health system because they frequently fall through the cracks that differentiate services for mental illness from services for people with developmental disabilities, substance abuse disorders, or general medical conditions. Frequently, dually diagnosed individuals are turfed to another service system; for example, the MISA patient is referred to substance abuse services by a mental health provider because the mental health agency is not able to deal with problems related to alcohol and other drugs. As a result, no one ends up serving the person. Alternatively, people with dual disabilities may enroll in a program that is sensitive to the problems related to one set of diagnoses (e.g., mental illness) but relatively oblivious to another (developmental disabilities). Public mental health systems are now calling for integrated services systems that are capable of serving multiply diagnosed individuals (Drake et al., 2001; Mueser et al., 2003). This means, for example, that interviewers with specialties in mental health will need to broaden their knowledge so they can also provide services targeting problems that result from other disabilities.

The Breadth of Disabilities

It is not the psychiatric diagnosis and associated symptoms per se that make a mental illness *serious*. Significant disability, typically in a number of areas of functioning, is a definitive component of serious mental illness (Corrigan et al., 1999). By saying people have "disabilities," we mean that people are not able to achieve significant life goals because of the primary symptoms and deficits that arise from the disorder (Anthony & Liberman, 1992). Individuals diagnosed with a serious mental illness typically have disabilities in one of two major life domains: finding and keeping a job or obtaining and maintaining independent housing. The nature of these disabilities significantly impacts interview goals. Individuals with serious mental illness may require the ongoing services of a job coach or a supported housing program in order to work and live independently. Hence, interviews need to assess the person's support system. Alternatively, individuals with serious mental illness typically lack social and coping skills that help them cope with the demands of work and housing. The clinical interview needs to assess for these skill deficits so appropriate treatment plans can be formed.

The Course of the Disorder

The third element that makes a mental illness serious is the course of the illness, particularly the potential for becoming chronic or recurrent. Research suggests that the illness course for many people with schizophrenia is progressively downhill (Harding, 1988); without aggressive intervention, most people will not be able to cope with their symptoms or address life goals blocked by their disabilities. Chronic course may appear as unchanging or undulating; in the latter case, periods of remission are marked by frequent episodes of acute symptoms and loss of functioning. In either case, people with serious mental illness typically present during interviews with a long history of psychiatric disorder and mental health care.

Note, however, that not all individuals with these illnesses experience a chronic or residual course of the disorder. For example, some individuals with schizophrenia have a single episode that, either with or without treatment, does not recur. Other individuals have recurrent episodes with full recovery between episodes (Harding, 1988). There are similar differences in course of the illness among individuals with schizoaffective disorder, major depressive disorder, and bipolar disorder (American Psychiatric Association, 2000). This bit of information often comes as a surprise to interviewers working with people with mental illness. This suggests one of the stigmatizing misconceptions that also include: individuals with serious mental illness are dangerous; they hold childlike views of the world; or they are rebellious, free spirits (Farina, 1998; Gabbard & Gabbard, 1992). These misconceptions lead to three stigmatizing beliefs about how individuals with serious mental illness should be treated (Corrigan & Penn, 1999): (1) they should be feared and excluded from most communities; (2) they are irresponsible and other people should make their decisions for them, and (3) they are childlike and need to be cared for by parental figures. Like much of the public, clinicians tend to endorse misconceptions of mental illness (Mirabi et al., 1985). Hence, clinicians need to be aware of these prejudices and make sure they do not bias the information-gathering process that occurs during interviews.

A Personal Empowerment Approach to Interviewing

In recognition of the pernicious effects of social stigma, psychiatric rehabilitation providers have defined a series of principles to guide the clinical relationship that are very useful for interviews that involve people with serious mental illness (International Association of Psychological Rehabilitation Services, 2003). Two superordinate rules for clinical relationships are recovery and personal empowerment. People with serious mental illness should be treated with hope; recovery is not only a possibility but a probability. Central to the clinical journey is the person with serious mental illness. Hence, he or she must have personal power over all facets of treatment and life decisions to achieve a quality life.

These rules generate three principles that are essential for effective interviewing. The first rule is that *people with serious mental illness have the right to direct their own affairs*, including the services they receive related to their psychiatric disability. This principle is meant to challenge authoritarian notions that have arisen in the mental health system that people with serious mental illness are incapable of making wise life choices. The second rule is that *all people are to be treated with respect and dignity*. Following up on the first principle, we need to respect a person's choices, even when it may vary with the interviewer's view of "good clinical practice." The third rule is that *interventions build on the strengths of each person and facilitate the process of recovery*. The client's goals for recovery are elicited early in treatment, for it is through these goals that problems are identified. In a recovery model, a problem is defined as something that interferes with achieving a goal (Ralph, 2000). In attempting to define these problems, interviewers also attempt to identify the client's strengths that will help them solve the problem. This task may be difficult early in treatment because individuals accustomed to dealing with psychiatric hospitals that focus on symptoms and deficits may have difficulty identifying their strengths (Pratt et al., 1999).

> Interviewer: Mike, you have told me about a number of problems that you have had with suspiciousness, hearing voices, problems sleeping, and urges to isolate. What I would really like to know is what your strengths are.
>
> Mike: I don't know what you mean.
>
> Interviewer: What skills and abilities do you have?
>
> Mike: I still don't know what you mean. I haven't really worked very much. Most of the time, I have been in programs or in the hospital.
>
> Interviewer: What are you good at? What do you like doing?
>
> Mike: Well, before I got sick, I did pretty well in school. I graduated from high school with an A- average, and I got mostly A's and B's my first year of college. My second year started out pretty good, but after I started hearing voices and feeling like people were laughing at me, I quit going to classes.
>
> Interviewer: What were your favorite subjects?
>
> Mike: I liked math and writing. I used to write short stories, and I thought some of them were pretty good.
>
> Interviewer: It sounds like you are creative, and if you wrote a lot, you must have known how to type. Is that right?
>
> Mike: My English comp prof thought my essays and stories were pretty good. And, yeah, I can type, and my grammar and spelling were pretty good, too.

These basic principles serve as the overall guides for various assessments that interviewers might adopt to understand the life problems that challenge people with serious mental illness.

ASSESSMENT STRATEGIES

Many of the traditional tests in the psychologists' armamentarium (such as the WAIS-III, MMPI, and sets of projective tests) are of little help in assessing the problems and strengths of people with serious mental illness (Corrigan et al., 1995). Instead, several semistructured interviews that most clinicians can easily learn provide information about the person's psychiatric disorder(s), as well the disabilities that arise from these disorders, only to interfere with accomplishing significant life goals. Semistructured interviews are preferred to pencil-and-paper tests for this population because people with serious mental illness frequently have significant cognitive dysfunctions that undermine reliable and valid responses to paper tests. The face-to-face interviewer can be sensitive to these cognitive dysfunctions and adjust questions as the person's deficits interfere with the quality of responses. Semistructured interviews are available to assess three areas that are especially relevant to the person with serious mental illness: diagnosis, symptoms, and social needs and competencies. We consider assessments in each of these domains more completely.

Diagnoses

Several interviews have been developed to guide clinical diagnoses. Typically, these interviews correspond with the *Diagnostic and Statistical Manual*, fourth edition (DSM-IV, American Psychiatric Association, 1994; 2000) or the DSM's European counterpart, the International Classification of Disease, 9th revision (ICD, World Health Organization, 2000). The Structured Clinical Interview for DSM-IV (SCID, First et al., 2001) is commonly used for the former and the Composite International Diagnostic Inventory (Robins, 1998) is used for ICD diagnoses. Of the various versions of the SCID, three modules from the Clinician Edition are most relevant for questions related to serious mental illness: Mood Syndromes, Psychotic Screening, and Psychoactive Substance Use Disorders. The Mood Syndromes and Psychotic Screening modules help interviewers differentiate among diagnoses within the schizophrenia spectrum, major depression, bipolar disorder, or psychosis not otherwise specified. Oftentimes, serious mental illness is either masked by or confused with some substance abuse disorder. Hence, the SCID Psychoactive Substance Use Disorders module is important to identify illnesses related to alcohol and other drugs. Finally, the SCID-II (First et al., 2001) assesses personality disorders; borderline personality disorder, in particular, is often included in the serious mental illness range.

Each module includes a series of items that, when answered affirmatively, lead to additional probes. Consider this example from the psychotic screen module:

> Did you ever hear things that other people couldn't hear, such as noises, or
> the voices of people whispering or talking? If patient answers "yes" ask, "Were

you awake at the time?" If patient answers "yes" code 1: Auditory hallucinations present when fully awake and heard either inside or outside of head. (First et al., 2001)

This kind of "developing question" process helps the interviewer to systematically guide patients through their experience of a symptom and related processes. Information from the SCID modules is then plugged into a decision tree that yields a differential diagnosis. Consider this tree that anchors the psychotic screen.

Schizophrenia Criteria:
Presence of characteristic psychotic symptoms in the active phase: either (1), (2), or (3) for at least one week (unless the symptoms are successfully treated).

(1) bizarre delusions (i.e., involving a phenomenon that the person's subculture would regard as totally implausible, e.g., thought broadcasting, being controlled by a dead person).

(2) prominent hallucinations of a voice with content having no apparent relation to depression or elation, or a voice keeping up a running commentary on the person's behavior or thoughts, or two or more voices conversing with each other.

(3) two of the following:
  (a) delusions;
  (b) prominent hallucinations;
  (c) incoherence or marked loosening of associations;
  (d) catatonic behavior; or
  (e) flat or grossly inappropriate affect. (First et al., 2001)

Structured interviews have several benefits. They are comprehensive, thereby assuring that the interviewer queries the person about all possible symptoms related to a specific disorder. They are systematic, so the complex components of a disorder can be presented to the person in a straightforward manner. They are fully developed, which assures more reliable implementation and subsequent interpretation of test items. In fact, interviewers with bachelor's level training can administer tasks such as the SCID with a couple of hours of training and yield fairly reliable results.

Symptom Levels

Diagnostic instruments typically yield a classification: for example, yes or no, does this person meet the criteria for schizophrenia? Although the diagnosis might have some implications for treatment, especially for appropriate psychopharmacological intervention, diagnosis does not suggest the person's current level of illness or how to titrate treatment given these current symptoms.

Structured interviews that yield symptom assessments for the serious mental illnesses include the Brief Psychiatric Rating Scale (BPRS, Ventura et al., 1993) and the Positive and Negative Symptoms Scale (Kay et al., 1988). The BPRS is a prototype symptom assessment scale. It includes twenty-four symptom areas, such as depression, unusual thought content, and hallucinations. Each of the symptom areas includes a clear definition, for example, unusual thought content is defined as,

> Unusual, odd, strange, or bizarre thought content. Rate the degree of unusualness, not the degree of disorganization of speech. Delusions are patently absurd, clearly false or bizarre ideas that are expressed with full conviction. Consider the patient to have full conviction if he/she has acted as though the delusional belief were true. Ideas of reference/persecution can be differentiated from delusions in that ideas are expressed with much doubt and contain more elements of reality. (Ventura et al., 1993, p. 17)

The BPRS also includes a set of probes that interviewers use to obtain information about the symptom; for example, probes for unusual thought content include,

> Have you been receiving any special messages from people or from the way things are arranged around you? Have you seen any references to yourself on TV or in the newspapers? Can anyone read your mind? Do you have a special relationship with God? Is anything like electricity, X-rays, or radio waves affecting you? Are thoughts put into your head that are not your own? Have you felt that you were under the influence of another person or force? (Ventura et al., 1993, p. 17)

The obtained information is used to rate each symptom on a seven-point Likert scale; 1 equals "not present" and 7 equals "extremely severe." Each of the seven anchor points is also defined with behavior characteristics to improve the reliability of rater judgments; a rating of 7 on unusual thought content is defined as "Full delusions present with almost total preoccupation or most areas of functioning are disrupted by delusional thinking" (Ventura et al., 1993, p. 18).

Items on symptom scales are typically collapsed into higher order factors to yield meaningful syndrome-level scores. For example, factor analysis of the BPRS has yielded four factors: psychotic behaviors, negative symptoms, depression, and mania (Ventura et al., 2000). The Positive and Negative Symptoms Scale yields two factors that have been hypothesized to fundamentally define schizophrenia: positive symptoms (e.g., hallucinations, inappropriate affect, delusions, bizarre behavior, and conceptual disorganization) and negative symptoms (flat affect, disinterest in others, and absent social interactions) (Kay et al., 1988).

Social Needs and Competencies

Understanding symptoms is by no means sufficient in trying to explain the problems of people with psychiatric disabilities. As we point out above, loss of important life goals is key to defining a mental illness as serious. Namely, people who are unable to attain significant social goals such as getting a job, living independently, or finding a life's mate—because of the symptoms of a mental illness—are psychiatrically disabled. Interviewers approach the assessment of social needs and competences from several directions (Dickerson, 1997; Scott & Lehman, 1998). Measures of psychosocial *need* assess the person's perceptions of life goals. Examples include the Medical Research Council's Needs for Care Assessment (Brewin et al., 1987; Brewin & Wing, 1993) and the Needs and Resources Assessment (Corrigan et al., 1995). What do individuals want to attain for themselves in the near future (frequently defined as the next few months) as well as long term (defined in three to five years)? This approach acknowledges that the person with mental illness has the best perspective on what are relevant disabilities and corresponding treatments for these disabilities. Need assessments typically consider the measurement question broadly, seeking to identify goals across the breadth of life domains.

The next two sets of measures attempt to identify barriers to obtaining life goals, proxies for the disabilities. A relatively direct way to measure social and community disability is to assess *functional skills*. This approach is fundamentally behavioral, resting on the assumption that life goals are achieved when persons have mastered the skills needed to accomplish these goals. Functional skills measures include the Independent Living Skills Survey (Wallace, 1986); the Multnomah Community Ability Scale (Barker et al., 1994); Rehabilitation Evaluation (Baker & Hall, 1988); and Social Behavior Schedule (Wykes & Sturt, 1986). In addition, researchers have adopted a variety of sampling procedures to identify the range of functional skills relevant to psychiatric disability (Corrigan & Holmes, 1994; Goldsmith & McFall, 1975; Holmes et al., 1995). These domains include interpersonal (basic conversation, assertiveness, problem solving, and dating), coping (medication and symptom management), and self-care (hygiene, money management, nutrition, work, and wellness) skills. Typically, overall functioning is tabulated as the total number of exhibited skills in the measure.

An alternative way to examine psychiatric disabilities is to determine whether the person has achieved *social roles*. According to social role theory, individuals achieve various roles and corresponding functions as they age and develop (Cohler & Ferrono, 1987). Although specific theme and time issues vary across cultures, there is consensus about common social roles within a group. For example, Western young adults (between ages of twenty and thirty) are expected to find and become successful vocationally, find and settle down with a life's mate, and establish a household that is independent from their family of origin. Social role theory is especially useful because it gives meaning to the discrete skills that make up a role. Hence, rather than assessing whether a person can get out of bed on time, ride public transportation, communicate clearly with others, and obey authority, assessing social roles indicates whether the person is likely to achieve goals related to work. Measures of social role attainment include the Role Functioning Scale (Goodman et al., 1993), the Social Adjustment Scale II (Schooler et al., 1970), and the Social Functioning Scale (Birchwood et al., 1990).

Absence of symptoms, presence of functional skills, and achievement of social roles is not sufficient to determine whether the individual's life is fulfilling. Consequently, clinicians have borrowed the concept of *quality of life* from medical researchers to measure the last domain related to psychiatric disability. Is the person satisfied with his or her life? Measures of quality of life attempt to assess this construct by asking persons to rate their satisfaction within the variety of domains that make up a full life in the community; they include the Quality of Life Interview (Lehman, 1983; 1988), the Quality of Life Self-Assessment (Skantze et al., 1992), and the Quality of Life Scale (Heinrichs et al., 1984).

SOME PROBLEMS THAT MAY IMPACT INTERVIEWS

People with serious mental illness often have two sets of dysfunctions that may interfere with the quality of the interview: cognitive and interpersonal dysfunctions. As a result of cognitive dysfunctions, some people may not be able to attend to interview items, may misunderstand these items, or may provide responses that seem off target. Alternatively, interpersonal deficits may undermine the interviewers' efforts to build an alliance with their clients so they can jointly investigate the clinical concerns that brought the person in for treatment. Understanding each of these dysfunctions is important for crafting a successful interview session.

Cognitive Dysfunctions

Since the time of Eugen Bleuler (1911), schizophrenia has been identified as a significant dysfunction in cognition. Many people with bipolar disorder and major depression show similar deficits. Cognitive dysfunction may alternatively manifest as a problem in content (the meaning of specific verbiage does not correspond with reality) or in process (the semantics and syntax of a message are disrupted). Cognitive dysfunctions have also been described as input deficits (information not attended to or misperceived) or output deficits (information stated nonsensically) (Corrigan & Yudofsky, 1996; Kingdon & Turkington, 1994). Clearly, these various forms of disrupted cognition may undermine the goals of the clinical interview. We provide a closer look at examples of each and ways in which they may interfere with the interview process.

Deficits in input. Sometimes, interview information is not correctly perceived by the person. This may occur because of deficits in information processing; for example, many people with serious mental illness have difficulties in sustained attention or short-term recall (Green, 1998). Other persons may be disoriented, seeming muddled in their responses and often asking that interview questions be repeated. In either case, clinicians need to determine whether interview responses are being affected by misperceiving the content or intent of interview questions. In cases where this seems possible, interviewers may wish to repeat items to make sure they are heard clearly. Moreover, interviewers should speak in short statements and avoid compound messages.

Deficits in output. The formal thought disorder that characterizes psychosis may interfere with the quality of responses provided to interview items (Kerns & Berenbaum, 2002). Formal thought disorder may diminish the syntax and semantics of responses. Loose associations and other forms of tangentiality may be evident. In formal thought disorder at its worst, the responses of some people may sound like word salad. As a result, little sense may be made of the answers to questions.

Alternatively, people with the negative symptoms of schizophrenia, as well as some people with major depression, manifest a significant impoverishment in cognitive processes (Andreasen, 1982). The cognitive processes of people with negative thought disorder are shut down. Some interviewers may misunderstand this kind of cognitive deficit as unwillingness to speak.

Interviewer: So Mr. Jones, how are you today?
Peter: OK.
Interviewer: What brings you here today?
Peter: Nothing.
Interviewer: Have you been having any problems you'd like to talk about?
Peter: Not really.
Interviewer: Well, your sister says you seem really depressed and sometimes
    she catches you talking aloud to yourself.
Peter: (No response.)
Interviewer: Is this a problem for you?
Peter: Not really.
Interviewer: Do you think you might benefit from a short stay in the hospital?
Peter: No.
Interviewer: What do you think would help?
Peter: (No response.)

The person in this situation is not being contrary or stubborn. Rather, these reactions are better viewed as the product of an empty set; the individual has nothing substantial to say.

The course of cognitive dysfunctions. Unlike mental retardation and more advanced forms of dementia, cognitive dysfunctions that result from serious mental illness often vary significantly within a similar group of diagnosed people, as well as within an individual (Green, 1998). Although the group of individuals as a whole falls in the deficient range of cognitive functioning, people with schizophrenia may vary from significantly below normal to the superior ranges in terms of specific information processes and intelligence (Spaulding et al., 1996). Moreover, the cognitive abilities of persons with serious mental illness may vary greatly, with significant lows evident when the individual is acutely ill and approaching normal levels when symptoms are remitted. Anxiety and arousal may be important mediators of cognitive functioning in people with serious mental illness. Hence, interviewers who note the person is less able to attend to items or clearly respond over the course of an interview should determine whether the person has become more anxious during that interview. Perhaps a short break in which arousal level can diminish will help the person regain cognitive abilities.

Problems with Interpersonal Relatedness

People with serious mental illness often have significant problems with interpersonal relations. This difficulty may manifest itself as a lack of appropriate social skills: intense shyness, inability to maintain a conversation, or lack of reciprocity (Corrigan et al., 1992). Alternatively, some people with serious mental illness may lack social interest. This kind of ahedonia or social autism is especially marked in people with schizophrenia who are showing the negative syndrome (Andreasen, 1982). In either case, the interviewer needs to determine whether poor responses to test items reflect the person's limited ability to interact. The general strategies for interviewing may help these folks become more engaged in the process.

GENERAL STRATEGIES FOR INTERVIEWS

As with most clinical interactions, fundamental strategies guide interviews with people with serious mental illness: identify the goals that will guide treatment, problems that block these goals, and resolutions to the problems. Interviewers might adopt two well-developed clinical skills to help the client achieve these aims: goal identification through motivational interviewing and personal problem solving. Each of these is well-suited to the interview needs of people with the kinds of cognitive deficits seen in serious mental illness, because they break relatively complex actions—such as goal identification and problem solving—into discrete, comprehensible bites. These two strategies are more fully discussed below. In addition, interviewers might want to consider two other rules when interviewing people with significant cognitive deficits. First, *keep it simple.* People with cognitive deficits may not be hearing messages correctly or may be misunderstanding key components. These individuals may find interviews easier if complex messages are divided into simple clauses. Hence, in cases where it is not clear if interview comments are being heard clearly, limit questions to single clauses that are meant to evoke simple answers. Instead of this,

> First, let's break the multifaceted day into essential components. This will mean carefully examining the hourly components of the day and documenting when key events are to occur.

try this,

> 1. List each hour of the day you are awake.
> 2. Let's start with 7A.M.
> 3. Now write one thing you want to do during that hour.

Another important rule here is not to use metaphor. Instead of,

> Clearly, the new work schedule is a winner. Let's now try flying it up the flag pole and see who salutes to it.

consider,

> Let's try out this new schedule with your roommate for one week beginning tomorrow when you wake up in the morning.

The second rule is equally important: *check it out*. If you are not certain the person heard or understood what you said, ask him or her to repeat the message. Sometimes, interview participants might appear to be insulted by multiple requests such as this. In those cases, own the request.

> Harry, we're talking about so much stuff I'm just having a hard time keeping track of it, so I'm asking you what we are talking about to make sure we are both understanding everything correctly.

Personal Goal Identification

Effective services begin with an assessment of the person's goals (Anthony & Liberman, 1992; Bachrach, 1992; Mosher & Burti, 1992). Goal assessment assures that the focus of treatment is driven by the individual's perceptions of important needs. A variety of methods have evolved to assess goals (Brewin & Wing, 1993; Corrigan et al., 1995; Marshall et al., 1995; Phelan et al., 1995); typically, they combine open-ended questions about the person's needs with Likert scale ratings about the importance of these needs. Unfortunately, these methods frame goal identification as a yes/no determination; for example, "yes, obtaining supported housing is important to me and I'd like some assistance in this area" or "no, I don't want to change my work experiences now." Rather than viewing a specific goal as a *categorical* decision, a more comprehensive picture may be obtained by considering the profile of factors that motivate and discourage a specific decision. For example, what are the advantages and disadvantages for an individual to change his or her current work setting?

This kind of assessment helps the person to identify specific barriers to achieving goals as well as the personal benefits related to that pursuit. *Motivational interviews* help the consumer consider the various costs and benefits of specific life goals (Corrigan et al., 2001). Motivational interviewing combines the fundamentals of behavior analysis with principles from Rogerian therapy (Miller & Rollnick, 2002). Behavior analysis is an assessment strategy in which

---

Name _____*Paul Simpson*_____ Date _____*May 14, 2002*_____

> **Personal Goal:**
> *Should I start dating again*

ADVANTAGES	DISADVANTAGES
He might have fun on a date.	*Women might make fun of him.*
He might meet a nice woman.	*He cannot monetarily afford it.*
He might meet someone he could marry.	*She might want to go some place he does not like.*
	He does not know how to ask women out.
	He might not be able to think of things to say during the date.

Figure 14.1. An example of the decisional balance that guides motivational interviews. In this case, Mr. Simpson is considering the advantages and disadvantages of dating.

the clinician identifies rewards (i.e., advantages) and punishers (disadvantages) that affect a specific behavior. The list of rewards describes reasons why the person might take on the effort of a new behavior. For example, Paul Simpson, forty-three years old, unmarried, and with an eighteen-year history of schizophrenia, is considering whether to date. Benefits of dating, identified by Mr. Simpson, are listed in figure 14.1. The list of punishers provides reasons why the person might not consider giving up the behavior. These are the barriers to taking on a new behavior such as dating.

In motivational interviewing, clinicians help the person identify the profile of rewards and punishers that affect the specific behavioral goal. The clinician might use a form like the one in figure 14.1 filled out for Paul Simpson. The list of rewards and punishers defines a decisional balance sheet. If the advantages of behavior change outweigh the disadvantages, the person will engage in activities that facilitate and overcome barriers to change; for example, Mr. Simpson might enroll in a dating group to improve his interpersonal skills. If the disadvantages outweigh the advantages, however, then the person will not be motivated to change.

The decisional balance also suggests ways in which the person might move toward adopting a behavioral goal. Remember that the disadvantages outlined in a motivational interview are the barriers to adopting that behavior. For example, Mr. Simpson identified five reasons why dating might be a problem for him, including the risk that women might make fun of him or that he cannot monetarily afford to take them out. Strategies that diminish these costs will predispose the person to pursue the goal. Hence, Mr. Simpson might be more likely to date if he could learn strategies for identifying women who are friendly and supportive rather than belittling and sarcastic.

Practitioners might mistakenly assume the purpose of motivational interviewing is to use the list of advantages and disadvantages to prove *logically* that the client's goal is attainable. Clinicians with this perception might unwittingly take a heavy hand, forcefully listing advantages when the person is unable to identify them. "C'mon Paul. You know dating is the only way to get out and meet people. Admit it!" Unfortunately, motivational interviewing has now become confrontational and suffers significant pitfalls as a result.

Miller and Rollnick (2002) believe the value of motivational interviewing lies in persons *discovering* the advantages and disadvantages for themselves. Therefore, they outline five principles to make sure the client's perceptions of a goal are obtained. The first is *express empathy*. Clinicians use the Rogerian skill of reflective listening to help clarify the person's experience of advantages and disadvantages. This method communicates acceptance of the client, which frees him or her from having to rationalize their reluctance to make change.

The second principle is *develop discrepancy*. Clinicians help clients understand how failing to change behavior blocks important personal goals. An attitude of discovery, rather than a confrontational approach, is encouraged. Mr.

Simpson discovers for himself the disadvantages of dating, especially in terms of life goals. The third principle is *avoid argumentation*. Even when a nondirective approach such as motivational interviewing is being used, clients are going to continue to deny the importance of behavior change. Clinicians need to avoid these traps and not engage the person in an argument about whether something is really a disadvantage.

The fourth principle is *roll with resistance*. Resistance is an indication that the clinician is addressing issues that the client does not perceive to be relevant or important. Miller and Rollnick remind the clinician that the client is an excellent resource for determining how to get back to addressing barriers to change. Have the client solve this kind of difficulty using his or her own resources. The fifth principle is *support self-efficacy*. The client is responsible for deciding to change. Clinicians should have confidence that their clients will decide to change when ready. Only then are persons able to participate in a program to reach their goals successfully.

Problem Solving

Problems are either internal or external factors that prevent people from achieving their goals. An example of an internal factor is social anxiety that interferes with a job interview; external factors might include a noisy roommate who prevents the person from getting a full night's sleep. The seven steps of problem solving, outlined in table 14.1, provide an excellent framework for interviewers to help clients make sense of their problems and develop plans to solve them (Corrigan et al., 1992; D'Zurilla, 1988). The first step is to develop a problem-solving attitude; specifically, the person needs to agree that solutions to the specific problem exist. Without this agreement, problem solving becomes a meaningless exercise because the person has no confidence in its results. Confidence in problem solving can be facilitated by asking clients to remember times in the past when they faced difficulties they were able to overcome.

The second step is to define the problem. This involves answering the *W* questions: Who is involved in the problem? What happens? When does the problem occur? Where does it occur?

Table 14.1.   The Seven Stages of Interpersonal Problem Solving

1. Develop a problem-solving attitude.
2. Define the problem.
3. Brainstorm solutions.
4. Consider the costs and benefits of specific solutions.
5. Pick one solution and plan out its implementation.
6. Try out the solution for a limited time.
7. Evaluate the solution and try another if the problem is not resolved.

Interviewer: Tell me more about your problem.

Frank: It's my roommate Harold. He's unbearable to live with.

Interviewer: What does he do that is such a problem?

Frank: He likes to play his stereo loud.

Interviewer: Is this more of a problem for you at certain times of the day?

Frank: You bet. I actually don't mind most of his music choices in the evening. But when I'm trying to get some sleep, he keeps it on and it disturbs me.

Notice that in the course of the interview, answers to who, what, when, and where may spontaneously emerge.

Once persons define the problem, they should brainstorm solutions. The goal at this stage is not to censor. A common mistake is for the client or interviewer to settle on a solution prematurely.

Interviewer: So what might you do about this problem, Frank?

Frank: It's clear. Move out. I don't have to put up with that.

Interviewer: Moving out is one option, but let's not censor ourselves. What else might you do?

Frank: I could talk to Harold; a lot of good that will do.

Interviewer: OK, you could talk to Harold. What else?

Frank: I could buy some headphones to drown out the noise.... I could just ignore it, though that's very hard. We could come up with some rules about when we could play music. I could tell the landlord on him.

A good rule of thumb is to gently push clients to generate at least five solutions (more is great), regardless of whether individual options seem relevant. In this way, clients have a chance to mull over ways to resolve their problem that they may not have considered.

The interviewer then helps the client consider the advantages and disadvantages of individual solutions. Some solutions will quickly emerge as yielding many costs for few benefits.

Interviewer: So let's consider the costs and benefits of each of these solutions. The first one was to just move out.

Frank: It would serve Harold right, but it would be kind of stupid for me to do. It took me six months on the waiting list to get this apartment. And it is fairly close to work.

Eventually, the client needs to wade through the costs and benefits of the various solutions and pick one to try out.

Interviewer: It seems like the best solution we have at this point is for you and Harold to sit down and discuss some plan for when he can and cannot play his music.

One of the overlooked secrets to problem solving is carefully planning out implementation of the chosen solution. Once again, the *W* words should guide the process:

> Interviewer: What are you going to do? When are you going to do it? Where and with whom?

The person needs to try out the solution for a limited period (such as a week). At the end of that time, the person should evaluate whether the solution has impacted the problem.

> Interviewer: Well, Frank, you've been trying out the music schedule with Harold for the past week. How did it go?

In cases where clients report the solution was beneficial, they should continue in this manner. If a person believes the solution did not have significant impact, he or she should either revise the plan for implementing the solution or consider implementing another on the list of brainstormed solutions.

Once again, note how problem solving, like motivational interviewing, facilitates the interview task for people with serious mental illness. It structures a relatively complex task into a format that is more accessible to people with cognitive deficits. Using structured interviewing techniques such as these greatly advances the goals of the clinical interaction.

CONCLUSION

As we have outlined in this chapter, people with serious mental illness experience a variety of problems that need to be assessed in an interview. Moreover, they are challenged by many deficits that can impede the quality of the interaction and the worth of the data. We outlined some of these problems as well as strategies that may help the interviewer overcome them. There is one last concern that may interfere with the interview, one we alluded to earlier in the discussion of stigma: artificial diagnostic expectations. The benefit of typologies such as the DSM-IV is that they provide terse information that helps interviewers to understand their clients quickly. The limitation of these typologies is that they might generate expectations about an individual that are not borne out by reality. For example, given that one of the common symptoms of schizophrenia is formal thought disorder, we may assume that the new client we are to meet in the interview with a chart diagnosis of schizophrenia will make little sense. We are surprised, however, to find him clear and easy to follow during the interview.

Although concern for false diagnostic expectations may apply to people with the entire breadth of child and adult disorders, research suggests that the stigma of mental illness may make these biases worse for individuals with the more serious disorders (Corrigan, 2000). The solution to this problem is easy: interviewers should remember the diversity of participants. We instruct our students on two rules that help to promote this diversity: (1) there are many, many more differences in a group with any specific diagnosis of serious mental illness than there are similarities and (2) people with serious mental illness share much more in common with the prototypical "normal" person than they differ. With these warnings in mind, clinicians need to learn for themselves about the strengths and weaknesses of the individual with whom they are engaged in the interview and not assume much about the person based on diagnostic labels. With this viewpoint, they should craft an interaction that generates the most useful information and that serves as the foundation for a subsequent treatment plan.

REFERENCES

American Psychiatric Association. (1994). *Diagnostic and Statistical Manual of Mental Disorders*, 4th ed. Washington, DC: American Psychiatric Association.

American Psychiatric Association. (2000). *Diagnostic and Statistical Manual of Mental Disorders*. 4th ed., text revision. Washington, DC: American Psychiatric Association.

Andreasen, N. (1982). Negative symptoms in schizophrenia: Definition and reliability. *Archives of General Psychiatry.* 39:784–788.

Andreasen, N. (1990). Schizophrenia: In *Positive and Negative Symptoms and Syndromes*. Basel, Switzerland: S. Karger AG.

Anthony, W., & Liberman, R. (1992). Principles and practice of psychiatric rehabilitation. In *Handbook of Psychiatric Rehabilitation*. New York: Macmillan.

Bachrach, L. (1992). Psychosocial rehabilitation and psychiatry in the care of long-term patients. *American Journal of Psychiatry* 149:1455–1463.

Baker, R., & Hall, J. (1988). A new assessment instrument for chronic psychiatric patients. *Schizophrenia Bulletin* 14:97–111.

Barker, S., Barron, N., McFarland, B., Bigelow, B. A., & Carnahan, T. (1994). A community ability scale for chronically mentally ill consumers: II. Applications. *Community Mental Health Journal* 30:459–472.

Bauer, M. S. (1997). Bipolar disorders. In *Psychiatry*.

Birchwood, M., Smith, J., & Cochrane, R. (1990). The Social Functioning Scale: The development and validation of a new scale of social adjustment for use in family intervention programs with schizophrenic patients. *British Journal of Psychiatry* 157:853–859.

Bleuler, E. (1911). *Dementia Praecox of the Group of Schizophrenias*. (J. Zinkin, trans.). Original work published 1911. New York: International Universities Press.

Brewin, C., & Wing, J. (1993) The MRC needs for care assessment: Progress and controversies. *Psychological Medicine* 23:837–841.

Brewin, C, Wing, J., Mangen, S., Brugha, T. S., & MacCarthy, B. (1987). Principles and practice of measuring needs in the long-term mentally ill: The MRC needs for care assessment. *Psychological Medicine* 17:971–981.

Bruss, G., Gruenberg, A., & Goldstein, R. (1994). Hamilton Anxiety Rating Scale Interview Guide: Joint interview and test methods for interrater reliability. *Psychiatry Research* 53:191–202.

Cohler, B., & Ferrono, C. (1987). Schizophrenia and the adult life-course. In *Schizophrenia and Aging: Schizophrenia, Paranoia, and Schizophreniform Disorders in Later Life*. New York: Guilford.

Corrigan, P. (2000). Mental health stigma as social attribution: Implications for research methods and attitude change. *Clinical Psychology-Science & Practice* 7:48–67.

Corrigan, P., Buican, B., & McCracken, S. (1995) The Needs and Resources Assessment interview for severely mentally ill adults. *Psychiatric Services* 46:504–505.

Corrigan, P., & Holmes, P. (1994). Patient identification of "Street Skills" for a psychosocial training module. *Hospital and Community Psychiatry* 45:273–276.

Corrigan, P., Holmes, P., & Luchins, D., Parks, J. (1994). Setting up inpatient behavioral treatment programs: The staff needs assessment. *Behavioral Interventions* 9:1–12.

Corrigan, P., McCracken, S., & Holmes, P. (2001). Motivational interviews as goal assessment for persons with psychiatric disability. *Community Mental Health Journal* 37:113–122.

Corrigan, P., & Penn, D. (1999). Lessons from social psychology on discrediting psychiatric stigma. *American Psychologist* 54:765–776.

Corrigan, P., Rao, D., & Lam, C. (1999). Psychiatric rehabilitation. In *Health Care and Disability Case Management*. Lake Zurich, IL: Vocational Consultants Press.

Corrigan, P., Schade, M., & Liberman, R. (1992). Social skills training. In R. P. Liberman (ed.), *Handbook of Social Functioning in Schizophrenia*. New York: MacMillan.

Corrigan, P., Schade, M., & Liberman, R. (1998). Social skills training. In *Handbook of Social Functioning in Schizophrenia*. Needham Heights, MA: Allyn & Bacon.

Corrigan, P., & Yudofsky, S. (1996). *Cognitive Rehabilitation for Neuropsychiatric Disorders*. Washington, DC: American Psychiatric Press.

Dickerson, F. (1997). Assessing clinical outcomes: The community functioning of persons with serious mental illness. *Psychiatric Services* 48: 897–902.

Drake, R., Essock, S., Shaner, A., Carey, K. B., Minkoff, K., Kola, L., Lynde, D., Osher, F. C., Clark, R. E., & Rickards, R. (2001). Implementing dual diagnosis services for clients with severe mental illness. *Psychiatric Services* 52:469–476.

D'Zurilla, T. (1988). Problem-solving therapies. In *Handbook of Cognitive-Behavioral Therapies*. New York: Guilford.

Farina, A. (1998). Stigma. In *Handbook of Social Functioning in Schizophrenia*. Needham Heights, MA: Allyn & Bacon.

First, M. B., Spitzer, R. L., Gibbon, M., & Williams, J. B. W. (2001). *Structured Clinical Interview for DSM-IV Axis 1 Disorders (SCID-1), Clinical Version*. Washington, DC: American Psychiatric Press.

Gabbard, G., & Gabbard, K. (1992). Cinematic stereotypes contributing to the stigmatization of psychiatrists. *Stigma and Mental Illness*. Washington, DC: American Psychiatric Press.

Goldsmith, J., & McFall, R. (1975) Development and evaluation of an interpersonal skill-training program for psychiatric inpatients. *Journal of Abnormal Psychology* 84:51–58.

Goodman, S., Sewell, D., Cooley, E., & Leavitt, N. (1993). Assessing levels of adaptive functioning: The Role Functioning Scale. *Community Mental Health Journal* 29:119–131.

Green, M. (1998). Schizophrenia from a neurocognitive perspective: In *Probing the Impenetrable Darkness*. Needham Heights, MA: Allyn & Bacon.

Harding, C. M. (1988). Course types in schizophrenia. *Schizophrenia Bulletin* 14:633–644.

Heinrichs, D., Hanlon, T., & Carpenter, W. (1984). The Quality of Life Scale: An instrument for rating the schizophrenic deficit syndrome. *Schizophrenia Bulletin* 10:797–801.

Holmes, P., Corrigan, P., Knight, S., & Flaxman, J. (1995). Development of a sleep management program for people with severe mental illness. *Psychiatric Rehabilitation Journal* 19:9–15.

International Association of Psychological Rehabilitation Services. (2003). IAPSRS Language Guideline (*http://www.iapsrs.org/pdf/langGuidelines.pdf*).

International Statistical Classification of Diseases and Health Related Problems. (2000 Revision). Geneva: World Health Organization, 1992.

Kay, S., Opler, L., & Lindenmayer, J. (1988). Reliability and validity of the Positive and Negative Syndrome Scale for schizophrenics. *Psychiatry Research* 23:99–110.

Kerns, J., & Berenbaum, H. (2002). Cognitive impairments associated with formal thought disorder in people with schizophrenia. *Journal of Abnormal Psychology* 111:211–224.

Kessler, R., Aguilar-Gaxiola, S., Berglund, P., Caraveo-Anduaga, J. J., DeWitt, D. J., Greenfield, S. F., Kolody, B., Olfson, M., & Vega, W. A. (2001). Patterns and predictors of treatment seeking after onset of a substance use disorder. *Archives of General Psychiatry* 58:1065–1071.

Kessler, R., McGonagle, K., Zhao, S., Nelson, C. B., Hughes, M., Eshleman, S., Wittchen, H. U., & Kendler, K. S. (1994). Lifetime and 12-month prevalence of DSM-III-R psychiatric disorders in the United States: Results from the National Comorbidity Study. *Archives of General Psychiatry* 51:8–19.

Kingdon, D., & Turkington, D. (1994). *Cognitive-Behavioral Therapy of Schizophrenia*. New York: Guilford.

Lehman, A. F. (1983). The effects of psychiatric symptoms on quality of life assessments among the chronically mentally ill. *Evaluation & Program Planning* 6 (2):143–151.

Lehman, A. F. (1988). A quality of life interview for the chronically mentally ill. *Evaluation & Program Planning* 11:51–62.

Levine, J., Schooler, N., & Cassano, G. (1979). The role of depot neuroleptics in the treatment of schizophrenic patients. *Psychological Medicine* 9:383–386.

Marshall, M., Hogg, L., Gath, D., & Lockwood, A. (1995). The Cardinal Needs Schedule: A modified version of the MRC Needs for Care Assessment Schedule. *Psychological Medicine* 25:605–617.

Miller, W. R., & Rollnick, S. (1991). *Motivational Interviewing: Preparing People for Change*. New York: Guilford.

Mirabi, M., Weinman, M., & Magnetti, S., et al. (1985). Professional attitudes toward the chronic mentally ill. *Hospital & Community Psychiatry* 36:404–405.

Mosher, L., & Burti, L. (1992). Relationships in rehabilitation: When technology fails. *Psychosocial Rehabilitation Journal* 15:11–17.

Mueser, K. T., Noordsy, D. L., Drake, R. E., & Fox, L. (2003). *Integrated Treatment for Dual Disorders: A Guide to Effective Practice*. New York: Guilford.

Narrow, W., Regier, D., Norquist, G., Rae, D. S., Kennedy, C., & Arons, B. (2000). Mental health service use by Americans with severe mental illnesses. *Social Psychiatry & Psychiatric Epidemiology* 35:147–155.

Opler, L., Kay, S., & Fiszbein, A. (1987). Positive and negative syndromes in schizophrenia. In *Typological, Dimensional, and Pharmacological Validation*. Hillsdale, NJ: Erlbaum.

Penn, D., Spaulding, W., Reed, D., & Sullivan, M. (1996). The relationship of social cognition to ward behavior in chronic schizophrenia. *Schizophrenia Research* 20:327–335.

Phelan, J., Link, B., Stueve, A., & Moore, R. (1995). Education, social liberalism, and economic conservatism: Attitudes toward homeless people. *American Sociological Review* 60:126–140.

Pratt, C., Gill, K., Barrett, N., & Roberts, M. (1999). *Psychiatric Rehabilitation*. San Diego, CA: Academic Press.

Ralph, R. (2000). Recovery. *Psychiatric Rehabilitation Skills* 4:480–517.

Regier, D., Farmer, M., Rae, D., Myers, J. K., Kramer, M., Robins, L. N., George, L. K, Karno, M., & Locke, B. Z. (1993). One-month prevalence of mental disorders in the United States and sociodemographic characteristics: The Epidemiologic Catchment Area program. *Acta Psychiatrica Scandinavica* 88:35–47.

Robins, L. (1998). An overview of the Diagnostic Interview Schedule and the Composite International Diagnostic Interview. In *International Classification in Psychiatry: Unity and Diversity*. New York: Cambridge University Press.

Schooler, N., Hogarty, G., & Weismann, M. M. (1970). Social adjustment scale II. In W. A. Hargraves, C. C. Atkisson, & J. E. Sorenson (eds.), *Resource Materials for Community Mental Health Program Evaluators* (No. ADM 79-328, pp. 290–330). Washington, DC: U.S. Government Printing Office.

Scott, J., & Lehman, A. (1998). Social functioning in the community. In *Handbook of Social Functioning in Schizophrenia*. Needham Heights, MA: Allyn & Bacon.

Skantze, K., Malm, U., Dencker, S., May, P. R. A., & Corrigan, P. (1992). Comparison of quality of life with standard of living in schizophrenic out-patients. *British Journal of Psychiatry* 161:797–801.

Spaulding, W. D., Reed, D., Poland, J., & Storzback, D. M. (1996). Cognitive deficits in psychotic disorders. In *Cognitive Rehabilitation for Neuropsychiatric Disorders*. Washington, DC: American Psychiatric Press.

Spitzer, R., Gibbon, M., Skodol, A., Williams, B., First, M., & Gibbon, M. (2002). *A Learning Companion to the Diagnostic and Statistical Manual of Mental Disorders*. Washington, DC: American Psychiatric Publishing.

Ventura, J., Green, M., Shaner, A., & Liberman, R. P. (1993). Training and quality assurance with the Brief Psychiatric Rating Scale: "The drift busters." *International Journal of Methods in Psychiatric Research* 3:221–224.

Ventura, J. Neuchterlein, K. H., Subotnik, K. L. Gutkind, D., & Gilbert, E. A. (2000). Symptom dimensions in recent-onset schizophrenia and mania: A principle components analysis of the 24-item brief psychiatric rating scale. *Psychiatry Reseach*, 97 (2-3), 129–135.

Wallace, C. (1986). Functional assessment in rehabilitation. *Schizophrenia Bulletin* 12:604–630.

World Health Organization. (2000). *The OCD-9 Classification of Mental and Behavioral Disorders*. Geneva, Switzerland: World Health Organization.

Wykes, T., & Sturt, E. (1986) The measurement of social behavior in psychiatric patients: An assessment of the reliability and validity of the SBS schedule. *British Journal of Psychiatry* 148:1–11.

IV

INTERVIEWING SPECIAL POPULATIONS

15

DIAGNOSTIC ASSESSMENT
OF CHILDREN

Nell Logan, Ph.D., ABPP

Children of all ages are referred to mental health professionals in schools, medical center clinics, other outpatient and inpatient facilities, and private practice for psychological evaluation and intervention. Most are four years of age and older, but developmental and psychological evaluations of children under four years, including infants, are occurring in increasing numbers. Children are referred for a variety of problems, including learning difficulties, fears, nervousness, depression, unhappiness, overactivity, disobedience, fighting, temper tantrums, eating problems, difficulty making friends, fire setting, stealing, lying, school truancy, excessive and unusual use of fantasy, and failure to reach developmental milestones.

The purpose of an assessment of a child is to arrive at an understanding of the child's presenting problems and the factors contributing to the difficulties. Problems may be manifestations of any number of physiological, psychological, and sociocultural variables. The assessment must include an understanding of specific psychological characteristics of the child, including strengths and difficulties. It must also look at the sociocultural background of the family, psychological characteristics of family members, the structure and dynamics of the family, and other life circumstances. Finally, it is important to assess the severity of the problem in the context of the child's age and the various contributing variables (Barker, 1990; Chethik, 2000; Eissler et al., 1977; Flapan & Neubauer, 1994; Goodman & Sours, 1967; Mishne, 1983; Morrison & Anders, 1999; Noshpitz, 1998). Several chapters in Noshpitz (1998) describe the OIM (Observation, Interview, and Mental Status) Assessment Guidelines developed by a number of researchers and clinicians. The OIM guidelines provide ideas for structured and unstructured observations, interviews, and mental status assessments with diverse populations and different problems.

This chapter will summarize important aspects of the diagnostic assessment of children. It will discuss diagnostic classification, assessment guidelines and format, work with parents, individual interviews with children, specialized evaluations, formulation of the problems, and treatment planning. The focus is on interviewing and observing children.

DIAGNOSTIC CLASSIFICATION OF CHILDHOOD DISORDERS

Most evaluations of children are conducted within the framework of a diagnostic classification system. The primary classification system currently in use for work with children is DSM-IV (American Psychiatric Association, 1994). This manual contains a section entitled "Disorders Usually First Evident in Infancy, Childhood, or Adolescence." Any other categories in DSM-IV that are applicable to adults may also be applied to children. The sections entitled "Mood Disorders," "Anxiety Disorders," "Schizophrenia and Other Psychotic Disorders," and "Adjustment Disorders," in particular, are fairly frequently applied to children.

Some authors (Mishne, 1983; Chethik, 2000; Sperling, 1982) still rely on more traditional categories. Chethik (2000), for example, has used the following categories: the neurotic child, character pathology, the borderline child, and the narcissistically vulnerable child.

ASSESSMENT GUIDES

Children seldom approach someone outside the family about their problems, although occasionally this happens, especially if the child has known someone who has received help in this way. A physician, teacher, parent, relative, or friend of the family is more often the one who initiates the referral. The parents usually bring the child for the evaluation.

Although evaluations occasionally occur in settings where it is difficult or impossible to obtain the cooperation of parents, it is important if possible to work closely with parents or guardians in order to establish rapport with them and to obtain information. When parents feel that the atmosphere is respectful and supportive, they are more likely to ally themselves with the interviewer, reveal important aspects of themselves and their child, keep appointments, and support the child's involvement in the process. One evaluator may work with parents, child, and other members of the family. In some settings, one therapist interviews the child while another interviews the parents. Sometimes, even a third person will see the family as a whole. All interviewers then collaborate closely.

An interviewer will achieve a deeper understanding of the problems by carefully listening to family members' communications, by noting the types of questions raised and the topics pursued, and by reflecting what is being said. *The interviewer wants to gain a sense of what it is like to be these parents with this child in this family and what it is like to be this child with these parents in this family.* The relationship between interviewer and family members develops as the interviewer tries to help them to clarify the nature of the difficulties. Family members should feel that they have been successful in communicating with the interviewer, have gained some new understanding, and have been validated as worthwhile people.

An important aspect of a child evaluation is to *place the problems within the context of the child's age and life circumstances* (Barker, 1990; Chethik, 2000; Eissler et al., 1977; Morrison & Anders, 1999). Childhood difficulties may reflect appropriate child developmental issues; common, transitory reactions to specific life circumstances; or more severe difficulties. Tantrums or clinging in a two-year-old child, for example, even after a relatively calm period in which the child seems cooperative and independent, are common developmental phenomena. Frequent crying in a five-year-old following the divorce of parents is a common reaction in children of this age to this trauma. These same behaviors, however, may reflect more severe difficulties, for example, if they are unusually intense or persist for a relatively long period of time. In assessing the severity of the problems, an evaluator especially looks at the extent to which the disturbances are interfering in important ways with play, learning, and interpersonal relationships and are slowing or impeding the development of important capacities.

Children are very involved in their families, and they trigger and react to many aspects of their families and of individuals within the family. However, they also have their own individual ways of coping with people and situations. *It is useful to begin to assess the contribution of their individual characteristics as well as the contribution of the characteristics of other family members and the family as a whole to the problems.* A child with severe asthma, for example, may have an intense fear of death, which partially arises from being near death. The anxieties, overprotectiveness, or underprotectiveness of other family members, however, may exacerbate this fear. The child's anger, depression, or loneliness may also increase the fear.

Interviewer Reactions

Children frequently act on their impulses, thus vividly manifesting their problems. They may be angry, destructive, sexually provocative, demanding, clinging, silly, passive, withdrawn, or inhibited. Parents also may react intensely to their children's problems with anxiety, anger, rage, shame, humiliation, guilt, self-criticism, demanding and controlling behavior, helplessness, and withdrawal. Such reactions may trigger strong responses in an interviewer.

A major hazard for interviewers is the somewhat common tendency to empathize with either a child or a parent and then to side with that person. One may think either that the parents have treated the child very poorly or that the parents have been stuck with a very difficult child. It is very important to gain a balanced view of the difficulties.

An interviewer's reactions to a child can provide important clues to the child's specific characteristics as well as suggest reactions that parents and others have to that child. An interviewer's reactions to a parent can also suggest reactions that a child or other parent may have to that particular parent. Remaining aware of and carefully thinking about one's own reactions are very important. An outside consultation may be useful in coping with very intense reactions.

EVALUATION FORMAT

Types of Data

An assessment must help one to understand factors that may be triggering and maintaining the current problems. The following list suggests possible types of data that may help in the assessment. Some evaluations will be briefer than others and will obtain less information. The data below thus will not apply to everyone or to every evaluation.

1. Identifying information
   a. Child's age, birthday, grade in school, gender, race
   b. Parents' ages, birthdays, occupations, and educational, socioeco-
      nomic, and sociocultural backgrounds
   c. Ages and relationship to child of siblings and others who live
      in the home
2. Referral information and presenting problems
   a. Referral source and nature of referral
   b. Description of presenting problems, with examples
   c. First appearance and history of problems
   d. Major precipitating and maintaining factors
3. Description of the child, parents, and other family members during the
   interview
4. Current physiological and psychological status of the child, including
   strengths and weaknesses
   a. Physiological status
      Physical appearance
      Vision and hearing
      Speech
      Overall health
   b. Physical difficulties
      Wishes, needs, affects, and defenses
      Predominant mood during interview

Important wishes or needs
Levels of anxiety and depression
Sources of anxiety and depression
Internal conflicts
Other specific affects
Frustration tolerance and affect tolerance
Regulation and control of affects
Methods of coping
Sources of pleasure and pain
c. Ideals, values, goals, and conscience
d. Interpersonal relationships
Quality and style of child's interaction with parents, siblings, teachers, peers
Child's perceptions of these other people
Specific conflicts with other people and methods of coping with conflicts
Communication patterns
Activities with others
Empathy for others
e. Perceptions of self and identity
Dependence, autonomy, and sense of self-efficacy
Gender identity
Racial, sociocultural, and religious identity
Interests and aptitudes
Self-confidence
f. Other capacities
Thought processes
Perceptual processes
Perceptual-motor skills
Overall intellectual capacities
Judgment
Sense of reality and reality testing
School achievement
Specific difficulties
g. Overall level of organization, integration, and rigidity
5. Developmental history
6. Parents and family
a. Personality functioning of each parent and sibling
b. Family structure and processes
c. Specific events in the life of the family
7. Other life circumstances
8. Formulation of problems
9. Treatment plan

Interview with Parents and Family

Interviewers frequently meet with parents either together or separately before seeing a child individually in order to obtain data on the presenting problems, history of the problems, past methods of coping with the problems, strengths of the child, physical problems or illnesses, and significant events or trauma in the life of the child, such as moves, a death, and physical or sexual abuse. Asking parents to present their memories of the child from pregnancy to the present may reveal important data on the child's development and parents' attitudes, feelings, and other reactions to the child. It is also useful at some point during an evaluation to gather information on discipline, emotional availability of the parents, legal problems, supports for the child, history of the parents' relationship, and characteristics of siblings and other members of the family. Observation of the parents during contacts with them will reveal information about the nature of the parents' interaction, roles played by each, sources of conflict, ways of handling conflict, attitudes toward each other and toward the child, and the nature of supports for each other and for the child. It may be useful to interview each parent separately, especially if there is some indication that a parent is having difficulty talking openly in the presence of the other parent.

The first interview or interviews may suggest that the family difficulties are as important as the child's specific problems or that data on the family as a whole will significantly enrich the evaluation. In these cases, an interview may be held with the entire family, including stepparents, foster parents, children, and sometimes others living in the home or relatives outside the home. An interviewer will ask specific questions and observe actual interaction during the interview.

Preparing a Child for an Evaluation

Children are usually at least somewhat anxious about an evaluation. This anxiety may be enhanced by a vivid imagination about possible dangers. If the problems are urgent, such as in the case of a suicide attempt, there may be little time for preparation. At least some preparation, however, can help to reduce anxiety to more tolerable levels. Interviewers can help parents think about ways of preparing a child for the evaluation.

Understanding a child's ambivalence about obtaining help can be useful in talking to a child. Children are at least somewhat aware that certain aspects of their lives are not going well for them. They may, for example, be fearful, worry a lot, feel rejected by others, or be doing poorly in schoolwork. They usually are aware that some aspects of their lives concern their parents or teachers. Obtaining help may provide some relief. The idea of receiving help may also be frightening. They may imagine that physical pain or increased psychological pain, such as rejection or criticism, will result.

Some parents and children discuss their concerns openly with each other. Parents sometimes sense a child's unhappiness and talk about it with the child. At other times, a child may talk to a parent, for example, about being teased and left out by other children. In some families, conversations about problems lead to heated arguments, criticisms, or angry outbursts. In other families, issues are not discussed openly.

Discussing problems and suggesting ideas about seeking help should be done as calmly as possible in language that is comfortable for a child. For younger children, the ideas may be very concrete or simple, such as "We feel bad that you are so unhappy so often" or "You have been getting into a lot of fights." It is easier for young children when the discussions do not occur too far ahead of the actual appointment. A few days to a couple of weeks ahead is usually sufficient. Discussions with older children may be more complex and may occur over a longer period of time. Parents may try to obtain their child's interest in an evaluation, or they may decide to state firmly that they plan to go with their child for help.

Confidentiality

Whether the same person or different people interview the child and other members of the family, the issue of confidentiality must be considered. The child may wonder what the interviewer has told the parents, and parents may wonder what has been told to the child. When two or more interviewers work with the family, some discussion of confidential information occurs between them. Parents also usually want some feedback on the nature of their child's problems, and most mental health professionals believe that parents in most situations are entitled to some feedback. The most general guideline is to *provide parents with a summary of the major problems and dynamics of the problems within the context of the child's strengths without divulging specific pieces of information.* An interviewer can state this guideline to both parents and child. Many interviewers also state briefly to the child the major ideas that will be presented to the parents and state to the parents ideas presented to the child. One may also give at least some feedback to parents and child together and to the family as a whole.

It is possible to base discussions with parents upon the nature of information that they provide, using interviews with the child primarily as general guides both to the types of information to elicit from parents and to the nature of the child's problems. Parents frequently can describe a child's behavior, including conversations with the child, in enough detail that the interviewer can use that detail as the basis for raising questions and providing feedback to the parents about the nature of the problems. Careful interviewing is important here. A parent, for example, may describe specific behaviors of a child that indicate depression, then describe significant strengths, such as good work in school, a close friendship, or specific hobbies, and then discuss some significant events, such as the recent death of a grandparent to whom the child was very close and several past family moves. An interviewer in this case, for example, might state that the child is doing very well in many respects but is experiencing a rather severe depression following the death of the grandmother. This child has had rather severe difficulties recovering from this separation because of several past separations and a tendency to react with depression following disappointments and separations. It is unnecessary, in this case, to tell parents what a child has said.

It is frequently useful to obtain information from teachers, physicians, and others who have previously worked with a child. It may also be important to provide information about the evaluation to people who will be involved with whatever treatment is pursued. Most interviewers discuss this issue carefully with parents and children. States, communities, and agencies have laws or policies governing such release of information and specific guidelines for what must be stated on forms. Parents must sign a statement granting permission for this transfer of information to occur. It is now common and sometimes legally required that children, especially older children, be asked to sign these statements along with parents. When children refuse to sign, the therapist and parents can usually sign the form and release information if they believe that it is in the best interest of the child.

INDIVIDUAL INTERVIEWS WITH CHILDREN

General Philosophy and Style

Since it may be difficult or impossible to converse directly with a child, especially a very young child, the term *interview* is used broadly in work with children to refer to interactions with and observations of children (Chethik, 2000; Greenspan, 1991; Mash & Terdal, 1997; Mishne, 1983; Noshpitz, 1998). The interactions may or may not include conversation. The purpose of such interviews is to learn as much as possible about the internal world and interactions of the child.

Sullivan's idea (1954) that the activity of the interviewer is "participant observation" is very relevant to work with children. As a participant, the interviewer must be aware of the child's potential and actual reactions to the interviewer and to the interview situation, respond in terms of these reactions, and help the child to feel comfortable, safe, and acceptable enough to reveal some important aspects of himself. *The interviewer as a participant also experiences what it is like to be with this child and, in a limited way, what it is to be this child.*

It is very important for an interviewer to know about communication styles and thought patterns of children of different ages with different cognitive capacities. Goodman and Sours (1967) recommend slow, concise, simple speech without too much direct questioning. One might say, for example, "All children

sometimes worry; I wonder what you worry about" or "We all sometimes remember a dream that we had at night; tell me about a dream that you have had."
Some people change their tone of voice when talking to a very young child.
This is not necessary and may sound patronizing or condescending to a child.
Therapists must respect children in the same manner as they respect peers and
convey this respect in the same way. Most interviewers of children keep some
toys and drawing materials in the interview room. This equipment may be used
primarily in the context of an unstructured play interview or may be available
in more structured interviews in the event that a child feels more comfortable
with the interviewer while using them.

Advantages and disadvantages of structured and unstructured interviews
have been discussed at some length in the literature (Goodman & Sours, 1967;
Greenspan, 1991; Mash & Terdal, 1997; Noshpitz, 1998). In structured interviews, the interviewer provides specific stimuli. For younger children, the stimuli may include concrete tasks with specific instructions, such as designs to be
copied and paper and markers with which to draw a person or family. The
structured stimuli for younger and older children may be specific questions and
self-report rating scales. The value of a structured situation is that some children
are more comfortable with at least some structure and that structure may help
to enhance the objectivity of the evaluation. The importance of unstructured
interviews is that the less the therapist intrudes into or structures a situation, the
more a child will project feelings, thoughts, and personal modes of action onto
the situation, thus structuring the situation in a personal manner. Many interviews contain both structured and unstructured features.

Children's Fantasies about Assessment Interviews

Young children in particular, but all children in some ways, view adults and
aspects of the adult world as large, powerful, omniscient, unpredictable, and
magical. They may view themselves as strong or weak, intelligent or stupid, controlling or controlled, vulnerable or invulnerable. They also in general view
themselves, others, and the world as good or bad without making the kinds of
more subtle discriminations that many adults make. These views all contribute
to anxiety, worry, ambivalence, and hesitation about interviews.

Some children are especially afraid that an interviewer will read their
minds, find out about their weaknesses, and then attempt to control them.
Other children are afraid that they are crazy, will be made to feel crazy, or will
be driven crazy or that parents or other people may abandon them. Still other
children are afraid of revealing "secrets" of either one or both parents or the
family, for example, about physical or sexual abuse, alcoholism, gambling, or psychiatric illnesses.

Probably the most intense and pervasive fears are of the exposure of personal weaknesses or "badness" and the resulting anxiety, embarrassment, shame,

humiliation, guilt, criticism, punishment, anger, disapproval, and rejection. Young children in particular, but also many older children, react with very intense, unmodulated affects, sudden mood swings, and sudden drops in self-esteem during interviews. Such reactions may be "normal" responses in children, especially young children, to specific unpleasant stimuli and may also occur in children with relatively minor as well as more severe problems.

Play Interviews

Interviews with children ten years of age and younger frequently are conducted as play interviews (Chethik, 2000; Gil, 1991; Greenspan, 1991; Mishne, 1983). Play interviews may be very unstructured, with children using the play materials in their own way with only occasional comments or questions by the interviewer. Play interviews may also be partially unstructured and partially structured. Such interviews frequently begin in a totally unstructured manner with the child allowed fairly free use of the materials. The interviewer then gradually begins to ask questions about worries, fears, dreams, friends, parents, and school. Some of these questions can be woven into ongoing play, while other questions may be related very little if at all to the play but are raised during the play with the idea that the child may be more comfortable answering questions while occupied with more pleasant activities.

Some interviewers watch the child but do not become involved in the actual play. Others follow the child's wishes and may or may not become involved in enacting stories or helping the child, depending on the child's wishes. Children vary in the amount and kind of talking that they do during play sessions. Their speech may be focused on the play or on other topics. Play equipment need not be elaborate but may include some or all of the following: wooden kindergarten blocks; a dollhouse; small, flexible dolls used sometimes in dollhouses, consisting of mother, father, boy, girl, and baby; a baby doll, perhaps with anatomically correct genitalia; small cars and trucks; toy soldiers, cowboys and Indians; puppets; small, light balls; modeling material; paper and markers; games; books; and a sand tray with various small play items. Many interviewers sit with the child on small chairs at a table designed for children. Some children prefer to play on the floor.

The major idea underlying the use of play interviews is that children will project their key issues into the content of the play and into the ways in which they use the play materials. Children frequently do not have the language, concepts, or introspective capacity to put their feelings and thoughts into words, and they may hesitate to discuss their problems or more actively resist such discussions. Children often use play, however, to master their concerns. They may indirectly reveal fears, sources of anger, sexual concerns, guilt, and conflicts with parents through their play. Such capacities as intelligence, creativity, spontaneity, defenses, perceptual-motor skills, thought processes, organization, perceptions of self and others, and nature of interaction processes can be assessed through observation of play.

Conversational Interviews

Children over ten years of age, but also some younger children, may prefer conversation to play and may discuss a variety of topics with the interviewer. They may especially enjoy talking about pleasant, safe topics. Topics considered nonthreatening will vary with the child but may include play activities, interests, classes in which they do well in school, favorite computer games or television shows, and family outings.

Some children will discuss at least some aspects of the problems fairly spontaneously without direct questioning, especially if these problems have been discussed with parents in a relatively safe manner. Other children will provide clues about the problems in the context of talking about comfortable topics. The therapist can then begin raising questions about the problems in the context of the safer topics.

Many children have difficulty discussing specific aspects of the problems for which they have been referred because of embarrassment, shame, humiliation, guilt, specific fears, or more generalized anxiety. Aspects of the conversation or interaction with a child may provide enough clues about the nature of the problem that direct questioning may be unnecessary. It is frequently useful, however, to probe gently into the subjects that evoke more intense anxiety and to find other ways of assessing the possible presence of such phenomena as substance abuse, suicidal potential, homicidal potential, traumatic memories, ongoing traumatic experiences such as sexual and physical abuse, and other dangerous or harmful behaviors. Various authors have described possible ways of evaluating the presence or absence and specific aspects of these difficulties (Briere et al., 1996; Noshpitz, 1998.)

Children through the ages of at least ten or twelve years are not very introspective and do not engage in the type of abstract thought that is a basic part of psychological understanding. They may, however, be able to label some feelings, describe dreams or play sequences, or tell about activities of friends and family members. Such discussions are often very concrete and contain specific descriptions of activities or statements of simple feelings rather than more complex elaboration of feelings or thoughts. In giving feedback, it is useful to present simple, concrete thoughts, reflecting the child's words or thoughts as much as possible.

Interview Process

Some children accompany the interviewer to the interview room fairly readily without a parent. Other children, especially very young children, are very hesitant about or resistant to parting from their parents. When this happens, the usual procedure is to talk to the child for awhile in the waiting room and then invite the child again to go into the interview room. If the child remains very reluctant to leave the parent, most interviewers invite the parent to accompany the child to the interview room. The parent may leave the room at some point or may remain throughout the interview.

Some children easily initiate play, conversation, or other interaction with the interviewer. When this happens, the interviewer then decides how much, when, and in what ways to structure the interview. Other children are very inhibited in thought and action in the interview room and may say or do little. The interviewer may remain quiet for awhile. It then can be helpful to make a simple comment such as "You may play with whatever toys you like" or "I would like to get to know you a little bit in here." Sometimes a simple question about what the child knows about why the child is there or a simple statement about what is already known about the child from the parents or teacher may help to initiate interaction.

The interviewer then usually follows the child's lead. The interviewer may remain silent, make comments, or raise questions, keeping in mind the presenting problems and data obtained from other sources. The specific data that emerge will provide clues about the child's strengths and weaknesses and the nature of the problems. The interviewer should guide the interview enough to communicate some understanding, acceptance, and respect and to obtain a deeper understanding of the problems that the child and family have.

One of the major questions raised by interviewers is how much freedom to allow a child during an interview. Interviews may trigger intense affect, and many children act upon impulses quite freely. The most common guideline is to allow quite a bit of freedom but to stop behavior that is destructive of property; physically hurtful to the child, interviewer, or another person; evokes an abundance of anxiety in the child; or interferes with the rights of others. The control of such behavior may involve physically restraining a child or terminating an interview. A sensitive interviewer, however, will often note signs of possible escalation of behavior before it occurs and will attempt to offer some calming comments.

Some children, however, are very inhibited during interviews. Sometimes it is possible with a few brief comments to help a child feel more comfortable. The child may remain very constricted, however. Even when a child says or does little in the interview room, there are clues about many facets of the child in the child's way of being with the interviewer from the time of the first introduction to the end of the interview. Nonverbal behavior as well as brief verbal communications are important data. The establishment of a relationship is also more important than the amount of data gathered.

Since children have a different sense of time than adults and often have difficulty with separations, it can be useful five to ten minutes before the end of an interview to mention the limited time available. Most interviewers also request the child's help in picking up play equipment, but allow the child some freedom to decline. At the end of the interview, some interviewers offer feedback to the child. Most interviewers also briefly discuss the nature of further contacts with the child and parents.

Unstructured Adjuncts to Play and Conversation

Drawings can be a rich source of data on a child. Many children spontaneously draw pictures during an interview. Other children readily draw when an examiner requests this. DeLeo (1973), Koppitz (1968), Malchiodi (1998), Naglieri (1988), Naglieri et al. (1991), and Thomas & Silk (1990) have discussed ways in which drawings reveal information on intellectual capacities, personality characteristics, family relationships, social attitudes and behaviors, attitudes toward physical impairments, and specific perceptual–motor and other learning problems.

Beiser (1979) describes ways in which playing games with children can provide data on attitudes toward rules, ways of coping with winning and losing, impulsiveness, dependent and independent behaviors, willingness to be taught, learning styles, risk-taking behavior, initiation of interaction, styles of interaction, and attitudes toward competition. Other techniques, such as the "mutual story-telling technique" (Gardner, 1985), the "squiggle game" (Winnicott, 1971), and statements about wishes (Winkley, 1982) may be especially useful in engaging more inhibited or resistant children.

Racial, Cultural, and Religious Diversity

There seems to be an important degree of commonality in psychological disorders across cultures in presenting problems, the nature and manifestations of disorders, and factors contributing to disorders (Silverman & McDermott, 1998). It is important, nevertheless, to learn about specific aspects of the cultural, racial, and religious backgrounds of specific children and parents. This background may impact values, ideals, ideas about personal difficulties, ways of expressing emotion, communication patterns, family structure, parental discipline, and personalities of the child and family members. Many families now consist of individuals of more than one racial, religious, and cultural identity, frequently contributing to interpersonal conflict, identity problems, anxiety, depression, and other personal difficulties. An evaluator may want to spend some extra time in forming an alliance and learning about these aspects of the family context. It may also be necessary or useful to use an interpreter during an interview.

A rather common problem in our contemporary society is for parents raised in one country to move to another country where they raise *their* children. One example of a clash of values is when the original country has emphasized close-ness to family and much respect for parents and family values, while the new cul-ture emphasizes independence and the development of personal values. It can be difficult for children and adults to decide what are reasonable expectations and values for themselves when they experience such conflicts.

Assessment of Infants and Very Young Children

The body of literature on normal and pathological development in in-fancy and early childhood and on assessment of these children has increased in the past thirty years (Brazelton, 1980; Flapan & Neubauer, 1994; Fraiberg, 1980; Greenspan & Lieberman, 1980; Noshpitz, 1997; Roberts, 1995). Interviewers typically rely heavily on interviews with parents in these assessments because of the nonverbal nature of very young children. Interviewers, however, may also interact with and observe the child and the child and a caregiver together. Such structured devices as the Brazelton Neonatal Behavioral Assessment (Brazelton, 1980), the Bayley Scales of Infant Development, and the assessment categories developed by Greenspan and Lieberman (1980) provide structured techniques for assessing various aspects of the development of infants and very young chil-dren. Many interviewers also conduct more unstructured observations. They may base their ideas upon their interactions with the child, a parent's caregiv-ing and play activities with the child, and the child's use of various objects, in-cluding play equipment. The interviewer, for example, notes affects, social in-teraction, use of play equipment, initiation of activities, responses to people and objects, or the use of sounds and language.

Many assessments currently rely on ideas about the nature of mother–child attachment. Such assessments may focus especially on observations of interac-tions between the child and a primary caregiver, usually the mother, and on in-terviews with the primary caregiver. These assessments developed from the work of Bowlby (1969) and Ainsworth et al. (1978). Research using the "Strange Sit-uation" originally developed by Ainsworth has repeatedly shown that the be-havior of young children is related to previous patterns of parent–infant interac-tion, is stable over time, and predicts later behavior in the same and other contexts (Lamb et al., 1985; Goldberg et al., 1995).

More recent neurophysiological and psychological research (Schore, 1994) has strongly suggested that physiological and psychological regulations of wishes, thoughts, affects, and behaviors occur concomitantly through mu-tual influences, begin prenatally, and continue through infancy and early child-hood. Such regulation of biopsychological processes seems to be influenced by an infant's early biological processes, parental interactions with the infant, and other aspects of the environment. These early processes become templates or "internal working models" (Cassidy, 1997, p. 240) for later behaviors and in-teractions. These ideas on attachment and neuropsychological processes are providing the basis for many assessments of the development of infants and young children.

Behavioral Assessment

Although much of the past literature on child assessment developed out of psychodynamic thought, behavioral assessment has been discussed more frequently over the past twenty-five years (Hughes & Baker, 1990; Mash & Terdal, 1997; Ramsey et al., 2002). These assessments focus on observable behavior but also may evaluate anxiety, depression, fears, anger, interests, perceptual and thought processes, expectancies, and standards of right and wrong. An evaluator may observe behavior in natural settings where it is a problem, such as school or home, or in an office, using specific categories for observation.

Behavioral assessments frequently use objective measures, quantify variables as much as possible based on research data, and rely on multiple sources of information. These assessments focus on delineating problematic behaviors, contributing environmental factors, personal variables, the contexts within which the behaviors occur, and consequences of the behaviors. Evaluators especially attempt to target behaviors that are essential for development, may be affecting the child's personal development and interactions with others, and are dangerous. It is useful also to highlight behaviors that are helping a child to adapt flexibly in order to suggest work on enhancing these behaviors. Some behaviors seem central to other problematic behaviors and then become the primary target behaviors. Hyperactive behavior, for example, may become a target behavior. Such behavior, however, may reflect other difficulties, such as intense anxiety or depression. These other difficulties and the behaviors associated with them then become target problems.

Structured Interviews and Rating Scales

Behavioral assessments often include one or more rating scale, although interviewers who conduct relatively unstructured interviews may also use structured interviews and rating scales. Some rating scales are designed for mental health evaluators, parents, and teachers to rate behaviors and characteristics of children, while others are for children to rate themselves.

Young et al. (1998) described the following two semistructured interview schedules that are frequently used with children: Kiddie-Schedule for Affective Disorders and Schizophrenia (K-SADS) and Kovacs Interview Schedule for Children (ISC). The K-SADS can be administered to parents and children and focuses on affective, schizophrenic, and anxiety disorders. Child and parent versions exist for the ISC, which assesses past and current symptoms in a way that is similar to the K-SADS. Hughes and Baker (1990) and Goldman and Rodrigue (1998) describe several additional rating scales.

New tests, rating scales, and interview schedules are being developed frequently. It is useful to review these in the literature.

Other Specialized Assessments

When children are experiencing difficulties in school, teachers are often willing to talk over the telephone or in person at the school about the child's socioemotional and cognitive functioning. Teachers are also usually willing to let an evaluator observe the child in the classroom. The school may also have results of more specialized evaluations of speech, language, perceptual–motor skills, intellectual abilities, achievement in school, and specific learning problems. If such evaluations seem important and have not been done, the school may be able to conduct these evaluations. Some evaluators will do psychological testing themselves; others refer the child to another psychologist for testing.

In gathering health history, a conversation with the child's physician and written data from the physician or other medical records may be useful. The evaluator may also refer a child for a thorough physical exam.

FORMULATION OF PROBLEM AND TREATMENT PLANNING

Information from an evaluation must be interpreted and integrated to provide a deeper understanding of the presenting problems. This formulation should include statements about specific personality assets and deficits and ways in which they are related to the problems; severity of the problems; physiological, psychological, family, and sociocultural variables contributing to the development and maintenance of the problems; consequences of the problems for the child and family; current means of coping with the problems; and vicious cycles that recur in interactions between parents and child.

The nature of the recommendations should flow from the formulation of the problems. Such recommendations might include one or more of the following: special classroom placement; remediation of specific learning problems; individual, group, parent, or family therapy; treatment of physical problems; hospitalization; and residential treatment.

It is important to provide adequate feedback to parents and child and to work with them around obtaining appropriate interventions. Some parents quickly understand and accept feedback and treatment recommendations and follow through with intervention on their own or with some help from the evaluator. It can be helpful with other parents to provide several interviews to describe the problems and treatment recommendations in a way that they can gradually understand and accept and to work more closely over an extended period of time with them in obtaining appropriate interventions. Some parents will obtain a second opinion before beginning interventions. Several chapters in Noshpitz (1998) provide guidelines for developing clinical formulations, making decisions, providing feedback to children and parents, and instituting interventions.

CASE HISTORY

The mother of an eight-year-old boy called an outpatient clinic about evaluating her son after his third-grade teacher expressed concerns about his difficulties interacting with other children. The teacher was also concerned about his poor handwriting, speech problems, difficulties learning arithmetic, and unusual behaviors. His school had recently begun speech and learning evaluations. This child's mother also described the teasing of her son by other children in the neighborhood.

An initial interview with the mother revealed that the boy was the oldest of four children and that the mother had enjoyed him during his first year of life but had become increasingly overwhelmed at the birth of each of the other children. She thought that he had developed well in his first year but began to have difficulties in his second and third years, when she became preoccupied with the younger children.

This child's father did not show up for any of the evaluation interviews, although the interviewer encouraged the child's mother to bring him along. The father would not talk to the interviewer on the telephone. The mother reported that she was depressed over the burdens of raising four children on little income and living with her husband's alcoholism and their marital difficulties.

The initial play interview with the child was difficult. He went rapidly from one toy or other object in the room to another and talked rapidly in an unorganized way, usually mumbling about such topics as our solar system, monsters, and evil in the world and rarely looking at the interviewer. During the second play interview, he seemed somewhat calmer, talked about topics in a somewhat clearer and more organized way, and drew some pictures that resembled aspects of our solar system. He seemed very afraid of possible dangers from outer space and on the earth.

Psychological testing through the school and interviews with the child and mother suggested that this child became very anxious very quickly, especially over harm to himself and members of his family, had a vivid imagination and at times thought what he imagined was real, and attempted to interact with other children by showing off his knowledge. He became quite disorganized and had difficulties concentrating and learning in school when he was anxious. He also was easily hurt and became very angry when other children taunted him. He was very dependent on his mother and at times had difficulty separating from her.

Psychological testing showed overall intellectual functioning in the high average range with verbal scores above average and perceptual–motor scores below average. A speech and language evaluation showed moderate enunciation problems and disorganized speech patterns.

The school agreed to provide speech therapy and learning disabilities help in the school. The child began play therapy with a therapist who also decided to begin seeing the family in the home.

Interviewing children is different from interviewing adolescents or adults. Children think about, perceive, react to, and speak about themselves in unique ways that may seem strange and unfamiliar to many adults, especially those who do not remember much about their own childhood or who have had little experience with children.

Children are usually brought for evaluation by others and thus frequently do not choose such an evaluation. Their anxiety and wishes to avoid the situation are frequently stronger than their wishes for help and may lead to withdrawal, inhibition, or aggressive actions that are strong resistances and may be difficult to surmount. When such actions are viewed as coping mechanisms for situations that evoke anxiety, however, rather than as resistances, they are easier to understand, tolerate, and handle in ways that have been suggested in this chapter. Mutual cooperation may develop slowly, however.

Children are quite influenced by their environments, especially home, school, and neighborhood. It is frequently difficult to understand and have an impact on the child unless work with the child is coordinated with work with the parents or family and sometimes also with the school or other groups that affect that particular child. Such work complicates therapeutic intervention.

Since issues in work with children differ from those in work with adults, it is important for clinicians to obtain specialized training in such work. It has been traditional in the past for most training programs to emphasize work with adults and to provide training for work with children as a subspecialty. In more recent years, some training programs have provided opportunities for study about and work with children that go hand in hand with training for work with adults. It is also possible for therapists to train primarily for work with children from the beginning of their studies.

Although work with children may be complex and difficult, it can also be very rewarding. Many children are eager for a good relationship with an adult, especially when they begin to trust the adult, and may be relatively flexible, which enables them to change in important ways. It is gratifying to the therapist when these children go on to lead more meaningful lives than they might have without clinical intervention.

REFERENCES

American Psychiatric Association (1994). *Diagnostic and Statistical Manual of Mental Disorders,* 4th ed. Washington, DC: American Psychiatric Association.

Ainsworth, M. D. S., Blehar, M. C., Waters, E., and Wall, S. (1978). *Patterns of Attachment: A Psychological Study of the Strange Situation.* Hillsdale, NJ: Erlbaum.

Barker, P. (1990). *Clinical Interviews with Children and Adolescents.* New York: Norton.

Beiser, H. R. (1979). Formal games in diagnosis and therapy. *Journal of the American Academy of Child Psychiatry* 18:480–491.

Bowlby, J. (1969). *Attachment and Loss: Attachment,* Vol. 1. New York: Basic.

Brazelton, T. B. (1980). Neonatal assessment. In *The Course of Life: Psychoanalytic Contributions toward Understanding Personality Development: Infancy and Early Childhood,* Vol. 1, ed. S. I. Greenspan and G. H. Pollock, pp. 203–233. Adelphi, MD: National Institute of Mental Health.

Briere, J., Berliner, L., Bulkley, J. A., Jenny, C., and Reid, T., eds. (1996). *The APSAC Handbook on Child Maltreatment.* Thousand Oaks, CA: Sage.

Cassidy, J. (1997). Attachment theory. In *Handbook of Child and Adolescent Psychiatry: Infants and Preschoolers. Development and Syndromes,* Vol. 1, ed. J. D. Noshpitz, pp. 236–250. New York: Wiley and Sons.

Chethik, M. (2000). *Techniques of Child Therapy,* 2nd ed. New York: Guilford.

DeLeo, J. H. (1973). *Children's Drawings as Diagnostic Aids.* New York: Brunner/Mazel.

Eissler, R. S., Freud, A., Kris, M., and Solnit, A. J., ed. (1977). *An Anthology of the Psychoanalytic Study of the Child, Psychoanalytic Assessment: The Diagnostic Profile.* New Haven: Yale University Press.

Flapan, D., and Neubauer, P. B. (1994). *The Assessment of Early Child Development.* Northvale, NJ: Jason Aronson.

Fraiberg, S., (1980). *Clinical Studies in Infant Mental Health.* New York: Basic.

Gardner, R. (1985). The initial clinical evaluation of the child. In *The Clinical Guide to Child Psychiatry,* ed. D. Shaffer, A. A. Ehrhardt, and L. L. Greenhill, pp. 371–392. New York: Free Press.

Gil, E. (1991). *The Healing Power of Play: Working with Abused Children.* New York: Guilford.

Goldberg, S., Muir, R., and Kerr, J. (1995). *Attachment Theory: Social, Developmental, and Clinical Perspectives.* Hillsdale, NJ: Analytic Press.

Goldman, J., and Rodrigue, J. R. (1998). Rating scales. In *Handbook of Child and Adolescent Psychiatry: Clinical Assessment and Intervention Planning,* Vol. 5, ed. J. D. Noshpitz, pp. 633–643. New York: Wiley and Sons.

Goodman, J. D., and Sours, J. A. (1967). *The Child Mental Status Examination.* New York: Basic.

Greenspan, S. I. (1991). *The Clinical Interview of the Child,* 2nd ed. Washington, DC: American Psychiatric Press.

Greenspan, S. I., and Lieberman, A. (1980). Infants, mothers, and their interactions: A quantitative clinical approach to developmental assessment. In *The Course of Life: Psychoanalytic Contributions toward Understanding Personality Development: Infancy and Early Childhood,* ed. S. I. Greenspan and G. H. Pollock, pp. 271–312. Adelphi, MD: National Institute of Mental Health.

Hughes, J. N., and Baker, D. B. (1990). *The Clinical Child Interview.* New York: Guilford.

Koppitz, E. M. (1968). *Psychological Evaluations of Children's Human Figure Drawings.* New York: Grune & Stratton.

Lamb, M. E., Thompson, R. A., Gardner, W., Charnov, E. L., & Connell, J. P. (1985). *Infant–Mother Attachment: The Origins and Developmental Significance of Individual Differences in Strange Situation Behavior.* Hillsdale, NJ: Erlbaum.

Malchiodi, C. A. (1998). *Understanding Children's Drawings.* New York: Guilford.

Mash, E. J., and Terdal, L. G., eds. (1997). *Assessment of Childhood Disorders,* 3rd ed. New York: Guilford.

Mishne, J. M. (1983). *Clinical Work with Children.* New York: Free Press.

Morrison, J., and Anders, T. F. (1999). *Interviewing Children and Adolescents: Skills and Strategies for Effective DSM-1V Diagnosis.* New York: Guilford.

Naglieri, J. A. (1988). *Draw a Person: A Quantitative Scoring System Manual.* San Antonio, TX: Psychological Corporation.

Naglieri, J. A., McNeish, T. J., and Bardos, A. N. (1991). *DAP: SPED, Draw a Person: Screening Procedure for Emotional Disturbance, Examiner's Manual.* Austin, TX: Pro-ed.

Noshpitz, J. D., ed. (1997). *Handbook of Child and Adolescent Psychiatry: Infants and Preschoolers. Development and Syndromes,* Vol. 1. New York: Wiley and Sons.

Noshpitz, J. D., ed. (1998). *Handbook of Child and Adolescent Psychiatry, Clinical Assessment and Intervention Planning,* Vol. 5. New York: Wiley and Sons.

Ramsey, M. C., Reynolds, C. R., and Kamphaus, R. W. (2002). *Essentials of Behavioral Assessment.* New York: Wiley and Sons.

Roberts, M. C., ed. (1995). *Handbook of Pediatric Psychology,* 2nd ed. New York: Guilford.

Schore, A. N. (1994). *Affect Regulation and the Origin of the Self: The Neurobiology of Emotional Development.* Hillsdale, NJ: Erlbaum.

Silverman, S. M., and McDermott, J. F. (1998). Observation, interview, and mental status assessment (OIM): Culturally different from clinician. In *Handbook of Child and Adolescent Psychiatry: Assessment and Intervention planning,* Vol. 5, ed. J. D. Noshpitz. New York: Wiley and Sons.

Sperling, M. (1982). *The Major Neuroses and Behavioral Disorders in Children.* New York: Jason Aronson.

Sullivan, H. S. (1954). *The Psychiatric Interview.* New York: Norton.

Thomas, G. V., and Silk, A. M. (1990). *An Introduction to the Psychology of Children's Drawings.* New York: New York University Press.

Winnicott, D. W. (1971). *Therapeutic Consultations in Child Psychiatry.* New York: Basic.

Winkley, L. (1982). The implications of children's wishes: Research note. *Journal of Child Psychology and Psychiatry* 23:477–483.

Young, J. G., Kaufman, D., and Nadrich, R. (1998). Structured interviews. In *Handbook of Child and Adolescent Psychiatry: Clinical Assessment and Intervention Planning,* Vol. 5, ed. J. D. Noshpitz, pp. 663–676. New York: Wiley and Sons.

16

CLINICAL INTERVIEWS WITH ADOLESCENTS

J. D. Ball, Ph.D., ABPP, Robert P. Archer, Ph.D., ABPP,
and Kathrin Hartmann, Ph.D.

Interviewing adolescents for detailed clinical information in preparation for mental health services that parents seek for them against their will may not sound to everyone like the easiest way to earn a living. Yet the authors, as a vast number of other clinical practitioners, have found it to be rewarding work. In the hope of bringing these rewards more quickly to those who aspire to interview adolescents more skillfully, this chapter will address several salient topics. We first review essential developmental considerations in working with adolescents. We then address ethical and legal concerns associated with gathering informed consent as a prelude to conducting the interview. We present newly emerging literature regarding structured clinical interviews, and we briefly review the advantages of using supplementary survey and test instruments and obtaining data from multiple sources. Finally, we turn to interview methods and strategies and walk the reader through an interview process. While space is too limited to provide a detailed skill manual, we offer time-tested ways of thinking about and working with this population, and we draw on a case example to illustrate the challenges and joys inherent to this endeavor.

As a prelude to a more complete discussion of developmental themes, it may be helpful first to address possible adolescent resistance to the interview. Even one-time assessment interviews require attention to the patient–therapist relationship as a first-order task. Of course, clinicians should begin by lowering personal defenses. Clinicians may express personal anxiety through stilted, intellectualized, rapid-fire questioning or through a passive, nondirective stance that yields too little data. Perhaps not surprisingly, the clinician's path to greater skill begins with increased empathy. Most of us can recall, from our own adolescence, a duality of thought we experienced in anticipation of being interviewed by a mental health professional. On one hand, we might have felt disdain and indignation and expressed these sentiments through wry humor with friends, sarcasm, or silence. On the other hand, we might have harbored a wish, or at least a private willingness, to connect to a caring adult who would be persistent enough to reach beyond our defensive ploys to earn our trust. Clinicians should begin with an appreciation for this duality, as it marks much of adolescence—apparent fierce independence (actually expressed through strong peer group identification) and underlying fragility (rarely expressed openly). By picturing the adolescent before his or her own peer group and appreciating the need to save face, adults are apt to take less personally the adolescent's bravado, provocative deception, or reticence. It may help to realize that some if not much of what adolescents do or say is an early draft of a script for an uncertain role in an unfinished play. Listen carefully for more genuine feelings and thoughts that tend to be at least partly disguised by a performance for a chorus of unseen peers. In fact, the peer-group influence on adolescent development is so critically important that psychotherapeutic interventions with adolescents are often most powerful from within a group therapy context (Ball & Meck, 1979).

RELEVANT THEMES DURING ADOLESCENT DEVELOPMENT

Some of the more serious errors that occur in the interviewing, assessment, and treatment of adolescents involve the failure to appreciate the extent to which adolescents present unique developmental themes and issues. The concept of adolescence as a discreet transitional period between childhood and adulthood is relatively recent, as prior to the twentieth century, many cultures recognized no formal transition between childhood and adulthood. Indeed, even during the early part of the twentieth century, most American and European adolescents went into the workforce rather than an educational setting.

An important feature of adolescence is the turbulence typically associated with meeting the demanding developmental tasks to be accomplished during these years. G. Stanley Hall (1904) was the formulator of the "Sturm und Drang," or "storm and stress," model of adolescent development. This view, consistent with the later views of Anna Freud (1958), suggests that the difficult challenges faced by the adolescent are typically mastered through a series of emotional and behavioral upheavals. Anna Freud's famous description of this process is summarized in her statement that "the upholding of a steady equilibrium during the process [of adolescence] is, in itself, abnormal" (Freud, 1958, p.275). Peter Blos (1962; 1967) also supported the view that adolescence was characteristically unstable and turbulent, underscoring the difficulty of identifying psychiatric illness from transient normative phenomena during this developmental period. Similarly, Eric Erikson (1956) proposed that adolescent struggles for self-definition frequently resulted in deviations from normal or expected behavior, which he termed "identity diffusion" or "identity confusion" and differentiated from symptoms of psychopathology. Thus, adolescents often report more erratic or undercontrolled behaviors and emotions than are typically reported in clinical interviews with either adults or children, and it is often more difficult to discern stable psychiatric symptoms from transitory adolescent turbulence. Nevertheless, the skilled clinician can make useful discriminations between psychiatric symptoms and normal developmental turbulence, and serious psychiatric illness does occur during this developmental stage. Prevalence studies, for example, indicate that between 12 and 22 percent of all adolescents display symptomatology that would warrant a DSM-IV diagnosis at some point during their adolescent development (e.g., National Institute of Mental Health, 1990; Powers et al., 1989). Thus adolescents do, in fact, suffer from psychiatric disorders that would not be expected to remit without active and effective treatment efforts. A useful way to facilitate the accurate identification of psychopathology during adolescence is to frame symptomatology within the context of major developmental challenges during this stage. Three major themes of development facing each adolescent during this period are sexual maturation, cognitive maturation, and psychological/emotional maturation.

Developmental Challenges

Many dramatic physiological changes occur during adolescence, and among the most important is the process of sexual maturation. Kimmel and Weiner define puberty as "the process of becoming physically and sexually mature and developing the characteristics of one's gender—female or male—such as physical build, genitals, and body hair" (Kimmel & Weiner, 1995, p. 60). Peterson (1985) has stressed that puberty is a process rather than an isolated temporal event. This process involves all the changes inherent in a sexually immature child achieving full reproductive potential. Kimmel and Weiner (1995) note that the timing and age of pubertal onset varies as a function of genetic inheritance, body weight and exercise, nutrition, and the potential effects of psychological trauma or physical disease. The course of pubertal development can have profound effects on the psychological functioning of the adolescent, especially self-identity and self-esteem, particularly in a precocious or early onset of puberty or an unusually late or delayed puberty. The successful mastery and incorporation of a rapidly changing and maturing body and emerging sexuality is a major developmental task for the adolescent.

Adolescents may also be defined in terms of changes that occur in cognitive processes. The work of Piaget and his colleagues (1975) postulates that qualitative changes occur in the cognitive processes of adolescents. Specifically, Piaget hypothesized that the individual typically makes the transition from concrete operations to formal operations during early adolescence. Typically, the latter stage is characterized by the capacity to manipulate ideas and concepts, to perform logical operations, to think about abstract ideas, and to draw logical conclusions. Thus, as expressed by Piaget (1975), the crucial difference between the child and adolescent is that the latter's capability to engage in abstract reasoning and to conceive of possibilities does not occur in younger children. However, not all adolescents, or even adults, achieve the cognitive stage of formal operations (Kimmel & Weiner, 1995). An important consequence of adolescents' attainment of formal operations relates to their ability to understand interview questions, as well as test items, such as those presented in one of the most commonly used assessment tools for adolescents, the Minnesota Multiphasic Personality Inventory for Adolescents (MMPI-A; Butcher et al., 1992). To the extent that the adolescent has not achieved formal operations, he or she will have significant difficulty in understanding questions requiring abstract reasoning or logical judgment, and individual responses will tend to be more concrete and directly related to an immediate experience of the physical world.

Finally, a host of psychological and emotional tasks, including the processes of ego identity or identity formation and the development of a sense of independence versus dependence, are typically accomplished during adolescence. Blos (1967), for example, describes individualization as a process involving the development of relative independence from family relationships and the increased capacity to assume a functional role as a member of adult society. Erikson (1956) describes ego identity formation during adolescence as the converging of various aspects of the self into a coherent sense of individual identity. Loevinger (1976) articulates a complex concept of ego development as a sequence of increasingly complex levels of functioning in terms of impulse control, interpersonal relationships, cognitive complexity, and personality development. At the lowest levels of ego development, collectively grouped into the preconformist stage, the individual may be described as impulsive, motivated by personal gain and the avoidance of punishment, and oriented to the present with limited ability to relate to the past or future. Cognitive styles during the preconformist stage are concrete and stereotypic; interpersonal relationships are exploitive and opportunistic. Most, although not all, adolescents reach the second broad stage of development described by Loevinger, referred to as the conformist stage. In this stage, the individual begins to identify his or her own personal welfare with that of his or her social group. Issues of social acceptability become important in the individuals' functioning, and the individual is able to adhere to expected group norms, standards, and behaviors.

STRUCTURED DIAGNOSTIC INTERVIEWS

As noted by Stein (1987), there has been a significant movement in psychiatry and psychology toward the development of more structured or semistructured interview formats. This movement has been in response, at least in part, to criticisms of unstructured clinical interviews in terms of significant limitations in reliability and validity (e.g., Matarazzo, 1983). Among the first structured interviews was the Diagnostic Interview for Children and Adolescents (DICA), originally developed by Herjanic and his colleagues (1975; 1977). The DICA was first designed to assess childhood diagnoses in pediatric and psychiatric samples for children ranging in age from six to seventeen. The DICA was subsequently modified in accordance with changes found in the DSM-III-R criteria, which resulted in the DICA-Revised or the DICA-R, and Reich (2000) notes that separate interview formats have been developed for children (six to twelve years) and adolescents (thirteen to eighteen years). The latest version of the DICA, the 1997 interview, can be used to derive either DSM-III-R or DSM-IV diagnoses.

The basic structure of the DICA-R is standard questions followed by occasional probes from a trained rater/clinician. The DICA is comprehensive in coverage, and items are presented in branching format, with screening questions for many sections. Rogers (1995) indicates that the DICA-R is typically administered in approximately forty minutes, and it is scored on a four-point scale that is organized by frequency of symptoms and, unless otherwise specified, for lifetime occurrence. The DICA-R is organized into fifteen sections, with the preliminary two sections covering general information and sociodemographic data. Other sections focus on psychosocial stressors and clinical observations. A total of eleven sections address a wide variety of mental disorders or symptomatology, including such categories as behavioral disorders, dysthymic disorder, gender identity disorder, and psychotic symptoms. Reich (2000) reports that rater training for the DICA is extensive, usually requiring two to four weeks of instruction and practice, and that interviewers are usually bachelor's or master's degree graduates. Parallel forms of the DICA exist for child, adolescent, and parent versions. There is also a self-administered computerized version of the DICA that was developed and pilot tested for adolescents and parents (Stein, 1987). Rogers (1995) indicates that until further research is done on the equivalency of the computerized format, this format should be used only for research purposes. Rogers (1995) and Reich (2000) concur that the available research suggests that the DICA has an acceptable interrater diagnostic reliability, but Rogers cautions that relatively few studies have examined the concurrent validity of the DICA, and these studies have yielded generally mixed results. With the exception of the DICA, most other structured diagnostic interviews have tended to focus on children rather than adolescents, and the few instruments that have been developed for adolescent respondents lack substantive reliability and validity data.

THE VALUE OF FORMAL TESTING WITH ADOLESCENTS

The clinical interview is probably the most widely used clinical assessment technique in the mental health field with patients of all ages. All types of mental health professionals, including psychologists, psychiatrists, and social workers, continue to employ the unstructured clinical interview as their primary means of assessing child, adolescent, and adult patient groups. There are, however, many reasons to believe that the accuracy and utility of these judgments are often enhanced through the use of additional test information. In 1991, Archer, Maruish, Imhof, and Piotrowski presented survey findings based on the responses of a national sample of psychologists who perform psychological assessment with adolescent clients. The results of that survey identify the Wechsler Intelligence Scales, the Rorschach, the Minnesota Multiphasic Personality Inventory (MMPI), the Bender-Gestalt, the Thematic Apperception Test (TAT), the Sentence Completion Test, Figure Drawings, and the Wide Range Achievement Test (WRAT) as the most frequently used instruments with this age group. In a subsequent survey, Ball et al. (1994) found similar rankings and further reported that, among personality instruments, the time demand for clinicians was substantially less when using the MMPI than when using either the Rorschach or TAT. Archer and Newsom (2000) conducted an updated survey in 1999 by examining the test practices reported by 346 psychologists who work with adolescents in a variety of clinical settings. In this most recent survey, respondents had a mean of nearly fourteen years of postdoctoral clinical experience in working with adolescents and spent an average of nearly half of their clinical time with this developmental group. Survey responses revealed a substantial degree of similarity in test usage between the 1991 and 1999 surveys. For example, the Wechsler Intelligence Scale was the most widely used assessment instrument with adolescents, underscoring the importance of the issue of cognitive functioning with this age group. The second, third, and fourth most frequently used tests were, respectively, the Rorschach Inkblot Technique, the Sentence Completion, and the Thematic Apperception Test (TAT); all are forms of projective testing that have withstood the pressures of both managed care as well as criticisms of projective assessment from parts of the academic community. The relative popularity of these projective instruments underscores the usefulness that clinicians find in these techniques and their utility in providing important personality functioning data with adolescents who have literacy limitations or reading disabilities. The fifth most frequently administered test for adolescents was the Minnesota Multiphasic Personality Inventory-Adolescent (MMPI-A), an objective self-report personality inventory. The MMPI-A (Butcher et al., 1992) is an adaptation of the original MMPI specifically created for use with adolescent respondents. Among the primary strengths of the MMPI-A reported by survey respondents were the ability to provide a comprehensive clinical picture, the availability of contemporary adolescent norms, ease of administration, and the psychometric soundness and research base of the instrument. Rounding out the top ten most frequently used tests were, respectively, the Child Behavior Checklist (Parent Report Form), the House–Tree–Person Technique (a projective technique), the Wide Range Achievement Test (WRAT), the Child Behavior Checklist (Teacher Report Form), and the Conners' Rating Scales-Revised. Three of these tests, (the Parent and Teacher Report Forms and the Conners' Ratings Scales) represent the increasingly critical role of rating scales in describing important attitudes, behaviors, and symptoms for adolescent patients. The data provided through these instruments by external informants often compliment and refine data provided through projective and objective self-report sources and other sources of information, including clinical interview findings.

A new instrument, the Stress Index for Parents of Adolescents (SIPA, Sheras et al., 1998), can be of considerable help to clinicians working with adolescents. This tool is applicable for parents of adolescents between eleven and nineteen years of age, and it requires only twenty minutes to administer. Of course, parent stress is directly related to the extent of adolescent stress, and this instrument provides important additional data regarding the quality or nature of the stress that parents experience. Subscales provide data regarding the degree to which parent stress is perceived to result from adolescent behavior, the parent's own behavior, or the interaction between parents and adolescents. Sheras (2002) has advised different ways of working with teens in therapy, depending upon the outcome of the SIPA. For example, when the Adolescent–Parent Relationship Domain reflects high stress, it may be best to work with the adolescent alone, as there may be too much anger within the family to work with parents and adolescents together. When the Parent Domain on the SIPA is exceptionally high, the principal intervention focus may need to be with parents, rather than with the adolescent. Subscale interpretations may offer still further treatment guidelines. By having each parent complete the instrument separately, the clinician can better understand how differing parent perspectives may influence the adolescent's problem presentation.

Achenbach (1999) has referred to the approach of combining assessment data from multiple sources as "multiaxial assessment." This approach clearly postulates that the accuracy and clinical utility of information concerning an adolescents' functioning will show incremental gains when multiple sources of information are gathered and skillfully combined. When information from a variety of sources converges on a similar conclusion, for example, increased confidence may often be placed on the diagnostic assessment developed for that adolescent. In contrast, however, variations in the perception of the clients' functioning that are reflected in different assessment sources may also prove very useful in underscoring the need for a variety of interventions to address each of the different problem areas that emerge from this type of evaluation. The instruments identified in the survey by Archer and Newsome (2000) have established popularity with clinicians because the combination of varied sources of information regarding adolescent functioning provide an enriched context in which to understand and interpret findings from clinical interview.

OBTAINING INFORMED CONSENT

Few adolescents seek treatment on their own, since they struggle to blend in with peers and to avoid being seen as different or especially, in their own vernacular, "mental." In a recent survey of forty-two outpatient children, Paul et al. (2000) found that one third reported not wanting to come to therapy and feeling coerced by parents. Just coming to a clinical interview is an act of bravery for adolescents, who are rarely interviewed for life successes. For these reasons and others, clinicians should give careful attention to the process of obtaining informed consent. Obtaining consent prior to interviewing the adolescent and his or her family is necessary from several perspectives: (1) legally in some states (e.g., Virginia), clinicians are required to provide enough information to prospective clients to enable them to give permission for treatment, before any treatment can begin; (2) ethically, the consent process is a critical means of protecting the client from blindly entering into a very personal and potentially life-changing activity; and (3) therapeutically, informed consent protects client trust, helps avoid potential pitfalls, and sets a serious, caring, and open tone.

The term "consent" derives from federal regulations regarding patients' participation in clinical research. It was later adapted for treatment issues as well (Koocher & Keith-Spiegel, 1990). Consent is the process by which clients give personal agreement to treatment, including even data gathering through clinical interview. Implicit in this process is the issue of whether the person giving consent is competent to do so, an especially important consideration for adolescents. As noted above, by age fourteen, most children have reached Piaget's formal operations stage and are capable of giving consent. They can attend to several ideas at once, entertain hypothetical possibilities, and use deductive logic in decision making. Clinicians can facilitate this process by presenting essential components of a problem and making the problem setting and its elements as familiar and meaningful as possible (Flavell, 1985). Several recent empirical studies suggest similarity between adults and adolescents in their decision making and in their knowledge of elements of informed consent (Leikin, 1993; Weithorn & Campbell, 1982; Susman et al., 1992; Ondrusek et al., 1998).

Weithorn and Campbell (1982) presented four hypothetical treatment descriptions to four age groups: nine year olds, fourteen year olds, eighteen year olds, and twenty-one year olds. Two of the case descriptions were based on psychological problems related to depression and enuresis. Subjects in this study were asked to put themselves in the place of the child described in the vignette and to choose one of several possible treatment alternatives. The fourteen year olds were as able as the older groups to consider several points simultaneously and to weigh risks and benefits, while the nine-year-old group failed to focus on more than one or two salient aspects of the problems presented.

Ondrusek et al. (1998) examined the quality of children's assent to a clinical trial by interviewing children after they had been given oral or written information about a nutrition research study they were joining. These authors' semistructured interviews about the children's decision-making processes suggested an age-related pattern to the children's understanding. Age nine seemed to be a pivotal age for an improved understanding of the purpose of the study, the procedures involved, the potential risks and benefits, and the right and inclination to withdraw. The authors concluded that children below age nine should not be expected to consent to clinical research in a meaningful way.

Throughout most of the United States, adolescents are recognized as legally competent to give consent, even though they are considered minors until age eighteen (unless emancipated). These standards are based on traditional British law, in which children younger than seven were considered irrebuttably decisionally incapable, children between seven and fourteen were presumed rebuttably decisionally incapable, and children above fourteen were presumed rebuttably decisionally capable (Glantz, 1998). In modern clinical practice, parents typically make decisions for their children under the assumption that they will act in the child's or adolescent's best interest (i.e., legal proxy decisions). In fact, to fulfill a legal requirement of parental consent, a parent of an adolescent signs the informed consent on behalf of the adolescent prior to a clinical interview. Legally, in most states, the adolescent's signature would not be recognized. While very few states permit minors to obtain psychotherapy without parental consent (Koocher & Keith-Spiegel, 1998), Virginia is an exception. The Virginia code, Section 54.1-2969 (D), reads, "A minor shall be deemed an adult for purpose of consenting to medical or health services needed in the case of outpatient care, treatment or rehabilitation for mental illness or emotional disturbance."

While legal consent may come from parents in most instances, clinicians are well advised to consider the Virginia example and recognize that adolescents are a vulnerable group, often lacking both legal and social power, even while they already possess the cognitive capacity to consent. Thus, practically, it is generally a good idea to invite the adolescent to be part of the formal consent process by asking directly whether the adolescent agrees to being interviewed or engage in treatment and whether they would like to cosign the consent form with the parent(s). At a minimum, the clinician should seek verbal consent from the adolescent. Ethically, this process meets professional obligations that are required and regulated in the ethical codes or professional standards of many disciplines. For example, the Ethical Standards of the American Psychological Association (1992) specify the clinician's obligation to act in the best interest of the client and to take the client's treatment preferences into consideration. As part of this obligation, clinicians should strive to present treatment information at a level the client can understand and should at least pursue the adolescent's "assent" (agreement) in lieu of legal consent. The essential components of informed consent should include a discussion of the type of any planned treatment, its benefits and risks, confidentiality and limits of confidentiality, fee structure, scheduling, and treatment alternatives (Gustafson et al., 1994).

When a clinical interview is a prelude to treatment, there should be a clear explanation of any planned course of treatment. For example, "talk psychotherapy" may be explained as a process by which clinician and adolescent will talk about issues in the adolescent's life that might benefit from change. Benefits might include (1) experiencing less emotional discomfort, such as anxiety, depression, alienation, or anger; (2) better understanding of personal feelings, thoughts, and behaviors; (3) discovering alternative ways of handling distressing situations; and (4) better relations with others. Risks are usually associated with external inconveniences such as giving up time and other enjoyable activities in order to be present and making and keeping a financial commitment. Internal risks might include feelings of embarrassment and shame about others knowing or learning about the treatment, feeling uncomfortable sharing personal information, and experiencing self-doubt and shame related to perceptions of personal shortcomings. There should be a discussion of cost specifics as they relate to fees, scheduling, and length of treatment. Alternative treatment offerings may include treatment with another provider who may be closer geographically or a better match with respect to age, gender, or cultural background. Alternative modes of treatment might include varying theoretical orientations and settings (inpatient vs. outpatient). In the event that an adolescent withholds consent, the clinician should take this seriously and consider possible reasons for this position, rather than go forward with the assumption that it is only the parent's consent that matters. The adolescent's dissent is grist for the therapeutic mill; it becomes important to explore whether it may represent oppositional behavior, anxiety, or some other basis of resistance.

Obtaining parental consent is important in its own right, especially since legal consent may rest with parents. Even when adolescents may legally consent on their own, American Psychological Association ethical guidelines (American Psychological Association, 1992) task clinicians with clarifying at the outset of treatment which persons within a family are being considered patients and what relationship each will have with the clinician. In general, clinicians should meet conjointly with adolescents and parents and, in that process, take pains to present the risks and benefits of treatment, treatment options, costs, and confidentiality boundaries. By beginning with the consent process, the clinician communicates respect for both the adolescent's dignity and the parents' authority.

CLINICAL STRATEGIES AND METHODS

Having properly obtained consent, the clinician next turns to interviewing strategies and methods. An early strategic decision is whether to interview the adolescent alone, with his or her parent(s) or within an even larger family group. There may be uncommon instances in which conflict between parents and adolescents is so intense that interviewing them together or including other family members serves only to drive everyone farther apart and yields so little data regarding historical information or symptom precipitants that joint interviews are destructive or entirely unproductive. Far more often however, there is a considerable advantage to interviewing adolescents and their parents together and even to including other family members in the room. It may be necessary sometimes, after beginning in this fashion, to break into separate sessions with parent(s) and the adolescent in order to afford each more personal time. While it is legally permissible in some states for adolescents to initiate treatment on their own behalf and to request that parents not be involved even in history taking, this places the clinician in a difficult circumstance, and the adolescent's wish to exclude parents should become a subject for further exploration. Generally speaking, the information that parents provide regarding health, early development, personal history, family dynamics, and behavioral descriptions outside of the clinical hour is critically important.

By interviewing parents and adolescent together, the clinician is well positioned to (1) communicate to all parties a direct interest in each person's feelings and perspective (Satir, 1964); (2) convey an interest in an open dialogue between parents and adolescent (Robin and Foster, 1989), (3) show respect for the adolescent as a principal player, but not necessarily the identified patient (Haley, 1976; 1980); and (4) make clear the therapist's perspective that parents are the executive subsystem of the family and should be in charge (Minuchin,1974). Of course, there is a need for clinician sensitivity with regard to how much and how long to allow parents to report on negative adolescent behavior while the adolescent twists and turns in silence or loud protest. Yet to exclude the adolescent from data gathering at the outset is to commit the more egregious error of placing the adolescent in an infantile role within the family system. Many adolescents will never forgive this insult and, once excluded as an active participant, will elect to remain peripheral to all further aspects of the assessment.

In terms of interviewing methods, it is usually best to begin with what is on everyone's mind—the reasons for the interview. To involve the adolescent from the beginning, the opening stance should be to ask the adolescent for a personal understanding of why he or she has come to the interview. Since this pressures the adolescent a bit, wise clinicians do not expect much information at this juncture. Most teens will remain noncommittal or even sarcastic. The typical response is, "I don't know," "I have no clue," "Ask them" (meaning the parents), or a shoulder shrug. However, the content of the response is not as important as the fact that this critical question was first directed to the adolescent. Asking this question first of the adolescent offers respect and initiates an important alliance. Even if little information is gleaned, the way is then cleared for the clinician to gather much more detail from parents, returning to the adolescent periodically to ask for agreement, disagreement, or a different perspective on specific information. Coming back to the adolescent also serves to break up any tendency the parents may have to be overly critical or verbose in their descriptions of the presenting problem. If parents persist in "piling on," it may be helpful to ask both parents and adolescent for their separate views on how others may see the problem—"others" possibly including other relatives (and they may be asked for this information directly if they are present in the room), teachers, the adolescent's friends, and the parents' friends. Avoid taking sides, and take care not to prolong a discussion of the presenting problem. Ten to twenty minutes on the "What do you think is wrong?" topic is generally ample time to gather a preliminary understanding of the essential facts about the referral concerns, while observing the nature of parent–child interactions. In most instances, parents will do most of the talking, making it necessary to turn next to the adolescent for information that only the adolescent can provide. This helps to block further parent diatribes, and by this time, most adolescents are eager to be heard.

The next interview phase may be an exploration of the adolescent's mental status. Mental status interviewing may be formal or informal, depending on what data have begun to emerge. Parents tend to understand that they are to be quiet during this period, unless a teenager fails to communicate critical information, such as self-destructive behaviors, threats against others, impaired thought processes, or symptoms that have not yet been discussed. It is often helpful to parents to witness a mental status process. They are often reassured that the clinician is addressing clinically important material that has concerned them enough to seek this professional opinion. Meanwhile, by responding openly to mental status questions, the adolescent may recognize that there is now an opportunity to enlist a professional's help in convincing parents that he or she is emotionally healthier than parents may have feared; or, alternatively, the adolescent may recognize that here help begins.

The clinician might begin with a general inquiry about mood, both now and in the recent past: "So, how does all this affect you? Do you find yourself angry or frustrated?" Follow this up, as necessary, with similar questions about other moods: "Depressed or bummed out?" "Really nervous or anxious?" Then try to learn how this individual expresses those feelings: "Different people express this feeling differently. Some cry? Yell? Hit people or get into fights? Just withdraw? Try to do harm to themselves? Feel like running away? Change eating or sleeping habits? Lose concentration for school?" It is often helpful for the interviewer to interject explanations for being so personal: "I need to gather all kinds of personal information, if I am to understand things well enough to be of help." Or the interviewer may make mention, perhaps in light of asking more intrusive questions than are typical of most social exchanges: "I ask a lot of questions, don't I?" or "Bear with me, I can sometimes ask a lot of questions when I am trying to learn so much in so short a time." The interviewer should take cues from the degree to which the adolescent is willing to answer these questions. When information is freely flowing and there is a very comfortable relationship between adolescent and clinician, the interviewer may be able to conduct the adolescent interview and many aspects of a formal mental status examination largely in the presence of the parents. At times, an adolescent is willing and able to talk honestly about even personal risk-taking behaviors (suicide ideation/intent, drug use, promiscuity, legal infractions, school disciplinary problems, peer group temptations, and so forth) in front of parents. When this occurs, it may be because these facts are well known to both parties already or because there are few risk-taking behaviors and the adolescent wants the parents to know this situation. Or the adolescent may speak freely as an opportunity to finally communicate information that has not been previously discussed with other family members. In any of these scenarios, this process has facilitated the conveyance of very constructive information, not only from the adolescent to the interviewer, but also within the family and, importantly, before a caring third party. New clinicians may be surprised by how frequently this level of communication can occur between all parties when the interviewer has shown respect for each person's thoughts and feelings and has pursued this information in a comfortable, natural fashion that communicates an expectancy that no one will have any reason to object (at least until someone offers verbal or nonverbal communications to the contrary). When information of this type is shared openly with parents in the room, the clinician is faced with many fewer ethical barriers or dilemmas regarding the confidentiality of adolescent communications. In the event that an adolescent appears unwilling to say very much about personal feelings or thoughts or about problem behaviors, the interviewer should take this cue to refrain from asking particularly personal questions, including especially those that might be outside of the parent's awareness. In these instances, the interviewer has learned of the need to make private time available to meet subsequently with the adolescent alone. Then, in the context of that closer, supportive relationship, the interviewer can renew a discussion leading to an informed consent to undergo the evaluation, with confidentiality protections and limitations made clear at the outset. It is usually best to indicate, at this point, an intent to gather this information in more detail in a private fashion with the adolescent later on, after first pursuing some further information that might be obtained while everyone is together.

Shifting back and forth between parents and teen takes pressure off the adolescent. So this is a good time to shift back to the parents to obtain a developmental history, essentially tracing the adolescent's early life, including prenatal or birth complications, early developmental milestones, medical problems (perhaps especially history of traumatic brain injury, seizures, or medical conditions that may be relevant to presenting concerns), school history (especially failed grades, special education needs, and prior formal psychological or psychoeducational evaluations), and psychological history (prior periods of inpatient or outpatient treatment, medication prescriptions, and so forth), pausing to explore in greater depth any unusual or relevant information that may emerge through this broad scan. This can be a constructive, family-rebuilding process, as it is often necessary for family members to help one another recall these details. If this aspect of the interview includes forays into recollections of fun things the family did together in the past or good feelings family members had for one another, it can serve to draw upon positive family experiences, facilitate rebonding, and locate areas of family resiliency of great use during times of stress. If there is clear tension about discussing specific problems in front of the adolescent, the astute clinician can make clear to parents that they, too, will have some private time available for further exploration.

To help bring all of the family together at the end of this interview and history taking, it is often helpful at this juncture for the clinician to collect information necessary to draw a family genogram. If there are siblings or grandparents present, this is a particularly good time to reinvolve them. Constructing this genogram in some way that allows everyone to see it coming together permits a sense of a group effort and ample opportunity again for each person to contribute. This provides critical information as to who is currently living in the home, what other relatives may have played important past roles and may still be influential, whether or not there are siblings (and how these relationships are characterized), who is in the extended family, and whether various family members are emotionally or physically close or distant. Depending upon parent willingness to explore this information with the adolescent present, this is also a good time to gather such related family history as marital divorce, separation, or remarriage; what parents do for a living; parents' education levels; and what genetic family history there may be for pertinent medical or psychological conditions (i.e., such specific conditions as attention-deficit/hyperactivity disorder, or ADHD, learning disability, affective disorders, alcohol or substance abuse, and neurological conditions).

In the ideal circumstance, parents and adolescent have been able to remain together and give a very detailed presentation of the presenting concern, circumstances leading up to this concern, and a very extensive personal and family history of a great deal of valuable information. Ideally, both parents and adolescent believe they were heard and understood and all are ready to engage in whatever further work the clinician may recommend. For this type of history taking, it is both necessary and appropriate for the interviewer to take extensive notes, as this not only ensures that no critical information will be forgotten but clearly conveys deep respect for the importance of this information and the emotional difficulties with which it may have been elicited. The vigilant interviewer will have been able to show empathy and compassion through intermittent eye contact, even amid this busy note taking. In the ideal situation, there may be little or no need for additional private contact with either adolescent or parents separately. However, in the less than ideal circumstance when it is necessary to meet alone with either party, the clinician should take care to meet with both parents and adolescent in two separate private sessions, even if one of these is only for a very few minutes. Again, balance and the notion that each have had an opportunity to speak in private may be most important. Interviewers who are concerned about time constraints may be partly relieved to hear that when it is necessary to meet with parents and adolescent in separate private sessions, it usually means that the joint meeting was made shorter by someone's need not to talk in so "public" a fashion. Thus, time saved in one part of this interview process can then be spent in another.

It is important for the interviewer to end this process by giving back some information. In fact, it may be helpful to summarize the process by saying something like, "I want to thank you for providing me with a lot of personal information. It will take me awhile to fully digest it. Even so, I want to give you some of my thoughts now, especially since you have shared so much with me." The interviewer can then note just a few highlights of what was said earlier, tentatively state a diagnostic suspicion (if a diagnosis has been formulated and giving one is not apt to intensify parent or adolescent defenses), and lay out a plan for how best to proceed—further formal assessment, recommendations for any treatment, or referrals to other providers.

A CASE EXAMPLE

William was a seventeen-year-old middle-class Caucasian boy whose parents were distraught over his declining grades, verbal outbursts at home, and indifference to their intense efforts to motivate him. They came into the initial interview collectively, and all three readily agreed to undergo a clinical interview as a prelude to formal psychological testing for William designed to provide information about his underlying cognitive abilities, specific academic skills, and personality functioning. Prior to the interview, William's parents signed formal papers to consent to this process, expressing detailed understanding of its fee structure and agreeing to the specific means by which it would be conducted, including test administration by a doctoral clinical psychology student and test interpretation by a licensed clinical psychologist. William agreed verbally to this process and understood that information he shared during the assessment would be relayed to him and his parents in as much detail as necessary in order to help determine what, if any, treatment was indicated and, if treatment was necessary, what might be an effective treatment plan.

As the interview began, William's answer to the question of what he thought led to his coming in was that his parents were upset over his grades. His parents agreed with this, of course, and they had much more to say about his poor use of time, rebellious defiance over curfews, poor choice of friends, rude and frighteningly angry behavior with his mother, indifference to academic achievement or earlier family goals regarding his future, and seeming unhappiness.

This led naturally to questions of William as to just how angry or sad he might be feeling. He denied being angry with anyone but his parents, and all agreed that he did not yell at others outside the home and had never been in fights, nor had he hit anyone within the home or hurt anyone physically. He was, however, prone to slamming doors and had once put his fist through a wall. He freely acknowledged that he was unhappy with his parents' restrictions and that he most enjoyed time with friends away from home, "hanging out." He denied problems sleeping or eating, and his parents confirmed that these were not concerns. He denied crying spells or feeling preoccupied by sadness while in school. He explained his poor grades by simply noting that he hated school, didn't like to study, and often failed to turn in assignments. He denied feeling suicidal or having ever planned or attempted to hurt himself. He denied taking drugs or using alcohol excessively but admitted to occasional beers when with friends. There were no indications of a thought disorder, as William relayed information logically and with affect appropriate to the situation at hand. His mood was angry and sullen, and he spoke willingly, if not spontaneously, answering frankly all questions put to him, without undue anxiety or apparent intent to deceive. He displayed stubborn defiance in his refusal to be as upset as his parents over his underachievement, and his explanations were provocative to them in that they were vague and communicated gross indifference.

All parties seemed relieved when questions were redirected toward prenatal development, birth, and early childhood, all of which had progressed normally. There had been no serious health problems, and school had generally progressed without difficulty, except that William experienced social difficulties in that he did not make friends easily and was often socially withdrawn. He had not shown symptoms of hyperactivity or distractibility in early school years, nor had there been any serious learning problems. He had never repeated a grade, nor had he received any special education assistance. His father had often been away in connection with his work for the Federal Bureau of Investigation, and while William was initially very sensitive about these deployments, he had grown accustomed to them and now expressed indifference to this, too. Discussions about various extended family members while constructing a family tree or genogram led to digressions about a paternal uncle with whom William had been very close who died in an automobile accident three years earlier. There was a strong extended family history of depression on the part of several maternal relatives, but there was no family history of ADHD or learning disability. Several extended family members had histories of alcoholism.

William and his parents were asked if either would like to meet privately to discuss information that was difficult to share openly, understanding that, except in the case where someone might be in danger, information shared privately would remain confidential. Because no one felt the need for this additional private time, the interviewer summarized what had been said and observed to that point. Recapping the parents' primary concerns and William's answers, and putting the presenting problem in the context of William's history and the family genogram, the interviewer observed that everyone appeared to be frustrated and a bit unhappy with the current situation. The interviewer reported being especially worried about William's unhappiness, noting that sometimes it feels safer to act mad than to acknowledge feeling sad. The interviewer hastened to add that it would be premature to draw final conclusions without being certain that William had the intellectual and academic ability to do work at the high school level and without more thoroughly evaluating his mood and personality. Again, with William's verbal agreement, concrete plans were laid to have William come back for a second appointment, during which he would undergo several hours of psychological testing while his mother completed questionnaires regarding his behavior and personality functioning. His father was to be away on another deployment by then, but would look forward to hearing from his wife and son regarding the outcome of this assessment and any plans for intervention.

During the course of testing about one week later, the doctoral clinical psychology student who was administering the tests brought to the interviewer's attention that William had made a suicidal reference when he responded to a written sentence completion test. The interviewer then met with William alone to inquire further about this response. William reported that the first interview together with his parents had helped him to realize that he was very angry over his father's frequent absences and his high expectations for William regarding school and other achievements. He was further enraged by his mother's inclination to look over all his schoolwork and nag him continuously about his studies. He had grown so impatient with this situation that he found himself becoming verbally abusive of his mother and spending as much time away from home as he could. School was just not a priority in this context. He acknowledged feeling as though he wanted to die but reported that he had no intent to hurt himself. He agreed with a plan to ask for help if he felt like hurting himself in any way. The interviewer proposed that he engage in psychotherapy with a professional and offered several referrals, but William protested that he did not want to seek therapy. A longer discussion ensued regarding the basis for those feelings, and the interviewer presented information regarding William's risk for serious depression, given his disappointment with his family, possible unresolved grief over his uncle's death, and a possible genetic predisposition toward biologically based depression related to the depression on his mother's side of the family. Arguing that William might find it very helpful to have someone to talk to who would not be judgmental and who might be able to help him understand how to make his own way amid strong expectations from others, the interviewer obtained William's agreement to see a therapist. After further discussion, William agreed to bring his mother into the room so that further plans could be laid for what to do in any emergency, pending arrangements were made for William to see a psychotherapist, and a third appointment was made with the interviewer to review formal testing once it had been scored and interpreted.

William's mother was initially shocked and frightened upon hearing of the extent of William's sadness, but she understood that these were not new problems and that, as William had been able to contract not to hurt himself, there was no imminent risk, provided that they each knew what to do should William feel worse and that they both agreed to follow the interviewer's recommendations. Arrangements were then put in place for what to do in an emergency scenario, and follow-up appointments were made for both the psychotherapy William had agreed to initiate and for a third visit with the interviewer to review test results when those findings were ready. William and his mother also agreed to contact his father to inform him that plans were already in place to act upon this new awareness of William's depression.

By the time of a third appointment to review test results, William had met once with the therapist. While he remained unenthusiastic about psychotherapy, he acknowledged that he liked this therapist and that he now had an appointment with a consulting psychiatrist to determine whether he might need antidepressant medication. Test results essentially corroborated clinical impressions to that point, showing William's intellectual abilities to be strong, his academic skills to be adequate, and his personality functioning to be marked primarily by depression and conduct problems. Testing lent support to an impression that the combination of William's rebelliousness and depression placed him at considerable risk to act out in escapist and self-destructive ways, perhaps including alcohol or substance abuse, which he had already experimented with and for which there was an extended family history. In light of William's feelings about his father's deployment and associated paternal losses, there seemed to be a particular need for William's father to be kept abreast of ongoing intervention efforts. On the father's return in several weeks, the family was to have at least one conjoint session with William's new therapist. The test interpretation process had the effect of intensifying the family's commitment to William's treatment, and plans were made to provide William's parents with a copy of the formal psychological report.

This case illustrates a few of the many complexities of interviewing adolescents. Some might argue that William's suicidal feelings might have been more quickly recognized had the interviewer spent time alone with William during the first appointment, rather than relying exclusively at that time on the family interview. This is certainly a fair criticism. Yet it is also possible that William needed the additional time after the interview to soften his defenses and recognize his own depression. In either case, the planned use of additional assessment tools gave an important safety net to the interview, providing another means of helping William self-disclose and stimulating both additional interview time and further data gathering in a thorough and comprehensive process. Of course, this case also demonstrates that interviewers of adolescents must be patient, flexible, and readily accessible. Adolescent timing, with respect to important self-disclosure, is apt to be substantially different from what adults might prefer (as are many other aspects of adolescent behavior).

SUMMARY

This chapter has presented an overview of many but not all of the considerations and possible strategies and techniques involved in interviewing adolescents. While other experienced clinicians might present different emphases and substantially different approaches, we have attempted to introduce the reader to some of the most salient issues. Understanding the context of adolescent development may be the most important preparatory activity. Attending to the legal and ethical aspects of informed consent helps to focus the interviewing process from the outset. Perhaps most controversial is whether to interview the adolescent alone or with parents and family. Given space restrictions, we have chosen to highlight one of several choices in this regard and to show, through case example, its strengths and limitations. While some may differ with the handling of the case example in this chapter, our principal hope is that it provides readers with a sense of the emotional charge and the interviewing skill that makes work with adolescents exciting. Even while we have striven to help readers interview more skillfully, it remains our premise that skillful clinical interviewing is a necessary but insufficient means of clinical assessment. Formal assessment with reliable, valid test instruments is often a critical adjunct activity.

REFERENCES

Achenbach, T. M. (1991). *Manual for the Child Behavior Checklist/4-18 and 1991 Profile.* Burlington: University of Vermont.

Achenbach, T. M. (1999). Child Behavior Checklist and related instruments. In *The Use of Psychological Testing for Treatment Planning and Outcome Assessment,* 2nd ed. Mahwah, NJ: Erlbaum.

American Psychological Association (1992). Ethical principles of psychologists and code of conduct. *American Psychologist* 12:1597–1611.

Archer, R. P., Maruish, M., Imhof, E. A., & Piotrowski, C. (1991). Psychological test usage with adolescent clients: 1990 survey findings. *Professional Psychology: Research and Practice* 22:247–252.

Archer, R. P., & Newsome, C. R. (2000). Psychological test usage with adolescent clients: Survey update. *Assessment* 7:227–235.

Ball, J. D., Archer, R. P., & Imhof, E. (1994). Time demands of psychological testing: A survey of practitioners. *Journal of Personality Assessment* 63:239–249.

Ball, J. D., & Meck, D. S. (1979). Implications of developmental theories for counseling adolescents in groups. *Adolescence* 14:529–534.

Blos, P. (1962). *Adolescence: A Psychoanalytic Interpretation.* New York: Free Press.

Blos, P. (1967). The second individualization process of adolescence. *Psychoanalytic Study of the Child* 22:162–186.

Butcher, J. N., Williams, C. L., Graham, J. R., Archer, R. P., Tellegen, A., Ben-Porath, Y. S., & Kaemmer, B. (1992). *MMPI-A (Minnesota Multiphasic Personality Inventory— Adolescent): Manual for Administration, Scoring, and Interpretation.* Minneapolis: University of Minnesota Press.

Erikson, E. H. (1956). The concept of ego identity. *Journal of the American Psychoanalytic Association* 4:56–121.

Flavell, J. H. (1985). *Cognitive Development,* 2nd ed. Englewood Cliffs, NJ: Prentice Hall.

Freud, A. (1958). Adolescence. *Psychoanalytic Study of the Child* 13:255–278.

Glantz, L. H. (1998). Research with children. *American Journal of Law and Medicine* 24:213–244.

Gustafson, K. E., McNamara, J. R., & Jensen, J. A. (1994). Parents' informed consent decisions regarding psychotherapy for their children: Consideration of therapeutic risks and benefits. *Professional Psychology: Research and Practice* 25:16–22.

Haley, J. (1976). *Problem Solving Therapy.* San Francisco: Jossey-Bass.

Haley, J. (1980). *Leaving Home: The Therapy of Disturbed Young People.* New York: McGraw Hill.

Hall, G. S. (1904). *Adolescence: Its Psychology and Its Relationship to Physiology, Anthropology, Sociology, Sex, Crime, Religion, and Education.* New York: Appleton.

Herjanic, B., & Campbell, W. (1977). Differentiating psychiatrically disturbed children on the basis of a structured interview. *Journal of Abnormal Clinical Psychology* 5:127–134.

Herjanic, B., Herjanic, M., Brown, F., & Wheatt, T. (1975). Are children reliable reporters? *Journal of Abnormal and Child Psychology,* 3, 41–48.

Kimmel, D. C., & Weiner, I. B. (1995). *Adolescence: A Developmental Transition,* 2nd ed. New York: Wiley & Sons.

Koocher, G. P., & Keith-Spiegel, P. (1990). *Children, Ethics, and the Law: Professional Issues and Cases.* Lincoln: University of Nebraska Press.

Koocher, G. P., & Keith-Spiegel, P. (1998). *Ethics in Psychology: Professional Standards and Cases,* 2nd ed. New York: Oxford University Press.

Leikin, S. (1993). Minors' assent, consent, and dissent to medical research. *IRB: Review of Human Subjects Research* 15:1–7.

Loevinger, J. (1976). *Ego Development: Conceptions and Theories.* San Francisco: Jossey-Bass.

Matarazzo, J. D. (1983). The reliability of psychiatric and psychological diagnosis. *Clinical Psychology Review* 3:103–145.

Minuchin, S. (1974). *Families and Family Change.* Cambridge, MA: Harvard University Press.

National Institute of Mental Health (1990). *National Plan for Research on Child and Adolescent Mental Disorders.* DHHS Publication No. ADM 90-1683. Washington, DC: U.S. Government Printing Office.

Ondrusek, N., Abramovitch, R., Penchartz, P., & Koren, G. (1998). Empirical examination of the ability of children to consent to clinical research. *Journal of Medical Ethics* 24:158–165.

Paul, M., Foreman, D. M., & Kent, L. (2000). Outpatient clinic attendance consent from children and young people: Ethical aspects and practical considerations. *Clinical Child Psychology and Psychiatry* 5:203–211.

Peterson, A. C. (1985). Pubertal development as a cause of disturbance: Myths, realities, and unanswered questions. *Genetic, Social, and General Psychology Monographs* 111:205–232.

Piaget, J. (1975). The intellectual development of the adolescent. In *The Psychology of Adolescence: Essential Reading*. New York: International Universities Press.

Powers, S. I., Hauser, S. T., & Kilner, L. A. (1989). Adolescent mental health. *American Psychologist* 44:200–208.

Reich, W. (2000). Diagnostic interview for children and adolescents (DIC). *Journal of the American Academy of Child and Adolescent Psychiatry* 39:59–66.

Robin, A. L., & Foster, S. L. (1989). *Negotiating Parent Adolescent Conflict*. New York: Guilford.

Rogers, R. (1995). *Diagnostic and Structured Interviewing: A Handbook for Psychologists*. Odessa, FL: Psychological Assessment Resources.

Satir, V. (1964). *Conjoint Family Therapy*. Palo Alto, CA: Science & Behavior Books.

Sheras, P. (2002). Tools and techniques for working with adolescents and their parents. Workshop presented to the Virginia Psychological Association 2002 Spring Convention, Virginia Beach.

Sheras, P. L., Abidin, R. R., & Konald, T. R. (1998). *Stress Index for Parents of Adolescents: Professional Manual*. Lutz, FL: Psychological Assessment Resources.

Stein, S. J. (1987). Computer-assisted diagnosis for children and adolescents. In *Computerized Psychological Assessment: A Practitioner's Guide*. New York: Basic.

Susman, E. J., Dorn, L. D., & Fletcher, J. C. (1992). Participation in biomedical research: The consent process as viewed by children, adolescents, young adults, and physicians. *Journal of Pediatrics* 121:547–552.

Weithorn, L. A., & Campbell, S. B. (1982). The competence of children and adolescents to make informed treatment decisions. *Child Development* 53:1589–1598.

17

CHILD AND ADOLESCENT ABUSE

Timothy J. Wolf, Ph.D.

The investigation of child and adolescent abuse and neglect has not always been the sophisticated and specialized process it is today. Beginning with the 1875 organization of the New York County Society for the Prevention of Cruelty to Children, voluntary societies began to take responsibility for the protection of children. These voluntary, private organizations were gradually replaced by public welfare agencies. Today, child social workers have broadened the scope of child abuse intervention to include not only the legal protection of the child but also the rehabilitation of the family. In the 1960s, beginning with Kempe's published report of the "battered child syndrome" (Kempe & Kempe, 1978), physicians, psychiatrists, psychologists, and social workers began to call attention to the special conditions surrounding physical abuse, neglect, and sexual abuse of children. Concurrently, legal developments have paved the way for greater professional involvement. The Federal Child Abuse Prevention and Treatment Act was passed in 1974, and by 1978 most states provided protective services and reporting laws for physical, sexual, and emotional child (and adolescent) abuse and neglect.

The developing fields of child psychiatry and child psychology during the past forty years have shed light on child abuse in terms of child development, child sexuality, and family dynamics. In that same period, the view of the credibility of children who report abuse has significantly changed. Until the 1960s, most perpetrators, especially if they were parents, were believed over the accusations of the child. In the case of sexual abuse, it was more likely that the child would be seen as inventing the allegation or encouraging the sexual abuse. During the 1960s and 1970s, it was believed that children rarely reported abuse unless it had actually occurred. This shift reflected the research in child development rather than reliance on Freudian theory. More recently, a middle ground seems to be emerging in which each case is judged individually, without presupposition. This may be partly due to a growing number of abuse accusations in custody cases that have been documented as false (Benedek & Schetky, 1985) and that were made in order to obtain custody or to terminate the accused parent's rights. Since there is often little evidence to document the cases of neglect or emotional or sexual abuse, and no reliable research indicates what percentage of child accusations are true, the clinical judgment of the therapist often becomes the critical criterion.

While the impact of child sexual abuse is highly variable, childhood sexual abuse is a risk factor for the development of psychiatric disorders and other forms of distress into adulthood, including the disorders of posttraumatic stress disorder and anxiety and depressive disorders. Abuse victims may continue to have other manifestations of emotional distress, heightened aggression, and sleep disorders (Kendall-Tackett, Williams, & Finkelhor, 1993; Saywitz et al., 2000). They have higher rates of personality disorders, substance abuse, binge eating, somatization, and suicide behaviors than a comparable group of nonabused children. They tend to report poorer social functioning, more problems with interpersonal relationships, greater sexual dissatisfaction, and greater tendencies toward sexual revictimization through partner sexual assault and partner physical abuse (Polusny & Follette, 1995). The impact of child physical abuse and neglect can be equally deleterious (Conaway & Hansen, 1989).

A virtual army of professionals is involved in the investigation of child abuse. It is therefore vital that the therapist or team conducting the interview and assessment of child or adolescent abuse have both an understanding of the process of child abuse reporting and specialized skills in investigation, as well as knowledge of the available treatment network. Sensitivity to other professionals involved may also be important to the success of the investigation and treatment. When this focus is maintained, psychiatrists, psychologists, pediatricians, social workers, marriage, family, and child counselors, child protective workers, teachers, clergy, police, and attorneys can maintain cooperation and professionalism and can work together successfully to support both the child or adolescent and the family.

GOALS FOR EVALUATION

Recently, there has been an interdisciplinary consensus on the investigation of child abuse that addresses the behavioral indicators of abuse, interviewing child victims, the use of dolls and other props, and the role of medical evaluations (Lamb, 1994). Before proceeding with any evaluation, the therapist should have specific goals. These goals should be determined by reviewing information already obtained in the investigation process, clarifying who is asking for the evaluation, and being cognizant of how the evaluation results will be used. Often, goals include such areas as protecting the community from danger, determining the risk of recidivism, assisting the court in the determination of guilt or innocence, and making recommendations in custody evaluations.

The interviewer must consider the following questions first: What happened to the child or adolescent prior to the clinical interview? Has the child been through a medical examination or legal investigation, or both? Has the child been removed from the home? Or is the interviewer in the position of being the person to initiate a suspected abuse report?

Second, the interviewer must ask: What are the dynamics of the allegations, and who is referring the child for evaluation? The court? One parent or both? A lawyer? Who are the other professionals with whom cooperation and exchange of information is necessary?

Third, the interviewer must ask: Who will use the information and for what purpose? Is there consideration of removing the child from the home? Is this a dispute about physical or legal custody? Who will see this child for psychotherapy? To what extent will the results be used in court, and will the interviewer be called upon to testify as an expert witness? To what extent is a family unification treatment plan necessary and appropriate?

When these kinds of questions are answered, the therapist can begin to formulate a direction for the interview. Since many professionals may be involved in each case, the interviewer will want to make the evaluation complement the information previously compiled so that the assessment is as comprehensive and nonduplicative as possible. Each clinician should strive to serve the best interests of both the child and the family with the least amount of trauma.

COUNTERTRANSFERENCE

Most clinicians will experience normal reactions upon hearing reports of essentially heinous behavior. The clinician is cautioned not to be judgmental, to hold his or her personal feelings in check, and not to allow these personal feelings to impair or interfere with the objectivity of the evaluation.

ESTABLISHING RAPPORT

Special attention should be given to establishing rapport with the child. This is especially critical for abused children who have experienced frequent violations of trust with adult figures. The therapist should not hurry the child, yet at the same time a specific agenda should be maintained. If a child should inquire, it is important to be honest with the child about the clinician's role and about how the information obtained will be used and with whom it will be shared.

Establishing rapport means entering the world of the child. I am reminded of the professional with whom I studied who would sit with legs crossed in a chair while the child played on the floor. It was not surprising that this professional did not elicit the information requested, since he was so out of sync with his patients.

The best way to enter the world of the child is to mirror the child. *Mirroring* is matching the child's behavior, including body posture, specific gestures, breathing rhythms, facial expression, activity levels, and voice tone and tempo (Cameron-Bandler, 1985). Mirroring enhances the child's trust in the therapist. Once this trust has been established, honest responses and significant information can be expected, and the credibility of the child is enhanced. For example, if the child's activity level is high, the therapist begins by mirroring the activity level, by sitting forward, playing on the floor, fingering an object. Once the child and therapist are in sync, the therapist can begin to slow down or alter the pace. This technique can be used to gain the child's confidence. Since parents who batter children are usually out of sync or rhythm with them, teaching parents similar techniques will be an important part of later therapy.

RECOGNITION OF PHYSICAL AND SEXUAL ABUSE

Most child abusers know their perpetrators and are members of the family. Most of the perpetrators live conventional, law-abiding lives, except for their child abuse. For the most part, they are not mentally or cognitively impaired. Their aberrations are accompanied by personality disorders and interpersonal problems.

The therapist should incorporate questions about physical and sexual abuse and neglect into all interviews with children, using the child's frame of reference and language that is age appropriate. Such questions might include the following: How did you learn about sex? Do parts of your body trouble you? Do you know other children who have been hurt by others? Do you know the difference between good touches and bad touches? Have you ever been touched by others in ways that make you feel bad?

Before beginning the interview, therapists must honestly assess whether his or her own discomfort with sexual or physical abuse investigation or reporting will interfere with the therapist's advocacy on behalf of the child. The child is not likely to volunteer the information, and unless the therapist is comfortably sensitive to the issues, the child may face additional trauma or withhold information.

An immense volume of literature has been generated in the past two decades regarding child and adolescent sexual abuse. Clinicians should familiarize themselves with current information as part of their continuing education. Federal, state, and local laws and guidelines cover the definition, reporting, and investigation of child abuse. These laws and guidelines vary from state to state, so we cannot address them specifically here. Any clinician who sees children is obligated to keep abreast of these changing laws and guidelines.

Within the context of evaluation and later psychotherapeutic treatment of the child, physical and sexual abuse is always an interactive process between adults and children. In cases of physical abuse, there is (1) the perpetrator, who may have some predisposition to act aggressively toward the child, (2) the child, who may be behaving in a way that triggers the perpetrator's aggressive feeling, and (3) a stressful context that aggravates the angry feelings of the perpetrator (Kadushin & Mortin, 1981). The research on physical abuse somewhat consistently identifies the perpetrator as having a history of childhood abuse or rejection; low self-esteem; a rigid, domineering, impulsive personality; social isolation; a history of inadequate coping; poor interpersonal relationships; high unrealistic expectations of children; and a lack of empathy (Kadushin & Mortin, 1981). In addition to these characteristics, the perpetrator in sexual abuse is more likely to have a personality disorder associated with sexual deviation (Craig, in press; Schetky & Green, 1988).

In studies of family dynamics of physical abuse, the parent–child interaction is less positive, less child-centered, and less tolerant, with more reliance on physical punishment for discipline than in nonabusive families (Kadushin & Mortin, 1981). The incestuous family has been described as rigid, patriarchal, and prone to secrecy, with the father maintaining his dominant, coercive position (Herman, 1981; Meiselman, 1978; Swanson & Biaggio, 1985). The marital relationship suffers from unmet dependency needs, with the mother often delegating marital and homemaking responsibilities to the daughter. The father may assume a nurturing role, which he enacts in a sexual context (Meiselman, 1978; Mrazch et al., 1981).

While clinicians should have a thorough knowledge of the foregoing research, they should also be cautious when evaluating a child from this perspective. There are few controlled studies that substantiate the universality of any of these hypotheses, including the concept of intergenerational abuse (Kadushin & Mortin, 1981). The therapist should strain to see each child and family within its own unique interactional context.

CLINICAL ASSESSMENT

During the assessment process, every effort must be made to avoid further traumatizing the child. Many children are more traumatized by parental rejection and medical, legal, and psychological intrusion than by the initial alleged incident of abuse. The clinician is in a unique position of being able to minimize further trauma while at the same time obtaining a detailed body of information. Care should be taken to avoid placing the dynamics of family pressures and the demands of other professionals ahead of the needs of the child. Further, child abuse cases are often highly emotionally charged, and therapists should be equally careful not to allow the demands or pressures of family members and of legal, medical, or child protective workers to cloud their objectivity or sensitivity to the child.

ELEMENTS OF ASSESSMENT

Ideally, the clinical assessment of the child should include interviews with the child, the perpetrator, and other family members or care-taking persons; a developmental history; and standardized measures. Assessment of the child includes cognitive, social, physical, psychological, and emotional information, as well as assessment of abuse.

Cognitive

In the cognitive assessment, special attention should be paid to questions of cognitive development that validate the child's verbal report. First, the child must be able to understand the concepts of who, where, and what. The clinician can determine the child's level of understanding by asking simple questions based on the child's developmental age. What is your name? Where do you live? For what reason are you here today? Second, the therapist must determine whether the child has a copy of a true statement versus a lie. Again, simple questions should be geared to the child's developmental level. Young children might be asked simple questions such as, If you ate a candy bar and said you didn't, would that be a lie?

When asking questions, the clinician must consider the child's developmental level. Questions for the preschooler should reflect the home environment and times and circumstances with which the child is familiar; questions to school-age children may reflect a more standardized developmental level. The therapist must be very careful to *avoid leading the child with questions that prejudice the answers or verbally or nonverbally rewarding the child for answers.* It is suggested that an audio- or videotape of the actual interview with the child be used to substantiate the impartiality of the nature of the questioning. This would be extremely important and relevant in subsequent litigation. The cognitive information in the interview may be compared to the information from the intellectual assessment for a more complete picture.

Emotional

The therapist should assess how the child is feeling about himself or herself. This assessment may include questions about the kinds of nurturing the child perceives based on parents' or care-takers' touches, feeding, time, and attention. What is the strength of attachments to various members of the family or outside care-takers? Does the child play a particular role in the family or outside the family?

Projective instruments, especially figure drawings, can be used to add validity to many of the child's perceptions.

Social

An examination of the child's social relationship will provide the therapist with many clues to the child's interaction with the world. Does the child have friends? Are they older, younger, or the same age? Is the child engaging in age-appropriate play? What characterizes the child's interactions with adults? Teachers and child-care workers are an important source of social information, since children often spend a significant part of each day with these persons.

Physical

Physical indicators are an important part of understanding the child. Is the child small or large based on current age? How does the child perceive his or her physical size or physical development? Are fine or gross motor skills developmentally appropriate? Are their soft neurological signs that may indicate sensory motor problems, or attentional deficits, or minimal brain damage as a result of abuse? If the child has not had a medical examination, is it necessary? Or is it necessary to reduce trauma from a medical examination that has already been performed?

In the case of sexual abuse in which a medical exam is necessary, special attention should be paid to the child's anxiety and fear. There may be a tendency for the child to interpret the physical exam as another aspect of physical intrusion or as a punishment. Young children may be able to work through this difficulty by acting it out using a doctor's play kit, in combination with the clinician's carefully prepared words of support, comfort, and encouragement. For the child who has not been physically examined, this play will pave the way for a less frightening experience. For older children, discussion of the medical examination in terms of their bodies and blossoming sexuality will help to lessen their fear and anxiety. Tedesco and Schnell (1987) suggest using a research-proven presurgical model in which parents are involved in preparing the child for the examination, thereby reducing anxiety for both children and parents.

CONTENT AREAS

The following questions should be included in the assessment of abuse:

1. What was the child's relationship with the perpetrator? Was the perpetrator a parent, relative, or neighbor, or a complete stranger?
2. What was the duration of the abuse? Was the abuse an isolated incident or did it occur over a long period or a short extended period?

3. How was the child violated? In the case of sexual abuse, was there penetration or fondling? In the case of physical abuse, how was the child hurt? In cases of neglect, what were the physical manifestations?
4. What kind of power did the perpetrator exercise? To what extent was there violence or manipulation of the child? (If the child is extremely withdrawn, the clinician may suspect that extreme violence has occurred.)
5. How long did the child keep the secret? Is this something that the child has been carrying around for years or did the child go straight to the parent(s)?
6. What is the level of the child's ego strength? Is the child well nurtured, independent, and psychologically healthy? Or is the child passive, dependent, undernurtured, and psychologically repressed?

These factors may be related to the length of time in treatment for sexually abused children (Hewitt & McNought, 1985). If the answers to the questions indicate severe abuse, a longer period of treatment may be necessary and the prognosis may be more limited.

A standard developmental history should be obtained, including the child's cognitive, social, emotional, and physical development since birth. The clinician may wish to use a standardized developmental form that the parent can complete while the clinician is interviewing the child.

STANDARDIZED MEASURES

The following are standardized tests that the clinician may find useful for gathering more information and validating findings:

Cognitive
    Wechsler Intelligence Scale for Children, Revised
Emotional
    Children's Apperception Test
    Roberts Apperception Test (for older children)
    Draw-A-Person Test
    Kinetic Family Drawing
    Rorschach
    Sentence Completion Test
Social
    Personality Inventory for Children
    Burks' Rating Scales
Family
    Minnesota Child Developmental Inventory
    Benet-Anthony Test of Family Relations

INTERVIEWING OTHERS

A complete evaluation includes data obtained from the perpetrator (whether from within or outside the family), from the parents, and from siblings, teachers, and child-care workers. Information obtained from the police report, medical examiner, child protective service worker, and attorney (if applicable) should also be reviewed to complete the evaluation.

In interviewing alleged perpetrators, the clinician should focus on the interaction with the child. When the parents are involved in the abuse, it is usually helpful to observe the perpetrator and spouse interacting with the child. Attention should be paid to the perpetrator's family and psychosocial history; the system of psychological defenses; the ability to abstractly or concretely react to the situation; the ability to assume responsibility; personality, thought, or mood disorders; drug or alcohol abuse; parenting skills (if the perpetrator is a parent); and personality strengths. If possible, such information should be validated with a standardized psychological instrument such as the Minnesota Multiphasic Personality Inventory.

When the abuse has occurred within the family, information about and observation of family dynamics will give the clinician a great deal of insight about prognosis and treatment. The spouse of the perpetrator should be interviewed to assess his or her role of support, denial, anger, or protection. The spouse's psychiatric and social history as well as current psychological functioning should be evaluated, along with substance abuse history and parenting skills. If the abuse has occurred outside the family, the clinician should deal with the family's anxiety and anger.

Siblings will also provide important, and often untarnished, information about the abuse and about family dynamics. It is important to rule out the possibility that siblings have been involved in the abuse.

Often overlooked are teachers and child-care workers. Since children often spend more significant time in these settings than in interaction with their parents, these persons become important evaluators of children's cognitive, social, emotional, and physical health.

INTERVIEW AIDS

Anatomically Correct Dolls

Anatomically correct dolls have become widely used for evaluation of physical and especially sexual abuse. Therapists who use these dolls should be cautioned about their validity. While White and colleagues (1986) and Jampole and Weber (1987) found that abused children displayed more sexually related behaviors than nonabused children, Jensen and associates (1986) and Gabriel

(1985) report that in their samples, one could not necessarily distinguish between abused and nonabused children. A California court has disallowed evidence obtained using anatomically correct dolls (in Amber B. & Tella B. 1987 191 Calif 3rd 682; in Christine C. & Michael C. 1987 191 Calif App. 3rd 676).

On the basis of these conflicting findings, it may be useful to adopt an objective procedure for the use of anatomically correct dolls such as that developed by White and her colleagues (1986). Schetky (1988) suggests that the dolls should not be used without guidelines or to contaminate the interview by teaching, coaching, or suggesting to the child what has happened. Also, the dolls should be visually pleasing to the child, they should be of the same race, and they should be integrated in a relaxed manner into the play interview. Children under the age of three appear to be confused by the family of dolls and should be given only the doll who represents the perpetrator.

Drawings

The Draw-A-Person test and the Kinetic Family Drawing may give the clinician some clues as to the extent or dynamics of abuse. According to DiLeo (1973), children do not usually draw genitalia or nude figures, and such drawings may be indicators of possible aggression or emotional disturbance (Koppitz, 1968). Hibbard and colleagues (1987) also found that sexually abused children were more likely to draw genitalia than were control subjects.

In addition to these more standardized drawings, time should be given to children to draw pictures of themselves, their families, or the abuse situation. Sgroi (1984) outlines a procedure in which the child draws a picture of the abuse situation, an activity that appears to help the child to describe the details of the abuse. Information can be obtained by having the children talk about their pictures or answer questions about the kinds of touches they have experienced on various body parts. Older children who are reluctant to draw detailed pictures may be more comfortable starting with a drawing of their room or the floor plan of the house (Goodwin, 1982).

Videotaping

There are numerous advantages and disadvantages to videotaping an interview with a child. The most obvious reason for videotaping is for courtroom procedures, yet videotapes are seldom admissible in trials (MacFarlane, 1985). Another reason for videotaping has been to minimize the frequency with which children must tell their story, thus saving them emotional trauma and preserving the affective component of the story, which may diminish with repetition. Tedesco and Schnell (1987) reported that children become more negative in reaction to the investigative process as a direct correlation to the number of interviews. Also, Hauggard and Repucci (1988) point out that, when a child initially denies that abuse occurred and later changes the story, the video-tape may provide evidence that the clinician did not encourage this change. The videotape may also be used as a therapeutic resource for the nonoffending parent or as an educational tool for the therapist. Videotaping often forces the clinician to begin the interview with a thorough case background and a structured strategy of assessment.

The disadvantages of videotaping are also numerous. For the videotape to be a professional product, technical and comfort factors must be optimal. Videotaping is not suggested for the novice. An unprofessional videotape will not serve the best interests of the child.

Another disadvantage of videotaping concerns confidentiality. The defendant and his or her attorney have rights to all evidence related to the case. This may include the videotaped interview. The videotape can become public and may be used out of context. Parents who are made aware of these confidentiality issues may refuse to permit videotaping. Lastly, if the clinician videotapes only part of the assessment, one must be able to support the selection of that position chosen. Ideally, the clinician should videotape all of the assessment interview or none of it.

It is suggested that videotaping decisions be made on a case-by-case basis in consultation with the assessment team and with legal professionals. Videotaping should also be used only when the clinician is skilled in and comfortable with the process.

Hypnosis

Although hypnosis for psychotherapeutic intervention is becoming increasingly accepted, its use remains controversial, especially in courts of law. While most clinicians have not been trained in hypnotic procedures, it is usually not necessary to employ formal hypnosis during the initial child abuse evaluation. Children spend a great deal of their time in natural trance states, especially in play. If the therapist establishes optimal rapport, children will use their natural trance states to answer questions or to interact in a comfortable, consistent, and candid manner.

ADOLESCENTS

Special attention should be paid to establishing rapport with adolescents, who are especially sensitive to the boundaries of social acceptability. Mirroring techniques, with special emphasis on language, are important. With the adolescent who uses slang, the therapist may evoke a more honest response by asking "what happens when the shit hits the fan at home?" rather than "What happens when you get in trouble?" Clinicians who are not entirely comfortable with such language should not risk alienating the adolescent by using it.

Adolescents may be particularly sensitive about confidentiality. A frank discussion about confidentiality within the context of the requirements imposed by the evaluation will set the stage for a respectful relationship. I can remember my own experience as a young therapist with an adolescent boy who offhandedly related that he was suicidal shortly after I explained confidentiality, neglecting to tell him the limits of a confidential relationship. It took about a year to win back his trust. Fortunately, he allowed the opportunity and time to redress my mistake.

It is also helpful if the therapist is comfortable talking to adolescents about their bodies and their sexuality. The therapist's comfort with this subject can help abused adolescents to gain or regain confidence in their physical and sexual selves. Adolescents may need reassurance that others have experienced and successfully conquered their fears and anxieties about the abuse.

FALSE ALLEGATIONS

False allegations of sexual abuse most often occur in the context of a custody dispute, and there are no reliable statistics to determine the overall prevalence of false allegations of child physical or sexual abuse. In custody disputes, estimates of allegations of sexual abuse have range between 1 percent and 10 percent, and between 20 percent and 80 percent have been determined to be false (Wakefield & Underwager, 1990; 1991). Also, there are few legal repercussions for making a false claim. Most complaints that emanate from children are probably true; false allegations of sexual abuse from a nonfamily member that emanate from adolescents tend to come from teenagers who are trying to cover their whereabouts after staying out all night. Occasionally, a woman who has herself been sexually molested as a child may misinterpret signs from a child and jump to conclusions, thereby filing a claim that, while made honestly, may be false.

GOING NOWHERE?

Despite the best plans and execution, there may be times when the clinician fails to receive the information necessary to complete the evaluation. The first question the clinician should ask is whether rapport has been established so that the child can address the questions being asked. Or is the clinician hurrying or using developmentally inappropriate language? If so, then the clinician may attempt to reestablish rapport by reentering the child's world.

If the therapist fails to obtain an answer to a particular question, he or she can incorporate it into a later phase of the assessment or schedule a later assessment time. The therapist can use questions or statements that bounce the issues back to the child, such as "I'm just trying to figure out what really happened," or "I don't understand," or "I'm curious about that." Keep in mind that many children fear even greater reprisals from a parent should they divulge their perverse "secret." Perhaps their biggest fear is that the parent will abandon them. And very young children may not even realize they have been abused.

If the clinician has exhausted these techniques without success, he or she must consider the possibility that the child is developmentally or traumatically unable to furnish detailed information. In this case, simply reporting this assessment may fulfill an important aspect of the evaluation.

The professional evaluation of child abuse and neglect requires knowledge of the syndrome's manifestations in the major spheres of functioning (intrapsychic, interpersonal, behavioral, and social). The detection of and therapeutic intervention into such abuse can forestall many of the deleterious consequences of abuse that could develop later in life.

REFERENCES

Benedek, E. P., & Schetky, D. H. (1985). Allegations of sexual abuse in child custody and visitation disputes. In *Emerging Issues in Child Psychiatry and the Law*, ed. D. H. Schetky and E. P. Benedek, pp. 98–133. New York: Brunner/Mazel.

Cameron-Bandler, L. (1985). *Solutions*. San Rafael, CA: Future Press.

Conaway, L. P., & Hansen, D. J. (1989). Social behavior of physically abused and neglected children: A critical review. *Clinical Psychology Review* 9 627–652.

Craig, R. J. (In press). *Personality-Guided Practice of Forensic Psychology*. Washington, DC: American Psychological Association.

DiLeo, J. (1973). *Children's Drawings as Diagnostic Aids*. New York: Brunner/Mazel.

Gabriel, R. M. (1985). Anatomically correct dolls in the diagnosis of sexual abuse of children. *Journal of the Melanie Klein Society* 3:41–49.

Goodwin, J. (1982). The use of drawings in incest cases. In *Sexual Abuse: Incest Victims and Their Families*, ed. J. Goodwin, pp. 268–334. Boston: Wright.

Hauggard, J. J., and Repucci, N. D. (1988). *The Sexual Abuse of Children*. San Francisco: Jossey-Bass.

Herman, J. (1981). *Father–Daughter Incest*. Cambridge: Harvard University Press.

Hewitt, S., & McNought, J. (1985). *Program in Human Sexuality*. Minneapolis: University of Minnesota Medical School.

Hibbard, R. A., Roghmann, K., & Hoekelman, R. A. (1987). Genitalia in children's drawings: An association with sexual abuse. *Pediatrics* 79: 129–137.

Jampole, L., & Weber, M. K. (1987). An assessment of the behavior of sexually abused children with anatomically correct dolls. *Child Abuse and Neglect* 11: 187–192.

Jensen, J. B., Realmuto, G. M., Wescoe, M. D., & Garfinkel, B. D. (1986). Are there differences in the play with anatomically correct dolls: Abused versus non-abused children. Paper presented at the annual meeting of the American Academy of Child and Adolescent Psychiatry, Los Angeles, October.

Kadushin, A., & Mortin, J. (1981). *Child Abuse: An Interactional Event*. New York: Columbia University Press.

Kempe, R., & Kempe, C. (1978). *Child Abuse*. Cambridge, MA: Harvard University Press.

Kendall-Tackett, K. A., Williams, L. M., & Finkelhor, D. (1993). Impact of sexual abuse on children: A review and synthesis of recent empirical literature. *Psychological Bulletin* 113:164–180.

Koppitz, E. M. (1968). *Psychological Evaluation of Children's Human Figure Drawings*. New York: Grune and Stratton.

Lamb, M. E. (1994). The investigation of child sexual abuse: An interdisciplinary consensus statement. *Child Abuse and Neglect* 18:1021–1028.

MacFarlane, K. (1985). Diagnostic evaluations and the use of videotapes in child sexual abuse cases. *University of Miami Law Review* 40: 136–165.

Meiselman, K. (1978). *Incest: A Psychological Study of Causes and Effects with Treatment Recommendations*. San Francisco: Jossey-Bass.

Mrazch, P., Lynch, M., & Bentovin, A. (1981). Recognition of child sexual abuse in the United Kingdom. In *Sexually Abused Children and Their Families*, ed. P. Mrazch and H. Kempe. New York: Pergamon.

Polusny, M. A., & Follette, V. M. (1995). Long-term correlates of child sexual abuse: Theory and review of the empirical literature. *Applied and Preventive Psychology* 4:143–166.

Saywitz, K. J., Mannarino, A. P., Berliner, L., & Cohen, J. A. (2000). Treatment for sexually abused children and adolescents. *American Psychologist* 55:1040–1049.

Schetky, D. H. (1988). The clinical evaluation of child sexual abuse. In *Child Sexual Abuse*, ed. D. H. Schetky and A. H. Green, pp. 57–81. New York: Brunner/Mazel.

Schetky, D. H., & Green, A. H. (1988). *Child Sexual Abuse*. New York: Brunner/Mazel.

Sgroi, S. (1984). Validation of sexual abuse. In *Handbook of Clinical Intervention in Child Sexual Abuse*, ed. S. Sgroi. Lexington, MA: Lexington Books.

Swanson, L., & Biaggio, M. (1985). Therapeutic perspectives on father–daughter incest. *American Journal of Psychiatry* 142: 667–674.

Tedesco, J. F., & Schnell, S. V. (1987). Children's reactions to sex abuse investigation and litigation. *Child Abuse and Neglect* 11: 267–272.

Wakefield, H., & Underwager, R. (1990). Personality characteristics of parents making false accusations of sexual abuse in custody disputes. *Child Abuse Accusations* 2:121–136.

Wakefield, H., & Underwager, R. (1991). Sexual abuse allegations in divorce and custody disputes. *Behavioral Sciences and the Law* 9:451–468.

White, S., Strom, G., Santilli, G., & Halpin, B. (1986). Interviewing young sexual abuse victims with anatomically correct dolls. *Child Abuse and Neglect* 10:519–529.

V

FOCUSED INTERVIEWS

18

THE MENTAL STATUS EXAMINATION

Eliezer Schwartz, Ph.D.

The phenomenological approach to the diagnosis of mental illness attained a credible position through the work of Emil Kraepelin (1856–1926). A compulsive and skilled observer, Kraepelin integrated findings of experimental psychology with confirmed observations to develop a psychiatric nosology. His systematized observations presented an accurate and sensitive picture of human suffering. The descriptions of manic-depressive patients that he presented to his students in the lecture hall are still valid today (Kraepelin, 1904).

Kraepelin's classic work was the genesis of a psychiatric nosology based on descriptive phenomena. These phenomena, which are sufficiently objective to allow easy and clear clinical inferences, include a variety of signs and symptoms presented by patients. Specific constellations of *signs* (observable patient behaviors) and *symptoms* (subjective experiences reported by the patient), with a particular and identifiable natural history (age of onset, life course, complications, and prognosis) ultimately define clinical entities (Spitzer, 1976). Consequently, the psychiatric diagnosis presents the psychopathology of the patient through its etiology, pathogenesis, and current behavioral manifestations.

Generations of physicians and psychiatrists, following in Kraepelin's footsteps, have maintained a tradition of assessment based on a structured diagnostic interview conducted rigidly and in a planned fashion:

> The student or physician who approaches the case without a definite plan in mind is certain to overlook important facts or permit the patient to lead too much in the examination, often with the result that the time is not spent to the best advantage or that he is misled into drawing false conclusions. (Lewis 1934, p. 11)

The emphasis on preselected topics considered crucial for accurate diagnosis makes the traditional psychiatric interview follow explicit, a priori guidelines, actively directed by the clinician and without regard for any demonstration of initiative on the part of the patient (Pope, 1979). Such initiative is considered irrelevant and quite disruptive, and the clinician might prefer to disregard the information presented by a verbose, undisciplined, or noncompliant patient in favor of the desired data obtained from relatives and friends.

The mental status examination, or MSE, was introduced to the American psychiatric community in 1917 by Adolf Meyer (Berrios, 1996). However, descriptive psychiatry, which has dominated European psychiatry from the beginning of the century to the present, suffered in the United States from the growing popularity and competition of a variety of psychological approaches to psychopathology and mental illness. For many decades, the descriptive approach to mental illness, which emphasized the *what* of observable behavior, was considered too narrow and at times too shallow in providing the necessary information toward a well-prognosticated treatment plan. These psychological approaches, with their focus on the *how* and the *why* of inferred dynamic forces and functions of personality structures, offered more attractive (and at times more seductive) promises for the diagnosis and the treatment of human psychopathology.

The introduction to the third official psychiatric nomenclature in 1980 by the American Psychiatric Association in the updated *Diagnostic and Statistical Manual of Mental Disorders* (DSM-III), formally revived in the United States the descriptive approach as a serious foundation for diagnostic work. Many factors contributed to this Kraepelinian revival and to the emergence of the DSM-III (Maxmen, 1986). Social, political, and economic forces joined clinicians' dissatisfaction with the biased and unreliable theoretical positions on mental health and illness and gave license to both psychiatrists and psychologists to at least recognize each other's approaches as viable alternative modes of diagnosis and treatment. Further, the emergence of specialties integrating and bridging medical and psychological processes (such as health psychology, neuropsychology, and rehabilitation), along with the increasing significance and use of psychotropic drugs, forced the proponents of traditional psychological approaches to study and use descriptive techniques in the investigation of psychological conditions. Consequently, psychologists have learned to appreciate the use of the nomenclature offered by the third and the fourth editions of the DSM (American Psychiatric Association, 1994), as well as the flexibility provided by the multiaxial system. The experience of using this classification of mental disorders for the past two decades promoted in clinical psychologists an appreciation of the MSE. They have come to recognize the considerable value that behaviors and complaints presented by patients during interview situations add to the latent content of their verbalizations.

MENTAL STATUS EXAMINATION

Spitzer (1976) discusses two main purposes for diagnostic work. The first is to *define clinical entities*, and the second is to *determine treatment*. Clinical entities are diagnostic classifications based on recognizable behavioral characteristics and enduring functional patterns. When several individuals present similar symptoms and signs, and when their emotional and cognitive distress is the result of a similar natural history, they are diagnosed as suffering from the same pathological condition and are considered candidates for the same form of treatment:

> How a diagnosis will define a disorder and guide treatment depends on its validity and reliability. When a diagnostic category represents a genuine entity—that is, when patients with the same diagnosis have similar clinical features, natural histories, etiologies, pathogenesis, and responses to treatment—the category is said to have *high validity*. The more clinicians agree on a diagnosis when examining the same patient, the greater its *(interrater) reliability*. (Maxmen 1986, p. 4)

The formulation of a treatment plan follows a formalized diagnosis and prognosis, which in turn are based on data collected systematically from a variety of sources. Psychological tests, laboratory findings, behavioral observations, and interviews with the patient and others provide valuable information toward diagnostic formulations. However, the formal descriptive assessment process considers the initial patient interview the most significant source of diagnostic material (Maxmen, 1986).

Levenson (1981) distinguishes between *subjective* and *objective* parts of an interview. The subjective component consists of information offered by the patient, but unwitnessed by the therapist. Such information typically includes psychosocial background and the events leading to the patient's current mental state. The objective component is that part of the interview that allows the therapist to observe (directly and indirectly) the signs and symptoms of the patient's mental state. According to Nelson and Barlow (1981), when therapists observe the behaviors emitted by the patient and categorize them toward a diagnostic definition of a clinical entity, they are engaged in a mental status examination (MSE).

The relative independence of MSE data from the verbalized content of the interview and the therapist's ability to observe and recognize known indicators of pathological entities allow for the validity and the reliability of this process as a diagnostic tool. The MSE is not necessarily a standardized test, and it is lacking rigidly planned guidelines. The validity and the reliability of the MSE are not based on its psychometric features, but on its simplicity and on its inherent ability to identify with clarity specific behaviors that are diagnostically significant and prognostically possible objectives for treatment. Rogers (2001) states that the diagnostic validity of structured interviews such as the MSE is in the language and the sequence of questions, which in the MSE is systematic and highly consistent. The MSE does not require a specific setting or the use of standardized questions. The MSE can be part of a diagnostic session, as well as part of a therapeutic one. It can be part of any event that requires observations and study of a patient's overt behaviors in interaction with others. The MSE is an ongoing process performed by clinicians and interviewers alike, as long as they observe interacting individuals (Nelson & Barlow, 1981).

The MSE is used by clinicians in need of specific behavioral targets for treatment. The ability of the MSE to identify relevant objectives for intervention allows clinicians from various theoretical and therapeutic orientations to adapt this diagnostic mode toward their own purpose. For example, traditional phenomenologists observe the flat affect of the individual suffering from depression, regardless of the presence or absence of verbalized morbid thoughts (Wing et al., 1974). From their perspective, pharmacotherapists are sensitive to loose associations or clang associations as psychopharmacologically responsive states for treatment with major tranquilizers, independent of reported delusions or hallucinations (Levenson, 1981). Furthermore, neuropsychologists pay attention to the patient's effortful speech production and slow body motion to differentiate between anterior and posterior cortical insults, without the administration of standardized tests (Strub & Black, 1993).

The operational criteria of major clinical entities presented by the DSM-IV make the MSE, in its phenomenological diagnostic approach, a useful instrument in the hands of behavioral psychologists. Nathan (1981) describes the significant contribution of the DSM-III toward increased accountability for assessment procedures. He concludes that behavioral assessment and symptomatic diagnosis have about the same level of reliability and utility, indicating the need for behavioral psychologists to learn how to use both. Twenty years later, the revised DSM-IV-TR (American Psychiatric Association, 2000) is considered a necessary tool in the hands of almost every mental health practitioner, and it is a regular topic of study in the curriculum and training of clinical psychologists.

CATEGORIES OF BEHAVIORAL OBSERVATIONS

The Present State Exam, a very detailed and elaborate standardized extension of the MSE, was published by Wing and colleagues (1974) with sample questions and data on reliability. Many writers have described and discussed the MSE, providing guidelines for the interview process and outlines to categorize the behavioral observations collected during such examination (Freedman et al., 1975; Maxmen, 1986; Morrison, 1997; Noyes & Kolb, 1963; Rosenthal & Akiskal, 1985; Slater & Roth, 1969; Taylor, 1981). The following categories of behavioral observations of an MSE are not as detailed as in the Present State Exam, but they provide the reader with the fundamental sequence of this inquiry. Each category of behavioral observations will also include examples of its clinical applicability.

General Appearance

Taylor (1981) considers appearance as the first topic to be addressed by the examiner. The patient's age, sex, race, body type, and quality of nutrition, health, and personal grooming are essential. Initiating a report of MSE findings with a paragraph describing the patient's appearance allows the reader to have a visual image of the patient. These observations enable the reader to distinguish the patient interviewed from others of the same age, economic background, and educational level.

This behavioral category also includes an assessment of the patient's *state of consciousness*. Consciousness is assessed on a continuum from *alertness* to *coma*. States of consciousness have important implications for the patient's ability to respond to environmental stimuli. In addition, the examination of general appearance includes an assessment of *manner* and *attitude*, which is based on the quality of the interaction with the examiner. Assessment of these parameters requires no specific inquiry, as the needed information is available to the observer throughout the interview period. Even seasoned clinicians are not immune to hostile feelings toward manipulative patients who endeavor to humiliate them; however, cooperative and grateful patients successfully reinforce examiners' self-perceptions of being caring and competent.

Behavior

This category of observations refers to the patient's overall profile of movements and motor activities. The examiner concentrates on the patient's gait, frequency and speed of movement, rhythm and coordination of movements, and the presence or absence of abnormal movements (Taylor, 1981).

Greeting the patient outside the office, shaking hands, and walking together toward the office are activities that allow the clinician to observe gait and overall coordination. Noted abnormalities (such as tics, twitches, favoring a foot, and so on) alert the examiner to points of inquiry and specific questions to be addressed with the patient. The patient's awareness of the abnormality is clinically significant, as well as the lack of such awareness. For example, it is expected that an individual with a vascular brain lesion within the right hemisphere will exhibit inattention or denial of left-sided motor losses. Without the etiology of an insult to the central nervous system, however, such denial can be indicative of strong psychological defensiveness.

Intense mood is usually expressed motorically through *agitation* (increased frequency of motor behavior). States of anxiety, depression, or anger result in such agitated behavior as pacing, foot tapping, restlessness, or jerky shifts of the body while sitting. Unlike agitation, *hyperactivity* is the term used to point out an increase in frequency of activities that are goal directed (or field dependent). For example, the agitation of an anxious patient will be demonstrated in his or her pacing in the room from wall to wall. The hyperactivity of a patient with a moderate degree of attention difficulties will be manifested by the inability to stay on task (while taking psychological tests) due to consistent reactivity to outside noises.

A decrease in frequency of activity is termed *hypoactivity*. The hypoactive patient who sits dejected in a corner, lethargic and rarely moving, might suffer from depression; but the patient who exhibits extreme hyperactivity or hypoactivity (excitement or stupor) might be exhibiting signs of catatonia.

Behavioral stereotypes (repetitive and nongoal-directed actions), frequently observed with catatonic patients, are often confused with obsessive-compulsiveness. The craft of the clinician in differential diagnosis and knowledge of psychopathology is demonstrated here in the ability to differentiate between the catatonic and the obsessive-compulsive. The catatonic patient with stereotypic behaviors is lacking the insight of the "ridiculousness" of such actions, while the obsessive-compulsive individual knows quite well how ridiculous and senseless repetitive behaviors are but is compelled to perform them to find relief from extreme anxiety.

Affect and Mood

The emotional coloration underlying the behavior of the patient during the MSE is called *affect*. Taylor (1981) discusses affect in terms of range, amplitude, stability, appropriateness and quality of mood, and relatedness. Morrison (1997) states that *mood* is the feeling state reported by the patient, while affect includes the physical appearance of the underlying feeling. Rosenthal and Akiskal (1985) also suggest that affect is the emotional tone as observed by the examiner, while mood is the self-reported and subjectively felt experience of the patient. Occasionally, there is a lack of congruity between affect and mood. For example, a patient may appear to the examiner to be quite excited and even joyful, but report being depressed for over a long period of time.

Subjective emotions are expressed in terms of sadness, happiness, anxiety, anger, or apathy (Taylor, 1981). These various types of affective messages indicate the *quality* of mood. The *amplitude* of emotions is ascertained by the patient's intensity in expressing a particular mood, while the variability of these expressions over a period of time—in this case throughout the MSE—is the *range* of affect. Normal expression of affect is expected to vary appropriately, according to the content of the diagnostic dialogue. *Inappropriateness* of mood (for example, laughing when reporting a recent death in the family), *constriction* in range of affect (when the interview is dominated by the expression of the same mood), or lability of affect (instability expressed in rapid and inappropriate shifts in mood) are signs of psychopathology.

The patient's *relatedness* during the interview is not only an important subject of investigation but also a difficult dimension of affect to assess and describe.

Relatedness involves the patient's capacity to interact emotionally, to establish rapport with the examiner, and to express warmth toward the examiner (Taylor, 1981). Clinicians' experience of two cooperative and task-oriented patients (similar in their attitude and manners) can be totally different if one of the patients appears to be blunt and cold, while the other seems warm and highly inquisitive. The examiner might feel that an unrelated patient is like a machine or an object. Individuals suffering from a schizophrenic disorder are known to respond to examiners in an unfeeling manner, frequently leaving the impression of talking to a computer or a mechanical voice.

Speech and Thought Processes

Thought disorders, which are communications based on pathological thinking processes, hold a central role in understanding and evaluating severe forms of mental illness. However, the term *thought disorder* has fallen out of favor with the third revision of the DSM, because of the term's nonspecificity and its failure to offer operationalized descriptions of pathological thinking. Consequently, Maxmen (1986) suggests four categories of observations, each dealing with a distinct aspect of thought processes and each sufficiently tangible to allow for descriptive specificity.

1. *The quantity of thought* is also referred to as *stream of thought*. For example, the patient whose speech pattern is slow and who utters very few words is exhibiting *poverty of speech*, a characteristic of depressed individuals or of those suffering from an organic impairment. A mute patient might suffer from a stroke or Huntington's disease. The regularity of spacing between words, or the *rhythm of speech*, is another target for clinical observations. Slurring of words can be a sign of intoxication or the manifestation of a more serious medical condition such as diabetes mellitus.

Pressure of speech can indicate underlying anxiety; together with *flight of ideas*, the feeling of being pressured to talk can be a strong differential sign for a manic episode.

2. *The quality of associations* between ideas communicated by the patient is referred to as *continuity of thought*. Disturbed associations manifest themselves in a variety of verbal idiosyncrasies, such as word salad, perseverations, neologisms, word approximations, paraphasia, echolalia, and clang associations. In addition, disturbed linkages between words and phrases are presented by the patient as looseness of associations, flight of ideas, and blocking. These signs are frequently indicative of psychopathology. The examiner must be sensitive to the difference between disturbances resulting from disorders of thought and the temporary consequences of humor, sarcasm, medical illness, fatigue, intense affect, differences in language and culture, and impoverished education or intelligence.

3. The content of thought refers to the patient's verbal expressions of experiences, perceptions, and feelings. Pathology of thought content is evident in delusions, illogical or magical thinking, overvalued ideas, incomprehensible speech, and obsessions.

Delusions are belief systems without cultural, social, or religious foundation. They present the patient as disowning his or her inner experiences (thoughts, perceptions, and feelings), which at times are considered externally imposed, mobilizing the patient to act as though against his or her will. The grandiosity evidenced in a paranoid patient's delusion that he is William Shakespeare is also an example of *illogical thinking* when in defense of this belief he states "we both are English." Persistent and disturbing thoughts that constitute *obsessions* are the ideational bases of *compulsive behaviors*, which are stereotypic and repetitive actions. Therefore, the presence of compulsions (when recognized by the patient as senseless) should alert the examiner to inquire about obsessions.

4. Abstraction is the ability to think symbolically, to conceptualize and generalize. Neurologically impaired patients, as well as those who suffer from psychosis, have impoverished abstractive abilities. Abstractive abilities or the lack of them are usually assessed by the examiner through specific requests to interpret proverbs or to identify similarities. Concrete or bizarre responses to these requests are usually very solid signs of psychopathology. For example, the expected answer to the question "What is the similarity between an eagle and a parrot?" is "They are birds." A concrete answer, however, would be "Both have feathers" or "They have two legs." A bizarre response would be "Both attack green-eyed and blond women." A concrete interpretation of the proverb "One swallow does not make a summer" would be "One swallow cannot bring the summer; you need more swallows." A bizarre interpretation of this proverb would be "In the summer you drink all the time."

Maxmen (1986) includes *abstraction* as a dimension of inquiry into thought process. However, many writers consider this abstraction a parameter of intellectual functioning, a category discussed later in this chapter. For the interested reader, an elaborate and detailed presentation of observable characteristics of speech and thought is presented by Taylor (1981).

Rosenthal and Akiskal (1985) discuss the need for every reported MSE to contain a statement about the presence or absence of suicidal ideas during the interview. Contrary to the popular belief that direct inquiry about suicide might aggravate or exacerbate a vulnerable emotional state, they advocate direct questioning about suicidal thoughts. They also indicate that failure to address suicidal ideation is frequently more dangerous than the remote risk involved in "putting ideas into patient's head." The gravity and seriousness of suicide potential must be assessed and, if necessary, treated immediately. Only direct and tactful questioning can provide the examiner with the diagnostic information necessary for proper intervention. Rosenthal and Akiskal (1985) also note that homicidal thoughts, if they emerge during the MSE, necessitate direct inquiry, proper documentation, and appropriate intervention.

Perceptual Processes

The impaired reality testing of patients who suffer from severe personality disorders, neurological dysfunctions, or psychosis is also manifested in sensory and perceptual disturbances. These phenomena may also occur temporarily in individuals who are without psychopathology but are in states of physical illness, fatigue, expectancy, or emotional arousal. However, persistent perceptual distortions and errors of sensation are pathognomonic, even in the absence of clearly evident corroborative signs and symptoms (Rosenthal & Akiskal, 1985).

Hallucinations are perceptions without external stimuli, while *illusions* are distorted perceptions of existing stimuli. These phenomena can involve all sensory modalities. *Auditory hallucinations* (hearing voices) are very common perceptual disorders found in schizophrenic disorders. Quite often, these disturbances are incorporated within a delusional system. Auditory hallucinations can also be observed in patients with major affective disorders, neurological insults, or intoxication. *Visual hallucinations* are more common with transient psychotic states, in depressive conditions, and in conjunction with auditory hallucinations in delirium. Such combinations are frequently quite frightening.

Haptic (tactile) illusions and hallucinations (such as sensation of bugs crawling on the body) are experienced by patients in states of delirium or drug-induced psychosis. Patients with delirium or psychosis induced by drugs can experience "flying" or *vestibular hallucinations*. In some organic conditions such as epilepsy, patients can also experience *olfactory hallucination*.

Depersonalization, derealization, and *déjà vu* are perceptual disorders found in both neurological disorders and intense affective states. For example, "out-of-body" experiences, distorted perception of physical distances from people, or misperception of depth are common in postsurgical periods as manifestations of masked depression.

Orientation

The patient's capacity to orient himself or herself is measured by most clinicians in three spheres: *person, time,* and *place.* Rosenthal and Akiskal (1985) add a fourth sphere: orientation to *situation.* Strub and Black (1993) include *spatial* and *geographic* orientations as significant fifth and sixth spheres requiring diagnostic scrutiny.

Specific questions about the identity of the interviewer and the patient such as, "What is your name?" and "Who am I?" provide an indication of orientation in *person.* Asking the patient to identify the day of the week, the full date (day, month, and year), and time of the day assesses orientation to *time.* An inquiry regarding the patient's address and the location of the interview provides clues to patient's orientation to *place*. The patient is considered disoriented to *situation* when he or she fails to recall or know the purpose of being in the examiner's office.

Spatial orientation is a fundamental ability of living in a three dimensional world, including such skills as knowing body parts, directionality, assessing distances and depth, and the overall cognitive ability to separate self from others. Various insults to the brain can result in such difficulties as problems with right–left differentiation (when language difficulties are ruled out), problems with constructional abilities (drawings or working with blocks), or difficulties avoiding a collision with objects while walking (due to errors in perception of depth or distance). Patients with *geographic orientation* (a more complex form of spatial orientation) have difficulties finding their way in a familiar neighborhood, cannot navigate with maps, and experience fear and severe anxiety when left alone in a new location.

Patients with neurological deficiencies are usually disoriented in one or more spheres. Similarly, drug intoxication and acute psychoses are characterized by orientation failures. However, most individuals suffering from schizophrenia or affective disorders are well oriented in all spheres, indicating clear sensorium and perceptual skills.

Attention and Concentration

Once the patient is found to be fully alert, the examiner has to observe the patient's ability to attend to a stimulus and to concentrate. The capacity to attend selectively and to concentrate on a task over time is a prerequisite for other cognitive abilities. Therefore, the examiner cannot adequately evaluate functions of memory, learning, language, or thinking without first establishing that the patient has attention and concentration skills.

Strub and Black (1993) define *attention* as "the ability to attend to a specific stimulus without being distracted by extraneous internal or external stimuli." They describe *concentration* or *vigilance* as "the ability to sustain attention over an extended period."

Strub and Black also discuss *alertness* as a fundamental ability of the awake individual to react to his or her environment. The attentive person is by definition alert and is able to "tune out" irrelevant stimuli. However, a patient can be alert but lacking in selective attention.

Distractibility or *inattention* are concepts that should be understood in the context of at least two clinical situations. The most commonly recognized clinical context is presented when the patient is unable to focus and attend to simple tasks due to distractibility by environmental stimuli. The other clinical scenario is found with the patient who suffers from specific inattention to environmental stimuli by the side of the body contralateral to the location of the neurological insult.

Both neurological/physiological and emotional disorders can impair attention and concentration. Careful observation and sensitivity are needed to differentiate between attentional deficiency and oppositional behavior. The former is involuntary, while the latter is a conscious, and possibly purposeful, attempt to manipulate the interview process.

Memory

Memory abilities are categorized as *immediate, recent,* and *remote.* Immediate or short-term memory is evident when the patient is able to recall information within seconds or minutes following its presentation. Often, failure of short-term (immediate) memory is mistaken for distractibility resulting from attention and concentration difficulties. The distractible patient tends to appear preoccupied, confused, or anxious and is unable to follow goal-directed tasks (Luria, 1973).However, while the patient deficient in immediate memory might be anxious, he or she is also aware of the problem and will try to perform to capacity (Taylor, 1981).

Short-term memory is also referred to as *working memory* (Strub & Black, 1993). The concept of working memory alerts the examiner to the functional value of short-term memory for other cognitive operations. Most cognitive processes are multistep operations, when short-term memory allows the individual to "work" with one step while temporarily storing the others. Therefore, difficulties with working memory interfere significantly with almost every cognitive task. Simple tasks such as asking the patient to repeat numbers (forward and backward) presented by the examiner, allow for the assessment of concentration and short-term memory. Simple arithmetic questions such as "How much is seventeen times three?" offer the opportunity to demonstrate working memory. In addition, the examiner might assess immediate memory by presenting a few cards with simple geometric configurations for the patient's visual inspection; the examiner then removes the cards and, following a delay of a few seconds, asks for the patient to reproduce these configurations (Strub & Black, 1993).

Recent memory refers to the ability to recall events from the past several days, weeks, or months, while *remote memory* involves events from many years ago. Inquiry into the patient's personal history allows for the assessment of recent and remote memory. *Confabulations* (recollections of imaginary events) indicate that the geriatric patient has memory deficits. The availability of collateral information (such as documents or data collected from family members or friends) may provide verification of the patient's recollections. Remote memory seems to be the most resilient in the face of neurological insults, while vigilance and working memory are affected by even mild trauma to the central nervous system. Individuals suffering from chronic schizophrenia might exhibit severe remote memory losses, while recent and immediate memory deficiencies are less pronounced (Mendel, 1976).

The ability to differentially diagnose between short-term and long-term (recent and remote) memory deficiencies is crucial for the neuropsychologist and the rehabilitation psychologist. Short-term memory losses are usually indicative of cortical damage, while long-term memory deficiencies are most likely the result of subcortical insults to the limbic structures and functions. Difficulties with immediate memory can also be part of a more complex language disorder, while patients with long-term memory problems implicating limbic systems might demonstrate intact working memory, with clear manifestations of lability of affect. For example, it is quite common to encounter patients working in sheltered workshops who demonstrate an excellent mastery of complex and multistep tasks (such as engine assembly), an achievement that lasts for the duration of one working day. However, by the next day, these patients have no recollection of this task. These patients suffer from subcortical losses.

Intellectual Functioning

True to the phenomenological approach and tradition, the mental status examiner approaches the assessment of intelligence by using a very pragmatic definition of this concept. *Intellectual functioning* refers to complex processes that are based on the integrity and the interaction of more basic skills (such as selective attention, perception, language, memory, and motor abilities). Many neurological and psychological deficiencies are evidenced by impoverished intellectual capacity, while the more basic skills remain intact.

The MSE evaluates intelligence through observations and assessment of the patient's vocabulary, general fund of knowledge, use of previously learned information, and abstract thinking. Most writers (Rosenthal & Akiskal, 1985; Strub & Black, 1993; Taylor, 1981; Wing et al., 1974) consider abstract thinking an important ingredient in the assessment of intellectual functioning, while Maxmen (1986) evaluates *abstraction* toward an understanding of *thought processes*.

In assessing intelligence, the examiner must consider the patient's age, level of education, cultural and ethnic background, socioeconomic status (access to resources), and past experiences. Such information allows the examiner to develop a set of realistic expectations with respect to the patient. For example, an academician would be expected to have a rich lexical stock, while a high-school dropout would probably be more limited in the abstract use of language. The socially exposed, well-traveled person is most likely quite informed, with a broad fund of general information; in comparison, the lifelong ghetto resident who rarely leaves the neighborhood is probably less informed in world affairs. Therefore, intelligence is measured relative to the patient's premorbid life experiences. Consequently, the examiner must be able to differentiate between inability and lack of opportunity. For example, a limited use of low-frequency words is usually the result of lack of education rather than intellectual deficiency. Therefore, a patient with only elementary education who demonstrates good abstractive skills is most likely highly intelligent.

The therapist's dialogue with the patient often provides a sufficient basis for the assessment of his or her *vocabulary, use of words,* and *fund of information.* When the therapist is in doubt, or when the patient is sparingly verbal, specific questions such as "Who is the mayor of this city?" or "How far is it from Los Angeles to New York?" can provide a reasonable estimate of the patient's knowledge.

Use of previously learned material is ordinarily tested through basic arithmetic calculations or simple problem-solving exercises. Completion of a conceptual series or a problem-solving exercise in an unfamiliar situation allows the assessment of *abstraction* abilities. For example, the patient is asked to complete a series of numbers (1, 2, 1, 4, 1, 8, 1, __, __, __.) or a series of letters (A, C, E, G, I, __, __, __.) by adding three numbers or letters, respectively.

Reliability

Throughout the diagnostic session, the examiner is also assessing the patient's prognosis. The value of diagnostic work is measured by its capacity to predict the outcome of therapeutic intervention. Therefore, clinical diagnosis must provide sufficient information on both pathology and prospects for treatment. The prognosis is based on, among other variables, the *reliability* of the patient's presentation. Many ingredients in the presentation by the patient contribute to reliability. General intelligence, clarity and chronology of background information presented by the patient, and the availability of alternative sources of information to validate accuracy of presented material are all significant. The confabulations of the chronic alcoholic with memory deficits, the confusion of the patient in an acute psychotic state, or the intentionally exaggerated and distorted report of the individual with antisocial tendencies are examples of unreliable presentations. The prognostic meanings of these situations are based on the patient's capacity for *insight* and *judgment* (Rosenthal & Akiskal, 1985).

Morrison (1997) considers *insight* in reference to "the patient's ideas as to what is wrong." When the patient is aware of his problems and exhibits an understanding of the causes and development of these problems, insight is considered good. Adequate intelligence is usually a prerequisite for insight, but intelligence does not ensure insight. Patients lacking insight are typically suffering from psychosis, severe depression, or cognitive losses. *Judgment,* according to Morrison (1997), "refers to the patient's ability to decide what course of action is appropriate to achieve realistic goals." Like insight, judgment is based on intellectual adequacy, but intelligence alone is not sufficient to guarantee good judgment. The patient's ability to adjust to social demands and to deal appropriately with social encounters is an excellent indicator of judgment (Strub & Black, 1993).

The examiner needs to evaluate judgment within the context of his or her own history. In addition, the examiner observes the patient's behavior during the MSE and assesses the appropriateness of his or her actions. The examiner asks questions that require the patient to relate to common social situations and to present an understanding of social cause-and-effect relationships. Hypothetical situations are presented to assess the patient's comprehension of the consequences of particular social actions. For example, the examiner might ask, "What would you do if you were the first person to see smoke in a movie theater?" or "What would you do if you lost a book that you had borrowed from a friend?" Patients suffering from delirium, dementia, or various psychotic states are among the individuals who will not demonstrate good judgment. Sudden changes in judgment can provide signs of a serious illness. For example, a recent onset of violent behavior can be a warning sign consequent to an aggressive metastatic brain tumor.

USE OF THE MSE

Kaplan and Saccuzza (2001) state categorically "There is no room for amateurs or self-appointed practitioners when a mental status examination is needed." The act of clinical diagnosis is, by definition, an act of expert decision making. Such an act is usually entrusted to the hands of professionals, individuals considered knowledgeable and able to use their knowledge to determine the nature of a clinical entity and the most profitable treatment approach. Knowledge in the field of mental health is very broad, based on a number of disciplines, a multitude of perspectives, and a variety of approaches to the understanding of human behavior. Consequently, a diagnostician not only considers the patient's presenting complaints, but also actively searches for a particular constellation of symptoms and signs that validates specific a priori assumptions about human behavior and psychopathology. These a priori assumptions are theoretically based; therefore, each diagnostician, regardless of the tools of investigation, is guided by a theoretical orientation and a philosophical inclination. The value of the MSE is demonstrated in its adaptability as a diagnostic tool in the hands of clinicians from various theoretical perspectives.

Psychiatry and psychology alike have accepted the practicality of the DSM-IV, recognizing the versatility of the multiaxial classification system. After a decade of extensive research, the Structured Clinical Interview for DSM-IV (SCID) was published by First and his colleagues (1997). The SCID is considered one of the best extensions of the MSE toward the diagnosis of Axis I disorders. Milton and coauthors (1997) consider the SCID as one of the most productive diagnostic tools for forensic purposes.

Folstein et al. (1975) were among the first to deviate from the traditional MSE and develop a brief test of cognitive functions. The resulting Mini-Mental

Status Examination is currently used quite extensively as a reliable screener for dementia and generalized progressive decline of cognitive skills. The development of the Neurobehavioral Cognitive Status Examination (NCSE) by Kiernan et al. (1987) has added to the diagnostic arsenal of the neuropsychologist a more elaborate structured screener of cognitive abilities, sensitive to mild dysfunctions, which are typically overlooked by the more traditional MSEs.

Morrison (1997) writes extensively about the use of the MSE in the overall assessment of health and the ability of the mental status examiner to identify specific medical conditions underlying psychological facades. According to Morrison, the MSE offers an "organizational framework for the observations we use to evaluate and reevaluate the health of our patients" (p.13).

The value of the MSE in working with children and adolescents was only recently recognized. Historically, diagnostic work with children is highly dependent on test data, reports and observations from parents and individuals with role relationships with the child (i.e., teacher), and narrative reports of facts and unstructured observations. Sabatino et al. (1998) have recognized in the clinical decision-making process of the MSE a "collaborative" and validating contribution to the diagnostic picture obtained from tests, reports, and informal observations. The interactive nature of the MSE is particularly adaptive to the clinical encounter with children.

The *Handbook of Diagnostic and Structured Interviewing*, by Rogers (2001), is one of the best overviews of the current use of the many variants of MSEs and the multiple adaptations of this phenomenological assessment tool to specific pathological populations. The interested reader will find Rogers's book a valuable resource for its comprehensive treatment of many forms of MSEs and structured interviews, in terms of their psychometric properties, clinical utility, and empirically established reliability and validity values.

This chapter is too limited in its space to allow for a comprehensive demonstration of the multiple clinical uses of the MSE approach. Nevertheless, it will review some of the more common uses of the MSE, along with clinical examples to demonstrate features that are unique to each of these approaches.

Toward a DSM-IV Diagnosis

The phenomenological approach to diagnosis considers, differentially, questions of *etiology* and *description* of a clinical entity. True to tradition, the etiological question differentiates between organic (physiological) and functional conditions (Levenson, 1981), while the descriptive question differentiates among known syndromes or recognizable constellations of signs and symptoms. Maxmen (1986), in discussing the DSM-III approach to assessment, has stressed two fundamental principles: *parsimony* and *hierarchy*. The first principle, that of parsimony, directs the diagnostician to look for "the single most elegant, economical, and efficient diagnosis that accounts for all the available data"

(p. 40); if one diagnosis does not explain *all* the available information, the clinician is directed to seek the fewest diagnostic possibilities. The second principle, that of hierarchy, "is that mental disorders generally exist on a hierarchy of syndromes, which tend to decline in severity from top to bottom" (p. 40). When both principles operate together, as when an individual presents symptoms indicative of several disorders, the most parsimonious decision is to diagnose the person as having the most severe syndrome.

The DSM-IV continues to maintain, both in spirit and practice, these two diagnostic principles. Practitioners are encouraged to avoid multiplicity of diagnoses on Axes I and II. In addition, the classification of clinical disorders and conditions intended to be reported on Axes I and II maintain a hierarchical sequence of declining severity. For example, on Axis I, psychotic disorders are listed before mood disorders, while the disorders on Axis II start with paranoid personality disorder. The Decision Trees for Differential Diagnosis suggested by the DSM-IV-TR are aimed "to aid the clinician in understanding the organization and the hierarchical structure of the DSM-IV classification." (American Psychiatric Association, 2000, p. 745). This hierarchy, the specific diagnostic criteria provided, and the decision trees provide the diagnostician with an agenda for inquiry, and a logic for diagnostic decisions.

Nelson and Barlow (1981) recognize several factors involved in deciding upon an appropriate diagnosis. First, the diagnostician needs a solid base of knowledge in abnormal psychology, and has to know the *response covariations* for clinical entities (a list of responses, cognitions, and emotions that tend to occur together and are distinctive features of a given pathological condition). For example, some of the typical signs of schizophrenia are delusions, auditory hallucinations, illogical thinking, inappropriate affect, and loosening of associations; however, the presence of these signs *together* with significant intellectual impoverishment might indicate a neurological condition. Second, the diagnostician has to have the skills to elicit in the patient sufficient responses to allow for a decision as to which of the known *response covariations* are present in this particular individual. Third, the diagnostician must be familiar with the specific diagnostic criteria of the DSM-IV.

The examiner actively elicits material that will help in the determination of whether the patient's signs and symptoms meet the DSM-IV criteria for particular diagnoses. For example, criterion 3 for the diagnosis of obsessive-compulsive personality disorder states: "is excessively devoted to work and productivity to the exclusion of leisure activities and friendships (not accounted for by obvious economic necessity)" (American Psychiatric Association, 2000, p. 729). Therefore, the examiner cannot be satisfied with the patient's presentation of his or her devotion to work, but will need to question the patient further to determine that indeed such devotion is not in response to economical hardship.

The hierarchical structure of the DSM-IV is another reason for the active nature of the diagnostic inquiry. The clinician needs to compare the presenting clinical picture with each possible syndrome, starting with the most severe. Therefore, the examiner must structure the interview so as to provide the data necessary for hierarchical diagnostic decision making. For example, reported delusions, which are included in criterion A for the diagnosis of schizophrenia (2000, p. 312), require an examination for possible signs of an underlying medical or neurological condition, because delusions are also predominant characteristics of syndromes with an underlying medical condition (such as delirium).

CASE HISTORY

Ms. E. was a thirty-six-year-old Caucasian, divorced mother of two teenagers who lived with her. She reported that she and her children "have regular and friendly contacts" with her ex-husband. Ms. E., who had been partially hearing impaired since early childhood, had been unemployed for the past twenty months, following a car accident in which she sustained head injuries. She was amnesic for the accident details, but recalled driving the car away from an unsuccessful job interview. Recent medical and neuropsychological tests found her physically and cognitively fully recovered from the accident, without any evidence of lasting brain dysfunction. She was referred by the rehabilitation services department for assessment of the possible cause for her failure to find a job. The MSE was recorded as follows:

Ms. E. was slim and petite. Her bright complexion was porcelainlike, giving her attractive facial features an aura of fragility and coldness. A noticeable small scar under her chin seemed like an intrusion to the symmetry and perfection of her facial lines (Ms. E. later explained that this scar, which "always reminds me how close I was to God," resulted from the car accident). Her well-styled hair and casual attire, along with her informal but haughty manner of relating, initially made the examiner somewhat uneasy and apprehensive. Ms. E. was an alert, compliant (but not quite cooperative), and seemingly open person, whose guardedness was manifested in her careful choice of words and frequent silent pauses. She sat rigidly in her chair, often "picking" nervously on her fingernails, the only significant bodily sign of tension. Her eye contact with the examiner seemed forced, giving the impression of a continuous "tug of war" with him; the examiner felt annoyed at times, when her penetrating eyes seemed to look not at him but through him.

Ms. E. was oriented to time, place, and person. Her intelligence, language skills, and ability to abstract were above average, commensurate with her college education. She spoke of her early childhood, her family, and her marital difficulties in an organized, chronological order. She related her history in a matter-of-fact tone, typifying the constricted range of affect that dominated the entire interview. Her vocal tone, along with her forceful and calculated verbal expression, alerted the examiner to consider her apathy a mask for underlying anxiety and anger. Similarly, the functional rapport established with Ms. E. was nothing more than a facade of cordiality, hiding a sense of seclusiveness and coldness. Ms. E.'s verbal expression was characterized by a slow and at times hesitant rate of speech, which became somewhat pressured when she responded to questions probing emotionally laden information.

She admitted having had periods of depression prior to the car accident, relating these feelings to specific difficulties she had had with her ex-husband. She impressed the examiner with her attentiveness, with the clarity and logic of her answers, and with her excellent memory. The intellectualized style of her presentation, her excellent command of the language, and the goal-directed nature of her answers seemed paradoxical to her claim to have "psychic powers." With the exception of this statement, there was no evidence for disturbed language functions or thought disorder. When asked to elaborate, Ms. E. claimed that she was able to communicate with dead relatives and to heal the sick. She also stated that the car accident was "God's way of granting me life" so that she could continue her "life mission." Such divine intervention was needed, according to Ms. E., because prior to the accident she had been lonely and desperate and felt useless, particularly as a mother. When questioned about suicidal ideation, she smiled (as if amused at such a ridiculous thought) and said, "It's against my faith; I wouldn't even think about such a cop-out." Ms. E. admitted to having difficulties falling asleep. When asked about her failure to find a job, she said, "I don't know . . . it's hard to find something in my neighborhood." Later she said, "I don't want to drive anymore." She rejected the examiner's suggestion that the car accident had made her fearful of driving, but she admitted that prior to the accident she had had no such inhibitions.

Ms. E. was a reliable interviewee in her ability to provide factual information. However, her judgment and insight were limited. When told that she would be referred for psychological testing, she seemed confused and surprised, stating, "I need a job. I don't understand why everybody thinks something is wrong with me."

This MSE is interesting because of the differential diagnostic possibilities and because the examiner's obvious countertransference reactions cast doubt on the objectivity of some of the observations. DSM-IV criteria guide the examiner to consider a posttraumatic stress disorder on Axis I, together with premorbid possibilities of a psychotic or affective nature. More information should be gathered to support a decision regarding an Axis II diagnosis.

Neuropsychological Evaluation

Traditional psychiatry and neurology have failed to provide sufficient understanding of cognitive and emotional consequences of brain injury. The general label of *organic brain syndrome* was used to differentiate conditions with an etiology of neurological losses from other clinical entities, without sufficient diagnostic specificity or pragmatic recommendations for treatment. The field of neuropsychology provided the paradigm and the knowledge necessary for the development of assessment techniques and the specific guidelines for functional management and rehabilitative intervention. The past two decades have witnessed a significant growth in the body of neuropsychological research and literature and the development of diagnostic tools and more productive treatment methods of many neurobehavioral disorders.

The MSE, with its sensitivity to pathognomonic signs and symptoms, has become a natural constituent of the comprehensive neuropsychological evaluation. Many writers consider the MSE a necessary addition to both neurological and psychiatric diagnostic assessments (Berg, et al., 1987; Strub & Black, 1993). Snyder and Nussbaum recommend to have the MSE as the first part of the diagnostic session "because it colors the remainder of the test in terms of reliability" (Snyder & Nussbaum, 1998, p. 12). The trained clinician, knowledgeable about brain functions and the characteristics of neurological disorders, can depend on MSE findings to help determine the need for and the direction of a more elaborate neuropsychological assessment.

Theories of brain functions present the central nervous system as a functional organ system, controlling interacting processes in a hierarchical fashion. The integrity of more complex functions (such as thinking and social judgment) is based on the integrity of simpler processes (such as movement, perception, and speech). Therefore, the MSE is conducted in a systematic and orderly fashion, starting with basic brain functions and working up to more integrative cognitive operations. For example, if a patient consistently fails to understand simple questions such as "Did you eat breakfast today?" or "Is it day or night now?" then a request for proverb interpretation is unnecessary.

The behavioral categories most commonly observed in the neuropsychological MSE are as follows, in order of assessment: level of consciousness, attention, language skills, amnestic abilities, constructional skills (drawings or working with three-dimensional configurations), and higher cognitive functions. More elaborate discussions of the MSE and its use in neuropsychology can be found in Berg and colleagues (1987), Strub and Black (1993), and Groth-Marnat (2000).

CASE HISTORY

A twenty-seven-year-old male with a short history of unusual behavior was brought to a local hospital by his roommate. Five days prior to the hospitalization, while intoxicated in a bar, the patient was involved in a brawl. In the days that followed, he seemed increasingly strange. He was confused, talked "differently," and seemed unable to relate appropriately to others. Routine medical and neurological exams found him healthy. When initially interviewed, he was found to be alert, but disoriented and not attentive. He manifested a number of signs of disturbed thought processes. His flat affect, inappropriate speech, and withdrawn manner led the medical staff to consult with a psychiatrist. The patient was admitted to a psychiatric unit, with a provisional diagnosis of schizophreniform disorder. Following several days without improvement, a neuropsychological assessment was ordered. The MSE report stated the following:

> The right-handed young male was awake and alert. He failed digit-repetition tasks, but seemed attentive, vigilant, and goal-oriented while copying geometric figures. His speech was fluent but tangential, with many paraphasic distortions. His comprehension was very limited: simple verbal instructions were not followed; he recognized very few common objects when asked to point to them; and he failed to repeat words or sentences. While he seemed to understand a few simple instructions, he had word-finding difficulties. Upon further observation, he was found to be quite efficient with constructional tasks, particularly when instructions were given nonverbally and he relied on mimicking or following the examiner's gestures.

The presence of many aphasic signs, as the single, most obvious cluster of disabilities, persuaded the examiner to direct further diagnostic efforts toward the left temporal lobe. More extensive neurological tests (including arteriography and a computerized tomogrophy scan) identified a left posterior temporal mass. Surgery confirmed a large subdural hematoma, consistent with an injury resulting from a violent blow.

Psychopharmacological Evaluation

Clinical psychopharmacology is by now a highly respected treatment approach to mental illness. In spite of philosophical and theoretical differences on psychopharmocology, and more than a century of animosity between the medical and the psychological models, the future clinical psychologist will advocate and even practice a combined mode of treatment. The paradigm of integrating psychotherapy with drug treatment is already an undeniable reality.

Levenson (1981) identifies the main objective for drug treatment as the remission of specific distressing states. He emphasizes that such intervention is not a cure. Alone or together with psychotherapy and other environmental changes, drug treatment can help sufferers improve the quality of their life. Levenson discusses the variables involved in the decision to use psychotropic drugs and the choice of the most appropriate drug and dosage: (1) the knowledge and experience of the clinician, (2) a physical and laboratory examination to assess the patient's physiological status, (3) the patient's medical and psychiatric history, and (4) "a working knowledge of psychopharmacologically responsive psychopathology" (Levenson, 1981, p. viii). This working knowledge includes the ability to recognize signs and symptoms of psychiatric states that are responsive to drug treatment and the capacity to assess these syndromes in a relatively rapid fashion. Levenson's Rapid Psychiatric Assessment is actually an elaborate MSE. Janick et al., while describing the psychiatric evaluation leading to psychopharmacological decisions, state that, "The mental status examination is the most important aspect of this phase and scrutinizes how an individual is feeling, acting, and thinking at the time of the interview" (Janick et al., 1993, p. 11). This structured interview consists of a subjective and objective component. In the subjective component, the examiner uses specific questions to guide the patient to describe past psychiatric history (including effectiveness of specific drugs) and recent or current symptoms (such as sleep disturbances or specific feelings or thoughts). The objective component consists of the examiner's observations of signs, which together with the presenting symptoms can indicate toward the presence of a drug-responsive syndrome. This objective component is a set of observations made by the examiner based on a priori expectations that certain aggregates of pathognomonic signs and symptoms are indicative of underlying mental disorders responsive to psychopharmacological treatment.

Disorders with or without a medical or neurological etiology often present similar symptoms. Acute states of brain trauma, for example (such as intoxication or lowered level of consciousness immediately following surgery or head trauma), are often contraindicative to drug treatment. Therefore, the differential diagnosis of these conditions is crucial to the pharmacotherapist. Consequently, the MSE utilized for drug treatment purposes is similar to that used by neuropsychologists. For example, the idiosyncratic production of word sounds can be part of a syndrome indicating a psychotic process. However, when the patient demonstrates partial loss of recent memory, impaired intellectual functions, an intact capacity to repeat digits forward but serious impairment in backward repetition, the presence of paraphasia is understood as aphasic reactions to brain trauma.

CASE HISTORY

A thirty-two-year-old male, recently admitted to a psychiatric inpatient unit, is examined by a psychiatrist, who recorded the following clinical profile:

Based on information from relatives, the patient has no psychiatric history. His wife recalls recent complaints (for the past seven to eight weeks) of sleep difficulties, periods of agitation, and irritability. She also reluctantly admitted being annoyed with the increased frequency of her husband's sexual advances. Physical and laboratory parameters were within normal limits. The review of symptoms found him somewhat concerned about initial and intermittent sleep disturbances, but he insisted that he has a positive outlook toward the future. He stated, "Doc, actually I feel great . . . never felt so energized in my life." The MSE found him alert, somewhat distractible, and quite euphoric, with an overall hypermotility. His speech was slightly pressured and at times incoherent, and his accelerated thought production included flight of ideas. There were no signs of neuropsychological losses.

This patient was diagnosed as having an acute hypomanic reaction, and he was judged a good candidate for pharmacotherapy with the drug of choice valproic acid. The observed agitation and hypermotility indicated the need to prescribe a major tranquilizer along with the valproic acid.

This chapter introduced the MSE as part of an initial diagnostic interview and as one of the most significant sources of data toward the formal description of a clinical diagnosis. The MSE was described as a set of systematic behavioral observations in pursuit of known manifestations of pathological conditions. The categories of behavioral observations collected during the MSE were outlined and discussed. The value of the MSE as a diagnostic tool was presented in terms of its adaptability to various theoretical perspectives and patient populations. Case examples were presented to demonstrate the uses of the MSE by clinical psychologists, neuropsychologists, and pharmacotherapists.

REFERENCES

American Psychiatric Association. (1980). *Diagnostic and Statistical Manual of Mental Disorders*, 3rd ed. Washington, DC: American Psychiatric Association.
American Psychiatric Association. (1987). *Diagnostic and Statistical Manual of Mental Disorders*, 3rd ed., rev. Washington, DC: American Psychiatric Association.

American Psychiatric Association. (1994). *Diagnostic and Statistical Manual of Mental Disorders*, 4th ed. Washington, DC: American Psychiatric Association.

American Psychiatric Association. (2000). *Diagnostic and Statistical Manual of Mental Disorders*, 4th ed., text revised. Washington, DC: American Psychiatric Association.

Berg, R., Franzen, M., & Wedding, D. (1987). *Screening for Brain Impairment: A Manual for Mental Health Practice*. New York: Springer.

Berrios, G. E. (1996). *The History of Mental Symptoms: Descriptive Psychopathology Since the Nineteenth Century*. Cambridge, England: Cambridge University Press.

First, M. B., Spitzer, R. L., Williams, J. B. W., & Gibbon, M. (1997). *Structured Clinical Interview for DSM-IV Disorders (SCID)*. Washington, DC: American Psychiatric Association.

Folstein, M. F., Folstein, S. E., & McHugh, P. R. (1975). Mini-mental State: A Practical Method of Grading Cognitive State of Patients for the Clinician. *Journal of Psychiatric Research* 12:189–198.

Freedman, A. M., Kaplan, H. I., & Sadock, B. J. (1975). *Comprehensive Textbook in Psychiatry*, Vol. 1. Baltimore: Williams & Wilkins.

Groth-Marnat, G., ed. (2000). *Neuropsychological Assessment in Clinical Practice: A Guide to Test Interpretation and Integration*. New York: Wiley and Sons.

Janick, P. G., Davis, J. M., Preskorn, S. H., & Ayd, F. J. (1993). *Principles and Practice of Psychopharmacotherapy*. Baltimore: Williams and Wilkins.

Kiernan, R. J., Mueller, J., Langston, J. W., & Van Dyke, C. (1987). The Neuro-Behavioral Cognitive Screening Examination: A brief but quantitative approach to cognitive assessment. *Annals of Internal Medicine* 107:481–485.

Kraepelin, E. (1904). *Lectures on Clinical Psychiatry*. London: Balliere, Tindall, and Cox.

Kaplan, R. M., & Saccuzza, D. P. (2001). *Psychological Testing: Principles, Applications, and Issues*, 5th ed. Belmont, CA: Wadsworth.

Levenson, A. J. (1981). *Basic Psychopharmacology*. New York: Springer.

Lewis, N. D. C. (1934). *Outlines for Psychiatric Examinations*. Albany: New York State Department of Mental Hygiene.

Luria, A. (1973). *The Working Brain*. New York: Basic.

Maxmen, J. S. (1986). *Essential Psychopathology*. New York: Norton.

Mendel, W. M. (1976). *Schizophrenia: The Experience and Its Treatment*. San Francisco: Jossey-Bass.

Milton, G. B., Petrila, J., Poythress, N. G., & Slobogin, C. (1997). *Psychological Evaluations for the Courts: A Handbook for Mental Health Professionals and Lawyers*, 2nd ed. New York: Guilford.

Morrison, J. (1997) *When Psychological Problems Mask Medical Disorders: A Guide for Psychotherapists*. New York: Guilford.

Nathan, P. E. (1981). Symptomatic diagnosis and behavioral assessment: A synthesis? In *Behavioral Assessment of Adult Disorders*. New York: Guilford.

Nelson, R. O., & Barlow, D. H. (1981). Behavioral assessment: Basic strategies and initial procedures. In *Behavioral Assessment of Adult Disorders*. New York: Guilford.

Noyes, A. P., & Kolb, L. C. (1963). *Modern Clinical Psychiatry*, 6th ed. Philadelphia: Saunders.

Pope, B. (1979). *The Mental Health Interview: Research and Applications*. New York: Pergamon.

Rogers, R. (2001). *Handbook of Diagnostic and Structured Interviewing*. New York: Guilford.

Rosenthal, R. H., & Akiskal, H. S. (1985). Mental status examination. *In Diagnostic Interviewing*. New York: Plenum.

Sabatino, D. A., Fuller, C. G., & Altizer, E. A. (1998). Assessing current psychological status. In *Psychological Assessment of Children: Best Practices for School and Clinical Settings*, 2nd ed. New York: Wiley and Sons.

Slater, E., & Roth, M. (1969). *Clinical Psychiatry*, 3rd ed. Baltimore: Williams & Wilkins.

Snyder, P. J., & Nussbaum, P. D., eds. (1998). *Clinical Neuropsychology: A Pocket Handbook for Assessment*. Washington, DC: American Psychological Association.

Spitzer, R. L. (1976). More on pseudoscience in science and the case for psychiatric diagnosis: A critique of D. L. Rosenhan's "On being sane in insane places" and "The contextual nature of psychiatric diagnosis." *Archives of General Psychiatry* 33:459–470.

Strub, R. L., & Black, F. W. (1993). *The Mental Status Examination in Neurology*, 3rd ed. Philadelphia: Davis.

Taylor, M. A. (1981). *The Neuropsychiatric Mental Status Examination*. New York: Spectrum.

Wing, J. K., Cooper, J. E., & Sartorius, N. (1974) *The Measurement and Classification of Psychiatric Symptoms*. Cambridge: Cambridge University Press.

19

ASSESSMENT OF
SUICIDE POTENTIAL

Robert I. Yufit, Ph.D., ABPP

A dvances in our attempts to assess suicide risk and suicidal behavior continue to be problematic. A major part of the problem is the complexity of the task. Suicide potential is a multidimensional problem, dealing with both internal vulnerabilities of the person and external stresses of daily life. The national tragedy of 9/11 and the periodic episodes of violence in our schools and in other environs tend to increase the intensity of daily life stresses. How can we best assess these vulnerabilities?

There has been an increase in the development of self-report questionnaires in recent years, but they are not in widespread use (Cull & Gill, 1986; Reynolds, 1987), and the clinical interview remains the most common means to assess suicidality and its many nuances.

A probable shortcoming of such assessment techniques is the lack of comprehensiveness of any single instrument, since no single method is likely to capture complex, multidetermined behavior (Maris et al., 1992). Few, if any, of these instruments include any attempt to measure immediate versus long-term risk or try to distinguish self-harm from self-destructive behaviors. Does the individual want to punish one's self or someone else? Does the person really want to die?

It is quite clear that attempts to assess self-harm and suicidal behavior need to be addressed by use of a battery of assessment techniques, which would include a clinical interview and would have a focus on assessing the intent of self-harm and self-destruction.

Ambivalence is an important variable to be explored in the assessment process. There is considerable ambivalence in almost all suicidal behavior, at all levels of intention (Beck et al., 1979; Menninger, 1938). Many persons are simply not certain what they want the outcome of their actions to be, but they do know they want to do *something* to themselves—or to *communicate* something to someone else. Thus we don't always know whether we are evaluating an attempt at communication or an act geared toward actual self-destruction.

385

Some suicidal patients' intentions are clearly manipulative. They may want to elicit sympathy from the clinician (or from a neglected loved one). They may mean to take into account the many variables related to suicidal behavior. The precipitating factors and the person's ability to handle change need careful exploration. These variables (objective and subjective) must be explored to see whether they are present (this is *screening*), and some kind of assessment of the current *degree* or *intensity* of these variables must be made. A clinical interview should permit such an assessment, but the interview needs to provide an answer to the ultimate question: How serious is this person's intent?

In other words, the interview should be quantified so that the degree of lethality of any present suicide potential can be determined. Such an assessment often helps to determine actual intention—whether the patient wishes to harm one's self, or harm others, or gain attention from inattentive others, or actually end life. Some overt behaviors are very obvious in their self-harm or self-destructive intent. Others are more indirect and may be distinguished by accident-proneness or as an abusive lifestyle (overeating, excessive drinking, smoking, illicit drug use, and overwork are examples).

THE QUANTIFIED FOCUSED INTERVIEW

To explore the important variables, a Quantified Focused Interview (QFI) format has been developed. The interview covers specific variables that are known to be correlated with suicide potential and are quantified by thirteen rating scales. A total score can be derived to provide an index of suicide potentiality. The goal is not to try to predict suicidal behavior as a specific act, but to establish some guidelines for assessing suicide risk or potential.

The task of suicide screening and assessment can be divided into two broad evaluation areas:

1. Is the person suicidal? (screening task)
2. If so, what is the *degree of lethality* that a suicide attempt may carry? (assessment task)

Will the suicide attempt be a bid for attention, an attempt to create shame, or a attempt to do limited harm? Or will the behavior be aimed at a level of lethality so high that death is the most likely outcome? A defined plan must be assessed in terms of its likely outcome. Some plans are definitely aimed at survival, not death. An example would be a person who turns on the gas stove, but turns off the pilot light, thereby ensuring no explosion, all while her family is sitting in the next room.) Of course, the survival plan may be based on miscalculation (medication dosage, hoped-for rescue), and death may result. Many completed suicides happen this way.

The *major indices of lethality* are defined by the

- Actual suicide behavior
- Likelihood that the plan that is being considered will be carried out
- Degree of ambivalence based on intention (unconscious versus conscious)
- Probability that the result will be death, and
- Method(s) available and finally chosen

Degree of lethality (in the former case of actual behavior) *is based on*

- Degree of reversibility of the act (for example, jumping from a high place versus superficial wrist cutting)
- Probability of rescue (Was the timing an attempt geared to coincide with being discovered?)
- Method chosen in the light of methods available (for example, taking several pills from a bottle of one hundred while at home in a tenth-floor apartment)
- Degree of medical injury resulting from the behavior (The more serious the injury, the greater the likelihood that lethality intent was high. The patient's physical health and intellect must also be considered.)

In assessing patients who are reporting suicidal ideation but who have not yet acted, the *plan* can be evaluated in similar terms. How reversible is the method being considered? What is the risk for rescue? How lethal is the method compared to others available?

Establishing the patients' *intention* along with the method chosen will allow for a measurement of *ambivalence*; both parameters are critical to evaluating the intensity of the patient's motivation (Yufit, 1992). An "accidental overdose" is rare. If intentions are explored in detail, it often becomes clear that unconscious desires have played a vital role in outcome.

While the QFI can be more useful than the more subjective nonfocused interview by providing some structure, the use of specific assessment scales directs the clinician's attention to exploring the intensity of suicidal ideation, by requiring the clinician to give weight in the rating of these relevant areas. The total score of the summed weighted ratings will indicate the degree of lethality of the patient's intentions.

SUICIDE ASSESSMENT CHECKLIST

Very few suicide screening or assessment scales have been universally accepted, mainly because most have a poor record of establishing acceptable validity and reliability (Lester, 1978). Follow-up studies have generally been adequate. They are few in number and often poorly designed. There is the added problem that effective treatment may "contaminate" the development of future suicidal ideation or acting out. Yet how are we to know whether a patient evaluated to have a high suicide potential is actually suicidal unless we have short-term and long-term follow-up?

This problem also brings up the issue of evaluating a patient for short-term risk—that is, the likelihood that suicidal behavior will occur within the next twenty-four to forty-eight hours. Longer-term suicide risk (that is, the risk that the patient will attempt suicide within the next thirty days or longer) may be indicated by particular characterological patterns, although research has not yet defined a specific "suicide personality." However, vulnerability to stress induced by loss and by change will give indications of long-term risk.

Definition of the anatomy of these vulnerabilities is a core task for suicide assessment research. We should also explore and define those coping skills that enable "healthy" persons to deal with loss and change so that we can use therapeutic intervention to develop these skills in our suicidal patients. A measure of coping skills is also needed and is being developed to incorporate the concepts of Seligman's Positive Psychology (Snyder & Lopez, 2002).

In some instances, the clinical judgment of the experienced clinician should supercede the results of an assessment technique that has low validity or reliability. Such assessment techniques should be improved, replaced, or supplemented by serial assessment or an assessment battery.

A useful procedure for establishing the utility of suicidal screening and assessment procedures is to develop such a procedure based on empirically established variables. Such variables are really correlates of suicidal behavior. If they are present, suicidal behavior can be considered more likely. Correlates can be presented in the form of a *checklist*, which can then be used to categorize interview data. The checklist instrument can be constructed around these empirical clusters of variables and can enable the clinician to do a more comprehensive assessment.

Such an instrument, called the Suicide Assessment Checklist (SAC), has been developed (Yufit, 1989), but has not yet been sufficiently researched to determine its validity (see figure 19.1). The SAC allows the interview data to be categorized based on empirical research. Such an assessment procedure is an abbreviation of the task posed by the more detailed clinical assessment by interview, the QFI. The SAC consists of sixty items, many of them numerically weighted on the basis of empirical evidence from formal research studies, and from accumulated "hands-on" knowledge of clinicians who have had extensive experience evaluating suicidal patients.

The SAC is now in its third revision, with more specific questions focused on empirical correlates of suicide. The SAC can be used with adolescents as well as with adults of all age ranges.

The SAC can usually be scored in about twenty minutes by the experienced clinician after asking the necessary questions, or it can be applied to the

Suicide Assessment Checklist

Rater _____

Patient Name: _____

Age: _____ Sex: M F Date _____

Estimate of Suicide Potential: H (high) M (medium) L (low) ? (uncertain)

Level of Confidence: H (high) M (medium) L (low)

Directions: Score each item on basis of interview responses or chart data. Verify
doubtful data with family members when possible. If no parenthesis after
item, score +1 for each "yes", or use listed weighted score in parenthesis.
"No" or "uncertain" scores = 0. Try to minimize "uncertain" scores. Sum
all scores and categorize as indicated. High total score is a danger sign.

Suicide History (max section score = 22):	Yes	No	Uncertain
1. Prior suicide attempt (×4); self-harm (×2)	___	___	___
2. Two or more highly lethal* attempts in past year (×4)	___	___	___
3. Prior suicide threats or ideation	___	___	___
4. Suicide attempts in the family (×2)	___	___	___
5. Completed attempts in family (×4)	___	___	___
6. Current suicidal preoccupation, threats, attempt (×2); detailed, highly lethal plan (×2); access to weapon, medication (×2); if all three "yes" = 6	___	___	___
7. Ongoing preoccupation with death	___	___	___

Psychiatric History (max score = 20):			
8. Drug, alcohol abuse (×6)	___	___	___
9. Dx of mental disorder (×2); Dx schiz. or bipolar (×4)	___	___	___
10. Poor impulse control; if current (×2)	___	___	___
11. Explosive rage episodes (circle: recent or past)	___	___	___
12. Recklessness/accident prone	___	___	___
13. Panic attacks (single (×3); recurrent (×5))	___	___	___

School (max score = 8):	or *Job* (max score = 8)			
14. Grade failure	14. Demotion (×2)	___	___	___
15. Rejection, poor social relations	15. Rejection	___	___	___
16. Probation or school drop	16. Fired (×2) out	___	___	___

(continued)

Figure 19.1. Suicide Assessment Checklist © 2000 Robert I. Yufit, Ph.D. (revision no. 3).

*Highly lethal: low risk for rescue; serious medical injury (comatose); irreversibility

17. Unwanted change   17. unwanted change   ___ ___   ___
    of schools
18. Unwanted change   18. unwanted change   ___ ___   ___
    of schools
19. Anticip. of severe   19. Criminal Act   ___ ___   ___
    punishment

Family (max score = 30):
20. Recent major negative change (loss: death,   ___ ___   ___
    divorce (×4) serious health problem); irrevers.
    loss (×4); both (×8)
21. Lack of emotional support, estranged (×2)   ___ ___   ___
22. Loss of job (parent, spouse) (×4)   ___ ___   ___
23. Major depression in parent, spouse, sibling (×2) ___ ___   ___
24. Alcoholism, other drug use in family   ___ ___   ___
    member (×2)
25. Psychiatric illness in family member (×2)   ___ ___   ___
25a. If 23 + 24 + 25 = 6, add 6 more   ___ ___   ___
26. History of physical or sexual abuse   ___ ___   ___
    (both = ×4)

Societal (max score = 8):
27. Contagion suicide in community (×3)   ___ ___   ___
28. Economic downshift in community;   ___ ___   ___
    financial loss
29. Loss of major support system (family; job,   ___ ___   ___
    career; both (×4))

Personality/Behavior/Cognitive Style (max score = 82):
30. Hopelessness (×6)   ___ ___   ___
31. Depression (intensely depressed (×2);   ___ ___   ___
    agitated depress. (×4); both (×6))
32. Anger, hostility, aggression (all = ×3); held ___ ___   ___
    in, all (×6)
32a. If 30 + 31 + 32 = 18, add 10 more   ___ ___   ___
33. Mistrust (×2); paranoid level (×4)   ___ ___   ___
34. Disgust or despair (both = ×2)   ___ ___   ___
35. Withdrawn, isolated (loneliness) (×4)   ___ ___   ___
36. Low or no future time perspective (×6)   ___ ___   ___
37. High or dominant orientation to the   ___ ___   ___
    past (×4)
37a. If 36 = 37 = 10, add 10 more   ___ ___   ___
38. Perfectionism, rigidity, obsessive/   ___ ___   ___
    compulsive (any = ×6)
39. Lack of a sense of belonging (×5)   ___ ___   ___
40. Indifference, lack of motivation   ___ ___   ___
    (boredom = ×2)
41. Worthlessness, no one cares (×2)   ___ ___   ___

Figure 19.1. *(continued)*

42. Shame or guilt (both = ×4)   ___ ___   _____
    (either one = ×2)
43. Helplessness   ___ ___   _____
44. Inability to have fun, lacks sense of humor   ___ ___   _____
45. Extreme mood or energy fluctuation   ___ ___   _____
    (both = ×2)
46. Giving away valuables   ___ ___   _____

Physical (max score = 14):
47. Male (×2); Caucasian (×2); both yes (×4)   ___ ___   _____
48. Markedly delayed puberty   ___ ___   _____
49. Recent injury leads to impairment,   ___ ___   _____
    deformity; permanent (×2)
50. Loss of appetite, disinterest in food   ___ ___   _____
51. Marked weight loss (more than 10 lbs in   ___ ___   _____
    past 6 months = ×2)
52. Sleep disturbed (onset, middle, early   ___ ___   _____
    awakening) hypersomnia
53. Ongoing physical pain (×2)   ___ ___   _____

Interview Behavior (max score = 16):
54. Pt. encapsulated, noncommunicative (×2)   ___ ___   _____
55. Negative reaction of pt. to interviewer (×3)   ___ ___   _____
56. Negative reaction of interviewer to pt.   ___ ___   _____
57. Increasing distance in interaction during   ___ ___   _____
    interview (×4)
58. Increasing hostility, noncooperation by   ___ ___   _____
    pt. (×2)
59. Pt. highly self-critical, self-pitying (×2)   ___ ___   _____
60. Discusses death; suicide is only way out (×2)   ___ ___   _____

                                      Sum   ___ ___   _____

Suicide Risk Potential Guidelines: Score Range
          Very high risk   150–200 (prob. hospitalize)
          High risk   100–149
          Moderate risk   50–99
          Low risk   below 50

Level of ambivalence: High
                         Low

Current Intention
Seeks attention   immediate risk (espec. 25a+32a=yes):   H   M   L
Escape pain   long term risk: H   M   L
Punish self/others
Harm/injure self   Confidence level: High   Low/Manipulating
Wants to die   reasons:

Figure 19.1. *(continued)*

existing data. The SAC is scored on the basis of presence (Yes) or absence (No) of data and by summing the separate item weighted scores. The total SAC score will provide an index to suicide potential, as indicated on the form. These ranges have not as yet been validated. The SAC can be considered a checklist interview, focused on significant variables. A disadvantage is that such an interview can become "mechanical" and can lack the richness of a more intensive exploration. The QFI, which is more loosely structured, allows for more data to be gathered than is required for the rating scales. Genuine rapport between the patient and the clinician should be established before inquiries into these variables are made. Emergency room personnel find this format useful, as do school counselors.

The SAC contains three cluster groupings of items known to highly correlate with suicide potential. Positive scores on these three clusters (25a, 32a, and 37a) merit an added weighting and are considered an index of high lethality attempts as well as an indication of *immediate risk*. These clusters relate to hopelessness, anger, depression, drug abuse, family history, and time perspective. The SAC can be used with adolescents and has a section on school experiences.

THE TIME QUESTIONNAIRE

Another dimension quite relevant to suicide screening and assessment is time perspective. The Time Questionnaire (TQ) has been developed to provide a time profile (Yufit & Benzies, 1973; 1978). The TQ consists of four sections: present, future, past, and an information sheet. Each section contains individual items, which are scored according to a scoring manual. The future section asks the respondents to select a future year and then answer a series of items as if they were living in that future year *now*. A total score is derived from the summed individual items and section scores. A "lie scale" is used to detect attempts to distort in either direction—to "look bad" or to "look good." Extreme high or low scores raise this possibility.

The suicidal patient appears to have a unique time profile, different from that of the nonsuicidal person. Most suicide-prone patients have a minimal involvement in the future, as might be expected. The involvement in the present is also minimal and usually quite negative in tone. The bulk of the suicidal patient's time perspective is in the past. This preoccupation with the past usually takes two forms. One is a nostalgia for the "good old days" that cannot be recaptured, which results in frustration, considerable psychological pain, and depression. There is often a key person from the past or a more coveted environment that appears to be (or may actually be) permanently lost in the present and difficult or impossible to reestablish in the future. Such past experiences are often distorted by idealization.

The second orientation to the past that characterizes the suicidal patient is less a regression and more an obsession. The obsession usually takes the form

Table 19.1.   Time-Perspective Profiles

	Suicide Prone	Nonsuicidal	
		American	European/Asian
Focus on	Most cultures	American	European/Asian
Past:	High	Minimal	Minimal
Present:	Low and/or negative	Moderately high	Very high
Future:	Minimal or none	Very high	Moderately high

of a preoccupation with a poor decision made in the past and the apparent irreversibility of that decision in the present (examples include a poor career choice or job choice or the selection of an incompatible marital partner). The patient wishes to go back and relive the past, in order to undo the present dilemma. Time profiles on over a one thousand patients who had considered or attempted suicide demonstrated a very strong preoccupation with the past and rarely more than a one-year projection into the future (Yufit & Benzies, 1973).

The time perspective of most (nonsuicidal) Americans is focused in the future and, to a slightly lesser degree, in the present, with minimal involvement in the past. In our study, several hundred subjects, grouped in matched "control" populations, reflected this characteristic profile of time perspective. Use of the TQ on some European and Asian suicide-prone populations (Belgians, Germans, and Japanese) reveals a time-profile pattern identical to that of suicide-prone Americans, except that the European and Asian control subjects were somewhat more focused on the present than on the future. The time profiles of suicide-prone persons versus nonsuicidal persons are presented in table 19.1.

These time profiles were consistent in five years of field testing of several matched populations of clinical and nonclinical samples totaling over 1,600 persons (Yufit & Benzies, 1973). Time perspective is a useful indicator, but it is too narrow in scope to be used by itself, and a clinical interview is recommended. The TQ is best used serially, or in combination with other assessment procedures, to more clearly encompass the need for comprehensiveness in the evaluation of suicide potential. The TQ can also be used with adolescents.

COGNITIVE STYLE

It has been found that there is a particular cognitive style that characterizes suicidal patients. First, their thinking tends to be rigid (Neuringer, 1964; Schneidman, 1985). Suicide-prone patients do not easily develop alternative solutions to problems. They are unable to "roll with the punches." They lack resiliency and perspective. Their rigidity leads to the use of a word that suicidologists dislike hearing: *only*. "It is the *only* way out, the *only* think to do."

When rigidity is accompanied by two other commonly found feeling states among suicide-prone persons—*hopelessness* and *helplessness*—there is cause for even greater concern about suicide risk. Hopelessness implies a lack of trust and a diminished expectation that future desires and goals can be attained. It implies a lack of optimism that bad situations will improve or that losses can be replaced. Vulnerability to suicide attempts has been a key concept for a number of authors (Beck et al., 1975; Menninger, 1938; Schneidman, 1985). Helplessness often indicates a deficiency of internal assets, a lack of confidence, underdeveloped autonomy, a poor self-image, overdependency on nongiving others, and doubt regarding one's ability to influence or control one's future. The result is usually a low achievement drive and inadequate energy levels, which can lead to fear, anxiety, stagnation, and depression. Consequent failure to attain desired goals adds to feelings of helplessness, creating a downward spiral.

Frustration often builds when these feelings of hopelessness and helplessness persist and predominate. The rigidity minimizes any shift in thinking and thwarts efforts to find alternative solutions. When the resulting psychological pain is too great, suicide can become the "only" way out, often to lessen the pain—a need that may be experienced as more critical than the wish to die. Identification and assessment of this pain is critical to timely intervention.

Excessive expectations can also increase the likelihood of failure and feelings of helplessness. Perfectionism frequently accompanies rigidity and is a characteristic commonly found in achievement-oriented young people who exhibit suicidal behavior, as well as in adults (Yufit, 1992).

Anger is a frequent result of continued feelings of helplessness and hopelessness. Because passivity is often a function of rigidity and helplessness, anger may not be overtly expressed.

Anger turned inward is probably one of the major psychodynamics that pulls the trigger of the suicidal impulse, wrote Menninger (1938) in his classic book *Man against Himself*. Suicidal persons may turn the anger onto themselves, after other outlets for this anger have been blocked by loss of control and by fear of the unknown response of the actual target of the anger, and "self-murder" can result. Danger to others is an additional concern, as the anger may not be entirely displaced toward the self.

The existence of a sudden, unexpected loss or failure requires considerable coping and adaptation after a variable period of mourning. A rigid person often lacks the skills necessary to cope and to adapt to change, or the resiliency to view the trauma in proper perspective. The uncovering of feelings of hopelessness, helplessness, and suppressed or repressed anger following sudden negative (and sometimes even positive) life changes is important in evaluating suicide potential. Guilt and shame can accompany these feelings and may create intolerable psychological pain (Vaillant & Blumenthal, 1990).

Another critical area for assessment is the *nature of the patient's support system*. Are there close friends available who can be trusted? What is the nature of the interpersonal relationships? Are previously nurturing persons now gone?

Are current relationships fulfilling and providing meaningful experiences? Isolation and alienation are ominous contexts that are often found in suicidal persons. The resulting loneliness often magnifies the loss and further distorts perspective. A good relationship with the self becomes critical, and is vital in establishing a solid identity (Erikson, 1950; 1982).

Does the patient have a sense of *belonging*—to someone, or to some place, or to a career or a leisure-time pursuit? Does the patient feel a sense of belonging to himself? Can he or she enjoy being alone? Is there intimacy with significant others and with enjoyed activities? Intimate relationships with valued others are especially important in helping patients cope with sudden negative life changes (Beck et al., 1979; Erikson, 1950; 1982). Such intimacy intensifies a sense of belonging. Feelings of belonging and intimacy are rarely found in suicidal personas. Their absence often precipitates emptiness, loneliness, and feelings of deprivation. Stagnation, boredom, and despair can result.

When internal resources are minimal, external support systems are crucial. When they are also absent, or worse yet, when support systems are experienced as hostile and withholding, the vulnerability of the isolated person increases exponentially. Suicidal behavior becomes a desperate means of finding a way out, again, often to end the psychological pain of rejection.

While cognitive rigidity is an ominous trait, the opposite extreme—manic behavior—can be of equal concern, as impulse control and thought regulation become loose or nonexistent. Bipolar disorders, along with schizophrenia, are associated with one of the highest suicide rates of any psychiatric diagnostic category. The poor impulse control of the manic patient minimizes the deliberation and reasoning necessary for effective problem solving. A thought flashes through the manic patient's mind—and why not act on it? Meditation and thinking through are not part of the problem-solving process. Do it, act fast; the impulsivity becomes a part of being. When these characteristics are noted in an assessment of personality and behavior, the patient should be considered a high suicide risk. Such impulsivity tends to compel quick and dramatic solutions, usually to distract from psychological pain by inflicting injury (self-harm behavior) or to end the pain permanently (suicide). Reckless behavior patterns may be related to manic behavior.

Depression is important in considering suicide potential, but some recent studies have indicated that as many as one-third of persons who completed suicide were not significantly depressed prior to their suicide (Paykel, 1989). Of course, any *psychotically* depressed patient should be considered a potential suicide threat, but the absence of clinical depression does not, in itself, mean that suicidal behavior is unlikely. Internalized anger and cognitive rigidity, all of which are common precursors of depression, are more critical to the evaluation of suicide potential than depression per se.

How important is s suicidal history? Extremely important! Despite some conflicting data, most research demonstrates that even a series of low-lethality suicide attempts are to be considered as an ominous likely forerunner to further suicidal behavior (Smith, 1985). The nature and frequency of the previous attempts, the methods used, an increasing gradient of lethality in recent attempts, and an existing life stress (or absence of stress) at the time all must be carefully explored and categorized during the clinical interview so that some estimate of the patient's vulnerability or coping skills can be made. Vulnerability is directly related to suicide risk when coping abilities are minimal.

The therapist must also note whether there is a progressive pattern in the suicide attempts. Have the physical injuries in a series of attempts been progressively more or less life threatening? Is there a seasonal pattern to the series of prior attempts? Are there significant anniversary reactions relating to prior attempts? Is there a common precipitating stress component to the previous attempts? Since the rate of completed suicides is so much higher for males, and the attempt rate is much higher for females, should we consider different factors to evaluate for suicide risk based on gender? Any one of the variables may give important clues to what has happened in the past and may allow a more comprehensive accounting of all current factors that must be considered in evaluating immediate as well as long-term risk.

At the same time, a long history of suicidal ideation, and no overt suicidal behavior, can be of equal concern. When a attempt is made, will it be of such magnitude that it will be fatal? Or is the pattern one of attention seeking, such as that represented by the dramatic behavior patterns of the hysteric. This may suggest low lethality. Some have argued that such patients should *not* be considered suicidal, even though their behavior may clearly be classified as attempts at suicide (Blumenthal, 1990). These patients *should* be considered suicidal.

From a clinician's point of view, the semantics are not important. Patients who make a suicidal gesture may miscalculate the lethality of the next attempt and may accidentally die. Terms such as *suicidal gesture* in reference to a low-lethality attempt, should be avoided, as they imply a lack of seriousness by the attempter and can result in an overly casual response in the plan of treatment.

RECOMMENDATIONS

Each suicidal patient is a unique individual, but the rules of assessment are standard and should be applied to all:

1. Listen with intensity and care. Developing a good rapport as quickly as possible is critical to obtaining genuine responses. Involved interaction reflects the capacity for intimacy. A good interview experience also helps to create a positive attitude toward subsequent psychotherapy and establish an effective therapeutic alliance.

2. Observe body movement and posturing as well as voice tone and facial expressions. Appropriate, animated responses are usually a better sign than flat, emotionless, remote or guarded responses.
3. Be compassionate and empathic in probing for information. Develop a "flow" by asking open-ended questions that also allow a chance to evaluate thinking, reasoning, and judgment.
4. Development of mutual trust between the patient and clinician is vital and should accompany good rapport.
5. Try to "reach" the patient behind the facade of defenses without destroying the protective covering needed to maintain adequate rapport.
6. Use other informants (or previously existing valid data) for information to corroborate questionable data, or when the patient appears to be manipulating.
7. Assess the critical correlates cited in the QFI and SAC, especially the Cluster Scales.
8. Derive a quantitative score to reflect the degree of suicide proneness, as well as a qualitative sense of the vital balance between the patient's assets (coping skills) and deficiencies (vulnerability).
9. Note the changes that occur during the course of the interview, especially increasing or decreasing cooperation and closeness in the interview dyad.
10. Be aware of countertransference reactions. Such reactions may be negative (anxiety and fear of what the patient might do) or positive (overly involved, "rescue fantasy" notions).

CASE HISTORY

Karen is a forty-five-year-old, divorced, employed white female who sought help following the suicide of her only son, an eighteen-year-old high school senior. She lives with her only other child, a single, twenty-year-old, employed daughter. Their relationship is poor, and the suicide made for considerably more tension and isolation at home. The loss drove a further wedge between mother and daughter, even though they both professed love for the deceased.

The presenting complaint was Karen's anger at what her son had done, her anguish at why she hadn't been more aware of his problems, and her own suicidal ideation, which was affecting her sleep and eating patterns. She was suffering from insomnia and anorexia and had lost several pounds.

Karen had made a suicide attempt several years earlier, following her husband's desertion, but she had led an uneventful life since then, being troubled only by her children's presumed drug use and by constant financial pressure.

Karen had dated, but she had been wary of men since her divorce and doubted that she would remarry. She overindulged in alcohol about once a month. Her work associates liked her, and she performed adequately at her job.

Karen was evaluated using a battery of assessment techniques, including the previously cited instruments. She was considered to be at moderately high risk for suicide. She scored fairly high on the TQ, with the cited characteristic time profile. She had considerable involvement in the past, the time when her son was alive, but she also had some hope for the future. Her QFI demonstrated high scores on anger and hopelessness, and the total score was moderately high, as was her score on the SAC. Her drinking behavior was of particular concern, as was the history of family suicide and her limited social support network.

Karen was verbal and very expressive in the opening individual therapy sessions. She was not clinically depressed, but she expressed doubts that anything could go right, and she was both angry and guilt-ridden about her son's suicide, which came on his second attempt. She was eating well but sleeping poorly.

As mentioned, her scores on the QFI and the SAC were in the moderately high range, and despite the added stress of the quarrelsome relationship with her daughter, which created an isolated home environment, it was decided to treat her on an outpatient basis, in twice-weekly individual psychotherapy. Medication was not prescribed.

A good rapport developed rapidly but unevenly, and this pattern was maintained throughout the early sessions, although Karen felt that therapy was "for the birds" and that it would not bring her son back. She was given optimal opportunity to express her anger and was offered much support to dilute her guilt feelings and reduce her shame and remorse over her son's suicide. Trust developed slowly but steadily.

Her suicidal obsession was addressed openly, and the effects of her son's suicide and her own potential suicide on her daughter's life were extensively discussed. We also discussed the lost opportunities to do some good things for herself in the future if she carried out her suicide threats. Efforts were made to set attainable future goals, increase her earning capacity and income level, and develop more effective communication with her daughter; the latter was the most difficult task.

She was encouraged to recognize her assets and to develop her social life. And after a year of therapy she ambivalently began to date a man regularly. She received a substantial salary increase at her job and developed some leisure-time pursuits to curb her frequent drinking. With my strong urging, she also joined a support group and developed some good relationships with other survivors of suicide, with whom she felt she had much in common. She had finally found a group to which she could belong.

While her early improvement in therapy had been very uneven, she began to explore herself more intensively, and she gained some important insights and understanding that the traumatic events in her life were not her punishments for being bad and that she had assets that she could develop to her future advantage. Her responses to individual items in the TQ and SAC served as useful guides to areas needing exploration.

Karen became quite depressed on the first anniversary of her son's suicide, but her own suicidal ideation had been markedly reduced by her new insights and the slow development of some future goals. Her anger was also diminished, but she continued to have communication problems with her daughter. She terminated therapy after two years, markedly improved, especially in her handling of her anger and controlling of her shame and guilt.

Reduced financial pressures, resulting from another salary increase, allowed more leisure time and a more rewarding lifestyle, and while she had dissolved the relationship with her boyfriend, she looked forward to a more involved social life in the future. Some men were not so bad, she now concluded, and some fulfilling relationships continued with female peers in the survivor's group.

A six-month follow-up revealed that Karen had attained a slightly improved level of functioning and a reasonable resolution of her son's death, which she finally admitted was his choice and not her doing. While Karen remains a somewhat higher-than-usual suicide risk, the therapeutic strategies worked reasonably well, and she is still working on a number of additional goals.

She was less vulnerable to suicidal ideation at termination than she had been at the onset of treatment, and she had learned to use her long-lost intellectual skills to improve her coping abilities and to adapt more realistically to the very difficult irreversible loss of a child.

Not only do effective assessment procedures serve to provide a picture of the patient's current balance of coping ability and vulnerability, but also the response patterns can be useful in governing the areas of focus for the treatment process.

Probably the most effective technique to evaluate suicide potential will depend on the development of a suicide assessment battery. Several assessment techniques can be used, either concurrently to provide a measure of construct validity or serially over several days to provide a minilongitudinal approach to assessing the balance between coping and vulnerability. Shifts in intention and degree of ambivalence can be evaluated in this manner. A funnel approach to help focus and pinpoint areas of concern for treatment can be performed by using such an assessment battery, which would include a clinical interview. Special training for clinicians would be imperative, to aid in this kind of optimal assessment procedure.

We are working on the development of these forms of assessment techniques, which will center around the major suicide correlates discussed in this chapter. The use of these techniques will greatly enhance the accurate assessment of suicide potential by providing a structured, quantified, empirically supported, supplemental assessment to the usual clinical interview, and should allow for more valid and reliable clinical decisions regarding management and treatment plans for suicidal patients (Bongar & Firestone, 2002).

REFERENCES

Beck, A. T., Kovacs, M., & Weussman, A. (1975). Hopelessness and suicidal behavior: An overview. *Journal of the American Medical Association* 234:1146–1149.

Beck, A. T., Resnik, H. L., & Lettieri, D. J., eds. (1979). *The Prediction of Suicide.* Bowie, MD: Charles Press.

Bongar, B., & Firestone, L. (2002). Understanding and treating the self-destructive process. Paper presented at the Annual Meeting of the American Psychological Association, Chicago. August 24.

Blumenthal, S. J. (1990). *An Overview and Synopsis of Risk Factors: Assessment and Treatment of Suicidal Patients over the Life Cycle.* Washington, DC: American Psychological Association.

Cull, J. G., & Gill, W. S. (1986). *Suicide Probability Scale.* Los Angeles: Western Psychological Services.

Erikson, E. (1950). *Childhood and Society.* New York: Norton.

Erikson, E. (1982). *Life Cycle Completed.* New York: Norton.

Lester, D. (1978). Attempts to predict suicide risk using psychological tests. *Psychological Bulletin* 74:1–17.

Maris, R. W., Berman, A. L., Maltsberger, J. T., & Yufit, R. I., eds. (1992). *Assessment and Prediction of Suicide.* New York: Guilford.

Menninger, K. A. (1938). *Man against Himself.* New York: Harcourt, Brace and World.

Neuringer, C. (1964). Rigid thinking in suicidal individuals. *Journal of Consulting and Clinical Psychology* 28:54–58.

Paykel, E. S. (1989). Stress and life events. In Report of the Secretary's Task Force on Youth Suicide, Vol. 2, ed. L. Davidson and M. Linniola. Washington, DC: U.S. Government Printing Office.

Reynolds, W. (1987). *Suicide Ideation Questionnaire.* San Antonio, TX: Psychological Corporation.

Schneidman, E. S. (1985). *Definition of Suicide.* New York: Wiley and Sons.

Smith, K. (1985). Suicide assessment: An ego vulnerabilities approach. *Bulletin of the Menninger Clinic* 48:489–499.

Snyder, C. R., & Lopez, S. J. (2002). *Handbook of Positive Psychology.* New York: Oxford University Press.

Vaillant, G. E., & Blumenthal, S. J. (1990). *Risk Factors and Life Span Development.* Washington, DC: American Psychiatric Press.

Yufit, R. I. (1989). Developing a suicide screening instrument. In Report of the Secretary's Task Force on Youth Suicide, Vol. 4, ed. M. Rosenberg. Washington, DC: U. S. Government Printing Office.

Yufit, R. I. (1992). Suicide, stress and coping with life cycle events. In *Assessment and Prediction of Suicide,* ed. R. W. Maris, A. L. Berman, J. T. Maltsberger, & R. I. Yufit. New York: Guilford.

Yufit, R. I., & Benzies, B. (1973). Assessing suicide potential by time perspective. *Journal of Suicide and Life-Threatening Behavior* 3:270–280.

Yufit, R. I., & Benzies, B. (1978). *The Time Questionnaire and Scoring Manual.* Palo Alto, CA: Consulting Psychology Press.

20

INTERVIEWING IN
MEDICAL SETTINGS

David Wakely, Ph.D.

The sorrow which has no vent in tears may make other organs weep.

—Henry Maudsley

I don't get mad, I grow a tumor.

—Woody Allen

INTERVIEWING MEDICAL PATIENTS

Clinical interviewing of medical patients encompasses skills that are in many ways similar to those required in traditional mental health assessment, as well as skills unique to the medical patient population. Many of the ideas, guidelines, and techniques in this book are directly relevant to interviewing patients across the range of problems that lead clients to an interview conducted either across a desk or next to a hospital bed. This chapter will also follow a broad definition of what constitutes a medical patient. It will focus on those problems and issues that apply to the patient who has a primary medical diagnosis as well as to the traditional mental health patient who has a concurrent medical disorder. Thus, in a sense, this chapter has two audiences—the traditional mental health professional who interviews a patient with a medical disorder and the interviewer who works directly with specific populations of medical patients. It will also offer suggestions for ways the interviewer can use traditional mental health interviewing skills, make some comparisons between interviewing the mental health and medical patient, and incorporate the new skills necessary when working with these patients.

It is beyond the scope of this chapter to provide specific information and recommendations regarding specific diseases, such as cancer or heart disease, except as they provide relevant interviewing examples. It is hoped the general principles and ideas presented here will motivate the reader to seek out specific materials as experience dictates. Also beyond the scope of this chapter is consideration of the various psychological assessment devices available to the interviewer, both traditional psychological test instruments and tests constructed specifically for use with medical patients. The interview is seen as standing alone in terms of clinical importance, and the interested reader is referred to other sources for testing issues (e.g., Sweet, 1991).

The reader who notes the variety of life problems faced by the medical patient will realize that models and techniques from areas such as mental status screening to screening for personality disorders and the family therapy interview are all relevant with regard to the medical patient. It is the contention of this chapter that medical illness and medical settings provide a context in which the patient operates and that clinical interviewing that understands and takes this context into account will be most successful in meeting its goals.

In recent years, there has been an explosion of awareness, research, and clinical work involving medical patients by mental health professionals. Traditionally, a variety of allied health professionals have had routine contact with medical patients. Clinical social workers and occupational, recreational, and physical therapists have long histories of professional interaction with medical patients, and they typically work in medical settings that provide daily contact with medical patients. Psychiatrists and psychologists, in contrast, have more traditionally been used in a consultant role, in which they are called in to interview, diagnose, and treat when medical providers suspect a mental health problem. Over the past twenty to twenty-five years, this traditional approach has significantly broadened with the advent of mind–body and "alternative" medical treatment as well as the rise of primary care medicine. The present chapter cannot hope to review this expanding field in depth, but a brief historical overview is necessary to put the process and goals of interviewing medical patients in proper perspective.

HEALTH PSYCHOLOGY

It was less than twenty-five years ago that the first text appeared in which the term *health psychology* appeared in the title (Stone et al., 1979). This marked the approximate end of an era when clinical interviewing of medical patients followed fairly rigid and simplistic thinking regarding the relationship of illness, disease, and personality. For example, for many years, attempts were made to delineate the personality characteristics of patients with specific medical disorders. This thinking owed much to psychoanalytic theory. Specific intrapsychic conflicts were seen as contributing to specific diseases, in what became known as the *nuclear conflict* model (Alexander, 1950). Indeed, considerable psychoanalytic elaboration was involved in explaining the psychological causes of various medical illnesses, with reasoning so far removed from biological functioning that some psychoanalysts termed them "organ neuroses" (Fenichel, 1945).

In a tautological manner, the interviewer's implicit job was to question the patient to "find" the intrapsychic conflict that was behind the medical condition. Not surprisingly, the interviewer who already held the belief that a patient possessed, for example, repressed hostility issues that led to blood-pressure problems or unresolved dependency problems that led to gastric ulcer formation was able to find evidence of just these problems in the clinical interview. Resolution of the conflict, typically by means of psychoanalysis, was hypothesized to lead to a cure of the psychosomatic condition. When research demonstrated that some medical patients failed to manifest the hypothesized personality traits, the findings were explained as the patients manifesting their unconscious motives in a subtler manner (Weiner, cited in Bakal, 1979).

As these assumptions were being questioned, reviews of relevant research found little evidence of any specific personality structure within groups of paraplegics, amputees, epileptics, and tuberculosis, heart disease, and multiple sclerosis patients, or among the blind or deaf (Schontz, 1971). Thus, the interviewer of these and other patients with medical problems who makes a priori assumptions regarding the personality structure of a patient does so without relevant research support.

Ironically, it was advances in medicine, more so than in psychology or psychiatry, that contributed to changes in these conceptualizations. With better understanding, diagnosis, and treatment of chronic conditions such as cancer and gastrointestinal and heart disease, awareness began to develop of the complexity of the mind–body interaction and of the large behavioral and environmental components of health and illness. Agras (1982) also notes that a confluence of events, including biobehavioral research and developments in applied behavior therapy and the identification of risk factors for illnesses of various kinds, all contribute to more sophisticated models of illness.

Responding to this new environment, Engel (1977) developed the holistic, *biopsychosocial* model of illness. Although written as a criticism of medicine's strict reliance on a biomedical model, its touting of the need for understanding the psychosocial factors in patients lives, not just as predictors of illness, but also as indicators of response to treatment, forced a change in the content and goals of clinical interviewing of medical patients.

With strict psychoanalytic thinking (and its interview techniques) seen as no longer relevant, the argument has been made (Turk et al., 1983) that a cognitive–behavioral orientation, with its emphasis on thoughts, feelings, and behaviors, is most consistent with the biopsychosocial conceptualization. Others (Melamed & Siegel, 1980; Tunks & Bellissimo, 1991) have termed clinical practice within this model *behavioral medicine*. Other chapters in this book outline the skills consistent with cognitive–behavioral interviewing.

Finally, Gatchel and Blanchard (1993) have noted that even psychoanalytic thinking underwent significant modifications when confronted with patient behaviors and disease courses that did not fit the older models.

As a result of this theoretical evolution, both the role and the settings in which the clinical interviewer operates have significantly expanded beyond traditional mental health. In some medical settings, inpatients and outpatients are almost routinely referred for psychological assessment, a testimony to the value placed on these skills. These services are sought across a variety of medical disciplines, not only to establish a mental health diagnosis, but also for assessment and treatment of a variety of psychologically mediated health problems. It has been estimated that between 50 and 90 percent of all physical problems have their origins in psychological issues (Hafen et al., 1996), and few medical disorders are now seen as entirely beyond the realm of the mental health professional. Public awareness has been fueled by articles in the popular press that inform patients in layman's terms about the importance of mind–body connections in health care (e.g. Beil, 2002).

Types of Interviews

Ironically, the same process that fostered a healing of the mind–body split has led to two distinct types of interviews: the mental health interview with the medical patient (mixing mental health and medical issues) and what this chapter terms the psychophysiological screening interview, conducted with a defined medical population such as dialysis patients, organ transplant candidates, and chronic pain patients, often to answer a specific question about the patient. These patients may, or may not, have a history of or current need for mental health treatment.

The term *psychophysiologic* (rather easily and literally interpreted as "mind–body") has largely replaced the term *psychosomatic* (Gatchel & Blanchard, 1993), which in common usage had begun to take on pejorative connotations (with its use as a description of a disorder leading to the implication that something is wrong with the patient's thinking or emotions). While all mental health professionals need to be aware of a patient's medical issues and problems, especially in this era of increased awareness of biological effects on mental functioning, the rise of health psychology and multidisciplinary medical treatment teams has led to a dramatic increase in the psychophysiological screening interview. Table 20.1 attempts to clarify this interaction.

Table 20.1.   Types of Interviews

	Mental Health Patient	Medical Patient
MH setting	MH Interview	Mixed interview
Medical setting	Mixed Interview	Psychophysiological interview

It could be argued that, given the theoretical outline presented above, *all* interviews are biopsychosocial interviews, a position with which this chapter agrees. However, it is the contention of this chapter that the purpose, setting, and context of the interview determine its content, structure, and methods. One straightforward example of differing contexts would be that of the patient who identifies himself as a mental health patient, versus the medical patient sent to the interview by his physician to answer a specific referral question. Indeed, while both patients may have the identical medical diagnosis, the interviews could easily unfold in quite different manners. Some of the settings in which clinical interviewing of medical patients occurs are listed in table 20.2. Note the discrepancy between the lengths of the mental health list versus the medical setting list.

Table 20.2.   Clinical Interview Locations

Mental Health Settings	Medical Setting
Public MH hospital	Public medical/surgical hospital
Public MH clinic/agency	Private medical/surgical hospital
Private MH hospital	Group medical/surgical practice
Private MH clinic/agency	Dialysis unit
Group/individual MH practice	Sleep disorders clinic
	Cardiac rehabilitation unit
	Sexual dysfunction clinic
	Spinal cord injury unit
	Weight loss program
	Biofeedback clinic
	HIV+ clinic
	Smoking cessation program
	Pain clinic
	Nursing home

Similarly, and consistent with the biopsychosocial model, the role in which the interviewer operates has broadened well beyond traditional screening for mental health problems. The interviewer of a patient with a medical diagnosis can no longer rely on familiar theories and procedures to provide all of the structure and content of the interview. With both the setting and the role of the interviewer of medical patients evolving, how is the interviewer to approach the patient? What are the medical patient's beliefs, attitudes, and behaviors that are of interest to the clinical interviewer, regardless of the setting?

PATIENT CHARACTERISTICS

In addition to a medical history, patients bring to the interview a host of needs, fears, thoughts, beliefs, predispositions, and a history of interactions with medical providers. The mental health patient typically comes to the interview in emotional distress and with the expectation of help. This sets the tone of the typical mental health interview, or as Gruba-McCallister (1989) has noted, "This expectation is often expressed as the desire for a remedy, a cure, a definitive answer to one's problems." While there are exceptions (e.g., court-ordered assessment), and as Craig (1991) has noted, hidden agendas or motives can certainly be brought to the session, in general, the interviewer can expect from the self-referred mental health patient a reasonably collaborative attitude that fosters the goals of the interview.

The medical patient brings to providers the prototypical expectations of a remedy or a cure, but the medical patient, due in part to the implicit threat of any illness, brings to the interview an even wider variety of attitudes, beliefs, agendas, expectations, hopes, and fears than the mental health patient does. Depending on the nature and chronicity of the illness, these patients also typically bring to the interview a wide variety of past medical experiences and interactions with medical providers. Consider the following list of patient characteristics in terms of these issues, all of which have been encountered by the author.

TYPES OF MEDICAL PATIENTS

- Chronic mental health patients recently diagnosed with a medical illness.
- Newly diagnosed medical patients, with no history of mental health treatment or problems.
- Patients with medical complaints but no clinical findings.
- Patients needing assessment of mental competence regarding medical treatment decisions.
- Workman's compensation patients.
- Patients with a history of poor adjustment suspected of a "somatization" disorder.
- Medical patients with chronic, progressive, debilitating conditions.

Even a brief reflection on the characteristics of and demands placed on these various patients points out the initial, daunting task for the medical interviewer: what (if anything) does the patient want from this encounter? Is the interviewer a potential ally helping to overcome a problem, or is the interview itself an obstacle to be overcome for emotional or financial gain or to fulfill some other agenda?

Some patients, revealing highly personal agendas, have written eloquently about the experience of illness, in ways that can help guide the interviewer to a deeper understanding of the emotional place in which medical patients find themselves and that reveal some of the underlying issues medical patients face. A young sociologist who suffered a mild myocardial infarction at the age of thirty-nine writes from an existential perspective that openly suggests areas of interview exploration:

> Heart problems teach you how quickly life can go out of a body. My fear was that I would go to sleep and not wake up again. Having a heart attack is falling over the edge of a chasm and then being pulled back. Why I was pulled back made no more sense than why I had fallen in the first place. Afterwards I felt always at risk of one false step, or heartbeat, plunging me over the side again. I will never lose that immanence of nothingness, the certainty of mortality. A heart attack is a moment of death. Once the body has known death, it never lives the same again. (Frank, 1991, p. 16)

Fear and worry are commonly seen among medical patients, and not just among the recently diagnosed, but also among the chronically ill patient who perceives a decline in health or functioning, or an increase in pain and discomfort. It is with these patient quality-of-life issues that the medical interview is most intimately concerned.

Had the young sociologist quoted above made his feelings known to the medical staff, he might well have been referred for depression screening by a mental health professional. Alternately, as his medical condition stabilized, he might have been interviewed as part of a screening process for admission to a cardiac rehabilitation program. The two interviews, conducted for different purposes, would have had different content and different structures, even though conducted with the same individual.

Patients are also quite capable of recovering from the shocking or depressing news a serious diagnosis brings, and they are capable of heroic acts in response. One of the best-known patient accounts of illness is by Norman Cousins, who in his classic *Anatomy of an Illness* was able to put his literary skills as editor of *The Saturday Review* to good use in describing the will to fight his disease.

> People have asked what I thought when I was told by the specialists that my disease was progressive and incurable.
>
> The answer is simple. Since I didn't accept the verdict, I wasn't trapped in the cycle of fear, depression and panic that frequently accompanies a supposedly incurable illness. I must not make it seem, however, that I was unmindful of the seriousness of the problem or that I was in a festive mood throughout. Being unable to move my body was all the evidence I needed that the specialists were dealing with real concerns. But deep down, I knew I had a good chance and relished the idea of bucking the odds. (Cousins, 1981, p. 45)

Cousins's quote also says much about the cognitive–behavioral approach as it relates to medical patients. He made a conscious decision to question a dire prognosis, and this cognitive act freed him from the negative emotions that commonly follow. It is important to note that he reached this conclusion only after considerable research and careful deliberation. To do otherwise would have placed him at risk of denial, another common patient coping strategy. Note that Cousins does not question the validity of his medical diagnosis, only its presumed course. Cousins's comment about relishing the fight also points to his shift from a passive victim of disease to an active participant in his health care. In all interview settings where physical illness is present, the difference is psychologically crucial, and much of health psychology would argue that it is equally crucial medically.

THE MENTAL HEALTH PATIENT

In a private practice office, a mental health professional meets for the first time with a couple that has requested help for a floundering marriage. As they discuss their conflicts and arguments, it is revealed that the husband suffers from advanced peripheral vascular disease, is often tired and depressed, takes multiple medications, and makes frequent visits to his physician. The mental health professional does not consider himself a health psychologist and has no special training in this area. What are the medical factors that should be considered and the questions that should be asked as a part of this patient's interview?

As other chapters in this book note, taking a thorough medical history has always been a part of the clinical interview process. What medicine gives the mental health practitioner is a body of knowledge regarding areas of exploration in the interview. Is the husband diabetic, and if so are blood glucose levels currently stable? There is considerable evidence that both hyper- and hypoglycemia contribute to mood and mental status changes (Aikens & Wagner, 1998). Is there a family history of vascular or other disease; that is, did the patient have an illness role model to observe? Taking the social role of a sick individual has clear interpersonal implications (Parsons, 1951). Is the patient impotent? This is a common finding in vascular disease (Wincze & Carey, 2001). Is he in pain? Is he sleeping well? Is the patient compliant in taking his medications? Is there a worsening of physical signs and symptoms during periods of marital strife? With what ethnic group, if any, does the patient identify, and what are that group's beliefs and attitudes regarding illness, death, and disability? What does the patient's wife know about peripheral vascular disease and it's presentation, course, and sequelae?

To the novice interviewer, the prospect of understanding the clinical presentation of patients with a complicated medical picture can be intimidating. Yet the family therapist above need not have a medical degree or familiarity with the pathogenesis of peripheral vascular disease to conduct a meaningful interview. Huszti and Walker (1991) have noted that there are a variety of good resources available to help the nonmedically trained professional decipher medical records and address medical issues. They also note that the more time psychologists spend in medical settings, the more comfortable they become with medical terminology, procedures, and common referral diagnoses. Often, some general knowledge of the symptoms, especially as they affect thinking, mood, and social behavior, as well as the course and prognosis of a disease, may be all that is required to begin asking some, if not most, of the questions listed above. The reader should consider the content of those questions in terms of a biopsychosocial perspective.

While the idea of "interviewing the whole person" is in keeping with this perspective, and while a major thrust of health psychology is the minimization of the mind–body dichotomy, patients themselves often act according to dichotomous diagnostic identities. Thus a current or former mental health patient diagnosed with a medical disorder is likely to approach the interview with a somewhat different set of predefined beliefs, expectations, and roles than the patient seen at his bedside on the medical/surgical ward who has never been interviewed by a mental health professional.

At some point, the patient with a history of mental health treatment sought help for symptoms that were found emotionally distressing, and a positive experience bodes well for the subsequent interviewer. In fact, a case could be made that there is an advantage to interviewing mental health patients in medical settings. On the one hand, the mental health patient has a history of taking the role of interviewee, which includes formulating answers to questions regarding thoughts, emotions, and behavior. Thus, in the medical treatment setting, both the role and the medical context contribute to the mental health patient's ability to achieve some reasonable sense of congruence regarding the biopsychosocial interview. On the other hand, to the medical patient, the same questions may appear unusual and "out of context"—they don't fit the patient's conceptualization of what occurs in a medical setting. The interviewer of medical patients often needs to spend some time explaining to the patient his presence and the meaning and purpose of the interview.

Incorporating Medical Findings

The mental health interviewer typically has a cognitive "map" to guide his judgment or some internal blueprint as to what constitutes mental health, such as the factors that indicate emotional maturity or a good marriage. The same competent interviewer may have no blueprint about what constitutes good physical health for a particular patient. For example, an interviewer might make predictions about a patient, including predictions about coping with illness, based on the good or poor emotional functioning inferred from interview data. The same interviewer may be unable to make predictions about the physical state of the kidney disease patient who is slipping into uremia or the liver disease patient exhibiting periodic hepatic encephalopathy. Even if this information were known, the interviewer would need the medical knowledge to be able to appreciate its meaning and significance. The former example is dependent on good psychological assessment, the latter on good medical assessment, yet both are certainly factors related to the patient's mental functioning.

As one example of the common "bidirectional" nature of medical interview findings, in heart transplant candidates there is often a marked mental slowing associated with, among other things, poor cerebral blood flow (perfusion). Following successful heart transplant, the author has observed significant and, at times, remarkable improvement in mental functioning due to the improved cardiac output a new heart brings. Assessing a pretransplant patient as unsuitable for the operation due to this factor alone would block the patient from receiving the one thing that would, in some cases, eliminate this interview finding!

The mental health professional, when faced with a patient diagnosed with a medical illness, has a responsibility to determine the extent to which that illness is influencing the current mental and emotional functioning of the patient. This may require permission from the patient for consultation with the patient's physician (in medical settings, it is typically the patient's physician who initiates the interview request) or some reading by the clinician about the effects of the particular disorder. Many clinicians keep a general medical textbook in their psychotherapy bookcase and turn to physician colleagues for consultation when needed.

Theoretical Issues

While contrasting the similarities and differences between mental health versus medical settings provides a context for the interview, it should not be construed as an endorsement of dichotomous thinking. The interviewer is typically directly confronted with a mind–body approach to interviewing when, for example, attempting to arrive at certain diagnoses based on the fourth edition of the *Diagnostic and Statistical Manual of Mental Disorders* (DSM-IV, American Psychiatric Association, 1994). Among others, these include "Mental Disorders Due to General Medical Condition," as well as the somatoform disorders. In attempting to negotiate mind–body issues, as the introduction to DSM-IV notes,

> It should be recognized that these are merely terms of convenience and should not be taken to imply that there is any fundamental distinction between mental disorders and general medical conditions, that mental disorders are unrelated to physical or biological factors or processes, or that general medical conditions are unrelated to behavioral or psychosocial factors or processes. (American Psychiatric Association, 1994, p. xxv)

While the criteria for making these diagnoses is outlined in DSM-IV and will not be repeated here, the point is that the interviewer must be aware of the various medical disorders that have been found relevant regarding mental functioning, as well as the impact any medical disorder can have on the psychological functioning of the patient. The quote also reinforces the idea put forth in this chapter that, with a blurring of mind–body distinctions, the context or setting of the interview comes to the forefront.

While this chapter points to a cognitive–behavioral orientation as consistent with a health psychology approach, it is not the only theoretical orientation applicable to the interview that addresses medical concerns. The neuropsychologist conducting an information/data gathering interview, for example, or the family systems therapist, when interviewing a patient with a medical diagnosis, can operate within their familiar frameworks while still incorporating the information, suggestions, and guidelines here. The medical setting does not dictate the interviewer's theoretical orientation; rather, any orientation must be able to incorporate the patient's relevant medical issues and problems.

In the example above, the couple sought out the interviewer, not for treatment of the medical condition, or even their reactions to it, but because of a disordered marriage. In this case, as in most where mental health and medical issues intersect, there is a reciprocal relationship between mental and physical illness. To the interviewer fishing for information, good mental health interviewing means casting as deep a net as possible, while good medical patient interviewing means casting as wide a net as possible. The mental health professional interviewing the medical patient needs to find an appropriate balance between the two.

THE MEDICAL PATIENT

When the interviewer identifies himself to the patient on a medical unit, he is frequently greeted by a narrow repertoire of responses, ranging from surprise through suspicion and fear. It is most likely a third party, typically the attending or resident physician, who initiates this contact. However, the contact may also be initiated by another medical specialist or by allied health professionals such as clinical social workers or nurse practitioners.

To the unprepared and unsophisticated medical patient suddenly informed he is about to be interviewed by a mental health professional, it can be as though his medical symptoms have been instantly invalidated and he has just been informed, "it's all in your head." In this case, the medical interviewer will need to overcome considerable psychological resistance. As noted earlier, it is entirely appropriate for the interviewer to spend time explaining the meaning and purpose for the interview, including the interviewer's role on the medical treatment team or relationship to the patient's physician.

Occasionally, a medical patient will flatly refuse to speak with a mental health professional, and in these cases insistence that the interview proceed typically leads to less than desirable outcomes. Contact with the referral source can lead to clarification with the patient regarding the reasons for the interview and, ideally, to a reframing that permits the interview to occur. It has long been recognized that successful referral of the patient to a mental health professional for physical problems with no observable organic basis depends on the patient's readiness and willingness to accept the referral and the physician's skill in initiating the interview request (Colby, 1951).

It is not unusual for the mental health professional, observing the typically sterile medical setting, to underestimate the emotional sensitivity of physicians or other primary care providers. As the preface to a popular medical textbook notes,

> This book begins with the assumption that the hospital is a dangerous place. It is the unusual patient who escapes without at least one scar: a phlebitis from an intravenous line, a miserable morning undergoing a poorly thought-out barium enema, anxiety over the when and why of the next blood drawing, the emptiness of disenfranchisement from decisions affecting his own integrity and sanity. One must therefore be sure the hospitalized patient belongs in the hospital; as soon as the patient can function at home safely and comfortably, let him go. (Fishman et al., 1991, p. ix)

The purpose of an interview with a medical patient can vary tremendously. While the depressed mental health patient may face life-and-death issues from his own hand, medical patients may face life-and-death issues from an alien organism, event, or disease process. The interviewer needs to keep in mind the altered perspective this notion of external versus internal threat brings to the patient's attribution of illness. In simpler terms, while the traditional mental health patient may send the message "My life's falling apart," the medical patient's message may more closely resemble "My body's falling apart." An ideal interview might begin by speaking to the medical patient at this level but proceed in a manner that helps the patient realize that both statements may be true. It has been suggested that beginning the interview with medical considerations before proceeding to emotional issues eases the course of the interview (Block, 1996), most likely by validating the patient's own perception regarding the cause of distress, which then allows the consideration of emotional factors and consequences.

While the mental health professional may work toward having patients take responsibility for the events in their lives, in the medical interview the goal is sometimes to help the patient come to terms with the impact of a new diagnosis or with the disabilities and limitations an illness imposes. This is especially true in traumas that lead to problems in daily living, such as spinal cord and closed head injury, but is also common in new diagnoses of diseases such as cancer or multiple sclerosis.

Medical illness may also have quite idiosyncratic meanings to a patient. For example, an often-neglected issue with medical patients is unexpressed guilt and shame. As the focus of medicine has shifted from the treatment of contagious diseases to lifestyle issues such as diet, smoking, and other health behaviors, the patient is confronted with the medical and life effects of, for example, forty years of smoking two packs a day. Medical disorders that result from poor judgment, habits, and behavior return the focus to the patient in terms of responsibility for health. As noted above, this may be more familiar territory to the mental health professional.

Particularly in the case of cancer, and more recently with HIV/AIDS but generalizable to other diseases as well, some patients focus on the societal aspects of illness, over which they have no personal control, going so far as to see the disease as a type of metaphor. In this form of stigmatization, there is an implicit flaw assumed on the part of the patient proven by the diagnosis itself. These patients may be convinced they have personally failed in some way, and that through the disease society has castigated them and, in effect, cast them out (Sontag, 1978). Patients who have based their self-esteem on the reactions of others are especially susceptible to the fear and withdrawal others may exhibit when a diagnosis is made public. Alternately, it cannot be emphasized enough that predictions of specific emotional responses to cancer, or any other disease, cannot be made on the basis of the medical diagnosis alone. A wide variety of sources are available to the interested reader that summarize relevant research findings and dispel the "uniformity myth" that all cancer patients, for example, face the same issues and can thus be treated in similar ways (Wakely, 2001).

Types of Medical Interviews

Some interviews with medical patients are screenings for the presence (and indications for treatment) of straightforward mental health problems and issues, based on complaints by or observation of medical patients, including issues of adjustment to illness. Others may be requests for very specific purposes such as screening for nursing home admission, for possible biofeedback training for a stress disorder, or for psychological screening prior to organ transplant. Such psychophysiological screening interviews will necessarily be structured by the needs and demands of the referral source. For example, among other factors, biofeedback patients need to be interviewed regarding the nature of the symptoms, motivation for behavioral self-management training, and previous treatments (Gaarder & Montgomery, 1977).

A relatively new type of medical interview could be termed the "risk-factor" interview. Recently, the author was asked to assist in screening HCV+ (hepatitis C) patients who are candidates for a new form of interferon therapy. Early treatment with interferon revealed that a number of patients fall victim to significant depression and other neuropsychiatric symptoms (Dieperink, 2000; Gleason & Yates, 1999) that affect treatment dropout rates. These patients typically have no mental health treatment history and usually have few complaints

---

HCV+ Treatment Compliance Screen

Name _____   Date _____

1) Current energy/fatigue level.

2) Depression/other MH history and current symptoms.

     CES-D =
3) Medical history w/ past treatment(s), side effects and toxicities.

4) Anticipatory anxiety re: proposed treatment.

5) Level of understanding re: purpose/goals of proposed treatment.

6) Patient/health care team communication issues or problems.

7) Family support.

Figure 20.1.   HCV+ treatment compliance screen.

of depression (not to be confused with the absence of depressive symptoms) at the time of the interview. For these brief assessments, a combination of a short screening instrument and the interview outline shown in figure 20.1 are used.

For medical patients who have not traditionally been interviewed by mental health professionals, the interviewer will need to use a combination of clinical judgment, medical literature review, and professional consultation to structure an interview that is appropriate and effective. The author used all of the above in constructing the brief HCV+ interview outline.

Practical Matters

The setting of the medical inpatient interview is not always conducive to patient privacy or confidentiality. The interviewer must first ensure that the patient is comfortable being interviewed on a medical ward with the potential presence of others. Nursing or other staff may arrive during the interview to take vital signs, administer medications, or perform other routine tasks. While medical treatment considerations always predominate, occasionally the interviewer must decide whether to permit such interruptions for any reason or to inform medical staff that they will have access to the patient at the conclusion of the session. At all times, patient confidentiality must take precedence.

The interviewer conducting a screening interview for admission to some specialized program, where the necessary information is largely demographic, historical, or routine, may decide to permit intrusions and interruptions. Alternately, the interviewer conducting, for example, a general mental health interview may decide to negotiate with medical staff regarding intrusions or to transport the patient to an office rather than conduct the interview on a privacy-compromised ward. Of course, many of these issues are ameliorated in the case of a medical outpatient.

Regarding these practical interview considerations, Van Egeren and Striepe (1998), in addition to the issues of lack of privacy and patient recalcitrance, list interview problems including patients' physical limitations (e.g., easily fatigued), the problem of the patient who is "somatically focused" regarding the source of distress, and sensory (eyesight/hearing) loss. Thus, somewhat paradoxically, the interviewer who attempts to speak softly to the patient in the medical inpatient room to maintain privacy may also find the hearing impaired patient unresponsive!

The interviewer confronted with a patient who in the course of the interview reveals an unfamiliar disease still has a multitude of options. What is the patient's understanding of the nature, causes, course, and treatments available? Has the patient questioned the physician or nurse, researched the disease through Internet or library readings, or avoided all thoughts of the problem? What threats does the patient perceive in terms of disability, death, or treatment side effects? How does the patient expect the disease to impact his ability to work or his relationships with family members? These cognitive–behavioral factors will likely be relevant for most medical disorders.

In the case of an interview conducted regarding coping with an unfamiliar disease, the interviewer may need to either research the disorder prior to the interview, if possible, or consider a two-part interview. In the latter case, after some consultation or research into the problem, the interviewer can return or reschedule the patient and address any misperceptions of the illness, or the interviewer can help the patient begin a process of appropriate grieving or adjustment to expected limitations, based on the particular disease presentation and course.

The range of problems and issues that prompt a request for assessment of a medical patient is large (see the list of "Types of Medical Patients," above). Some interviews by their very nature suggest their own content and structure. For example, an interview to determine mental competency typically includes cognitive, neuropsychological, and even ethical considerations. While specific laws may vary from state to state, good general guidelines are available (Grisso & Applebaum, 1998) to assist the interviewer in conducting such assessments. It should be noted that some assessments, for example, those involving extensive neuropsychological skills, might call for the examiner to seek out or refer to other professionals with appropriate training.

Among all medical patients, however, are commonalities this chapter has attempted to explore. An interview that addresses these points will at least begin to adequately meet its objectives. One such structured interview outline (Block, 1996) is presented in figure 20.2 as encompassing most of the relevant issues in interviewing medical patients. This example not only provides an outline for interviewing chronic pain patients who are candidates for surgery, but it also illustrates the structure needed for obtaining comprehensive information from patients who have a variety of medical disorders.

Note that this interview combines historical and present-time data as well as including behavioral observations of the patient during the interview. The astute reader will note the various biopsychosocial considerations this interview incorporates, as well as its causal bidirectionality. That is, both the effects of pain on emotional functioning and the effects of emotional state on pain are questioned and worked into the assessment process. Interviewers in medical settings often devise their own means of structuring the interview content and process for their particular work. As they are published and this literature base expands, they become resources for those who routinely interview medical patients.

Reporting Results

Since interviews with medical patients are typically requested by medical treatment personnel, the interviewer needs to ensure that a mechanism is in place to provide feedback to the requester. While this will often take the form of a note in a patient medical chart, in other cases, including those involving medical outpatients, the interviewer will need to make direct contact with the referral source and convey the findings. At the same time, the medical professional typically wants only a specific answer to a specific question, and psychological jargon should be avoided in the report. Sweet (1991) has noted that the exact form of feedback can range from a brief verbal report (usually followed by at least a brief written summary) all the way to a formal, multipage, typed assessment.

PPS Interview Form (with questions identified).

Name _____   Date _____
Age _____ Marital Status _____   Occupation _____
Referring MD _____   Education Level _____
Insurance Type _____   Medical Diag. _____
Surgery Planned _____   Height _____ Weight _____

Onset
  Date of onset,
  Circumstances
  Remissions & exacerbations
Pain Site
  Primary & secondary pain sites
  Sensations other than pain

Past Procedures
  Medical & rehab procedures
  Number of previous spine surgeries
  Other procedures
Blame for injury
  Employer
  Self, other, no one

Pain Increasing Conditions
  Activities, environmental conditions
  Psychological states
  Times of day
Pain Decreasing Conditions
  Medications
  Self-regulation techniques
  Positions, modalities
Medications
  Narcotic medications
  Nonnarcotic pain medication
  Psychotropics, non–pain-related meds.
Nonspine Medical Problems
  # of non spine hospitalizations
  Current vs. past medical problems

Pain Ratings   Least: Now: Worst: Average:

Rating Scale: 0 = no pain to 10 = worst pain ever.
Indicate if sensation is not pain but some other sensation.

Typical Day
  Uptime general activities, naps
  Exercises
  Feelings about average day
Sleep
  Total hours sleep
  Periods of sleeplessness
  Reasons for sleep disturbance
Appetite
  Desire for food last 30 days
  Weight change since injury
  Reasons for weight change

Concentration & Memory
  Long- vs. short-term memory
  Pain vs. nonpain disruptions

Effect on Family
  Marital problems (preexisting vs. reactive)
  Solicitousness in response to pain
  Spouse's emotional condition
Sex
  How often, how satisfying?
  Adjustments made. Partner's reaction
  Sex before injury
Mood
  Depression, anger, irritability
  Frustration & tension
  Emotional state before injury
  Cognitions accompanying emotions

(continued)

Figure 20.2. PPS Interview Form.
From Block, A. R. (1996, pp. 52–53). Copyright 1996, Lawrence Erlbaum Associates. Reprinted by permission.

Stresses	Abuse History
Financial difficulties	Physical, mental, or sexual abuse
Recent losses or changes	Current or past?
Does pain vary with stress?	
Vocational History & Attitude	Vocational Plans
Employment duration before injury	Return to same employer planned?
Job satisfaction	Light duty available?
Past employment history	Concrete alternative job plans?
Current Income Source	Litigation Pending
Worker's comp	Does patient have attorney?
Social Security disability	Actions planned or pending
Other income sources	Settled cases in regard to injury
Coping	Self-Statements
Activities that reduce or control pain	Has pain changed self-image?
Use of self-hypnosis, relaxation	Perceived strengths & weaknesses
Hoping and praying?	Other self-observations
Past Psych Problems	Substance Use History
Inpatient vs. outpatient	Prescription medication abuse
Reasons for treatment	Alcohol. Street drugs.
Outcome of treatments	Smoking?
Recreational Activities	Expectations for outcome
Current enjoyable activities	Pain relief: complete, moderate, none
Pre-injury enjoyable activities	Return to work
Does patient have fun?	Self-responsibility for improvement
Worst Effect of Injury	Positives in Current Situation
What is most upsetting about the injury?	What is patient happy with?
Who does the patient blame for this?	How can this not change?

Observations: Recommendations:

Behavior	Rating (1 to 5)*	Surgical prognosis
guarding	_____	Facultative treatments needed?
bracing	_____	Alternatives to surgery?
grimacing	_____	
rubbing	_____	
standing	_____	
shifting	_____	

Actions Taken:

Inconsistency	_____	
Bad rapport	_____	General notes of referrals, assignments or
La Belle Ind	_____	follow-up needed

1 = none to 5 = extreme

Figure 20.2. *(continued)*

In general, reports of interviews with medical patients will vary in length and complexity depending on the specific questions asked and the manner in which the findings potentially impact the course of treatment. For example, if the referral question was some variation of, "Are the patient's symptoms and presentation consistent with emotional factors influencing the course of the disease or interfering with treatment?" negative interview findings could be briefly summarized. It is rare for medical personnel with requests such as this to require an extensive or exhaustive report on the patient's psychosocial history. Alternately, an interview with, for example, a chronic pain patient that reveals an extensive history and ongoing problems with substance abuse might warrant a more lengthy report cautioning the medical provider regarding the use of narcotic pain medications and assessing the likelihood of abuse or relapse.

Since interviews for these various, but specific, purposes may have widely varying content and take a variety of courses, no one outline of an interview with all medical patients can be presented, nor can one set of guidelines be recommended. To the novice interviewer of medical patients, this can appear to be an interviewing "Tower of Babel." The best this chapter can hope to do is present some general principles and examples that can help the professional structure and conduct an interview that takes into account the varying mental and physical issues and suggests ways for the interviewer to integrate the two. The work involved in doing this helps ensure that the patient, the interviewer, and the referral source are all speaking the same language.

SUMMARY

An interview with a medically diagnosed patient, in either the mental health or the medical setting, challenges the interviewer in several ways. It demands a general appreciation for the factors common to all patients with disabling and possibly life-threatening disease, as well as the need to continually update a fund of relevant medical information about specific diseases. It is the purpose, the setting, and the context in which the interview occurs that determine the manner in which the interview with a medical patient is conducted. The biopsychosocial model is consistent with this conceptualization, but the issues and problems medical patients face can be considered within most theoretical models. Collaborations with physicians and other health care providers enrich the interview/assessment process and are entirely consistent with the biopsychosocial approach.

THE FUTURE

This is a dynamic field, and the learning curve for the interviewer of medical patients is only likely to increase. With awareness of psychological effects in most illness, including the effects of psychological interventions, there has been a significant increase in research and some surprising findings regarding mind–body connections. For example, recently researchers have discovered a signaling system between the brain and the immune system (Sternberg & Gold, 2002), opening the door to interventions at an even earlier stage of treatment and prevention in cancer, inflammatory disease, and a host of other disorders.

CONCLUSION

In the course of clinical interviewing, the professional who encounters patients with diagnosed medical disorders will need to use skills both familiar and new. These skills, and the level of complexity and judgment in applying them, are undoubtedly challenging to even the experienced practitioner, but the rewards are in the knowledge that the interviewer is functioning in the truest sense as a "scholar–practitioner" and providing medical patients the most competent and comprehensive treatment possible.

REFERENCES

Agras, W. S. (1982). Behavioral medicine in the 1980s: Nonrandom connections. *Journal of Consulting and Clinical Psychology* 50:797–803.

Aikens, J. E., & Wagner, L. I. (1998). Diabetes mellitus and other endocrine disorders. In *Clinical Handbook of Health Psychology: A Practical Guide to Effective Interventions*, ed. P. M. Camic & S. J. Knight, pp. 191–225. Seattle: Hogrefe & Huber.

Alexander, F. (1950). *Psychosomatic Medicine: Its Principles and Applications.* New York: Norton.

American Psychiatric Association. (1994). *Diagnostic and Statistical Manual of Mental Disorders*, 4th ed. Washington, DC: American Psychiatric Association.

Bakal, D. A. (1979). *Psychology and Medicine: Psychobiological Dimensions of Health and Illness.* New York: Springer.

Beil, L. (2002, July 15). Head over healing. *Dallas Morning News*, pp. 1–2C.

Block, A. (1996). *Presurgical Psychological Screening in Chronic Pain Syndromes: A Guide for the Behavioral Health Practitioner.* Mahwah, NJ: Erlbaum.

Colby, K. M. (1951). *A Primer for Psychotherapists.* New York: Ronald.

Cousins, N. (1981). *Anatomy of an Illness as Perceived by the Patient: Reflections on Healing and Regeneration.* New York: Bantam.

Craig, R. J., ed. (1989). *Clinical and Diagnostic Interviewing.* Northvale, NJ: Jason Aronson.

Dieperink, E. (2000). Neuropsychiatric symptoms associated with hepatitis C and interferon alpha: A review. *American Journal of Psychiatry* 157:867–876.

Engel, G. L. (1977). The need for a new medical model: A challenge for biomedicine. *Science* 196:130–136.

Fenichel, O. (1945). *The Psychoanalytic Theory of Neurosis.* New York: Norton.

Fishman, M., Hoffman, A., Klausner, R., & Thaler, M. (1991). *Medicine*, 3rd ed. Philadelphia: Lippincott.

Frank, A. (1991). *At the Will of the Body: Reflections on Illness*. Boston: Houghton Mifflin.

Gaarder, K. R., & Montgomery, P. S. (1977). *Clinical Biofeedback: A Procedural Manual*. Baltimore: Williams & Wilkins.

Gatchel, R. J., & Blanchard, E. B., eds. (1993). *Psychophysiological Disorders: Research and Clinical Applications*. Washington: American Psychological Association.

Gleason, O. C., & Yates, W. R. (1999). Five cases of interferon-alpha-induced depression treated with antidepressant therapy. *Psychosomatics* 40:510–512.

Grisso, T., & Applebaum, P. S. (1998). *Assessing Competence to Consent to Treatment: A Guide for Physicians and Other Health Professionals*. New York: Oxford University.

Gruba-McCallister, F. (1989). Phenomenological orientation to the interview. In *Clinical and Diagnostic Interviewing*, ed. R. J. Craig, pp. 18–31. Northvale, NJ: Jason Aronson.

Hafen, B. Q., Karren, K. J., Frandsen, K. J., & Smith, N. L. (1996). *Mind/Body Health: The Effects of Attitudes, Emotions and Relationships*. Boston: Allyn & Bacon.

Huszti, H. C., & Walker, C. E. (1991). Critical issues in consultation and liaison: Pediatrics. In *Handbook of Clinical Psychology in Medical Settings*, ed. J. J. Sweet, R. H. Rozensky, & S. M. Tovian, pp. 165–185. New York: Plenum.

Melamed, B. G., & Siegel, L. J. (1980). *Behavioral Medicine: Practical Applications in Health Care*. New York: Springer.

Parsons, T. (1951). *The Social System*. New York: Free Press.

Schontz, F. C. (1971). Physical disability and personality. In *Rehabilitation Psychology*, ed. W. S. Neff, pp. 33–73. Washington, DC: American Psychological Association.

Sontag, S. (1978). *Illness as Metaphor*. New York: Ferrar, Straus & Giroux.

Sternberg, E. M., & Gold, P. W. (2002). The mind–body interaction in disease. *Scientific American* 12:82–89.

Stone, G. C., Cohen, F., & Adler, N. E., eds. (1979). *Health Psychology: A Handbook*. San Francisco: Jossey-Bass.

Sweet, J. J. (1991). Psychological evaluation and testing services in medical settings. In *Handbook of Clinical Psychology in Medical Settings*, ed. J. J. Sweet, R. H. Rozensky, & S. M. Tovian, pp. 291–313. New York: Plenum.

Tunks, E., & Bellissimo, A. (1991). *Behavioral Medicine: Concepts and Procedures*. New York: Pergamon.

Turk, D. C., Meichenbaum, D., & Genest, M. (1983). *Pain and Behavioral Medicine: A Cognitive–Behavioral Perspective*. New York: Guilford.

Van Egeren, L., & Striepe, M. (1998). Assessment approaches in health psychology: Issues and practical considerations. In *Clinical Handbook of Health Psychology: A Practical Guide to Effective Interventions*, ed. P. M. Camic & S. J. Knight, pp. 17–50. Seattle: Hogrefe & Huber.

Wakely, D. J. (2001). [Book review on cancer patients and their families]. *Biofeedback* 29(2):28–29.

Wincze, J., & Carey, M. (2001). *Sexual Dysfunction: A Guide for Assessment and Treatment*. New York: Guilford.

21

THE FORENSIC INTERVIEW

J. Reid Meloy, Ph.D.

In 1924, the lord chancellor of England said "Psychology is a most dangerous science to apply to practical affairs" (Overholser, 1953, p. 109). Nowhere is this more apparent than in the forensic arena, through which clinicians walk as invited but not necessarily welcomed guests. The dangers to the professional, moreover, in such an adversarial and public system are legion, yet the opportunities are challenging and exciting.

A forensic interview is a clinical interview conducted in the context of a legal process or pertaining to a psycholegal question. This chapter will present six distinguishing characteristics of the forensic interview. Focusing on the core dimensions of the forensic interview naturally leads to thoughts about specific knowledge, skills, attitudes, approaches, and techniques that clinicians can apply to the forensic interview and clinical services to these patients/clients.

THE COERCIVE CONTEXT

The term *forensic* is derived from the Latin *forensis*, meaning "the forum" (Webster, 1977). The forum is commonly understood as a public, or legal, forum, hence the application of the term to describe those professionals who practice in a legal context, whether they be psychologists, psychiatrists, or other mental health professionals. Inherent in this forensic context is the *element of coercion, the first core characteristic* that distinguishes forensic interviews from other interviews. Complete voluntariness should never be assumed. Rather, it should be assumed that the interviewee is being either partially or completely forced to do something against his or her will.

The element of coercion is often obvious. A criminal defendant's attorney recognizes that the client can cooperate neither with the attorney nor with the legal proceedings. The attorney therefore enters a motion for the client to be evaluated to determine whether the client is competent to stand trail (*Dusky v.*

United States). The defendant, by virtue of the case and statutory law surrounding procedures to determine competency to stand trial, can refuse the evaluation only if the client is willing to risk being held in contempt of court (Melton et al., 1987). Yet the client's Fifth Amendment right against compulsory self-incrimination is also protected if he or she should give evidence during the competency evaluation that is further incriminating. Even though a competency motion granted by the court usually benefits the defense due to a complete suspension of the criminal proceedings, a seriously mentally disordered defendant, perhaps with a paranoid delusional system, would probably irrationally, but strenuously, resist answering questions in a forthright manner. One defendant who was brought to me for a competency evaluation while in custody angrily accused me of being a "school-worm." Intrigued by this neologism, I asked him what that meant. He replied, "an educated person trying to worm his way into my mind."

A more subtle form of coercion may be present in a civil custody dispute. A mother of a four-year-old daughter accuses her ex-husband of violating certain visitation terms in the divorce decree. A psychologist is appointed by the court to evaluate the situation and make recommendations to the court. The forensic psychologist, seasoned to the inherent distortions that occur in custody disputes, insists that the entire family be evaluated, both individually and as a unit, including the individual parents' new live-in companions, consistent with guidelines from the American Psychological Association pertaining to custody evaluations. The mother, who initiated the proceedings through her attorney in the hope of reducing her ex-husband's visitation, is now in the uncomfortable position of being interviewed by a psychologist and probably completing certain psychological tests. To her relief, she is initially asked only about her parenting attitudes and beliefs, but she suddenly feels coerced and invaded when the psychologist begins the process of psychological testing.

Coercion may also be an internally perceived process, such as the case of a paranoid schizophrenic who is compelled by command hallucinations to confess to a murder. Such intrapsychic coercion, although no longer recognized by the U.S. Supreme Court as a legal basis for compulsory self-incrimination (*Colorado v. Connelly*), may still be quite clinically salient to the forensic interview.

How should the forensic interviewer respond to this ubiquitous core characteristic? First, this question should be considered prior to the evaluation: What are the legal and clinical factors in this particular interview that could be perceived as coercive? Second, once these factors are identified, the clinician should consider ways in which coercion will affect the interview. One of the major ways is through malingering or dissembling (concealment) of symptoms, a separate core characteristic that I will consider later. Third, the clinician should tailor the interview to minimize the impact of coercive factors: (1) conduct the interview in a neutral setting if at all possible—evaluations in custody settings *must* be done in a private, soundproof interview room, although security personnel may insist, for good reason, that they be able to visually observe the interview—(2) ask that the interviewee not be physically restrained during the interview unless there is imminent risk to your safety, which there may be; (3) inquire about the reasons for restraints before requesting their removal; and (4) discuss your speculations abut the coercive elements of the interview directly and empathically with the interviewee. This brief, but frank discussion will help establish rapport without misleading the interviewee and should predict the extent to which the evaluation will be reliable and valid.

> A female superior court judge had been verbally threatened by a defendant, now in custody, and asked me to evaluate him. Supported by civil and case Law (*Tarasoff v. Regents of the University of California*), I agreed. The defendant was brought to me while in custody. He sat and glowered at me, remaining mute. I explained to him the nature of my interview and made several empathic statements about the obvious coercion he must be feeling. He stared at me. I then asked him if he understood my statements but was voluntarily choosing not to answer me, he should nod his head. He did. I then told him that if he wanted to end our brief encounter, he should nod his head. He did. The deputy escorted him, at my request, back to his cell.

All criminal defendants should be allowed an opportunity to consult with counsel before they participate in a forensic psychological interview. This protects the defendant's Sixth Amendment right to counsel, shields the clinician from inadvertently giving legal "advice" concerning the defendant's choice to participate in the interview, and may attenuate the felt concern during the interview. In civil proceedings, such as personal injury and custody cases, a right to consult with counsel is usually a moot issue, since no criminal process is involved and both parties have usually retained their own counsel prior to any request for a psychological interview.

THE ABSENCE OF PRIVILEGE

Mental health professionals are ethically trained to value and protect the confidentiality of patient care and its written products. The legal correlate of confidentiality—privileged communication—is also considered an essential right held by the patient. In forensic interviews, however, there is virtually always a partial or complete waiver of privilege. This is often quite unsettling to the clinician first entering the forensic arena, because it jostles the heretofore sanctified belief in the inviolate nature of the patient–therapist relationship. Also, the professional's behavior is no longer as insulated as one would like it to be.

The nature and degree of waivers of privilege are quite variable. Criminal defendants entering a plea of not guilty by reason of insanity automatically waive all privilege since they are introducing their mental state at the time of the alleged crime as a complete defense. The court forces a partial waiver of privilege when it finds reasonable doubt that a criminal defendant is competent to stand trial, even if the prosecution enters the motion; yet the forensic examination is limited to evaluation of the defendant's psychological processes relevant only to his competency, and incriminating evidence uncovered during the examination is protected. Depending on the jurisdiction, clinicians retained by the defense in a criminal trial and then subsequently not used as experts may or may not be called as witnesses by the prosecution (*United States ex. Rel. Edney v. Smith; United States v. Alvarez*). The judicial rule of thumb in most criminal litigation is balancing of the individual's rights to privileged communication and the public safety. In civil litigation, waiver of privilege is often carefully controlled by the court. California, for example, established a constitutional basis for privileged communication between therapist and patient.

How should the forensic interviewer respond to this core characteristic? First, therapists should be thoroughly familiar with their jurisdiction's penal code, civil code, and evidence code concerning privileged communication. There may be contradictions among these codes, and subsequent case law may have been written to clarify or delineate the nature and extent of privilege in certain representative cases.

Second, the clinician should be quite familiar with one's profession's code of ethics, and should ponder potential areas of conflict in a particular case between professional ethical principles and the jurisdiction's settled law. For example, the American Psychological Association states that psychologists have an ethical responsibility to "avoid undue invasion of privacy" (American Psychological Association, 2002). However, ethical principles generally carry little weight in court.

Third, the legal context of a particular case, and its impact upon privilege, should be thoroughly assessed and understood before the forensic interview. A legal consultation with an attorney *knowledgeable in this areas of law* may be quite propitious.

Fourth, at the beginning of the interview, forensic clinicians should spend as much time as needed to explain to the interviewee who they are, what they are doing, why they are doing it, how they are going to do it, what will be produced, and where the product will be used. The interviewee must be fully informed. For example, I might conduct this portion of the interview as follows:

Hello, Mr. Smith. My name is Dr. Reid Meloy. I am a psychologist hired by your attorney [who] to meet with you this afternoon. I am here to learn as much as I can about you, and the crime you are charged with [what]. As you know, the reason I am here is that you and your attorney are considering an insanity defense. This means that because of a mental disorder at the time of the crime, you were not responsible for your behavior [why]. Any questions?

I will be talking with you and asking you lots of questions. You do not have to answer any of them, and can ask me to repeat or clarify any questions you don't understand. I'll also be asking you to fill out some questionnaires, and I may ask you to respond to certain objects, drawings, or pictures that I'll show you [how]. Any questions?

When we're finished, I will be thinking about everything you've told me and studying all the other information I've received from your attorney. Then I will write a report [what]. This report, which I expect to have finished one week from today, will be sent only to your attorney. But if you plead insanity, my report will go to the court, the judge, and the district attorney [where]. I can then be forced to testify truthfully and completely about anything you've told me or any opinions that I've formed. Any questions? Do you understand? Can you tell me briefly what I've told you so I know you understand.

The disclosure of such information, although it appears tedious, is generally expected behavior in forensic interviews. It is consonant with ethical principles wherein psychologists must fully inform consumers as to the nature and purpose of evaluation procedures (American Psychological Association, 2002) and with case law (*Estelle v. Smith*).

The doctrine of informed consent is not as germane to a forensic interview as it is to treatment, since most forensic evaluations are court ordered. However, the clinician should be sensitive to the possible need for informed consent prior to a forensic interview and should seek it in writing if necessary. Three elements are considered to determine whether informed consent has been obtained: (1) the adequacy of disclosure from both the clinician's and the patient's perspective, (2) the patient's competency to give consent, and (3) the voluntariness of the consent (*Salgo v. Leland Stanford Jr. Univ. Bd. of Trustees*; Grisso, 1986). Informed consent is more likely to be a requirement in civil work (personal injury, family, and custody cases) than in criminal work.

A LAY COMMUNICATION TOOL

Unlike other mental health interviews, *the forensic interview is essentially a means to gather information that can then be communicated to nonmental health professionals.* The product of the forensic interview, whether it be a written report or an oral testimony, is only valuable if it is understandable to educated lay professionals, usually attorneys and judges. The clarity, simplicity, and thoroughness of the work product not only will determine its usefulness in a particular case, but it also will either enhance or discredit the forensic clinician's reputation. In no other mental health specialty is one's "paper trail" more important to professional standing in the community. Even if the report does not become a matter of public record, it may be exhumed years later in another legal matter concerning the same individual. The forensic report, and to a lesser degree forensic testimony, is the legacy of the forensic clinician.

Clarity means that the written and oral communication about the forensic interview is free of technical jargon or that technical terms, if they are necessary, are carefully defined throughout the report or testimony. For instance, delusions are defined as "fixed and false beliefs."

Simplicity means that any individual of average intelligence can understand what the report means. This is a measure of external validity or utility. It is the mandate that one must expose one's ideas and opinions to their reflections in the variously shaped mirrors of others (Gill, 1967). Projection as a psychological defense, for instance, can simply be understood as the attribution of one's thoughts and feelings to others. If the psychological concept is too esoteric or complex, it is useless in the forensic context. It may be ambiguous to begin with, or it just may need to be further analyzed, or broken down for intelligent consumption. Forensic communication requires disciplined and analytic thought, often anathema to clinicians who are trained only to be synthetic or empathic.

Thoroughness means that every issue is explored if it is relevant to the forensic issue being addressed. Forensic interviewing usually requires additional corroboration of the data gleaned from the interview. Nothing discredits a forensic clinician more than mere regurgitation of the interviewee's perspective in the report or through testimony. It is evidence of the clinician's laziness and naïveté, and may be very embarrassing if easily contradicted by information that was available but was not sought.

How should the forensic clinician manage the forensic interview as a means of communication? First, the forensic interviewer's written and oratory skills should be reasonably good. Close attention should be paid to one's writing skills, and much can be gained by reading books devoted to improved writing. Second, forensic report writing should be addressed as a specialized skill through some excellent texts (Blau, 1984; Curran et al., 1986; Melton, et al., 1987; Rogers, 1986; Shapiro, 1984). Most forensic reports, regardless of legal context, should include the following content, in this sequence:

1. Legal reason for evaluation
2. Complete database used in the evaluation
3. History of defendant/patient
4. Clinical observations during the interview
5. Mental status exam
6. Interpretation of psychological test findings
7. DSM-IV diagnosis
8. Clinical findings
9. Clinical opinion
10. Recommendations

Third, note taking during the forensic interview should be sufficient to ensure reliability and validity and may be protected as the clinician's "work product."

Test protocols and answer sheets may be sought by attorneys for either side, however, despite the clinician's ethical obligation to protect such data (American Psychological Association, 2002). Although case law in this specific area has not developed, the forensic psychologist should refuse to turn over any "raw data" such as test answer sheets and protocols, except to another qualified psychologist, usually retained by the other side. Psychiatrists are generally not qualified to interpret raw psychological test data. It has been my experience that if the court orders the raw data to be produced through *subpoena duces tecum*, then a letter to the court accompanying the data, explaining the ethical violation of such conduct on the part of the psychologist and requesting that the court turn over the data to another qualified psychologist retained by the other side, will suffice in protecting this important professional privilege (*People v. Laws*).

If this argument fails, it may be useful to distinguish for the court the difference between the psychologist's "work product" (notes, scoring, interpretations) and the interviewee's "raw psychological test data" (answer sheets, drawings, projective responses). Dr. Sherry Skidmore (personal communication) has suggested that a set of *unscored* answer sheets and responses sent to the opposing psychologist can be a useful way of demarcating "work product" from "raw data," since a *scored* Rorschach protocol, for example, is a combination of both raw data from the patient and "work" done by the psychologist. Unscored and uninterpreted data also protect the patient.

Fourth, the forensic interviewer should strive to be both an empiricist and a humanist in the communication to others concerning a particular case. The presentation, whether oral testimony or formal report, should be a complete behavioral science document, but it should also communicate an *experiential feel* for the interviewee. This is the science and art of forensic psychological communication.

DISTORTION

The fourth core characteristic of the forensic interview is the *conscious distortion of information provided during the evaluation*. This is a direct outgrowth of the first core characteristic, coercion, but it is also spawned by the general presence of external factors that would be considered "secondary gain" in most forensic settings, such as monetary settlement, movement to a less restrictive level of care (prison to a hospital), or mitigation of a criminal offense.

Although there are a wide variety of forms of distortion, I will limit the discussion to conscious, willful distortion by the interviewee. Other forms of distortion that have more symbolic and unconscious meanings, such as factitious disorder, must be clinically ruled out in forensic evaluations, but they are not as prevalent as intentional distortion. This core characteristics *must be assumed to exist* in all forensic interviews until it is disproven.

Distortion in the interview usually takes one of two forms: *simulation* (malingering), which is the feigning of symptoms that do not exist, and *dissimulation* (dissembling), which is the concealment or minimization of symptoms that actually do exist. Other combinations are possible. Garner (1965) defines pure malingering as the feigning of disease where none exists, partial malingering as the conscious exaggeration of symptoms that do exist, and false imputation as the ascribing of actual symptoms to a cause consciously recognized as having no relationship to the symptoms.

Malingering is listed as a "V Code" in DSM-IV (American Psychiatric Association, 1994). It should be strongly suspected in any medicolegal setting if any combination of the following are noted: marked discrepancy between claimed symptoms and objective findings, lack of cooperation during the diagnostic evaluation, and a diagnosis of antisocial personality disorder. This "suspicion index" would also apply to dissimulation.

How should the forensic clinician respond to the core characteristic of distortion? Prior to any forensic evaluation, whether civil or criminal, one should construct the hypothesis that *distortion will be present in this evaluation.* Once this particular perspective is taken, *disproving* this hypothesis then becomes the clinical task. In order to accomplish this, the clinician must be familiar with the research literature on simulation and dissimulation (Adelman & Howard, 1984; Gorman, 1984; Resnick, 1984; Rogers, 1984a). Rogers (1984a) constructed both heuristic and empirical models of malingering and deception, and I have adapted and combined them in table 21.1.

All indicators have heuristic support among a group of experienced forensic clinicians that Rogers (1984a) surveyed. This table also covers the three data sources for the clinician to consider in determining whether an interviewee is distorting: the clinical interview, psychological testing, and independent corroborative information. A judgment of distortion should not be made without corroboration of all three data sets, if available.

The clinical interview's contribution to the distortion hypothesis can be viewed from the dual perspective of observation and intervention. Observations of an individual attempting to distort or deceive find direction in the following research conclusions: increased body movements and postural shifts are more indicative of deception than is facial expression (Ekman and Friesen, 1969; McClintock & Hunt, 1975; Rogers, 1984a); visual clues serve more as a distraction than as a facilitation in the detection of deception (Littlepage & Pineault, 1978; Rogers, 1984a); verbal content is a primary determinant in the direction of deception (Maier & Thurber, 1968; Rogers, 1984a); intuitive assumptions concerning an individual's veracity may lead to misjudgments in the face of actual honesty or dishonesty (Zuckerman et al., 1979); and clinical research of distortion in psychiatric populations is extremely important, but very limited (Rogers, 1984a).

Interventions during the clinical interview to ferret out distortion include purposeful lengthening of the interview to induce fatigue; varying of the pace

Table 21.1. Clinical Indicators of Distortion

Indicators	Response Styles		
	Reliable	*Simulated*	*Dissimulated*
Severity of symptoms	variable	severe	minimal
Selectivity of reporting symptoms	selective	overendorsed	underendorsed
Consistency of self-report	consistent	consistent	consistent
Contradictory symptoms	unlikely	likely	unlikely
Rare symptoms	unlikely	likely	unlikely
Sequence of symptoms	consistent with diagnosis	inconsistent	inconsistent
Obvious v. subtle symptoms	balanced	more obvious	more subtle
Appearance of symptoms	gradual onset & resolution	sudden onset	sudden resolution
Memory of past psychological problems	normal memory	heightened memory of impairment	heightened memory of adjustment
Potentially self-damaging statements	likely	unlikely	unlikely
Random response pattern	no	unlikely	no
Self-report consistent with clinical observation	no	unlikely	unlikely
Endorsement of highly specified symptoms	unlikely	likely	unlikely

Adapted by permission of van Nostrand Reinhold from Rogers (1984a). Underlines denote indicators that are empirically supported in the literature (a five-year search of *Psychological Abstracts*, PsyInfo, and NCMHI databases).

and speed of questioning; confrontation of the interviewee with the suspicion that he or she is distorting; repeat questioning with sufficient time and interference to increase the difficulty of remembering prior deceptions; suggesting the need for twenty-four-hour hospitalization to thoroughly assess the clinical situation (and sometimes carrying out the suggestion); in criminal settings, evaluation of the defendant as soon as possible after the crime was committed; avoidance of leading or suggestible questions about symptoms; use of open-ended questions to inquire about symptoms (for example, "Can you describe to me what it is like to be depressed?"); intentional mixing of symptoms from various diagnostic categories that are usually mutually excludable (for example, "Do you ever have auditory and visual hallucinations right after you've had a drink of alcohol?"); linking of preposterous symptoms to complaints ("Have you noticed a change in your hat or glove size since you started hearing voices?"); purposeful inducing of stress ("I don't want you to be anxious about what I am going to ask you next"); and expanding on details at random without following a detectable sequence. I always try to present myself as an "ambiguous stimulus" to the interviewee, especially at the beginning of the evaluation, after the initial legal and ethical introductions. This minimizes clues to which the interviewee can consciously adapt if he or she is planning a distortion strategy. If he is not planning to distort, the presentation should be quite reliable and valid without needing me to provoke the antecedents for the behavior.

Thorough knowledge of the nature and expression of certain commonly feigned symptoms is also very important. Hallucinations, for instance, are a troublesome symptom in a forensic setting because they cannot be absolutely disproved or objectively measured. Yet clinical research has given the clinician a wealth of information about hallucinations, particularly in schizophrenia. Command hallucinations are experienced by only a small proportion (less than 20 percent of schizophrenic patients) and are successfully resisted by most patients who hear them. Command hallucinations do not significantly increase the risk of inpatient violence (Hellerstein et al., 1987). Hallucinations are usually accompanied by delusions, and are usually related to some psychic purpose (Resnick 1984). Voices speaking directly to the patient or commenting on one's behavior are characteristic of schizophrenia, but are less easily discussed than alcohol-induced hallucinations (Alpert & Silvers 1970; Resnick 1984). Schizophrenic hallucinations are usually intermittent and rarely continuous (Goodwin et al., 1971). The majority of schizophrenic patients, when asked if their hallucinations could be the product of their imagination, will say yes (Goodwin et al., 1971). Most auditory hallucinations will be heard "outside" the head and will contain both male and female voices. The message is usually clear, and it is accusatory about one-third of the time (Goodwin et al., 1971). Hallucinating patients should be asked what they do to make the voices go away. Common coping strategies include specific activities, changes in posture, seeking out others, and taking medication (Resnick, 1984).

Patient A complained of continuous auditory hallucinations telling him to kill his sister. He was absolutely sure that the voices were a product of his schizophrenia, which he gladly talked about with any clinician. He said that they were always "inside" his head, especially when one of the clinicians suggested that this location of hallucinations was "much more serious" than if they occurred "outside" his head. He had not thought of any strategies to alleviate the "voices." The clinical staff concluded that he was malingering (simulating) the symptom of auditory hallucinations, and his motivation to deceive became a focus of treatment.

The use of psychological tests to ferret out distortions in a forensic setting is the second source of data to be considered by the clinician. It is beyond the scope of this chapter to review all of the psychological tests commonly used to detect distortion, so I will briefly comment on two of the most widely used tests: the Minnesota Multiphasic Personality Inventory-2 (MMPI-2, Butcher et al., 1989) and the Rorschach.

Self-report measures in clinical populations are inherently unreliable (Hare, 1985a). Yet the MMPI-2 should be considered the clinician's "workhorse" in adult forensic interviews due to the enormous amount of research available concerning its clinical use and the sensitivity of its various indicators of distortion.

The most commonly used indicator of distortion, whether simulation (fake bad) or dissimulation (fake good) is the configuration of the validity scales L, F, K. Since the early work of Hunt (1948) and Gough (1950), the F-K index has been confirmed as a reliable indicator of distortion (Baer et al., 1992; Berry et al., 1991; Green, 1990; Osborne et al., 1986; Rogers, 1984a).

The Wiener (1948) Subtle-Obvious items on five scales of the MMPI also appear to be useful in forensic settings. A difference of greater than 1 standard deviation between subtle and obvious items on any one of the scales should alert the clinician to the possibility of simulation or dissimulation around the particular symptom complex that is measured by the scale, depending on the direction of the difference (subtle items greater than obvious items suggests dissimulation; obvious items greater than subtle items suggests simulation). Rogers (1983) notes, however, that specific indicators of randomness should be measured before distortion conclusions are drawn from the Wiener-Harmon subscales. These might include VRIN, TRIN, F(B), and Fp scales.

The Rorschach remains the second most widely used psychological test (Piotrowski et al., 1985) by members of the Society for Personality Assessment, and it is popular with other clinicians as well (Lubin et al., 1984). The Comprehensive Scoring System (Exner, 1993) is now the only scoring system that is in frequent use.

Controversy surrounds the vulnerability of the Rorschach to distortion (Perry & Kinder, 1990). Albert and coworkers (1980) found that a group of untrained subjects could successfully simulate paranoid schizophrenia and fool a group of expert clinicians who were given their Rorschachs to interpret. This study has been criticized, however, for its small sample size (six subjects in each group), blind analysis, and unknown methods of scoring (Exner, 1978; Ziskin 1984). Exner (1993) and others (Seamons et al., 1981) have found that standardized administration and scoring of Rorschach protocols did allow for respectable discrimination between faked and genuinely psychotic Rorschach protocols.

The heart of Rorschach distortion appears to lie in the difference between content and structural analysis. Both Exner (1993) and Seamons and associates (1981) have noted that the layperson's idea of "faking psychosis" is to give dramatic and fantastic content responses. Blind content analysis of such data would be misleading in the absence of other behavioral data. Structural analysis of the same protocol would probably yield nonpsychotic indices, however, since these would be much more difficult to compute and distort, even with prior knowledge of their meaning. In the Exner (1993) system, such indices as X+%, X-% and Special Scores, as indicators of reality convergence, reality distortion, and cognitive slippage, would be very difficult to intentionally distort.

I would suggest that interpretation of the Rorschach in a forensic setting begin with the Comprehensive System (Exner, 1993) to determine whether the protocol is valid, with a particular focus upon number of responses and lamda (see Meloy, 1988, for Rorschach criteria with psychopathic individuals). The Exner (1993) scoring system is also the most defensible in court (Meloy, 1991) due to the extensive empirical studies that have been done. Once validity has been established, content analysis of the Rorschach can then proceed so that certain object relational and psychodynamic patterns are fully apprehended. I think this multidimensional analysis of the Rorschach is most revealing and useful in forensic settings (Meloy, 1988). My clinical experience suggests that the best way to "beat" the Rorschach is to refuse to take the test, but this behavior is also diagnostically and behaviorally revealing.

The third source of data to be considered in distortion is collaborative information on the individual. This source is crucial to disproving the distortion hypothesis and should be aggressively pursued by the forensic examiner. One very useful forensic instrument, the Hare Psychopathy Checklist (Hare, 1991), a trait measure of psychopathic disturbance completed by the forensic clinician, has *greater* reliability and validity when based upon only corroborative information than when based upon only the clinical interview (Hare, 1985b).

The following behaviors are useful in increasing the amount of available corroborative information: obtain all records on the patient (school, medical, psychiatric, psychological, criminal history, arrest, prosecution, defense, archival court, and so on) and read them before the examination; meet with the patient at least twice and consider administering some tests twice, to measure temporal reliability; audiotape or videotape the evaluation, always with the patient's permission, and review it later; conduct collateral interviews, using the efficiency of the telephone to do so; and gather data on the patient in as "naturalistic" a manner as possible. The latter method might include observing the patient approaching and leaving the office; observing the patient's interactions with others; asking the secretary about the individual's behavior in the waiting room; or visiting the individual's home (or jail module) for a portion of the evaluation. It can also be useful at the end of the evaluation for the clinician to lay paper and pencil down, sit back, and ask the patient, "Now, is there anything else you'd like to tell me?" The obvious nonverbal clues here suggest to the patient that the clinician may be receptive to some "off the record" comments, without actually saying so. It is a misleading, and some would consider deceptive, gesture, but it may yield important new information.

When evaluating for criminal responsibility, it is especially important to talk to individuals who observed the defendant just prior to, during, or right after the offense. The reconstruction of an offense is central to the task of inferring the defendant's state of mind, and therefore criminal responsibility, in all insanity evaluations (Rogers 1986).

DISAGREEMENT AND SCRUTINY

Regardless of the clarity, simplicity, and thoroughness of the work product of the forensic interview (oral testimony or written report), it will usually be *disagreed with by opposing* counsel. This is the nature of the adversarial system wherein the two sides of any legal question advocate as strongly as possible for their opposite positions. The judicial hope is that the trier of fact, whether judge or jury, will then be better able to discern the truth.

The forensic clinician must prepare himself or herself for this adversarial reality, being careful not to personalize and feel narcissistically insulted by disagreements from "the other side." It is less usual to have both legal counsels to stipulate (accept) the forensic work product, and this most commonly happens when the forensic psychologist is appointed as *amicus curiae* (friend of the court) to conduct the evaluation. Such consensual gifts are the exception, not the rule.

Disagreement by opposing counsel is therefore accompanied by careful scrutiny of the work product to ferret out mistakes; such errors of omission or commission during the forensic interview then serve as points of attack during cross-examination if the case goes to trial.

Such disagreements and scrutiny are the fifth distinguishing core characteristic of the forensic interview. How should the forensic clinician prepare for this core characteristic? *Most fundamentally, forensic clinicians should advocate for their data and interpretations based upon sound scientific reasoning.* This should take precedence over all personal philosophy, political views, social reformist ideals, and therapeutic goals for the patient. The forensic interview is not the place to develop a social advocacy or psychotherapy treatment plan for the interviewee.

This principle is most easily followed when the clinician is appointed by the court, since it presents major difficulties when the clinician is retained by counsel and the forensic interview findings are not what the counsel wants. The attorney will likely seek another examiner, reluctantly pay the clinician's bill, and not call that psychologist again. This may be quite economically damaging in the short run, but in the long run it will build the clinician's reputation among attorneys and judges as a professional who *cannot be bought*. It takes great integrity and resolve to maintain a neutral, behaviorally scientific position in an adversarial system that is continuously attempting to distort the facts and findings of every scientific investigator and may initially punish by not referring more cases.

Moreover, the ability to advocate successfully for a forensic database depends upon the reliability and validity of the content of the database. Certain steps can be taken to ensure that the forensic interview is both reliable and valid.

First, attorneys should be excluded from observing or participating in most forensic interviews. The one exception may be during an evaluation for competency to stand trial, when the interactions between the attorney and client are crucial behavioral samples used to correctly answer the legal question. This exclusionary position finds case law support at both the federal and state level for both criminal and civil evaluations. Despite the opposing Sixth Amendment right to counsel, most courts have deferred to the request of the clinician that attorneys be excluded in both civil and criminal proceedings when the examiner is court appointed (*United States v. Byers, Durst v. Superior Court, Taratino v. Superior Court, In re Spencer, Rollerson v. United States, Edwards v. Superior Court, Vinson v. Superior Court*). The American Bar Association (1984) also supports the exclusion of counsel from clinical interviews in most cases. However, attorneys do not like to be excluded from anything. Such a clinical position may raise the ire of counsel, particularly opposing counsel, but when faced with such a demand it is very important not to capitulate. The clinician should allow the attorney to take the demand to court in the form of a motion and let the court rule on the appropriateness of attorney presence.

Second, it is most wise to use structured interview formats when conducting forensic interviews. Such formats demonstrate to anyone who scrutinizes clinicians' work that they do have a "standard of care" and are interested in their own clinical reliability. It also ensures that crucial areas to be probed will not be overlooked because of momentary anxiety or distraction.

Structured interview formats may range from the clinician's own list of questions that he or she repeatedly uses when certain psychological questions are addressed, to much more formalized structured interviews that have both reliability and validity in the larger scientific community.

One such instrument, the Rogers Criminal Responsibility Assessment Scales (R-CRAS), is an excellent example of a structured interview for evaluating insanity at the time of the criminal offense (Rogers, 1984b). The R-CRAS

is a systematic and criterion-based instrument. It consists of a fifteen-page examination booklet that is organized into two parts. Part 1 consists of twenty-five
assessment criteria that are each quantified into four to six gradations of increasing severity. They address patient reliability, organicity, psychopathology, cognitive control, and behavioral control. Part 2 consists of three decision models that
operationalize the American Law Institute Guilty But Mentally Ill and Mc-
Naughten standards of criminal responsibility. The structured instrument has a
moderate degree of internal consistency and a high degree of interjudge reliability (Meloy, 1986).

A second example of a structured interview, this time used to assess competency to stand trial, is the Interdisciplinary Fitness Interview (IFI) by Golding and associates (1984). Ideally used as a joint interview by both a mental
health professional and an attorney, the IFI covers the joint domains of psychopathology and law from an explicitly functional perspective. It consists of
three sections: legal items (for example, "quality of relationship with one's attorney"); psychopathological items (for example "delusional processes"); and an
overall evaluation ("overall fitness judgment").

Interjudge agreement yielded a kappa coefficient of .93 in one study
(Golding et al., 1984). It appears to have both a low false positive rate and a low
false negative rate, but additional validity studies are needed (Meloy, 1985).

A third example of structured interviewing, although not standardized, is the
"structural interview" developed by Kernberg (1984). In Kernberg's own words,

> The structured diagnostic interview . . . combines a psychoanalytic focus on
> the patient–interviewer interaction with a psychoanalytic technique for inter-
> preting conflictual issues and defensive operations in this interaction in order
> to highlight the classical anchoring symptoms of descriptive psychopathology
> and the underlying personality structure. (Kernberg, 1984, p. 30)

Kernberg's interview begins in a traditional manner with a history taking
and mental status examination, but then probes more deeply into the patient's
personality by focusing on questions that are bound to elicit certain transference and countertransference reactions: emotions perceived by the examiner
that may be crucial to identifying underlying Axis II disorders that are endemic
in forensic settings. Kernberg begins his investigation of pathological character
traits with the following questions; "You have told me about your difficulties,
and I would now like to hear more about you as a person. Could you describe
yourself, your personality, what you think is important for me to know so that
I can get a real feeling for you as a person?" (p. 33). Such a structured interview
that combines both descriptive-symptomatic and object relational areas of inquiry can be particularly useful in assessing psychopathically disturbed individuals (Meloy, 1988).

A third method to ensure the reliability and validity of the forensic interview is always to address the psychological question—nothing more and noth-

ing less. The design of the forensic interview should be a logical outgrowth of the psychological question to be answered, and the database produced by the interview should build inferences that logically answer the psychological question. Anyone scrutinizing the forensic clinician's work should not be surprised by the interview methods or tests chosen to address a particular question, and subsequently should not be taken aback by the conclusions drawn from the accrued database.

I am always amazed at the frequency with which this seemingly simple and direct proposition is not followed by forensic clinicians. One way this commonly occurs is by what I call the "Oh, no!" technique (rather than the "Ah ha" experience). One is carefully reading forensic evaluation that appears to be accumulating more and more information supporting a particular legal opinion (for example, the individual did not know the difference between right and wrong at the time of the offense). Suddenly, on the last page, the evaluator renders the *exact opposite* opinion and the reader is left feeling surprised and confused. Reasons for such Aristotelean failures abound, but the essential problem is that the logical progression has been negated and reversed.

Another common way this occurs is by what I call the "leap-before-you-look" technique. One begins by reading a forensic evaluation that is supposedly addressing a psychological question. As the report proceeds, the reader waits expectantly, and more impatiently, for the forensic interviewer to *do* something or *say* something that is relevant to the psychological question. Then the report is finished with an opinion and a recommendation.

Something has been lost; the structure of the interview, the questions asked, the test administered, the database collected, and the resultant conclusions *had nothing to do with the psychological question*. I have read reports that addressed competency to stand trial when the psycholegal question was insanity at the time of the offense. I have seen psychiatrists render opinions of dangerousness based solely upon a diagnosis of schizophrenia. The forensic interview must be scientifically relevant and therefore a valid measure of the psychological question.

The courts have long recognized the importance of reliability and validity in expert testimony, and the admonition set forth in *Frye v. United States* is also applicable to the structuring of the forensic interview:

> Just when a scientific principle or discovery crosses the line between the experimental and demonstrable stages is difficult to define. Somewhere in this twilight zone the evidential force of the principle must be recognized, and while courts will go a long way in admitting expert testimony deduced from a well-recognized scientific principle or discovery, the thing from which the deduction is made *must be sufficiently established to have gained general acceptance in the particular field in which it belongs*. (*Frye v. United States*; italics mine)

This admonition, known as the "Frye test," is usually understood to mean that the particular scientific technique in question must be accepted by a majority of the profession, usually through authoritative scientific writings and other judicial citations.

The mental status examination, for example, would successfully pass the Frye test because it is used by most clinicians in conducting diagnostic evaluations. In fact, the *absence* of a mental status examination during a diagnostic evaluation could call into question the interviewer's competence. But forensic clinicians using the Piotrowski method for interpreting the Rorschach could be seriously challenged using the Frye test, since only 5 percent of survey respondents espouse this method of Rorschach interpretation (Piotrowski et al., 1985). The Exner Comprehensive System has now gained acceptance among clinicians (Watkins et al., 1995) and is probably the only Rorschach interpretive method that will pass the Frye and Daubert (see below) standards.

In 1993, the Supreme Court changed the rules of evidence. In *Daubert v Merrell Dow Pharmaceuticals*, the court ruled that the trier of fact (e.g., judge, jury) must make a preliminary assessment as to whether the expert's reasoning and methodology are *scientifically valid* and *can be properly applied to the facts at issue* in the court. This new standard now compels the forensic psychologist to pay far more attention to issues of reliability and validity and to other psychometric properties and psychological tests on which the testimony is based (Craig, in press).

In California, *People v. Kelly* established a two-prong test for admissibility of new scientific technique. The reliability of the method must be established, usually by expert testimony, and the witness so testifying must be properly qualified as an expert to give an opinion on the subject. The court also noted, however, that this "Kelly-Frye rule" applied to novel devices or processes, not to medical expert testimony: "Such a diagnosis need not be based on certainty, but may be based on probability; the lack of absolute scientific certainty does not deprive the opinion of evidentiary value" (*People v. Mendibles* at 557).

One can therefore conclude that the forensic interview should be conducted in a manner and with certain assessment techniques that would be accepted by a majority of the forensic psychology community. The opinion rendered on the basis of the forensic interview would not have to be accepted by a majority of the professional community to have evidentiary value, however. Such planning should ensure the reliability and validity of the forensic interview and should protect the forensic clinician, who continually faces scrutiny and disagreement.

FORENSIC PSYCHOLOGICAL INVESTIGATION

The final distinguishing core characteristic of the forensic interview is the attitude and expectation of the interviewer. Forensic interviews compel the forensic clinician to assume the role of a *forensic psychological investigator*. The attitude is one of impartiality and objectivity. The expectation is that data will accumulate that will eventually answer the psychological question that prompted the evaluation. The "client" may be a government agency, a private attorney, a referring professional, or the judiciary. It is rarely the interviewee. Monahan (1980) has edited an excellent compilation of papers about the ethics of psychological intervention in the criminal justice system.

The role of the forensic psychological investigator precludes certain other expectations that are often deeply embedded in the clinician's professional training; the role of healer, therapist, helper, and patient advocate *must be abdicated* if forensic psychological investigation is to occur in a reliable and valid manner. This does not mean, however, that respect for the dignity and worth of the individual, protection of the person's civil rights and welfare, or awareness of the person's legal rights should be ignored. In fact, these ethical imperatives must be vigilantly pursued, since forensic investigation, by its nature, may tempt the clinician to violate or compromise them.

The role of the forensic psychological investigator is fully consonant with the psychologist's ethics. Nothing in the ethical principles implies that all professional interactions must be "therapeutic" or "helping." There are limits, however, to psychological investigation.

I have occasionally seen role confusion lead to contrived ethical conflicts for the clinician and, in some cases, defensive and angry posturing under cross-examination. When this happens, the clinician's credibility as an expert witness is usually lost, and the courtroom experience becomes an unpleasant, if not painful, emotional memory.

How does the clinician prepare to assume the role of a forensic psychological evaluator? First, the clinician must be comfortable with the goal of understanding, rather than changing, human behavior. If this is not the case, and the clinician's primary identification is with the role of therapist or "healer," he or she should not undertake the role of forensic psychological investigator.

Second, careful thought must be given to potential ethical problems that may arise with each forensic case. The ethical caveat concerning dual relationships (American Psychological Association, 2002) is most germane to this consideration. For instance, if at all possible, a clinician should avoid conducting a forensic psychological investigation of a patient he or she has seen in psychotherapy, regardless of whether the treatment has ended. Sometimes, a court order will make this virtually impossible, but the clinician is ethically obligated to inform the court of the professional imperative to avoid such dual relationships. Clinicians should avoid serving as experts for attorneys who are also friends or social acquaintances. This can be particularly difficult in small communities, but may be considered a violation of the dual-relationship clause if ethically challenged. The assessment of competency for execution is another area of professional concern that raises profound ethical problems for clinicians who believe in the primacy of individual life (Heilbrun, 1987). Such an evaluation may violate several ethical principles (American Psychological Association, 2002).

And third, clinicians should be knowledgeable about the other core characteristics that I have outlined and should prepare themselves with the requisite skills, attitudes, approaches, and techniques that I have suggested accompany each characteristic: the coercive context, the absence of privilege, a lay communication tool, the presence of distortion, and disagreement and scrutiny. Such preparation for the forensic interview should foreshadow success in the forensic area.

REFERENCES

Adelman R., & Howard, A. (1984). Expert testimony on malingering: The admissibility of clinical procedures for the detection of deception. *Behavioral Sciences and the Law* 2:5–20.

Albert, S., Fox, H., & Kahn, M. (1980). Faking psychosis on the Rorschach: Can expert judges detect malingering? *Journal of Personality Assessment* 44:115–119.

Albert, S., & Silvers, K. (1970). Perceptual characteristics distinguishing auditory hallucinations in schizophrenia and acute alcoholic psychosis. *American Journal of Psychiatry* 127:298–302.

American Bar Association (1984). *Criminal Justice Mental Health Standards.* Chicago: American Bar Association.

American Psychiatric Association (1994). *Diagnostic and Statistical Manual of Mental Disorders,* 4th ed. Washington, DC: American Psychiatric Association.

American Psychological Association (2002). Ethical principles of psychologists and code of conduct. *American Psychologist* 57, 1060–1073.

Baer, R. A., Wetter, M. W., & Berry, D. T. (1992). Detection of underreporting of psychopathology on the MMPI: A meta-analysis. *Clinical Psychology Review* 12:509–525.

Berry, D. T., Baer, R. A. & Harris, M. J. (1991). Detection of malingering on the MMPI: A meta-analysis. *Clinical Psychology Review* 11:585–598.

Blau, T. (1984). *The Psychologist as Expert Witness.* New York: Wiley and Sons.

Butcher, J. N., Dahlstrom, W. G., Graham, J. R., Tellegen, A., & Kaemmer, B. (1989). *Minnesota Multiphasic Personality Inventory-2: Manual for Administration and Scoring.* Minneapolis: National Computer Systems.

Colorado v. Connelly, 107 S. Ct. 515 (1986).

Craig, R. J. (In press). *Personality-Guided Practice of Forensic Psychology.* Washington, DC: American Psychological Association.

Curran, W., McGarry, L., & Shah, S. (1986). *Forensic Psychiatry and Psychology.* Philadelphia: F. A. Davis.

Daubert v Merrell Dow Pharmaceuticals, Inc., 113 S. Ct. 2786 (1993).

Durst v. Superior Court, 35 Cal. Rptr. 143 (1964).

Dusky v. United States, 362 U.S. 402 (1960).

Edwards v. Superior Court, 16 cal. 3d 906 (1976).

Ekman, P., & Friesen, W. (1969). Nonverbal leakage and clues to deception. *Psychiatry* 32:88–106.

Estelle v. Smith, 451 U.S. 454 (1981).

Exner, J. (1978). *The Rohrschach Comprehensive System: Current Research and Advanced Interpretation*, Vol. 2. New York: Wiley and Sons.

Exner, J. E., Jr. (1993). *The Rorschach: A Comprehensive System. Vol. I: Basic Foundations*, Vol. 2, 3rd ed. New York: Wiley and Sons.

Frye v. United States, 293 F. 1013 (D.C. Cir. 1923).

Garner, H. (1965). Malingering. *Illinois Medical Journal* 128:318–319.

Gill, M. ed. (1967). *The Collected Papers of David Rapaport*. New York: Basic.

Golding, S., Roesch, R., & Schreiber, J. (1984). Assessment and conceptualization of competency to stand trial. *Law and Human Behavior* 8:321–334.

Goodwin, D., Alderson, P., and Rosenthal, R. (1971). Clinical significance of hallucinations in psychiatric disorders: A study of 116 hallucinatory patients. *Archives of General Psychiatry* 24:76–80.

Gorman, W. (1984). Neurological malingering. *Behavioral Sciences and the Law* 2:67–74.

Gough, H. (1950). The F-K dissimulation index for the Minnesota Multiphasic Personality Inventory. *Journal of Consulting Psychology* 14:408–413.

Green, R. J. (1985) Comparison of procedures for the assessment of psychopathy. *Journal of Consulting and Clinical Psychology* 53:7–16.

Green, R. J. (1990) *The MMPI–2/MMPI: An Interpretive Manual*. Needham Heights, MA: Allyn & Bacon.

Grisso, T. (1986). *Evaluating Competencies*. New York: Plenum.

Hare, R. (1985a). Comparison of procedures for the assessment of psychopathy. *Journal of Consulting and Clinical Psychology* 53:7–16.

Hare, R. (1985b). *The Psychopathy Checklist*. Vancouver: University Press of British Columbia.

Hare, R. D. (1991). *Manual for the Revised Psychopathy Checklist*. Toronto: Multihealth Systems.

Heilbrun, K. S. (1987). The assessment of competency for execution: An overview. *Behavioral Sciences and the Law* 5:383–396.

Hellerstein, D., Frosch, W., & Koenigsberg, H. (1987). The clinical significance of command hallucinations. *American Journal of Psychiatry* 144:219–221.

Hunt, H. (1948). The effects of deceit and deception on the Minnesota Multiphasic Personality Inventory performance. *Journal of Consulting Psychology* 12:396–402.

In re Spencer, 63 D. 2d 400 (1964).

Kernberg, O. (1984). *Severe Personality Disorders: Psychotherapeutic Strategies*. New Haven: Yale University Press.

Littlepage, G., & Pineault, T. (1978). Verbal, facial, and para-linguist cues to the detection of truth and lying. *Personality and Social Psychology Bulletin* 4:461–464.

Lubin, B., Larsen, R. M., & Matarazzo, J. D. (1984). Patterns of psychological test usage in the United States: 1935–1982. *American Psychologist* 39:451–454.

Maier, N., & Thurber, J. (1968). Accuracy of judgment of deception when an interviewer is watched, heard, and read. *Personnel Psychology* 21:23–30.

McClintock, C., & Hunt, R. (1975). Nonverbal indicators of affect and deception in an interview setting. *Journal of Applied Social Psychology* 5:54–67.

Meloy, R. (1985). *The Fitness Interview Test*, by R. Roesch, C. Webster, and D. Eaves (book review). *Bulletin of the American Academy of Psychiatry and the Law* 13:419–420.

Meloy, R. (1986). *Rogers Criminal Responsibility Assessment Scales*, by R. Rogers (book review). *Bulletin of the American Academy of Psychiatry and the Law* 14:99.

Meloy, R. (1988). *The Psychopathic Mind: Origins, Dynamics, and Treatment*. Northvale, NJ: Jason Aronson.

Meloy, J. R. (1991, Fall–Winter) Rorschach testimony. *Journal of Psychiatry and Law*, 221–235.

Melton, G., Petrila, J., Poythress, N., & Slobogin, C. (1987). *Psychological Evaluations for the Courts*. New York: Guilford.

Monahan, J., ed. (1980). *Who Is the Client?* Washington, DC: American Psychological Association.

Osborne, D., Colligan, R., & Offord, K. (1986). Normative tables for the F-K Index of the MMPI based on a contemporary normative sample. *Journal of Clinical Psychology* 42:593–595.

Overholser, W. (1953). *The Psychiatrist and the Law*. New York: Harcourt Brace.

People v. Kelly, 17 Ca. 3d 24 (1976).

People v. Laws, San Diego County Superior Court, MH 74987, Honorable J. Perry Langford, June 17, 1987.

People v. Mendibles, 245 Cal. Rptr. 553 (1988).

Perry, G. G., & Kinder, B. N. (1990). The susceptibility of the Rorschach to malingering: A critical review. *Journal of Personality Assessment* 54:47–57.

Piotrowski, C., Sherry, D., & Keller, J. (1985). Psychodiagnostic test usage: A survey of the Society for Personality Assessment. *Journal of Personality Assessment* 49:115–119.

Resnick, P. (1984). The detection of malingered mental illness. *Behavioral Sciences and the Law* 2:21–38.

Rogers, R. (1983). Malingering or random? A research note on obvious vs. subtle subscales of the MMPI. *Journal of Consulting and Clinical Psychology* 39:257–258.

Rogers, R. (1984a). Towards an empirical model of malingering and deception. *Behavioral Sciences and the Law* 2:93–112.

Rogers, R. (1984b). *Rogers Criminal Responsibility Assessment Scales*. Odessa, FL: Psychological Assessment Resources.

Rogers, R. (1986). *Conducting Insanity Evaluations*. New York: Van Nostrand Reinhold.

Rollerson v. United States, 343 F. 2d 274 (1964).

Salgo v. Leland Stanford Jr. Univ. Bd. of Trustees, 317 P. 2d 170 (1957).

Seamons, D., Howell, R., Carlisle, A., & Roe, A. (1981). Rorschach simulation of mental illness and normality by psychotic and non-psychotic legal offenders. *Journal of Personality Assessment* 45:130–135.

Shapiro, D. (1984). *Psychological Evaluation and Expert Testimony*. New York: Van Nostrand Reinhold.

Strunk, W., Jr., & White, E. (1979). *The Elements of Style*, 3rd ed. New York: MacMillan.

Taratino v. Superior Court, 48 C.A. 3d 465 (1975).

Tarasoff v. Regents of the University of California, 118 Cal. Rptr. 129, 529 P. 2d 553 (1974); 17 Cal. 3d 425, 551 P. 2d 334 (1976).

United States v. Alvarez, 519 F. 2d 1036 (1975).

United States v. Byers, 740 F. 2d 1104 (1984).

United States ex. Rel. Edney v. Smith, 425 F. Supp. 1038 (1976); affirmed 556 F. 2d 556 (1977).

Vinson v. Superior Court, 43 Cal. 3d 833 (1987).

Watkins, C. E., Campbell, V. L., Niebording, R., & Hallmark, R. (1995). Contemporary practice of psychological assessment by clinical psychologists. *Professional Psychology: Research and Practice* 26:54–60.

Webster, N. (1977). *The Living Webster Encyclopedic Dictionary.* Chicago: English Language Institute of America.

Wiener, D. N. (1948). Subtle and obvious keys for the Minnesota Multiphasic Personality Inventory. *Journal of Consulting Psychology* 12:164–170.

Ziskin, J. (1984). Malingering of psychological disorders. *Behavioral Sciences and the Law* 2:39–50.

Zuckerman, M., Larrance, D., Hall, J., DeFrank, R., & Rosenthal, R. (1979). Posed and spontaneous communication of emotion via facial and vocal cues. *Journal of Personality* 47:712–733.

AUTHOR INDEX

SUBJECT INDEX

EDITOR BIOGRAPHY

Robert J. Craig, Ph.D., ABPP, studied clinical psychology at De Paul University and at the Illinois Institute of Technology. He is the director of the Drug Abuse Program at VA Chicago Health Care System and is an Adjunct Professor in Psychology at the Chicago School of Professional Psychology and at Roosevelt University. He is a diplomate (board certification) in both clinical psychology and administrative psychology, a fellow in the American Psychological Association and in the Society for Personality Assessment. He is a consulting editor to the *Journal of Personality Assessment* and has published over one hundred professional articles in peer-reviewed journals. This is his eighth published book.

CONTRIBUTORS

Pamela Pressley Abraham, Psy.D., NCSP
Coordinator, Psy.D. Program in School Psychology
Immaculata College
Immaculata, Pennsylvania

Robert Archer, Ph.D., ABPP
Department of Psychiatry and Behavioral Sciences
Eastern Virginia Medical School
Norfolk, Virginia

J. D. Ball, Ph.D., ABPP
Department of Psychiatry and Behavioral Sciences
Eastern Virginia Medical School
Norfolk, Virginia

Daniel A. Beach, Ph.D.
Department of Psychology
Rosary College
River Forest, Illinois

Patrick Corrigan, Psy.D.
Center for Psychiatric Rehabilitation
University of Chicago

Robert J. Craig, Ph.D., ABPP
Director, Drug Abuse Program
VA Chicago Health Care System – West Side Division, Chicago
Chicago School of Professional Psychology
Chicago, Illinois

Kathrin Hartmann, Ph.D.
Department of Psychiatry and Behavioral Sciences
Eastern Virginia Medical School
Norfolk, Virginia

Carl Isenstat, Ph.D.L.P., MBA
Coordinator, Addictive Disorders
VA Minneapolis Health Care Center
Minneapolis, Minnesota

Salvatore Maddi, Ph.D.
Professor and Director, Social Ecology Program
University of California, Irvine
Irvine, California

Cheryl Marshall, Psy.D.
Coordinator, Eating Disorders Program
Lutheran General Hospital
Park Ridge, Illinois

Frank Gruba-McCallister, Ph.D.
Adler School of Professional Psychology
Chicago, Illinois

Stanley G. McCracken, Ph.D.
Center for Psychiatric Rehabilitation
University of Chicago
Chicago, Illinois

J. Reid Meloy, Ph.D.
Chief, Forensic Mental Health Services
San Diego County
Clinical Professor of Psychiatry
University of California at San Diego
San Diego, California

Nell Logan, Ph.D., ABPP
Private Practice
Chicago, Illinois

Peter E. Nathan, Ph.D.
Department of Psychology
University of Iowa
Iowa City, Iowa

Nicole Pizzini, Ph.D.
Department of Psychology
University of Iowa
Iowa City, Iowa

Sheila A. Rauch, Ph.D.
Center for the Treatment and Study of Anxiety
University of Pennsylvania
Philadelphia, Pennsylvania

Deborah A. Roth, Ph.D.
Center for the Treatment and Study of Anxiety
University of Pennsylvania
Philadelphia, Pennsylvania

Bonnie Rudolph, Ph.D.
Texas A&M International University
Laredo, Texas

Eliezer Schwartz, Ph.D.
Illinois School of Professional Psychology at Argosy University
Chicago, Illinois

Anne H. Skinstad, Ph.D.
Department of Psychology
University of Iowa
Iowa City, Iowa

David Wakely, Ph.D.
VA North Texas Health Care System
Dallas, Texas

Timothy J. Wolf, Ph.D.
Private Practice
San Diego, California

David van Dyke, Ph.D.
Director, Family Therapy Program
Illinois School of Professional Psychology at Argosy University
Chicago, Illinois

Jed Yalof, Psy.D.
Professor and Chair, Department of Graduate Psychology
Immaculata College
Immaculata, Pennsylvania

Robert J. Yufit, Ph.D., ABPP
Northwestern University
Evanston, Illinois